STILL THE BEAST IS FEEDING
FIFTY YEARS OF
ROCKY HORROR
Revised, updated & expanded

STILL THE BEAST IS FEEDING FIFTY YEARS OF ROCKY HORROR
Revised, updated & expanded

Rob Bagnall and Phil Barden

First published in the UK in 2013 by
Telos Publishing Ltd
www.telos.co.uk

This revised and expanded edition 2023
This edition has a black and white photo section.

Telos Publishing Ltd values feedback. Please e-mail us with any comments you may have about this book to: feedback@telos.co.uk

ISBN: 978-1-84583-224-7

Research and text by Rob Bagnall
Research and new interviews by Phil Barden

Still the Beast is Feeding: Fifty Years of Rocky Horror
© 2013, 2023 Rob Bagnall and Phil Barden

The moral right of the authors has been asserted.

British Library Cataloguing in Publication Data.
A catalogue record for this book is available from the British Library.

This ebook is sold subject to the condition that it shall not by way of trade or otherwise, be lent, resold, hired out or otherwise circulated without the publisher's prior written consent in any form of binding or cover other than that in which it is published and without a similar condition including this condition being imposed on the subsequent purchaser.

This Book Is Dedicated To:

DAD:
For introducing me to the joys of late night monster movies at a very early age; and for those very first *Rocky Horror Show* tickets.
You definitely started something.

And To:

ROCKY HORROR FANS – ALL OVER THE WORLD:
For continuing to 'Dream it' and 'Be it' in equal measure.
'Let The Party and the Sounds Rock On …'

Rob Bagnall

Acknowledgements

For kindly consenting to be interviewed, and for being so generous with their time and precious memories, special thanks must go to: Daniel Abineri, Perry Bedden, David Bedella, Jay Benedict, Peter Blake, Zalie Burrow, Ziggy Byfield, Ellie Chidzey, Clare Clifford, Tom Crowley, Derek Griffiths, Anthony Head, Kara Lane, Kristian Lavercombe, Christopher Luscombe, Neil McCaul, Richard Meek, Yasmin Pettigrew, Christopher Porter, Belinda Sinclair, Anthony Topham, Mark Turnbull and Toyah Willcox.

For their indispensable contributions, support and advice, heartfelt appreciation is gratefully extended to the following individuals: Stewart Bagnall, James Bainbridge, Peter Cliff, Rob Cope, Bruce Cutter, Dawn Evans, Marty Fairgrieve, Graham Fletcher, Norman Forster, David Freeman, Stephanie Freeman, Vicky Hawkins, Mark Jabara, Tony Johnson, Kieran Kimberley, Geoff Legan, Edward Marlowe, Kevin McEwen, Carol Mulhern, Jayson Noble, Tony Pazuzu, Claire Potter, Justin Ward and Jessica Woods.

Contents

Author's Note: This Wasn't Simply A Chance Meeting	9
Prologue: And the Void Would Be Calling	13
Introduction: At The Late Night Double Feature Picture Show	16
Chapter 1: They Came From Denton High	26
Chapter 2: You're The Product Of Another Time	56
Chapter 3: They Got Caught In A Celluloid Jam	95
Chapter 4: Don't Judge A Book By Its Cover	129
Chapter 5: Madness Takes Its Toll	158
Chapter 6: I Wanted To Be Dressed Just The Same	202
Chapter 7: Let's Do The Time Warp Again	229
Chapter 8: I'm Sure You're Not Spent Yet	280
Chapter 9: Sensual Daydreams To Treasure Forever	344
Chapter 10: And I Realise I'm Going Home	407
Bibliography and Selected Sources	439
Gallery	445
Index	509
About the Authors	530

… ROB BAGNALL AND PHIL BARDEN

Author's Note: This Wasn't Simply A Chance Meeting

While it may be true that life is full of coincidence, accidents and random encounters, the evidence for hypothetical predestination is occasionally hard to dismiss for even the most rational of thinkers.

For instance, having grown up (in the loosest sense of the term) watching vintage science fiction and monster movies, most often in the company of my dad, on late night television in the 1970s – the original version of *King Kong* (1933) and the intellectually stimulating *The Day the Earth Stood Still* (1951) were much-loved favourites from a very young age – I strongly believe that it was inevitable that I should discover *The Rocky Horror Show* just as adolescence was beginning to tighten its hormonally confused grip on my youthful mind and body.

For a lover of tacky sci-fi, horror movies, comic books, juvenile rock 'n' roll, 1950s Americana and camp comedy – never feeling obligated to bow to peer pressure by robotically following the contemporary youth trends, modern music and sporting pursuits dictated by my classmates – *Rocky Horror* (already more than a decade old before I encountered it) was a revelation.

It was (quite unfeasibly) geeky and sexy in equal measure – a rather epic paradox in itself – and with teenage hormones racing, and even the briefest glimpse of a lady's stocking tops under a short skirt having a profound effect on my horny young desires, I found that *The Rocky Horror Show* skilfully and uniquely merged these newfound urges with the puerile pop-culture pursuits of my childhood. It stamped its spangled platform heels all over tiresome stereotypes and somehow made being a movie geek, comic book fan and sci-fi aficionado cool and sexy – although these weren't the only barriers that this amazing work of contemporary entertainment helped to relax of course – which would never have seemed possible before.

When I first heard the mesmerising lyrics to 'Science Fiction Double Feature' – sung by an alluring 1950s style cinema usherette in a local performance of a mid-1980s touring production – I did so in open-mouthed wonder. Here was a witty and touching tribute to those late night monster flicks I had adored as a child. The song, and indeed the show, spoke to me like nothing I had ever seen before.

AUTHOR'S NOTE

Who could possibly have tapped into my psyche and envisioned a work of entertainment so deeply personal to me and so perfectly in tune with my obsessions and enthusiasms?

Only someone who shared those same passions of course; an unashamed eternal adolescent by the name of Richard O'Brien – a man who, along with Jim Sharman (director of the original stage production and subsequent film version) and, as I learned shortly thereafter, countless others (both fans and contributors to the show itself), helped prove that I wasn't alone. That it was okay to be yourself and dance to your own tune, and yet still be socially accepted and confident.

A long time coming, the book you hold in your hands is largely the result of two things. Firstly, my unending thirst for more and more reading on the subject began to reveal that, while other authors may have covered the humble origins of *The Rocky Horror Show* and, in particular, the development of its celluloid adaptation – most notably Jim Whittaker in his excellent self-published 1998 book *Cosmic Light: The Birth of a Cult Classic* – writers rarely chose to continue the story beyond the late 1970s and the early stages of the film's belated cult success as an interactive midnight matinee.

The reason for this, in my opinion, is that a lot of people probably do not even realise that there is a story beyond the late 1970s, and assume, erroneously, that the show simply rattled along in its original form for revival upon revival in the decades that followed. The truth however, as we shall discover, is that, while its classic story and utterly timeless music have, quite rightly, remained unaltered, the ways in which the show has been presented and even the manner in which audiences have responded to it have continued to evolve, constantly transcending current trends and keeping a 50-year-old rock musical fresh and exciting for new generations of followers.

Secondly, when I met Phil Barden (at first online via the UK *Rocky Horror* fan club's discussion forums and later in person at performances of *The Rocky Horror Show* itself) I was instantly thrilled and entranced by his memories of seeing the original London stage production years before I had even become aware of the show's existence.

Phil had started to satisfy some of the nostalgic yearnings he was feeling for countless nights spent in the darkened confines of the King's Road Theatre by tracking down a number of previous cast members from the show's early days and conducting his own personal informal interviews with these fascinating individuals.

When I revealed my desire to see a book that chronicled the entire history of the *Rocky Horror* phenomenon – taking in the touring productions and revivals of the '80s and '90s, not only in the UK but around the world, the making of the film version and its subsequent cult success, spin-offs, homages and parodies, in addition to the show's own impact upon 20th Century popular culture – ultimately bringing the story completely up to date for the very first time, Phil realised that such a volume might be a way of getting the enthralling memories and innumerable anecdotes revealed by his more than accommodating interviewees into the open, and he suggested that I should write the book myself.

Initially I took some persuading – no matter how much I had wanted to see such a work in print, it had never been my intention to attempt such a vast undertaking personally – but, as Phil widened his search and began talking to cast members from every era of the show's history, he began to convince me that it might actually be fun.

It was my goal to tell the story in detail, with abundant reference to the rock 'n' roll music, late night B-movies and other pop-culture trends that had influenced the show and its eternally youthful author-composer. As a major sci-fi and horror movie buff, as well as a deeply passionate *Rocky Horror* devotee, I was keen to include the kind of encyclopaedic minutiae that I personally revelled in whilst reading about my passions; the kind of things that to the uninitiated might be considered irrelevant detail, but real enthusiasts devour avidly.

While the likes of Richard O'Brien, Tim Curry, Rayner Bourton and Patricia Quinn – all present at the show's inception – have often aired their views and had the chance to recall their *Rocky Horror* memories, we realised that so many of the show's other (lesser known but no less integral) collaborators had never been heard; and, as devoted fans of the show and its history, these were the individuals that we decided we particularly wanted to hear from.

Once Curry's groundbreaking and acclaimed performance had grabbed headlines, and the attention of the critics, the bright young star left the original production and went on to recreate the role of Frank-n-Furter in LA and on film, leaving actors such as Ziggy Byfield, Peter Blake and Daniel Abineri with the seemingly impossible task of following in his high-heeled footsteps. On the London stage, each would bring something of his own to this extraordinary role; and yet, until now, none has been afforded the opportunity openly to share his vivid memories and, often very strong, personal opinions about the show itself.

Likewise, while facing the new and unprecedented challenges of audience participation, talented performers such as Anthony Head and David Bedella would help keep the character and the piece fresh and relevant for the next generation of fervent fans – many of whom had not been born when *The Rocky Horror Show* first made theatrical history in the early 1970s – and their voices and contributions to its enduring legend would be equally important.

In addition to the abundant interview material collected from those involved in various productions of the show itself, a significant quantity of the anecdotal reminiscences contained herein has been garnered from personal memory; firsthand recollections of incidents and occurrences

AUTHOR'S NOTE

witnessed at the countless number of *Rocky Horror* performances Phil and I have independently attended over the years.

Nevertheless, as with any work of this nature, there will always be a certain amount of conflicting accounts, strained memories, unsubstantiated rumour, personal opinion, speculation and hyperbole. I have, in such instances, attempted to make this clear; just as I have acknowledged whenever and wherever I have quoted from other sources.

This book has been a genuine labour of love; a comprehensive and engaging account of a truly incomparable work of contemporary entertainment.

In many ways, the story encapsulates the latter half of the 20th Century (and the beginning of the 21st) according to *Rocky Horror*. As major historical events – both good and bad – unfolded around the world, *The Rocky Horror Show* always seemed to be there, making its own small but significant contribution to global affairs; often by breaking down barriers, easing tensions and uplifting the mood ('A light in the darkness of everybody's life'), and I wanted to reflect that.

Above all, Phil and I agreed that the book should be a celebration. A celebration of the show, the film and the unparalleled music of *Rocky Horror*; a celebration of the gifted artists who conceived and created it, and those who continue to keep its legend alive and kicking (the lasting enthusiasm and adoration that so many actors and previous contributors noticeably feel for the show proved particularly touching and pleasing to both of us, not least because we feel the same love for it ourselves); and a celebration of the dedicated supporters and faithful followers whose ceaseless loyalty to *Rocky Horror* on stage and screen has ensured its status as an everlasting theatrical legend.

The Rocky Horror Show had an enormous impact on me as a teenager – it boosted my confidence, it helped me make friends, it gave me a sense of purpose and a feeling of belonging – and my unending devotion to it has continued to play an essential role in my life on a daily basis ever since.

No matter how many times I see it – even after many hundreds of performances – *The Rocky Horror Show* still gives me the same overwhelming feelings of exhilaration and fulfilment. Whenever I hear the opening chords of 'Science Fiction Double Feature', I get the same electrifying buzz; and as soon as the show ends, I can't wait to see it again – every time.

I can only hope that this book conveys at least some of the passion and everlasting affection that I feel for this very special work of entertainment, as well as my eternal gratitude to the highly talented individuals who masterminded its creation.

Rob Bagnall

Prologue:
And The Void Would Be Calling

A vibrant and diverse municipal area, boasting a population in excess of 130,000 residents – nearly half of whom are reportedly under the age of 30 – the thriving township of Hamilton is New Zealand's largest inland city.

According to historical records and local tourist information, while it was later renamed after Captain John Charles Fane Hamilton – a Scottish-born military hero who fought in the famous New Zealand Wars and died at the 1864 Battle of Gate Pa in Tauranga – the region was known to early Maori settlers as Kirikiriroa; a moniker that, by all accounts, translates literally into English as 'Long stretch of gravel'.

Though the accuracy of the translation might seem a tad questionable after more than 150 years of urbanisation and technological advancement, this somewhat unromantic title has remained the city's Maori name to this day.

One of Hamilton's most outstanding tourist attractions is a larger-than-life bronze sculpture of a man who clearly means a great deal to the city and its people. Unveiled at the south end of Hamilton's Victoria Street, during a massive midnight street party in November 2004, this impressive erection bears the likeness of a slim, shaven-headed figure. A figure dressed – a little unconventionally some might say – in a futuristic quilted tunic, high-heeled ankle boots and ladies' stockings, whilst clutching a rather formidable triple-pronged extraterrestrial ray gun in his gauntlet-clad hand. Thankfully, this eccentrically-attired monument does not represent the late Captain Hamilton, or even a historical world leader, pioneering scientist or great politician. It is in fact an individual who, despite being born thousands of miles away in England, is regarded by many as one of Hamilton's favourite sons.

The man in question is Richard O'Brien; actor, singer, songwriter, and, most importantly for the purposes of this book – and legions of adoring fans – the individual who conceived *The Rocky Horror Show*.

Unlike any other work of contemporary entertainment, *The Rocky Horror Show*, with its mythical tale of a naive young couple seduced and tormented by a maniacal, sex-crazed, cross-dressing scientist from another planet, has, over five decades, evolved from a low budget experimental piece of fringe theatre – expected to be forgotten once it had completed its original three-week engagement at a tiny London playhouse – into a global event with a truly unparalleled cult following.

Experimentally assembled by a maverick director and a hitherto unproven writer-composer – together with an energised and eager troupe of players and behind-the-scenes talent – *The Rocky Horror Show* defied all expectations. It tapped a particularly potent nerve, and grew from an imaginatively stimulating zero-budget piece of cheap and cheerful rock 'n' roll tat into a full-blown, persistently fashionable, polished and sophisticated cultural tour de force.

Since its most humble of beginnings – before an audience of just 63 astonished spectators – the phenomenon spread, like the inescapable crawling red weed of H G Wells' *The War of the Worlds* – inexorably and exponentially – exploding like a jubilant theatrical orgasm, joyfully defiling the pure but willing face of an entire planet. Australia; New Zealand; Germany; Austria; Brazil; Argentina; South Africa; Japan; South Korea; Poland; Norway; Denmark; Iceland; Finland; Mexico; Canada and the United States of America; *Rocky Horror* conquered them all, and more. Productions worldwide have boasted such luminaries as Anthony Head, Russell Crowe, Jason Donovan, Tracey Ullman, Julie Covington, Joan Jett, Jonathan Wilkes, Craig McLachlan, Jerry Springer, Nicholas Parsons, Darren Day, David Arquette and Alvin Stardust among their illustrious ensembles; while the 1975 screen version helped launch the film careers of Tim Curry, Susan Sarandon, Barry Bostwick and legendary rock megastar Meat Loaf.

Although admired by critics, musical aficionados and regular theatregoers, the show also attracts members of the general public, many of whom might never dream of entering a playhouse to see any other dramatic presentation. A local press advertisement for the latest *Rocky Horror* touring production will immediately provoke excited preparations for a joyful evening out, as regular citizens from all walks of life begin to contemplate what bizarre, tacky and skimpily erotic outfits they should wear for the occasion. Surely no other trip to the theatre is likely to incite such an unusual dilemma.

A night at *The Rocky Horror Show* is a ready-made party – an exciting, naughty and liberating night out – where even the generally unremarkable fellow selling souvenir merchandise in the foyer will often be considered a star in his own right. Its lively, colourful and often sensationally-dressed audience frequently competes with the outrageous antics of the onstage performance; so much so that critics have found it increasingly difficult to review the production in question without focusing upon the unique cult following and extreme audience participation rituals that have spontaneously grown up around it.

Sadly, this rather apathetic journalistic approach does the show itself an enormous disservice; as, despite being described by its overly modest author as a work of 'ephemeral juvenilia', *The Rocky Horror Show* is, at its heart, a rather dark, poignant and sophisticated little story; one that works on numerous levels, both superficial and intellectual. Not only does it send up the conventions of old science fiction films and kitschy entertainment – skilfully framed around the wittiest collection of catchy rock 'n' roll show tunes ever written – it cleverly reworks well-known fables such as *Babes In The Wood*, classic mythology and the biblical story of Genesis and the fall from Eden, while saying a significant, though perhaps subliminal, amount about life, death, love, lust, obsession, betrayal, sexual diversity and the very nature of the human condition.

Unashamedly derivative, and yet, at the same time, remarkably unique and groundbreaking on its 1973 debut, *Rocky Horror* emerged as a deliciously oxymoronic paradox; borrowing extensively from all areas of trashy popular culture – from rock music and B-movies to comic books and pop-art – and blending them, seamlessly and ingeniously, to fashion a landmark of unequalled originality and non-conformity.

Rather than remaining stuck in a 1970s time warp like most other, now hideously dated, musicals of the glam rock era, the show developed its own timeless charm, brilliantly beguiling each successive generation. From a cheap and tacky little rock show in the tiniest of venues, it steadily grew into a massive mainstream musical event; to such an extent that today a passionately protective '*Rocky Horror* then versus *Rocky Horror* now' attitude exists amongst many of its early contributors.

There are no doubt those who would dismiss it instantly; probably on the grounds that it is not Shakespeare. This, of course, is true. But that is not to say that *The Rocky Horror Show* is not a hugely important theatrical landmark in its own right. And it really should be respected as such.

Introduction:
At The Late Night Double Feature Picture Show

Without Richard O'Brien, *The Rocky Horror Show* would not have existed. There are those who seek to refute this, arguing, perhaps not entirely unreasonably, that the original production was the result of a collaborative effort, brought to life by a group of abundantly talented and creative individuals; and that O'Brien has, somewhat unfairly, taken all of the credit.

While it is undeniable that any theatrical work of this kind could not possibly have been produced by one person alone, it is nonetheless upsetting that some of the people who unquestionably helped to develop the show – contributing ideas, evolving characters, structuring plot and refining the script – all of whom remain heroes in the eyes of every genuine *Rocky Horror* fan around the world, now seem to find it increasingly difficult to acknowledge the fact that without the man who conceived the initial spark of an idea for a rock 'n' roll horror musical – and, most importantly, composed all of its songs – it would never have happened in the first place.

He was born Richard Timothy Smith in Cheltenham, England on 25 March 1942, as the Second World War relentlessly continued its course of global devastation. The youngest of four children – with two brothers and a sister – Richard was, by all accounts, a rather sickly child, not actually expected to survive his very first night on the planet. He has on occasion related the story of how the family doctor apparently expressed obvious surprise at finding the baby still alive the following morning; clearly a practitioner with a deeply compassionate bedside manner.

When his accountant father decided on a complete change of career and suddenly took up sheep farming, the family moved to New Zealand in 1952; originally settling briefly at a beautiful house in the suburbs of Hamilton – where the sound of the rain rapidly pelting down against the old tin roof would often frighten the impressionable ten-year-old as he lay awake at night; a particularly vivid memory that he would touchingly share many years later during a visit to his childhood home for a New Zealand television programme – and then moving to Tauranga the following year.

Growing up on the farm, Richard spent his formative years learning to ride the neighbour's horse – becoming extremely proficient in the saddle – a skill that would later prove invaluable as he took his first steps into the movie business. A fantasist from an early age, he found himself easily distracted at school, although a keen interest in literature, fantastic adventure stories and make-believe developed swiftly. At the age of 15 ½ he dropped out of high school and headed back to Hamilton, having already decided that, although bereft of any kind of long-term life plan, his ultimate destiny did not involve sheep farming. An interest in comic books gave the pubescent dreamer the idea that a career as a graphic artist might stimulate his blossoming creativity – although this was rather vague and uncertain, and not really a passionate or serious goal – while his practical but unimaginative family seemed convinced that a future in dairy farming might be an ideal vocation.

Directionless and with no real sense of purpose – like so many adolescent romantics of any generation – Richard would fill the void with trashy juvenile distractions.

The 1950s was the era of the teenager – the word having been invented to describe the youth of that very decade – and, for the first time in history, young people had their own culture and a legitimate sense of identity. For teens living before or during the War, the world had been a considerably darker and more serious place in which to grow up; but with the post-war economy at last beginning to strengthen and an optimistic future ahead, teens began to distance themselves culturally from their parents in an effort to augment their newfound independence; and, unlike any previous generation, they had their own fashions, entertainment and music.

The music in question was, of course, rock 'n' roll. An exciting amalgamation of assorted musical styles (including jazz, folk, rhythm and blues, gospel and country and western), this exhilarating musical sub-genre captivated the youth of America and soon spread worldwide, helping to cement the generation gap. Many judgemental adults, particularly those who objected to its roots in what was generally considered to be predominantly 'black' music, thought it subversive or even destructive. While the thought of this rather innocent trend being labelled 'the Devil's music' may seem almost comical today, it was accepted as a serious problem by countless adults at the time. Rock 'n' roll was cited as the major cause of teenage rebellion and the corruption of youth in much the same way that future generations of adults would point accusing fingers in the direction of horror comics, television, 'video nasties', violent computer games and the internet without worrying too much about providing reasonable evidence to endorse such knee-jerk allegations.

While England famously had its Teddy Boys, and the coolest American

INTRODUCTION

teenagers became leather-clad Greasers, the young Richard Smith found himself part of the Bodgie crowd – New Zealand's equivalent 1950s youth culture – daydreaming about becoming a rock 'n' roll idol, while incessantly playing the latest hits of Elvis Presley and Little Richard on his mother's record player. If the world saw Presley as the King of rock 'n' roll, then, in the eyes of this Brylcreemed New Zealand tearaway, the flamboyant Little Richard (born Richard Wayne Penniman), with his flashy onstage theatricality, was undoubtedly the Queen.

With television in its infancy, and yet to establish itself in New Zealand, the awkward adolescent romantic found escape from the mundane banalities of everyday life in the darkened auditorium of Hamilton's Embassy Theatre, a wonderful smoke-filled flea-pit that presented late night screenings of American drive-in 'classics', B-movies and cheesy atomic age monster flicks.

The likes of *Invasion of the Saucer Men* (1957), *I Was a Teenage Werewolf* and its trashy follow-up *I Was a Teenage Frankenstein* (both 1957) and the original version of *The Blob* (1958) epitomised the American teen movie of the 1950s, and Richard found himself captivated by the stilted dialogue and wooden acting of deadly earnest players who seemed blissfully unaware that their overly dramatic straight-faced performances were in fact quite terrible.

Immortalised by Johnny Depp in the film *Ed Wood*, Tim Burton's acclaimed 1995 black and white biopic, one particular director from this era, whose name has become synonymous with film-making at its absolute worst – garnering him an unlikely cult following in the years since his death – is the now legendary (mostly for the wrong reasons) Edward D Wood Jr. Wood – who died of a heart attack in 1978 at the age of only 54, never knowing that, just a couple of years later, he would gain such affectionate notoriety – made one of the 'greatest' bad movies of all time, the infamous *Plan 9 from Outer Space* (aka *Grave Robbers from Outer Space*). With its laughable flying saucers – aficionados generally accept them to be commercially available plastic model kits, although cynical viewers over the years have identified them as everything from automobile hub-caps to painted paper plates – dangling unconvincingly from obvious wires, wobbly cardboard grave stones and the last footage ever shot of 1930s horror star Bela Lugosi, *Plan 9* (released in 1956) is – despite its shoddy visual effects, abysmal acting and incoherent dialogue – a rather fun and immensely watchable film, with a plot that, when examined more closely, is not too dissimilar to that of the highly respected *The Day the Earth Stood Still* (1951).

Aside from making dreadful – but somehow enjoyably camp – science fiction romps, Ed Wood was an unashamed cross-dresser (giving him another slightly tenuous, but definitely relevant, link to the origins of a certain little rock 'n' roll musical). His well-documented penchant for angora sweaters and ladies' underwear was addressed not only in his films, but also between the pages of the pulp exploitation novels he wrote during the 1960s; books that boasted such unsubtle titles as *Black Lace Drag* and its sequel *Death of a Transvestite* (also known as *Let Me Die in Drag*), the cover of which bore an image of a masculine middle-aged gentleman wearing sheer nylon stockings and a bra. Wood's bizarre 1953 film *Glen or Glenda* (released with various alternative titles, including *I Led Two Lives, He or She?* and *I Changed My Sex*), a semi-autobiographical piece, in which the director also starred (under the pseudonym Daniel Davis) as a morally-tormented transvestite desperately agonising over the right way to declare his fetish to his beloved fiancée, was partly a means of publicly addressing this side of his personality. It was also the peculiar manner in which he apparently chose to announce his compulsion to his unsuspecting actress girlfriend Delores Fuller, who was, by all accounts, not too comfortable with this disturbing revelation.

Edward D Wood Jr made exactly the kind of films that would later be celebrated on stage (in a suitably irreverent manner) in *The Rocky Horror Show*; but their brand of particularly poor B-movie acting was certainly not exclusive to pictures dismissed at the time as forgettable trash. Many monster movies destined to be acknowledged by film buffs as *bona fide* genre classics featured less than Oscar-worthy performances, by actors who perhaps should have had the good sense to fire their agents as soon as the audition was over.

Even the great Steve McQueen, at the beginning of his career and evidently taking his first dramatic screen role very seriously indeed (despite the ridiculous premise of the movie itself), was uncomfortably wooden and over-the-top as the well-meaning teenage hero of *The Blob*; a situation that proves typical when examining any number of comparable sci-fi movie performances of the period. Actors would invariably appear totally committed to the script and their character, never consciously sending themselves up or metaphorically winking at the camera in any way; which is chiefly the reason why so many of these performances are so unintentionally hilarious today. The irritated frustration of Charles Drake's cantankerous Sheriff's at the scorching heat of a small town in the middle of the Arizona desert in Jack Arnold's 1953 classic *It Came from Outer Space* should be powerfully dramatic and full of conviction. But due to the nature of the speech – ranting about why 'More murders are committed at 92 degrees Fahrenheit than any other temperature' – and the film's absurd scenario, the actor's excessively passionate delivery comes across as hysterically hammy and laughable. As much as anything, these cheerfully cheap and tacky movies and their distinctive brand of acting definitely had an enormous influence on what would become *The Rocky Horror Show*.

INTRODUCTION

A certain British production company, which became almost solely associated with horror during the 1950s and '60s, was Hammer Films. Based primarily at Bray Studios in Windsor, England, Hammer made other kinds of pictures, notably Dick Barton detective stories and big screen versions of popular 1970s British TV sitcoms, including *Love Thy Neighbour*, *Nearest And Dearest* and a successful trilogy of *On the Buses* spin-offs (amusingly described by Sinclair McKay in his 2007 book *A Thing of Unspeakable Horror: The History of Hammer Films* as 'The most gothically awful productions that the studio made'), but it is for its abundant blood-drenched and bare-breasted horror offerings that Hammer continues to be remembered and adored.

Universal Studios had set a precedent for cinematic horror during the 1930s with two hugely important pictures. Their 1931 adaptation of Irish novelist Bram Stoker's influential vampire yarn *Dracula*, starring Bela Lugosi in his prime (long before he became an impoverished drug addict, reduced to appearing in Ed Wood's horrendous efforts) and directed by Tod Browning, an ex-sideshow barker who also made the seminal cult classic *Freaks* (1932), and James Whale's immortal 1931 version of Mary Wollstonecraft Shelley's *Frankenstein*, with Colin Clive in the title role and a groundbreaking performance from Boris Karloff as his persecuted and misunderstood creature.

The studio churned out numerous sequels to these instant classics, as well as a multitude of similar monster movies, throughout the '30s and '40s. 1932 saw the release of *The Mummy*, with Karloff again, now billed on the posters as 'Karloff the Uncanny'; while *The Wolf Man*, starring Lon Chaney Jr as the tragic Lawrence Talbot and Claude Rains as his father Sir John Talbot, hit movie theatres in 1941. Universal's long and profitable horror series came to an end in 1948 with probably one of the best examples of horror-comedy ever made. While most popularly known as *Abbott and Costello Meet Frankenstein*, the picture's on screen title was actually *Meet Frankenstein* with the full names of its two stars – Bud Abbott and Lou Costello – appearing above it. The film was released in the UK as *Abbott and Costello Meet the Ghosts*, and the British title probably made a little more sense (although not much), as the hapless pair never actually encountered the titular doctor during the movie at all; although they were menaced repeatedly by his infamous creation (this time played by Glenn Strange), along with Lon Chaney Jr's Wolf Man, Lugosi's Count Dracula and an unseen Vincent Price voicing the Invisible Man at the film's final fade out (Price had played the lead in *The Invisible Man Returns* in 1940.) Quite rightly, all of the mirth was provided by the popular comic duo, as, in a shrewd move by director Charles T Barton, the monsters were played straight – providing the perfect balance of scares and laughs – making it not only a fitting end to Universal's Frankenstein series but probably Bud and Lou's most memorable film as well.

Although the Universal monster pictures had been made in black and white, by the time Hammer obtained the rights to remake *Frankenstein* and *Dracula*, as well as other familiar horror titles, colour film made one vital element absolutely essential to creating an unforgettable impression on unsuspecting audiences – blood. Generous amounts of bright red theatrical blood, as well as ample gratuitous close-ups of heaving cleavages and naked nubile breasts, ensured that, thanks to Britain's fairly new X certificate for films of a horrific or sexual nature, Mary Shelley's obsessed scientist and Bram Stoker's un-dead Transylvanian Count could go about their monstrous mayhem in ways that James Whale and Tod Browning could only have dreamed of.

While the methods by which Frankenstein actually constructed his wretched creature were left somewhat vague in Mary Shelley's novel (first published anonymously in 1818), most film-makers understood the fun that this part of the tale in particular could offer to a visual medium. Delightful innovations such as grave robbing, roughly sewn- together body parts and the harnessing of elemental electricity featured heavily in most screen adaptations; while, in contrast to the book's dedicated young medical student, Frankenstein himself was typically depicted on film as a crazed middle-aged doctor.

Released in 1957, *The Curse of Frankenstein*, Hammer's first official horror picture – although 1955's *The Quatermass Experiment* (known in the US as *The Creeping Unknown*), the studio's big screen adaptation of Nigel Kneale's classic science fiction television serial, contained its fair share of scares – became the most financially successful British film of the year; and while many critics were repulsed by its graphic representation of violence and grisly horror, audiences obviously lapped it up.

In the role of Baron Victor Frankenstein was Peter Cushing – who would later play Count Dracula's nemesis, Professor Van Helsing – while the Baron's tragic creation was brought to hideously unnatural life by another distinguished British character actor, Christopher Lee.

Designed by make-up artist Phil Leakey and featuring a milky white eye and pale green facial swelling, the gruesome prosthetic worn by Lee as the cumbersome creature, though not nearly as iconic as Jack Pierce's unparalleled visage for Boris Karloff's 1931 portrayal of the monster (a design stringently copyrighted by Universal), was nevertheless strikingly creepy and unsettling on screen.

The film was a box office sensation in 1957 and quickly permeated the public's consciousness, as instantly recognisable properties often do. A slew of knowing pop-culture references soon followed. A particularly memorable example in the 1975 British sex farce *Confessions of a Pop Performer* features a character played by much-loved actress Rita Webb –

INTRODUCTION

known at the time for her depiction of ghastly old cockney battleaxes – approaching a group of wannabe rock stars in search of her pubescent groupie daughter. 'Have you seen my Fanny?' the hatchet-faced harridan enquires coarsely, in a voice that could curdle milk. Misunderstanding the question, as the great tradition of double entendre-based comedy demands, Robin Askwith's aghast Timothy Lea immediately snaps back, 'Blimey, I saw *The Curse of Frankenstein*; that was enough.' Audiences are left in no doubt as to what he means.

With Hammer keen to replicate the film's astonishing success, and realising that its stars were now box office gold, it was not long before Christopher Lee and Peter Cushing were facing each other again, in the studio's colourful reworking of *Dracula* (re-titled *The Horror of Dracula* for its American release). Like *The Curse of Frankenstein* before it, this 1958 version of Bram Stoker's famous vampire story was an enormous hit, many critics agreeing that Lee's momentous performance eclipsed even that of Bela Lugosi. The picture firmly established Hammer as a significant force to be reckoned with in the field of cinematic terror, subsequently securing it various dubious but affectionate nicknames, including the Studio that Dripped Blood and Hammer House of Horror. The latter was actually used as the title of a short-lived television series, co-produced by Hammer and ABC, which ran for 13 self-contained episodes in 1980.

During its bloody reign of terror, Hammer contributed gallons of the red stuff, oodles of naked flesh and more than a dash of camp to the world of exploitation cinema. Surely though, not even in his worst nightmares could Peter Cushing have imagined Mary Shelley's obsessed scientist slipping into a lace corset, fishnet stockings and six-inch high heels, regularly bursting into song and lasciviously seducing all unfortunate outsiders who happened upon his castle of debauchery. But someone else certainly could.

Sitting in the shadowy gloom of Hamilton's Embassy Theatre, bombarded with unforgettable images of plastic flying saucers, alien invaders in moth-eaten gorilla suits and deep-sea diving helmets, man-made patchwork monsters and spacemen with cheap, toy-store ray guns had a profound impact on Richard Smith's impressionable young mind. It was his first experience of the late night double feature picture show, and it would subsequently provide not only the basis for the plot, characters and overall style of his rock 'n' roll opus, but also the touchingly nostalgic lyrics of its opening number.

By the time he had spent two years working as an apprentice in Stan Osborne's hairdressing salon – conveniently situated next to the Embassy Theatre on Victoria Street – Richard was beginning to feel slightly disenchanted with New Zealand, and, at the age of 22, he decided that the land of his birth, a land he scarcely knew, was starting to beckon. He would, nonetheless, proudly consider himself a Kiwi for the rest of his life, retaining an intense spiritual and emotional connection with the beautiful country that had tenderly nurtured him through his formative years, and the persistent lure of his adopted homeland would ultimately prove irresistible before his journey on the planet was over.

He flew back to England in 1964, moving in with his grandparents in Cheltenham, with a view to making those idle adolescent dreams of rock 'n' roll stardom into a reality. Already a talented and prolific songwriter, with a particular flair for pastiche, simple catchy melodies and deliciously witty lyrics, Richard figured that a career as a singer-songwriter might be a fitting outlet for his talents; although, with his delicately slight frame and already receding hairline (by the mid-1970s he would be routinely shaving his head), he did not really fit the Elvis mould. Brimming with youthful verve and innocent exuberance, he soon concluded that naively walking uninvited into the London-based offices of record companies, with guitar in hand, and announcing that he had come to play them some of his material, was maybe not the best way to break into the notoriously cut-throat music business.

Realising that veteran genre stalwarts Peter Cushing and Christopher Lee would possibly be getting on a bit (the phrase 'long in the tooth' for a man best known for playing Count Dracula on screen would be far too cheap and obvious a pun to use here of course), thus necessitating a new generation of horror stars, and that his quirky looks and eccentric personality might conceivably help to secure him the offbeat screen roles they were used to monopolising, he decided to try his hand at acting. However, upon discovering that there was already a Richard Smith on the books of the British actors' union Equity – probably not the most shocking revelation of all time – he promptly adopted the surname of his maternal grandparents, and henceforth became known professionally as Richard O'Brien.

Unfortunately, principal character roles were not immediately forthcoming; and, even though he did not relish the physical dangers associated with being a stunt man, O'Brien was aware that his considerable horse riding skills, mastered whilst idling away his childhood on the farm in New Zealand, might prove to be an easier way into the movies. He thus became a registered stunt performer and soon found himself in the saddle (on horseback that is) at Pinewood Studios, on the set of *Carry On Cowboy* (released in 1965). This was the eleventh entry in producer Peter Rogers' long-running series of saucy comedy romps, which had begun with *Carry On Sergeant* in 1958 and had quickly become as much of a beloved British film institution as the Hammer horrors. Indeed the *Carry On* team's next effort, merely a year later, would be *Carry On Screaming*, an uproarious, affectionate and occasionally quite creepy

INTRODUCTION

parody of the Hammer oeuvre.

Carry On Cowboy featured many of the series' regulars – Sid James, Kenneth Williams, Jim Dale, Charles Hawtrey, Joan Sims, Peter Butterworth and Bernard Bresslaw among them – while O'Brien can be recognised clearly (in at least one moment) by eagle-eyed viewers, as an incredibly skinny American Indian, attacking a stagecoach that is being defended by *Carry On* starlet Angela Douglas as crack shot Annie Oakley.

Other films to which O'Brien contributed as a stunt performer were Disney's *The Fighting Prince of Donegal* (1966) and 1967's colourful James Bond spoof *Casino Royale*, a big budget shambles that showcased (and wasted) a host of Tinsel Town's finest, including David Niven, Peter Sellers, Woody Allen, Orson Welles and Peter O'Toole.

On 27 September 1968, the Broadway musical sensation *Hair*, with book and lyrics by Gerome Ragni and James Rado and music by Galt MacDermot, opened for what would become a five-year run at London's Shaftesbury Theatre. Billed as 'The American Tribal Love-Rock Musical,' it captured the very essence of the peace and love flower-power culture of the late 1960s and generated high-profile controversy because of its infamous (though fairly innocuous) nude scene, images of hallucinogenic drug use and anti-establishment protests about the Vietnam War. It was originally produced Off-Broadway in October 1967 and opened on Broadway itself the following April. One of the first rock musicals, it, along with its memorable songs 'Aquarius' and 'Let The Sun Shine In', became a celebratory anthem for the, by then declining, hippie culture.

O'Brien appeared as a member of the show's original British touring company – or the Tribe, as it famously labelled its ensemble. He also joined the London cast, which featured amongst its players a noticeably talented up-and-coming young triple-threat by the name of Tim Curry. Other names that appeared at various times during the musical's long-running engagement at the Shaftesbury Theatre (which eventually played for 1,998 performances; 256 more than the New York version) included Kimi Wong, Belinda Sinclair, Angela Bruce and Peter Blake. A then unknown rock singer by the name of Marvin Lee Aday, known professionally as Meat Loaf, had already made his mark in the 1968 Los Angeles production.

It was while touring with *Hair* in 1970, as revealed in 2000 on the audio commentary for the twenty-fifth anniversary DVD edition of *The Rocky Horror Picture Show*, that Richard O'Brien recalled being part of the small audience one wet Wednesday afternoon for a matinee performance of *The Resistible Rise of Arturo Ui* – the 1969 English adaptation of Bertholt Brecht's *Der Aufhaltsame Aufstieg der Arturo Ui* – which had played at the Playhouse Theatre in Nottingham in April 1969 before transferring to London's Saville Theatre in July the same year. The production starred respected British character actor Leonard Rossiter in the title role, a character that satirically paralleled the dangerous ascent of Adolf Hitler. Inspired both by Rossiter's dedicated professionalism in giving a deeply committed performance in spite of the minuscule attendance, and by the eternally pertinent messages about the constant threat of fascism in Brecht's allegorical fable, O'Brien quickly wrote a song that evocatively echoed the play's warning, 'Do not rejoice in his defeat, you men; for though the world has stood up and stopped the bastard, the bitch that bore him is in heat again.' These sobering words, also used in Sam Peckinpah's 1977 film *Cross of Iron*, were, consequently, the direct influence for O'Brien's unforgettably thought-provoking lyric, 'And superheroes come to feast; to taste the flesh not yet deceased; and all I know is still the beast is feeding,' later to become the haunting second verse of a light-hearted rock musical's unexpectedly bleak denouement.

Although he was now in his late twenties, Richard O'Brien's juvenile obsessions, and constant need for escapist fantasy, continued to play an important role in his adult life. At the time he may not have been consciously aware of it, but with *Hair* – his first foray into the world of musical theatre – as well as a ceaseless pre-occupation with rock 'n' roll, B-movies, pop-art, horror films and comic books (particularly *Doctor Strange*, a character created in 1963 by Marvel Comics gods Stan Lee and Steve Ditko), it is more than likely that the seed of an idea for a gender-bending science fiction rock 'n' roll horror musical had already been planted and was slowly beginning to germinate in his creative brain.

Just as *Hair* had come along towards the end of the 1960s and triumphantly defined the entire decade for a whole generation, Richard O'Brien would, just a few years later, write the show that would ultimately do exactly the same for the '70s.

1
They Came From Denton High

Following the introduction of the Theatres Act in 1968, the duty of licensing scripts for performance on the London stage was suddenly no longer the responsibility of the Lord Chamberlain's Office, as it had been since 1737. The immediate result was the abolition, or at least a huge relaxation, of restrictive theatrical censorship in the UK, and a predictable explosion of moral ambiguity, liberalisation and experimentation on the British theatre scene of the early 1970s.

Originally presented Off-Broadway in 1969, Kenneth Tynan's infamous revue *Oh! Calcutta!* opened at London's Roundhouse Theatre on 27 July 1970 and transferred to the Royalty Theatre in September of the same year. It instantly generated fierce debate and public outrage due to its unrepressed depiction of explicit male and female nudity and blatant sexual content; none of which adversely hindered its box office or stopped it from chalking up over 2,400 performances.

Unsurprisingly, *Hair*, the 1968 London opening of which had been briefly postponed until after the Theatres Act had been officially passed, continued to draw big crowds; and other shows saw composers and lyricists turning to the Bible – not for spiritual guidance (although some of them probably did that too, in addition to a multiplicity of other relaxants and stimulants, both prescribed and un-prescribed), but as an abundantly fertile, albeit rather obvious, muse.

John-Michael Tebelak and Stephen Schwartz conceived *Godspell*, a feel-good (despite its unavoidable crucifixion finale) collection of pleasantly memorable sing-along songs, loosely strung together to recount the gospel of St Matthew. Andrew Lloyd Webber and Tim Rice followed *Joseph and the Amazing Technicolor Dreamcoat* – expanded into a full-length musical from a well-received 15-minute school concert piece they had presented in 1968 – with another Christian-based musical, this time using the New Testament as its source. A colourful, vibrant rock opera, the influential *Jesus Christ Superstar* chronicled the last few days in the life of Christ – with the help of some undeniably hummable show tunes. Available first in 1970 as a best-selling concept album, *Jesus Christ Superstar* had opened on Broadway the following year, and had taken London's Palace Theatre by storm a few months later with a young Paul Nicholas in the title role.

During his time with the UK touring company of *Hair*, Richard O'Brien had fallen for a spirited young South African-born actress by the name of Kimi Wong. Raised by her Chinese father and African (Mauritius born) mother – who moved to England (and later Ireland) when the menacing shroud of apartheid engulfed South Africa – Wong had grown up on a diet of rock 'n' roll and old movies. Consequently, this fresh-faced young ingénue felt an acute spiritual and emotional connection with the man who had idled away his adolescence watching science fiction films in Hamilton and dreaming of becoming the next Elvis Presley. The couple married in December 1971. Their son Linus was born the following May, although Wong continued to perform nightly in *Hair* until she was very heavily pregnant.

Actress Belinda Sinclair – a former fellow *Hair* tribe member – affectionately recalls an informal get-together one evening at the flat O'Brien and Wong had in Oakington Road in the affluent London district of Maida Vale: 'I clearly remember what I now realise was the night *Rocky* was conceived,' she reveals. Through a haze of smoke, alcohol, and perhaps other intoxicating substances, O'Brien drew everyone's attention to the flickering screen in the corner of the room. A long-forgotten black and white B-movie was playing on late night television, and its typical brand of poor production values, coupled with laughably wooden yet totally straight-faced performances, led him to express, for the first time, a yearning to see a rock 'n' roll horror show on the London stage. With his childlike creativity already stimulated, the wannabe rock star picked up his guitar and instantly invented the enticing first line of an irresistible chorus, 'Science Fiction double feature ... Doctor X will build a creature ...'

That very moment, a seemingly insignificant instant in time – a few friends enjoying a drink, some laughs and a rock 'n' roll jam session – became an epoch-making historical event. 'We stayed all evening, all chipping in ideas,' Belinda Sinclair remembers affectionately. 'John Sinclair, who went on to found Sarm Studios, was my boyfriend at the time, and he contributed lots of thoughts and ideas that evening.'

In fact, being a close friend of O'Brien and Wong, John Sinclair actually suggested that he and O'Brien have a crack at writing the script together, but the aforementioned commitment to the opening of his own recording studio would ultimately thwart this proposed collaboration. 'John Sinclair was very angry that he'd never got any credit for his input into *Rocky*,' Belinda adds wistfully. 'In those early days it was all still work in progress, and we re-rehearsed it and everyone contributed.'

Never a huge fan of the musical genre *per se*, O'Brien became increasingly irritated with numbers that invariably sounded like show songs rather than a style of music more suited to the setting and plot of the piece in question. He has on occasion singled out Rodgers and Hammerstein's much lauded *Oklahoma* as a prime example of such creative misconduct and questioned why cowboys in the 19th Century mid-West of America would be using 'an elephant's eye' as a point of reference for the impressive stature of the latest corn crop. Would not a country or cowboy song with a more pertinent Wild West simile be far more apposite?

O'Brien concluded that he would like to fashion a genuine rock 'n' roll show; with a score made up of actual rock 'n' roll songs. Something that would incorporate his adolescent obsessions of horror, sci-fi and comic books, along with the beloved music of his youth; something he could be a part of and relate to. Fittingly, the eventual progeny of these speculative daydreams would one day be described in the programme notes for the show's 21st Century Broadway revival as, 'The anti-musical; an antidote to the big scale blandness permeating the London theatre scene.'

Staging *Jesus Christ Superstar* in London was Jim Sharman, celebrated director of the acclaimed Sydney productions of both *Hair* and *Superstar* itself, a man described by Australian luminary Barry Humphries in his 1973 review of *The Rocky Horror Show* as, 'Unarguably the second most gifted Australian in London'; high praise indeed!

A native of Randwick, just outside of Sydney, Sharman, like O'Brien, had endured a seriously complicated birth, surviving his first few hours on the planet against considerable odds. While working with his father's (formerly his grandfather's) travelling sideshow boxing booth – the legendary Jimmy Sharman's Boxing Troupe – from an early age, he developed a deep-rooted admiration for theatre, opera and the arts, as well as an equally enthusiastic pubescent passion for rock 'n' roll and American movies.

In 1971, with his friend and eventual long-term collaborator Brian Thomson, Sharman made his first feature film; a little seen, low budget 16mm science fiction musical with the delightfully kitschy title *Shirley Thompson Versus the Aliens*. Sharman had met Thomson, a talented and inventive architectural student, while standing in line at a fast food restaurant on Sydney's Oxford Street during the rehearsal period for the 1969 Australian premiere of *Hair*. Despite a lack of experience and a self-proclaimed dislike of traditional theatre, Thomson had gone on to create imaginatively innovative sets for the director's subsequent Melbourne and Tokyo productions of the show.

Featuring Thomson's art direction, music by Ralph Tyrell and a screenplay by Sharman and Helmut Bakaitis (who also appeared in the movie itself), *Shirley Thompson Versus the Aliens* was the everyday story of malevolent extraterrestrial invaders taking over Sydney's Luna Park by disguising themselves as a motorcycle gang and communicating through an animated waxwork of the Duke of Edinburgh. Nothing strange or mind-boggling about that of course; although, rather astonishingly, and while none could have predicted it at the time, for Sharman and Thomson, as well as two of the film's female stars – Jane Harders and Kate Fitzpatrick (who portrayed the title character and a nurse respectively) – *Shirley Thompson Versus the Aliens* would not be the final expedition into the unusually potent world of musical 1950s science fiction satire.

For the London ensemble of *Jesus Christ Superstar*, Jim Sharman initially cast Richard O'Brien in the minimal chorus role of Apostle/Leper, and their shared interests and juvenile passions, as well as a mutual antipodean upbringing, made them kindred spirits. Assuming the show-stopping role of King Herod was New Yorker Paul Jabara, a powerfully charismatic actor and well-known singer-songwriter, who had played the part particularly effectively as a camp tap-dancing vaudevillian in the New York production. With Jabara's three-month contract in the London run scheduled to end in October 1972, Sharman gave O'Brien a chance to take over the role, suggesting he use his love of rock 'n' roll – especially Elvis Presley – to create a markedly different interpretation and make the part his own. Unfortunately, O'Brien had only a couple of rehearsals to develop the character before having to present his performance for the approval of producer Robert Stigwood during a Friday afternoon matinee. In spite of the actor's genuine exhilaration at being entrusted with a prestigious West End role – not to mention fervent support from Sharman and choreographer Rufus Collins (who would later play the supporting role of a Transylvanian in the *Rocky Horror* movie) – Stigwood hated O'Brien's rock 'n' roll Teddy Boy translation of the character and demanded it be returned to the established (and audience-approved) style of Paul Jabara.

In retrospect, there is probably more than a little irony in Stigwood's excessively negative reaction. While *Superstar*'s Herod is traditionally interpreted as a foppish 1930s tap-dancing variety act, the equally crowd-pleasing role of Pharaoh in Rice and Lloyd Webber's previous biblical toe-tapper, *Joseph and the Amazing Technicolor Dreamcoat*, is most often played as a hip-thrusting Elvis impersonator, complete with rhinestone encrusted Vegas jumpsuit and slurred vocalisation.

Released from his *Jesus Christ Superstar* contract, despondent and discouraged, and with Kimi Wong – now the family's sole breadwinner – back onstage in *Hair*, O'Brien found himself, quite literally, at home with the baby. For a while, he even considered admitting defeat, quitting showbusiness and returning to New Zealand. When invited to entertain the staff of EMI studios with a few songs at their Christmas party, his immediate response, given the downhearted melancholic state he found himself suffering, was to decline. At a UK *Rocky Horror* fan convention in 2006, Wong recalled how she had insisted that he accept the EMI gig, and lovingly attempted to snap him out of his despondency by encouraging him to write a song about his passions: something he knew and genuinely enjoyed.

1: THEY CAME FROM DENTON HIGH

Once again the idea for a musical homage to vintage science fiction movies came to the fore. O'Brien reached for his treasured guitar and surrendered to half forgotten memories of the beautiful Fay Wray, caught in the clutches of a gigantic love-struck ape, and the heroic Flash Gordon, regularly thwarting the devious plans of the evil Ming the Merciless. The melodious outcome of these blissful daydreams was 'Science Fiction Double Feature', a sci-fi aficionado's wet dream, bursting with geeky references to the likes of Michael Rennie, Dana Andrews and Claude Rains, as well as the tacky celluloid treasures in which they starred.

Both the song and O Brien's appealing stage persona went down well at the EMI Christmas party, giving a much-needed boost to his deflated ego and self-worth, and impelling him to spend the long dark winter evenings a lot more productively than he had been. At last, suppressed yet unquestionably fertile ideas for a horror-musical-comedy, for which 'Science Fiction Double Feature' would make an ideal mood-setting prologue, began to take shape.

O'Brien has often reiterated that he did not view the process as writing, insisting it was more akin to making a collage or putting together a jigsaw puzzle, sketching out a basic structure, adding a few jokes and some intentionally corny dialogue. 'I had written several of the songs before and all I had to do was slot them in,' he revealed to Patricia Morrisoe, during an interview for the *Rocky Horror Picture Show Official Magazine*, a one-off 1979 tie-in publication. 'I didn't start at the beginning and develop the plot from there. I started at both ends and then filled in the middle.'

Nevertheless, as his hastily scribbled, handwritten notes – some of which were reproduced in Brian Thomson's *The Rocky Horror Scrapbook* in 1979 – would confirm, his use of the open-ended phrase 'Story resolves itself' implied that the author was initially uncertain of a fitting conclusion for his camp musical adventure. The ending he and his original creative team eventually fashioned would be perfect, giving the plot a genuinely satisfying beginning-middle-and-end formation, while combining the superficial – yet genuinely affecting – pathos of *King Kong* (1933) and *Bride of Frankenstein* (1935) with the intellectually acknowledged cathartic fulfilment of Shakespeare's *Hamlet*.

O'Brien's early list of scenes, each punctuated with a song and/or the introduction of a new character, involved an Eisenhower-era all-American couple subjected to an unforgettable night of scientific experimentation, sexual depravity and self-discovery. The newly engaged couple – identified as Brad Majors and Janet Weiss – suffer the indignities of a flat tyre on a deserted country road. As evidenced by O'Brien's reprinted annotations in *The Rocky Horror Scrapbook*, other names may have been briefly considered for the characters; Carol Hayman (a schoolboy play on the word 'hymen' maybe) being one such possibility. Braving an obligatory late night thunder storm, during which they find time to sing a catchy little song about their plight, our heroes seek help at an archetypal horror movie castle. Amid this woolly outline appeared vague and indecisive comments about the characters and their predicament, such as 'Explain relationship' and 'Reason for traveling' [sic]. Arriving at the castle, the contemporary Hansel and Gretel are greeted by a creepy, hunchbacked minion called Joe Vitus (irreverently incorporating 1960s British rock singer Joe Cocker and the spasmodically erratic muscular convulsions associated with Sydenham's chorea, a neurological disorder more commonly known as Saint Vitus Dance). This Igor-like creature – inspired by the malformed underlings of such films as Universal's *Frankenstein* series and, in particular, Boris Karloff's drunken manservant Morgan in James Whale's darkly satirical film version of J B Priestley's *The Old Dark House* (originally published as *Benighted* in 1927) – would in due course be renamed Riff Raff.

The Old Dark House is yet another movie with which *The Rocky Horror Show* intentionally shares more than a few plot and style similarities, thanks to the sensibilities of the film's playfully rebellious director. Born in the West Midlands town of Dudley, England, in July 1889, and remembered primarily for his four landmark horror pictures, *Frankenstein* (1931), *The Old Dark House* (1932), *The Invisible Man* (1933) and *Bride of Frankenstein* (1935), in addition to the luxurious 1936 adaptation of Jerome Kern and Oscar Hammerstein's Broadway musical *Show Boat*, James Whale had an extensive background in live theatre that gave his films a characteristically showy demeanour. Openly gay throughout his life and professional career, at a time when homosexuality was widely regarded as depraved and unacceptable, Whale had a practice, now legendary amongst film historians and his many fans, of knowingly inserting subversive imagery – both sexual and religious – into his work, elusively and joyfully sneaking it past the censors (hidden in plain sight as it were). While the overtly effeminate Ernest Thesiger, an early proponent of camp comedy (and horror), as *Bride of Frankenstein*'s Dr Septimus Pretorius, is a none too subtle example, the persistent persecution of Boris Karloff's pitiable creature has also been interpreted as a symbolic reaction to Whale's feelings of social and sexual segregation.

The hapless Brad and Janet enter the foreboding fortress, and its intimidating door is slammed shut behind them. The sinister servant introduces his dictatorial master, who invites the reluctant house guests to his bizarre laboratory. Here, the disturbingly attractive doctor is (rather worryingly) playing God by creating life according to the laws of Mary Shelley. A practice that – as most will verify – rarely turns out well.

So far, so run-of-the-mill monster movie plot. The basic premise was certainly not entirely new. A few years earlier, for instance, Bobby 'Boris'

1: THEY CAME FROM DENTON HIGH

Pickett (along with Sheldon Allman) had reworked his popular 1962 novelty hit single 'The Monster Mash' into a similarly themed stage play, with the unfeasibly longwinded title *I'm Sorry, The Bridge is Out, You'll Have to Spend the Night*. Opening at the Coronet Theatre in West Hollywood, California, on 28 April 1970, the musical had a madcap plot involving Pickett's Dr Frankenstein (articulated in the singer's trademark Boris Karloff imitation, as heard on the original record); his clumsy, though endearingly childlike, creation; a deformed assistant; Count Dracula; a reluctant werewolf and his over-protective mother; a seductive vampire Countess; and a naive teenaged couple who are forced to spend a stormy night in the professor's castle. A movie version, entitled *Monster Mash* (aka *Frankenstein Sings*), again starring Pickett as the Karloff-esque scientist, would be released in 1995.

The Rocky Horror Show's unique ace-in-the-hole, apart from its immaculate and extraordinary musical score, was Richard O'Brien's glorious twist on the conventional Frankenstein figure. His translation of this well-worn horror movie stereotype would be no over-emotional Colin Clive, scenery-chewing Peter Cushing or rambling Lionel Atwill; no crusty old scientist with wild and crazy grey hair and the sex appeal of an aging bank manager. Christened Frank-n-Furter, the character envisioned by O'Brien was a dynamically alluring, peacock-strutting, fishnet stocking-clad, lace corseted Glam Rocker; an insatiable sex-crazed alien with a vampire-like bisexual thirst for carnal gratification.

O'Brien has repeatedly cited Walt Disney's Cruella De Vil from *One Hundred and one Dalmatians*, *Snow White and the Seven Dwarfs*' Wicked Queen, Sergei Eisenstein's *Ivan the Terrible Part I* (1944), Shakespeare's *Richard III* and even Loki, the Norse god of mischief, as direct influences for the character. However, Frank-n-Furter also encompassed essential and eclectic ingredients audaciously purloined from a diverse assortment of rock stars and Hollywood leading ladies. These influences included Alice Cooper, Lou Reed, Joan Crawford, Gloria Swanson, Bette Davis, Marc Bolan and David Bowie in full-on Ziggy Stardust mode. At the time, as O'Brien recalled in 1999, Bowie was successfully adding theatrical elements to rock 'n' roll, and the idea for *Rocky Horror* was to try it the other way round; the vibrant energy and pulsating effervescence of a rock concert but with a structured story and clearly defined characters.

As previously noted, the author-composer, an accomplished songwriter with a not inconsiderable repertoire, already had a generous head start on the score. He realised that a mixed bag of unrelated, previously written material would be totally in keeping with the tone of the piece. Chosen songs from his existing gamut of work included 'Once in a While', a touching 1950s style love ballad; 'I'm Going Home', a supercharged emotional swansong, which would end up as Frank-n-Furter's heartrending farewell; 'Superheroes', the evocative anti-fascist warning he had written after seeing Brecht's *Arturo Ui* a few years earlier; and of course 'Science Fiction Double Feature'.

Speaking on *Let's Do the Time Warp Again* – a twenty-fifth anniversary *Rocky Horror* retrospective first broadcast on BBC Radio 2 in 1999 – the composer recalled that, not knowing how to tune his first guitar, he would simply compress the strings with the fingers of one hand and beat it like a drum with the other to get a suitable rhythm. 'My guitar playing hasn't improved,' he confessed modestly, claiming that he knew only three chords, which, quite fortuitously, was enough to create the characteristic rock 'n' roll sound. Though typically his songs tended to invoke a '50s vibe, O'Brien insisted that was due purely to his background as a teenager of the period. He was simply writing what he knew, and never consciously parodying the era at all.

Rock 'n' roll, which continued to inspire O'Brien's own compositions, had progressed rapidly since Elvis's suggestive gyrations first shocked bourgeois middle class America. In a quantum leap from the three chord innocence of Bill Haley, Little Richard and Buddy Holly, the 1960s and early '70s had given rise to the likes of the Beatles, the Beach Boys, the Rolling Stones, Jimi Hendrix, Alice Cooper, Roxy Music, the New York Dolls, T-Rex and Bowie. Heavy metal line-ups, such as Black Sabbath and AC-DC, would continue this movement; while the notable American rock band Ramones – whose influence on the 1970s punk scene is widely recognised – first made their presence known in 1974.

Comparable to his comments about the works of Rodgers and Hammerstein and other respected theatrical composers, Richard O'Brien's attitude to so-called rock musicals of the early '70s – including those in which he had appeared – was that the songs still sounded like show tunes and had very little to do with rock.

The only true example of traditional rock 'n' roll being embodied unpretentiously in theatre at the time was perhaps *Grease*, a cheerful, crowd-pleasing appropriation of 1950s teenage sensibilities. Written by Jim Jacobs and Warren Casey, *Grease* had struck a chord with Broadway audiences, many of whom would have been '50s adolescents themselves and were now probably young or middle-aged parents with a wistful longing for rose-tinted nostalgia. The show's catchy collection of simple rock 'n' roll tunes would bear the test of time and remain popular for decades to come. The lead character, Danny Zuko, was played in the 1973 London production by an unknown Richard Gere, and in the 1978 screen adaptation by John Travolta, flavour of the month and fresh from his star-making turn in John Badham's gritty urban fable *Saturday Night Fever*. Originally, however, the role had been created on Broadway in 1972 by Barry Bostwick, a handsome and engaging leading man whose name will

1: THEY CAME FROM DENTON HIGH

turn up again in a far more relevant capacity before this story concludes.

Even today, *Grease*, which offers audiences an entertaining, though arguably shallow, view of the rock 'n' roll era, remains something of a conundrum. In the face of its reputation as a gentle, inoffensive family show, it delivers constant sexual puns, teenage violence and gang culture, references to contraception and unwanted pregnancy, and a debatable finale in which its sweet middle class heroine feels duty bound to abruptly (and somewhat unconvincingly) cast aside her virtuous moral upbringing and become a spandex and leather-clad maneater in order to win the affections of her wrong-side-of-the-tracks macho beau. Even the popular film version, with its occasional expletive and fairly innocuous back-seat-of-a-car sex scene sometimes removed in edited-for-family-viewing daytime television screenings, slyly gets away with what some might consider less-than-family-friendly dialogue and suggestive lyrics. That is if they understood the references in the first place of course. At times, the blissful ignorance of both censor and viewer can be a useful and convenient tool to an artist.

Like the rock scene, the face of fantasy cinema, chiefly the horror genre, had also matured since Richard O'Brien's countless hours in the darkness of Hamilton's Embassy movie house. The world was on its way to becoming inexorably desensitised by television, uncensored videos, violent computer games, and, as a new millennium dawned, the impossible-to-monitor joys of the internet. Within this new context, once-chilling low budget science fiction shockers would become harmless and laughable enough for unedited broadcast on afternoon television. By the early '70s, the fanged visage of Christopher Lee and Peter Cushing's sloppy DIY organ transplantation, considered upon their initial exhibition to be way beyond acceptable limits of taste, now seemed non-threatening, melodramatic and even camp. This was especially apparent when comparing such films to the new precedent for cinematic horror set by William Friedkin's much discussed adaptation of William Peter Blatty's 1971 supernatural horror novel *The Exorcist*. While enduring a personal crisis of faith, a young Catholic priest battles for the demonically-constrained soul of an innocent child. At its heart, *The Exorcist* is a typical good-versus-evil story, not unlike *Dracula* in many respects, but its contemporary urban setting, as well as Friedkin's unflinching direction and totally serious approach to an inconceivable premise, made it something quite different; fresh and frighteningly real.

Opening in December 1973, the film, with its powerful script, unnerving photography and credible central performances, ushered in a new era of straight-faced, disturbingly plausible screen terror. Along with Tobe Hopper's unsettling (though surprisingly non-bloody) *The Texas Chain Saw Massacre* (1974), Brian De Palma's film version of Stephen King's

Carrie (1976), John Carpenter's trend-setting *Halloween* (1978) and George A Romero's *Dawn of the Dead* (1978), *The Exorcist* challenged the public's perception of what might be considered shocking or unacceptable, and completely pushed the endurance levels of movie audiences. As a direct consequence of these uncompromising new cinematic terrors, Hammer Studios' comparatively quaint brand of fright would be forever relegated to the realm of comfortable, innocent, misty-eyed nostalgia.

In 1973, fresh from his success with *Jesus Christ Superstar*, director Jim Sharman was casting a new production of *The Unseen Hand*, an allegorical one act play by prominent American writer and actor Sam Shepard, at London's Royal Court Theatre. Feeling sorry – maybe even a little guilty – about the way Richard O'Brien had been treated by Robert Stigwood, Sharman decided that the actor would be perfect for one role in particular. The character – for which O'Brien certainly did seem tailor-made – was Willie (the Space Freak), an extraterrestrial primate from the planet Nogoland, on a mission to free his enslaved race from the Orwellian oppression of an imperceptible hand (represented by a painted five-fingered blemish on the actor's hairless cranium). One of Willie's lines, 'This is your world; do what you want with it,' aimed at the play's human characters, effectively reversed the sentiment of Klaatu's message to mankind at the climax of *The Day the Earth Stood Still* (1951). Indeed, thanks largely to Brian Thomson's typically quirky set design, showcasing a performance space made up of real grass and incorporating the gutted shell of a classic American car, and Sharman's intuitive understanding of Shepard's material, the whole style of the piece owed much to the pop-art and B-movies that fuelled Richard O'Brien's eternally youthful imagination. Spurred on by the reassuring presence of like-minded individuals, O'Brien reservedly disclosed to Sharman that he had been composing his own musical. Understandably cynical in the face of London's seemingly endless stream of Bible-based rock shows, the director had an initially flippant reaction to this uninspiring revelation, saying simply, 'I hope it's not religious.'

Such offhand scepticism was to be short-lived. The mesmeric melody and razor-sharp lyrics of 'Science Fiction Double Feature', persuasively performed by O'Brien on his precious acoustic guitar, immediately enthralled Sharman, Thomson and Richard Hartley, composer of *The Unseen Hand*'s score. A handsome, softly spoken and almost horizontally laid-back Englishman, Hartley had recently assisted musical director Anthony Bowles with *Jesus Christ Superstar*'s music auditions. All three instantly understood where O'Brien was coming from (and hoping to go) with his skeletally vague outline of a plot and paradoxically unique concoction of clichéd rock 'n' roll lampoonery. Interviewed by Patricia Morrisoe for the 1979 *Rocky Horror Picture Show Official Magazine*, Thomson referred to his and Sharman's aforementioned 1971 sci-fi movie *Shirley Thompson Versus the Aliens*, which Morrisoe's article described as having been 'Almost *Rocky Horror* in embryo form.' Of the film's entirely coincidental similarities to Richard O'Brien's concept, Thomson mused, 'It's interesting that we were developing the same ideas on different continents.'

Although he had already won them over easily, O'Brien was nonetheless compelled that night by his captivated audience to sing his hypnotising science fiction homage again – twice.

London's unassuming Royal Court Theatre is something of an understated focal point of Sloane Square, in the trendy Royal Borough of Kensington and Chelsea. Located on the East side of the square, the building faces the fashionable King's Road (historians and purists constantly dispute the apostrophe), which by the early 1970s had already usurped the famous Carnaby Street as the chic, hip and happening place to be. Thanks to the worldwide repute of the Beatles and their like, Carnaby Street had lately become regarded as a little ostentatious, brash and touristy. It would later be satirised to uncomfortable perfection in Mike Myers' Austin Powers film franchise.

The Royal Court Theatre had effectively replaced the Belgravia Theatre, converted from the Ranelegh Chapel on Lower George Street in 1870, which despite a number of critically acclaimed productions had been unable to attract sizeable audiences and thus closed its doors within a few months of opening. A London newspaper report from 20 November 1870 announced: 'Another New Theatre – The new West-end Theatre building in Sloane Square, from plans by W Emden, Esq, architect, is to be called the Royal Court Theatre, and will open in January next with an original comedy by W S Gilbert, Esq, supported by a very strong cast.'

Walter Emden's playhouse, on the West side of Sloane Square, was indeed unveiled to the public on Wednesday 25 January 1871. A presentation of the popular one-act Strand farce *Turn Him Out* was quickly followed by inaugural speeches and a new three-act comedy, *Randall's Thumb*, written especially for the evening by W S Gilbert. When the venue was later demolished, in the summer of 1887, in order to be replaced by another Emden-designed edifice, the extraordinary circumstances surrounding its original construction were brought to light by the *ERA*, a weekly theatre-specific London newspaper (a predecessor of modern publications such as *The Stage* and *Variety*), which was published between 1837 and 1939: 'It may interest theatre-going people to know that the Court Theatre, now being demolished, was erected in the shortest space of time on record for such an undertaking,' announced the *ERA*'s 13 August 1887 edition. 'It was commenced November 3rd 1870, and was ready for opening on January 25th 1871. This was accomplished by working day and night, and, as no builder could be found to execute the work in time, Mr Wybrow Robertson became his own builder, his architect Mr Walter Emden taking the entire superintendence. The new Court Theatre will be erected on the other side of the road, next to the railway station, so that visitors will be under cover from the station to the theatre doors. The plans for the new theatre have been deposited by Mr Walter Emden, the architect, with the Board of Works.'

Under the management of Arthur Chudleigh and Mrs John Wood, Emden's new theatre finally welcomed its first audience on 24 September 1888. Its opening night presentation consisted of the customary speeches, a single act play by Charles Thomas entitled *Hermine*, and *Mamma*, Sydney Grundy's English adaptation of Alexandre Bisson and Antony Mars' *Les Surprises du Divorce*, which featured Mrs John Wood herself in a principal role.

Following several years as a picture house in the late 1930s, the structure was badly damaged in a 1940 Luftwaffe bombing raid and closed to the public for over a decade. It finally reopened as a place of live entertainment, with a completely reconstructed interior, in 1952. In 1956, artistic director George Devine secured the Royal Court as a permanent home for the newly-formed English Stage Company, with a continued commitment to producing contemporary and experimental new works and encouraging fresh writing for the theatre. With the debut of John Osborne's seminal *Look Back in Anger* the same year, not to mention a notorious censorship battle and subsequent prosecution surrounding the controversial 'stoning of a baby' scene in Edward Bond's *Saved* in 1965 – a situation that contributed significantly to the formation of the 1968 Theatres Act – the Royal Court made a decisive and long-lasting impression on modern theatre.

After receiving critical acclaim for *The Unseen Hand* at the Theatre Upstairs – the Royal Court's minuscule 63-seat attic studio, which had opened in 1969 – Jim Sharman was asked to direct *The Removalists*, a new Australian play by David Williamson, in the venue's considerably larger (439-seat) main house. Given the Court's rather stuffy self-imposed pledge to turn out stern and sombre contemporary works, it was not prone to deliberately letting its hair (or its guard) down with something a little more light-hearted and superficial. Sharman felt it was high time it did, and he agreed to stage *The Removalists* on the proviso that he first be allowed a 'bit of fun' at the Theatre Upstairs.

Interviewed for a *Rocky Horror* retrospective on US music channel VH-1's *Behind the Music* programme in 2000, Nicholas Wright, director of the Royal Court Theatre, recalled, 'I had a policy that the most interesting subjects in the world were sex, politics, drugs and rock 'n' roll.' *Rocky Horror* therefore appealed to him instantly. Scottish-born theatrical impresario Michael White, co-producer of the London productions of the scandalous *Oh! Calcutta!* and, another controversial Off-Broadway import, Tom Eyen and Jeff Barry's *The Dirtiest Show in Town*, also perceptively detected a palpable potential after hearing only a brief plot outline and a couple of songs, and agreed to finance a three-week run. Thus the creative team of Sharman, O'Brien, Thomson and Hartley began shaping a vague handwritten outline into a tangible structure for a full blown rock musical.

In the text for the souvenir booklet accompanying *The Rocky Horror Picture Show*'s fifteenth anniversary CD box set in 1990, Michael White explained his involvement with the project: 'I received a phone call from the director of the Royal Court Theatre, who said they were doing a new musical in the Theatre Upstairs and were looking for a producer to put up £3000 towards the cost of production in return for the West End rights.' White would subsequently declare that, of the countless productions he financed during his illustrious career, *The Rocky Horror Show* was the only one he never tired of seeing again and again.

Unable to actually write music, Richard O'Brien instead opted to compose everything on his faithful guitar. Thus he and Richard Hartley worked on the compositions together. From demo tapes of O'Brien's raw unaccompanied performances, Hartley arranged the songs for guitar, keyboard and percussion, and recruited musicians to make up the show's band. A small group with a big sound, the four-piece consisted of Ian Blair (known as the Count) on electric and acoustic guitar, Dave Channing playing saxophone and bass, Martin Fitzgibbon at the drums and Hartley himself playing piano and synthesiser.

Another early recording – featuring O'Brien's unrefined solo performances of the songs and a basic outline of the plot and its characters – was purportedly used to help explain the proposed show to producer Michael White and the Royal Court Theatre. This demo – which would eventually become available on the internet as a digital download recording in 2015 – demonstrated brilliantly how lyrics and dialogue were constantly being reworked as the score began to take shape. For example, the momentary spoken section in the middle of the song 'The Sword of Damocles' originally seemed to take the form of a hallucinatory inner monologue:

'Hey there, I'm your mind; And I wanna tell you that you're doing just fine; You were born under a groovy sign; And feeling down, well that ain't no crime.'

This brief interlude would be partially rewritten for the show itself – giving it a different context – and spoken by the Narrator to Frank-n-Furter's newborn creation:

'Rocky Horror, you need peace of mind; I wanna tell you that you're doing just fine; You're the product of another time; And, so feeling low, well that's no crime.'

O'Brien's hastily scribbled plot notes initially amounted to little more than a few basic B-movie situations, deliberately hackneyed dialogue, suitably corny jokes and suggestions for appropriate character names. His initial scene index simply listed Scene Three as 'Entrance of Frank-n-Furter', the character described in the notes as an 'Alice Cooper type Frankenstein', and Scene Four as 'Laboratory and meeting of Rock Horroar'; but references to 'Janet & Frank-n-Furter (impersonating Brad)', 'Brad & Frank in Frank's room (Rock breaks out)' and 'Dr Evrett [sic] Scott' seem to suggest that, apart from the lack of a fitting conclusion, much of the show's final composition remained unchanged from this preliminary outline.

The show was provisionally labelled *Rock Horroar* but would begin its rehearsal period with O'Brien's favoured working title *They Came from Denton High*, which Jim Sharman openly disliked. In spite of the title's trite B-movie appropriateness, the intuitive director felt that the author's intended double-level meaning – a mischievous drug pun on top of an innocent and obvious small town high school interpretation – did not translate. After the name of Frank-n-Furter's man-made Adonis evolved from Rock Horroar to Rocky Horrific and finally Rocky Horror, Sharman suggested *The Rocky Horror Show* as a more suitable alternative. Again, this worked on two levels; by incorporating the recognisable words '*Rocky*' and '*Horror*', it not only divulged the name of the title character, but blatantly indicated two of the show's primary ingredients – rock and horror – in a way that the invented word '*Horroar*' did not.

With limited finances, Brian Thomson struggled with the considerable conundrum of how to stage a piece that begged for some kind of flashy (even cinematic) theatricality. Any thoughts of creating an elaborate and convincing laboratory set were swiftly scuppered by a lack of funds, but Thomson's ingenious compromise would ultimately set the whole tone of the show. 'We wanted a hardware science fiction look,' he told Patricia Morrisoe in1979, 'but could hardly afford it on a set design budget of $600. Suddenly I remembered an image I had stored away. A few months before, I had gone to the cinema and seen an usherette selling ice-cream on the side of the stage with a spotlight shining on her. I thought it was one of the most theatrical things I'd ever seen.'

After that epiphany, as Frank-n-Furter would say, 'All the pieces seemed to fit into place.' Thomson proposed that 'Science Fiction Double Feature' should be sung by a cinema usherette, dressed in a suitably plain uniform and carrying an old-fashioned refreshments tray. The minimal and inexpensive set could then be dressed as a dilapidated old picture palace – long abandoned and scheduled for demolition – with little more than a few moth-eaten drapes, a section of Odeon carpet and a big white movie screen in the middle. The implication that the Usherette might possibly be the cinema's resident ghost, lovingly lamenting the forgotten movies of a simpler time, would be there for those who wished to perceive it.

Frank-n-Furter's (and perhaps Richard O'Brien's) sensual appreciation of ladies' intimate apparel provided the catalyst for the show's 'The Floorshow' finale, inspired by the big scale musical extravaganzas of MGM and parodying the sophisticated choreography of Bob Fosse and Busby Berkley (even to the point of including a tacky burlesque underwater ballet in the subsequent film version). With Frank indulging a multitude of fantasies by presenting both male and female participants of his chorus line in sexy female lingerie, O'Brien spawned what became the show's catchphrase, 'Don't dream it, be it,' a slogan he borrowed from a most apposite source.

Founded by Frederick Mellinger in 1946, world-renowned underwear store Frederick's of Hollywood opened its doors the following year. Years later, Frederick's unveiled its Lingerie Museum and the Celebrity Lingerie Hall of Fame, displaying the alluring undergarments of numerous Hollywood greats. Today, Greta Garbo, Ava Gardner, Elizabeth Taylor and Ethel Merman (star of many a Broadway musical spectacular) are showcased accordingly; while more contemporary icons are represented by the likes of Tom Hanks' boxer shorts from the film *Forrest Gump* (1994) and Madonna's famously recognisable Jean Paul Gaultier bustier. With memories of thumbing through old Frederick's underwear catalogues (unquestionably the conduct of a horny pubescent boy), O'Brien felt that there was something strangely masculine about the simple yet memorable line drawings of curvy female models wearing the company's latest products; a look he would bluntly describe years later as 'Men in drag with tits.' He therefore concluded that much of the company's business would probably have come from transvestites. Evidence suggests that the Frederick's of Hollywood's advertising slogan may actually have been 'Don't dream it; *live* it'. It is possible that they may have occasionally used variations, but equally likely that O'Brien (who always claimed that he found the words in the Frederick's catalogue) simply decided that a slight paraphrase might better fit the song and Frank's mindset.

Another significant purveyor of saucy scanties was The Undie World of Lili St Cyr. St Cyr, born Willis Marie Van Schaack in Minneapolis, Minnesota on 3 June 1918, was a celebrated stripper and burlesque artist in the 1940s, and opened this popular mail order lingerie company after she retired from performing in the late '60s. Artistic renderings of St Cyr personally modelling the sexy items on offer would frequently appear in her catalogues, and these evidently made an impression on Richard O'Brien, as he had an enraptured Janet Weiss evoke her memory as *The*

Rocky Horror Show's erotic 'Floorshow' reached a sensual crescendo. While St Cyr herself passed away in 1999, it is likely that this flippant, yet unmistakably reverential, lyrical reference may well help immortalise her name for generations to come.

Deciding that he might as well indulge in a little bit of harmless, free-spirited titillation by way of the casting process, O'Brien took it upon himself to scout local gymnasiums for a suitably beefy candidate to play Frank-n-Furter's perfectly-proportioned creation; a role eventually filled with great aplomb by a fair-haired, fittingly toned, relatively inexperienced young actor from Birmingham by the name of Rayner Bourton. Ironically, despite being a comparatively limited role, the show's integral title character is often the most difficult to cast. It would seem that finding an athletic bodybuilder who can act, sing and dance in spiked stiletto heels, is – for some baffling reason – no easy task. And it was even harder in the 1970s.

The character is described in Samuel French's 1983 published edition of *The Rocky Horror Show*'s libretto as, 'Rather vain – very beautiful.' Many actors grasp the childlike innocence of the role and then fail to convey his primping narcissism, but Rayner Bourton clearly understood both aspects and nailed the character right away. In *The Rocky Horror Show: As I Remember It*, his 2009 book of personal *Rocky Horror* recollections, the actor recounted what happened at his original audition for the show. With his singing experience until then limited to a spirited rendition of Little Jimmy Osmond's 'Long Haired Lover From Liverpool' in a 1972 pantomime, Bourton decided to revive the number for his *Rocky Horror* try-out. Confident that he knew the song well enough to forego the customary last minute rehearsal and nervous pacing, he awaited his turn by casually staring out of the window and absently twirling his long blond hair. The actor subsequently learned that, when asked by Jim Sharman which role he was auditioning for, casting director Gillian Diamond had answered, 'Frank-n-Furter.' Observing Bourton's outwardly relaxed and apparently self-absorbed demeanour, the perceptive director had immediately responded, 'No, he's not. That's Rocky.'

Leaving a gym on Paddington Street one day, during his quest to find a suitably strapping contender to play the object of Frank-n-Furter's obsessions, O'Brien bumped into an old friend from the London cast of *Hair*. The son of a Methodist Royal Navy Chaplain, Timothy James Curry was born on 19 April 1946 in the civil parish of Grappenhall, a suburb of the Borough of Warrington in Cheshire, England. Upon moving to London after his father's death in 1958, he developed an adolescent interest in acting, for which he exhibited a natural flair; although frustrated, and never fully realised, rock star aspirations were always abundantly apparent too. When asked by Mark Caldwell, host of a little seen 1975

1: THEY CAME FROM DENTON HIGH

British programme called *Film Talk*, how he had originally broken into acting, Curry gave a frank and direct reply that proved equally amusing and enlightening. 'I lied and cheated, basically,' he smiled sneakily. 'I left Birmingham University in '68 and I came down to London. And I met an agent who said that *Hair* were looking for somebody; and I told them that I had a full Equity card and that I'd done tours of *Cabaret* in the North, both of which were untrue. And by the time I'd done three auditions and they asked me to do it, they discovered both of these things to be false … but went ahead anyway.'

In the summer of 1974, Curry was living in a small Paddington Street apartment above the Speed Queen launderette, and, by a sheer twist of fate, happened to be appearing in *Give the Gaffers Time to Love You* by Barry Reckford, the current production at the Theatre Upstairs – and the actor's fourth Royal Court engagement to date – which was due to close on 4 June. Explaining his motives for furtively cruising London gymnasiums, Richard O'Brien suggested that Curry audition for *Rocky Horror*.

According to O'Brien, the first choice to play Frank-n-Furter had actually been Jonathan Kramer, an American actor who had appeared in the Broadway production of *Hair* between 1968 and 1972 and had played supporting roles in a number of films, notably *Women in Revolt* (aka *Andy Warhol's Pigs*, *Andy Warhol's Women*, and *Andy Warhol's Women in Revolt*), released in 1971 and directed by Paul Morrissey, and the Oscar-winning *Midnight Cowboy* (1969), starring John Voight and Dustin Hoffman. Nevertheless, the moment Tim Curry arrived at the Royal Court Theatre, purportedly to try-out for the role of Rocky, and belted out a classic rock 'n' roll number with vociferous verve and vigour, Jim Sharman knew at once that he had found his Frank-n-Furter. It is most commonly reported that Curry auditioned with an uproarious rendition of 'Tutti Frutti', even the actor himself having said so on occasion. Sharman, on the other hand, persistently maintains (in interviews as well as in his published memoir) that the song in question was actually another Little Richard number, 'Rip It Up'; a perfect example of how conjecture and discrepancy can regularly occur with the search for facts in such circumstances, thanks to people frequently remembering things differently. Either way, the pivotal role of the swaggering, supercilious scientist was filled, and poor Jonathan Kramer – who sadly passed away in 1976 – missed his opportunity to create a genuine legend of musical theatre.

'When I read it, I just thought it was very, very funny and the most kind of economical script that I'd read for a very long time,' Curry told Mark Caldwell for *Film Talk* in 1975. 'I was hesitant in that if it worked it might be a difficult image to shake off,' he then confessed, quite matter-of-factly; words that would prove rather prophetic in the years that followed. 'But really I have always thought that it wasn't worth doing unless you took a risk really; so I just took the risk.'

Yasmin Pettigrew – an actress who had recently returned to London (after being in the Norwegian cast of *Hair*), and would subsequently join *The Rocky Horror Show*'s backstage team, providing vitally important daily costume maintenance – recalls Curry's astutely prophetic optimism about the show: 'I remember having a cup of tea one day with Tim, and he told me that he'd just had an audition for *Rocky*, and he said "I've got a little feeling about this".'

As well as Tim Curry, the Theatre Upstairs cast of *Give the Gaffers Time to Love You* featured a surrealist artist and sometime actor by the name of Jonathan Adams. Hearing that the *Rocky Horror* producers were looking for a number of peculiar characters, including 'A mad professor' that he thought might suit his client, Adams' agent persuaded him to go along and audition. O'Brien and Sharman both liked Adams – who reportedly auditioned with an old nightclub routine he had devised in the '50s; a quirky rendition of 'Baa Baa Black Sheep' sung at the piano in the style of assorted composers – and felt that his ironic wit and deadpan delivery would be perfect for the show's Narrator. This character, who appeared at the beginning of the show, would set the scene in the style of Edgar Lustgarten, a famous British writer who had hosted late night crime dramatisations such as *Scotland Yard* and *The Scales of Justice* on UK television in the 1950s and '60s. Once Adams was cast, the Narrator's role – at first just a single scene-setting monologue – was significantly expanded, in order to utilise the actor's talents more fully. As new songs and scenes were added during rehearsal, the Narrator acquired more lines to link them together; the character now appeared periodically throughout the story, commenting on the action and ultimately judging the whole of society in a condescending, maybe even hypocritical, manner.

Playing the part of a resurrected cowboy called Sycamore in Jim Sharman's production of *The Unseen Hand* was Scottish-born and Canadian-raised Christopher Malcolm. The tall, rugged, unmistakably masculine actor looked every inch the square-jawed American movie hero, and he was quickly offered the part of Brad Majors in *Rocky Horror*. Speaking on the 1999 BBC Radio documentary *Let's Do the Time Warp Again*, Malcolm confessed that, the story having been described to him from the perspective of Brad and Janet, he was under the impression that Brad was the central character. Only during rehearsals, when he first witnessed Tim Curry's vibrant performance, did he realise, 'Uh oh, there's a better role than this.'

Julie Covington, an already prominent young diva with naturally strong vocal ability who had recently left the London production of *Godspell*, was cast as Janet Weiss. Upon finding an abundantly talented impending star amongst the ensemble of their cheap and tacky little rock show, Jim Sharman and Richard O'Brien thought it would be a crying shame to deny her a solo number. According to Rayner Bourton's book of *Rocky* memories, the issue was eventually addressed when producer Michael White expressed concern at the show's then scant running time – a mere 80 minutes – prompting O'Brien to speedily write 'Touch-a Touch-a Touch-a Touch Me' as an addition. As Rayner recalled, the consummately professional Covington learned this new song, a joyous declaration of sexual freedom – which unforgettably validated Janet's emancipation from demure 1950s stereotype to liberated young woman – in just 30 minutes.

Particularly in view of her later success with a 1976 recording of 'Don't Cry For Me Argentina', which achieved number one status in the UK singles chart in February 1977, from Tim Rice and Andrew Lloyd Webber's musical *Evita*, it is sad to reflect that Covington never had the opportunity to record any of her songs from *The Rocky Horror Show*, as, due to previously contracted work commitments, she left the production before its cast album was produced.

It had always been O'Brien's intention to appear in the show, so he added an incidental character – a ghoulish delinquent delivery boy called Eddie – with the objective of playing the part himself. This minimal role (an ex-lover of both Frank-n-Furter and Columbia, and an unfortunate victim of Frank's deranged experiments), described in the published edition of the script as 'A 1950s type rocker from the locker', would give O'Brien the chance to burst onto the stage midway through the show. Having indulged his teenage rock 'n' roll fantasies by belting out one of his own compositions – the high energy rock anthem 'Hot Patootie – Bless My Soul' (aka 'Whatever Happened to Saturday Night') – he would then be quickly and bloodily dispatched at the hands of a murderously enraged Dr Frank-n-Furter, understandably unimpressed at being upstaged.

Uncertain of the show's success, O'Brien viewed the role of Eddie as an opportunity to fleetingly live out his dreams of being Johnny Devlin, Elvis Presley, Eddie Cochran or Little Richard – with a little bit of Frankenstein's monster thrown in for good measure – and then shamelessly 'run away', leaving the rest of the cast to face any potential audience hostility. Jim Sharman, on the other hand, thought differently and, no doubt recalling the actor's interpretation of Willie (the Space Freak) in *The Unseen Hand*, felt that O'Brien would be perfect as Frank-n-Furter's devious hunchbacked minion Riff Raff. At first reticent about taking on such a pivotal role in his own script, O'Brien soon concluded that, had he not been involved in the show's conception, and a director of Sharman's stature had offered him the chance to create such a choice part in a brand new work, he would have been overwhelmingly flattered. Hence, he promptly accepted the challenging role.

In his autobiography *Blood & Tinsel: A Memoir* (2008), Sharman admitted that casting the show's author as the master's subservient manservant created an unmistakable air of tension between Richard O'Brien and Tim Curry, which the director later fully exploited whilst shooting the film version.

The part of Eddie, which would now be doubled with that of his inscrutable uncle Dr Evrett Scott (the spelling would eventually change to Everett) to flesh out the actor's role from a solitary rock number half way through, ultimately went to Paddy O'Hagan. A bright young performer, O'Hagan founded the Pip Simmons Theatre Group and later became a cast member on ATV's fondly remembered children's series *Pipkins*, a rather unassuming British answer to Jim Henson's groundbreaking *Sesame Street*, which had originated as *Inigo Pipkin* on 1 January 1973. As recounted in Jim Whittaker's 1998 book *Cosmic Light: The Birth of a Cult Classic*, the smart advice O'Hagan was given by his agent to take his saxophone along to the *Rocky Horror* audition – in case Jim Sharman and his associates were also recruiting musicians – resulted in him jamming with O'Brien and Hartley and chatting about rock music and science fiction movies. Engaging their enthusiasms – always a wise move where those guys were concerned!

Legend has it that, when considering a suitable performer to play Columbia – originally intended to be Frank-n-Furter's only female servant – Jim Sharman remembered an effervescent, pink-haired, squeaky-voiced tap-dancer he had seen busking outside London's Palace Theatre whilst he was putting together *Jesus Christ Superstar*. Born Laura Campbell, Little Nell had acquired her stage name from her father. An eminent Australian journalist, Ross Campbell used his daughters as inspiration for characters in his *Sydney Herald* newspaper column, giving each of them a well-known pseudonym from literature. For Laura's *nom de plume* he chose the tragic heroine from Charles Dickens' 1841 novel *The Old Curiosity Shop*.

Sharman, Thomson and Hartley tracked Nell down to Smalls – the Knightsbridge restaurant where she waited tables, while reportedly tap-dancing as she did so. Presently, the vivacious young Australian was offered the part of Columbia; a role she would expand in order to exploit her trademark tap skills, with a scene-stealing dance break during the show's most popular crowd-pleaser.

Each member of *Rocky*'s original cast brought elements of themselves – which then became synonymous with the characters – to the roles they created. Like Little Nell's tap-dancing ability, a similarly significant upshot of Paddy O'Hagan's audition was that his saxophone would be irrevocably incorporated into the character of Eddie.

The rumour that 1960s singer Marianne Faithful, one time squeeze of Mick Jagger, expressed a short-lived desire to be in the show and sing its opening song has become the stuff of *Rocky Horror* folklore. Although exact timelines and details differ from one account to another – time, old age and other mind-altering cruelties make a relentless mockery of the human memory – it seems that the thought of possibly securing a prominent pop idol to open the show may have led Jim Sharman to advocate the creation of a completely new role to accommodate her. Frustrated by the suggestion and totally perplexed about how to invent a whole new character and magically integrate her into the proceedings, O'Brien decided to simply split the female servant's role (and dialogue) into two separate parts. From this was born Magenta, a sultry domestic servant and sister of the devious Riff Raff; an implied incestuous relationship between them would be expanded and played upon by the actors as the show continued. Magenta (as the Usherette) would now sing 'Science Fiction Double Feature' at the top of the show, a number originally assigned to Columbia in the early draft notes.

When Marianne Faithful ultimately declined the role, the part of Magenta went to Patricia Quinn, an elegant, flame-haired actress from Belfast, Northern Ireland, whom Richard Hartley had spotted playing celebrated French actress Sarah Bernhardt in a recent production of Tom Eyen's *Sarah B Devine*.

Always openly honest about her limited singing ability, Quinn nevertheless charmed Hartley, Sharman and O'Brien at her audition, at the Irish Club on Sloane Street, with a sweetly naive rendition of Harry M Woods' 'Over My Shoulder' – a number made famous by Jessie Matthews as the theme from the 1934 film *Evergreen* – claiming that it was the only song she knew all the words to. With the director recognising a certain irresistible quality in her innocently unrefined singing voice, which he thought would fit the romantic reminiscences of the Usherette, Quinn was offered the part.

Having heard Richard O'Brien sing 'Science Fiction Double Feature' – 'I thought, "That's the most wonderful song I've ever heard",' she recounted dreamily in interview material included in a documentary for the 1995 laserdisc release of *The Rocky Horror Picture Show* (which subsequently showed up again on the widescreen VHS and DVD editions of the movie) – Quinn was eager to accept the role. Her agent, on the other hand, recommended caution, in case the character was 'just a four-line part', and advised that she first take a look at the script before making a decision. Upon collecting the script, Quinn was thrilled to see the song in all its glory. Closer inspection then revealed that Magenta did indeed have only four lines of dialogue. 'I said: I don't give a shit, I'm going to do it,' the actress squealed in the aforementioned documentary, 'because it's the best song I ever heard.'

In an interview for US music channel VH-1's twenty-fifth birthday celebrations for the movie in 2000, Quinn admitted that, due to the limitations of having just four lines, playing Magenta on stage had actually held very little excitement for her. 'Considering I was playing Lady Macbeth and things like that at the time,' she clarified. 'She did have to hang about a lot, Magenta.' She went on to say that, as she was an actress used to playing parts already established by other performers, the opportunity to create a whole new character did have its appeal. 'It's really wonderful to create something, because you're *it*,' she declared. Then, of those who followed her into the role, she added, 'They're just pretending to be *it*,' with a diplomatic and sincere afterthought of, 'Some of them have been awfully good.'

Jim Sharman appreciated that, with the show being something of a strange costume piece, the impact of the characters would rely very much on their initial appearance. He implored Harriet Cruickshank, manager of the Theatre Upstairs, to find him a costume designer willing to manufacture the production's entire wardrobe on a meagre budget of just £200. At the end of her tether, having been turned down by just about every possible candidate in London, Cruickshank contacted Sue Blane, a young designer from Wolverhampton, with whom she had worked at the Citizens Theatre in Glasgow. After learning her craft at Wolverhampton's College of Art and the Central School of Art and Design, graduating in 1971, Blane had been working as assistant designer at the Glasgow Citizens for a year or so.

Like every designer before her, Blane thought *Rocky Horror* sounded terrible and decided at once that she was not interested. 'I had no desire to design a lot of drag costumes for no money,' she told Patricia Morrisoe in 1979, disclosing that she had not been short of work at the time and would not have accepted any job unless it was particularly well paid or it sounded like fun. 'And from what I imagined, *Rocky* didn't promise to be fun at all.'

Pretty desperate by this stage, Cruickshank begged Blane to meet with director Jim Sharman, as a personal favour to her, so that it would look as though she had at least tried to find somebody. Blane politely acquiesced to her friend's request. Sharman took her to dinner and they hit it off immediately. 'While he was outlining the plot, we got incredibly drunk and then went round to the Royal Court Theatre,' she confessed to Morrisoe. Upon learning that Sharman's cast included Tim Curry and Julie Covington – friends she had enjoyed working with previously – Blane gradually warmed to the idea. 'By three o'clock and the start of a terrible hangover,' she admitted, 'I was doing *Rocky*.'

In his published memoir, *Blood & Tinsel*, Jim Sharman mused, 'When Richard O'Brien conceived Frank, I'm sure he had in mind a lovely dress, an elegant staircase and possibly himself.'

Sue Blane however had other ideas.

Tim Curry had previously appeared as Solange in Lindsay Kemp's 1971 production of *The Maids* by Jean Genet, for which Blane had provided costumes (again with very little money), at the Close Theatre Club, a small studio venue attached to Glasgow's Citizens Theatre. Genet's melodrama, originally produced as *Les Bonnes* in April 1947 at the Theatre Athenee in Paris, tells the story of two Parisian housemaids who fantasise about killing their younger mistress. The play's themes of fantasy role-play and subterfuge are often emphasised by casting male actors as the titular maids. For Kemp's production, Blane dressed Curry accordingly in an extremely shabby Victorian corset she had found on Paddy's Market in Glasgow's East End; and she decided to save money by recycling the same corset for Frank-n-Furter. There would be a credit in *The Rocky Horror Show*'s programme thanking the Citizens Theatre for the loan of various items of costume. But while most tellings of the oft-repeated story of the origin of Frank's corset have used the term 'borrowed', Kemp might have chosen a stronger word. In an interview for actor Daniel Abineri's 1999 television documentary *Walk on the Wild Side*, the director animatedly recalled his reaction to unexpectedly seeing the familiar garment adorning the alluring frame of Tim Curry's outrageous extraterrestrial scientist: 'Mortified,' he squealed. 'Mortified when the curtain went up and there was the bloody costume. I mean, Tim Curry or Sue Blane I think had just kind of popped it in their bag.'

Recycled from another production it may have been, but expert opinion will never be required in order to point out which of Tim Curry's stage personas made that corset a theatrical fashion icon.

Curry spared the costume department yet more expense by offering to wear his own leather jacket for the scene in which Frank, having previously dubbed Riff Raff his 'faithful handyman', viciously whips him for allowing Rocky to slip his leash; a rather harsh punishment for what would arguably seem a negligible misdemeanour.

For the laboratory scene and the birth of Rocky, both Frank and Riff Raff would don green surgical gowns, Frank's with an upward pointing red triangle over the left breast. There has been much debate as to the meaning of this odd little insignia. Some have argued that it is a reference to the Nazi concentration camps of World War II, whereby civilian prisoners would be categorised according to various symbols – a red triangle for example represented political prisoners, green would indicate habitual criminals, and the badge for homosexuals and sex offenders would be pink – although, unlike Frank-n-Furter's emblem, these badges typically pointed downwards. Sue Blane has continually downplayed such theories, insisting that she just liked the triangle's quirky, alien appearance, and claims that she knew nothing of the symbol's alleged darker significance until years later.

Variations of the same idea occasionally attempted by subsequent costume designers have included pink triangles, red triangles, other geometric shapes and even stylised splatters of blood.

Along with a suggestion of drug addiction emphasised by crossed Band-aids on his inner arms, Tim Curry's Frank also displayed a couple of faux tattoos. Emblazoned on his right upper arm was a skull with a vertical dagger through it (later replaced by the more familiar 'Boss' heart and horizontal dagger, made famous by the film version), while the number '4711', the branding of a famous German cologne, was clearly visible on his outer thigh.

Recognising the enormity of the task at hand, Sue Blane frantically recruited Colin MacNeil, an acquaintance from her time at the Glasgow Citizens, to be her assistant costume designer on *Rocky Horror*. Between them, Blane and MacNeil spent an additional £50 design budget renting a sewing machine and purchasing other essentials; then, working from Jim Sharman's and Richard O'Brien's clearly detailed character descriptions, they set about dressing the entire ensemble of a rock 'n' roll show for £200. Unfamiliar at the time with comic books or the genre of film that had influenced the piece, Blane sketched a number of stunning character designs that, purely from instinct, captured the required look perfectly. She and MacNeil then bought, begged and borrowed from junk shops, flea markets and various other sources.

As the show's programme would attest, hospital gowns for the lab scene, as well as surgical gloves and masks, were loaned by Hammersmith Medical School, while Bill Lewington supplied the Usherette's Lyons Maid ice-cream tray; a prop that, thanks to its prominent 'Strawberry Time' logo, would lead to Patricia Quinn's otherwise unnamed Usherette sometimes being referred to as Miss Strawberry Time.

In 1973, Blane had not yet visited the United States, but had, as she later told Patricia Morrisoe, 'a fixed idea of how people looked there. Americans wear polyester so their clothes won't crease and their trousers are a bit too short. Since they're very keen on sports, white socks and white T-shirts play an integral part in their wardrobe.' She admitted that these assumptions later turned out to be a huge generalisation, but insisted that her ideas had worked perfectly for the look of Brad and Janet. According to Jim Whittaker's *Cosmic Light: The Birth of a Cult Classic*, so as not to confuse the audience, Blane wanted to make the show's protagonists a little more contemporary and identifiable than the typically 1950s twosome Richard O'Brien had envisioned. She decided to costume them as a trendy 'middle of America' couple whose dress sense was maybe six or seven years behind the times. Hence Brad sported a white turtle-neck sweater, dark trousers, a dark blue plaid jacket, glasses and peace medallion (shades of *Hair*?), while Janet wore a pretty pink dress with a pleated skirt (a look that would resurface in untold revivals of the show) and a simple

1: THEY CAME FROM DENTON HIGH

white sweater.

While this made Brad and Janet look slightly more fashionable, Blane admitted to Patricia Morrisoe that *Rocky*'s eccentric blend of styles and periods resulted in costumes that covered several different eras. 'I thought Brad and Janet were supposed to be mid-'60s, while Eddie was straight out of the '50s. He was a mixture between a Hell's Angel and a Teddy Boy,' she said; which, with his Bodgie background, would no doubt have been Richard O'Brien's inspiration for the unfortunate corpse-like delivery boy. The hunchbacked Riff Raff was attired in ill-fitting black tails, a scruffy grey waistcoat and tight black trousers, while his mysterious sister wore a revealing wrap-around dress of sheer silk chiffon, over a black bra, g-string, suspenders and stockings.

Blane confessed to Jim Whittaker that she designed Columbia's look around Little Nell's already colourful persona. 'I kept the theme going,' she proclaimed, 'but there was no question once you met Nell: you go with what Nell is.' The vivacious young groupie was dressed in dazzling striped trousers, rolled up to mid-calf, revealing socks and sock suspenders, to deliberately evoke the look of 1930s tap-dancing star Ruby Keeler. A glittery waistcoat, which dipped exceptionally low to intentionally expose the actress's rouged nipples; outrageous eye make-up (which got progressively more elaborate as time went by); facial sequins; glitter; and of course Nell's trusty tap shoes finished the look.

'Nell was larger-than-life even when she wasn't being Columbia,' Yasmin Pettigrew declares, 'She used to walk down the King's Road, wearing a tutu and not giving a fuck.'

In comparison to the rest of the line-up, the Narrator and Dr Scott appeared somewhat more conservative, wearing smart conventional suits, with a trilby hat for Dr Scott that gave him the look of a 1940s newspaper reporter. By contrast, in just a tiny pair of trunks, leather sandals and a generous quantity of body glitter, Rocky Horror himself had the skimpiest costume of all. The sandals, which brought to mind the Greek and Roman heroes often portrayed on film by bodybuilder Steve Reeves (1926-2000) – one of Frank-n-Furter's fixations – were later replaced with a pair of silver boxing boots, commissioned from Lonsdale's, a company specialising in boxing wear and equipment.

Other costumes included the Usherette's uniform, with a large button badge of Elvis Presley (a tribute to one of Richard O'Brien's rock 'n' roll heroes) and a hat embroidered with the legend 'Sloane Cinemas'; white 1950s-style underwear and lab coats for Brad and Janet; silver tunic space outfits with black shoulder wings and stockings for Riff Raff and Magenta to wear when executing their ultimate *coup d'état*; and a magnitude of tawdry burlesque lingerie for 'The Floorshow'. Columbia's and Janet's 'Floorshow' outfits consisted of high heels, red panties, fishnet stockings and red push-up bras that unashamedly revealed their bared nipples. Brad and Rocky wore panties, stockings and suspenders for this number, with Brad still sporting his beloved peace medallion; but were both bare-chested until the show's success allowed the purchase of additional plus-size lingerie items. Sue Blane could not find high heels to fit the burly Christopher Malcolm's sizeable feet, so, in keeping with Brad's self-conscious reaction to his symbolic emasculation, the actor would stagger onstage *sans* footwear, awkwardly clutching just one shoe in his hand.

'Above all, Sue knew how to make everyone look and feel rock star sexy,' Jim Sharman astutely observed in his book *Blood & Tinsel*.

Without doubt, along with Brian Thomson's inventive set designs, Sue Blane's remarkable costumes for the Theatre Upstairs production of *The Rocky Horror Show* contributed enormously to its extraordinary success. Her creations set an unmovable precedent for the look of almost every production that followed; a massive testament to the fact that the show's original designer got it absolutely right first time.

On 1 January 2007, Sue Blane was justifiably awarded an MBE (Member of the Order of the British Empire) for her services to the theatrical industry; a worthy honour to which Jim Sharman bestowed appropriate respect in his book: 'I privately hoped it was in acknowledgment of her innate skill in understanding the right gap to leave between stockings and crotch when arranging fetishist underwear.'

To a considerable degree, the director workshopped the production in rehearsal, as he had done with *Hair* in Australia, encouraging his fresh-faced, eager cast to contribute inventive staging ideas, come up with jokes and lines of dialogue to embellish the slender script and essentially create their characters from the ground up. It was a technique he had favoured since his directorial debut at the age of 21; a radical reinterpretation of Mozart's *Don Giovanni* that divided audiences and angered blinkered critics.

Director and author concurred that the acting approach to *Rocky* should be straight and sincere, like that of the doggedly determined B-movie performers they affectionately appreciated. '*Peyton Place* acting,' Richard O'Brien often called it; a reference to the deadly earnest performances that peppered the sensationalist 1960s American soap opera, itself inspired by the melodramatic 1956 novel by Grace Metalious and its subsequent film adaptation. It is a technique that has continued to suit the show best in subsequent revivals, with O'Brien persistently urging directors and performers not to play for laughs. 'Play it like Shakespeare,' he advises, incisively noting that the jokes are already there and will take care of themselves and insisting that, like that of a poor B-movie actor, the more serious and committed the performance, the funnier it will be.

In the BBC Radio 2 documentary *Let's Do the Time Warp Again*, Tim

1: THEY CAME FROM DENTON HIGH

Curry remembered Jim Sharman taking his cast to see *Beyond the Valley of the Dolls*, a lurid 1970 offering by celebrated director of American sleaze Russ Meyer. Curry chuckled as he admitted that being shown this recent opus from the acknowledged king of cinematic sexploitation as their primary piece of research should have been a huge clue as to the tone Sharman was hoping to achieve for *Rocky Horror*.

Possibly influenced by the classic German Expressionist picture *Nosferatu* (1922), directed by F W Murnau, a film-maker Jim Sharman openly admired, Curry at first interpreted Frank-n-Furter as a sinister European horror figure with a clipped German accent. After also experimenting with an American inflection for the character, the actor confirmed that the voice he eventually settled on – a distortion of London's ostentatious upper-class Kensington accent – was influenced by a woman he heard talking on a bus. The exaggerated affectation and overstated vowel sounds resulted in words such as 'house' and 'town' sounding like 'hice' and 'tine', which, with Curry's expressively accentuated mouth movements and sensually enticing pout, fitted Frank to immaculate perfection.

As an influence on Frank's physical deportment, the actor cited a Japanese Kabuki dance production he had seen during rehearsals for *Rocky*. He expressed a fascination with the way performers would make high-speed entrances in a crouched position, before striking an effective pose and holding it for what felt like minutes. 'That kind of physical boldness very much went into Frank,' he confirmed.

Like many actors, Curry reputedly had difficulty finding his character until he first put on the shoes. Hardly surprising, given the character in question; especially when said shoes are glittered platform sandals with five inch heels. He also held a cast meeting and stressed the importance of Frank being seen to be in control. For the production to work, he strongly believed that the minions would have to willingly submit to their master's power and allow him to take charge. 'If you don't allow me to dominate you,' he told them, 'then we don't have a show'.

Deciding that Frank-n-Furter's trio of servants needed some form of routine to augment their connection to one another and endear them to the audience, Jim Sharman requested a dance number and gave Richard O'Brien a fitting point of reference; a scene from director Jean Luc Godard's 1964 French film *Bande a Part* (*Band of Outsiders*). A routine, generally described as the Madison, although its choreography bears little resemblance to the famous novelty dance, is performed in a café by three of the film's characters, Arthur (Claude Brasseur), Franz (Sami Frey) and Odile (the director's then wife, Anna Karina). An early form of line-dancing created in Columbus, Ohio in 1957, the Madison became fashionable with the increasing number of teenage dance shows on US television in the 1960s. One such programme, *The Buddy Deane Show*, would be the direct inspiration for *The Corny Collins Show*, the fictional – but brilliantly observed – send-up in John Waters' 1986 cult film *Hairspray*.

Richard O'Brien's response to Jim Sharman's request was suitably apposite. With its thumping rock beat, infectiously catchy chorus and uncomplicated, easy to follow dance steps (printed instruction sheets would be distributed to the audience), 'The Time Warp', purportedly invented overnight (Sharman's typical deadline) by O'Brien and Kimi Wong – the youthfully keen Mr and Mrs O'Brien – was *Rocky Horror's* unforgettable answer to the endless list of silly 1960s dance crazes: the Twist, the Hucklebuck, the Pony, the Watusi, the Mashed Potato and, as popularised by Little Eva's 1962 hit of the same name, the Loco-Motion, to name but a few. Initially conceived as a spoof of such undemanding participatory pop crazes, 'The Time Warp' – vigorously demonstrated by its composer to his receptive director in a cold rehearsal room early one morning in 1973 – would prove its mettle by ironically becoming an enduring party dance in its own right, often valiantly attempted at weddings, birthdays and drunken family get-togethers by revellers who possibly have never seen or even heard of *The Rocky Horror Show*.

As the production took shape, O'Brien's proposed intermission was removed in order to make the piece more cinematic. The director meanwhile demanded more songs to expand the short running time. He felt that Brad and Janet needed a number at the beginning, comfortably sandwiched between the Usherette's song and the Narrator's first expository speech, to establish the couple's relationship and delay Frank-n-Furter's introduction until around the 15-minute mark, the traditional entrance point for a major player. This time, O'Brien met Sharman's overnight deadline with 'Damn it. Janet' (aka 'Dammit Janet' and 'Wedding Song'), a fun, up-tempo parody of '50s and '60s declarations of teenage love. This song, which *Plays and Players'* critic W Stephen Gilbert would call 'A monstrous rock-a-ballad that makes 'Hey Paula' seem like high art', slickly advanced the plot, as, by way of the lyrics, Brad not only proposed to his beloved but also advocated a visit to their old high school science teacher; the all-important motivation for their fateful journey.

The final score would also include 'Wise Up Janet Weiss' (aka 'Planet Schmanet Janet') and 'I Can Make You a Man' (aka 'Charles Atlas Song'), the latter being an affectionate homage to the world famous bodybuilder, born Angelo Siciliano in 1894, who had recently passed away on 23 December 1972. Atlas's trademark Dynamic Tension programme was memorably endorsed amongst the pages of Richard O'Brien's cherished comic books, and the song would make playful allusions to his renowned fitness techniques and advertising slogans: 'In just seven days, I can make you a man,' sings Frank-n-Furter, after proudly declaring that his creation carries 'the Charles Atlas seal of approval.'

Though he advocated a relaxed and enjoyably experimental working environment for much of the five-week rehearsal phase, Sharman eventually recognised the time to adopt a more 'tough love' approach with his cast, in an effort to give performances their necessary edge. In his book *Blood & Tinsel*, the director admitted being deliberately unsupportive of Tim Curry's efforts, no matter how impressive, and consciously making the actor feel anxious, uneasy and exasperated. When Curry finally accused him of being unhelpful and called him a bastard, Sharman's cool and insightful response was, 'If only the character you're playing was an even bigger bastard.'

With the production scheduled to open officially on 19 June 1973, after two initial preview performances on 16 and 18 June, Richard O'Brien made use of his artistic talents and drew a suitably simple programme cover for the show. Along with the title, opening dates and cast list, the author's illustration, which subsequently found its way onto the 1983 published edition of the show's libretto, featured a long-haired muscular Adonis with outstretched arms in front of a winding mountain road with a castle at the end. A cartoon approximation of an imposing Riff Raff, firing a ray gun, with the words 'Thrills, chills and spills' and the production credits incorporated into its blast of energy, dominated to the left of the phrase, 'Brad and Janet found it was a night they were to remember for a very long time.' To the right of this slogan, which ran across the bottom of the picture, stood a tiny-waisted, immaculately coiffured blonde bimbo (presumably the author's own fantasy interpretation of Janet Weiss), wearing a coned 1950s bra, suggesting more than a hint of a Frederick's of Hollywood catalogue model, while a quiff-headed rocker rose chillingly from a box clearly labelled 'Eddie'. Appropriately, this rather busy cartoon prominently bore the legend 'Something for everyone'.

As opening night drew inexorably closer, a tricky problem presented itself, the solution to which would become another of the show's memorable trademarks. Due to the pulsating rock 'n' roll sound, which permeated through the entire building, Sharman's production at the Theatre Upstairs would not be permitted to commence until 10.30 pm, after the curtain had fallen on the evening's main house performance of Edward Bond's *The Sea*, directed by Bill Gaskill and starring renowned stage diva Coral Browne. This in turn meant that the show would not finish until after local bus services had ceased operation for the night. However, as the theatre's management refused to pay their cab fairs, front-of-house staff refused to work late. Since their characters were not needed on stage for at least the first ten minutes, Sharman hit on the inspired notion of dressing Richard O'Brien, Little Nell and Paddy O'Hagan in what actor Perry Bedden describes as 'scarlet nylon jackets, black trousers and eerie, semi-translucent masks that had a fixed grin'. These creepy Ushers could then act as genuine front-of-house personnel, while effectively freaking out punters at the same time and putting the audience suitably on edge. They quickly became an integral ingredient of the show, and could achieve a genuine sense of unease by showing people to the wrong seats, uncomfortably separating someone from the safety of their group or silently and secretly positioning themselves behind or to the side of an unwary victim.

On the night of Tuesday 19 June 1973 – with preview performances on the preceding Saturday and Monday evenings having been promisingly well-received – the unsuspecting audience for *The Rocky Horror Show*'s first official performance prepared to witness theatrical history. Brian Thomson's brilliant derelict picture palace design theme cleverly added to the ambience by taking over the entire auditorium, incorporating shabby Odeon seating and a large notice announcing: 'The Sloane Cinema regrets the inconvenience caused to patrons during renovations. A modern three-screen cinema centre will open shortly.'

Fresh from her performance downstairs in the Royal Court's main house, actress Coral Browne settled into a seat beside her imposing partner (and future husband), the eminent star of *House of Wax* (1953), *House on Haunted Hill* (1959) and *The Abominable Dr Phibes* (1971).

As the musicians assumed their positions and Patricia Quinn crouched motionless in the gloom, her face obscured by a large shroud of pasty white gauze, the searing sticky humidity of a prolonged English heatwave suddenly broke in the most spectacular fashion. Like a scene from the show itself, ominous and threatening grey clouds gathered in the London sky, signalling the imminent onslaught of a dramatic seasonal storm. Maybe the eternal spirit of Emperor Ming the Merciless, tyrannical ruler of the planet Mongo, had an insatiable yearning to appraise a project which flippantly evoked the memory of his noble arch nemesis. Or perhaps the ghosts of Michael Rennie, Claude Rains and Charles Atlas were keen to offer their collective seal of approval to such an affectionate homage.

The three disturbing Ushers crept silently towards the stage, slowly uttered the unsettling words 'Glad … you could … come … tonight,' and unveiled the gauze-covered figure of the Usherette.

As thunder rumbled noisily over Sloane Square, and the band struck the first startling chords of 'Science Fiction Double Feature', an unscripted flash of shocking white lightning unexpectedly lit the auditorium, fleetingly illuminating the unmistakable visage of horror icon Vincent Price.

2
You're The Product Of Another Time

'Dear Richard O'Brien. I am delighted to inform you that as a result of *Plays & Players* annual poll of London Theatre Critics, *Rocky Horror Show* has been voted Best New Musical of the year.'

A particularly pleasing item of morning mail, dated 27 December 1973. This charming communication from Peter Ansorge, editor of *Plays and Players* magazine, no doubt made breakfast at the O'Brien residence particularly fulfilling. When added to a similar epistle announcing that the production had also won the prestigious London *Evening Standard* Drama (Opera & Ballet) Award for Best Musical of the Year, it would surely have placed an understandably self-satisfied grin on the face of its contented author-composer.

'The choice of best musical produced a unanimity as rare as it was sweet among members of the Drama Panel,' proclaimed Antonia Fraser in the pages of the *Evening Standard*'s edition of Monday 21 January 1974. 'It did bring forth some dewy-eyed confidences from sophisticated critics who spoke, nay boasted, of visiting their choice two or three times, even at their own expense. One distinguished member actually touched his breast pocket in which it appeared there resided yet further tickets for a potential fourth visit.'

In the presence of Her Royal Highness Princess Alexandra, the lunchtime award presentation, which Richard O'Brien reportedly attended wearing, rather aptly, 'white vest and a leopard skin,' took place at London's Savoy Hotel the following afternoon, Tuesday 22 January 1974.

From struggling actor, unceremoniously fired (though he seems to prefer the more diplomatic term 'let go') from the ensemble of a major West End show, to dining in the company of British royalty and celebrating the overwhelming success of his own highly praised musical hit. Few would argue that it had been a truly exhilarating, destiny-changing year in the life of this former Hamilton hairdresser's apprentice.

Months earlier; on a stormy summer evening, whilst anxiously awaiting his first entrance as the sinister alien manservant Riff Raff, the author of a show not ten minutes into its first official performance had listened intently to the reactions of its inaugural audience. Already an atmosphere of edgy electric excitement had been skilfully fashioned by creepy, unpredictable, featureless Ushers – behind the masks of which lurked actors Paddy O'Hagan, Little Nell and O'Brien himself – as they disturbingly prowled the auditorium like silent, sleazy, fixed-grinned vampires, while naive spectators took their seats. Yet no-one had any real concept of how the outwardly strait-laced British public would react to such a radical, innovative and sensuous work of experimental theatre.

Would they boo?

Throw things?

Walk out?

'There's a light …' sang a hopeful Brad and Janet, presumptuously (and foolishly) assuming that the occupants of a nearby gothic mansion would hold the key – or more specifically the telephone – to their salvation.

'Over at the Frankenstein place,' intoned ominous ghoulish offstage voices.

And the audience laughed.

They got it.

They instantly understood the irony; the macabre satirical wit; the wonderfully warped, B-movie-addled imaginations of Jim Sharman and Richards O'Brien and Hartley.

Upon hearing this gleeful laughter, the author, now secreted nervously behind the centre-stage screen, allowed himself a moment of relief. If they laughed at that, then surely Frank-n-Furter's jaw-dropping entrance would slay them. As would the unveiling of his perfect, baby-oiled, muscular sex slave and the sinful, worse-than-death fates he would deal his uninvited guests.

In truth *The Rocky Horror Show* had made an indelible connection with its audience long before its creator was in a position – prior to Riff Raff covertly monitoring the approach of Brad and Janet to his master's castle – to gauge personally their unmistakable delight. They had already been easily and willingly seduced by Patricia Quinn's alluring Usherette, the catchy melody and irresistible lyrics of 'Science Fiction Double Feature', and a pitch-perfect Edgar Lustgarten caricature delivered with masterful aplomb by the marvellous Jonathan Adams.

Scrutinising and assessing the gleeful reactions of the opening night audience – including those of horror film veteran Vincent Price, whose imposing presence occupied the seat next to his own – producer Michael White was quick to deduce that Mr O'Brien and Mr Sharman might already have something of a hit on their hands. Notwithstanding White's proven experience and firmly established credentials, O'Brien himself decided to remain sensibly cautious at first and take nothing for granted. It was a healthy attitude, and one that would later prove correct when

2: YOU'RE THE PRODUCT OF ANOTHER TIME

bombastic American producers rather foolishly decided to try to tell New York critics that they had a guaranteed box office triumph heading for Broadway.

All that, and much more, was still to come.

Right now, in the cramped confines of a poky attic theatre, in the company of 62 other fortunate souls, on a hot and sticky stormy night in Chelsea's fashionable Sloane Square, White's insightful and proficient judgment was about to prove absolutely spot on.

Before the opening night party (held, according to Rayner Bourton's recollections, in a shabby London furniture warehouse) was even in full swing – during the small hours of Wednesday 20 June 1973 – critics hastily began plundering their thesauruses in search of fitting superlatives to convey the theatrical bliss they had just witnessed.

Probably the production's most famous review – which achieved a form of pop-culture immortality of its own after it was reprinted on the back cover of the original *Rocky Horror Show* cast LP – was that of *Daily Mail* theatre reviewer Jack Tinker. Immediately recognising Richard O'Brien's diverse musical and trash culture influences, the noted critic observed, 'He has taken all the kitsch fantasies of the '50s – horror movies, Charles Atlas muscle-bound ads, sequined pop stars – and turned them into the high camp sensuality of the '70s,'; while, of the show's pastiche of rock's high speed history, he enthused, 'From Bill Haley to David Bowie is one hell of a time leap. Mr O'Brien measures it effortlessly, illuminatingly and wittily.'

Clearly this was a man who understood the show from the outset; in addition to its unconditional thumbs-up, Tinker's astute appraisal suggested that the piece was, 'so funny, so fast, so sexy and so unexpectedly well realised that one is in danger of merely applauding it without assessing it.' He felt that this would be a shame, as it was his genuine belief that, 'Mr O'Brien has something quite nifty to say about the present state of nostalgia.'

In addition to being the first impartial perceptive examination of *Rocky Horror*'s more subtle connotations, Tinker's comments elicited their own thoughtful debate. A light-hearted nostalgia trip the show may be, but the inevitable emancipation of Brad and Janet, as well as Frank-n-Furter's precarious lifestyle, could be viewed as a caution about the dangers of living permanently in the past and refusing to yield to the inevitability of progress. By seeking out this joyous caper, might audiences have been expressing a similar (albeit short-term) need for frothy nostalgic escapism? With a global energy crisis, a lengthy, pointless and unwinnable war in Vietnam, and cinema screens soon to flaunt graphic scenes of a possessed pre-pubescent girl projectile vomiting, spouting obscenities and viciously masturbating with a crucifix, a mass craving for undemanding humorous diversions such as *The Rocky Horror Show* was perhaps understandable.

Frank-n-Furter's ultimate fate might also be deciphered as a warning against the dangers of taking the rock star existence too far. Though fans of both stage and screen incarnations of *Rocky Horror* often adopt Frank's dubious advice to decadently 'Don't dream it, be it' – questionably interpreting it as a legitimate message – it is worth remembering that this excessively hedonistic outlook is ultimately the character's undoing and he dies at the hands of those he has haughtily abused and manipulated. Such illuminating symbolism is surely a metaphor to which numerous self-destructive celebrities could relate.

In contrast to most of the decade's self-proclaimed serious dramatic works and biblically-inspired rock musicals – all of which seemed to bubble with significant issues and seemingly important ideas, but on reflection turned out to be little more than entertaining shallow diversions – *The Rocky Horror Show* emerged as the complete opposite. On the surface, an unashamedly inconsequential and superficial pop-art comic book, with no intentional message and a playful desire simply to please and amuse, it revealed a delicious multitude of hitherto hidden layers – some of which even its author remained unconscious of – only after repeat viewings, deep thought and a lot of studious stripping and probing (of the text that is).

At the very moment *The Rocky Horror Show* first took hip and trendy 1970s Chelsea by storm, glam rock was making its brazenly bold and unforgettable mark on the British music scene.

Primping, pouting and prancing before audiences, in a manner that, paradoxically, seemed to accentuate their self-assured, undoubted heterosexuality, men in outrageous make-up, platform boots and effeminate clothing certainly found no shortage of sexually excited young girls throwing themselves (and various, probably still warm, intimate undergarments) eagerly at the stage in response to such flagrantly flamboyant behaviour.

Although the psychological rationale behind them remains a constant, youth trends, by necessity, grow more extreme and mutinous with each successive generation, as society becomes desensitised and broadminded. Adolescent behaviour deemed unacceptable in the 1950s would almost certainly be viewed as agreeably twee to many 21st Century parents. The natural progression for rock 'n' roll – itself born out of a post-war need for teenage identity – was the peace-loving 1960s hippie culture. Early '70s androgyny then gave rise to the sequins, glitter, lipstick and eyeliner of glam; and, while this most British of rock sub-cultures – epitomised by the likes of Marc Bolan, Gary Glitter and David Bowie – never really thrived on the other side of the Atlantic, shock rockers such as Alice Cooper were very much the darker, moodier, less glitzy American equivalent.

Before long, the ever-changing face of rock transmogrified yet again;

2: YOU'RE THE PRODUCT OF ANOTHER TIME

this time into punk. A relatively short-lived (particularly in the UK), but nonetheless significant, chapter in the history of popular music, punk rock confirmed that from the 'peace and love' flower-power ideology of the 1960s had developed a frustrated, angry and rebellious youth culture with flagrant anti-establishment attitudes. Not only did *Rocky Horror* bridge the gap between 1950s rock 'n' roll and the glittered, glamorous, grandiose pop icons of the '70s, it foresaw and incisively spoke to the subsequent punk generation too.

Consequently, some have claimed that the real secret to the show's sensational success was nothing more than the old dictum (steady on, it's nothing rude), 'right place, right time.' With the relaxation of British theatre censorship just five years earlier – as well as Stanley Kubrick's controversial 1971 film version of Anthony Burgess' dystopian novel *A Clockwork Orange*, and porn chic becoming momentarily fashionable amongst the bourgeois middle classes thanks to director Gerard Damiano's (aka Jerry Gerard) notorious hardcore blockbuster *Deep Throat* (1972) – the consensus amongst certain pop-culture theorists is that, by sheer coincidence, the world just happened to be ready for *The Rocky Horror Show*.

It is, nonetheless, far too easy and convenient simply to attribute all of the accomplishments of any major contemporary triumph to the turbulent state of the world in which it was born. The decade that spawned *Rocky Horror* also witnessed the original theatrical release of *Star Wars* (1977), a movie that promptly broke box office records to become the most lucrative and iconic motion picture in the history of cinema, generating an unstoppable franchise, global hysteria and a multi-million dollar merchandising empire. Historians and socio-political analysts were quick to pin the unprecedented success of George Lucas's colourful, mythological space adventure on volatile world politics, economic instability, the Vietnam War, rising unemployment, the gloomy seriousness of the decade's previous cinematic efforts and the entire bleakness of existence.

It's all so depressing.

The politicians don't have a clue.

The military want to destroy us.

The lunatics are running the asylum; and the world could end at any moment.

A despondent public is desperately in need of pleasant, jolly diversions.

Then suddenly, along comes a perfectly-timed, joyous, escapist romp to cheer everybody up and take their minds off the world's insurmountable problems.

Of course the irony is that there is probably nothing coincidental about such timing at all.

It is always the right time.

Be it war, famine, economic meltdown, climate change, international terrorism or a global pandemic; whatever the decade, there will constantly be dismally frightening headlines, necessitating the need for something a little more frivolous and cheerful. Consequently, while a certain amount of lucky timing may indeed be a deciding factor in the success of any contemporary entertainment, it is likely that the work itself needs to have something far more substantial going for it than just 'right place, right time'; particularly when the popularity of that work transcends its own time and continues to endure well beyond the era in which it was born.

Inspired by Jack Tinker's *Daily Mail* review, 1960s music mogul Jonathan King was compelled to book tickets for the show's next performance. As he explained in his CD liner notes for a 1996 re-release of the first *Rocky Horror Show* cast album, 'There was nothing in the write-up to indicate this was a musical' – although one would have thought that the words 'Book, music and lyrics by Richard O'Brien' as well as references to Bill Haley and David Bowie might have been a slight clue – so the surprises began the moment the show commenced.

King recalled that he and a friend both, 'rocked with laughter and fell in love with the performance.' So much so in fact that he felt immediately obliged to go backstage and announce his desire to invest in the show and produce a recording. 'They gasped,' he remembered. 'It was unheard of for a play to make and release an LP until it had at least transferred to a real theatre.'

One critic's 1973 review of the resultant cast album – recorded, at the suggestion of Richard O'Brien, at John Sinclair's recently opened Sarm Studios – perceptively concluded, 'It was a pity Jonathan King didn't think of putting out an LP of the show recorded live on stage. Audience reaction is essential to a lot of the lyrics in *The Rocky Horror Show*'; intuitively prophetic words indeed, given the show's unexpectedly interactive future.

Thanks primarily to word of mouth, *Rocky* promptly became (to employ an over-used – but far too good to miss – cliché) 'the hottest ticket in town,' and, with the nine-strong cast elevated to celebrity status, quite literally overnight, and the initial three week run hastily extended to five, Michael White sought a suitable venue in which to re-house his unforeseen new hit for an extended engagement.

A couple of locations were briefly considered, including the Gaumont Cinema in Notting Hill Gate, where – according to Rayner Bourton's book – the cast had recently been cajoled by Jim Sharman into viewing a double feature of *Valley of the Dolls* and its satirical semi-sequel *Beyond the Valley of the Dolls* (purely in the name of character research of course). However, the insightful producer eventually decided to keep the production within the fashionably sophisticated Royal Borough of Kensington and Chelsea, and

2: YOU'RE THE PRODUCT OF ANOTHER TIME

settled on the Classic cinema at 148 King's Road. A derelict picture-house, scheduled to be unceremoniously demolished later in the year and situated just a few hundred yards from Sloane Square and the Royal Court Theatre, the Classic was an ideal choice for *Rocky*'s temporary new home.

With a suitable venue secured for the transfer, *The Rocky Horror Show*'s five-week engagement at the Royal Court's Theatre Upstairs was scheduled to end on 21 July 1973. However, thanks to what could best be described as a fundamental – although extremely painful – performer *cock-up*, the final Theatre Upstairs performance never actually took place.

It is an anecdote that, whenever he gets the chance, Rayner Bourton gleefully relates – in the most explicit and excruciatingly eye-watering detail – so much so that it has become widely acknowledged as the world's most famous 'glass splinters in the bell-end' story. (Well, be honest, how many others spring readily to mind?) With Mick Jagger already ensconced in the auditorium, and more than a buzz of excitement backstage, tormented moans of anguish, emanating from the not-so-little boys' room, alerted the company to a rather unique and unfortunate problem. A quantity of the theatrical glitter, in those days made from crushed glass (gentlemen, you may want to stop reading here and skip to the next paragraph), which Rayner used to give Rocky's body beautiful its alluring sparkle, had mischievously found its way into his shorts during the previous evening's performance. Unbeknownst to the actor at the time, his hasty post-show shower had failed to remove these razor-sharp shards, which had rapidly embedded themselves in his manhood and caused it to swell considerably (unfortunately not in a good way) overnight. It has often been chronicled that the offending particles had sneakily crept beneath the actor's foreskin, but whenever Rayner himself recounts the tale – usually with a glint in his eye as he no doubt observes his male spectators simultaneously crossing their legs and wincing in empathetic agony – he often states that he is circumcised; and, let's face it, apart from a plethora of nubile blonde female groupies (who seem to liberally pepper his published *Rocky* memoir), he should know his personal equipment better than anyone. The minuscule grains of broken glass had actually entrenched themselves inside the actor's excruciatingly enlarged penis, now oozing blood and pus profusely as it became nastily infected.

Legend has it that Little Nell, desperate for the show to go on – particularly with a rock god of Jagger's stature in the audience – offered to play Rocky; not really a practical option, especially with no time available to adapt the script accordingly. It was therefore decided that, with Rocky Horror himself unarguably incapacitated – although receiving very little sympathy from an enraged cast and director, not to mention Harriet Cruickshank who, as house manager of the Theatre Upstairs, was obliged to break the news to the disappointed audience – the evening's performance would, regrettably, have to be cancelled.

Had Nell actually gone on as Rocky, enquired David Evans in his co-authored (with Scott Michaels) 2002 book *Rocky Horror: From Concept to Cult*, with the low budget production having no understudies at the time, who would have played Columbia that night? 'They'd have just cut Nell, easily cut Nell,' Rayner replied flippantly; meaning the character she played of course, not the actress herself. 'Don't forget, she was only ever an appendage anyway.' This comes across as a rather harsh and unfair assessment, given that very few *Rocky Horror* fans would ever accept the suggestion that any of the show's characters is in any way less important or unessential to the story.

Thanks to a combination of an extremely painful penis lancing (a medical first, according to the doctor who administered it); prescribed tablets of pethidine – a strong painkiller, which induced memorably metaphysical out-of-body experiences – and good old-fashioned sleep, Rocky would be fully recovered and ready to take his rightful place upon Frank-n-Furter's laboratory slab when the show opened at the Chelsea Classic on 14 August 1973.

With only one production taking place on the premises, the band's booming acoustics would no longer be the issue they had been at the Royal Court. Therefore, earlier performance times – and even two shows a night – suddenly became feasible.

Michael White was keen to run the show on Sunday evenings, giving the cast Mondays and Tuesdays off, and actually released a number of early press ads to this effect. As Rayner Bourton explained in his book, however, this plan was swiftly compromised when actors' union Equity demanded White pay everyone in the company double time for working on a Sunday; an expense the producer was unable to justify. 'With Michael accepting defeat on the issue of Sunday performances,' recalled Bourton, 'our new contracts were for eight shows a week, Monday to Thursday at 9.00 pm, Friday and Saturday at 8.00 pm and 10.00 pm, no performance Sunday, with everyone being on the going West End rate of £60 a week, although I do believe Tim Curry was on £65 a week.' With this pay increase – a massive leap from the basic rate of £18 a week at the Royal Court – the original cast of *The Rocky Horror Show* signed lucrative one-year contracts.

Well, most of them did. There were in fact two notable exceptions.

Eager to become established as a serious actor, Bourton had already decided to return to the Citizens Theatre in Glasgow – where, earlier in the year, he had enjoyed a particularly agreeable repertory season – and, despite much persuasive wrangling by Michael White, could not be convinced to remain with *Rocky Horror* in the King's Road for any longer than a further seven weeks. Meanwhile, director Tony Richardson's high-

2: YOU'RE THE PRODUCT OF ANOTHER TIME

profile production of William Shakespeare's *Antony and Cleopatra* was scheduled to open at the Bankside Globe Playhouse on 9 August, with Julie Covington in the role of Charmian. Even though this contract – which had been agreed prior to her accepting the planned three week run of *Rocky* at the Theatre Upstairs – was unaffected by the show's unexpected two-week extension, it would be impossible for Covington to stay with the production for its King's Road transfer.

'Julie was pre-contracted to do *Antony and Cleopatra* on the South Bank, so they had to find a replacement quickly,' recalls Belinda Sinclair – one of two former *Hair* cast members brought to the attention of Jim Sharman by *The Rocky Horror Show*'s author – who, having been present at a certain party in Maida Vale on the very night that the idea for the show was first conceived, was, in the eyes of many, already a member of the original *Rocky* family. 'Richard suggested me and Elaine Paige. Jim Sharman auditioned both of us and I got it. I'm proud that I beat Elaine to a role. We re-rehearsed the show between the Pheasantry and the Classic in the King's Road, and some more money got put into the show, and I opened in the role of Janet at the Classic. It was amazing at the time; I remember one night we had Mick Jagger, David Bowie and Claire Bloom all together in the communal dressing room.'

It could be argued that Sinclair – who immediately made the part her own – actually better suited the role of Janet Weiss than the actress who had created it. Unlike Sandy in the musical *Grease*, Janet's transformation from seemingly squeaky clean, prim and proper mama's girl to man-eating sex kitten should not be played as a sudden illogical change of character for the sake of cheap laughs or an easy shock. Depending on the actress's talent and understanding of the role, Janet's repressed sexuality ought to be subtly perceptible throughout, slowly bubbling beneath the surface, ready to explode like a pressure cooker once encouraged. As Frank throws off his cloak to expose lacy black lingerie and a brazenly hedonistic outlook on life, Janet Weiss is in a state of alarm, astonishment and unexpected arousal. By the time Rocky's flawlessly formed physique is revealed to the world, this wholesome American girl's virginal white panties are practically sopping wet and steaming hot.

Despite her strong acting ability and incredible singing voice, Julie Covington gave the impression of a naturally demure person, possibly not fully at ease with the skimpy outfits or the show's shamelessly adult themes. Belinda Sinclair, on the other hand, appeared to have no such reservations. Even with a naive, pubescent schoolgirl look – complete with painted facial freckles and her hair in cute little bunches – the feeling that a sultry, sleazy, predatory nymphomaniac might be burgeoning beneath that innocent facade was ever apparent.

Even now, Sinclair is amusingly and light-heartedly open about one of her fondest memories of appearing in the production: 'Having Tim Curry on top of me was pretty damned good,' she giggles, with more than a hint of Janet's coquettish wickedness, 'Tim was unique. He had this incredible sexual magnetism. [He] was suggestive but coy with it, so that both men and women fell for him. He was absolutely fabulous in the role and everyone adored him. I had a crush on him for two years. Once he took me to see the *Snow White* cartoon at the Hammersmith Odeon, and we even held hands. I was willing him to get closer, but after a nightcap I just got a taxi home.'

Despite the show's future status as a *bona fide* theatrical milestone, Sinclair is quick to point out that being cast in *Rocky Horror* was at the time not nearly as thrilling as being in another recent landmark musical: 'It felt like we were just doing a job, to be honest. I didn't feel particularly lucky to be in it. I was young and took everything in my stride. Sometimes we didn't get a full house, so it didn't feel anywhere near as special as being in *Hair*, which was iconic and groundbreaking. But *Rocky* didn't feel like that. The audiences were pretty stiff; the Ushers spooked everyone out before the show. The show looked like it had been thrown on, like the aliens had just fallen into what was going on.'

The look in question was entirely intentional of course. While the Chelsea Classic could seat around 270 people – a substantial increase on the Theatre Upstairs' meagre capacity of 63 – it had been decided that Brian Thomson's ingenious abandoned cinema concept fitted the show perfectly, demanding little in the way of change. In fact, given the nature of the building and its already determined fate, Thomson's shabby drapes – which now had the words 'Acme Demolition Co' stencilled across them; a reference to the fictional gadget company seen in Warner Bros' Looney Tunes, particularly their Wile E Coyote and Road Runner cartoons – and related signage would have a much more literal connotation at the Classic; and even though the earlier curtain meant that genuine ushers would this time be on hand to perform all the traditional front-of-house duties, the creepy pre-show Ghouls, by now considered an essential part of the show itself, would be retained.

While the sinister Ushers were never actually written into the libretto itself, actors would throw themselves wholeheartedly into these fun pre-show roles, delightedly chasing frightened women into the lavatories or standing perfectly still like statues, giving the appearance of weird masked mannequins, and then terrifying their next unsuspecting victim by suddenly 'coming to life' as they walked by. The shrieks of alarm elicited (from both men and women) by these disturbing dwellers of the dark became an acknowledged element of *Rocky*'s pre-show atmosphere. Individual recollections tend to differ of course, but some audience members from the time seem to recall that genuine mannequins were

2: YOU'RE THE PRODUCT OF ANOTHER TIME

employed as well, turning the proceedings into an entertaining game to try and spot which ones were the actual flesh and blood actors, although actress Clare Clifford – who would join the production as an understudy and backing vocalist later in the run – is quick to refute this theory:

'No mannequins,' she states, definitively, 'You're just standing stock still and then just suddenly move, and that was enough. I also remember some hiding in rows – empty rows of seats – as well, and then just sort of slowly appearing. And the shrieks of laughter and horror.'

'People want to be scared,' she suggests, 'Isn't that why horror films are the biggest genre across cultures?'

'There wasn't much briefing,' the actress confirms, elaborating on what she describes as an 'active interactive prologue' to the show: 'I think it was, "Put on a mask. Just scare people. Just go 'boo'." And I had a ball. I remember someone fled the cinema because I'd been sitting very, very still, and then suddenly moved. I discovered I was quite good at being a statue, and then all you had to do was turn your head. This woman left and refused to come back. It was a challenge, and we certainly didn't take it lightly. It was about setting the tone, bringing the audience into that space, shutting off whatever they were doing. Remember, there were no people looking at their mobiles back then. The act of going to a theatre back then was like you gave yourself up, and we were there to take them captive and get them ready for the show.'

This practice became as much fun for the actors as it was for the audience, as actor Perry Bedden cheerfully remembers: 'The audience didn't know if you were real or not. You'd stand in the shadows and move when you were sure you weren't being watched; then, if someone in the audience had been watching you, by the time they looked again you'd moved position, and that really spooked them.'

Whereas the overall look of the set would not be changed for the Classic transfer, however, the significantly larger playing area still required considerable expansion and adaptation. According to Rayner Bourton's book of *Rocky Horror* recollections, the tiny space at the Theatre Upstairs had in effect trapped the audience in place, making it impossible for them to leave once the performance commenced: 'Seated in two blocks either side of the ramp, they were confined on each side by the laboratory and freezer platforms, from the rear by the back wall and from the front by the stage. Effectively they had no escape.'

Talk about a captive audience.

This and Rayner's impressive acrobatics – swinging like Tarzan from the overhead scaffolding during the Narrator's dialogue break in 'The Sword of Damocles' – was no doubt the reason Jack Tinker's *Daily Mail* review noted that Jim Sharman's direction took the action 'round, up and over his audience.'

For *Rocky*'s transfer to the Classic, the central ramp was widened to the breadth of three seats, making it, in the words of Bourton, 'like an airport runway in comparison to what had gone before'; and, while the considerably larger centre stage screen still dominated the set – in compliance with Brian Thomson's simple yet inventive design – it now featured a curved ladder behind it, which could be lit to evoke a rainbow effect, most memorably during the dreamlike climactic crescendo of the song 'Superheroes'.

This effect, remembers Perry Bedden – who played Riff Raff a couple of years into the run (and appeared as a Transylvanian in the 1975 *Rocky Horror* film adaptation) – took a sizeable chunk of the production's still relatively shoestring budget: 'The most expensive thing in the production was the rainbow that slowly, colour by colour, lit up behind Brad and Janet as they climbed from opposite sides. The rainbow, which was no more than coloured light bulbs, came on during the "ahhs" before the Narrator's final piece.'

Bedden recalls another unforgettable effect, which was achieved without the need for expensive apparatus or complicated trickery: 'For Riff's piece in "Over at the Frankenstein Place", which is my favourite song in the show, I climbed a painter's ladder behind the screen. The ladder was painted black; so it wasn't visible from the audience. At the top of the ladder was a light box with a flap over it. For Riff's appearance, I pulled the flap, and the light shone onto my face from below. There was a green gel over the lamp, so my face was lit from below with a green light. The effect from the audience was of a disembodied head, floating about 15 feet in the air; simple and effective.'

As professional scaffolding erectors set about constructing the impressively bigger set, a fledgling company – later to become a leading supplier of theatrical lighting equipment in the UK – began the unenviable task of installing the extensive equipment required to illuminate the newly expanded production. 'Our heritage is in theatre,' White Light's official website now announces proudly. 'Our first job was the transfer of *The Rocky Horror Show* from the Royal Court Theatre to the King's Road Theatre; even now, we regularly supply productions of the show! We remain as happy to supply two lights to a school play or fringe production as we are to supply a complete West End lighting rig.'

Meanwhile, whereas budgetary constraints and technical limitations at the Theatre Upstairs had required the nine-strong ensemble to share a single microphone – often passing (or even throwing) it to another member of the cast mid-song (a necessity that somehow added to the show's base rock 'n' roll sensibilities) – the number of these handheld cable-mics would increase (initially to three) once the production transferred to a larger venue.

2: YOU'RE THE PRODUCT OF ANOTHER TIME

With the show attracting fervent critical and public acclaim, producer Michael White decided that, while Richard O'Brien's memorable cartoon programme cover was completely in keeping with the B-movie spirit of the piece, a more eye-catching, professionally-illustrated poster should be commissioned for *Rocky*'s engagement at the Classic. At his request, 31-year-old photorealist artist Michael English – who had previously designed an unused, overtly risqué poster for White's infamous production of *Oh! Calcutta!* – took a look at rehearsals for *Rocky Horror* to get a flavour of the show; and then airbrushed his now familiar face graphic onto a piece of ten-inch square card. A classic theatrical poster, without doubt as recognisable and iconic as *The Phantom of the Opera*'s red rose and white mask, English's open-mouthed androgynous visage – generally accepted to be that of Columbia, despite only a negligible resemblance to actress Little Nell – with its shocked, wide-eyed expression, slicked black hair and enormous hooped earrings, was to become the official poster phizog for most *Rocky Horror* productions throughout the 1970s and '80s. Supposedly, English intended the design to be in grainy black and white, in accordance with the cheap pulp comic book style he had in mind when he painted it, but White favoured a full colour version. Nevertheless, while colour posters did indeed adorn billboards throughout the city, the face was printed in black and white on press ads and programmes; and some black and white posters were eventually used (with the show's title and the parted lips gaudily printed in red to make them stand out), especially when the production transferred to the Comedy Theatre towards the end of its original London run in 1980.

More money to spend on wardrobe meant that Sue Blane could tweak and improve on her original shoestring costume designs. The embellishments included a suitably kitschy pair of sparkly silver trunks for Rocky to replace the plain briefs Rayner Bourton had purportedly worn for the five-week Theatre Upstairs run; while, for their 'Floorshow' entrance, the initially bare-chested Brad and Rocky could now be more modestly attired in front-laced corsets. Intimate apparel was not the only character change for Rocky though, as, according to his book, Rayner Bourton now decided to try a different voice for the show's titular Adonis. Having hitherto used his native Birmingham accent, which gave the mad doctor's creation a sweetly comic innocence, he decided to switch to a clichéd American surf-bum twang that emphasised the muscular hunk's characteristic vanity and was immediately approved by Jim Sharman.

Unlike at the Theatre Upstairs, when the show had, for the most part, been moulded and workshopped by Sharman and the cast during rehearsals – scenes constantly added, lines dropped and dialogue hastily scribbled down by hand – the actors at the Chelsea Classic found themselves presented with professionally-bound copies of an actual typed script. These impressive-looking documents seemed to be let down only by the words *The Rocker* [sic] *Horror Show* prominently presented on the front cover; possibly the only known example of a typographical error on a libretto's title page.

Furthermore, with a view to minimising the risk of cast indisposition – particularly with Rayner's painfully inconvenient glitter incident still fresh in everyone's minds – the increased budget allowed for the employment of understudies – one male, one female – who would also cover backing vocals as Ushers. Later productions (especially those of the '80s and early '90s) would utilise similar 'characters', though often excessively, almost making them principal parts in their own right and contentiously allowing them to hog the limelight. Jim Sharman's far more understated, and consequently more effective, approach was to suggest that these cadaverous creatures were in fact the cinema's phantom employees, economically assisting with backstage duties because of budgetary restrictions – even to the extent of 'becoming' scenery and props, standing in for the castle doors and the like – thus adding immeasurably to the cheap and tacky feel of the piece.

'I first met Richard O'Brien when we were both touring the UK in *Hair*,' recalls Ziggy Byfield, the artiste hired to understudy the show's male roles. 'I remember he was always doodling and writing, and I'm sure that he sketched out some initial ideas for *Rocky* in comic strip form in a big book. He used to write the songs and thoughts around them on big illustrated pages. That book would be worth a bit now. I think he lost it, or it got stolen.'

Born Trevor Byfield in Preston, Lancashire in 1943, the actor points out that his professional name was not, as some believe, a reference to a certain well-known alter-ego of David Bowie: 'No, it actually came from a guy who used to drive me. His name was Zeke, but I heard his wife on his radio calling him something. I thought it was Ziggy, but she was actually calling him Zekey.'

Byfield is also candid about how being cast in *Rocky Horror* salvaged him from the all too familiar pitfalls of a rock 'n' roll lifestyle, and full of heartfelt gratitude to Richard O'Brien for rescuing him from a very real abyss: 'My background was as a rock 'n' roll singer. I'd done cabaret and the usual stuff, and then, by some fluke, I got a part in *Hair*. After that I did *Jesus Christ Superstar* and *Mother Earth*; but I'd got addicted to drugs and was drinking heavily, so I was a bit of a mess and not really able to work. Richard actually saved my professional career by offering me a job as the first male understudy in *Rocky*. Thanks, Richard.'

According to Rayner Bourton's book, the honour of understudying Frank-n-Furter was originally reserved exclusively for the show's author. As a result, it was not long before the newly appointed understudy was

2: YOU'RE THE PRODUCT OF ANOTHER TIME

required to step into the breach and play one of the show's most prominent characters. 'As soon as I started I had to play Riff, because Tim had a sore throat, so Richard took over the role of Frank,' Byfield remembers clearly. Of his interpretation of the character – in many ways already defined by Richard O'Brien – he recounts, 'I always played him as Igor – i.e. the master's servant – but ... more dangerous than that. You had to give the impression that Riff always knew too much.'

Selected to cover the three principal female parts was yet another former *Hair* tribe member, Angela Bruce, a Yorkshire born actress in her early twenties, who would become a familiar face on British television in the 1980s and '90s with prominent supporting roles in episodes of popular series such as *Red Dwarf, Only Fools and Horses* and *Bad Girls*. The progeny of mixed parentage, a West Indian father and a white mother who had put her up for adoption at the age of three, the striking actress gave Magenta in particular the fitting appearance of a stunning dark-skinned Amazon, and the role became hers full time when, later in the year, Patricia Quinn left the production to play famed suffragette Christabel Pankhurst in BBC TV's *Shoulder to Shoulder*.

Bruce being the name of her much-loved adopted parents, her extremely brief biography in the *Rocky Horror* programme stated, rather intriguingly, 'Only Elvis Presley knows her real name.'

With Dr Everett Scott conspicuously the only major protagonist without a character-defining musical moment (even though actor Paddy O'Hagan performed 'Hot Patootie' as Eddie) and with the show still running at only around 80 minutes, Richard O'Brien added another song to the score for the production's transfer. Although not included on the original cast album, 'Eddie' (aka 'Eddie's Teddy') – a bouncy rock number, with more than a hint of gospel, in which the mysterious scientist laments his tragic juvenile delinquent nephew – was recorded and released as the B-side of one of several singles by Kimi and Ritz; a vocal duo comprising O'Brien and his wife Kimi Wong.

The inside cover of Ziggy Byfield's copy of the *Rocky Horror* script still includes his own unfinished handwritten lyrics for this song. Unfinished because, as the actor recalls, while he was actually writing out the words, somebody came into the rehearsal room waving typewritten copies for everybody, making it no longer necessary for him to finish transcribing the number by hand.

With the addition of 'Eddie' (aka 'Eddie's Teddy') the complete list of the show's songs – as well as the order in which they were originally performed – was as follows:

- 'Science Fiction Double Feature'
- 'Damn it. Janet' (aka 'Dammit Janet' and 'Wedding Song')

- 'Over at the Frankenstein Place'
- 'Sweet Transvestite'
- 'The Time Warp'
- 'The Sword of Damocles'
- 'I Can Make You a Man' (aka 'Charles Atlas Song')
- 'Hot Patootie – Bless My Soul' (aka 'Whatever Happened to Saturday Night')
- 'I Can Make You a Man: Reprise' (aka 'Charles Atlas Song: Reprise')
- 'Touch-a Touch-a Touch-a Touch me'
- 'Once in a While'
- 'Eddie' (aka 'Eddie's Teddy')
- 'Wise Up Janet Weiss' (aka 'Planet Schmanet Janet')
- 'Rose Tint My World' (aka 'The Floorshow')
- 'I'm Going Home'
- 'Superheroes'
- 'Science Fiction Double Feature: Reprise'

Byfield's preserved copy of the first typed version of the libretto also reveals how dialogue and even character names were continually evolving at an early stage. The name of the (not seen on stage) newly married high school friend of Brad and Janet is typed as 'Frank Hapschatt' but has 'Ralph Hapschatt' handwritten over the top, as it was felt that 'Ralph' sounded more of a stereotypical American class president type, and also that 'Frank Hapschatt' might be confused with 'Frank-n-Furter'.

One thing that did not change when the show transferred was the enthusiasm with which critics praised the production and its performances. '*Rocky Horror* is a lewd and lovable show, reeking with grume, gunpowder and gusset,' raved Barry Humphries for *Punch* magazine, 'and the laughter flows with haemophiliac abundance.' One of *Rocky*'s earliest and keenest supporters, Humphries also declared, 'The musical theatre is now surely the richer for Mr Curry's phantom fellatrix.'

'Tim's performance was fearless,' director Jim Sharman would later affirm in his 2008 published memoir, 'He was the man every woman wanted to be, and the woman every man wanted to be – or secretly wanted. A remarkable and inventive actor and singer with the swagger of a rock star.'

Not everybody got the sophisticated depths of O'Brien's and Sharman's smutty send-up though, as Belinda Sinclair poignantly recalls: 'I always remember wanting my dad to love the show,' she proclaims sadly. 'He came to see me in it, and walked out. When I asked him why, he simply said, "Once you've seen the man in stockings, that's it; you've seen the whole joke."'

2: YOU'RE THE PRODUCT OF ANOTHER TIME

As *Rocky* continued to prove a word-of-mouth juggernaut, the stars of London's numerous West End productions – among them such luminaries as Angela Lansbury and Lauren Bacall – were anxious to see for themselves what all the fuss was about. Consequently, the producers organised two midnight matinees, exclusively for those unable to make it to a regular performance because of their nightly commitments to other shows (proof of which was required when booking tickets, which promptly sold out).

In his book, Rayner Bourton joyfully recollected, 'Performing those two midnight pro matinees so early in the run firmly established us as being London's number one show, and we, the cast, were established as being London's number one cast, placing us firmly on the theatrical celebrity "A" list.'

A much more solemn affair was the midnight benefit performance for Roy Truman, a 32-year-old part-time technician who had been blinded in one eye and left partially deaf when an explosive effect (known in the theatre world as a maroon) – used to signify the climactic return of Riff Raff and Magenta to their home planet – had detonated prematurely.

In 1972, paramilitary faction the Provisional IRA (Irish Republican Army) had conducted its first offensive operation on the British mainland. With the intention of ending British rule in Northern Ireland, the organisation's prolonged violent and bloody campaign would continue for the next two and a half decades, and the possibility of busy public meeting places such as theatres being attacked was an ever-present danger. As a consequence, it was certainly not difficult to accept that London's trendiest show – currently residing on London's trendiest street – would be a potential bombing target, and several telephoned warnings were made during *Rocky*'s engagement at the Chelsea Classic. As much as loss of life, the objectives of such action are to cause maximum disruption to public order, generate self-publicity and cause feelings of panic and unease. Most often this is achieved satisfactorily because any bomb threat (including all suspected hoaxes) has to be treated seriously and investigated accordingly. Therefore, on three known occasions, the denizens of the Classic – staff, audience and cast alike – found themselves hastily evacuated into the street, while appropriate counter measures were taken.

The British, with their famed stubbornness, dogged determination and stiff upper-lip mentality, not to mention something of a characteristic apathy, have never been a race to allow their spirits to be easily dampened or their morale broken. Consequently, as Rayner Bourton recalled in his book, the evacuees, including the scantily-clad actors, soon decided – at the suggestion of Ziggy Byfield – to temporarily relocate to a nearby pub and make the most of this minor inconvenience; whilst presuming, quite rightly, that should the theatre be razed to the ground by a colossal explosion or, as was the actual outcome, the sniffer dogs find nothing (thus allowing the evening's performance to continue after all), they would all soon hear about it one way or another.

Thus, the prospect of a large destructive incendiary device ticking away in their place of employment had indeed caused the desired disruption and publicity, but nothing even remotely approaching panic.

Another memory of such an occurrence, this time from Paddy O'Hagan, was revealed in Jim Whittaker's 1998 book *Cosmic Light: The Birth of a Cult Classic*. In O'Hagan's account, while a highly trained anti-terrorist unit presumably searched the theatre for alleged explosives, and the performers once again found themselves shivering on the King's Road pavement on a breezy late summer evening – most probably before someone again recommended the pub as a convivial sanctuary of warm refuge and welcome refreshment – a passing old lady expressed her disgust at Tim Curry's sleazy attire. To which, her equally disgruntled companion apparently sneered the addition, 'Well, I'm not surprised. I mean, if she looks like that, it's no surprise she's not getting any trade.' It is the kind of hilarious anecdote that, while containing all the hallmarks of a classic urban myth, one desperately hopes is true.

Indeed, wonderful anecdotes such as this – unquestionably worthy of time-capsule immortality – help put everything that *The Rocky Horror Show* ultimately spawned into perspective. Little over a decade later, provincial streets would become awash with half naked theatregoers, temporarily giving even the most conservative urban area the dubious appearance of a bustling, squalid red-light district, while, ironically, raising very few eyebrows and rarely upsetting little old ladies. Without such retrospective knowledge, it might be difficult for today's jaded and increasingly desensitised youth to believe that an actor bedecked in Frank-n-Furter's traditional tacky regalia could have possessed the power to astonish or offend. As Bob Dylan had prophetically declared in 1964, 'The times they are a-changing.'

In 1973, however, *Rocky*'s journey from cutting edge, avant-garde entertainment to mainstream theatrical establishment was only just beginning, and no sooner had the production settled into the Classic than the 'Acme Demolition Co' again necessitated a speedy relocation. Okay, maybe it wasn't actually Acme, but certainly somebody's wrecking ball was poised, like the rogue planet Bellus in George Pal's *When Worlds Collide*, to obliterate *Rocky*'s existence, reduce the building to rubble and force the hippest show in town to find another new residence.

Having been aware of the Classic's impending demolition since before the show had even opened there, Michael White, *Rocky*'s cunning and ever-resourceful producer, hastily secured another abandoned cinema, the 400-seat Essoldo at 279 King's Road, in which to continue the run for an

2: YOU'RE THE PRODUCT OF ANOTHER TIME

indefinite period.

Actor Jay Benedict, hired as male understudy when Ziggy Byfield was promoted to a principal role during the run, remembers that not only was the building aesthetically fitting in its capacity as a genuine decaying movie house, but it was also a perfect home for *Rocky Horror* because of its somewhat macabre history. As Benedict explains, one day, as he was practising to walk in high heels at his apartment on Tite Street: 'Weatherly – the family retainer, who'd never done a day's cleaning in his life – came unexpectedly into my room with a broom; and, without batting an eyelid when I told him what I was doing, said, "Oh yes, I remember the Essoldo all right. That's where they used to keep the dead bodies during the war." The Essoldo had been a cinema, was then a theatre, and now in 2008 it's once more a cinema; but during World War II it was a temporary morgue.' Perhaps the spirits of the Usherette's favourite movie stars would no longer be the only ghosts watching over *The Rocky Horror Show* as it continued its inexorable voyage through the King's Road's dilapidated picture palaces.

And so, when Chelsea's Classic cinema, *Rocky*'s faithful second home, was at last pummelled into particles of pulverised powder, the show itself, like Victor Frankenstein's indestructible creature, lived on. The last performance at the Classic was on Saturday 20 October 1973, but the first at the Essoldo (renamed the King's Road Theatre shortly thereafter), planned for just over a week later on Monday 29 October, had to be postponed when the Greater London Council's performing licence failed to come through in time; a behaviour it seemed they were in the habit of, as purportedly their licence for the Classic had arrived just two hours before curtain up on opening night. Finally, on the evening of Saturday 3 November 1973, *The Rocky Horror Show* opened at its third venue in less than five months.

With the show originally booked for a mere three-week run at the Theatre Upstairs – with its subsequent transfers and extensions surprising most of those involved – its short-sighted producers had not secured anyone to manage its rather important costumes. Tim Curry and Yasmin Pettigrew were, at the time, sharing accommodation with Peter Straker – a mutual friend who had been in both the London and Norwegian productions of *Hair*. Interestingly, for the purposes of this story, the Jamaican-born Straker – an already acclaimed singer and stage performer – would later play Frank-n-Furter in a regional UK production of *The Rocky Horror Show* in 1983. Whilst employed as Lauren Bacall's dresser for the West End production of *Applause*, a hit Broadway musical reworking of the acclaimed Oscar-winning 1950 Bette Davis film *All About Eve* (itself based on a short story by Mary Orr), at the Talk of the Town – a cabaret venue situated at London's converted Hippodrome theatre – Pettigrew was asked by Tim Curry to take on the crucial task of maintaining *Rocky*'s costumes:

'Tim and I had been put up in Straker's flat, and Tim knew I could manage a wardrobe,' she proclaims merrily, 'I did their washing in the afternoon, then went off to my regular job with Bacall in the evening.' For *Rocky*'s latest transfer (from the Classic to the Essoldo), Pettigrew found herself officially listed under the programme's stage management credits as Wardrobe Mistress: 'There was only one set of underwear, so it had to be washed every day,' she confirms, further underlining the shoestring nature of the show's inaugural production, 'In fact everything was a one-off, and lots borrowed and old, requiring lots of daily care.'

Due to their very nature of being close to the cast and their most intimate apparel, a laundress might encounter the occasional delicate situation, and Pettigrew recalls one of the show's actresses approaching her with a rather embarrassing problem: 'She'd found little things crawling in her underwear. It turned out that she'd caught crabs from another cast member. Obviously, they'd been intimate.'

This forthright openness is typical, and Pettigrew's memories from the three and a half years she remained with the production are numerous and enlightening, perfectly illustrating both the sex, drugs and rock 'n' roll core of the show and the care-free era in which it was born:

'I remember after the show had opened at the Essoldo – which by then was the King's Road Theatre – Michael White sent loads of booze in for us after the second show on the first Saturday we were there. The band started playing and we ended up having a great party. There was also a funny moment once when the Company Manager had been trying to clamp down on dope smoking. He put loads of 'No Smoking' signs up around the place and said he wanted to speak to us all in the dressing room. So, everyone was there waiting for him and, when he arrived, he walked in – expecting to give us all a bit of a lecture – but he found Michael White sitting cross-legged on the floor of the dressing room, smoking a big spliff, surrounded by the cast. He could hardly lay the law down after that.'

'I also remember helping to hide the dope from this guy who used to visit the theatre. He searched high and low for it, but never found it. I'd sewn it into the hem of the stage curtain. Back and forth nightly it went,' Yasmin continues, cheerily, also revealing a little naughtiness of her own during the famously hot British summer of 1976:

'Caroline Noh [Magenta] and I used to get up onto the roof of the King's Road Theatre and sunbathe naked,' she confesses freely, 'If only the boys in the cast and crew had known about that.'

Actress Clare Clifford – one of the King's Road production's hard-working understudies and backing vocalists – vividly recalls the first time she saw the show at the Theatre Upstairs in 1973:

2: YOU'RE THE PRODUCT OF ANOTHER TIME

'Patricia [Quinn] came out as the Ushherette, in the pink costume, pulled off the veil, and I just remember sitting there, literally thinking, "Well that's one part I won't have to worry about ever playing."'

'It was just so out of my orbit at that time.' However, after auditioning at the King's Road Theatre in late 1974, the actress soon found herself covering that very role.

'I went in as chorus with Jay [Benedict], and understudying Magenta,' she explains, 'And then, not long after that – I suppose late January or February maybe – Anna Nicholas did her back in, and so I did three, nearly four, weeks as Magenta in the spring of '75.'

Due to another unforeseen indisposition – that of actress Linda Dobell – shortly thereafter, the routinely uncertain nature of an understudy's role would see Clifford unexpectedly stepping into Columbia's tap shoes, a situation for which she was initially quite unprepared.

'They rang me up in the morning at 10.00 am, unusually early for *Rocky*. They said, "Linda's off, so for the 7.30 show you're doing Columbia and then you're going back to do Magenta for the 9.30." And I said, "But I haven't rehearsed Columbia." And they said, "Yeah, I know; that's why I'm ringing you now to come in for 11.00."'

As any actor who has been in this all too familiar situation would no doubt confirm, this level of sudden 'seat-of-the-pants' flexibility is to be expected in the precarious world of an understudy or Swing.

'I'm not the greatest tap-dancer,' Clifford admits, 'My head does not connect to my feet. Nevertheless, somehow we made it. A bonkers night.'

'But yeah, I got the benefit of a few hours' rehearsal.'

As if to further highlight the hands-on nature of the production, the actress also points out that her role within the company continued backstage too: 'Part of my duties in the show was bandaging up Rocky and helping Yasmin Pettigrew as Wardrobe Mistress,' she smiles, 'She's been a friend now for fifty years, ever since.'

Shortly before she had been cast in *The Rocky Horror Show* in the King's Road, Clare had begun a series of auditions for *Angels*, a forthcoming BBC medical drama centred around a group of student nurses. This show would become a hit – eventually running for nine series and a total of 220 episodes between 1975 and 1983 – and, amongst its young ensemble, would also feature former *Rocky Horror* cast member Angela Bruce in one of her earliest TV roles.

'I had three meetings about that,' declares Clifford, recalling the programme's quite lengthy audition process, 'And then I heard that I'd got it the day before my birthday in February, and was told that I would be starting in May. The female BBC booker, with whom I had to negotiate because I had no agent, was incredibly rude, and when I very nervously asked for £10 more than the minimum salary she was offering, she said,

"Who do you think you are? We've picked you out of the gutter for this part." That was my introduction to the wonderful world of telly.'

Despite the opportunities that such a role in a major BBC TV series would open up, the actress is wistfully honest about the bittersweet feelings she felt at the time:

'I was sort of distraught because I didn't want to leave *Rocky*. Hardly surprising really,' she confesses, 'We started rehearsing *Angels*, and I was going, "I don't want to go, I don't want to go,"; and everyone was saying, "Clare, you've just landed a television series, don't be so absolutely stupid."'

Despite Richard O'Brien's narrative touching on such sombre themes as gender confusion, seduction, murder, betrayal and man playing God, the show's tongue-in-cheek tone and refusal to take itself seriously undoubtedly played a significant part in its popularity; and this playful irreverence was often reflected by the mischievous behaviour of the company. Derek Griffiths, who joined the five-piece *Rocky Horror Show* band at the King's Road Theatre in September 1976, taking over from the show's original electric and acoustic guitarist Ian (The Count) Blair, fondly recalls some of the blatant shenanigans: 'You'd never get bored because there was always something going on. The cast were always fun; Columbia came over to the band one night and pulled down (saxophone player) Geoff Driscoll's trousers while he was playing. Another night, just for fun, I played the intro to "Time Warp" on a banjo. It didn't put Riff Raff off though –we had more respect for the show than that – but we did have a good laugh.'

Griffiths openly confesses his good-humoured attempts to make performers laugh during songs: 'We used to try to make the cast corpse,' he chuckles. 'One time when Ziggy sang "Whatever happened to Fay Wray?" we changed key just before the word "Fay," just to annoy him. The good thing was that there was never an overbearing MD or fixer.'

A professional freelance session musician, Griffiths not only stayed with *The Rocky Horror Show* until the end of its run in the King's Road and ensuing transfer to the Comedy Theatre in 1979, but also returned for its high-profile West End revival a decade later (more of that to come), as well as subsequent UK and European tours. A *Rocky* veteran in every sense, he is humorously unambiguous about which was his favourite part of the original production and why: 'Definitely the fuck scene,' he declares, alluding to Frank-n-Furter's prolonged seduction of Janet and Brad, the script's longest section without a musical number, 'because it meant that Geoff Driscoll and I had time to sprint down to the Cross Keys pub and down a pint before coming back. The landlady there was a very Chelsea type, probably been to Roedean, and she always had our pints waiting for us.'

2: YOU'RE THE PRODUCT OF ANOTHER TIME

With a reference to the band's position at the King's Road venue, 'Stage left, about a quarter of the way down the auditorium, up behind some drapes,' Griffiths describes how he and his thirsty colleague made their regular mid-show dash in search of precious alcoholic stimulation: 'We could get from our seats, round the back of the screen on stage and down the walkway behind the drapes on the left-hand side of the auditorium, out of the doors and into the lobby, then race down the street to the pub. We could then be back in our places in time for the next number.'

By the time the production transferred again the practice had obviously become something of a tradition; a tradition that the boys were not keen to renounce. 'We made it our business to sort out the nearest decent local to where we were playing,' Griffiths admits. 'When we were at the Comedy, we'd go to The George in Brewer Street or the Tom Crib pub in Panton Street. At the time, I had a Cocker Spaniel who used to sit by my side when I was playing and then come to the pub with me and Geoff when we snuck out. The landlord always used to have our beers ready and also some chipolata sausages for my dog; he'd made them into the shape of a dog, using cocktail sticks to keep them together.'

Ziggy Byfield also recalls such playful tomfoolery being enjoyed by the company, in addition to his understandably unreserved response to the band's aforementioned deliberate key change in the middle of a song. 'I remember looking over at them and giving them the middle finger,' he laughs. 'Overall though it was a fantastic team. We were a bunch of ragamuffins, all helping to put it together. We didn't realise that it would become a worldwide cult.'

Corroborating the cast camaraderie recalled warmly by others, the actor attests: 'Ninety percent of those who joined the cast were great people; there were no prima donnas there.

'We had two dressing rooms, a big one and a small one, so we all mucked in; it was like a party every night. We were all pros; we all worked hard to make it a good show. I was evangelical about the philosophy of *Hair* – i.e. work hard and mean it. You should never complain about the audience and the only time you don't appear is when they carry you out in a box.'

Everybody involved with *The Rocky Horror Show* at the King's Road has their personal memories about what made it so special, not least the sense of family experienced by its close-knit ensemble of players.

'As a cast we all mucked in,' recalls Jay Benedict. 'There was one dressing room with one long mirror and we all shared that. It was a unique atmosphere. Also, what was appealing for the cast at the time was the fact that it ran for 90 minutes with no break, which meant time in the pub and parties afterwards. We used to go to the Roebuck and Water Rat pubs; it was party time every night.

'Playing Eddie was great fun. There are a lot of words in "Hot Patootie"; it was a bit like the one hundred yards dash. You just had to throw yourself into it, and do a lot with your diaphragm. Breathing is the key. I came out of the freezer every night, climbed down the fire escape-type stairs, rushed to centre stage, grabbed the mic, sang the song, was chased back upstairs by Frank and stabbed through the heart with the mic stand.'

As Benedict reveals, this murderous moment would allow the actor playing Frank-n-Furter a rare opportunity to deviate slightly from the scripted dialogue, by inserting his own variations of the mad doctor's post-homicide quip: 'Then he slammed the fridge door shut down on my head, and turned to the audience with, "One from the vaults," or on some nights, "A rave from the grave." I used to love trying to guess which line Frank would use after he'd despatched Eddie. Would it be "A greaser from the freezer," "A rocker from the locker," or "A blast from the past"? It changed every night.'

Given the profusion of skimpy knickers and lace corsetry on display, it is probably no great revelation that the production enjoyed more than its share of embarrassing wardrobe malfunctions, even in the early days; one of which remains eternally imprinted in Derek Griffiths' memory: 'I'll never ever forget the night when Brad was stripped down to his underwear by Magenta and Columbia, and he stood there with one bollock hanging out of his Y-fronts. The band and the audience were peeing themselves, and poor old Brad didn't know why.'

Another comically awkward costume gaffe – this time involving Perry Bedden – not only underscored the show's rock gig associations, but resulted in one jubilant audience member being on the receiving end of a very special rock 'n' roll memento, undoubtedly the *Rocky Horror* equivalent of being thrown one of Elvis Presley's iconic silk scarves, as the actor elaborates: 'I had a quick costume change from Riff as manservant to Riff as spaceman. I walked down the side passage – behind the Acme Demolition Co drapes – from backstage to the point where Riff makes his entrance from a black velvet curtain on to the catwalk. I was carrying the space gun, which was made by the designer Andrew Logan, mostly out of broken mirrored glass, and which was very heavy. I made my entrance singing "Frank-n-Furter, it's all over ..." and I felt that something wasn't quite right with my costume. It turned out that the elastic had broken on my suspender belt and, as I walked down the catwalk – which by this time had been moved from the centre of the auditorium to the side – my fishnets slipped down around my ankles. The rest of the cast and the audience were all laughing; so I ripped them off and threw them and the suspender belt into the audience to awaiting outstretched hands.'

The Cavern, the celebrated Liverpool nightclub famous for having

2: YOU'RE THE PRODUCT OF ANOTHER TIME

cultivated the Beatles as well as numerous other successful British recording artists during the 1960s, had gone into receivership in May 1973; but, as Bedden's story helps to confirm, even as that legendary venue was being demolished the following month, its legacy of revolutionary rock 'n' roll madness was being reborn in, of all places, the cramped 63-seat loft of an unassuming Chelsea playhouse; an interesting, and rarely acknowledged, appendix in the history of rock music.

Having endured an uncomfortably long overnight flight from Los Angeles to London in January 1974, American record producer Lou Adler wanted nothing more than to crawl into bed and sleep off the unavoidable jet-lag; jet-lag no doubt exacerbated by the sleeping pills he had taken in order to relax for the duration of the journey; a plan well and truly scuppered by the subsequent announcement of a six hour flight delay. To his dismay, however, his then partner (and mother to their infant son), actress Britt Ekland, had tickets for that evening's performance of a rock 'n' roll musical that she said had been wowing London's theatre crowds. Ekland – who, a few months earlier, had made her own significant mark on the world of British horror cinema with her appearance (and unforgettable nude scene) in *The Wicker Man* (1973) – had seen *The Rocky Horror Show* several times already and was keen to share the experience with her partner.

Inevitably, the show had much the same impact on Adler as it had had on Ekland, and in his booklet notes for *The Rocky Horror Picture Show*'s fifteenth anniversary soundtrack box set in 1990, the producer concisely and effectively expressed his emotions at experiencing *Rocky* for the first time: 'No sleep!! Jet-lag!! BAM!!! *The Rocky Horror Show*. It cut like a knife. From the first moment I entered the theatre, cob-webs, flash-lights, white-faced Ushers and the opening chord of "Science Fiction", I had the feeling you get when you see or hear something very special for the first time.'

At the time, the Chicago-born impresario seemed somehow to be tapping into cynical youth trends, which, thanks to the likes of the Vietnam War and race-related civil disorder, were beginning to grow from the impracticable idealism of the dissipating hippie era. In 1967, he had presented the Monterey International Pop Festival – which pre-dated the legendary Woodstock by two years – and the tie-in movie version (released the following March). He also managed cult stoner comedy double act Cheech and Chong and '60s pop duo Jan and Dean. It therefore seemed fitting that the man who produced the Mamas & the Papas, Sam Cooke and Monterey Pop should take this groundbreaking pastiche of deliberately clichéd rock conventions on to the next stage of its incredible journey. Allegedly, a number of top producers were by now vying for the show's worldwide rights; but a chance meeting with Michael White, at a party thrown by a mutual friend a couple of nights later, allowed Adler swiftly to strike a deal that would take *The Rocky Horror Show* to the United States.

'So thank you Britt, and I guess thank you British Airways for the delay,' Adler's 1990 box set notes concluded. 'Because Richard O'Brien, not Tim Curry, played the lead that night and I didn't even notice how skinny his legs were in high heels. And that must have been jet-lag.'

Along with a small consortium of producers and promoters, Adler had recently taken over the Largo, a former burlesque club situated at 9009 W Sunset Boulevard in Hollywood, and re-opened it on 23 September 1973 as a 500-seat theatre-cum-nightclub called the Roxy. With the Roxy facing stiff competition from a plethora of local clubs and discotheques – which were fast becoming commonplace as the mid-'70s disco boom took hold – Adler at once saw the potential for *Rocky Horror* to provide his venue with a definite quirky edge. Authentic rock 'n' roll theatre.

While the show's understated satire had been an instant winner with London's sophisticated, culture-drenched theatregoers, the American production was given a flashy and extravagant make-over to appeal to the swanky, fast-living LA crowds. This included 'rocking up' some of the musical arrangements; giving 'Sweet Transvestite' an attention-grabbing brass-heavy intro; speeding up 'The Time Warp' from the medium rock beat of the London production; giving the Usherette, now christened Trixie for American audiences, a much more upbeat, effervescent and ostentatious persona than the starry-eyed, dreamy nostalgia of Patricia Quinn's interpretation; and adding a few layers of Hollywood glitz and glamour. A little bit of polish and shine.

Aside from seasoned film and television actor Graham Jarvis, who was hired to play the Narrator, and Tim Curry, whose performance it was decided would be essential to the show's US success, the Los Angeles cast of *The Rocky Horror Show* was made up of eager youngsters. After an intense two-week audition period, Jamie Donnelly – who would later be known to cinemagoers as Jan in the 1978 movie version of *Grease* (having previously played the role on Broadway) – and Boni Enton were cast as Usherette (aka Trixie)/Magenta and Columbia respectively. In the role of Brad Majors was a fresh-faced TV actor called Bill Miller, billed as B Miller to distinguish him from another actor with the same name, while a husky-voiced, experienced brunette singer by the name of Abigail Haness became his willingly corruptible fiancée Janet Weiss, for whom Sue Blane designed an appealing, light-coloured '60s-style dress with a mid-thigh length skirt, which would be developed further as a smart mauve two-piece for the film version. Unlike Christopher Malcolm's original Brad, Bill Miller did not wear glasses for the role – it was not, after all, a scripted requirement for the character – although Barry Bostwick's bespectacled jock look in the subsequent movie adaptation would become fairly definitive and set the

2: YOU'RE THE PRODUCT OF ANOTHER TIME

tradition for most future stage Brads.

As Rocky Horror himself, 23-year-old Kim Milford, a statuesque, long-haired actor with an athletic Grecian god-like build of which Rayner Bourton could merely have dreamed, was the perfect embodiment of Frank-n-Furter's man-made Adonis; while an as-yet unknown Meat Loaf – a best-selling rock album entitled *Bat Out of Hell* would make him a household name just four years later – secured the dual role of Eddie and Dr Scott.

Having been told only that the show had been a huge hit in England, the Texas-born rock star-to-be signed his contract without seeing a script and knowing very little about the production itself; as did the rest of the enthusiastic American cast. Therefore, after spending the first few days of rehearsal singing pleasantly satirical horror movie homages such as 'Science Fiction Double Feature' and 'Over at the Frankenstein Place', but with no knowledge of the show's plot, it came as something of a shock to all when, upon his arrival in LA, Tim Curry was immediately coerced by Jim Sharman into belting out 'Sweet Transvestite' in full costume for his new cast mates, without prior warning.

As the nature of the show now slowly dawned on the rest of the company, the genuinely horrific realisation that he was part of a 'drag show' impelled the naive young Meat Loaf to storm out of the rehearsal room, vowing never to return. It is a tale he has told excitedly, vividly and amusingly many times since. 'We're finally ready to rehearse Curry's entrance, but we still haven't seen him,' the singer recalled in his 1999 published autobiography *To Hell and Back*. 'Doors in the back of this little theatre open up and a guy with big black hair and a leather jacket comes walking down the aisle singing "Sweet Transvestite". As he gets closer we see that he's got a garter belt, fishnet stockings and enough make-up for a cosmetics counter.

'I'm sitting next to Graham Jarvis, the show's Narrator. I turn to him and say, "I'm leaving!" I walk across the street against the light and get a ticket for jaywalking. Graham followed me out and I asked, "What is this? What's going on? These people are nuts. I'm not doing a drag show."'

The older and more experienced Jarvis managed to convince his freaked-out colleague not to make any impetuous decisions until he had at least seen a script. While said script, when it finally arrived, did indeed convince Meat that the show was witty and clever and musically first-rate, the idea of having to don ladies' hosiery for Dr Scott's final reveal filled him with dread: 'I'm saying, "Listen guys, I can't do this drag part. I'd feel silly." They're telling me it's not drag. "Read the script and see what's going on here. Just trust us." "Okay, but no way am I doing drag."'

Eventually, it was only the contemplation of a huge laugh from an hysterical audience at the sight of his enormous thigh clad in (presumably extra-large) hosiery that convinced the would-be comedian that it would be all right to slip into the stockings and stiletto heels. 'Cut to: me in fishnet stockings; which stopped the show,' he recalled in his book. 'Sometimes even Curry would start laughing; the whole cast would break character. Some nights I'm laughing too. And guess what? I'm doing drag,' He expanded on the anecdote in his interview for BBC Radio 2's *Let's Do the Time Warp Again* retrospective: 'To this day, I will tell you, that it is probably the biggest laugh that I have ever heard in theatre in my life. I would lift my leg as Dr Scott from underneath this blanket, with this fishnet stocking on and this shoe and the place would fall apart. Because I weighed about 60 pounds more than I do now. So here's this hulking giant in a fishnet stocking, with a garter belt on; but I had nothing to do with it, other than it was my leg. I mean it wasn't like I had told this great joke; the joke was my leg in a fishnet stocking.'

In approaching the role of Riff Raff, Bruce Scott chose to eschew the slow-moving subtlety and almost imperceptible facial tics of method actor Richard O'Brien's sinister, slithering, minimalist interpretation. Instead, he made him an unpredictable, slavering, wild-eyed, maniacal madman. At first, O'Brien and Jim Sharman were apparently unmoved by Scott's reinterpretation of what they saw as an already clearly defined character, especially when the actor threatened to hijack the limelight (and audience attention) from Tim Curry's Frank-n-Furter; something akin to the subservient Renfield attempting to steal Count Dracula's thunder. However, as Scott explained to Jim Whittaker in 1998, once it became abundantly clear that audiences were revelling in his and Curry's onstage rivalry, Curry simply focused his performance, upped his game and embraced this light-hearted conflict. Audiences witnessed another Renfield-like piece of creative characterisation when Scott spontaneously pretended to catch flies out the air and eat them during Riff's melodically haunting 'Over at the Frankenstein Place' interlude, a move copied over the years by more than one subsequent Riff Raff.

Although he did not get to play the part in the film version of *Rocky Horror* – that honour, quite rightly, going to Richard O'Brien – Bruce Scott revisited his interpretation of Riff Raff, in all but name, when he portrayed with obvious relish the sleazy perverted manservant Master Bator in director Howard Ziehm's 1989 soft porn sci-fi spoof *Flesh Gordon Meets The Cosmic Cheerleaders* (known on video as *Flesh Gordon 2: Flesh Gordon Meets The Cosmic Cheerleaders*), for which he also performed and co-wrote the bouncy theme song. A penis-shaped rocket ship, extraterrestrial turd people, a field of farting ass-teroids (you heard), sub-par porn movie acting, and a giant grinning ape (imaginatively named King Dong) gleefully peeing on passers-by from the top of a skyscraper, featured amongst the film's 'highlights', making Scott's stand-out performance and

2: YOU'RE THE PRODUCT OF ANOTHER TIME

the catchy opening song two of its (very few) redeeming qualities.

With Tim Curry relocating his Frank-n-Furter to Lou Adler's Roxy Theatre in LA, the role in the London production was assumed by Philip Sayer, a tall, long-limbed actor whose skeletal frame, angular, emaciated features and straight, shoulder-length hair were remarkably different from the look established by Curry. Though some sources maintain that Sayer played the character for eight months, Ziggy Byfield remembers it being for a much shorter period, asserting that the actor left the production, due to alleged back problems, after just a few weeks, thus allowing Byfield to step into the prestigious heels full-time: "I don't think he was all that happy with the part, to be honest. I think the back problems were an excuse; but anyway it gave me my chance because I took over from him as Frank. I used to look at it as a rock 'n' roll show with Frank as the star, and I loved to sweat. Singing "I'm Going Home" with make-up dribbling down your face, you can't beat that feeling.'

Meanwhile, on the other side of the world, self-made mogul Harry M Miller was fast becoming Australia's most prominent showbiz promoter and producer. Like Michael White and Lou Adler, the New Zealand born Miller possessed an uncanny knack for spotting the 'next big thing'; and with successful international tours by the likes of Louis Armstrong, the Rolling Stones and the Beach Boys already under his belt, not to mention the smash hit Australian productions of *Hair* and *Jesus Christ Superstar* – both of which had been directed by Jim Sharman – he set his sights on successfully transplanting *The Rocky Horror Show* onto its third continent.

'A transvestite-science-fiction-rock 'n' roll B-movie award winning musical!' declared local newspaper ads for the show, prior to its Australian debut, just about covering all the bases in one broad statement and surely arousing the interest of even the most apathetic of readers.

Although the much-in-demand Jim Sharman was the obvious and only real choice to direct the Australian version – which premiered at the New Arts Cinema (later renamed the Valhalla Cinema) in the Sydney suburb of Glebe on 15 April 1974 – it did mean that he would now be helming his third production of this exciting new musical; and with Tim Curry kicking up his spangled heels on the Los Angeles stage, an electrifying new Frank-n-Furter would have to be found.

Selected for the role, and seizing it fervently with both hands, was Reg Livermore. Already a hot talent, well on the way to becoming an Australian theatrical legend, Livermore had recently played Herod in Sharman's Australian premiere of *Jesus Christ Superstar* and, like many other *Rocky Horror* performers, had also appeared in *Hair*. The actor welcomed the chance to recreate what Tim Curry had effectively made an instantly iconic role. It was undeniable that, in originating and defining the character, Curry had set the bar exceptionally high. But Livermore dared to be different, and boldly decided to interpret the character his own way. He elaborated on his approach to the character in his fascinating 2003 autobiography *Chapters and Chances*: 'Jim agreed to let me model my Frank-n-Furter on Hollywood's legendary Bette Davis; it quickly opened the right doors, filling out the performance in ways that had been eluding me. It was the licence to kill; it gave me the walk, the strut, the stance, the voice, the delivery, and I think in the end I took the venerable Miss Davis where even she hadn't dared to go.'

He explained that much of this creative reinterpretation of the role was necessitated by a lack of awareness about *Rocky*'s British incarnation: 'Nobody knew anything much about the show; reading the script didn't help, and the scant information dribbling our way only added to the intriguing sense of bamboozlement.

'Cautiously, we dipped our feet into the murky waters of sleaze and tack, Jim Sharman all the while ranging about with a glint in his eye; he certainly knew something we didn't, but wasn't letting on.'

Livermore confessed that, although for the first couple of months he played the role as written – 'to the dot and the comma,' as he put it – he later began to 'take unpardonable liberties with Richard O'Brien's script' in ways that today's protective *Rocky Horror* fans, not to mention O'Brien himself, would undoubtedly consider profane: 'I thought Frank so fabulous, such a fascinating creature that I wanted the audience to know more about him; I wanted them to know *everything* about him, indeed I wanted to know more myself. I started inventing stuff, a line here and a line there, the occasional improvised monologue, an occasional "excursion" into the audience.

'When invention was flying I just had to go with it; I couldn't help myself most of the time. It was all part of the fun, and for the percentage numbers who came to see *Rocky* many times over, it meant there was always a surprise no matter how well acquainted they thought they were with the piece.

'The role of Frank is obviously a gift for the right actor. I took it with both hands and shook the life into it.'

Furthermore, Livermore was generous and candidly open with his counsel to all successive actors who might take on this inimitable force of nature. 'My advice to any prospective Frank is this,' he announced in his book. 'If you're remotely concerned about whether the audience thinks you're really like that, if you care at all what an audience thinks about you as a person, you'd be well advised to take off the corset and head home. Frank *is* like that; he's worse, his behaviour is scandalous, and must be played that way. Frank is the fearless embodiment of all that's unspeakable, let alone the unnatural; his antics encourage many laughs, but first and foremost he presents real and terrible threat. Never forget, the

2: YOU'RE THE PRODUCT OF ANOTHER TIME

audience must be wary of him, they should never take their eyes off him, and if they do it's at their peril.'

With those well-founded points made, however, it seems that the ever unpredictable Dr Frank-n-Furter still had one last bombshell in store for Mr Livermore himself, as the actor revealed in his concluding comments: 'Some years after I'd quit the show, I finally succumbed and saw the movie version; I was shocked and surprised to observe how beautiful Tim Curry was. Nobody ever told me Frank-n-Furter was supposed to be attractive. I went out of my way to make myself as grotesque as possible.'

'I've seen only two people play the transvestite Frankenstein to perfection,' stated Jim Sharman in his 2008 autobiography, 'Tim Curry, who created the role, and Reg Livermore in Sydney. Reg was a tough cookie, Bette Davis style. Tim was on the sweeter side of Frank's bittersweet equation. He developed the character through his South Kensington accent and his walk, courtesy of Sue Blane's extra-high heels. Like Dorothy's ruby slippers in *The Wizard of Oz*, the sequinned stilettos held some magic for this character.'

'I think Tim, in many ways, did do a definitive performance,' Richard O'Brien told Rob Cope in 1990. 'I've seen it done better – but that's without denigrating Tim, because the guy that did it better couldn't have done it better unless Tim had set the seal first.'

While tactfully mentioning no names, the show's author went on to elaborate profusely: 'What the guy did was steal everything that Tim did well and add on top of it. But he did it blatantly; he was knowledgeable about it. He didn't do it because that's the way Tim did it and it's got to be done that way. He said quite deliberately, "That's good, I'll steal that, that's great."

'And he was quite open about it, even to me. He said, "That's brilliant. Why throw it away? I fucking like that." He said, "I know it's what Tim did, but it's great, I'm going to hang onto that." But he built on top of what Tim did; and it was Tim – Tim's basic framework of performance if you like – with this great dynamic platform on top of it, which was exhilarating.'

While it is impossible to do anything but speculate as to whom he may have been referring to (one of the later London Franks maybe), and even though Reg Livermore never saw Tim Curry's interpretation on stage, it is worth noting that O'Brien told Alan Jones, in an interview for a 1981 issue of *Starburst* magazine: 'Tim's was the definitive performance (although some say Reg Livermore's performance in Sydney, Australia, was the best).'

In addition to Reg Livermore, the first Sydney production also featured Jane Harders and Kate Fitzpatrick (as Janet and Magenta respectively), both of whom had appeared in Jim Sharman's 1971 celluloid science fiction send-up *Shirley Thompson Versus the Aliens*, a film that no doubt gave them a head start when it came to *Rocky Horror*'s required B-movie acting style.

With Sue Blane and long-time Sharman and Miller collaborator Brian Thomson again handling the design, *Rocky* was assuredly in safe hands for its opening 'down under'.

On the first night, Thomson received a heartfelt telegram from the producer, courtesy of the Australian Post Office. It read: 'Dear Brian. What can I say except that tonight is just another great night in our long past and long future collaborations? You are the only person in the world who gets his sets applauded. Sincerely, Harry.'

More than two decades later, as if to emphasise this most deserved praise, Thomson's scene-stealing titular bus for *Priscilla: Queen of the Desert*, the hit musical stage version of Stephan Elliot's 1994 camp cult road-movie *The Adventures of Priscilla: Queen of the Desert*, would indeed elicit nightly spontaneous ovations from joyfully wowed audiences as it made its first appearance onstage.

The Rocky Horror Show was a considerable hit in Sydney, earning over a million Australian dollars. It played at the New Arts Cinema for 18 months – Trevor Kent assumed the role of Frank mid-run, with several other cast changes occurring along the way – and spawned a successful cast album (with Michael English's Columbia face on the cover) featuring Reg Livermore and the original company. The production transferred to the Regent Palace in Fitzroy, Melbourne in October 1975, with Max Phipps taking the role of Frank-n-Furter, and finally moved to Adelaide in August 1977.

Strangely, the look of Frank-n-Furter for the Australian production – particularly Max Phipps' interpretation, with his slender facial structure and slicked short black hair – gave him more than a passing resemblance to Michael English's now instantly recognisable poster artwork. This resulted in confusion amongst some viewers as to whether the image was, in fact, intended to represent Frank rather than Columbia.

In his programme notes for the Melbourne run, Harry M Miller set the scene for the tone of the production: 'Here at the Regents Palace in Fitzroy, which Eric Dare and I have had made over into the beautifully dilapidated setting Brian Thomson created for it, Melbourne can now see and hear the '50s sent up as they were never sent up before, never so brashly or with such wit and satire.

'After I first negotiated for an Australian production of *Rocky*, it was judged the Best Musical of 1973 by critics of the London *Evening Standard* (it is still playing there) and has been staged in Los Angeles, New York, Paris and Japan. Jim Sharman declares the Australian version his favourite. He and Brian returned to Australia to stage this Melbourne production. We hope it will match the Sydney season, which was second only to

2: YOU'RE THE PRODUCT OF ANOTHER TIME

London. Their visit renews my professional association with two young Australians who have spearheaded the advance of Western theatre for the past decade, with their exciting productions and designs for *Hair* and *Jesus Christ Superstar*. Sue Blane has come from London to costume our production, but otherwise we have drawn entirely on the talents of Australians.'

While Meat Loaf recalled that American singer-songwriter Carole King (another artiste produced by Lou Adler) attended *Rocky* performances in LA costumed as Magenta, it would be a number of years until audience participation and dressing up became an established by-product of the *Rocky Horror* phenomenon. Nevertheless, it quickly became apparent that the London production was gaining a dedicated following, with fans returning to see the show on a regular basis. Those arriving early enough might have had the added thrill of seeing one of their heroes, the brawny, leather-clad Christopher Malcolm, wheeling his enormous motorcycle into the foyer of the King's Road Theatre, which (being a converted cinema) lacked the customary stage door facility to allow actors access to the building and dressing rooms.

'*The Rocky Horror Show* is fast becoming a new generation's *The Sound of Music*,' declared a local mid-'70s newspaper report. 'At least one hundred people are believed to have been to see it more than 20 times. One girl claims she has seen it 50 times.'

Early devotees included the late British punk pioneer Malcolm McLaren (who would later manage the Sex Pistols), rock legend David Bowie and actor Daniel Abineri (destined to become one of the show's longest playing Frank-n-Furters just a few years later). McLaren's partner, fashion guru Vivienne Westwood, peddled her wacky new wave clothing creations from their shop Let It Rock, periodically known by various other names such as Sex, Too Fast To Live Too Young To Die, and finally Seditionaries. Located at 430 King's Road, the store was just a few hundred yards from the King's Road Theatre; and, in the 1999 TV documentary *Walk on the Wild Side*, Richard O'Brien stressed his opinion that *Rocky Horror* had undoubtedly influenced the look of punk rock. 'Malcolm McLaren used to come along to the King's Road Theatre to see how it was done,' he stated unequivocally. 'Little Nell for instance, with her brightly coloured socks and tap shoes with glitter on, and fishnets and striped shorts. That look is pre-punk.'

Another fan of the show was prolific freelance photographer Mick Rock. Frequently labelled 'the man who shot the '70s,' Rock – who passed away on 18 November 2021 at the age of 72 – was an artist whose work – which includes iconic images of David Bowie, Iggy Pop, Queen and Debbie Harry – is widely recognised even by those who might not know his name; while his famous, intentionally out-of-focus cover shot for Lou

Reed's *Transformer* album is an image recurrently cited as an influence for the look of Tim Curry's Frank-n-Furter.

At the behest of Bowie, Rock attended an early performance of *The Rocky Horror Show*, the result of which was a long and happy association with the show and its creators. He later shot several images of the King's Road cast and would eventually be invited by director Jim Sharman to serve as special photographer on the set of the movie version.

As loyal and adoring as *Rocky*'s London following may have been, however, it was overwhelmingly eclipsed when the show had its unforeseen Japanese premiere in the summer of 1975. 'There was a guy called Yuzuro Koga, who had seen the show at the King's Road Theatre,' explains Ziggy Byfield. 'He was the son of a wealthy Japanese businessman, and decided that he wanted to put the show on in Japan.'

Rather than cast the production with local actors, it was decided to employ British performers, many of whom – including Christopher Malcolm (Brad), Belinda Sinclair (Janet), Rayner Bourton (Rocky) and Ziggy himself (Frank) – had already played in the London version and knew what worked best for the characters. 'Several of us volunteered to go,' Byfield recalls. 'We needed a new Eddie/Dr Scott, Riff Raff, Magenta and Columbia; so these were auditioned and Neil McCaul, Des McNamara, Jeanie MacArthur and Judy Lloyd were cast in these roles.'

Before heading for the mystical East, Byfield had his legs insured (as a publicity stunt) for £50,000. 'I remember a *Daily Express* article of 14 June that year quoting me saying, "I've got better legs than Danny La Rue",' he smiles whimsically.

The cast flew via Moscow on Russian airline Aeroflot, and Byfield recalls the consumption of vast amounts of alcohol *en route*, as well as the (probably quite sobering) experience of suddenly being on the other side of the Iron Curtain during a very different period in world history: 'I remember getting off at Moscow and walking into the terminal building. This was still during the Cold War don't forget, so we had to walk between two white lines that were taped to the floor. You could walk from the plane straight into the terminal, round to the bar – which was extortionately expensive – and back out again. There were armed guards everywhere to stop you straying outside the lines; what an eye-opener for us. I still have the sick-bag from that flight; I've tended to keep loads of mementoes from my career, and that's one of them.'

Opening at the Concert Hall of the Japanese Labour Party Headquarters, the production debuted successfully. It then moved to Osaka before travelling back to Tokyo.

'We must have done well,' observes Byfield, 'because we then played in the HQ of the ruling Conservative Party. We played in the Shakai Bunka Kaikan Hall in the Miyakezaka area of Tokyo. It was funny, because obviously the Japanese didn't understand the dialogue, and they all thought that we were putting on a rock concert with the dialogue being the introduction to the next number. So we printed a new programme with an explanation of the plot and the lyrics of the songs.'

In the three decades since the Second World War, the youth of Japan had enthusiastically embraced certain aspects of Western pop-culture – rock 'n' roll music in particular. Hence, rather appropriately, the *Rocky Horror* cast began to attain almost rock star status, with many of them receiving handmade gifts from excited young devotees.

'We got spoilt rotten,' says Byfield. 'There were loads of fans and parties; and fans used to make us things, little presents like paper fans and paintings, which they'd leave outside the stage and dressing room doors.'

'I received a beautiful kimono,' reveals Belinda Sinclair, whose funky disco version of 'Touch-a Touch-a Touch-a Touch Me' went to number three in the Japanese singles chart.

'There's a lovely quotation in *Mainichi Daily News* in Japan from 10 July 1975,' recalls Ziggy Byfield, who also had a Japanese hit single with his recordings of 'Sweet Transvestite' and 'I'm Going Home', Frank-n-Furter's two biggest showstoppers, 'which says, "'Time Warp' incidentally might lead to the introduction of a new dance here." How right they were.

'We had such a fabulous time. We were wined and dined all the time and got on so well with each other. In fact a couple of marriages grew out of that time; Chris Malcolm married Judy Lloyd and Yuzuro Koga married Jeannie MacArthur.'

After his extended period with the show in both England and Japan – between 1973 and 1979 – Byfield would return to the world of music, forming Ziggy Byfield and the Black Heart Band with a number of musicians from the King's Road production – Derek Griffiths on guitar, Dave Johnson on bass and Chris Parren on keyboards – before taking on the role of Eddie/Dr Scott opposite Daniel Abineri's Frank-n-Furter for *Rocky*'s very first UK tour.

In the wake of its astonishing triumphs in England, Australia and Japan, *The Rocky Horror Show* was lucratively staged in other territories, including Brazil, Mexico, Norway and New Zealand. The latter famously featured 1970s glam star Gary Glitter as Frank-n-Furter, along with Rayner Bourton – who also directed the production – once again reprising his original role of Rocky (this time without the Jimmy Osmond falsetto).

Vinyl cast albums were produced for most of these productions, including the Los Angeles Roxy cast (released on Lou Adler's own Ode Records label) – with Tim Curry, Meat Loaf and Bruce Scott – and the Sydney cast (on Festival) – with Reg Livermore; meaning that – with the 1975 movie soundtrack – no fewer than eight *Rocky Horror* recordings had already been made available in the space of just six years.

Although released in 1975, making it officially the first non-English language *Rocky Horror* recording, the original Brazilian cast album, entitled *Rock Horror Show*, was for some reason unknown to most international fans for well over two decades; and although copies occasionally surface on internet auction sites, it is still a much sought-after Holy Grail amongst serious *Rocky* memorabilia collectors. The record's front cover sported a large close-up of Eduardo Conde as Frank-n-Furter (listed as '*o vampiro Frank-n-Furter*' in the gatefold sleeve's cast list), wearing outrageous (even for Frank) glam style eye make-up, rather reminiscent of Gene Simmons from the American rock band Kiss. The recording was inexplicably missing both 'Sweet Transvestite' and 'The Time Warp', two of the show's most popular and well-known songs, making it even more of an oddity.

For the 1976 Mexican interpretation, performed at Teatro Bar Salon Versales and Teatro Venustiano in Mexico City, the show's title became *El Show De Terror De Rocky*. The script and songs were translated into Spanish by Julissa, a fashionable actress and pop diva of the time, who also translated the Mexican productions of *Jesus Christ Superstar* and *Grease* (for which the title translated as *Vaselina*). Julissa furthermore produced and directed *El Show De Terror De Rocky*, took the role of Janet (renamed Chelo here) and got her name featured prominently above the title on the album cover. In addition to Julissa, the production starred Gonzalo Vega as Frank and Hector Ortiz as Brad (or Carlos as the character became known), while the cast album, recorded at Mexico City's Churusco Studios in February 1976, boasted similar musical arrangements to those of Lou Adler's 1974 LA cast recording and a memorable cover image of Boris Karloff's Frankenstein monster wearing bright red lipstick.

The original Norwegian (Norsk) production – starring Knut Husebo as Frank, Ivor Norve as Jan (Brad) and Kari Ann Grosund as Janne (Janet) – opened at the Oslo Nye Centralteatet on 11 October 1977 and ran until 18 March the following year, playing a total of 129 performances. Responsible for translating Richard O'Brien's script into Norwegian were Johan Fillinger and Ole Pars, while the beautifully produced and polished cast recording has since become a favourite version amongst fans and collectors.

As *The Rocky Horror Show* set about conquering the globe – something its creators could never have envisioned when they first set about staging their 'bit of fun' for three weeks at the Royal Court in 1973 – the original London incarnation, with various cast changes along the way, continued to please the crowds at the King's Road Theatre.

Belinda Sinclair's successor in the role of Janet Weiss was her friend Susie Blake, a pretty young actress with a flair for comedy. After *Rocky Horror*, Blake would become a recognised face on British television in such comedy shows as *Russ Abbot's Madhouse* and *Victoria Wood: As Seen on TV*,

2: YOU'RE THE PRODUCT OF ANOTHER TIME

and later as Bev Unwin in the long-running soap opera *Coronation Street*.

Replacing Ziggy Byfield as Frank was Peter Blake (no relation to Susie). An imposing, charismatic, Scottish-born character actor, Blake had appeared in *Hair* with Byfield and Richard O'Brien before assuming the role of Pharoah in *Joseph and the Amazing Technicolor Dreamcoat* at the Albery Theatre. It was while playing Pontius Pilate in the London production of *Jesus Christ Superstar* that he was offered the role of Frank-n-Furter. 'When I was playing Pilate, who really only has two big scenes and songs in *Superstar*, I practised walking in Frank's high heels,' the actor reveals. 'There was a long catwalk backstage, which was ideal for me to use between scenes. The shoes were custom made for me, and four-inch heels and platforms take some getting used to if you're not going to do yourself an injury. I found the only way to walk properly, if you wanted to keep your spine intact, was to place one foot directly in line in front of the other as if you're walking a tightrope.'

Although he had seen and loved Tim Curry's performance at the Theatre Upstairs, Blake had no desire to copy it; he had clearly defined ideas of his own about who Frank-n-Furter should be. While still seductive and compelling, Blake's interpretation was much more aggressively arrogant – sometimes even vicious and unpleasant – than the Franks who had preceded him. 'You've got to realise that Frank's a space pirate who'll fuck anyone or anything that takes his fancy,' he declares. 'He's a complete psycho, a hedonist. When he's bored, he's dangerous; and woe betide anyone who fucks with his "toys". I believe that Richard intended there to be a lot of Alice Cooper in Frank.'

Delving deeply into the psyche of the character, exploring Frank's personality and developing his own back stories, Blake even came up with his own bizarre and fascinating origin for one of the extraterrestrial scientist's tattoos: 'As well as the tattoos that have become part of the make-up – i.e. the "Boss" and "4711" ones – I added a "666" one as a symbol; you know, the mark of the Beast. Incidentally, everyone wonders where the "4711" tattoo originated. You know that it's been part of the Eau de Cologne logo for years, but my belief is that it comes from an episode when Frank, in an effort to lose weight, travelled back in time to Belsen, and that was his concentration camp number. The only thing I copied from Tim were the heroin tracks visible on Frank's arm.'

Blake maintains that his nightly transformation into Frank-n-Furter would take place as soon as he had applied his third coat of lip-gloss. 'Always; that did it. At that point I was Frank.' Very much a red-blooded heterosexual male, the actor also recalls, frankly and amusingly, his body's not entirely surprising response the first time he slipped into his character's sensual attire. 'It was fantastic,' he laughs. 'In fact I was obliged to have myself away.' A liberating experience with which many other men will have no doubt been familiar; though few might be quite so openly honest about it.

In 1971, singer-songwriter Don McLean coined the term 'The Day the Music Died' in his folk-rock classic 'American Pie'. While, for the most part, the song's lyrics remain intentionally unclear and open to interpretation, its most memorable phrase is generally recognised to be an allusion to McLean's grief over the untimely death of rock 'n' roll pioneer Buddy Holly; an artist mentioned by *Rocky Horror*'s Eddie in his vigorous rock anthem 'Hot Patootie – Bless My Soul'. On the morning of 3 February 1959, a plane carrying 22-year-old Holly (born Charles Hardin Holley on 7 September 1936), Jiles Perry Richardson (more popularly known as the Big Bopper) and Ritchie Valens crashed *en route* to a concert venue in Minnesota, killing all on board, including pilot Roger Peterson. During *The Rocky Horror Show*'s engagement in the King's Road, the world witnessed the passing of a number of the eminent rock stars who had inspired it, and for whom the expression 'The Day the Music Died' was just as pertinent.

Marc Bolan (born Mark Field), whose cosmic rock – his self-termed brand of free-spirited rock 'n' roll androgyny – helped define the early '70s glam scene, was killed in a car crash at the age of 29 on 6 September 1977, when the purple mini in which he was a passenger collided with a tree in London.

Three weeks earlier, on 16 August 1977, 42-year-old Elvis Aaron Presley – known the world over as the King of rock 'n' roll – had suffered a fatal heart attack at Graceland, his famous home in Memphis, Tennessee, prompting a sorrowful phase of genuine international mourning. Derek Griffiths fondly remembers the *Rocky Horror* band's personal heartfelt tribute on that fateful night: 'I remember the day that Elvis died in '77 because our sax player just started to play "Love Me Tender" at the end of the show, and most of the audience stayed to listen. They gave him a standing ovation and quite a few of them were crying.'

In various interviews, Meat Loaf recalled Elvis attending a performance of *The Rocky Horror Show* at the Roxy Theatre in Los Angeles in 1974, after which he had held court, inviting both Meat and Tim Curry to meet with him; a situation that, according to the story, resulted in a rare moment of speechlessness from the starstruck Meat Loaf.

Growing up in 1950s New Zealand, Richard O'Brien had always been a huge Elvis fan, while it is beyond doubt that the legendary star influenced every rock 'n' roll artist, including Buddy Holly, throughout the '50s and '60s.

Presley's mark had of course been all over *Rocky Horror* in a number of ways since the very beginning. As previously noted, Patricia Quinn's Usherette had proudly displayed a large conspicuous button badge of Elvis's face on her uniform at the Theatre Upstairs, while – as also mentioned earlier – the programme biography for Angela Bruce, the actress who succeeded Quinn as Magenta, had declared cryptically, 'Only Elvis Presley knows her real name.' If this – likely tongue-in-cheek – statement is in fact true, then it can be surmised that on 16 August 1977, the King took her secret with him to his grave.

After six years as a successful fringe production in the King's Road, Jim Sharman's original incarnation of *The Rocky Horror Show* opened at London's 820-seat Comedy Theatre on Panton Street on Friday 6 April 1979; an event that marked its long overdue West End debut. While once again the set remained true to Brian Thomson's modest original, this final transfer – from converted bijou movie houses into a traditional proscenium arch theatre – began the show's evolution from the grungy little rock show it had thus far been into a legitimate mainstream musical.

As a stage play, *Rocky Horror* unquestionably helped to define musical theatre in the 1970s; but it would be the extraordinary way in which audiences responded to the tale in another medium that would ultimately make what could have remained a quirky, kitsch, and all-but-forgotten period piece into an indisputably timeless and immortal one-of-a-kind icon.

3
They Got Caught In A Celluloid Jam

Ever the entrepreneurial visionary, from the moment he secured the rights to stage the first US production of *The Rocky Horror Show* at his Roxy theatre on LA's Sunset Strip, Lou Adler was aware of the potential for a film version.

At Adler's behest, Gordon Stulberg, then president of 20th Century Fox – the studio that a few years earlier had released Russ Meyer's profitable exploitative sleaze-fest *Beyond the Valley of the Dolls*, the very film recommended by Jim Sharman to *Rocky*'s original London company in order to illustrate his required flavour and ironic acting style for the show – attended a *Rocky Horror* performance during the first few weeks of its Los Angeles run; a performance to which Adler cunningly invited some of the show's more exuberant early supporters in order to help ensure the necessary atmosphere. Also in attendance were Stulberg's teenage children, and while the 48-year-old studio head may not have been able to comprehend fully what it was he was watching, his kids' youthful enthusiasm for the piece, as well as Adler's unmistakable gusto, helped to convince him of its merits. While recent disaster epics such as *The Poseidon Adventure* (1972) and *The Towering Inferno* (1974) had proved lucrative for Fox, the studio was aware of rapidly changing trends and the fickleness of public tastes. Hence, when it came to selecting future projects, a healthy and plucky attitude towards diversity – including musicals, trendy comedies and teen exploitation pictures – was being maintained.

Having already stamped their collective mark on three productions of the stage incarnation, Jim Sharman (director), Brian Thomson (set designer) and Sue Blane (costume designer) were the obvious choices for bringing *Rocky Horror* to the screen. In addition, the show's London and Los Angeles musical director Richard Hartley would supervise the score, compose a number of incidental music cues for the movie – as well as attaching Felix Mendelssohn's famous 'Wedding March' from *A Midsummer Night's Dream* to the reprise of 'I Can Make You a Man' – and recruit the five principal musicians required for the soundtrack recording: guitarist Mick Grabham (aka Mick Graham) and drummer Barrie James Wilson (both members of the early UK progressive rock band Procol

Harum), acoustic guitarist Ian (The Count) Blair, saxophonist Phil Kenzie and keyboard player John Douglas Bundrick (credited as Rabbit).

With *The Rocky Horror Picture Show*'s eight-week shoot scheduled to commence on Monday 21 October 1974, after two weeks of rehearsal at the Whitehouse Hotel in Earl's Court, the band and cast recorded the soundtrack sessions, produced and mixed by Richard Hartley, in Studio Two of London's Olympic Studios over a two-week period in September.

It might seem obvious that the slight title variation of adding the word '*Picture*' just for the screen adaptation would forever distinguish the movie from its stage counterpart. Paradoxically, however, the move would elicit eternal confusion amongst uninformed critics, dim-witted journalists and ignorant viewers; with regular references to 'a cinema screening of *The Rocky Horror Show*' or 'the latest stage production of *The Rocky Horror Picture Show*' causing genuine fans to grit their teeth in infuriated despair. It is surely not that difficult to deduce that *Show* and *Picture Show* signify a perfectly simple distinction between stage and screen.

With Michael White credited as producer and Lou Adler as executive producer, the opening title cards on British prints of the movie would read 'Twentieth Century Fox presents – A Michael White-Lou Adler Production,' with the order of Adler's and White's names being switched for the US edition.

In *The Rocky Horror Double Feature Video Show*, a retrospective documentary included on the 1995 laserdisc of the film (and subsequently on the widescreen VHS and DVD releases), Jim Sharman recalled being offered a choice of financial options. Initially it was suggested that a considerably more substantial budget would be made available if he was to populate the movie with currently fashionable (and bankable) rock stars. There would certainly have been no shortage of interest amongst the contemporary music community. Keith Moon, the wildly erratic drummer for legendary British rock band the Who, was an early devotee of *The Rocky Horror Show* and developed his own peculiar 'calling card' to alert the cast to his presence whenever he was in the audience. Moon, who saw the show several times in both London's King's Road and at the Roxy in LA would, as Meat Loaf has often recalled, place nine bottles of champagne, one for each member of the cast, across the front of the stage every time he was in attendance. The Roxy's Riff Raff, Bruce Scott, disclosed to author Jim Whittaker in 1998 that Moon had approached him backstage one night and drunkenly announced, 'You know, I'm gonna do your part in the movie.'

It was also no secret that Mick Jagger had expressed an interest in portraying Frank-n-Furter on the big screen. Tim Curry's performance as the flamboyant, cross-dressing alien scientist at the Royal Court Theatre had been compared (somewhat unconvincingly) by some critics to Jagger's offbeat, reclusive rock star in Donald Cammell and Nicolas Roeg's *Performance* (1970); although his less-than-lauded depiction of the legendary Australian outlaw in Tony Richardson's *Ned Kelly* (1970) had done little to strengthen the reputation of the Rolling Stones' front-man as an actor.

Sharman, however, felt that his original troupe of talented performers, who had created their characters for the stage and therefore knew them personally and profoundly, would be an essential element in transferring *Rocky Horror* to celluloid. For that reason, he opted for the meagre budget of $1,000,000 (although it would eventually be exceeded by another $250,000 before the shoot was over), which allowed him to retain his ensemble of relative unknowns. 'It was made on a Fox executive's lunch money and shot on a tight schedule,' the director quipped many years later in his published memoir.

Having initiated the much-admired abandoned cinema concept for the Royal Court and King's Road productions of *The Rocky Horror Show*, Brian Thomson was now faced with the question of how the film version should look. One possibility was to set the action in a deserted drive-in movie theatre, an idea that would have given the picture a romantic (as well as an artistic) connection with its theatrical precursor. Director David Greene had used a similar premise for his 1973 film version of the hit Broadway musical *Godspell*, in which a group of contemporary citizens assumed the roles of the apostles, acted out the gospels and performed the show's songs whilst using modern day New York City as a backdrop. However, while he intended to retain the rough rock 'n' roll energy and overall feel of the show, Jim Sharman was keen for the *Rocky Horror* movie to have an authentic, reality-based look, similar to that of the motion pictures it was satirising; and, as both director and designer quickly discovered, with the production being shot on the compact soundstages of England's Bray Studios – significantly the home of the Hammer horror productions that had fuelled Richard O'Brien's adolescent imagination and been a key inspiration for *The Rocky Horror Show* itself – the perfect, almost too-good-to-be-true, location was, by some extraordinary coincidence, sitting right next door.

Located in the most beautiful, idyllic setting on the banks of the River Thames, just a few minutes' drive from the town of Windsor in Berkshire, stands Oakley Court. This magnificent gothic mansion, constructed on a stretch of the Thames known as River Oakley, was originally built in 1859 for Sir Richard Hall-Say, who, so local tourist information proclaims, had married Ellen Hannah Evans – only daughter of Edward Evans Esq of Boveney Court, Buckinghamshire – in 1857. According to these same reports, Sir Richard became High Sheriff of Berkshire in 1864 and Justice of the Peace a year later. The property then changed owners a number of times before the turn of the century. It was sold in 1874 to Lord Otto Fitzgerald and subsequently John Lewis Phipps, and in 1900 to Sir William Avery of Avery Scales, before being purchased, along with 50 acres of local woodland, for £27,000 in 1919 by Ernest Olivier. Known for his quirky behaviour, Olivier would purportedly entertain foreign diplomats whilst flying the flag of their nation over the house as a courteous mark of respect. Local history claims that the building became the English headquarters for the French resistance during the Second World War, during which time President Charles De Gaulle is also believed to have stayed there.

Hammer Films and Oakley Court became neighbours – and thus irrevocably entwined – in the early 1950s when Bray Studios moved into the adjacent Down Place. The imposing edifice then became the distinctive locale for over two hundred British films, horror movies and television productions.

As Brian Thomson would later explain in *The Rocky Horror Double Feature Video Show*, although the structure stood empty in 1974, its most recent owners had removed the lead from the roof, with the intention of side-stepping an already in-place preservation order, so that they could demolish the building and free up the land for development. Consequentially, the wooden floors and interiors of the building had rotted, and the constant rain of a typical British autumn incessantly poured in through the damaged roof. While this did not make for very comfortable filming conditions, it did evoke perfectly the essential appearance of a mad scientist's ramshackle old residence.

For the film, costume designer Sue Blane was able to refine her original conceptions of the characters from her three stage productions (London, Los Angeles and Sydney) of *Rocky*, while enjoying the freedom to give some of them, particularly Columbia, a bit of a make-over. The striking gold sequined tailcoat and top hat, pink bow tie and multi-coloured striped shorts ensemble created for Columbia especially for the movie emphasised the character's vaudevillian tap-dancer roots and suited Little Nell perfectly.

Frank-n-Furter's look stayed true to that of the stage version, with a beautiful silver-lined, high collared black cloak for his entrance, the traditional green surgeon's gown for the creation sequence, the addition of a stunning rhinestone-decorated velvet and chiffon corset and knee-high platform boots for a couple of the later scenes, and a more extravagantly detailed translation of his outfit for 'The Floorshow', for which the screenplay described him as being 'Reminiscent of a '30s film star.'

Riff Raff also remained close to his original look from the show (although, unlike Frank, he would no longer wear surgical scrubs in the lab), while Magenta's costume became more that of a household domestic (black button-through uniform and white apron) for the early scenes and then reverted to her see-through chiffon negligee for much of the second half.

The Narrator (renamed the Criminologist for the film) wore an elegant grey velvet smoking jacket, dark trousers, a white waistcoat and a wide red cravat with intricate black beading.

Blane dressed Brad and Janet formally for the film's opening scene – Brad in a black tuxedo, white shirt, plaid cummerbund and bow tie, and Janet in a smart lavender two-piece with a white hat – but they would change into travelling clothes for their fateful car journey. Once Frank-n-Furter's cronies got their grubby hands on them, Brad's grey slacks, sleeveless pullover, striped shirt and tan jacket (with a 1963 Denton High School patch on the left breast) and Janet's short informal pink dress and white cardigan would be discarded in favour of the customary white underwear, covered by laboratory coats for the main lab scene.

Subsequent to the bedroom scenes, Brad donned a light blue satin kimono. Frank-n-Furter would also wear a robe (his being black with a stunning gold embroidered dragon on the back) immediately prior to 'The Floorshow'. The kinky burlesque corsetry, fishnet stockings and stiletto heels of the stage version's 'Floorshow' were refined and revisited for the film. After all, if it ain't broke, why fix it?

'Sue Blane again created the incredible costumes,' Jim Sharman enthused in his published memoir. 'She knew exactly how to frame a face with the perfect collar and how to create a great silhouette, something I emphasised in my shooting approach by choosing frontal angles and echoing the composition of pop-inspired paintings.'

In the years following production, Richard O'Brien would stress repeatedly that, while he, Tim Curry, Patricia Quinn and Little Nell all reprised their original stage roles for the film, he understood that the decision to cast American actors as Brad and Janet was a stipulation made by 20th Century Fox in order to help boost US interest when the movie opened on the other side of the Atlantic. 'It was a perfect idea because it allowed them to become the strangers,' the author stated in his interview for the 2005 documentary feature film *Midnight Movies: From the Margin to the Mainstream* (this interview was included as a bonus feature on the documentary's DVD release). 'Because all the rest of us had worked together and we were all kind of English; and so everything inside the house allowed that to be slightly alien, and they were the constant Americans.'

One person who was, unsurprisingly, extremely unhappy with this turn of events was the show's original Brad Majors, Christopher Malcolm. On the BBC Radio 2 documentary *Let's Do the Time Warp Again* in 1999, the actor expressed his lingering bitterness at the decision, saying he felt as

3: THEY GOT CAUGHT IN A CELLULOID JAM

though there had been lots of shady, secretive whisperings going on in corridors behind his back.

'I was asked to dub Janet for the movie soundtrack,' reveals Belinda Sinclair. 'However, I was sad not to have been asked to play the role, so I declined. I was offered the part of Betty Monroe and Chris was offered the part of Ralph Hapschatt, but we both declined.'

American casting for the film was handled by Otto & Windsor Ltd – the agency that, along with Joel Thurm, had overseen the casting process for Lou Adler's stage production of *The Rocky Horror Show* in Los Angeles – and the pivotal roles of Brad Majors and Janet Weiss were filled by Barry Bostwick and Susan Sarandon, a pair of extremely talented up-and-coming stars, both of whom instinctively understood the satirical nature of the piece and its characters right away, and were able to pitch their faultless performances accordingly.

Barry Knapp Bostwick was born on 24 February 1945 in San Mateo, California, and studied acting at the California Western University School of the Arts. Following a number of other stage roles, the charismatic young performer originated the part of Danny Zuko in the New York production of *Grease* in 1972, for which he received a Tony Award nomination.

With his truthful representation, in spite of the obligatory B-movie trappings, the 29-year-old Bostwick made *Rocky Horror*'s Brad Majors believably real and vulnerable, and, in the process, fashioned a characterisation from which subsequent stage Brads would find it hard to deviate.

The eldest of nine children, Susan Sarandon was born Susan Abigail Tomalin in Jackson Heights, New York City on 4 October 1946 and grew up in Edison, New Jersey. While studying at the Catholic University of America – eventually graduating with a BA in drama in 1968 – she met fellow student Chris Sarandon and they married in 1967. The actress would retain her married and professional name when she and Chris divorced in 1979. Her illustrious film career began in 1969 with John G Avildsen's *Joe* (released in 1970); and after numerous acclaimed acting roles and four previous nominations – for *Atlantic City* (1981), *Thelma and Louise* (1991), *Lorenzo's Oil* (1992) and *The Client* (1994) – she was finally presented with an Academy Award in 1995 for her performance as Sister Helen Prejean in *Dead Man Walking*, a film directed by Tim Robbins, Sarandon's long-term partner from 1988 to 2009.

In his 2008 published memoir, Jim Sharman had nothing but the highest of praise for Sarandon and her faultless performance as the delectable Janet Weiss. 'How does a small town girl greet an illustrious transvestite scientist?' he pondered. 'Does she shake hands, or curtsy? It's played to perfection by the flirtatiously shrewd Susan Sarandon. Likewise, Janet's seduction of wide-eyed Rocky, involving jump cuts, ripped petticoats, sex-with-the-neighbours fantasies and her understated rendition of Richard's brilliant ode to the eternal itch, "Touch-a Touch-a Touch-a Touch Me."'

'More than Rocky or any other character, it's Janet Weiss that develops through her exposure to Frank and the haunted house,' Sharman continued, citing the series of jump cuts – during Janet's anxious 'If only ...' moments – as his favourite sequence of the film, 'probably because it is the most cinematic.

'The camera is an amoral beast and it loved Susan Sarandon. Through the view finder, it was obvious she would enjoy a great career.'

'Janet was kind of the *Saturday Night Live* version of all the ingénues I'd been doing,' Sarandon told VH-1 in 2000. 'I mean, she was kind of a take-off on myself in a way, because I was making films since I was 20, and so it was a chance to do the ingénue with a little bit of a twist.

'No-one had ever found a way to make Janet funny. Being the straight person and being so straight that you're funny is difficult.'

While her intuitive understanding of the role's comic irony swayed the film-makers, Sarandon admitted that an inherent fear of singing had almost stopped her from auditioning in the first place: 'I thought if I did this, then I'd have to sing, and I'd have to get over this whole ego-involvement that was keeping me so self-conscious that I wouldn't even hum out loud.

'I decided just to jump in, trusting that they would give me drugs or alcohol or something to get me through the recording session; which of course they didn't.'

Meat Loaf, who had already made a big impression on stage in the Los Angeles production of *The Rocky Horror Show*, was cast as Eddie, the unfortunate juvenile delinquent delivery boy; although, with the part of Dr Everett Scott being assigned to the show's original Narrator, Jonathan Adams, the up-and-coming rock star would be denied the chance to reprise the other half of his dual persona for the screen. As he recalled to VH-1 in 2000, Meat felt the decision to split the roles – which deprived cinemagoers not only of his larger-than-life portrayal of Dr Scott but also his enormous fishnet-clad thighs – was a serious misjudgement on the part of the film-makers: 'Even though the actor was fine, I think they made a huge mistake. Because the way it was in the play, Eddie and Dr Scott really looked alike, and so you knew it was his nephew. And I was a very good Dr Scott.'

As Tim Curry candidly divulged on BBC Radio 2's 1999 retrospective *Let's Do the Time Warp Again*, when the opportunity to recreate his groundbreaking role on film presented itself, pride of ownership was a key factor in his decision to accept. 'My agents didn't want me to do the movie at all,' he revealed bluntly, 'but I was buggered if anybody else was going

3: THEY GOT CAUGHT IN A CELLULOID JAM

to play it.'

The UK side of the casting process was the responsibility of the Celestia Fox agency; and with the parts of Frank-n-Furter, Riff Raff, Magenta, Columbia and Dr Scott already being assumed by members of the original Theatre Upstairs ensemble, their primary task, at least as far as principals was concerned, was to find suitable candidates to play the Criminologist and Rocky Horror himself.

As the Criminologist, distinguished English character actor Charles Gray wonderfully embodied every ounce of aloof charm and stuffy superiority that the Edgar Lustgarten-inspired authority figure required. Born Donald Marshall Gray in Bournemouth, Hampshire on 29 August 1928, the softly spoken thespian was probably best known for his portrayal of Ernst Stavro Blofeld, arch nemesis of Sean Connery's James Bond, in *Diamonds Are Forever* (1971), in addition to his appearance as ill-fated British agent Henderson in *You Only Live Twice* (1967), an earlier Connery-starring Bond movie that also featured choreographer David Toguri – who staged *The Rocky Horror Picture Show*'s dance numbers – in the supporting role of an assassin. Due to the similarity of his soft velvety voice to that of eminent Hollywood leading man Jack Hawkins, Gray also became one of two actors (the other being Robert Rietty) to regularly dub Hawkins' vocal performances after the throat cancer-stricken star had his larynx removed in 1966.

Among his innumerable stage, film and television roles, Gray turned up in a couple of memorable, though slightly kitschy, supernatural offerings, which may have subliminally prepared him for his *Rocky Horror* experience. As Mocata, the leader of a satanic sect in *The Devil Rides Out*, Hammer Films' impressive 1968 foray into the world of the occult (based on Dennis Wheatley's 1934 novel), Gray starred with Hammer regular Christopher Lee (cast as the good guy for a change, in the role of the authoritative Duc de Richleau). He then later appeared opposite another genre stalwart, Peter Cushing, along with Michael Gambon and Anton Diffring, in a rather ropey werewolf-whodunit in 1974. *The Beast Must Die*, from Amicus Productions – a studio whose chiller-thrillers often evoked the look and feel of a poorer man's Hammer – was noteworthy primarily for a much-publicised gimmick: a 30 second 'Werewolf Break' in the final reel that gave the audience the opportunity to guess the human identity of the film's lycanthropic antagonist.

The Criminologist's scenes in *Rocky Horror* would be filmed during the last week of production in December 1974, thus allowing black and white stills of previous shots from the movie to be inserted into the case file (a large extravagant dossier labelled 'The Denton Affair') to which the character regularly referred during his monologues. Charles Gray did not meet the rest of the cast, as none of his segments required their presence, and, in accordance with his aversion to watching himself on screen, he reportedly never saw the finished film.

When Gray himself succumbed to cancer on 7 March 2000, many newspaper obituaries cited *The Rocky Horror Picture Show* alongside his high-profile appearances in the James Bond movies as his most significant screen roles.

Of finding the right performer to embody the show's title role, director Jim Sharman had this to say in his 2008 published memoir *Blood & Tinsel*: 'The problem of finding a great body and voice was tricky in the days before gym culture – a culture that *Rocky Horror* might have inadvertently encouraged. On stage it was less important than the charismatic rock star element, captured so well by Rayner Bourton in the original and Kim Milford in Los Angeles. For the film, the muscularity had to survive close-ups.'

Ultimately cast as Frank-n-Furter's man-made hunk was photographer and professional model Peter Hinwood. Hinwood's only previous big screen role had been in Roddy McDowell's *Tam-Lin* (aka *The Ballad of Tam-Lin*, *The Devil's Widow* and *The Devil's Woman*), starring Ava Gardner, in 1970, although he had also played Greek messenger god Hermes in *L'Odissea* (aka *The Adventures of Ulysses*), Italian producer Dino De Laurentiis's 1968 television mini-series adaptation of Homer's *The Odyssey*. A little more than window-dressing role in Derek Jarman's controversial *Sebastiane* in 1976 – which also featured Patricia Quinn, Little Nell and the King's Road Theatre's second Frank-n-Furter Philip Sayer in blink-and-you'll-miss-them appearances – would bring Hinwood's short-lived screen career to an end. He later went into the antiques business.

In a departure from the stage version, Rocky Horror had no dialogue in the film and became audible only for his songs. An un-credited Australian singer by the name of Trevor White provided the character's vocalisation, although it would seem that the involvement of a former King's Road cast member was prohibited by a badly-timed bout of seasonal sickness: 'I narrowly missed out on being the voice of Rocky on the *Picture Show* soundtrack,' explains Peter Blake rather philosophically. 'I was invited to do it, but had flu when they were recording and couldn't sing.'

Richard O'Brien left the UK production of *The Rocky Horror Show* – with Robert Longden replacing him as Riff Raff at the King's Road Theatre – at the same time Tim Curry flew to America to commence rehearsals with the Los Angeles company. Subsequently supplanting Curry as Frank on the LA stage, once shooting began on the movie, would be none other than Paul Jabara, the actor O'Brien had failed to replace as Herod in Jim Sharman's London incarnation of *Jesus Christ Superstar*. It is quite possible that, had O'Brien successfully managed to wow producer Robert Stigwood and been offered that part full time, *The Rocky Horror Show* might never

3: THEY GOT CAUGHT IN A CELLULOID JAM

have happened; a thought that gives Jabara's assumption of Frank-n-Furter, a dream role for any musical theatre performer, a kind of poetic resonance.

Jabara's biography in the *Rocky Horror* programme ended with a rather whimsical paragraph: 'Paul looks like a cross between Dustin Hoffman, Barbra Streisand and Harpo Marx, speaks three languages, loves travelling, Rio de Janeiro is his favourite city, is very lonely, and is dying to fall in love. If you are interested, please write c/o his mother ... but be careful what you write ... Olga opens the mail.'

In June 1974, Richard O'Brien played the part of Crow, a one-eyed assassin with a pirate-style eye-patch, in a Royal Court Theatre production of Sam Shepard's 1972 play *Tooth of Crime*. Also featuring Christopher Malcolm and Jonathan Adams, the production, directed by Jim Sharman – with contributions from the usual team of Richard Hartley, Brian Thomson and Sue Blane – failed to repeat the critical success of *The Unseen Hand* and ran for just over a month.

Meanwhile, with *The Rocky Horror Show* attracting enthusiastic crowds in both London and LA, O'Brien and Sharman withdrew to the seclusion of a hotel room (a regular habit with writers) to work on the screenplay. 'I allowed myself to be creative secretary,' O'Brien confessed in his *Midnight Movies* interview in 2005. 'I thought, "He's going to shoot the movie; why should I write the screenplay and write scenes he doesn't want? He's got his own vision of this." So I just let him sit there and tell me how he saw he was going to shoot it, and I dutifully shaped the screenplay to suit his shooting needs.'

Accordingly, the film's on screen writing credit would list Sharman's name before O'Brien's, although the fact that it was based on O'Brien's original stage play would also be duly acknowledged; and while he was allowed to express a personal opinion on set, O'Brien would later divulge to Patricia Quinn on *The Rocky Horror Picture Show* DVD's audio commentary that he actually had very little power or influence over creative decisions.

It was Jim Sharman's film.

There were, therefore, a number of developments with which O'Brien did not concur. One of these was the controversial addition of the Transylvanians – an assortment of oddball alien party guests (known in the film's shooting script as the Transylvanian Secret Agents), of various shapes, genders, ages and ethnicities – an aspect of the film that continues to irritate previous cast members and admirers of the stage show.

'The Transylvanians in the *Picture Show*; what are they all about?' asks an exasperated Peter Blake with typically animated annoyance. 'Why put them in? They ruin what is a very scary plot development. Imagine you're Brad and Janet; you break down miles from nowhere in the middle of a storm and seek shelter in a place that's so scary even Satan would shit his pants. It's a castle straight out of Hammer House of Horror; the door is answered by a complete weirdo of a butler who looks like he might jump you at any moment. You enter and are quickly confronted by two more creatures; a maid who is totally spaced out and looks like a vampire, and a groupie who's obviously high on drugs too. Then, as if that wasn't enough to make you turn and run, their master appears and completely dominates proceedings, and within minutes has revealed himself as, in your eyes, a sexual deviant.

'That whole sequence in the original script takes about five minutes, and the audience, like Brad and Janet, are swept along and reeling from one shock after another.'

Blake concludes that the inclusion of the colourful, larger-than-life Transylvanians, as well as an incompatible party atmosphere, destroys the continuity and 'dumbs down the terror.'

While it is undeniable that the presence of the Transylvanians does weaken an important plot point – it is unquestionably more sinister for Brad and Janet to be the only outsiders to see Frank's lab and witness the birth of Rocky – this was Jim Sharman's first 35mm film, and he found himself faced with the dilemma of how to fill cavernous sets and a 30-foot screen; a far cry from the postage stamp dimensions of the Royal Court's Theatre Upstairs. Therefore, while relating to them as strange 1970s descendants of the Munchkins from *The Wizard of Oz* (1939) – Richard Hartley sped up their backing vocals accordingly – Sharman saw the Transylvanians as a way of opening up the film and giving 'The Time Warp' in particular a more energising visual impact.

While the film's closing credits would list only 18 Transylvanians – Perry Bedden, Christopher Biggins, Gaye Brown, Ishaq Bux, Stephen Calcutt, Hugh Cecil, Imogen Claire, Tony Cowan, Sadie Corre, Fran Fullenwider, Lindsay Ingram, Peggy Ledger, Annabelle Leventon, Anthony Milner, Pamela Obermeyer, Tony Then, Kimi Wong and Henry Woolf – there were in fact 19. Despite Tony Cowan being credited even though he replaced the no-longer-available Henry Woolf for only a couple of days during the shooting of 'The Time Warp' sequence, Rufus Collins, who was present throughout, was inexplicably and unforgivably omitted from the on screen cast roster.

Some of these supporting players, cult figures in their own right amongst many of the film's devotees, were hired through an organisation in London with the most wonderfully politically incorrect name of the Ugly Agency – a modelling company specialising in unique looking individuals – while others, including Perry Bedden, Christopher Biggins, Rufus Collins and Richard O'Brien's wife Kimi Wong, were already acquaintances of the film-makers.

3: THEY GOT CAUGHT IN A CELLULOID JAM

'Casting, down to the last hand-picked Transylvanian, was a key element in the film's success,' Jim Sharman affirmed in his 2008 book *Blood & Tinsel*. 'Many of our cross-cultural Transylvanians were partners, friends and extended family of the cast and creative team. I often think of *The Rocky Horror Picture Show* as one big home movie.'

In addition to being on set at Bray for 12 long hours between 6.00 am and 6.00 pm – for the daily rate of £100 – shooting his scenes as a Transylvanian, the much-in-demand Perry Bedden was also appearing nightly in *Jesus Christ Superstar* at London's Palace Theatre. A free-spirited adolescent at the time, Bedden has rather hazy memories of the shoot itself, for reasons that remain perfectly clear: 'I honestly can't remember much about it, as we were on a planet of our own most of the time. In fact, I don't remember filming 'The Time Warp' at all. We used to smoke a lot in those days. I remember one night at the King's Road Theatre when I'd smoked some particularly strong stuff and I was struck by paranoia; so much so that I couldn't open the castle "doors" (two Ushers, each holding an arm out).'

In addition to the sped-up vocals of the Transylvanian extras, further allusions – some of them rather obscure – to a certain 1939 Judy Garland-starring classic would pop up throughout the film. All of them, as Jim Sharman clarified in his book, were intentional: '*Rocky Horror* celebrates movie references, and my contribution to the screenplay was to propose a dark underbelly version of *The Wizard of Oz*.'

One such parallel, which ultimately proved too costly and technically ambitious to realise, was the notion of beginning the movie in black and white after a set of red theatrical curtains had first opened to reveal an old-fashioned, standard-sized screen. This idea was detailed in the final version of the film's screenplay (which included two pages of script amendments dated '9/12/74'):

THE FIRST IMAGE IS A SET OF RED VELVET CINEMA CURTAINS.

Soft drum roll.

THEY SPLIT OPTICALLY TO REVEAL THE DISTRIBUTION COMPANY LOGO.

Fanfare.

A SMALL WHITE SCREEN – ACADEMY SIZE – APPEARS IN THE MIDDLE OF THE WIDE SCREEN FORMAT.

On the sides of the image are stationary sprocket holes of celluloid. SCIENCE FICTION DOUBLE FEATURE * Musical introduction. Film head runs down numbers: 10, 9, 8, 7, 6, 5, 4, 3, 2, 1, START. Very scratched. During the SONG we see snatches of the films mentioned in the SONG. They look old and scratched and they are INTERCUT with flashes of white screen, burnt celluloid, etc.

The movie would then continue in black and white – the format opening to widescreen once Brad and Janet entered the castle – until Frank-n-Furter's pulsating entrance. A rapid zoom would isolate his bright red lips, the first shocking burst of colour in an otherwise monochrome scene, before going completely to colour at the moment the wayward scientist threw off his cloak to expose his outrageous transvestite finery.

As evidenced by the final film, Brian Thomson's set reflected the black and white concept. Apart from any colour that was added to the scene solely by lighting, the interiors of the castle ballroom were dull and grey, while, probably most noticeably, the copies of Leonardo Da Vinci's 'Mona Lisa' that adorned the walls were also reproduced in black and white.

The expansion of the wedding sequence at the beginning of the film was another way in which the screenplay opened up the action of the original show. On stage, Brad and Janet had made their first entrance with Janet having already caught the bride's bouquet and referring to an unseen Ralph and Betty. But the happy couple (played by Jeremy Newson and Hilary Labow) and members of their congregation were added for the movie, creating a more streamlined introduction to the film's lead characters and allowing the audience to witness that all-important bouquet moment.

A number of the actors who would later turn up at the castle as Transylvanians also appeared, somewhat more conventionally attired, in this first scene. Though most assumed the roles of wedding guests and family members, Henry Woolf played the photographer, with Perry Bedden as his assistant, and Rufus Collins portrayed the newlyweds' chauffeur.

Sharman explained this innovation in his 2008 book *Blood & Tinsel*: 'The small town church congregation being Transylvanians in disguise, or *vice versa*, has its roots in Shakespeare's *A Midsummer Night's Dream* where the real world inhabits a parallel universe with the fairytale kingdom.'

This theme was further highlighted by the inclusion of a dog-collared Tim Curry representing the parish minister; while a pitchfork-wielding Richard O'Brien, in dungarees and wire-rimmed rounded spectacles, and Patricia Quinn as his grey-haired dowdy wife, flanked the doorway of the generic small town white church. This image deliberately called to mind the peculiar couple in 'American Gothic' – the famous 1930 painting by

3: THEY GOT CAUGHT IN A CELLULOID JAM

Iowa artist Grant Wood, which would later turn up in the hallway of Frank-n-Furter's creepy abode – although the duo in the painting (for which the artist famously asked his sister and their family dentist to pose) are generally considered to be father and daughter. As these characters, along with Little Nell as their own similarly-attired daughter, O'Brien and Quinn would provide backing vocals for 'Damn it. Janet'.

With Richard O'Brien, Jim Sharman and Brian Thomson completely immersed in popular culture and film lore, cinematic references, both conscious and unconscious, seem to seep through every pore of *The Rocky Horror Picture Show*. One such visual allusion that, though less frequently documented, has been perceived by speculative fans, is Brad's and Janet's stroll through the Denton churchyard being analogous to that of brother and sister Johnny (Russell Streiner) and Barbara (Judith O'Dea) at the beginning of George A Romero's pioneering 1968 apocalyptic zombie picture *Night of the Living Dead*. While this may be thanks partly to Sue Blane's use of late 1960s styles for *Rocky Horror*'s fated young couple – both Brad's and Johnny's trousers appear to be slightly too short, both wear dark suits and spectacles, and both have comparable side-parted haircuts – some have noted subliminal similarities between the opening scenes of the two films. Two films that became phenomenally successful midnight movies.

The church's exterior facade, conceived by Brian Thomson to represent an outsider's clichéd view of middle-America, was built in a paddock on the studio lot. Its interior – in which the scenery of the preceding wedding would be flippantly and literally turned around, during the song, in preparation for a subsequent unseen funeral – was constructed on Bray's minuscule Stage Two.

The church was referred to as the 'Denton Catholic Church' in the screenplay but became the 'Denton Episcopalian Church' for the actual film; while a huge billboard – bearing the pretentious slogan 'Denton: The Home of Happiness!' against a large red heart with an arrow through it – overlooked the church's quaint cemetery, underlining the insular naiveté of 'wholesome' small town ignorance.

For Oakley Court's iconic appearance in *The Rocky Horror Picture Show*, Thomson erected an enormous geodesic dome – constructed from metal and fibreglass – on the roof, to represent Frank-n-Furter's attic laboratory; while Ernest Olivier's famous flagpole, having previously borne the colours of numerous international ambassadors, would reverentially fly a stylised cartoon lightning bolt on a black and white background, the RKO-inspired flag of the galaxy of Transylvania.

With Thomson drawing inspiration from Brad's description of the house as 'Probably some kind of hunting lodge for rich weirdoes,' many of the building's existent rotting interiors were also used and decorated accordingly by set dresser and prop master Ian Whittaker. A large upright clock, made from a converted coffin (and containing a real human skeleton); an unusual array of stuffed animals; Greek statues; classic paintings; and reproductions of the location's existing stone griffins were but a few examples of the more memorably unusual items that showcased Thomson's obsession for quirky details while simultaneously suggesting that the alien Frank-n-Furter was a collector of eccentrically eclectic Earth artefacts.

'Brian Thomson's brilliant design embodies a thousand film and art references that multiple-viewing audiences enjoy picking up on,' Jim Sharman wrote in his book. 'His work on the film is incredibly detailed, bold and inspired.'

Young Frankenstein, a well-observed send-up of Universal Studios' 1930s monster pictures, was released by 20th Century Fox in 1974. This much-lauded comedy, director Mel Brooks' follow-up to his irreverent Wild West spoof *Blazing Saddles* (released earlier the same year), starred Gene Wilder, Madeline Kahn, Marty Feldman, Cloris Leachman, Teri Garr and James Boyle, and famously utilised the actual laboratory equipment designed by Kenneth Strickfaden for James Whale's horror classics *Frankenstein* (1931) and *Bride of Frankenstein* (1935). By contrast, stimulated by Hammer's more lurid versions of Mary Shelley's enduring tale rather than Universal's gloomy black and white interpretation, Brian Thomson envisaged Rocky being nurtured inside an iron-framed glass water tank, in accordance with the formation of Christopher Lee's monstrous abomination in *The Curse of Frankenstein* (1957). With Frank-n-Furter's ostentatiously tacky tastes in mind, Thomson painted the tank's frame, as well as other lab equipment and trimmings, a retina-scorching bright red; and – remembering the bathroom of a sleazy Amsterdam hotel he had recently visited – decorated the entire set with pale pink tiles, with various scientific formulae (scribbled, it would appear, in red lipstick) on the wall next to the main control panel. According to the 2017 book *The Art of Illusion: Production Design for Film and Television* by Art Director Terry Ackland-Snow, the tiles were made from lightweight hardboard squares, painted in different shades of pink and applied at random to the walls of the set. With a raised dais – from which Frank would deliver his speech – and a balcony for the Transylvanians, this gave the lab, in accordance with its description in the shooting script, a look somewhere between a Greek gymnasium and an operating theatre's observation gallery.

Reproductions of Michelangelo's statue 'David' and Myron's 'Discobolos' ('The Discus Thrower'), which adorned the unashamedly kitsch set, were given a camp twist with the addition of painted red nails and lips. The large speakers, used to broadcast Frank's words to the assembled throng, which hung from the 'David' statues had the words

3: THEY GOT CAUGHT IN A CELLULOID JAM

'Acme Sound' stencilled on them (one of several appearances of the 'Acme' name in the film); a nod to the 'Acme Demolition Co' tarpaulins Thomson had used as part of the sets for the Chelsea Classic and King's Road Theatre productions of *The Rocky Horror Show*.

Nevertheless, as Jim Sharman confessed in his published memoir: 'The sequence involving the birth of Rocky became a personal testament to James Whale, the originator of the *Frankenstein* films. We were able to do what Whale and earlier generations couldn't – reveal that the creator loves his creation and vice versa.'

Tightly wrapped in bandages and suspended in a container of unidentified liquid (amniotic fluid perhaps) like so many Frankenstein monsters before him, Rocky Horror was brought to life in the film through a combination of weird and wonderful apparatus, and a perfect spectrum formed by a mixture of coloured chemicals discharged into his birthing tank from a giant overhead 'cocktail mixer'. As Brian Thomson explained in *The Rocky Horror Double Feature Video Show*, Tim Curry's manically confused fumbling as he searched for the correct liquids was instigated by his ignorance of their required sequence: having purposely tricked Curry by failing to inform him of the order of the colours, Jim Sharman was then able to yell them out and enjoy the actor's frantic searching, scrabbling and groping.

The interior of the gigantic deep freeze, from which Meat Loaf's Eddie appeared astride his US Army Harley Davidson motorcycle, was described in the shooting script as 'A wall of ice and many Coca-Cola bottles.' On the actual set, the cola bottles – an allusion to the fact that, in Thomson's stage productions, Eddie emerged from a 'fridge' emblazoned with the world famous Coca-Cola brand logo – would be replaced by giant blocks of artificial ice; thus the prominent product placement never made it to the screen.

In the *The Rocky Horror Show*'s published libretto, with a cry of, 'Hi Ho Silver,' from Columbia – a reference to the famous yell made by the Lone Ranger to his trusty steed in radio series, film serials and television shows during 1930s, '40s and '50s – Dr Scott's wheelchair was rapidly propelled onto the stage, ensuring the character a memorably strong first appearance. The logistics of this had initially caused a few headaches for Sharman at the Theatre Upstairs; and when it came to getting the wheelchair-bound scientist into the movie's laboratory, the director found himself faced with a curious case of déjà vu. This time, however, the blame was aimed squarely at Brian Thomson. The film's screenplay specified that Frank-n-Furter's powerful Triple Contact Electro Magnet speedily impelled Dr Scott's wheelchair through various rooms and corridors – the shoestring nature of the budget and shooting schedule would be apparent in the final version, as a section of carpet clearly flips up to reveal the lo-tech wire used to actually pull the chair along – and into the laboratory. However, a key design flaw had resulted in the impressive set having no discernible access other than its centrepiece lift – a custom-built (with the cooperation of the Otis Elevator company), art-deco, three-storey high, working pneumatic elevator – which had until then proved a practical and straightforward method for getting characters up to the castle's upper level. The builders of Frank's top floor laboratory had obviously not taken disabled access into account!

Frustrated with the quandary of how to achieve another dynamic entrance for Dr Scott, the resourceful director suggested simply crashing his wheelchair through the wall. An access was quickly cut and hastily tiled over, while ramps were laid to facilitate the chair's ascension of the staircases, and the undignified – yet unquestionably dynamic – entrance worked brilliantly on screen.

After completion of filming in the laboratory – which was constructed on Stage One at Bray Studios (the company's only full sized soundstage) during the picture's eight week pre-production period by a team headed by art director Terry Ackland-Snow and construction manager Dick Frift – the magnificent lift (the set's crowning glory) was reinstalled at Oakley Court for its required location scenes, including Frank-n-Furter's unforgettable first appearance.

With Patricia Quinn's Magenta sliding backwards down its actual banister, the reception area of the old house itself provided the tailor-made setting for the fearful entrance of Brad and Janet into the dingy domicile. Riff Raff's inaugural verse of 'The Time Warp', including his and Magenta's trademark extraterrestrial greeting (lovingly referred to by *Rocky Horror* fans as 'elbow sex') would also take place in the mansion proper, with the action cutting to the ballroom set for the Transylvanians' first chorus of: 'Let's do the Time Warp again.'

The ballroom, in which 'The Floorshow' and most of 'The Time Warp' and 'Sweet Transvestite' would be filmed, was built (also on Bray's main soundstage) in place of the swiftly dismantled laboratory during the ensuing location shoot that took place between Friday 8 November and Wednesday 20 November 1974 at Oakley Court. For 'The Floorshow', the stage's water tank, which on the laboratory set had accommodated the elevator, was converted into a full-sized practical swimming pool.

Exterior shots, involving the fateful journey of Brad and Janet on a narrow country road near the house, were filmed throughout a very cold night on Thursday 21 November. According to the screenplay, a rusted sign on the castle gate was supposed to read 'FRANK N FURTER – SCIENTIST,' but by the time the scene was shot this had evolved into a wooden notice bearing the ominous warning 'ENTER AT YOUR OWN RISK!!'. Also involved in the night shoot were several of the actors

3: THEY GOT CAUGHT IN A CELLULOID JAM

portraying the Transylvanians who, despite being completely unrecognisable beneath their motorcycle helmets, were required to ride pillion on the bikes seen approaching the castle.

The following day – Friday 22 November 1974 – was labelled clearly in the shooting schedule as 'REST DAY AFTER NIGHT SHOOTING.'

Riff Raff, Magenta, Columbia and the Transylvanians were then called at 2.00 pm on Saturday 23 November for dance rehearsals, with the next two weeks to be spent filming on the ballroom set.

Another example of Frank's irreverent misuse of classical art, again instigated by the fastidious Brian Thomson, was a reproduction of Michelangelo's 'The Creation of Adam' on the bottom of the ballroom's swimming pool. Aside from providing an impressive backdrop for Jim Sharman's tacky reinterpretation of a Busby Berkley/Esther Williams underwater ballet, its depiction of God transferring the spark of life into an anatomically immaculate Adam was an echo of Rocky's blasphemous birth at the hands of the self-important and delusional Frank-n-Furter. In addition, the painting's location on the bottom of a pool in a festering old dilapidated mansion – rather than in its rightful place on the magnificent ceiling of the Sistine Chapel – might be construed as a subliminal indication of Frank's subversive outlook on life; literally turning the world (and convention) on its head.

The style of acting required for film is naturally markedly different from that for live theatre. Without the necessity of projecting every word and translating each facial expression to a spacious auditorium of several hundred people, the intimate in-your-face nature of the camera generally demands a more subtly nuanced performance. Having trained as a method actor when he arrived in London during the 1960s, Richard O'Brien was able to translate his already minimalist interpretation of Riff Raff onto film fairly easily – it is indeed an often overlooked masterpiece of understated brilliance. Tim Curry, meanwhile, for what was his first screen role, worked on making his over-the-top gestures a little more restrained for the camera, while preserving the spontaneous energy that had made his stage performance such a triumph.

As he later told *Film Talk*'s Mark Caldwell, Curry intended to give the villainous alien scientist a more malevolently sinister edge for the celluloid version. 'It got quite night-clubby on stage,' he explained. 'It got sort of quite Las Vegassy on stage, which I kind of regretted; and I wanted to make him a bit more evil on film than he had been on stage.' Hence, while it retained much of the mischievous humour, theatrical flamboyance and charismatic allure that had made the character so wholly irresistible to theatregoers, Curry's expertly judged performance in the finished film would exhibit several examples of this added menace. Whether sadistically thrashing his 'loyal' minion with a cat o' nine tails, callously prodding

Brad while angrily interrogating him about his alleged affiliation with the newly-arrived Dr Everett Scott, violently slapping Janet across the face or obviously relishing his brutally gruesome murder of Eddie with an ice pick, the movie's Frank-n-Furter displayed an unmistakable and entirely fitting mean streak that would influence subsequent stage interpretations.

Although the film had a real-world look, Jim Sharman kept the tale firmly rooted to its stage show origins by intentionally retaining a measure of deeply embedded theatricality. As well as in the staging of the musical numbers, much of this was achieved through performance. In addition to the Criminologist, Tim Curry's Frank-n-Furter in particular shamelessly delivered lines of dialogue into camera, as though addressing the viewer directly. Likewise, Dr Scott jokily broke the fourth wall during the dinner scene with his line, 'I knew he was in with a bad crowd, but it was worse than I imagined.'

'The Floorshow' sequence in particular begged to remain theatrical in nature. To that end, Frank was given a proscenium arch stage in order to indulge his showbiz fantasies, as well as an auditorium of seaside or cruise liner-style deck chairs. These would be occupied during 'I'm Going Home' by a crowd of extravagantly attired sycophantic senior citizens (played by supporting artists wearing their own evening dress) in accordance with the decadent scientist's hallucinogenic reverie. These apparitional delusions during Frank's swansong were reminiscent of those experienced by big screen has-been Norma Desmond (played by Gloria Swanson) in director Billy Wilder's 1950 Hollywood horror story *Sunset Boulevard*. Sharman also included another prominent visual reference to this multi-Oscar winner. Shot from below, Frank-n-Furter's corpse floating face down in the pool consciously provoked memories of murdered writer Joe Gillis (William Holden) in a comparable position from the classic film's opening moments.

With *The Rocky Horror Picture Show* being distributed by 20th Century Fox, Brian Thomson had envisaged a gigantic plywood replica of the instantly recognisable Fox searchlight logo as a backdrop for Frank-n-Furter's 'Floorshow' entrance. With Fox patently anxious about the content of the film, however, Gordon Stulberg forbade the use of the studio brand in such a way. That said, the larger-than-life monochrome mock-up of the RKO Radio Pictures radio mast, which Thomson and Sharman ultimately settled on as a compromise, probably suited the essence of the movie even more. After all, while Fox had released *The Day the Earth Stood Still* in 1951, RKO had produced 1933's legendary *King Kong*, so the latter studio's logo was no less apposite. In addition, the presence of the familiar RKO mast allowed Sharman to stage a fishnet-clad parody of *King Kong*'s iconic Empire State Building finale, with Rocky as Kong and Frank representing Fay Wray; and the studio itself – the other notable genre efforts of which included *Cat People* (1942), *I Walked With a Zombie* (1943), *Mighty Joe Young*

3: THEY GOT CAUGHT IN A CELLULOID JAM

(1949) and producer Howard Hawks' *The Thing From Another World* (1951) – was actually referred to by name in the song 'Science Fiction Double Feature'.

A favourite story of Richard O'Brien's – recalled in several interviews, as well as in his audio commentary on *The Rocky Horror Picture Show* DVD – involves the stuntman hired to double Tim Curry's Frank-n-Furter for his climactic fall from the radio mast. Upon discovering, to his horror, that he would be required to wear Frank's lace-up corset, suspenders and fishnet stockings for the role, the uncomfortable performer began to noticeably overcompensate. Much to O'Brien's delight, in an effort to dispel any ambiguity about his sexuality, the poor fellow became more and more comically macho, which paradoxically made him appear even more camp.

Resplendent in their gold-quilted tunic spacesuits, accessorised with heeled pixie boots, matching gauntlets and black nylon stockings – evoking everything from *Flash Gordon* serials to Roger Vadim's psychedelic 1968 science fiction camp-fest *Barbarella* – Riff Raff and Magenta stopped the party dead in the true spirit of *coitus-interruptus*. Magenta's stunning beehive hairstyle with a striking white streak lightning bolt up each side was blatantly evocative of Elsa Lanchester's unforgettable shock-headed locks in James Whale's *Bride of Frankenstein* (1935), while Riff Raff's triple-barrelled chrome ray gun not only suggested a devil's trident but was also purposely reminiscent of the old man's three-pronged pitch fork in Grant Wood's aforementioned 'American Gothic' seen on the castle wall and recreated by Richard O'Brien and Patricia Quinn during the film's opening scene.

The stage direction in the published edition of *The Rocky Horror Show*'s libretto specified that on stage Columbia valiantly threw herself between Riff Raff's laser and Frank. However, the nature of Jim Sharman's character blocking on the film set – with Columbia having positioned herself at the other end of the ballroom in order to operate Frank's spotlight for 'I'm Going Home' – left her too far away to make the same noble gesture. This was in no way an indication that the effervescent groupie would be spared in the movie; the director simply found another way of placing her in the line of fire. Rapid edits and intense close-ups of eyes and mouths – as well as Riff's fingers firmly grasping his gun – brought to mind comparable showdowns in 1960s Italian Westerns directed by Sergio Leone. An ear-piercing scream would distract the trigger-happy homicidal handyman for the briefest of moments, causing him to whirl around and discharge his weapon, sealing Columbia's fate.

As is the norm, the screenplay had undergone a number of drafts over a short period of time. Even the final shooting script differed from the finished film, as well as the original stage version, in various ways. Frank's 'Unlock a mind, un-mind a lock' and 'I wonder, may I offer you something refreshing?' word-play with Brad and Janet was absent from the movie, but the shooting script's version of his laboratory speech was, aside from the odd turn of phrase, pretty close to the one in the live show. It read:

> 'It was strange the way it happened. One of those quirks of fate really; one of those moments when you seem irredeemably lost. You panic, you're trapped, your back's against the wall. There's no way out; and then suddenly you get a break. All the pieces seem to fit into place. What a sucker you've been; what a fool. The answer was there all the time. It took a small accident to make it happen; an accident.'

This monologue, which was delivered much faster and with a lot more energy on stage, would eventually be pared down considerably in the film as released. In the final version, Frank would go immediately from 'It was strange the way it happened' into 'Suddenly you get a break', while a cutaway to one of the speakers craftily obscured the edit.

Another scripted line removed from the finished film was Frank-n-Furter's odd but revealing 'And so perish all those who reject my love,' which replaced the stage show's brief dialogue between Rocky and his creator after the slaughter of Eddie. In the completed film, Frank's 'One from the vaults' would eventually be followed by nervous obsequious laughter from the Transylvanians, Magenta dutifully and silently removing her master's bloodied rubber gloves, and Frank rushing to console his distressed creation: 'Oh, baby. Well, don't be upset. It was a mercy killing; he had a certain naive charm, but no muscle.'

According to Richard O'Brien on *The Rocky Horror Picture Show*'s DVD commentary, the close-up of Tim Curry delivering this particular line was filmed after the lab set had already been dismantled – in order for the ballroom to be constructed on the same soundstage – hence the tightness of the shot. The line of dialogue as written appeared at the end of the amendments pages in the shooting script as:

> Sc. 77 pt. C.S. FRANK
> FRANK: Oh no my baby – don't be upset – it was a mercy killing.
> He had a certain naive charm – but no muscle.

Also in the shooting script, an exchange between Columbia, Janet, Magenta and Riff Riff, which on stage had explained Eddie's identity as the castle's delivery boy ('His delivery wasn't good enough') and introduced 'The Time Warp', was rephrased slightly and transplanted to the moment Eddie burst from the freezer, only to be ultimately dropped from the film completely in order for the intro to 'Hot Patootie' to kick in

3: THEY GOT CAUGHT IN A CELLULOID JAM

as soon as the ragged biker emerged.

The screenplay also alluded to Magenta vacuuming and a live band playing during 'The Time Warp', neither of which would make it into the final film; while probably one of the director's wisest decisions was to delete the shooting script's weird and outrageously out of place insinuations that Dr Scott could somehow miraculously walk again during and after 'The Floorshow'.

The most significant omission of all, however, would be that of an entire song; the film's only real deleted scene. Although Barry Bostwick had recorded 'Once in a While' during the initial studio sessions, it was felt that his sensually breathy version of the number – a lot slower and more dreamlike than the way it was performed on stage – severely slowed the pace of the picture. Bostwick found his vocal talents pruned even further when 'Over at the Frankenstein Place' was truncated to the extent of Brad's whole verse being removed.

The words of Richard O'Brien's Charles Atlas tribute song 'I Can Make You a Man' were revised and, to a degree, rewritten for the film. 'His girl split on him, so soon in the gym' was changed to 'And soon in the gym, with a determined chin,' for example, and the lyric 'Then a magazine advert with a new muscle plan' – an unconcealed (and perhaps slightly inaccessible for the '70s youth crowd?) reference to the Charles Atlas ads in 1950s comic books – was replaced with 'Such an effort, if he only knew of my plan.'

Filming on the laboratory set on Wednesday 30 October 1974 coincided with what would have been Charles Atlas's eighty-second birthday. Facsimiles of the shooting schedules for that day confirm that Jim Sharman was filming Eddie's entrance from the deep freeze, involving most of the principal players as well as Meat Loaf's stunt double and the 18 Transylvanians; and according to *Rocky Horror* folklore (and cast recollections) the company performed an on-set rendition of 'I Can Make You a Man' in honour of the legendary late bodybuilder.

During the seduction scene, the shooting script's dialogue had the silhouetted Frank – disguised as Janet – at first protesting Brad's amorous advances ('Oh Brad. Oh no; not 'til after the wedding') before rolling over and explicitly suggesting 'Maybe we could try it this way.' The screenplay then stated: 'BRAD switches on the bedside lamp and realises he is making love to FRANK wearing a JANET wig.' This exchange, possibly deemed a little too risqué for a mainstream motion picture in 1974, was ultimately dropped in favour of Brad unwittingly pulling the loose-fitting wig from the head of his devious bedfellow, thus revealing it to be Frank. In accordance with the film's recognised cheapness, the bedrooms assigned to Brad and Janet were in fact the same room with nothing but different coloured filters over the camera lens to distinguish them.

Riff Raff's provocative reference to 'Our androgynous planet' as written in the shooting script was altered to the broader 'Our beloved planet' for the film itself; while other dialogue that would fail to make the final cut included: 'Do your worst, inferior one,' Frank's defiant stand when confronted by the ray gun-toting Riff Raff; Riff's arrogantly delusional response of 'Yes' to Brad's 'Good God,' immediately after the assassination of Frank and Rocky; the Narrator's 'If and only ...' speech; Janet's subsequent words of comfort to Rocky, 'Yes. There you see, it's instinctive, this room is your womb. You returned here for one thing – security'; the Narrator's dialogue break during 'The Sword of Damocles'; and Frank inviting Dr Scott to 'Sample the speciality of the house; roast loin of pork,' prior to the macabre dinner scene in which the sadistic host serves up pieces of the murdered Eddie to his unaware guests. This added sequence – shot on location at Oakley Court, rather than in the studio – served the purpose of relieving monotony with a change of scenery, momentarily taking the characters out of the lab for Dr Scott's musical number.

'He was the thorn in his mother's side,' Scotty's less than flattering, but no doubt accurate, assessment of his nephew was illustrated with another famous artwork – this one in the Criminologist's dossier – a reproduction of 'Arrangement in Grey and Black: The Artist's Mother' by James McNeill Whistler (more commonly known as 'Whistler's Mother'), albeit with Meat Loaf (in drag again) representing Eddie's poor mom. Leonardo Da Vinci's 'The Last Supper' was also used by the Criminologist to foreshadow Frank's gruesome feast.

According to some sources, it was while Jim Sharman was shooting this rather weird banquet on Friday 8 November and Monday 11 November 1974, during the third and fourth weeks of production, that a contingent of 20th Century Fox executives famously visited the location; although, in his *Midnight Movies* interview, Lou Adler remembered that this visit actually occurred on set at Bray during the filming of the swimming pool scene. Another case of conjecture and conflicting memories. If they had been present on the day of the dinner scene shoot, the grisly tableau – which involved, amongst other things, such strange sights as transvestism, partial nudity, a mutilated corpse, non-consensual cannibalism, incompetent domestics, excessive cutlery and a hospital specimen bottle being used as a receptacle for table wine – would undoubtedly have given the toffee-nosed bosses perceptible cause for concern about the horrors they were witnessing (and, more importantly, financing).

A putrid location with no heating and a leaking roof, along with the persistent heavy drizzle of a typically cold British autumn, helped make the eight weeks of principal photography more than a little uncomfortable for all concerned, with several members of the company falling victim to colds and other seasonal unpleasantness. As Richard O'Brien intimated on

3: THEY GOT CAUGHT IN A CELLULOID JAM

the DVD commentary and in his *Midnight Movies* interview, Sharman's hasty shooting pace, dictated largely by studio pressure to wrap the picture and vacate the lot before Christmas, left very little time for relaxation and niceties on the set. Although the long-suffering players soldiered on like troupers – consummate professionals each and every one of them – being subjected to a very cold (and wet) late November night shoot, coupled with being constantly in and out of the swimming pool, dancing on a treacherously slippery floor and remaining wet between shots, no doubt contributed to Susan Sarandon's much-publicised pneumonia and resultant health problems.

As the actress revealed to UK chat show host Clive Anderson in 1999, even though she made only two movies in England – the other being Tony Scott's 1983 vampire thriller *The Hunger* (starring David Bowie, Catherine Deneuve and Cliff De Young), a film notable for its brooding cinematography, impressive special make-up by Dick Smith and the sensually erotic lesbian scene between Sarandon and Deneuve – she actually caught pneumonia on both occasions.

In preparation for the stage version of 'The Floorshow', the characters had simply been drugged by Riff Raff's atomiser and led off stage, whereas the movie would see them turned into marble statues via Frank's Medusa machine. This particular plot development called for each of the relevant cast members to undergo a full body cast – suffering yet more indignity and discomfort – in order for their plaster doppelgangers to be constructed.

Principal photography on *The Rocky Horror Picture Show* wrapped on Friday 13 December 1974 with a bedraggled Brad, Janet and Dr Scott, their clothing tattered and scorched, at the bottom of an enormous crater on the Bray soundstage surrounded by a fog of dry ice, 'Lost in time, and lost in space, and meaning.'

Despite the frenetic nature of the shoot, which also left little time for retakes – another benefit of using actors who already knew their roles inside out – Sue Merry (continuity) and Graeme Clifford (film and music editor) did a sterling job of assembling and making sense out of Jim Sharman's footage.

The quick-fire succession of names ('Dr Scott!', 'Janet!', 'Rocky!') at the moment Frank becomes aware of Rocky's infidelity with Janet had been punctuated on stage with an insolent exclamation of 'Piss off!' from Rocky towards his flabbergasted creator. But with Rocky being all but mute in the movie, this crowd-pleasing joke was lost. Director Sharman and film editor Clifford therefore created an equally amusing and memorable moment by cleverly repeating the sequence of names, as yelled out by Jonathan Adams, Susan Sarandon, Barry Bostwick and Tim Curry, with a silent scowl from Rocky ending each one. Subsequent *Rocky Horror* stage productions would invariably combine both versions; the thrice repeated cartoonish exchange of names being stopped by Rocky's exasperated expletive, to inevitable applause.

Amongst the clever editing and camera techniques used to give the film a genuinely tacky old school look was the employment of comic book-style shaped frame wipes between scenes. These included a lightning bolt, a key hole and a question mark, while a torrent of dripping cartoon 'water' introduced the storm scene. Aesthetically similar editing techniques would later be used by George Lucas to underscore scenes in *Star Wars* (1977) for precisely the same reason; *Star Wars*' primary influences being 1930s *Flash Gordon* serials, golden age science fiction, vintage Westerns and pulp adventure stories.

While the talent of the *Rocky Horror* editors was never in doubt, a number of bloopers and continuity blunders unavoidably made it into the final cut. Most added to the film's surreal qualities and rough-around-the-edges charm, and were ultimately embraced as beloved flaws by devoted fans.

In the wake of the infamous Watergate scandal, Richard Milhous Nixon, the thirty-seventh president of the United States, had resigned from office on 9 August 1974. Ostensibly to set the movie in history – a move Richard O'Brien disliked – Jim Sharman made the creative decision to have Nixon's infamous speech made on 8 August, the eve of his resignation, clearly playing on the radio in Brad's and Janet's car. This resulted in a glaring continuity error, as, in accordance with O'Brien's original script, Charles Gray's Criminologist had already stated in the previous scene that the story took place on a 'late November evening.' Eagle-eyed viewers have also pointed out that *The Plain Dealer* – the Cleveland, Ohio newspaper Janet is reading in the car – does not actually appear to be the 8 August 1974 edition. While generally considered a monumental gaffe, the use of Nixon's speech in this context has been justified in a number of intriguing ways by fans. Some simply rationalise that the radio station is playing a re-run of the 8 August broadcast, while others have speculated that it may be a conscious indication that time has somehow already been warped and that normal laws of physics no longer apply. In other words, Brad and Janet are literally in the wrong place at the wrong time.

This particular theory further emphasises the popular premise that the film's young protagonists can be viewed as emblematic remnants of outmoded 1950s naiveté, taking their first tentative steps – along with the rest of humanity – into adulthood and the brave and uncertain new world of the 1970s. In addition, if one accepts that they are indeed listening to the broadcast's original live transmission, then the couple's blissful indifference to the monumental world-changing events unfolding on the radio – Janet is contentedly nibbling on a Hershey bar while Brad smiles

3: THEY GOT CAUGHT IN A CELLULOID JAM

inanely – might be construed as a further indication of their insular and petty small town attitudes.

Other discrepancies, resulting from the breakneck shooting schedule, include examples of the same actions from close-ups being immediately repeated in subsequent long-shots, while Frank-n-Furter's 'Boss' tattoo seems to have been partially washed away in the swimming pool, only to reappear as good as new for the next scene. A quick touch-up by the make-up artist is just one of the perks of acting on film.

A conspicuous incongruity occurs when Brad and Janet clearly appear to assist Dr Scott out of the castle on his feet, and yet his broken wheelchair somehow ends up underneath him in the smouldering crater. Viewers might also question why Frank and his servants decide to serve dinner in the middle of the night, despite having already packed their guests off to bed earlier in the evening, but such illogicality ultimately adds to the movie's quirky sense of fun.

Another alleged 'blooper', even mentioned by Richard O'Brien on the DVD commentary, is the supposed shadow of a boom microphone against the church door. While this may well be present in the film – along with the occasional reported sighting of the camera crew reflected in the wedding car's windscreen – closer inspection reveals the most noticeable shadow to be merely that of the lantern hanging in the porch.

An unconscious undercurrent of sadomasochistic perversity amongst the players might even be detected by overly analytical fantasists, thanks to a couple of evidently painful slip-ups. As confirmed by Richard O'Brien, again on the film's DVD commentary, Frank-n-Furter (an overzealous Tim Curry) actually caught his faithful handyman with the whip several times; and the momentary look of contorted anguish on Barry Bostwick's face, as Riff Raff and Magenta burst through the ballroom doors to break up 'The Floorshow', is a clear indication that Susan Sarandon staggered backwards and inadvertently jammed her spiked stiletto heel into the soft bare flesh of her co-star's foot.

While the initial proposal of opening the movie with a montage of scratchy black and white film clips from the science fiction pictures named in the show's opening number would have been in keeping with the B-movie spirit of the piece, Brian Thomson in particular had always found the idea a little obvious and unimaginative. Inspired by a 1966 image of disembodied lips he had seen on a painting by American surrealist Man Ray, displayed on the wall of Thomson's studio, as well as the opening titles of Alfred Hitchcock's *Vertigo* (1958) and, most notably, *Not I*, a 1972 dramatic monologue by playwright Samuel Beckett performed at the Royal Court Theatre by the 'floating' mouth of its sole actress lit only by a single spotlight on an otherwise pitch black stage, Jim Sharman decided that a similarly incorporeal oral orifice, sensuously enunciating the words of the song, might prove a suitably eccentric alternative.

As he clarified in his 2008 book *Blood & Tinsel*, however, Sharman's motivation for fusing Richard O'Brien's singing voice with the glossily rouged mouth of Patricia Quinn actually went a lot deeper than mere visual imagery. 'The seductive title sequence has Pat Quinn's luscious lips syncing with Richard O'Brien's falsetto, establishing a disorientating sense of ambivalence and androgyny,' he explained, further elucidating that it had been his intention to, 'celebrate incestuous twins Riff Raff and Magenta, played by Richard and Patricia, and to see them eternally morphed together in image and song.'

As she is fond of recounting at *Rocky Horror* fan conventions, having already lost the chance of recreating the opening number she had delighted in singing on stage – in favour of its composer's own interpretation – Patricia Quinn reacted to her director's request that she instead portray the scene's ethereal lips with a single dry enquiry: 'My mouth and his voice? How much?'

The question of Quinn's fee notwithstanding, the unforgettable representation of singing red lips – an effect achieved (according to interviews with director of photography Peter Suschitzky and make-up artist Peter Robb-King in Jim Whittaker's *Cosmic Light: The Birth of a Cult Classic*) through the use of polarised filters, blacking out the actress's entire face and attaching a mouth-shaped cardboard stencil to the front of the camera – would come to symbolise the movie just as Michael English's Columbia painting (seen on T-shirts worn by the *Rocky Horror* film crew during production) had represented the stage show.

The use of a similar mouth on the film's theatrical trailer, announcing, in a softly sexual voice, that 20th Century Fox had never before unleashed anything like *The Rocky Horror Picture Show*, had strait-laced company execs fearing for the studio's wholesome image and demanding that the marketing people immediately remove 'Those lewd and lascivious lips mouthing the words "20th Century Fox".'

A replacement trailer, in which the still 'lewd and lascivious lips' gently spoke the amended, and presumably less offensive, phrase 'You've seen all kinds of movies, but you've never seen anything like *The Rocky Horror Picture Show*' was approved by the studio.

In addition, posters and press advertising, also inspired by the film's opening sequence, featured what is probably now the best known and most recognisable version of this extraordinary image. The teasingly sensual mouth, with its upper teeth erotically nibbling on the lower lip, provocatively displayed on *Rocky Horror* film posters, T-shirts and all manner of merchandise, is generally acknowledged to be that of model Lorelei Shark, who purportedly received the then standard rate of $60 per hour for two hours modelling work in order to provide the poster's iconic illustration. It seems wholly appropriate that these famous lips, often accompanied on posters by the slogan 'A different set of Jaws' (in reference to Steven Spielberg's rampaging Great White summer blockbuster, which came out the same year), should belong to a model named Shark.

Immediately prior to filming, a management restructure at Fox in October 1974 had caused a stir, with the new administration wanting to review the budget; although, with principal photography about to begin and Michael White and Lou Adler in a position to fund the venture themselves, they were unable to stop production. When Gordon Stulberg resigned two months later, Alan Ladd Jr was appointed senior vice president (in charge of worldwide production) by the studio's new president Dennis Stanfill.

The new regime did not like *The Rocky Horror Picture Show* at all, right down to Richard Hartley's cheesy piano rendition of their beloved brassy fanfare that introduced the movie. As the film's premiere – at the Rialto Cinema on London's Coventry Street on Thursday 14 August 1975 – slowly approached, studio heads feared they had an authentic turkey on their hands.

And, for a while, it would appear that their concerns were well-founded.

With the stage version of *Rocky Horror* already a roaring success in Los Angeles, Lou Adler decided to take the show to Broadway, with a view to using its success as a means of promoting the film.

Designed by George Keister, the magnificent Belasco Theatre at 111 West 44th Street, New York City had been opened by producer-playwright David Belasco as the Stuyvesant in 1907. When in 1910 he surrendered ownership of the New Victory Theatre (formerly the 42nd Street Playhouse) – a venue that had hitherto borne his name – the eccentric impresario transferred his moniker to the Stuyvesant, and took up residence in a gothic apartment above it. As Bruce Scott told Jim Whittaker in 1998, following Belasco's death in 1931, at the age of 77, his ghost was thought to haunt the site, causing many a superstitious actor to believe that it was an unlucky location to stage a production. The Shubert Organisation became the new proprietors of the Belasco in 1948, and, after innumerable conventional plays and theatrical works throughout the '50s and '60s, their 1971 production of the sensationalist nude revue *Oh! Calcutta!* was thought by some to have finally frightened away the restless spirit of the building's previous owner.

As the home of *The Rocky Horror Show*'s first New York engagement, the 967-seat Belasco was renovated and themed as a cabaret venue in the style of an old-fashioned nightclub; while the show's scene-setting Usherette (rechristened Trixie for the Roxy in LA) became known here as the Belasco Popcorn Girl.

With Jim Sharman again directing the production, a number of minor amendments were made to some of the lyrics and dialogue in order to match those of the upcoming film, while the control panel from the movie's laboratory was incorporated into the Belasco's set.

With the movie already in the can, Tim Curry was secured to make his Broadway debut – mere months before his film debut – in the role that had thoroughly enraptured audiences and critics in London and LA. Meanwhile, following the closure of the Los Angeles production on 5 January 1975, after a successful nine-month engagement, many members of the Roxy cast – including Jamie Donnelly, Boni Enton and Meat Loaf – also reprised their roles for the New York production. Due to the indisposition of Bruce Scott, Richard O'Brien was invited by Lou Adler (by arrangement with actor's union Equity) to return to the familiar role of Riff Raff, making his own Broadway debut in the process; while William Newman, although initially cast as the Narrator for the entire Belasco run, was replaced (for undisclosed reasons) by the Roxy's original Narrator Graham Jarvis after the first preview.

Lou Adler's decision to highlight Curry's name above the title on the ads and posters, over a black and white (with red lips) reproduction of Michael English's enduring Columbia face illustration – with no mention of any other players or even the show's author-composer – would apparently cause periodic resentment from Richard O'Brien. But, as Curry poignantly disclosed in an interview for *The Sunday Times* Culture supplement in September 2006, he never attempted to claim any kind of ownership of the piece: 'One of the things I terribly regret that he doesn't understand is that I've never, ever given an interview about *Rocky Horror* where I didn't say "You're talking to the wrong person. Please remember who wrote every single note and every single word and imagined this whole extraordinary grab bag of the zeitgeist of 1973." But they never print that, so Richard doesn't know.'

Preview performances for 7 March 1975 (the 20th Century Fox preview), 8 March (the Ode Records preview) and 9 March (the public preview), as well as the show's grand premiere on Monday 10 March, quickly sold out; and, after a rest day, the Broadway production officially commenced its run of public performances on Wednesday 12 March.

Much to the producer's alarm and dismay, however, although the show gained the odd favourable review and acquired a faithful following – particularly on Saturday nights – most New York critics mercilessly panned the production.

With such a voluminous auditorium and only a nine-strong cast, sound levels were amplified to such a degree that the show's all important razor-sharp lyrics became virtually unintelligible; while, as Graham Jarvis recalled in Jim Whittaker's *Cosmic Light: The Birth of a Cult Classic*, the

3: THEY GOT CAUGHT IN A CELLULOID JAM

removal of Frank-n-Furter's central entrance ramp after the first preview – due to the balcony audience being unable to see it – which resulted in a more routine entrance from the wings, substantially compromised the impact of his first appearance.

Considered a disappointing flop, the 1975 Broadway production of *The Rocky Horror Show* never recovered from its poor reviews. It limped through the ensuing month before closing, after just 45 performances (in addition to the three previews) on Sunday 6 April 1975.

Richard O'Brien would repeatedly blame Lou Adler's overconfidence, as well as the cabaret nature of the venue, for the show's failure in New York. Audaciously declaring to notoriously blinkered and self-important Broadway critics that a sure-fire hit was heading their way might not have been the shrewdest marketing strategy in the world. Written in the style of lipstick on a dressing room mirror, a bright red slogan on posters for the Belasco production had forcefully announced 'Give our regards to Broadway and tell them we're on our way! Rocky,' with Adler's full page ad in the 26 January 1975 edition of the *New York Times* asserting that the show was already 'Acclaimed on two continents.'

It soon became evident that an atmosphere of dinnertime conversation, raised glasses and clinking cutlery in a cavernous auditorium was not the ideal setting for a character-based, story-driven musical, especially one that, as had been repeatedly confirmed, clearly thrived in the more intimate and personal setting of a derelict cinema.

After the Belasco fiasco, the film's UK and US releases – in London on Thursday 14 August and LA on Friday 26 September 1975 – were remembered by many as rather lacklustre, sombre affairs; and, while the picture was quite well received by Los Angeles audiences, it was deemed a monumental dud almost everywhere else it played.

Compared with the frenzied, non-stop rhythm of the stage productions, the unhurried, almost dreamlike, quality of the film came as a shock, and many of those involved in its execution felt let down by the end result. 'We all went to the premiere of the film and were disappointed,' says Perry Bedden. 'I find it too slow. It lacks the pace of the stage show, and I think the Narrator character breaks up the continuity rather than providing it.'

While Patricia Quinn and Little Nell liked the picture, Richard O'Brien was uncomfortable with its sluggish dialogue and protracted pauses between some of the lines. In his audio commentary for the film's twenty-fifth anniversary DVD release, he expressed confusion as to why the picture felt so long and unexciting when Jim Sharman had insisted on it being the same length as the fast and furious stage version. In actual fact, depending on the varied running times of different formats – 35mm film for example runs at a speed of 24 frames per second whereas standard VHS (PAL) video tape runs at 25 frames per second, imperceptibly affecting the duration of any movie – *The Rocky Horror Picture Show*'s run time has been variously specified between 94 minutes and 100 minutes. The UK Region 2 edition of the DVD for example came in at exactly 96 minutes, including the end credits; six minutes longer than Sharman's specified duration.

As it happens, the film's final length – both actual and perceived – was inevitably dictated by a number of factors that separated it from the stage show. While the whole of 'Once in a While' and Brad's verse of 'Over at the Frankenstein Place' were taken out to tighten the pace of the picture, O'Brien's interpretation of 'Science Fiction Double Feature' as a wistful, tantalising ballad over the opening titles was slower, and therefore longer, than the Usherette's sprightlier version on stage. The extended wedding scene at the beginning added a couple of minutes, as did the change of setting from the lab to the dining room for Dr Scott's number. This brand new scene had to be established – first with dinner being served by Frank's comically incompetent staff and then by the shocking revelation as to the origin of the meal's meat – before Scotty could even begin the song he had launched into almost immediately on stage. On top of this, many of the film's lines were interspersed with thoughtful glances and calculated pauses and delivered at a more leisurely pace – with far more emotional and cinematic intensity – than their snappier theatrical predecessors.

Tim Curry felt less than satisfied with the slick, polished nature of the movie compared to the shoddy, rough-around-the-edges charm of the show; feelings he freely expressed on BBC Radio 2's *Let's Do the Time Warp Again* in 1999: 'I think it became a little self-congratulatory, the movie, and I was pushed to make Frank-n-Furter a lot more kind of camp than I'd played him on stage. I mean, I played him much more like a truck driver on stage. And it kind of got a bit kind of *Vogue*. Because the great thing in the show was that most of the make-up had gone in about 20 minutes; it had all sweated off my face. And that was part of the look of it, it was grungy and punky; and the movie was all a bit kind of Hollywood for me.'

As Richard O'Brien pointed out in his interview for the film *Midnight Movies: From the Margin to the Mainstream* in 2005, 'The biggest problem was, on stage we were parodying B-movies. [In the film] we had a problem [as to] whether we would be seen to be a parody or just another B-movie. Could we introduce a note of – not cynicism so much – but satire perhaps, something to allow us to comment upon the B-movie without appearing to be unintentionally funny?'

Attempting to justify the film's initial failure to connect with its audience, O'Brien elucidated that, with so many dreadful (supposedly straight) films being lampooned, the line between bad drama and knowing send-up had become increasingly fuzzy: 'To do a medieval film today for instance, you find it very difficult to bring authenticity to it that doesn't make us laugh, now we've seen *Monty Python's Holy Grail* [sic] and that kind of stuff. It's been parodied so many times and it's been bad so many times. And we had this; that we were stealing from the B-movies and yet we were making a B-movie, and intentionally making a B-movie. Would it work? Would our audience understand what we were doing? That's what we were facing. And then when we opened of course and it was quite clear that the audience didn't understand what we were doing – and certainly Fox didn't understand what we were doing – I wondered if we'd screwed it all up.'

With the show failing to illuminate Broadway and the film's investors reaching for the anti-depressants, Richard O'Brien surrendered to the notion that the *Rocky Horror* story was all over, while a more philosophical Tim Curry mused that the whole three-year experience had in fact been a 'great ride.'

In the aftermath of the film's failure, Richard O'Brien's marriage to Kimi Wong sadly collapsed. His subsequent marriage to costume designer Jane Moss – with whom he had two children, Joshua (born in 1983) and Amelia (born in 1989) – would likewise end in divorce in 2006.

With the *Rocky Horror* movie in the can, O'Brien began adding a string of memorable theatre, television and motion picture acting credits to his résumé. In 1980 he appeared as Fico, pipe-playing henchman to Timothy Dalton's flamboyant Prince Barin, in producer Dino De Laurentiis's and director Mike Hodges' colourfully enjoyable reworking of Alex Raymond's *Flash Gordon* comic strips. Considering O'Brien's affectionate allusion to the *Flash Gordon* serials of the 1930s within the lyrics of *Rocky*'s opening number, it seems rather fitting that he then appeared in the '80s incarnation. Other notable movie appearances included John Dee in Derek Jarman's *Jubilee* in 1977; a seedy undercover paparazzo on the trail of 1990s pop sensation the Spice Girls in *Spiceworld* (1997), a film that also featured Meat Loaf as the driver of the band's tour bus; Mr Hand, a parasitic alien humanoid, in writer-director Alex Proyas's 1998 futuristic neo-noir fable *Dark City*; and the despicable Pierre Le Pieu, opposite Drew Barrymore and Anjelica Huston, in *Ever After: A Cinderella Story* (1998).

In 2001, director Sam Irvin and writer-actress Cassandra Peterson cast O'Brien as the mysterious and histrionic Lord Vladimere Hellsubus in the second big screen outing for Elvira, Peterson's voluptuous wise-cracking alter-ego. With an amusing script, co-written by Peterson and John Paragon, *Elvira's Haunted Hills*, a non-sequential follow-up to 1989's *Elvira: Mistress of the Dark*, took the form of a good-natured parody of Roger Corman's popular series of kitschy Edgar Allan Poe adaptations from the 1960s – movies such as *House of Usher* (1960), *The Pit and the Pendulum* (1961), *The Raven* (1963) and *The Tomb of Ligeia* (1965) – of which Peterson was a huge admirer, and all of which had starred larger-than-life horror icon Vincent Price.

A considerable improvement on the first Elvira film, *Haunted Hills'* clever lighting and inventive set design genuinely evoked the required look, while O'Brien's role at last allowed him the opportunity to portray the kind of melodramatic horror character once played by the likes of Christopher Lee, Peter Cushing and especially Vincent Price, whose presence had added immeasurably to the very pictures being sent up.

Subsequently on stage, O'Brien garnered overwhelming acclaim when he played a role that could have been tailor-made for him, that of the loathsome Child Catcher – a character first created on film by Robert Helpmann in 1968 – in the original West End production of *Chitty Chitty Bang Bang*, which opened at the London Palladium on Tuesday 16 April 2002.

Having wrapped the film version of *Rocky Horror*, director Jim Sharman returned to the world of Australian theatre. The rest of the cast meanwhile resumed their respective film, television, theatre and music careers – with an Oscar-winning future ahead for Susan Sarandon and rock superstardom just around the corner for Meat Loaf. None could have suspected that they had just been involved in one of the most unusual 'sleepers' in motion picture history.

While clearly not the greatest film in the world – its budgetary constraints and hectic shooting schedule definitely showed on screen – *The Rocky Horror Picture Show*, unlike many musical screen adaptations, remained completely true to its source. By contrast, the hit 1978 film version of *Grease*, starring John Travolta and Olivia Newton-John, for example, concentrated almost solely on the teen romance between its two lead characters, whilst adding several new songs and radically altering much of the dialogue, whereas the original stage incarnation had been very much an affectionately tongue-in-cheek parody of the rock 'n' roll era as a whole. Although Jim Sharman had restructured and tightened the script a little, his movie was still unmistakably *Rocky Horror*. It was intelligently directed, imaginatively lit and stylishly edited with cannily economical panache. Each and every one of its meticulously-pitched central performances was played to sardonic perfection.

Most up-to-the-minute, hip and groovy, particularly youth-orientated films of the late hippie and early glam rock era made the mistake of being conspicuously fashionable and contemporary, especially in terms of production design, art direction and costume. In retrospect, this would seem a sure fire way to ensure that a film becomes dated in the shortest possible time frame. The clothing, hair, sets, and even the lighting of *Performance* (1970), *Phantom of the Paradise* (1974), *Tommy* (1975) and the film versions of *Godspell* (1973) and *Jesus Christ Superstar* (1973), all made in the early '70s, inevitably root those films in history.

3: THEY GOT CAUGHT IN A CELLULOID JAM

Despite making a self-aware 1950s B-movie homage, Brian Thomson and Sue Blane did not give *Rocky Horror* a fashionably '70s – or even a noticeably '50s retro – look. Consequently, while they may not have been overly conscious of it at the time, the film's astute designers cleverly bestowed upon it a timeless quality that would help to ensure its endurance way beyond that of its contemporaries.

Over a year after it first launched, and with memories of the film's production beginning to fade, Richard O'Brien began to hear interesting stories. People would ask if he was aware of what was happening with his movie in the United States. 'It's opened and closed, as far as I know,' he would reply innocently, blissfully unaware that, in the days before the 1980s home video boom, 20th Century Fox's embarrassing little flop – derided on its initial release by critics and audiences alike – was beginning to make quite a noticeable mark on the alternative midnight movie circuit.

As if raising an impudent middle finger to snooty New York critics who had panned the show and driven it from their short-sighted city, insomniacs and anti-establishment cultists began to embrace the film version, take it to their collective hearts and ultimately heap unprecedented devotion and worship upon it.

Like no other work of cinema, *The Rocky Horror Picture Show* affected its fans on such a personal level that they began to dress as the characters, mimic the on screen events and shout their own independently-invented dialogue between the lines of the script that they now knew word for word. O'Brien now found himself being asked by American fans if those absurdly long drawn-out pauses – which, upon seeing the film for the first time, he had found so disagreeable – had actually been left intentionally by the director in order to try to encourage audience interaction. Of course they hadn't.

In the decades that followed, *Rocky Horror*'s final irony would be that the offbeat, inaccessible little oddity, which Fox had immediately realised was not the mainstream musical they had been coerced into making, would slowly grow from an underground cult into the longest continually playing film in cinema history. It would gradually become a box office hit of modern blockbuster proportions, an unparalleled audience participation experience and the ultimate cross-generational rite-of-passage movie, reverently adored by millions of dedicated fans the world over.

4
Don't Judge A Book By Its Cover

A self-confessed eternal adolescent, Richard O'Brien has frequently insisted that *The Rocky Horror Show*'s plot is simple, unsophisticated and juvenile; little more than a nostalgic musical comic book or a tacky science fiction B-movie for the stage.

To the outsider, though, all this talk of glam rock fused with B-movie horror, cross-dressing extraterrestrials, gender confusion and the creation of artificial life – not to mention mythological, metaphysical and even religious connotations – might sound rather complicated and pompous. In truth, while these elements definitely exist on a number of levels within the show's narrative, most – apart from sex, rock 'n' roll and the transparent horror movie conventions – are rarely more than hinted at. Such subtle undertones may often bypass the perception of the average viewer, yet without alienating them or diminishing their enjoyment of the show as a whole. Much of this can be attributed to a smartly accessible multilevel script structure, which is happy to appear outwardly shallow and fun with no pretentious desire to show off how clever it actually is. It may seem infantile or superficial at its surface, but *Rocky Horror* can be viewed as a modern myth – the relevant ingredients are certainly all present – and, like all myths, it is open to individual interpretation.

'One could say it's the work of genius,' its author and composer suggested nonchalantly on VH-1's *Behind the Music* in 2000, 'but it isn't the work of genius. It's probably the work of somebody that should've been on a couch somewhere, talking to an expensive psychiatrist.'

An examination of the work itself – its characters, its songs, and a few of its influences, in-jokes and pop-culture references that have not yet been covered herein – would seem to be in order.

As already documented, Brian Thomson's original minimalist set (enforced chiefly by the production's minuscule financial resources) represented a crumbling old 1950s movie-house. Although later productions would proudly show off their more substantial budgets by adding grandiose laboratory equipment, foreboding castle walls, real cars and working spaceships, keeping the show innovative and fashionable for increasingly demanding and sophisticated audiences, Thomson's original – a faultless example of unsophisticated brilliance – perfectly suited the ambience of the piece, shrewdly allowing the simplistic excellence of the material as written to work its magic, without need of elaborate scenery or complicated special effects.

Though they do not appear in every production – due to the personal preferences of individual directors – the show's ghastly, ghoulish Ushers (aka Ghouls or Phantoms) create a creepy unsettling atmosphere with their unpredictable antics and irreverent interaction with the audience, while setting the scene for the appearance of the Usherette. As created on the London stage by Patricia Quinn, and traditionally played by the same actress who portrays Magenta, the character as conceived is a dreamy innocent, poignantly mourning the forgotten celluloid treasures of a less complicated time.

While there is often a palpable sexiness to the Usherette, with her short button-through uniform and the occasional involuntary flash of stocking top, it is more a sweet unknowing naiveté than anything approaching explicit exhibitionism. Many subsequent productions, however, surrendered to impulse and gave the character a raunchier temperament. Jamie Donnelly's interpretation – glitzy extravagant make-up, wild hair and a hand-microphone themed to look like a large ice-cream cone – for the Los Angeles and New York productions in 1974 and 1975 flaunted a flashy flamboyance not seen in the London version, and the phrase 'Hi, I'm Trixie', audaciously emblazoned across the front of her refreshments tray, hardly helped to curb such ostentation. While either approach works, it is without question that a degree of restraint during the early scenes will massively amplify the impact of Frank-n-Furter's entrance.

Actress Kara Lane, who portrayed the Usherette for the 2009/10 UK touring production, remembers being directed to approach the character as if she were 'a 1950s housewife whose form of escapism is working at the local cinema so she can watch her heroines on screen.' She explains that the tour's director, Christopher Luscombe, expressed a belief that the Usherette should be a bit more 'real' than the show's other characters. 'Sue Blane is so precise with her costume design that she'd even designed the Usherette's dress to be tacked up higher than the usual 1950s style knee length uniforms,' Lane reveals, 'I think the tacking could only be seen from the first couple of rows, but the overall effect was to see the tops of the Usherette's stockings.'

That this woman's slight rebellious streak – as well as a yearning for the fantasy and glamour of the silver screen to supplant her dreary daily existence – could be palpable simply by crudely stitching up the hem of her workwear by a couple of inches is a prime example of the designer's ingenious eye for detail and the importance of logical realism within a surreal fantasy environment.

During the 1930s and '40s, the likes of Universal Studios' *Dracula* (1931), *Frankenstein* (1931) and *The Wolf Man* (1941) had been suitably chilling for their time, filling audiences with dread and causing many a sleepless night. The detonation of two atomic bombs over the Japanese cities of Hiroshima and Nagasaki by the US Air Force in 1945 abruptly awakened the world to the threat of brand new – all too real – horrors, and (in the cinema) ushered in an era of radioactive mutations and alien invaders from outer space, effectively laying the traditional Universal monsters to rest; at least for the time being. These atomic age terrors, frequently symbolising the dangers of nuclear conflict or exploiting the West's fearful ignorance of international communism, would continue to dominate the science fiction fantasy genre for the next decade. That is until Britain's Hammer Films came along, and, with the help of Peter Cushing and Christopher Lee, began to infuse new life – and a new look – into a few old friends.

Technically, most of the films referenced in the song 'Science Fiction Double Feature' would not classify as B-movies in the truest sense of the term, as most of them were reputable and respected on their initial big screen releases. By definition, B-movies were often intended as speedily produced supporting features to play on the same bill as a more popular mainstream presentation in order to flesh out the programme – without spending much money on trivialities such as decent actors, coherent scripts, impressive sets or expensive locations. Latterly the term has come to encapsulate a broader category of film, often being used to describe any low budget or badly acted picture. Genres most commonly associated with it are crime thrillers, Westerns, horror and, most notably, science fiction.

While he could have name-checked any number of movies, from an unlimited back catalogue of memorable possibilities, those Richard O'Brien chose for his tribute song (probably for reasons no more significant than to find a necessary rhyme or whimsical lyric) have become 'the hallowed few', with countless *Rocky Horror* fans owning video or DVD copies of them in their treasured collections.

The song's opening allusion to distinguished British actor Michael Rennie in Robert Wise's genre-defining *The Day the Earth Stood Still* (1951) not only establishes the spirit of *The Rocky Horror Show* itself with a simple yet ingeniously effective epigram – typical of O'Brien's song writing – but effectively condenses into two lines the entire plot of an admired science fiction classic. Mortally wounded by the paranoid and trigger-happy US military on the eve of a crucial universal ultimatum, compassionate alien ambassador Klaatu (Rennie) imparts his decisive warning to assembled representatives of the human race.

In the once golden age of Hollywood, inferior even to the lowly B-picture was the Saturday morning serial. Running week by week – in an unapologetic bid to generate repeat trade – in the form of cheaply made (in most cases *very* cheaply made) 15-minute episodes, the serials would pack

4: DON'T JUDGE A BOOK BY ITS COVER

in the action and adventure with little or no time for character development or narrative logic. Each chapter would then invariably end with an impossible-to-escape cliff-hanger, leaving its heroes in horrendous peril for an agonisingly long week. The technique practically dared audiences to miss the next instalment, only to blatantly cheat – once viewers had had seven days of real life to forget exactly how the previous sequence had unfolded – as usually nothing more heroic than tricky editing came to the rescue.

Of the abundant celluloid serials of the 1930s and '40s, none was more enduring than Universal's *Flash Gordon* (aka *Space Soldiers*) in 1936, starring Larry 'Buster' Crabbe in the valiant title role, along with Jean Rogers as his plucky love interest Dale Arden, Frank Shannon as brilliant scientist Dr Hans Zarkov and a deliciously histrionic Charles Middleton as the evil Ming the Merciless, launching his planet Mongo, quite literally, against the Earth. Despite Richard O'Brien's cheeky song lyrics, however, thanks to monochrome film, the colour of the fearless space adventurer's underwear (or indeed his other garments for that matter) would forever remain a mystery.

The first *Flash Gordon* adventure proved so popular with audiences that it spawned two sequels, with Crabbe (who also played *Buck Rogers*, another famous science fiction hero, in a 1939 Universal movie serial) reprising his role. *Flash Gordon's Trip To Mars* (aka *Deadly Ray from Mars* and *Mars Attacks the World*), which first hit movie screens in 1938, featured the unforgettably menacing Clay People, while 1940's *Flash Gordon Conquers the Universe* (aka *Space Soldiers Conquer the Universe*, *Perils from Planet Mongo* and *Purple Death from Outer Space*) saw mankind threatened once again by the tenacious Emperor Ming, this time dispatching his lethal Purple Death plague into Earth's atmosphere. Tune in next week to see if Flash can save the day.

On the strength of his distinctive voice alone – his face remaining transparent or completely concealed by surgical bandages until the film's final few moments – 1933's *The Invisible Man* made a star of English character actor Claude Rains. James Whale's darkly comic melodrama, based on H G Wells' cautionary tale of a scientist driven criminally insane by his own extraordinary discovery, showcased some astounding (for the time) visual effects and an abundance of delightfully camp and subversive humour (a Whale staple). It is also fondly remembered for a renowned and much-loved blooper, as the bare-footed invisible protagonist appears to leave very obvious shoe imprints in the snow.

Never less than a compelling, though softly spoken, presence on screen, Rains subsequently played the sympathetic father of Lon Chaney Jr's cursed Lawrence Talbot in *The Wolf Man* (1941) and the title role in Universal's 1943 colour remake of *The Phantom of the Opera*, directed by

Arthur Lubin. In addition, he appeared in a number of noteworthy non-genre pictures, including Frank Capra's *Mr Smith Goes to Washington* with James Stewart in 1939, and the enduring propaganda classic *Casablanca* in 1942.

In 1933, a studio makeover turned natural brunette Fay Wray into cinema's definitive blonde scream queen, and the character of aspiring Hollywood actress Ann Darrow not only captured the heart and imagination of Skull Island's colossal ape deity *King Kong* but became almost as iconic as the gargantuan gorilla himself. An authentic movie phenomenon, *King Kong*, boldly released by RKO at the depth of the Great Depression, even assisted the ailing US economy by reviving public interest in previously unoccupied office space at the top of the recently completed Empire State Building. It skilfully utilised all known visual effects techniques of the time, including the pioneering stop-motion work of effects innovator Willis O'Brien, and carried them to dizzying new heights; while Max Steiner's majestic music set the standard for all future orchestral film scores. *King Kong* had the added distinction of being the first motion picture in history to play simultaneously at New York's two largest movie theatres – Radio City Music Hall and RKO's Roxy Theatre – reportedly selling out every performance. Kong himself may have been just 18 inches (45cm) tall in reality, but fantasy cinema owes him the biggest debt of eternal gratitude.

As reflected by the decade's never-ending slew of thought-manipulating alien invasion pictures, Cold War tension and anti-communist scaremongering in the United States had reached fever pitch by the mid-1950s. Directed by Jack Arnold from a story by Ray Bradbury, *It Came from Outer Space* (1953) wove into its routine plot a curiously fitting 'don't judge a book by its cover' message, as – despite their weird appearance – the film's otherworldly cyclopean visitors turn out to be benign, temporarily employing human slaves out of necessity to help unearth their crashed spaceship. Exhibited in 3-D – a trendy movie gimmick at the time – the film featured genre stalwarts Richard Carlson (who played the male lead again the following year in *Creature from the Black Lagoon*, another 3-D monster flick by the same director) and Barbara Rush, as well as Arnold's typically eerie desert photography.

The infectious chorus of 'Science Fiction Double Feature' additionally makes reference to 1932's *Doctor X*, a mixed-up hybrid of the mad doctor genre, horror-comedy and a straight detective thriller, starring Lionel Atwill and Fay Wray (a year before *King Kong*) and directed by Michael Curtiz; although the song's implication that Atwill's insane Doctor Xavier 'will build a creature', a plot device missing from the film in question, suggests that O'Brien may have jokily used the name as a general term for all mad movie scientists; perhaps the name Frankenstein would not scan

4: DON'T JUDGE A BOOK BY ITS COVER

within the melody.

'See androids fighting Brad and Janet,' continues the Usherette's touching tribute, knowingly name-checking *The Rocky Horror Show*'s young protagonists and categorising them generically as the charmingly formulaic innocents abroad (whatever their names) in so many a clichéd B-movie script.

A futuristic version of Shakespeare's *The Tempest* with state-of-the-art high-tech visuals, a mature dialogue-heavy screenplay and a mechanical Ariel may have sounded like an offbeat pitch for a major studio project, but that's exactly what MGM delivered with the groundbreaking *Forbidden Planet* in 1956. In spite of its interplanetary rocket ship, sparking ray guns and an invisible monster – manifested from the twisted subconscious of the villainous Dr Morbius (a space age Prospero) – the story pioneered a realistically believable human outlook towards a career in space exploration. Subjected to a daily mind-numbing routine and tiresome working environment, the film's 23rd Century astronauts have long since developed a jaded world-weary attitude toward the exotic wonders of the universe. An entirely justified approach, which was borrowed and used even more effectively for future genre efforts such as John Carpenter's darkly satirical *Dark Star* in 1974 and Ridley Scott's 1979 science fiction blockbuster *Alien*.

With an attractive human ensemble, including Walter Pidgeon, Leslie Nielsen and Anne Francis, relentlessly upstaged by scene-stealing automaton Robby the Robot – later the star of his own spin-off movie *The Invisible Boy* (1957) – and its stimulating premise, *Forbidden Planet*, like *The Day the Earth Stood Still* before it, set a significant new standard for science fiction cinema; one that would remain intact until Stanley Kubrick's *2001: A Space Odyssey* re-wrote the rule book in 1968.

Known primarily as *The Man from U.N.C.L.E.*'s Alexander Waverley between 1964 and 1968, eminent British thespian Leo G Carroll, a method actor before the phrase was invented, played an extensive range of characters during an abundantly prolific stage, film and television career, and his turn as Professor Gerald Deemer in Jack Arnold's 1955 creature feature *Tarantula* remains as memorable as any. An experimental growth serum – intended to solve the world's food crisis by enlarging animals and plants to gigantic proportions – results in the escape of a monstrous arachnid (inaccurately described as an insect in the film's uninformed 1955 trailer). The creature terrorises the countryside, devouring people and livestock and depositing puddles of a disturbing sticky white discharge (thankfully identified as venom) until, in an impressive climax, it is finally napalmed by a squadron of jet fighters led by pilot Clint Eastwood in a minuscule early appearance. A memorable subplot, in which Carroll's aging scientist is injected with his own serum by a disgruntled former lab assistant and falls victim to a prematurely advanced form of acromegaly – a genuine disfiguring disease, caused by an over-production of growth hormones – showcases an impressive 1950s prosthetic make-up, more creepy and unsettling in many ways than the film's titular arachnid.

Of course, while increasing the size of cattle and poultry might make sense, the logistics of why the creation of a monstrous tarantula would be a requirement of any research to help feed the starving would never stand close examination. Of the countless atomic-age giant bug pictures however, *Tarantula* transcended its unashamedly implausible B-movie premise, thanks to honest performances, an intriguing story and Arnold's well-paced direction and editing.

Adapted from a 1951 novel by John Wyndham, director Steve Sekely's *The Day of the Triffids* (1963) told the sensational story of a poisonous species of sentient plant life that malevolently threatens to dominate the Earth after most of humanity has been irreversibly blinded by a spectacular meteor shower. Much of the paper-thin plot centres on the characters Bill Mason (Howard Keel), his sight spared thanks to the hospital bandages that temporarily sheild his vision after an eye operation, and Christine Durrant (Nicole Maurey) as they flee the ghastly vegetable menace. An unrelated, often criticised (and marginally more interesting) subplot, involving a married couple (played by Kieron Moore and Janette Scott) defending their besieged vulnerable lighthouse from a frightening assault by the blood-thirsty Triffids – shot by a completely different director, Freddie Francis – was added late in production to extend the slender running time, and was ultimately responsible for the film's uneven feel.

Another renowned actor was Dana Andrews, who played sceptical paranormal investigator John Holden, struggling to pass on a cursed runic parchment believed to bestow a diabolical demise upon whoever should inherit it, in the 1957 British chiller *Night of the Demon*. The film, which has since acquired cult classic status amongst fright film aficionados, was severely truncated and re-titled *The Curse of the Demon* for its American release a year later, where it formed half of a double bill with Hammer's *The Revenge of Frankenstein*. Based on M R James's 1911 short story *Casting the Runes*, director Jacques Tourneur's film is an intelligent, sophisticated, suspenseful and plausible horror offering, making Richard O'Brien's playful suggestion 'Dana Andrews said prunes gave him the runes, and passing them used lots of skills' – which again served the purpose of providing an essential rhyme – suitably insolent.

In 1951, two years before presenting director Byron Haskin's influential big screen translation of H G Wells' *The War of the Worlds*, producer George Pal delivered a visually impressive, well-crafted work of apocalyptic sci-fi hokum entitled *When Worlds Collide*. Spectacular in its day, the film was the natural precursor to similarly-plotted modern blockbusters such as 1979's *Meteor*, an ill-conceived run-of-the-mill disaster flick that featured big name stars Henry Fonda, Natalie Wood and a clearly uncomfortable Sean Connery all wrestling with a ludicrous script; Michael Bay's deliberately over-the-top *Armageddon* (1998) with Bruce Willis, Ben Affleck, Billy Bob Thornton and Liv Tyler heading a glamorous all-star cast; and the far more plausible, but financially less successful, *Deep Impact* (also 1998).

With him having his amorous eye on astronomer's daughter Joyce Hendron (portrayed by the rather striking Barbara Rush), the irksome news that wayward planet Bellus is on a collision course with Earth was probably not the kind of bang that pilot Dave Randall (Richard Derr) was hoping for; although the impending threat of global destruction rarely deterred horny '50s B-movie heroes from the pursuit of hanky-panky. After depicting a controversial lottery to determine who should survive, amid widespread panic and pandemonium, Rudolph Mates' film adaptation of the 1933 novel by Philip Wylie and Edwin Balmer develops into a gripping struggle to evacuate the chosen few to nearby planetoid Zyra in a huge interstellar ark before the cataclysmic finale. Sadly, Pal's plan to film the same authors' follow-up book *After Worlds Collide* (1934), chronicling the survivors' exploration and colonisation of their new home, was abandoned when his 1955 science fiction epic *Conquest of Space* failed to conquer the box office.

Having firmly established the mood with her witty melodic prologue, the Usherette promptly exits. Wedding bells then signal the arrival of Denton High School's Brad Majors and his exuberant young sweetheart Janet Weiss. The wedding in question is not their own, but that of their close friends Ralph Hapschatt and Betty Monroe (identified with spelling variations as Ralf Hapshatt and Betty Munroe in the published version of the show's script), the teenaged quintessence of the American dream. The engagement ring in his pocket is weighing heavily on Brad's mind; and so, inspired by his friends' nuptials, he decides to surprise his beloved by whipping it out, slipping it on her finger and manfully declaring his feelings; by way of a song of course.

Their symbolic debt to the likes of Adam and Eve, Hansel and Gretel and the Babes in the Wood has been repeatedly emphasised, but for the most part Brad's and Janet's character origins stem from the world of classic science fiction monster movies.

Creature from the Black Lagoon's Richard Carlson (also the leading man of *It Came from Outer Space*) has been referred to by Richard O'Brien as the archetypal Brad Majors; but a rugged, square jawed, bespectacled Gene Barry as astro-nuclear physicist Dr Clayton Forrester (that's a real sci-fi hero name right there) in George Pal's *The War of the Worlds* must undoubtedly rate as a worthy contender. Embarrassed after failing to recognise Forrester from his cover picture on a recent issue of *Time*, Ann Robinson's Sylvia Van Buren blushes and decides that it must be because he was photographed without his glasses for the magazine. 'Well, they're really for long distance,' the handsome scientist explains, slickly removing said specs as he turns to gaze into her eyes. "If I want to look at something close I take them off.' It may be only ten minutes into the film, with the menacing Martian death machines yet to make their first appearance, but after a smooth speech like that, the coy smile on Robinson's face informs the viewer that this courageous hero has already scored. She'd be a push-over for Dr Frank-n-Furter.

The aforementioned scene is a fitting illustration of why the temptation to play Brad as a wimpy nerd (as some actors mistakably do) is to seriously misjudge the character, and ought to be resisted. Brad's predecessors, the self-assured male protagonists of the atomic age monster flicks, were often scientists, yet none was ever portrayed as an awkward, geeky, buck-toothed buffoon. Academically gifted, every one of these guys may have been a high school science major (Brad's surname is typical of Richard O'Brien's drollness), and yet it would be no stretch whatsoever to imagine them as both the handsome class president and captain of the football team as well.

'Some of the characters have got way out of hand,' states actor Peter Blake, evidently infuriated at the way certain productions have inexcusably diluted the material. 'Brad, for example, has turned into a Jerry Lewis type of idiot, a wimp. He's not that at all. He's a red-blooded all-American regular guy. He's horrified by what he's confronted with and should defend Janet like a caveman.'

Addressing an assemblage of *Rocky Horror* fans at London's Hard Rock Cafe in October 2007, Blake made similar observations, positing that the idea of Frank-n-Furter being able to seduce an unquestionably masculine high school jock is not only funny but has, at the same time, an uncomfortably dangerous edge. He argued that, conversely, the notion of Frank deflowering Jerry Lewis's typically timid and feeble screen persona was neither dangerous nor amusing in any way.

Having seen one of the show's earliest performances at the Theatre Upstairs, Blake considers that the best performance overall was that of Jonathan Adams as the original Narrator, who he insists was the perfect embodiment of the role as envisioned: 'He was superb. He held the audience spellbound as he conjured up the scene with his opening lines of, "I would like ... if I may ... to take you on a strange journey." The audience were right there with him, they wanted to go on that strange journey with him from that moment.'

Initially, the same approach was adopted by most performers who assumed the role – not least Charles Gray, whose dignified presence and

4: DON'T JUDGE A BOOK BY ITS COVER

velvety cadence memorably graced the film version – although some gave it the occasional inventive slant, such as a precocious librarian, a stuffy professor, a condescending college lecturer, a perverted headmaster or a haughty school ma'am.

Circumstances – primarily audience behaviour – would later dictate major revisions to the Narrator's responsibilities, and the character regrettably changed from a scholarly storyteller into a cheesy MC; Edgar Lustgarten's gracious aristocratic decorum sadly replaced by the uncouth deportment of a vulgar game show host.

Even if Brian Thomson could not afford or even dream of such extravagance at the Royal Court Theatre in 1973, *Rocky Horror*'s newly affianced couple (in the guise of countless different actors over the years) would, in the lavish productions that followed, find themselves embarking on their momentous journey in style; their vehicle being represented by a variety of real automobiles (or parts thereof), wooden cars, cardboard cars, projected images or even a hand-held facsimile of a windshield. While larger budgets would ultimately allow such creativity to be expressed, nothing more elaborate than a mimed journey – improvised by the ever-resourceful Jim Sharman and his imaginative cast – was all that the Theatre Upstairs and King's Road versions required. Janet mimicking the action of a windshield wiper with one arm and a finger while Brad clutched an invisible steering wheel simply added to the show's intentional cheap B-movie charm.

The ensuing tyre blow-out has been achieved in a number of inventive ways, including a comic-book style explosive flash (with the word 'bang' written across it) held up behind the car at the appropriate moment; a balloon popped with a pin by one of the production's gruesome Phantoms; or even by having a Phantom, kneeling on all fours to symbolise a car seat, slowly sinking to the ground (with a bemused Brad on his back) as the hypothetical tyre rapidly expels its air.

In the publicly available edition of the show's libretto (published by Samuel French in 1983), when Riff Raff confronts Brad and Janet at the castle door, the accompanying stage direction indicates that he is looking past them as if expecting someone else; an excellent illustration of O'Brien's brilliantly understated read-between-the-lines script complexities. While the viewer has no definite clues as to the identity of Riff's anticipated visitor – they might not even perceive such a slight nuance in the actor's performance – could it possibly be surmised from his earlier allusion to morphia (during the song 'Over at the Frankenstein Place') that the emaciated, pasty-faced butler might have an addiction to pain-killing drugs such as morphine? Indeed Frank-n-Furter, who is often depicted as having crossed Band-aid plasters on his inner arms, no doubt to hide tell-tale needle marks, implies that his servant may be a little out of sorts because he had been awaiting a visit from his dealer: 'He's just a little brought down because, when you knocked, he thought you were the candy-man.' Can it not, therefore, be further presumed that Eddie, the unfortunate delivery boy in the laboratory freezer, was couriering something a little more dubious than a pizza?

At the Theatre Upstairs, as well as in most *Rocky Horror* stage productions before 1990, Frank-n-Furter made his startling entrance – with a unified cry of 'Master!' from his servants – almost immediately after Brad and Janet entered the castle. 'The Time Warp' then followed 'Sweet Transvestite' once Frank left the stage and our docile duo had been divested of their rain-drenched clothing. When Jim Sharman and Richard O'Brien wrote the *Rocky Horror* film screenplay, they revised scenes and amended some of the dialogue; the most instantly noticeable change being the switched order of these two songs. While purists and admirers of the stage version might deride this creative decision, it does, when examined objectively, make a certain logical and narrative sense.

As with Dorothy Gale's arrival over the rainbow in *The Wizard of Oz* (1939), Brad Majors and Janet Weiss enter an entirely new world the very moment they accept Riff Raff's invitation to cross the castle's threshold. As already noted, an initial proposal to present *The Rocky Horror Picture Show*'s early scenes in black and white – effectively making Brad's and Janet's Denton the equivalent of Dorothy's Kansas – and not turning to colour until Frank-n-Furter shamelessly threw off his cloak proved unfeasible and was dropped during production. Despite continued fan debate, however, just as the eye-popping Technicolor of Oz indicated Dorothy's coming of age after a dull and sheltered childhood in monochrome Kansas, the lyric 'Let's do the Time Warp again' occurring as soon as the characters (and the audience) find themselves inside Frank-n-Furter's castle can be seen to symbolise a literal leap in time from the innocent naiveté of Brad's and Janet's (and Richard O'Brien's) 1950s to the free-thinking liberalism of Frank's permissive new world.

Furthermore, while Magenta and Columbia appear to make their entrances rather unceremoniously, the only motivation seeming to be that they need to get on stage – either to introduce Frank or to perform 'The Time Warp', according to which incarnation of the script is being presented – it can be argued that the movie version presents a more linear sequence for these events. On film, the journey of Brad and Janet takes the audience directly to Riff Raff, who, by way of a skilfully-tossed and expertly-caught feather duster, introduces Magenta, an action that initiates 'The Time Warp', then reveals Columbia (appropriately seated on top of a retro jukebox), and ultimately allows the imposing master of the house to make his magnificent entrance.

'So come up to the lab, and see what's on the slab,' Frank purrs invitingly at the climax of 'Sweet Transvestite'. 'I see you shiver with anticipation; but maybe the rain is really to blame, so I'll remove the cause but not the symptom.' While it may seem unimaginable for such an obvious and delightful joke to be overlooked, and even though it features on subsequent recordings, neither the published script nor the original London cast album include Frank's signature pause between 'Antici ...' and 'pation,' indicating that small, character-defining idiosyncrasies were constantly evolving as the show developed.

Transsexualism and gender confusion aside, there are a number of reasons why an individual may indulge in the act of cross-dressing. Some might be transvestites or transvestic fetishists – frequently heterosexual men (typically married with otherwise completely conventional lifestyles and occupations) whose penchant for feminine clothing may be psychologically inherent or habitual, and rarely an indication of homosexual leanings. Female impersonators or drag queens, on the other hand, are more often (though not exclusively) gay men with a taste for showy theatrics – heightening or parodying the feminine persona with the masquerade of an overly confident and excessively glamorous diva – many of whom make use of outrageously overstated female attributes such as false breasts, extravagant make-up and flashy costumes in order to entertain, amuse or titillate; but off stage might have no cross-dressing cravings whatsoever. While a typical transvestite male might harbour aspirations to be ostensibly indistinguishable from a real woman, with no desire for detection (though in some cases the danger of possible discovery might actually add to the thrill of such behaviour), the female characteristics of a drag artiste are often intentionally grandiose in order deliberately to attract attention.

From the character of Old Mother Riley, created in 1934 by actor and Musical Hall performer Arthur Lucan, who appeared in 16 successful comedy pictures between 1937 and 1952 – the last of which, *Old Mother Riley Meets the Vampire* (1952), featured Bela Lugosi in another of his humiliating final film appearances – to Rupert Everett's sweetly appealing headmistress Camilla Fritton in the 2007 reboot of the *St Trinian's* franchise, cross-dressing has been a staple of stage, film and television for decades. In practically every instance, the objective of the proverbial 'cock in a frock' (a common and charmingly eloquent definition of a man in ladies' attire), including the ludicrously grotesque dame of the traditional British pantomime, is to infer a feminine facade. Whatever the motive – disguise, humour or erotic arousal – the character being portrayed, whether convincingly feminine or suspiciously macho, is invariably supposed to be female. Even Norman Bates, the horror genre's predominant dress-wearing mama's boy, as played by Anthony Perkins in Alfred Hitchcock's *Psycho* (1960), has no incentive for donning his long-dead, though perpetually over-bearing, mother's clothes other than to assume her personality for the purpose of murder; an incentive that indicates, according to the dialogue of Joseph Stefano's tight screenplay (adapted from Robert Bloch's novel), that Norman is in fact *not* a transvestite.

The primary exception has always been *Rocky Horror*'s Dr Frank-n-Furter, who, despite an unmistakable and self-confessed proclivity toward female undergarments, implies not the slightest intention of feminine pretence; and whose affinity for such attire by no means betrays his unquestionable masculinity. He is not pretending to be a woman; he is simply a very sensual and seductively charming man clothed in garments customarily associated with the opposite sex.

This was clarified particularly wisely in an especially succinct and adroit character description for Frank-n-Furter which appeared on the website of theatrical producer Toby Simkin:

'This is not about camp or drag; it is about manly bisexuality and transvestism in a way which allows everyone to question quite which sex he prefers.'

An uncompromising and unethical sexual predator with no preference between genders – or even, given his unearthly origins, between species – Frank has a fondness for such apparel that is stimulated by decadent self-indulgence and the hope of enticing his next conquest. While he often exhibits a decidedly hedonistic, self-centred and thoroughly amoral persona – a brutally out of control homicidal seducer with a dangerously delusional God complex – Frank-n-Furter has been perceived by many as a shameless and liberating role model, largely because of the revolutionary manner in which the character seems to challenge increasingly passé conventional attitudes towards sexuality.

Even as fashionable rebellious playwrights such as Joe Orton were sneaking sexually subversive material under the noses of inattentive theatre censors – as James Whale had done with prohibited religious imagery in his 1930s horror films – homosexual characters in mainstream entertainment were predominantly depicted throughout the 1960s and '70s as overtly effeminate and unthreatening comedy figures. The colourfully carefree Mr Wilberforce Claybourne Humphries, played to limp-wristed perfection on British television by John Inman in the BBC's long-running department store-based sitcom *Are You Being Served?*, was adored by audiences and became a national (and later international) treasure. On BBC Radio, Julian and Sandy, a pair of camp out-of-work actors, brilliantly realised by Hugh Paddick and Kenneth Williams, were two of the most instantly popular characters on the hugely successful comedy show *Round the Horne* (originally broadcast between 1965 and 1968). Their flamboyant theatricality, naughty ad-libs, double-entendre laden language and blatant use of Polari – a coded lingo used by gay men at a time when homosexuality was illegal in Britain – endeared them to the general British public.

It is reasonable to suppose that presenting such characters as seemingly exaggerated caricatures might have helped a deliberately ignorant (and fearfully intolerant) conservative society to view them as something alien or imaginary – and thus accept them as figures of fun and amusement – rather than as a proportion of their own community.

In a very real sense, Frank-n-Furter helped to stamp a huge platform heel over the image of this mincing gay stereotype, simply by refusing to conform to such outmoded *fairy-queen* type-casting.

Although he went along with encouragement to camp it up a bit more for the film version, Tim Curry's periodic assertion that, in spite of the character's chosen attire and indiscriminate sexuality, his interpretation of the role on stage was 'more like a truck driver' reiterates early US *Rocky Horror* enthusiast Dori Hartley's insightful description of Frank-n-Furter as 'a faggot Clint Eastwood' [sic]; while 'I'm just a Sweet Transvestite, from Transsexual, Transylvania,' his brazenly bold introduction to a couple of outwardly clean-cut strangers, is an empowering declaration of unashamedly arrogant supremacy. Although he is evidently not averse to the odd effeminate tantrum or an occasional bout of sheer unadulterated camp (primarily when comedy demands it), it remains abundantly clear that Frank-n-Furter is powerful, controlling and attractively masterful. 'Everyone in the audience should not mind being seduced by him,' Richard O'Brien told Rob Cope in 1990. 'It's not a rape fantasy; but they really shouldn't mind being seduced by him.'

The performance of the actor remains crucial in establishing character, but the essential symmetry between feminine and masculine qualities – a major justification for why Frank provoked unexpected feelings of arousal in both female and male members of 1970s audiences, much to the astonishment of the show's creators – can be augmented through seemingly indiscernible use of make-up and costume. Citing, with unmistakeable reverence, the genius of Sue Blane, performer David Bedella presented a practical demonstration of such techniques, via communal video website YouTube, to all would-be Frank-n-Furters in 2009. From his dressing room, the actor candidly revealed how cosmetic embellishments such as heavy eye shadows, dark shading under the nose and lips, and a prominent cleft in the chin, all achieved through the skilful application of theatrical make-up, could add essential hints of masculinity to an evidently feminine visage. These refinements – along with costume minutiae, such as a delicate lace glove adorning one arm and a more basic and manly equivalent on the other – can all help to make Frank-n-Furter who he is. 'Constant balance,' Bedella emphasised. 'That's what makes him sexy.'

Flirtatiously admiring their 'charming underclothes,' the eccentric doctor, by now adorned in a strangely alluring green surgical gown, offers his young guests blood-stained laboratory coats to spare them any blushes. 'It'll make you feel less vulnerable,' he drools salaciously. Impressed by Brad's manly assertiveness (in response to the household's hitherto lack of telephonic assistance), Frank playfully articulates his approval and probes mischievously about the possibility of body art residing beneath the aforementioned underwear: 'Tell me, Brad, do you have any tattoos?' In his book *The Rocky Horror Show: As I Remember It*, Rayner Bourton related Richard O'Brien's amusing account of this particular line's origin. Purportedly, in response to the wearily predictable cries of 'blasphemy' from members of the church when *Jesus Christ Superstar* first opened in London, the show's press office proposed a clever publicity stunt. They organised a tea party at St. Paul's Cathedral; to be attended by members of the cast (including Paul Jabara, the production's memorable King Herod) and a group of church leaders.

'Conversation between cast and clergy had been going as one might expect; polite, conservative and a little strained,' Bourton recounted. 'Tea was being served by some of the lower ranking younger priests, when Paul Jabara turned to one of them and asked in an extremely loud voice so everyone present could hear, "Do you have any tattoos?". It was a showstopper of a line and caused an embarrassing silence before the young priest, whom Paul had addressed his question to, managed to utter an embarrassed and rather mumbled "Certainly not".'

Completely unfazed, Jabara apparently then turned at once to the Archbishop ('or whatever high rank he held,' as Bourton put it) and asked, 'Oh well, how about you?'

The very thought of the actor's delightfully brazen irreverence – a classic example of the term 'culture clash' – cannot fail to raise a satisfied smile, making it completely understandable why Richard O'Brien felt the need to immortalise the whole uncomfortable exchange in Frank-n-Furter's laboratory. Brad, like that immature young priest before him, is duly appalled at the suggestion; whereas Janet becomes giggly and joyfully coy.

The audience is given no time, though, to contemplate the possibility that Frank's next enquiry might have been about piercings, as, prompted by Riff Raff, the enigmatic scientist proceeds to divulge the secrets of his latest experiment. Following a dramatic, attention-grabbing monologue, containing all the confusingly vague spin of a slippery political speaker – compelling and charismatically delivered, while in actual fact explaining very little – the postmodern Prometheus unveils the sinful fruits of his impious labours.

Taking into account his fervent showy theatrics, the scarcity of detailed information within Frank's over-the-top lab speech (nothing more definite than an undisclosed *accident* is revealed to be the sacred 'secret' of creation) suggests that – rather than a legitimate desire to advance bio-chemical science – narcissistic praise and self-absorbed worship (not to mention carnal gratification) are the real motives behind the dubious doctor's reprehensible experiments.

Interviewed by Rob Cope in 1990, Richard O'Brien confirmed that the implication that an unacknowledged and unappreciated Riff Raff might actually have been responsible for these experiments – a fact which would explain his unmistakable underlying bitterness – had been deliberate: 'I always said this in the subtext to myself when I was playing Riff. I built Rocky, Frank didn't; he was having champagne and smoking joints and fucking people. I was doing all the work in the laboratory.'

'He's got all the glamour, he's got all the chat, everybody thinks he's fucking wonderful,' the author exclaimed passionately, the line between Riff's attitude toward his master and the opinion of their flesh and blood creator almost seeming to blur for the briefest of moments, 'but actually I'm wonderful, but nobody can see it.'

In addition, having had the experience of playing both parts, O'Brien expressed the inherent challenges he felt the role of Riff Raff offered an actor:

'In many ways, it's the best part. Frank gets all the adulation; but to play a good Riff is a bit daunting really, because you have to have a lot of the power behind the throne.

'Resentment and an incestuous relationship (which isn't spoken about) with Magenta; it's subtext, subtext, subtext. And this quiet, pulsating resentment that's there; so that when the worm turns, he wants to be in control. It builds on the fact that when Magenta says "But I thought you'd liked them, they liked you" we get this paranoid little human being, which you know is a weak human being, revealing himself. I think it's actually a great part to play. However it's not seen to be so, because Frank steals all his glory. But the more Frank steals the glory, the better the part it is to play.'

Far from the monstrous, mismatched, crudely-constructed abomination decreed by formulaic cinematic convention, Rocky Horror is a lot more pleasing on the eye than anything ever stitched together by Peter Cushing or any of his celluloid contemporaries. Although, with that said, Cushing did have a little more luck (at least as far as looks were concerned) with Susan Denberg, a former Playboy pin-up who portrayed the rather more aesthetically pleasing product of the Baron's ill-fated experiments in director Terrence Fisher's *Frankenstein Created Woman* (1966).

Sporting a flawless physique, evoking the classical heroes played by Steve Reeves in the sword and sandal genre favoured by Frank-n-Furter –

and preceded by that of bodybuilder (and future Darth Vader) David Prowse as another monstrous creation in *The Horror of Frankenstein* (1970) – the newly unbandaged Rocky instantly rocks the house with a fast and furious musical number, astutely equating his own precarious situation with that of fabled Greek courtier Damocles.

As if to illustrate the seamlessness with which O'Brien's score cleverly blends scholarly sophistication with trashy 20th Century pop-culture, the razor-sharp lyrics leap swiftly from the highbrow mythological references of 'The Sword of Damocles' into a cheerful tribute to a contemporary bodybuilder, who famously advertised his fitness programme in 1950s comic books, and then straight into a kick-ass rock 'n' roll anthem, with nary a join in sight.

Much like Columbia – who, in addition to the familiar sequined get-up of the tap-dancing Ruby Keeler figure, has had numerous other costumes through countless productions (a PVC-clad fetishist, an '80s pop groupie, and a Shirley Temple lookalike being just a few examples) – Eddie has been attired with similar creative flexibility. Even within the parameters of the archetypal retro rock 'n' roller, definitively described in the published libretto as very much a 1950s British Teddy Boy in skin-tight drainpipe trousers and crepe-soled shoes, the character has been adapted into an Elvis Presley clone, a leather-jacketed biker, and a '70s punk rocker among others. Thanks largely to the film, and in spite of the libretto's specific outline for the character, the leather-clad biker interpretation largely replaced the Teddy Boy look for most subsequent productions.

Sinisterly, the unfortunate delivery boy's introductory stage direction concludes with 'He has a hint of Frankenstein's monster.' Whether the evoked visage is that of Boris Karloff's classic flat-headed hulk or the blistered fetid facial flesh of Christopher Lee's radical reinvention, hazily derived from a subconscious filled with half-remembered movie images, the picture painted by these seven simple words is perceptibly clear. 'He is battered and shows the occasional seam,' the script states, as the ghoulish juvenile delinquent, originally conceived to satiate O'Brien's personal rock star fantasies, is typically presented with a botched and bloody lobotomy scar across his forehead. Just as the show's swift-paced second half lets slip that the castle's occupants are of extraterrestrial origin (from the planet Transsexual in the distant galaxy of Transylvania), that Dr Scott is Eddie's uncle and that Frank's peculiar domestic personnel are siblings, it also divulges that half of Eddie's disruptive brain was transplanted into the head of Frank's muscular new playmate (who, somewhat curiously, displays no visible scars). This rather questionable organ relocation is deemed by the increasingly infuriated scientist to be the root of Rocky's insubordination.

In the published script, Frank stabs Eddie to death with the microphone stand while pushing him back into the freezer, although it should come as no surprise to learn that the delivery boy's unfortunate demise has often been imaginatively reworked by directors. Strangled with a microphone cord, dismembered via chainsaw, repeatedly stabbed with a butcher's knife and even sliced and diced with a razor-fingered glove, resembling the one worn by *A Nightmare on Elm Street*'s Freddy Krueger in the popular '80s slasher franchise, are just a few of the inventive ways in which the psychotic scientist has summarily despatched his former dispatch rider. In the film version, the deranged doctor's formidable ice pick actually makes fast work of Eddie off-camera, but brutal sound effects and a bloody aftermath are suggestively graphic in the best Hammer horror tradition.

'Normally I find camp exploitations of old movies highly resistible because they imply a wholly unjustified feeling of cultural superiority,' wrote the *Guardian*'s Michael Billington in his 1973 review of *The Rocky Horror Show*. 'But this show won me over entirely because it achieves the rare feat of being witty and erotic at the same time.' A salient observation indeed, endorsing just how daringly cutting-edge *Rocky* was for its time; particularly when taking into account the notoriously prudish British attitude toward sex as a spectator sport. Explicit publicity stills and posters shamelessly adorn cinema frontages in the liberal city centres of Scandinavia and mainland Europe, and yet the comical image of dirty old men in grubby brown raincoats, furtively sneaking into a seedy, dimly-lit establishment on a squalid London backstreet, still endures.

Although the lampooning of homosexual characters on television no doubt abetted their acceptance amongst repressed middle class audiences in the 1970s, a similarly uncomfortable response toward the portrayal of even the most conventional sexual act as entertainment could be easily deduced from the slew of farcical sex comedies dispensed by the UK film industry at that time. The likes of *Eskimo Nell* (1974), *Come Play With Me* (1977) and *The Playbirds* (1978) – promoted with lurid exploitative posters, proudly displaying their 'X' certificates and false promises of deliciously dirty delights – may have starred Mary Millington (known at the time as Britain's sex superstar) and featured an ample abundance of gratuitous nudity, but the presence of Alfie Bass, Henry McGee, Irene Handl, Rita Webb, Windsor Davies and other familiar names of mainstream British comedy on their various cast lists betrayed them as the innocuous slapstick romps they actually were. *Rocky Horror* luminaries Jonathan Adams, Rayner Bourton, Christopher Biggins and even choreographer David Toguri – hardly typical porn stars – all turned up in *Eskimo Nell*.

Whereas Bernado Bertolucci famously shocked cinemagoers with the notorious *Last Tango in Paris* in 1972 and Dutch-born starlet Sylvia Kristel set pulses racing in the French soft-porn classic *Emmanuelle* (1974) a couple of years later, a brief (unintentional by all accounts) flash of Barbara

Windsor's breasts in *Carry On Camping* (1969) or the unsophisticated sex scenes of the popular *Confessions* films, pitched towards smutty comedy rather than actual titillation – Robin Askwith's pale bare arse continually going above and beyond the call of duty for the sake of a cheap laugh – are probably the UK's foremost contribution to cinematic eroticism.

The permissive society it may have been, but the inhibited British public clearly didn't want it rammed down their throats.

The Rocky Horror Show, on the other hand, as Michael Billington's review indicated, although rich in laughs, was also genuinely and undeniably sexy, from Frank-n-Furter's appearance and general demeanour; Janet's spirited seduction of Rocky, while still wearing her virginal white underwear and effectively obliterating the wholesome 1950s 'mom and apple pie' tag with a single song; and Frank's pleasurable unveiling and breathless appraisal of his physically immaculate creation; to the copious exhibitionistic display of saucy lingerie; Magenta's tiny black panties, stockings and bra, teasingly exposed through the sheerest chiffon; and the principal cast dressed in seamed fishnets and burlesque corsetry for Frank's hedonistic 'Floorshow'. 'Probably every man's sexual fantasy, and some women's,' *Time Out* magazine declared provocatively. Whatever the sexual preference, it could probably be found amongst *The Rocky Horror Show*'s eclectic collection of characters; an overview of which substantiates the assurance of 'Something for everyone' on Richard O'Brien's original Theatre Upstairs programme cover.

The prim and proper girl next door type, with a veiled yet unmistakable wicked streak, is intrinsically embodied by the delightfully corruptible Janet Weiss; a profusion of feisty, youthful kookiness is relentlessly and exhaustively expressed by the roguishly naive Columbia; and the domineeringly sultry Magenta oozes cool, no-nonsense womanly experience.

While the strait-laced dependability of Brad Majors might suit those not euphorically enraptured by the prospect of surrendering to the hard-to-resist, self-gratifying wiles of the seductive Dr Frank-n-Furter or the primordial allure of rebelliously delinquent bad boy Eddie, there are those who might prefer a home-made, dumb blond, muscle-bound hunk. Even the twisted, seething, resentful Riff Raff has an appealing vulnerability that some find oddly attractive.

The show's impeccably balanced fusion of comedy and erotic sensuality is best exemplified by the unforgettable bedroom scenes, in which Frank flagrantly deceives and seduces both female and male visitor consecutively. It is here that the narrative, which has thus far borrowed extensively from the likes of *The Old Dark House* and *Frankenstein*, throws a welcome dose of *Dracula* into the mix, with Frank now representing the role of Bram Stoker's voracious vampire Count, whose lust for blood –

often perceived by vampire aficionados as a metaphor for sexual gratification – was seldom gender specific. It is never open to question though that Frank-n-Furter will opt to suck something a lot more pleasant (for both parties) than mere arterial fluid.

Eliciting uproarious laughter and flabbergasted astonishment – even amongst today's harder-to-shock audiences – the inevitable raucous reaction to the revelation that Brad is actually getting it on with a burly transvestite (with remarkable impersonation skills), and not his petite young fiancée as he had presumed, can usually indicate just how many *Rocky Horror Show* first timers are in the crowd on a particular night.

The tradition, established by Jim Sharman, of playing the scene in silhouette works twofold. It cleverly allows the undeniably Shakespearean motif of deception and mistaken identity to be played to its full comic potential, while also cunningly maintaining a semblance of tasteful decency. Having experienced fairly sheltered, small town, antipodean childhoods, open-minded big city liberalism and wanton depravity had proved an invigorating eye-opener for both Sharman and Richard O'Brien, and yet both had managed to retain a degree of shy, reserved – in some ways almost prudish – restraint. 'Everyone assumes *Rocky Horror* is just pantomime camp,' Sharman wrote in his published memoir, 'but it's subtler than the cliché suggests. The secret isn't in the outrageousness but in the fact that Richard O'Brien created a skilful comedy of manners – a tradition as old as 18th Century Restoration plays or Mozart and Da Ponte operas. This is often overlooked in revivals, and the results can be grotesque. The cult audience engaged with the cast and the characters but also with the style in which it was played.'

Time Out's 1973 review labelled the original production 'provocative rather than permissive,' an adroit summing up of Sharman's *modus operandi*; and O'Brien has since criticised other directors for approaching the show in an inappropriately crude and vulgar way. Speaking on *BBC Breakfast* in 2009, he disclosed that, during filming of *The Rocky Horror Picture Show* in 1974, associate producer John Goldstone pointed out that the two most successful film series to emerge from British studios were the Hammer horrors and the *Carry On* movies, and suggested that at least some of *Rocky*'s appeal might be attributed to its being a kind of next generation combination of the two. Although brimming with grisly mayhem and blatant naughtiness, both Hammer and the *Carry Ons* managed somehow to exude a quaint, inoffensive and quintessentially British demeanour.

The script is indisputably rude (there is never any doubt, even in silhouette, that Frank is indeed fellating Brad behind the screen), but it is generally accepted that, in much the same way that a saucy hint of stocking top or a naughty glimpse of nipple can be frequently more stimulating than full frontal nudity, an approach somewhat more akin to *Carry On Camping* (1969) than *Debbie Does Dallas* (1978) usually best befits the teasingly sinful tone of *The Rocky Horror Show*.

'If I was to believe that everybody went home from that show and had the most wonderful night's sex, and that the show had just been little more than foreplay, that's fine by me,' Richard O'Brien quipped mischievously on VH-1's *Behind the Music* in 2000, as the wickedest of impish smiles slowly crept across his cheeky face. 'As long as they screamed my name at the optimum moment.'

According to *The Rocky Horror Show: As I Remember It*, Rayner Bourton's book of personal *Rocky* recollections, the nature of the Theatre Upstairs' tiny performance area presented director Jim Sharman with a slight dilemma concerning the dynamics of one entrance in particular. Frank-n-Furter's dialogue stipulates that Dr Scott has illegally penetrated the sordid stronghold of his arch rival via 'the Zen room'; although, rather than signifying a genuine understanding of age-old Buddhist wisdom or a profound yearning for inner enlightenment, the latter is more likely a chamber reserved for the likes of drug-induced mind-expansion and psychedelic out-of-body experimentation (a theory to which the movie version's sly candid cutaway of the newly arrived Dr Scott examining an iffy-looking cigarette butt, his wheelchair parked next to a conspicuously smoking hookah, would appear to add validity). 'There were only two places Dr Scott could make his entrance from,' Bourton elucidated, 'Through the double doors that were the main entrance to the auditorium or from the back of the central walkway.'

Sharman's appeal for suggestions apparently drew a plethora of ideas – both sensible and outrageously bizarre – from cast and crew. These included parachuting the doc in from above, launching him through the floor by way of a trap-door and spring, magically materialising him out of thin air, rolling him out of a carpet in the tradition of Cleopatra, or (Rayner's own proposition) firing him from a cannon. These were all rejected, as was the possibility of him staggering onto the stage as Columbia whipped him from behind, although the latter did result in the idea of a sadistic whipping being retained for the scene in which Frank reprimands Riff Raff.

Bourton revealed that, inspired by the rolled carpet image, Sharman particularly liked the thought of Scotty falling prostrate at Frank-n-Furter's feet: 'Then Jim came up with what was to prove to be a crippling decision for Dr Everett Scott; a wheelchair. Entering through the double doors, opened by our two assistant stage managers, Columbia propelled him onto the stage at high speed, bringing him to a sudden halt by tipping him out of the chair at Frank's feet. Undignified; but extremely effective.'

This memorably dramatic entrance, used impressively throughout the

4: DON'T JUDGE A BOOK BY ITS COVER

Theatre Upstairs and King's Road era, would unfortunately prove far less powerful once the show transferred to a more traditional auditorium with a proscenium arch stage and no practical central runway, such as the Comedy Theatre in London's West End.

After the Second World War, a number of Germany's most brilliant rocket scientists were recruited by the USA – by way of a government programme known as Operation: Paperclip – to work on various space and military programmes; while any supposed former Nazi associations remained tactfully unmentioned. Actor Peter Sellers took the idea to ludicrous extremes when creating the sinister title character of Stanley Kubrick's satirical Cold War classic *Dr Strangelove: Or How I Learned to Stop Worrying and Love the Bomb* (1964). Although generally accepted to be based, at least in part, on famed physicist and astronautics engineer Werner von Braun, Sellers pushed his characterisation beyond the very boundaries of absurd, setting a benchmark for preposterous parody in the process. Consequently, the urge to ape such a comic masterpiece, by playing *Rocky Horror*'s Dr Scott as an over exaggerated, barking mad professor, has proved irresistible to countless actors.

In a lot of ways, the wheelchair-bound boffin is probably the only character, other than Frank-n-Furter, who – by being so far removed from recognisable reality – can be plausibly sent-up without violating Richard O'Brien's '*Peyton Place* acting' rule. With that said, however, many have also played the part extremely effectively as a more subtle, snooping and mysteriously unreadable character. The published libretto makes references to him sneakily snapping covert photographs of Frank-n-Furter's curious laboratory equipment, evidently suggesting a hidden agenda.

As Rayner Bourton's book revealed, the obvious *Dr Strangelove* parallel was certainly not lost on the movie-savvy Sharman, and Dr Scott's persona was quickly developed accordingly: 'Sellers' character spoke with a strong cod German accent and was confined to a wheelchair. So, with the seeds of that parody firmly sewn, Dr Scott was given a little more character background with the addition of a line for Frank-n-Furter: "Or should I call you Dr von Scott?"' And with Paddy O'Hagan instinctively raising his arm in a customary fascist salute, with an accompanying cry of '*Sieg heil*,' Bourton continued, 'it was a natural progression for Dr Scott to have a German accent.'

Nevertheless, as Richard O'Brien explained on *The Rocky Horror Picture Show* DVD's audio commentary, Frank-n-Furter's provocative insinuations that Dr Everett Scott may have Nazi affiliations ought really to come as a shocking revelation to an audience; and the impact is severely lessened if Scotty already has perceptibly Germanic intonation. Whilst clearly admiring Jonathan Adams' talent, O'Brien expressed a disappointment at his being allowed to use the German inflection for the character on screen.

To those familiar only with the cinematic incarnation of *Rocky*, Dr Scott's accent has become definitive, almost to the point of confusion. Actor Nathan Amzi divulged to *Rocky Horror* convention attendees in 2006 that, having been cast as Eddie/Dr Scott in the 2006/07 UK touring production, and with viewings of the film as his only template, he eagerly honed a suitably stereotypical Nazi accent in preparation, only to be told during his first rehearsal that, in fact, Dr Scott should speak with an American accent. This initially led him to fear that audiences would hate him for going against the expected, and it was only reassurance from the show's most ardent devotees, with their comprehensive knowledge of its characters and traditions, that ultimately helped put his mind at rest before his first performance. After all, Meat Loaf – a proud Texan born and bred – had played the wheelchair-restricted scientist with his own unmistakable Southern drawl in the 1974 Los Angeles production, with great success.

Dr Scott having been exposed as a governmental UFO investigator, and having recognised Frank's Sonic Transducer as a perfected version of the much sought after Audio Vibratory Physio-molecular Transport Device, the secret of which has long eluded Earth's brainiest boffins, the petulant transvestite tyrant drugs his uninvited human visitors (along with Columbia and Rocky, with whose dissension he is fast becoming bored) in preparation for 'The Floorshow'; a decadently self-indulgent late night musical extravaganza.

Dressed – presumably by Frank (behaving in the manner of an arrogant Greek god, manipulating human beings for perverse personal pleasure) – in high heels, fishnet stockings and lace corsetry, the partakers lyrically express innermost feelings relating to their plight. With their behaviour no longer dictated by bourgeois middle class convention – an upshot of their fateful encounter with the free-spirited personification of a permissive society – Brad's and Janet's conformist roles have been effectively inverted. Janet it appears has been refreshingly born anew, a strong-willed contemporary young woman: 'I feel released, bad times deceased; my confidence has increased; reality is here.' Conversely, Brad, his hunter-gatherer status outmoded and his sexuality suddenly open to question, is reduced to a state of meek, self-conscious perplexity: 'It's beyond me, help me mommy; I'll be good, you'll see; take this dream away.'

On film, Jim Sharman and his editor Graeme Clifford cleverly illustrated Brad's discomfort in the scene by shooting Barry Bostwick from the rear (stumbling clumsily on his stiletto heels) for part of his verse, in complete contrast to his more confident fellow partakers in 'The Floorshow'.

'Although I have seen productions where this scene has been nothing short of consenting onstagecast groping, in those early days the scene was certainly played for sensuality,' Rayner Bourton declared in his book, in reference to the orgiastic group love-in, tenderly prefixed and accompanied by Frank's persuasive pleas to 'Give yourself over to absolute pleasure' and 'Don't dream it, be it,' during which the priggishly aloof Dr Everett Scott finally loses all self-control and unveils stocking-clad legs from beneath his blanket.

Any promise of climax (sexual, musical or otherwise) is suddenly cut short by the no longer subservient Riff Raff and Magenta – now resplendent in spectacularly kinky extraterrestrial space outfits – gate-crashing the party and executing an extraordinary *coup d'état*.

As revealed by Jim Whittaker's 1998 book *Cosmic Light: The Birth of a Cult Classic*, the confusion of actor Bruce Scott (Riff Raff in the first US production) as to why Riff displayed no hump when wearing his spacesuit was met with a hastily indefinite response from Jim Sharman: 'That's the way we do the show.' A more logically judicious explanation might be that Riff Raff has at that point simply cast off his submissive servant disguise, adding to the plot's recurring themes of betrayal, subterfuge and deceit.

Nit-pickers have insisted that Riff's assertion of his laser's ability to discharge a beam of pure anti-matter scientifically contradicts its status as a laser. But surely, aside from the obvious – a weapon so technologically advanced would likely have various settings, anti-matter being but one of them – O'Brien was just having fun with his own quirky, nonsensical, pseudo sci-fi jargon, as he did with the laboratory's Sonic Oscillator and Sonic Transducer? After all, *Rocky Horror* is not *Star Trek*; it's a tacky, whimsical 1950s B-movie spoof.

'What's his crime?' Brad demands, as self-appointed judge, jury and executioner Riff Raff's plan to terminate his sadistic tormentor becomes evident. This is a particularly revealing line, speaking volumes for the way in which the evening's experience has challenged Brad's viewpoint. It is not unthinkable that the very notion of Frank-n-Furter's *avant-garde* lifestyle would previously have constituted a crime in the eyes of the staid and conservative Brad Majors.

Columbia – in many ways the only character to express unabashed defiance toward Frank, with an eleventh-hour rant in the previous scene – now valiantly takes the 'bullet' for him; a courageous and selfless act that at last penetrates Frank's pomposity and opens his eyes to the very real danger he faces.

'The master is not yet married,' Riff tells Janet in an earlier scene. 'Nor do I think ever will be.' At face value, the line is typically read as a jokey throw away reference to Frank-n-Furter's sexual proclivities and unconventional way of life. However, the luxury of foresight, a benefit of repeat viewings, can add complexity, and effectively alter its meaning. Given his ultimate demise at the hands of his vengeful 'faithful handyman,' the snide insinuation that Frank will never marry – coupled with a knowing glance between Riff and his conniving sister – could be construed as a clue that the misshapen minion has already planned his master's fate.

Understated facial expressions and subtle nuances in a talented actor's performance can further expand an audience's understanding of Riff Raff, often revealing unexplored depths of a fascinating, multi-layered individual. Some play it stone-faced and unwavering – bitter, obsessed, fanatical – so that Columbia's sacrifice seems a minor, almost unnoticeable, inconvenience to his single-minded plan. Some adopt a manic, wide-eyed grin, as if thoroughly enjoying the chance to finally unleash psychotic judgment upon humanity. Others choose to convey a conspicuous look of regretful dismay as the twisted handyman inadvertently shoots the bubbly household groupie (an innocent bystander, whose only crimes appear to be idealistic naiveté and misplaced trust), hinting that he might actually be horrified by what he has done. Something he knows he must now see through to the finish.

'Columbia should die quickly,' stresses the stage direction in the 1983 published edition of *The Rocky Horror Show*'s script. 'Frank should enjoy it more.' Unfortunately, rather than read this as an intimation that an actor ought to make more of the moment dramatically and emotionally, innumerable performers and directors seem to have interpreted the word 'enjoy' in this context far too literally. Pleasing though it may be for an undemanding and uninitiated audience to witness Frank ludicrously sending up his climactic death scene – unimaginative histrionic melodrama and outrageously camp dying swan impressions being all too common – both the character and the show deserve something a lot more sincere and affecting.

In spite of his selfish and iniquitous ways, as he yields to Riff Raff's laser, Frank-n-Furter, like every great villain, should elicit a degree of sympathy from his audience. As with all genuine tragicomedy, unashamedly playing the scene for poignant, heartfelt pathos can pack a powerful punch, which endows the camp buffoonery of previous scenes with an uncomfortably edgy sense of balance. It also has the power to shock an audience who, as well as being a little afraid of sentimentality or of having to confront their own feelings, may have been lulled into believing that they had been watching just an inconsequential comic sex-farce for the last 90 minutes.

In many ways, Frank's inevitable downfall is made all the more tragic because of his earlier upbeat and optimistic outlook, which contrasts with that of such perpetually tortured souls as the eternally morose title character of *Hedwig and the Angry Inch*, an angst-ridden resentful transsexual who spends much of that musical bewailing their tormented existence. A far cry from such melancholic anguish, Frank-n-Furter's early declaration of 'I'm just a Sweet Transvestite …' is unashamedly joyous. He delights in the mischievous seduction of his naive young guests and the unveiling of his hunky new plaything, while his 'Wild and Untamed Thing' climax to 'The Floorshow' is a blissfully unapologetic celebration of a hedonistic lifestyle.

Only when he feels let down or betrayed does Frank appear to get upset (in the face of his creation's illicit liaison with Janet), peeved (Riff Raff's incompetence in allowing Rocky to slip his chains), afraid (facing imminent death at the hands of his seditious servant) or downright psychotic (when annoyingly upstaged by an unexpectedly defrosted Eddie); all of which make his fear and sadness at the end infinitely more heartbreaking than if he had spent the whole show woefully bemoaning the wretchedness of a dismal existence.

That Richard O'Brien left the question of what might become of Brad and Janet (and indeed Dr Scott) unanswered is somehow deliciously satisfying in its uncertainty. While Riff Raff leaves a *Hamlet*-style bloodbath in his wake, before blasting off from Earth in the castle (now revealed to be a disguised alien spacecraft) along with his strange incestuous sister, he allows the human visitors to live. Undoubtedly changed and psychologically scarred by their experience, they are left to ponder not only their own infidelities, and the feasibility of redeeming a severely tarnished relationship, but their very existence in an infinite cosmos.

This deliberately ambiguous denouement notwithstanding, a different directorial approach can imply potentially diverse futures. The character arc suggested by the attitudes of Brad's and Janet's 'Floorshow' verses is emphasised by 'Superheroes'. Brad is melancholic, pitiable and submissive, while Janet, supported by punchier percussion and a throbbing bass line, although anxious and bewildered (for the moment), is perceptibly stronger and emotionally empowered.

'I think the last half hour is magical – you almost can't go wrong – and it's great that it finishes so strongly,' declares Christopher Luscombe, director of the 2006/07 and 2009/10 UK touring productions. 'Some of the writing is genuinely poetic and has a profundity that surprises those who don't know the piece … "Superheroes" for example was actually written before *Rocky Horror* and Richard always said that it works because of that; much better than trying to write a number to provide a neat finish and tie it all up with a bow. The end's great because it's open to interpretation. Which one of [Brad and Janet] should stand up first? Who should take whose hand?'

In the published libretto, the song culminates with a separated Brad and Janet futilely reaching for each other across the stage, while the cast assembles between them for the Narrator's closing assessment.

In accordance with personal interpretation – of a script already rich in subtexts – various directors have intimated differing levels of hope or despair. In some productions Brad and Janet have left the stage separately, without physical contact; while in others they have tenderly held hands or embraced. In several versions Janet has protectively supported Brad, now a frightened, broken and confused young man, the conventional gender roles, exhibited at the beginning of the evening, now unmistakably reversed. Although often they have remained in their skimpy 'Floorshow' attire, occasionally the couple has been fully clothed again at the end of the show, possibly wondering whether or not the whole experience was simply a rather bizarre dream. Sometimes Janet has been wearing Frank-n-Furter's leather jacket for the scene, categorically ruling out the dream theory and symbolically substantiating her newfound empowerment, while Brad has been back in his conventional mens' jacket from the beginning of the show, possibly signalling his subconscious desire to return to the way things were. Other variations have included a moment in which Brad, upon rediscovering the engagement ring in his pocket, has offered it to Janet again. Sometimes she has sorrowfully refused. On other occasions she has accepted. The outcome of such an instance, unspecified by the script and left to individual creativity, is enough to dictate very disparate levels of gloom or optimism at the show's conclusion.

'I think that, ultimately, they do stay together, and they have a good marriage because they've achieved self-knowledge,' suggests Christopher Luscombe, revealing his own hopeful approach to show's closing moments. 'Because of what they've been through, they're stronger people and better partners. I wanted the show to end optimistically too, so that, as an audience member, you feel you've got somewhere.'

'And crawling on the planet's face; some insects called the human race. Lost in time and lost in space and meaning.' With many contemporary audiences, the Narrator's condescending judgment on society as a whole might as well be directed specifically at the loutish, moronic spectators who incessantly heckle the characters and care nought for the metaphysical conundrums posited by a cleverly insightful script. In many ways, this makes his despairing observations even more perceptive and immediately pertinent, while Richard O'Brien's intuitively wise warnings about the ever-looming shadow of tyrannical oppression – conceived years earlier during that rainy afternoon matinee of *Arturo Ui* – remain eternally relevant.

As ghostly smoke swirls and the lights begin to fade, the quietly haunting final chords of the song 'Superheroes' bring forth a becalming ambience across the auditorium.

Backstage, on the other hand, the atmosphere can often be one of chaos.

4: DON'T JUDGE A BOOK BY ITS COVER

With the same performer usually playing both Magenta and the Usherette, a swift costume change is crucial in order for the actress to divest herself of a cumbersome extraterrestrial space outfit – complete with an elaborate Elsa Lanchester-style hairdo – and step back into her drab 1950s cinema uniform in time for the melancholic closing reprise of 'Science Fiction Double Feature'. 'We had it down to perfection,' smiles actress Kara Lane. 'I had someone taking my space wig off while someone else took my boots off, and I undid and took off the silver spacesuit. Then I'd slip my white heels on, while doing up the buttons of my Usherette dress. Finally I'd take off my purple Magenta eyelashes and purple lipstick, and put on pink lips while someone put my blonde wig on; and then I'd run to the wings while putting my belt and earrings on. It took about 60 seconds. The fastest quick change I've ever done was 11 seconds.'

Of how the melancholic despair of the show's final moments made her feel, Lane – who played the dual role of the Usherette/Magenta for the 2009/10 UK tour – says sincerely: 'That was emotional, but in a way I think it makes you feel a bit empty inside as well. Everything's gone wrong at the end,' she laments, recalling the Narrator's deeply profound closing words. 'It's very thought-provoking and always made me feel a bit lonely. But I loved that it had that effect.'

Bookending the proceedings perfectly, the Usherette's reflective reprise of the show's opening number allows the audience to leave the theatre pondering the profundities of the universe. Or just humming some excellent tunes. Either way, it's been fun.

'I sound as if I'm singing my own praises here, and please forgive me, I'm not,' implored the show's author during an unused portion of his interview for the 2005 film *Midnight Movies: From the Margin to the Mainstream* (included on the DVD as an insightful bonus feature), 'but every character comes on the stage at the correct time. Every joke falls into the script at the correct time. Every song occurs at the correct time.'

Every actor with whom he had worked, O'Brien declared, had expressed the opinion that no other show was as enjoyable to be a part of as *Rocky Horror*: 'It's such a joy to walk onto the stage and know the audience is going to love you and love the show; and know that it's the easiest show you can do, because all you've got to do is play it for real. The jokes are there and the songs are there; and all you have to do is play it for real.'

'It's almost seamless and flawless, this show,' he asserted, attempting to fathom its secret. 'It's almost fool-proof. I've seen it under dreadful, dreadful conditions; with dreadful actors. And I'll be sitting there groaning, watching this show, and the performances perhaps, and maybe the paucity of musicianship, or whatever. But at the end of it, I've always gone, "Well actually, it wasn't that bad," because it somehow rather saves itself.'

Of the oft-proposed hypothesis that *The Rocky Horror Show* is a 20th Century reworking of *Babes in the Wood* or the Garden of Eden story, O'Brien wrote in the 4 March issue of *The Oldie* magazine in 1994: 'It is my belief that in the (naive) gathering and selection of elements for this musical collage, I chose, unwittingly, many of those that were already locked into both our conscious and subconscious memory.

'Am I deluding myself with this theory? Becoming pretentious? Perhaps so; perhaps it simply provides a childishly good toe-tapping time for those of an arrested development who are not too dissimilar from myself.'

The author-composer explained that his discovery of *Shadow and Evil in Fairy Tales*, a collection of transcribed lectures by Swiss scholar and Jungian psychologist Marie-Louise von Franz in which, in an effort to elucidate the continuous cross-generational appeal of classic myths and fables, she disassembled and examined their psychology, archetypal symbolism and recurrent allegorical themes, had added weight to his suppositions: 'After reading this treatise, I applied her theory to my show, and found – surprise, surprise – that it was chock-full of your actual psychological motifs and symbolism, which just goes to show that there are perhaps greater depths and rewards in the artless approach than there might be from a more knowing course of action. Rock 'n' roll, baby!'

5
Madness Takes Its Toll

It looked like a war zone. Toilet paper strewn like carnival bunting between rows of seating; chocolate bars scattered liberally across a desecrated floor; exploded bags of flour and copious amounts of white rice further defiling an already waterlogged carpet. Utter devastation, suggesting the consequences of wanton mob-handed violence, the destructive handiwork of a professional demolition company or the aftermath of some strange military operation, rather than the opulent magnificence of a beautiful Victorian playhouse.

And yet, thanks to the shameful exploits of over-excited – not even hostile – spectators, a performance of the 1985 UK touring production of *The Rocky Horror Show* was brought to a premature close in the interests of performer safety. The unavoidable decision was made by the theatre's management due to a ceaseless bombardment of missiles – rice, chocolate bars, toilet rolls and, most perilous of all, water – being hurled onto the stage by an increasingly frenzied crowd. With the production's electrical equipment in hazardously close proximity to a soaking wet stage, it was eventually deemed unsafe to continue with the performance.

For anyone who had been in the audience at the King's Road Theatre just a few years earlier, this incarnation of *The Rocky Horror Show* – already becoming something of a Frankenstein monster in its own right – would have seemed almost unrecognisable in comparison with the modest, understated, sharply satirical send-up created by Richard O'Brien, Jim Sharman and their talented associates.

So, how had it come to this?

The 1975 British cinema poster for *The Rocky Horror Picture Show* had borne the legend 'A musical dream come true.' Something the show had certainly granted actor Daniel Abineri. An adolescent penchant for early '70s glam rock – Lou Reed and David Bowie were big influences – led to Abineri's first *Rocky Horror* experience at the Chelsea Classic in 1973. 'I didn't know what the hell it was all about, but I absolutely loved it,' he confesses. 'There was a lot of pressure on me becoming an actor, as both my father and brother were in the business, but I just wanted to be a pop star; and it seemed to me that *Rocky* provided the perfect combination.'

Abineri's obsession with the show grew when, upon leaving school at the age of 15, he regularly attended performances at the King's Road

Theatre:

'Effectively I became a groupie. I got to know Perry Bedden and Chris Malcolm, and I used to hang out at the Cadogan with the cast after the show.

'The stage show was punk before punk,' he announces confidently, evidently still very clear and excited about what made the piece so appealing. 'It was dark, it was vulgar, yet it had these plaintive, melodic, beautiful songs. My favourites are "Science Fiction", "Over at the Frankenstein Place" and "I'm Going Home". It's a delicate balance of fear and comedy. The audience must worry about what's going to happen next. The original Ushers got the audience feeling uneasy before the show started and that contributed to the atmosphere. There's something about the absurdity of the situation and the characters that emerge from it.

'All the props were simple and in keeping; a hospital trolley, neon tubes rather than fancy lights, a curtain drape to shut off a piece of the action like the lab,' the actor expounds fondly, citing the eccentric eclecticism and fastidious attention to detail of the show's designers as a vital part of its initial charm. 'The rainbow across the screen when Brad and Janet are climbing the frame behind the screen during "Superheroes" was made out of neon tubes and Perspex; so simple but so effective, and all adding to the feel of the piece. You know the bulbs that we were set around the screen? Brian Thomson used to smash the odd one to make it look like a few random bulbs had blown and not been replaced. He also jammed a pink sling-back shoe into the fake proscenium arch. Everything was very precise. Brian and Sue had this great skill; they organised the chaos. It looked rough and ready, but the feeling of being in a zoo has to be carefully rehearsed.

'I think the whole sexual thing is a key ingredient. Having seen it first as a hormonal teenager I know just how important black stockings and suspenders are. All in all I think it was serendipity, but all the factors in the show just clicked together and worked.'

Once his own acting career took off – he starred opposite Arthur Lowe in three series of the LWT sitcom *Bless Me Father* between 1978 and 1981, and appeared in the film *International Velvet*, the 1978 sequel to the fondly-remembered 1944 classic *National Velvet* – Abineri did not resume his association with *The Rocky Horror Show* until 1979, by which time it had left the seedy converted flea-pits of the King's Road for the luxurious auditorium of a genuine West End theatre. Keen to revisit the show that had made such a memorable impression during his formative years, he accompanied his younger brother to a performance – starring Peter Blake as Frank-n-Furter and Neil McCaul as Riff Raff – at the Comedy Theatre. He remembers that, while his brother loved it, he personally felt that it was no longer the same show he had fallen in love with back in '73:

5: MADNESS TAKES ITS TOLL

'I remember saying to my then wife, "My obsession with *Rocky Horror* is over." It had lost something in the transfer from the King's Road to an established theatre with a proscenium arch. However, the very next morning my agent called me to go for an audition for the first British tour of the show. How spooky. I later discovered that the wardrobe mistress had heard me at a party, singing a very drunken version of "Sweet Transvestite" and had put my name forward.'

Producing the tour in collaboration with Michael White was British theatrical impresario Cameron Mackintosh, who, along with Richard O'Brien, oversaw Abineri's audition for Frank-n-Furter.

'They gave me a script to run over the lab scene, but I already knew the lines by heart, which I think impressed them,' smiles the actor, who also sang 'I'm Going Home' and 'I Can Make You a Man' for his meticulously thorough interviewers. 'Richard said to me, "You really want to play Frank, don't you?" I told him that I wanted it like an actor wants to play *Hamlet*, to which he replied, "I should think so too, it's a better part".'

Directed by Julian Hope – the programme would also acknowledge Jim Sharman as the show's original director – the very first UK tour opened on Daniel Abineri's twenty-first birthday, 8 August 1979, and co-starred Amanda Redman as Janet, Terence Hillyer as Brad, Brett Forrest as Riff Raff and Ziggy Byfield, already a veteran of several *Rocky Horror* roles, as Eddie/Dr Scott.

'One of my great pals was Ziggy Byfield,' recalls Abineri. 'He auditioned to play Frank in the first UK tour, but ended up with the part of Eddie, which of course he'd already played in the King's Road. He became my mentor for the character of Frank. He taught me how to walk in high heels, how to lock the legs, and made me run fast in heels for practice and to gain confidence. I can remember the first time I threw off Frank's cloak, standing in front of eight hundred people and thinking, "Oh fuck".'

Abineri unreservedly acknowledges the influence Tim Curry's Frank had on his own interpretation of the character: 'I'd seen Tim, Philip Sayer, Ziggy Byfield and Peter Blake. Of all those, I preferred those whose performances were closest to Tim's. His was a proper acting performance. It was insane but believable.

'I started off imitating him and then went off and improvised. His was such a powerful performance. He was a shaman, androgynous, and appealed to both sexes. He really made the most of Frank's entrances, which have to rank amongst the most powerful in theatre, especially his opening number.'

When the tour concluded, Abineri was invited to reprise his performance in the London production, which was still playing at the Comedy Theatre. 'I was offered the part and did an interview with the *Daily Mail*, which published that I was taking over the role. This was a bit unfortunate since Robert Fox, who was managing for Michael White at the time, had not yet told Neil McCaul, who was playing Frank.' This awkward situation at first caused a little friction between Abineri and members of the existing cast, which included an as-yet-unknown Tracey Ullman in the role of Janet. 'I took over; and then, two weeks into the role, Tracey Ullman led a posse to Robert and gave him an ultimatum; either he got rid of me or the rest of the cast would walk out. Robert, fortunately, thought that I was strong in the role, so his response to Tracey was, "See ya".'

Having had her bluff well and truly called, Ullman chose to remain with the *The Rocky Horror Show* for the remainder of her contract. Following appearances in two UK comedy sketch shows – *A Kick Up the Eighties* (which ran between 1981 and 1984, and featured Robbie Coltrane and Rik Mayall) and three series of *Three of a Kind* with Lenny Henry and David Copperfield between 1981 and 1983 – the popular actress-singer-comedienne played the role of Candice Valentine, alongside Ruby Wax, Dawn French, Jennifer Saunders and Joan Greenwood, in the first series of ITV's all-female sitcom *Girls on Top* in 1985, before relocating to the United States and making a name for herself with her own top-rated TV show. *The Tracey Ullman Show*, which lasted for four seasons between 1987 and 1990, was perhaps most notable for first showcasing the original animated shorts that famously unleashed Matt Groening's *The Simpsons* – America's most popular dysfunctional cartoon family – upon an unsuspecting society on 19 April 1987.

Amongst Daniel Abineri's abundance of memories from his time with *Rocky Horror* in the West End is the reaction of his doting family to his electrifying performance as Frank-n-Furter. 'My little brother and sister loved it. My older brother thought it was just gay. And my dad was confused by it all,' he smiles contentedly.

The original London production of *The Rocky Horror Show* finally closed at the Comedy Theatre on 13 September 1980, having played a total of 2,960 performances over seven eventful years. A considerable achievement for a shoestring show, initially scheduled to run for less than a month in a 63-seat attic. When the 1970s drew to a close, *Rocky Horror* was thought by many to have run its natural course. After all, a camp glam rock horror musical, which in many ways played like a celebration of liberal sexual attitudes and the permissive society – themselves no longer regarded by the mainstream as radically shocking or subversive by the decade's conclusion – would surely be confined to history and remembered through rose tinted eye-wear as a quaint, but no longer pertinent, product of a simpler time.

The '70s had left their indelible mark on the world of popular culture with such unforgettable fashion nightmares as glam rock, seen on the surface to be largely made up of androgynous men strutting around in effeminate clothes and make-up, and punk, a viciously rebellious and intentionally misunderstood musical movement, which effectively came to an end with the break-up of the Sex Pistols on 17 January 1978. In his 2008 book *Blood & Tinsel: A Memoir*, Jim Sharman remembered an incident, witnessed first-hand by himself and Richard O'Brien, that appeared adroitly to underscore this significant epoch in rock history.

From the window of a Chelsea coffee shop, opposite Seditionaries – the alternative fashion boutique owned by Malcolm McClaren (manager of the Sex Pistols) and his partner Vivienne Westwood – the creative forces behind *The Rocky Horror Show* observed a ferocious horde of punk rock disciples descending like a crowd of torch-wielding angry villagers in a Universal monster movie. Feeling bitterly betrayed by McClaren for having broken up the band, the rampaging rabble violently overwhelmed the unassuming edifice, spouting aggressive abuse and hurling bricks through the windows. As the situation escalated into a full scale riot, with the humble British police force powerless to curtail hostilities, the irony of this manufactured mob rising up with insatiable rage against its creator was not lost on the typically cynical O'Brien, as Sharman recalled: 'Richard turned to me, shook his head, and wryly observed, "I think Frankenstein's monster has just turned".'

Like the deaths of Buddy Holly and Elvis Presley, the passing of the Sex Pistols' second bass player Sid Vicious (real name John Simon Ritchie) – the very embodiment of the British punk scene – from a heroin overdose in the early hours of 2 February 1979 marked the culmination of a pop music zeitgeist.

Surely the 1980s would prove to be a considerably more sophisticated era, both culturally and technologically, and the savvy new generation would not make such toe-curlingly horrific lifestyle choices in the never-ending quest to stick it to their terminally square and embarrassingly uncool parents?

However, this bright new decade had scarcely begun when along came the New Romantic scene. Epitomised in the UK by popular bands such as Spandau Ballet, Culture Club, Flock of Seagulls, Duran Duran and Ultravox – and seen on the surface to be largely made up of androgynous men strutting around in effeminate clothes and make-up. The more things change, the more they stay the same, as the saying goes.

An applicable observation about both glam and this new youth trend was that the clothing and use of cosmetics were not construed as effeminate. A lot of young men actually used their flamboyant attire and elaborate make-up in peacock-like, and often successful, attempts to attract the opposite sex – once again evoking memories of Frank-n-Furter's surprising impression on his first, unexpectedly titillated, 1970s audiences.

At the same time, another youth subculture, known as goth (aka gothic rock or death rock) was also evolving. Usually considered a natural progression from the 1970s post-punk fad, the goth scene – represented musically by the likes of Bauhaus, the Cure, the Damned and Siouxsie and the Banshees – embraced the darker side of life and popular culture, including horror movies. Like the New Romantics, goths – both male and female – wore make-up and extravagant outfits to make their statement, but of a much darker and more mournful kind, typically employing a deathly white pallor along with heavy black eyeliner and dark shadows. These young people may not yet have seen or even heard of Dr Frank-n-Furter, but they already had a close affinity with him nonetheless.

While the anarchic excess of the Sex Pistols had proved a relatively short phase in the history of music, the spirit of rock 'n' roll rebellion, once emblematic of 1950s teenage independence, continued to fuel youth trends and adolescent frustration into (and beyond) the '80s.

The policies of Britain's Conservative Prime Minister Margaret Thatcher and America's newly-elected Republican President Ronald Reagan did not suit the socialist ideals of an increasing number of young people in the West, many of whom viewed the stationing of US nuclear missiles in mainland Europe, along with their governments' outspoken opinions against the political strategies of the Soviet Union and the Eastern Bloc, as dangerously antagonistic.

As supported by the publication of the infamous *Protect and Survive* pamphlet in 1980 – a British answer to the US government's laughable *Duck and Cover* procedures of the '50s and '60s – as well as Raymond Briggs' darkly satirical 1982 graphic novel *When the Wind Blows*, TV movies *The Day After* (1983) and *Threads* (1984), and even pop anthems such as Frankie Goes to Hollywood's controversial 'Two Tribes' in 1984, fears that world leaders were aggravating an already precarious situation, and steering the superpowers towards the unthinkable – an all out nuclear confrontation – were obviously frighteningly real; and such concerns crossed over into every aspect of entertainment.

Alternative comedy – typified by *The Comic Strip Presents...*, which debuted on 2 November 1982 (during the inaugural night of UK television's Channel 4), and BBC 2's *The Young Ones* (named, with knowing irony, after the 1961 film and title song by Cliff Richard), also first broadcast in November 1982 – and similarly subversive TV programming, obviously pitched towards the angry and aggravated young teen market, became very much the comedy equivalent of rock 'n' roll. Along with the popularity of politically motivated cutting-edge comedians, this revolutionary brand of radical humour clearly reflected the subversive attitudes of punk; it provided a voice for those with an anti-establishment viewpoint, and encouraged them to communicate their anxieties and express their frustrations. In the midst of global volatility, political unease, rising unemployment and economic uncertainty the necessity for outwardly superficial recreational diversions becomes ever more prevalent.

It is not unlikely that, while some might have made a defiant stand by participating in pro-disarmament marches or anti-government rallies as a means of relieving such socio-political frustrations, others might simply have chosen to buck (and fuck) the system by strapping on a pair of high heels, slipping into sensuous lingerie, getting stoned and shouting obscenities at a movie screen. God bless rock 'n' roll.

With *The Rocky Horror Picture Show* gathering momentum on the US midnight movie circuit, its reputation as a cult phenomenon spreading steadily, and current musical trends again tapping into the natural and necessary need for young people safely to explore and express confused gender issues and sexual identities, it was apparent that there might yet be life in a gender-bending 1970s gothic rock musical, whose messages were clearly still relevant after all.

Though the scale of its impact would never reach that of *Star Wars* (1977), *Saturday Night Fever* (1977) or *Grease* (1978), by 1980 *The Rocky Horror Picture Show* was beginning to make its own small but significant mark on the world of popular culture. Shooting his latest motion picture – with the working title of *Hot Lunch*, eventually released in 1980 as *Fame*, a vibrant, sassy and often surprisingly edgy look at the trials and tribulations of the student body at New York's famous High School for the Performing Arts – prominent British film-maker Alan Parker, director of lightweight kiddie gangster musical *Bugsy Malone* (1976) and the groundbreaking *Midnight Express* (1978), needed an integral rite-of-passage sequence for one of the film's ensemble. The character of Jewish mama's girl and aspiring actress Doris Finsecker (played by Maureen Teefy) required a life-affirming epiphany as a symbol of her having blossomed from awkward adolescent into a self-assured young woman. *Rocky Horror* not only fitted the needs of the scene perfectly – it was, after all, performing that role in real life for seemingly directionless and gender-confused teenagers every Friday and Saturday at midnight in the very city in which Parker's film was set – but it was also a movie that the director himself personally admired. Years later, on his audio-commentary for the DVD release of *Fame*, Parker would describe *The Rocky Horror Picture Show* as one of his favourite films.

An extended sequence for one of *Fame*'s key scenes was shot at the 8th Street Playhouse featuring some of New York's *Rocky Horror* regulars, along with extras making up the rest of the audience; principals Maureen Teefy as Doris and Barry Miller (who had played Tony Manero's naive young friend Bobby C in *Saturday Night Fever*) as Ralph Garcie; and *Rocky*

Horror fan club president Sal Piro in the not-so-demanding role of himself. The scene, which culminated with the previously plain and timid Doris throwing off her blouse (along with her inhibitions) and leaping in front of the screen to dance 'The Time Warp' with other *Rocky Horror* revellers, fulfilled its requirements by showing Doris' metaphorical ascension into womanhood (itself rather aptly tapping into *Rocky*'s 'Don't dream it, be it' and 'Fantasy free me' themes). It also included a tantalising montage of images from the first few scenes of *The Rocky Horror Picture Show* itself, giving the uninitiated a titillating idea of what a late night *Rocky* screening felt like. One of the scene's outstanding moments, where during his pre-show warm-up Sal Piro silenced an irate heckler's 'Get on with the show' with a ferociously quick-witted 'Hey, this is the fucking show, buddy; and if you don't like it, you can go see the movie in Staten Island,' was a word-for-word reconstruction of a genuine incident that had occurred on the night that *Fame*'s location and casting scouts attended the 8th Street Playhouse on a reconnaissance quest. Impressed with Piro's handling of the situation, they quickly decided on a small rewrite to immortalise the episode.

Fame was a substantial box office hit, winning Academy Awards for its music and spawning a popular television series, which ran for six seasons between 1982 and 1987. For the movie version of *Rocky Horror*, previously regarded by many as an oddity with little or no appeal beyond a white gay minority audience, the success of *Fame* would arouse the interest of a more conventional, multi-racial and straight youth market, promptly giving *Rocky*'s devoted following and midnight revenue a considerable boost.

In a blatant effort to ride on the back of the film's unprecedented (albeit belated) success, producers Michael White and Lou Adler presented a major North American tour of *The Rocky Horror Show* between 1980 and '81. Many of the ads slyly inserted the word '*Original*' between '*The*' and '*Rocky Horror Show*', while others read 'Alive on stage from London!', as the tour would give fans of the movie their first chance to see the original stage version since the disastrous Broadway incarnation had disappeared with an embarrassing whimper in 1975.

Directed by Julian Hope, who had helmed the 1979 UK tour, the 1980/81 American production employed the film's celebrated choreographer David Toguri – and also retained Brian Thomson, Sue Blane and Richard Hartley in their usual creative roles – keeping the feel of the show true to the original, along with a few nods to the film in some of the costume designs. A definite 'if it ain't broke, don't fix it' approach to the overall design and staging has always served *Rocky Horror* very well, even though an imaginative injection of creativity occasionally helps to keep it fresh.

Riff Raff was played by songwriter and popular Broadway performer

5: MADNESS TAKES ITS TOLL

Pendleton Brown, Frank Gregory seized the role of Frank-n-Furter with relish, Kim Milford (the much-loved Rocky from Lou Adler's 1974 Los Angeles production) briefly recreated his original role mid-run, and the tour proved popular with audiences. However, while the stage version continued to be successful in almost every other part of the world, the screen adaptation always dominated the US *Rocky Horror* scene. Many people even assumed erroneously that the movie came first, making it increasingly difficult to stage the piece in its original form for a sustained mainstream run. In 2000, the amateur performance rights were made available in the United States (currently the only major territory where they legally exist; Richard O'Brien and the show's controllers remain fiercely protective of *Rocky*'s artistic quality), allowing colleges, local drama groups and other non-professionals to legitimately stage their own interpretations of the show. Sadly, a lot of these productions merely resembled unimaginative carbon copies of the film, sometimes to the point of adding wedding guests and Transylvanians, and even omitting Brad's solo number 'Once in a While'.

As the show's London engagement came to an end, provincial British theatres quickly seized the rights to mount their own professional productions of *The Rocky Horror Show*, with varying degrees of quality and success, in the early 1980s. The first official UK repertory production was that of the Coliseum Theatre in the northern town of Oldham near Manchester, which played between 24 January and 14 February 1981, just four months after the original London run ended. Lurid pink, red and purple posters, featuring a cartoon back view of Frank-n-Furter with the show's title emblazoned in a stylised font across his jacket, declared it to be the 'Regional premiere' of 'The Outrageous Hot Rock-musical by Richard O'Brien.' Directed by Dion McHugh, the show starred a young actor by the name of Jeffrey Longmore, a permanent member of the Coliseum's rep company since 1978 (having appeared in most of their productions), as Frank-n-Furter. Apart from a few black and white out-of-costume rehearsal photos, the song lyrics and cryptic small print notes in the programme – listing such curiosities as 'Lift gates by J&H Lowe (Cranes) Ltd, Rochdale'; 'Rocky's tan courtesy of Outline Figure Salon, Oldham'; 'Wheelchair courtesy of Oldham & District General Hospital'; and 'Motor Scooter courtesy of Horner's, Old Trafford' – the cartoon stocking tops and red panty-clad male buttocks on the ads were the only clues as to the show's content. It is therefore reasonable to assume that *Rocky* would have had quite an impact on its unsuspecting Northern audience, most of whom would not have seen the London production (or recent tour) and would have been blissfully ignorant of its reputation.

Daniel Abineri, meanwhile, was already reprising the role of Frank-n-Furter on stage, this time in an incredibly well-received Australian tour, which stuck pretty closely to the London original as far as sets, costumes and staging were concerned – thanks to another perceptive reunion of the design team of Brian Thomson and Sue Blane, and musical arrangements by Richard Hartley.

'You know the plot of *Priscilla: Queen of the Desert*?' Abineri smiles. 'Well, I've been there. I was that transvestite in the outback.' The actor highlights the *Priscilla* comparison by recounting his experiences of playing a small (undisclosed) mining town in the middle of the Queensland desert: 'The audience comprised rock-hard miners, all dressed in their wives' bras. They arrived, pulling in cases of beer with them, and loved the show way too much. I decided that I should beat a hasty retreat, and I locked the door in my hotel room that night.'

The '80s Australian revival, directed by *The Rocky Horror Picture Show*'s choreographer David Toguri, spawned a lively six-track cast recording. This album, released in 1981 as a rather eye-catching red vinyl record, not only captured Abineri's rich and distinctive voice – singing the role he was born to play – but featured, amongst its other highlights, Perry Bedden as Riff Raff.

Following his supporting role in the movie, and having played Riff on stage for two years in the King's Road and 12 months at London's Comedy Theatre – and also in a short-lived German tour – Bedden had thought, not unreasonably, that *Rocky Horror* was finally behind him. So, when Wilton Morley (son of veteran English actor Robert Morley), producer of the Australian revival, approached him to reprise yet again the role of Frank-n-Furter's embittered handyman, the actor attempted to out-price himself. 'I made him an offer I thought he would refuse,' confesses Bedden, 'but he didn't.'

Nervous because he was not a member of Australian Equity, the actor was rumbled by an inquisitive reporter while attending Columbia's casting session: 'It was embarrassing, but I needn't have worried. When I'd arrived in Australia, "Time Warp" was number one in the charts. I thought I'd got away from *Rocky*, but it was hugely popular there. I remember the opening night in Sydney, Sue Blane sent me a card of one of Riff's boots; it is so beautiful, I had it framed and still have it.'

After a nine-month engagement at the Theatre Royal, Sydney, the production transferred to Melbourne's Comedy Theatre, once again playing to packed houses. 'This was supposed to be six weeks, but it turned into six months,' Bedden recalls. 'We were supposed to have done a national tour by then, but, as the dates for this were now screwed, we had to reschedule; so I re-contracted for a further 18 months. It broke all box office records in Australia, and made me the longest-playing Riff.'

Of the character itself, Bedden says: 'I always played him for laughs, but only up until his entrance in the space costume when he confronts

5: MADNESS TAKES ITS TOLL

Frank; then I played him as a serious character, as he changes so much at that point. I based his facial expressions on my dog's; he always threw me sidelong guilty looks, as if anticipating that he's about to be found out.' Bedden also gave Riff Raff a pronounced limp, which he says vanished, along with his hump, when he appeared in the spacesuit: 'I think Riff's the last person you would expect to come from Transylvania, so I liked the change to a very controlled, frightening, fearful alien.'

Having modestly confessed to a reporter for Australian *Woman's Weekly* magazine that he did not think himself good enough for the role, he admits that he was terrified about what the published article might divulge. 'Again I needn't have worried,' he concedes, 'as we got great reviews wherever we went.'

Despite critical acclaim and sell-out crowds, however, the production was not without incident. 'I do recall throwing a fit when we did a technical run-through in Australia,' Bedden admits. 'They wanted Riff to climb a ladder on stage whilst singing, "The darkness must go ..." It was way too elaborate, compared with the original, and I didn't like it.'

On another occasion, understudying an absent Daniel Abineri – who had lost his voice – Bedden delivered Frank's customary creation speech from a centre-stage ramp, which protruded several rows into the stalls: 'I spun around on the ramp to walk back upstage, but I fell off sideways into the pit. I cracked a rib and was off for two months.'

The 1984 Australian tour, which also marked Daniel Abineri's directorial debut, saw the great Reg Livermore, Australia's very first sweet transvestite, return to the role in Brisbane ten years after he'd worn the heels in Jim Sharman's Sydney production. As he gleefully recalled in his autobiography *Chapters and Chances*, Livermore slid back into his mischievous and unpredictable interpretation of the role with ease:

'I did again the Bette Davis jump into the auditorium that had been a defining moment in the original Sydney show: responding to mocking and derisive laughter brought on by one of Frank's more emotionally charged and self-indulgent moments, I would suddenly hurl myself into the audience, via a flight of conveniently placed stairs, to seek out the offending culprit. I'd push and shove my way along a row of seats until I found a suitable victim, usually somebody I guessed would be willing to go along with the joke, and when I had my pawn I'd lift him up bodily and shake the shit out of him, and not stop until he was man enough to apologise.'

As Livermore subsequently explained, however, while in complete accordance with Frank-n-Furter's subversively unpredictable nature, such crazed behaviour could occasionally backfire spectacularly: 'In Brisbane one night, I made the wrong choice. The man I picked was a part-time reporter, also a part-time model. In the scuffle he cut his beautiful face on my jacket belt buckle. He wasn't very pleased, believing the minor scratch would almost certainly put paid to chances in the fashion world, so he sued. I didn't personally end up in court over the matter, but I was more cautious thereafter.'

Two years later, Abineri – who by now seemed to be making something of a career out of *The Rocky Horror Show* and was reported to have played Frank more times than any other actor – helmed yet another production, touring Richard O'Brien's beloved New Zealand. The casting process for this initially proved rather challenging. After several non-productive days of auditions, during which he declares he must have seen the entire New Zealand acting fraternity try-out for at least one role or another, Abineri suggested to producer Wilton Morley that they re-use the Australian cast:

'He didn't want to do that, so the only option was to hold open auditions, which we did in Auckland over a period of three days. By the end of this I was getting really fed up and had only Eddie left to cast. So, instead of seeing them all individually, I went outside where there was a queue of wannabe Eddies waiting. I went down the queue and picked out a youngster who had a quiff and was obviously trying his best to be Elvis.'

This young rock singer, whose only previous theatrical acting experience had been in a 1983 production of *Grease* and who had recently been fired from his job as a bingo caller, went by the name of Russ Le Roq; a name Abineri was keen for him to change.

'I offered him the part but told him that his stage name was naff,' Abineri reveals. 'I quizzed him about his real name. He said he was reluctant to use it, as his cousin had exactly the same name and was a famous New Zealand cricketer; but I pressed him and he reluctantly agreed to use his real name: Russell Crowe.'

Even though Crowe would still be credited under his original stage name in some of the production's programmes, Daniel Abineri – and *The Rocky Horror Show* – had unknowingly given a future Academy Award-winning Hollywood heavyweight one of his first big breaks.

Directing the show that had been such an important part of his life from both sides of the curtain, Abineri was keen to retain the elements he felt had made it so remarkable. 'I knew the piece so well that I knew how to bump it up without losing the atmosphere, which a lot of other productions had done,' he declares openly, while conveying nothing but praise for the way in which its original director had, along with his gifted cast, moulded it into something extraordinary. 'It was all very experimental in those early days. It's like a piece of sinful alternative theatre; David Bowie meets rock theatre. Jim Sharman brought his considerable genius to bear and his experimentation was like casting a fishing line. The hook caught in the audience's collective cheek and he reeled them in.

5: MADNESS TAKES ITS TOLL

'I think the simple set was brilliant, as it accentuates the characters and fits perfectly with the parody elements. If you use real props, you lose the bizarreness; it loses the "What's happening here?" element that forces the audience to use their imagination. It also focuses and puts the emphasis on the bodies and costumes on stage. When I was directing it, I fought to keep the cable mics in the show and not go for radio mics. Cable mics are in keeping with the '50s rock 'n' roll feel and are a great prop in themselves. There's a lot you can do with them; for example whipping Riff and putting a noose around his neck.

'The show was a huge hit in New Zealand. We even got the ex-Prime Minister, Sir Robert Muldoon, as the Narrator for two weeks. We did a 17-week tour and then I went back to Sydney.'

In 1987, Wilton Morley asked Abineri to reprise the role of Frank in the Australian production one more time: 'I said no, but he offered me silly money – two thousand dollars per show – so I agreed. By this time, Russell had come to Sydney and he stayed at a friend's flat. I fed and watered him while he was there, and he expected to be offered the part of Eddie again. I told him that it was not guaranteed, so he embarked on a campaign to get the part. He snuck into auditions, and eventually we gave in and he got the part.'

The latest incarnation toured twice around Australia to the usual fervour. Amongst its fans it boasted pop sensations Kylie Minogue and Jason Donovan – most famous at the time for their roles in the popular Australian daytime soap opera *Neighbours* – who asked to meet Abineri in his dressing room after the show to express their gratitude and personally praise his performance. The show obviously struck a chord with Donovan in particular, as he fervently assumed the role of Frank-n-Furter to widespread acclaim for touring productions in Australia, New Zealand and the UK during the 1990s.

As long as *The Rocky Horror Picture Show* was a box office flop, any notion of a sequel would have been inconceivable. Success however (especially of the financial variety) often begets greed in the minds of those who control the money, and, once the film began raking in millions at its weekly midnight screenings, it was probably no surprise that studio executives began to consider the possibility of a follow-up.

By the end of the 1970s, 20th Century Fox already owned several profitable movie franchises. *Planet of the Apes* (1968) had swiftly spawned four successful sequels and a TV series between 1970 and 1974; *Damien: Omen 2* (1978) had witnessed its predecessor's devil child causing death and disorder in a military academy as he continued his diabolical quest for satanic supremacy over the Earth; the first sequel to *Star Wars* (1977), at the time the most lucrative movie in history, was released to record-breaking business in the summer of 1980; and director James Cameron would unleash an all-action follow-up to Ridley Scott's 1979 science fiction horror hit *Alien* in 1986. Although something of a slow-burner in terms of worthy box office receipts, *The Rocky Horror Picture Show*'s success would eventually be comparable to those of such aforementioned blockbusters, and a sequel to this kinky late night, low-budget cult movie was suddenly no longer such an outlandish idea.

As far as Richard O'Brien was concerned, continuing the plot would simply be a case of resurrecting the tried and tested 'monster rises from the grave' formula of the classic science fiction creature features that had inspired *Rocky Horror* in the first place.

With all evidence of his dreadful experiments being conveniently dissolved in an acid bath at the close of 1957's *The Curse of Frankenstein*, it had been up to Peter Cushing's fanatical Baron to escape the guillotine – his seemingly inevitable fate at the climax of the first picture – and, having apparently learned nothing from his mistakes, obsessively patch together even more horrendous horrors, with equally disastrous results, for each successive sequel in Hammer's gaudy take on Mary Shelley's enduring tale.

A couple of decades earlier, it had been the wretched creature, rather than his titular creator, who had survived throughout Universal Studios' popular series of Frankenstein films.

Using this age-old tradition as his starting point, O'Brien surmised that, like Universal's iconic Frankenstein monster, the blond-haired and muscular Rocky Horror might be similarly indestructible, and would consequently have survived Riff Raff's deadly laser blasts. He began working on a treatment, tentatively titled *Rocky Horror Shows His Heels* (another witty title, somewhat akin to the ultimately unused *They Came from Denton High*), in which a not-quite-as-dead-as-first-supposed Rocky, still wearing his battered and torn 'Floorshow' lingerie, emerged from the smouldering crater left by the space-bound castle. Carrying the lifeless body of Dr Frank-n-Furter and singing a defiant rock song called 'Breaking Out', the distraught creation would take the corpse of his maker to Dr Everett Scott (now cohabiting with Brad Majors) in an effort to persuade him to try to resurrect the deceased alien scientist.

'Janet is having a baby,' O'Brien explained to *Fangoria* magazine in 1981. 'It's not Brad's, and we discover it isn't Rocky's, but it is in fact Frank's, so we now have "son of Frank". There is a big party, the baby's brought in and Janet is wheeled in from the hospital. We discover that the orderlies who have wheeled her in are in fact Riff and Magenta. They steal the baby, go off in an ambulance and off into the future.'

With this story outlined in detail and a collection of characteristically catchy new musical numbers already composed by O'Brien and Richard Hartley, director Jim Sharman threw a large spanner in the works by stating that he had absolutely no intention of merely continuing the plot of the original and instructing the author to write an entirely new story.

'I said, "I've no interest in writing another story",' O'Brien told *Fangoria*'s Mike Conroy. '"What I will do is adapt this as a framework. I have done ten songs already; we are going to have 15 songs – I have written ten of the songs and I have no interest in throwing all that away; let's use it as a framework, as a basis."

'We went through five drafts. A university should study this – how you can adapt one story, it's most extraordinary. Eventually there was no Frank, there was no Rocky. Brad became the focal point; much the same story, taking *him* through that. Then Jim and I were about to go up and have a committee meeting, sitting around with the producers discussing the script – what did we think, did it say enough?

'Jim said we made one mistake. I said, "What's that?"

'"We should have made Janet the lead character."

'I said, "Of course we should have done. Let's change the names around on all the dialogue."

'"You can't do that," said Jim.

'"Yes you can."

'But of course you *can't*. It simply doesn't work that way. It seemed simple at the time in the King's Road on a sunny afternoon – it seemed fine. Three drafts later, we finally got it together.'

With the Frank-n-Furter and Rocky Horror characters no longer involved, the film's new working title became *The Brad and Janet Show*, with the original's once-innocent young lovers now married (though not entirely happily) and embarking upon a completely different journey of discovery, totally unrelated to their experiences in *Rocky Horror*.

The plot cleverly satirised the American public's fixation with television, and in particular its obsession with the likes of insipid daytime soap operas and quiz shows. Richard O'Brien's and Jim Sharman's screenplay also examined the shifting of gender roles in modern society, far more blatantly than *Rocky Horror* had done. An early gag in the new movie would have a self-assured Janet comforting her hesitant husband in an emasculating echo of his dialogue to her in the original: 'It's all right, Brad, everything's going to be all right.'

O'Brien elaborated on his thoughts about these themes in his 1981 interview with *Fangoria*'s Mike Conroy: 'The only thing that provoked thought about *Rocky* was, "Let's look at our sexuality. Are we right to condemn the hedonists of society, and, if so, how do we condemn them? What is the value of the hedonistic outlook on life and do you have to pay the price for living that sort of life?"

'This deals with modern neuroses in the modern marriage in the same way that *Kramer vs Kramer* dealt with the same problem, but this is dealt with differently. How do we operate as individuals within the framework of the family? The woman says "I refuse to be locked and chained to the house and the kids. I want to be recognised as a human being and as a person," which is quite right, and in so doing emasculates the man ... "Where does that leave me?"'

Taking place in the fictional picturesque town of Denton (with actual US location filming planned), the now radically altered (from *Rocky Horror Shows His Heels*) story saw Janet Majors – described in the draft script as, 'Attractive suburbanite in her twenties. Recently established a promising career and is adapting accordingly' – seduced and manipulated by the promise of instant fame, as she was groomed for stardom by the charismatic and calculating Farley Flavors – 'Local boy made billionaire' – and a still wheelchair-bound Everett Scott, now the scheming manager of the local TV station. A troubled and possibly mentally unstable Brad – 'Recently unemployed and is not adapting accordingly' – is meanwhile committed to the care of professional (though hardly ethical) neuro-specialists Cosmo and Nation McKinley for treatment. As the plot unfolds, Oliver Wright (a later rewrite would make him Judge Oliver Wright, Denton's leading social scientist) and recently divorced current affairs host Betty Hapschatt uncover a conspiracy that sensationally reveals Flavors to be Brad's bitterly resentful long lost twin brother, his sights set on Janet and revenge for all he was denied during an underprivileged upbringing.

With the script and songs in place, Lou Adler and Michael White again sharing the producer credit (as with *The Rocky Horror Picture Show*, the order in which their names appeared on screen would be switched accordingly between the US and UK prints) and cameras set to roll, the film-makers' plans were unexpectedly scuppered by an industry-crippling 1979 strike by the Screen Actors Guild; a situation that resulted in the promised $5,000,000 budget being frozen and location filming in the US no longer feasible.

As Richard O'Brien revealed to *Fangoria*, rather than lose two years of work and some very strong material, the ever-resourceful Jim Sharman suggested mounting the new musical as a stage play in London: '"It would be quite exciting and I could film the stage show, take cameras into the theatre," said Jim. I said, "In that case, if we're going to do that, why don't we do it as a stage show, but do it under controlled conditions in a controlled environment; do it on a soundstage somewhere and cast the audience just the same as we are casting the play".'

Though initially reticent, the producers ultimately agreed to the plan, which would in fact cut the proposed budget by nearly a third; the estimated final cost of the picture was around $3,500,000, a fairly modest sum for a major motion picture but still almost three times that of *The Rocky Horror Picture Show*.

5: MADNESS TAKES ITS TOLL

Instead of building a facsimile of a realistic town, the film-makers and set designer Brian Thomson – who, in recognition of his creative input into the film's narrative and visual style, would be given an on screen 'Additional ideas' acknowledgment at the end of the movie, immediately after O'Brien's and Sharman's 'Screenplay' credit – decided to utilise the in-built look of the soundstage itself, using the boundaries of its gloomy cramped interiors to their advantage. Hence, the plot now centred on this completely confined environment, as if – like willing slaves – the entire community had somehow become passively trapped forever within the confines of their own hum-drum, television-obsessed existence.

When Janet's parents (Harry and Emily Weiss, played by Manning Redwood and Darlene Johnson) enter a televised contest, for example, they win 'A delicious stay in that evergreen series *Happy Homes*, with unlimited use of a new dream kitchen.' In this way, the script combined the typical prize of a luxury holiday with the bizarre idea of winning a starring role in one's own television series; blatantly commenting on the questionable priorities of contemporary Western society (with unlimited use of the kitchen being emphasised as a key selling point of the prize's appeal) and the increasing thirst for instant fame along the way. For instance, when Janet (now a rising star in her own right) visits her parents at their new home, Sharman and O'Brien presented it – along with cheesy narration and the added voyeuristic intentions of the ever-present studio audience – as if she were having a guest shot on her mother's daytime TV show.

With the script reworked yet again in order to accommodate the new, totally enclosed setting, cameras finally rolled in the middle of November 1980. The movie's title was changed to *Shock Treatment* and the character of Dr Everett Scott replaced by a bizarre Viennese game show host, gourmet chef and sometime psychiatrist by the name of Bert Schnick. With a change of name, the nature of the character's disability was also revised, so that Schnick – played to perfection by Australian actor-comedian and satirist Barry Humphries – would (at least at first) appear to be blind rather than confined to a wheelchair. Best known to theatre and television audiences as the talent behind legendary comic creations Dame Edna Everage and Sir Les Patterson, Humphries had also aided *The Rocky Horror Show*'s initial word-of-mouth success with his rave review of the original production for *Punch* magazine in 1973.

While Jeremy Newson (as Ralph Hapschatt) had the distinction of being the only actor to play the same role in both movies – his now ex-wife Betty (played by Hilary Labow in *Rocky*'s opening wedding scene) was portrayed by American comedienne Ruby Wax in the sequel – many of *The Rocky Horror Picture Show*'s original line-up returned as different (though oddly familiar) characters for its follow-up.

As Judge Oliver Wright, the distinguished Charles Gray actually got to interact with the rest of the cast this time, while enjoying a charming on screen chemistry with Wax's Betty Hapschatt; Richard O'Brien and Patricia Quinn became the strange and incestuous Cosmo and Nation McKinley – Riff Raff and Magenta had been described as being disguised as medical staff when they came to kidnap Janet's newborn baby in O'Brien's early treatment for *Rocky Horror Shows His Heels* – and Little Nell (listed in the credits as Nell Campbell) played the squeaky and vivacious Nurse Ansalong.

Sue Blane again worked her inimitable magic and made the costumes sexy and memorable, despite a distinct lack of the sexual aspect that had undoubtedly added to *Rocky*'s appeal. Nell, for instance, actually looked far sexier and more beautiful as Ansalong – with her long auburn hair, bright red lipstick and impossibly short green nurse's uniform (seizing every opportunity to flash her little black panties) – than she had as Columbia. The alluring doctors-and-nurses look also provided an obvious outlet for saucy *Rocky Horror*-style dressing up possibilities and proved just as flattering on the cast as Blane's flawless designs for Frank-n-Furter had done on Tim Curry.

With work commitments preventing Barry Bostwick from returning as Brad Majors, Curry was reportedly considered for the role, but did not feel that he would be able comfortably to pull off a believable American accent. Jim Sharman then offered the part to Cliff De Young, an actor he had originally considered for the role in the first film. In *Shock Treatment*, De Young would show his remarkable versatility both vocally and physically by convincingly portraying the twin brothers – Brad Majors and Farley Flavors – completely differently. With dark-rimmed spectacles and casual attire, Brad appeared timid and endearingly vulnerable, while the devious, cigar-chomping Flavors exhibited slicked black hair, a nervous eye twitch (complete with facial scar), tailored suits and a slimy Jack Nicholson grin.

Supplanting Susan Sarandon – who had purportedly asked for $500,000 to reprise the role of Janet – was a brown-haired, wide-eyed, spirited young actress-singer by the name of Jessica Harper. Without bettering Sarandon's interpretation in any way, the talented Harper, who had already played leading roles in two recognised cult films – Brian De Palma's colourful camp rock 'n' roll extravaganza *Phantom of the Paradise* in 1974 and Dario Argento's admired 1977 psychological Italian horror opus *Suspiria* – would take the character of Janet in a totally different direction, wholly appropriate for O'Brien's and Sharman's new story.

Shock Treatment would also be notable for the appearances of a few before-they-were-famous names in supporting roles. A pre-*The Young Ones* Rik Mayall – whose regular comedy partner Adrian Edmondson would later assume the part of Brad Majors for the 1990 London revival of *The Rocky Horror Show* – played hospital orderly 'Rest Home' Ricky; while, as a member of the on-set rock band Oscar Drill and the Bits, American-born pop singer Sinitta Renet (who shortly thereafter would begin her solo career with such hits as 'So Macho' and 'Toy Boy') played one of two Denton cheerleaders (the other being actress Claire Toeman) in the opening scene's musical celebration of Brad's and Janet's home town.

Assuming the role of lead singer Oscar Drill was British actor Gary Shail, known primarily for appearances in the popular children's TV show *Metal Mickey* (which ran for four series on ITV between 1980 and 1984) and Franc Roddam's 1979 debut feature *Quadrophenia*. Based on the classic 1973 concept album by the Who, Roddam's powerfully frank examination of 1960s British gang culture and teen psychology featured Phil Daniels, Leslie Ash, Ray Winstone, Toyah Willcox and (on the very brink of rock stardom) Sting, and became an enduring cult hit with adolescent audiences during the early '80s.

As *Shock Treatment*'s Oscar Drill, Shail would sing 'Breaking Out' – the song initially composed by Richard O'Brien for Rocky himself at the beginning of *Rocky Horror Shows His Heels*. A personable and refreshingly blunt and forthright actor, Shail would later become a popular guest at *Rocky Horror* fan conventions, where he would often oblige with a live rendition of the number to the collective delight of an infatuated crowd.

Amongst *Shock Treatment*'s on screen audience, Jim Sharman was keen to cast as many members of the core *Rocky Horror* family as possible – from both the film and the King's Road stage production – in fun cameo roles. Perry Bedden and Rufus Collins appeared as the hard-working sound and camera crew of probing TV reporter Neely Pritt (Betsy Brantley), while another of the first film's Transylvanians, Imogen Claire, was cast as the TV station's wardrobe mistress. Christopher Malcolm, *The Rocky Horror Show*'s original Brad Majors, played studio security cop Vance Parker; US *Rocky Horror* fan club president Sal Piro could be glimpsed briefly in shadow (talking on a telephone) in an early shot; and, as well as Rayner Bourton and Ziggy Byfield as singing GIs, a number of *The Rocky Horror Picture Show*'s Transylvanians (along with Diane Langton, who had appeared in O'Brien's and Sharman's *T Zee* at the Royal Court in 1976) would also be glimpsed in the crowd as townsfolk and chorus members.

In accordance with Richard O'Brien's predictions, shooting the whole film on a soundstage at London's Lee International Studios in Wembley actually allowed Sharman far greater control and the chance to be a lot more artistically imaginative and experimental than location filming would have permitted. His meticulously-planned and brilliantly-executed opening long-take for example – lasting close to two and a half minutes and slowly showcasing a full 360° panoramic view of the entire soundstage, introducing various characters and observing the on-set 'audience' excitedly taking their seats – predated the celebrated

Copacabana Club tracking shot in Martin Scorcese's 1990 gangster epic *Goodfellas* by almost a decade.

Brian Thomson's characteristic attention to detail again provided much to admire within the set designs. Partitioned and padded white walls symbolically implied that the entire town (maybe even the whole of society) was actually a madhouse, while overhead shots suggested the populace might be little more than rats in a laboratory maze, and a host of familiar props and images would be recycled not only to amuse and delight legions of *Rocky Horror* fans but also to verify that, despite its dissimilar visual style, the film's action definitely took place in the same world.

A large neon version of the instantly recognisable 'Denton: The Home of Happiness!' billboard dominated the soundstage (behind which an unobserved Farley Flavors could keep a deviously twitching eye on important plot developments), Grant Wood's 'American Gothic' painting appeared on a wall in the fictional TV studio's wardrobe department, Frank-n-Furter's throne from *The Rocky Horror Picture Show*'s 'Sweet Transvestite' scene was painted bright red and occupied by Jessica Harper's Janet; and the number '4711' could be viewed clearly on both a computer screen and the microfilm detailing the plot's crucial familial connection between Brad Majors and Farley Flavors.

In addition, the assemblage of permanent spectators – once allowed into the studio (from an unseen exterior world) during the picture's opening title sequence, the voyeuristic audience would never leave the building, even sleeping (fully clothed) through the night in their seats – could be seen as a sly commentary on the obsessive over-involvement of modern television viewers. There remains the further possibility that the film-makers might even have been acknowledging a phenomenon a little closer to home, and perhaps making an appreciative jokey reference to *Rocky Horror*'s passionately devoted midnight revellers and their peculiar participatory practices.

Shock Treatment had its US premiere at the United Artists (UA) cinema in Fresno, California, in August 1981, and this was followed by a limited general release from December the same year.

In addition to dazzlingly bright red posters, featuring a head-shot of Richard O'Brien's sinister Dr Cosmo McKinley, 20th Century Fox's primary promotional campaign for the film included *The Rocky Horror Treatment*, a short television documentary hosted by Sal Piro that chronicled both the history and rising cult following of *Rocky Horror* and the making of the follow-up – now being labelled as 'Not a sequel, not a prequel, but an equal.'

Unfortunately, Fox's efforts knowingly to manufacture an instant cult movie proved as fruitless as they had in 1974 with Brian De Palma's

5: MADNESS TAKES ITS TOLL

Phantom of the Paradise. *The Rocky Horror Picture Show* had found an enthusiastic and devoted audience completely by accident, nearly a year after its disastrous cinematic debut; and, while many *Rocky* fans applauded and admired *Shock Treatment* – it would achieve cult status, albeit on a much smaller scale than its predecessor, in the years that followed, with audience participation and the occasional fan 'shadow cast' performances taking place at *Rocky Horror* convention screenings – they were not about to abandon their weekly midnight subversions in order to become slaves to the conformity of studio marketing. There would, after all, be nothing rock 'n' roll about that whatsoever.

It could also be argued that *Shock Treatment* was in many ways a little too clever for its own good. Whereas *Rocky Horror* had multiple layers – and mainstream audiences who did not get its copious retro pop-culture references and mythological motifs could still enjoy it on its more easily accessible 'comedy, sex and rock 'n' roll' level – the follow-up was undeniably profound and cerebral even at its surface.

In his 2008 autobiography *Blood & Tinsel: A Memoir*, Jim Sharman adroitly and concisely summed up *Shock Treatment* as being 'Set in a desperate future, where the only currency was fame and the media-dominated population had become slaves to the banal values of reality television.' With the benefit of hindsight – that eternal provider of retrospective wisdom – this typically on-the-nail assessment by the film's co-writer and director astutely identified one of the primary reasons for its failure at the 1981 box office. In short, the movie had been ahead of its time.

Long before Peter Weir used similar themes in his critically-acclaimed postmodern cautionary tale *The Truman Show* (starring Jim Carrey) in 1998, *Shock Treatment* served as a thought-provoking warning of the dangers of overnight manufactured celebrity and the perils of believing one's own publicity, while perceptively predicting the disturbing rise of undemanding and unimaginative reality TV and insipid talent shows – not to mention the excessive Orwellian CCTV culture of the early 21st Century – by nearly two decades. These themes would appear infinitely more relevant 20 years later, prompting many to re-evaluate the film's merits.

Technically a more refined production than the shoestring-budget *The Rocky Horror Picture Show*, *Shock Treatment* reveals Sharman's talents and confidence as a film director to have matured and improved exponentially in the intervening period. It showcases a range of ingenious camera angles, clever use of crane and tracking shots and inventive editing, as well as charming performances from all concerned.

Richard O'Brien would on occasion single out his turn as Cosmo McKinley as the worst acting of his career. On the evidence of the film itself, however, this would appear a somewhat harsh and unfairly self-deprecating verdict. Although devoid of Riff Raff's between-the-lines bitterness and subtle nuances, Cosmo is memorably amusing and creepily unsettling nonetheless. His polished cranium and huge eyes, magnified unnervingly behind enormous octagonal spectacles, gives him the look of Albert Dekker's deranged Dr Thorkel in Ernest B Schoedsack's 1940 mad scientist movie *Dr Cyclops*; and his impeccably timed self-conscious micro-pause between the words 'sister' and 'colleague' when first introducing Patricia Quinn's Dr Nation McKinley implies volumes about the true nature of their unspoken relationship.

While the inspired advertising slogan 'Trust me, I'm a doctor' – accompanied by Richard O'Brien's creepy visage on all of the film's promotional material – was never actually heard in the movie itself, *Shock Treatment*'s final line of dialogue, the off-screen Narrator's smug declaration 'The sun never sets on those who ride into it,' is easily as profound as *Rocky Horror*'s immortal catchphrase 'Don't dream it, be it.'

Its soundtrack (recorded at Regent's Park Recording Studio in London) – with compelling melodies, clever lyrics and delightful song titles such as 'Bitchin' in the Kitchen', 'Look What I Did to My Id', 'Little Black Dress' and 'Looking for Trade'– was of O'Brien's and Hartley's customary high standard, and the chance to see most of *The Rocky Horror Picture Show*'s cast enjoying themselves in another colourful escapade was an absolute joy.

The picture lampooned the seductive lure of television in much the same way as *Rocky Horror* had paid homage to 1950s monster movies and popcorn cinema, and, at the time of its release, Richard O'Brien hinted that, should the new film prove successful, there might always be the possibility of placing Brad and Janet in a theatrical setting for a third bout of madness.

In this way, the author-composer saw his star-crossed young couple as having parallels with the famous hero of Jonathan Swift's 1726 fantasy satire *Gulliver's Travels* (the complete title of which, *Travels into Several Remote Nations of the World, In Four Parts, By Lemuel Gulliver, First a Surgeon and Then a Captain of Several Ships*, has to be a contender for the most ridiculously pointless and long-winded title in the history of ridiculously pointless and long-winded titles). In the event, however, the failure of *Shock Treatment* to attract a significant mainstream audience ended (at least for the time being) the prospect of further *Rocky Horror* follow-ups, and its limited theatrical engagement was followed by a swift home video release.

The Rocky Horror Picture Show itself was released for home rental on VHS and Betamax by CBS/Fox video in Australia and the UK in 1984, although it would be a further six years before the film made its US video cassette debut; a conscious effort by Lou Adler to help preserve its lucrative and unique midnight community. While future releases would favour variations of the traditional 'lips' poster, the original UK edition's rather unorthodox cover illustration featured an odd, though strangely appropriate, stylised artistic rendering of Frank-n-Furter, Riff Raff and a scantily-clad female character – who seemed to be a peculiar amalgam of Janet, Columbia and Magenta (with maybe even a hint or two of the Transylvanians thrown in). The image was accompanied by the provocative phrase 'Wonderfully weird, fabulously freaky and the cast is completely crazy,' which had been previously used in Fox's original theatrical trailer for the film. Drawn in the same distinctive pseudo-realistic style, the back cover showed an exceptionally young Brad and Janet (clearly not old enough to be out at night without a chaperone) dressed in rather natty outfits that resembled nothing they wore on screen at any time – Janet's smart little black and red number was especially appealing – alongside a battered brown suitcase, which they must have decided to leave in the car during the movie itself.

A year later, *The Rocky Horror Show* spawned a popular computer game (a claim very few other musicals could make), created by software company CRL and available for a number of formats, including Sinclair ZX Spectrum, Commodore 64 and Amstrad. Basically a variation of the standard platform adventure, the game cleverly incorporated ideas from both the stage and film versions of *Rocky*, as players (adopting the role of either Brad or Janet) tried to rescue their incarcerated (never as painful as it sounds) sweetheart from the evil clutches of Frank-n-Furter and his demented servants. Facing the ever-present danger of being zapped by Riff Raff's ray gun, along with the relentless countdown to the castle-cum-spaceship being blasted into the stratosphere, players might also suffer the indignity of being 'taken' by Frank himself. At this point, their character's clothes would immediately disappear and have to be located from a secret hiding place somewhere in the building. The game was repackaged and re-released (with updated game-play and radically improved graphics for the 21st Century PC generation) on a number of occasions, and remains an enjoyable and quirky *Rocky*-related item.

As news of *The Rocky Horror Picture Show*'s growing popularity as a midnight attraction became more widespread (thanks in no small part to its prominent scene-stealing role in Alan Parker's *Fame*), Lou Adler decided to capitalise on the unique nature of its cult success by releasing a second soundtrack album. The new record would feature the entire film (including dialogue), as well as audience responses and American fan club president Sal Piro (already a rising *Rocky Horror* celebrity and PR guru in his own right) performing his obligatory MC duties. A hit with fans, the one-of-a-kind soundtrack was a well-crafted mix of both studio recorded talkback and a genuine 8th Street Playhouse audience; the latter was added late in production to give the recording an air of spontaneity, similar to that of a real midnight screening, which it seemed to be lacking with just the studio-based verbiage on its own.

The Rocky Horror Picture Show Audience Par-tic-i-pation Album was released in the United States as a double LP with a gatefold sleeve (plus a 'Rules of *Rocky Horror* Etiquette' insert) in 1983. It was available elsewhere as an import, making the fans' hit-and-miss, and often vulgar, retaliations to the film's dialogue accessible to a worldwide audience and opening up the *Rocky* cult; just as a major new touring production of the stage show was about to hit British theatres.

If ever a UK touring musical deservedly earned the term 'legendary' it is the controversial 'Mesmeric laser production' of *The Rocky Horror Show* presented by the Theatre Royal in Hanley, Stoke-on-Trent, in the mid-1980s. It elevated a low budget independent musical to the position of second most successful touring show in the country; eclipsed only by Bill Kenright's long-running version of Rice and Lloyd Webber's ever-popular *Joseph and the Amazing Technicolor Dreamcoat*, which had the added box office allure of being categorised as a more family-friendly show than *Rocky*. This production was also responsible for irrevocably instilling the American style of audience participation, until then associated primarily with screenings of the film version, into *Rocky Horror* stage productions, and finally turning a cult curiosity into an interactive mainstream sensation.

Such was its repute that, to this day, certain less-informed denizens of Stoke-on-Trent – at one time the beating heart of England's once thriving pottery industry – still believe that *The Rocky Horror Show* itself actually originated in their fair city, a 'fact' of which they are fiercely proud.

As is frequently the case with the history of this unique work of entertainment, the words 'humble beginnings' are again the right ones to describe the origins of the production that would ultimately prove something of a box office juggernaut. It began as just another of the innumerable independent *Rocky Horror* productions that appeared, and inevitably disappeared once their two or three-week contracts came to an end, at repertory theatres all over Britain in the early '80s. The 365-seat Kenneth More Theatre (KMT) in Ilford, Essex, first opened on 31 December 1974 with a commitment to serving professional (both in-house and visiting) and amateur productions, dividing its annual programme equally between the two. The company produced an acclaimed 26-week national tour of *Hair* in 1978, but their greatest touring success was yet to come.

Directed by Vivyan Ellacott, the theatre's artistic director, who also assumed the role of the Narrator, the KMT's production of *The Rocky Horror Show* opened in March 1983. Starring Jeffrey Longmore – who had previously played Frank-n-Furter in the Oldham Coliseum's 1981 production – and the theatre's choreographer Loraine Porter as Columbia, *Rocky* was a hit for its two-week run, and the KMT quickly revived the production in May of the following year; this time at the Theatre Royal in

5: MADNESS TAKES ITS TOLL

Stoke-on-Trent's Hanley city centre.

The beautiful Victorian building, which stood in an area known as Pall Mall, had been converted from a Methodist Chapel in 1840 and experienced a turbulent life as a place of live entertainment, including a devastating fire in 1949 and various financial difficulties, before becoming a bingo hall in 1961 and finally closing 20 years later due to a decline in business. Former local solicitor Charles Deacon had, as a young boy, enjoyed Christmas pantomimes at the theatre and dreamed of seeing the venue reliving its glory days. His beloved Stoke-on-Trent was, at the time, the largest UK municipality that did not boast a traditional touring theatre within its limits. In the hope of rectifying this, Deacon set up the Theatre Royal Restoration Trust with a view to re-establishing the city's oldest theatre as a thriving palace of entertainment. In December 1982, the venue re-opened its doors to the public with the pantomime *Babes in the Wood*; but, left to the cruel cold realities of a typically harsh British winter, the building itself had fallen into serious disrepair.

The Trust leased the venue from Mecca, the bingo company that still owned the property, in 1983, with an option to buy it for £246,000. This option, however, would expire in August 1984 if not fully exercised, and it was calculated that a further £300,000 would be needed to carry out the crucial repair work and rewiring required to make the venue fully functional again, as well as necessary aesthetic work and redecoration. Thanks to the patronage of the Earl of Lichfield, the trust purchased the building well before the deadline and restoration was completed in time to welcome audiences for the theatre's 1983 pantomime *Aladdin*. Charles Deacon and the venue's management team then began to pursue popular and profitable shows with which to try to draw the public away from their new video cassette recorders, home entertainment's latest innovation, and the oh-so-thrilling popularity battle between the VHS and Betamax formats.

Vivyan Ellacott's production of *The Rocky Horror Show* - starring Jeffrey Longmore, now completely familiar and comfortable with his celebrated performance as Frank-n-Furter - enjoyed an outstandingly successful week at Hanley's Theatre Royal during May 1984. Longmore's experience and all important respect for the character - a trait forgotten by some actors - allowed him to experiment with the dangerous diva to great effect, teasing and toying with the audience, while, most importantly, never allowing them to take control. The sustained thunderous cacophony that inevitably erupted at the end of the final chorus of 'Sweet Transvestite' demonstrated this perfectly, as, momentarily denied the opportunity to deliver the script's customary 'Come up to the lab,' Longmore would, in true Frank style, bask imperiously in the incessant ovation, exhibiting a crowd-pleasing, self-satisfied pout, before calmly and demurely announcing 'I haven't finished yet' with exquisite timing.

Encouraged by the show's remarkable reception in Stoke, the venue's managing director Paul Barnard, an influential entity in the theatrical world, quickly booked it again for later the same year; and he was already drawing up plans for a UK tour, to be mounted as a co-production between Ilford's Kenneth More Theatre and the Theatre Royal Hanley. The striking posters for the show's Stoke-on-Trent engagement prominently featured the words 'Alive on Stage,' with Michael English's familiar Columbia face against a black background and a short tally of *Rocky*'s international conquests to date: 'London, Los Angeles, Frankfurt, Brazil, New York, Tokyo, Paris, Oslo, and now alive in Stoke-on-Trent.' Ads for subsequent venues would rectify a glaring omission by adding Australia to the list. After all, the stage version of *Rocky Horror* had been embraced a lot more warmly down-under than it had in New York.

Joining the production as Janet Weiss for its short run in Hanley was Sally Ann Triplett, a strong, confident young singer who had recently appeared in the Kenneth More Theatre's 1983 production of *Godspell*. As a vocalist, Triplett twice represented the UK in the Eurovision Song Contest – first in 1980 as part of the six piece Prima Donna, who disbanded after their second unsuccessful post-Eurovision single, and again in 1982 as half of pop duo Bardo. After her brief stint in *Rocky Horror* – which also featured her Bardo partner Stephen Fischer as Brad – the talented actress saw her theatrical career bloom, with celebrated performances in a multitude of West End, national and international musical productions.

Another early Hanley standout was Keith Burns, an elegant and agile young performer, whose dementedly energetic and scene-stealing depiction of Riff Raff as a twisted, insect-like alien sociopath quickly became a fan favourite. At the tender age of 21, Burns left *Rocky* to join the original 1985 company of *Les Miserables*, and four years later created the role of Thuy in the premiere production of *Miss Saigon* at the Theatre Royal, Drury Lane. He also contributed his vocal talents to the cast recordings of both those influential modern musicals. A number of iconic roles followed – the swanky self-assured Rum Tum Tugger in Andrew Lloyd Webber's *Cats* and Judas in an acclaimed concert version of *Jesus Christ Superstar* among them – and, rather appropriately, Liverpool-born Burns later carved something of a comfortable niche for himself in both the West End and UK touring productions of Willy Russell's *Blood Brothers*, deftly making the role of its mysteriously omnipresent Narrator his own.

'Back by public demand,' announced the posters, 'prior to tour,' as producer Paul Barnard prepared to take *The Rocky Horror Show* on the road. With the Kenneth More Theatre and Vivyan Ellacott retaining artistic control of the production (along with the director's credit in Ellacott's case), all financial dealings and general management for the touring version were handed over to the Theatre Royal, Hanley, with Malcolm Sircom replacing the KMT's Laurence Payne as musical director.

Sircom, who died at the age of 73 on 11 June 2008, enjoyed a lengthy theatrical career that spanned more than 50 years. In addition to being an accomplished musician and musical director, he was a talented writer whose works included a hit stage adaptation of Roger Hargreaves' popular *Mr Men* childrens books and a female twist (pun acknowledged) on Charles Dickens' *Oliver Twist*, appropriately named *Olivia!*

As the curiously familiar title of one of his musicals for schools suggested, Sircom's cherished years with the 1980s *Rocky* tour clearly inspired at least one of his own concoctions. Described as 'A riotous mix of *The Addams Family, Young Frankenstein,* and *The Phantom of the Opera*, with *Rebecca* and *The Rocky Horror Show* thrown in for good measure,' his *The Rocky Monster Show* – in which a singing descendent of Baron Frankenstein creates a genetically engineered rock band, fronted by a clone of Elvis Presley – was made available in separate editions for both senior and junior schools, giving such institutions the chance to enjoy a little irreverent *Rocky Horror*-type fun at their end-of-term concerts without fear of copyright infringement or having surreptitiously to navigate *Rocky's* naughty bits past apprehensive parents.

Malcolm Sircom so enjoyed his time with *Rocky Horror*, self-assuredly strutting onto the stage each night in high heels, black fishnet stockings and an official tour sweatshirt to take his finale bow, that he joyfully shared a number of stories and experiences in his text for the 1987 edition of the souvenir tour brochure. One such amusing anecdote concerned Julia Howson, a confident and appealing young actress playing the part of Janet, who, upon reaching the moment where she and Brad are stripped of their clothes by Frank-n-Furter's seedy servants, suddenly realised during one performance that she had forgotten to put on her most intimate of undergarments. The mind boggles as to where her thoughts must have wandered in the dressing room for such an oversight to have occurred. Modestly hiding her blushes – plus everything else, apart from the all too obvious truth of the situation – from the hysterical audience by dexterously manoeuvring herself behind the laboratory set's prop freezer, she carefully removed her dress. Eventually the stage manager waved a familiar frilly white flag rather indiscreetly from the wings, saving the poor girl from having to reveal far more than Richard O'Brien's script ever intended. Sircom ended his delightful retelling of this unforgettable incident perfectly with a final amusing quip: 'The visiting theatre managers fell over themselves to book the show for the following year.'

On another occasion, vividly recalled by Sircom, Judith Eyre, a memorably larger-than-life Magenta in every sense of the expression, sustained an eleventh-hour pre-show injury and, with her understudy also absent, was unable to perform. Incredibly, with just a few modifications to the text – and David Dale (Frank-n-Furter) valiantly slipping into the Usherette's frock to sing the opening number – the show transpired without Magenta. An interesting occurrence serving as an intriguing reminder that, while every character is absolutely integral to *The Rocky Horror Show*'s final structure, Richard O'Brien initially conceived the plot with only one female servant (Columbia) and added Riff Raff's sister Magenta only when Marianne Faithful reportedly expressed a fleeting desire to play one of the roles.

After two more performances in Hanley in November 1984 ('At your further insistence,' the posters now declared), followed by encouraging engagements at the Alexandra Theatre in Birmingham and Glasgow's Pavilion, a full scale tour was scheduled to commence in Edinburgh the following February.

With the tour having no predetermined end date, and cast members tentatively contracted for just three months at a time, new faces regularly assuming the primary roles became the norm as the run gained momentum. Richard O'Brien and Samuel French Ltd., who then held the professional performing rights to the show, eventually granted the Theatre Royal Hanley an exclusive *Rocky Horror* touring licence for 1985; themselves taking a 'suck it and see' attitude as to the tour's staying power.

With worldwide cinema audiences having been privy to a suggestion of this unique new cult, thanks to *Fame* and a brief background scene of New York's 8th Street Playhouse crowd performing 'The Time Warp' in line outside a movie theatre at the end of Paul Mazursky's *Willie & Phil* (1980), Hanley's theatre management made water pistols and small bags of rice available in the foyer. Their hope was that a little of the fun enjoyed at US screenings of the movie might cross over to the stage version, adding a new dimension to the theatrical experience. This decision would soon come back to haunt them (and the managers of almost every major UK theatre), as it quickly became obvious that audiences were already way ahead of the game.

A number of independent productions had already been subjected to a limited amount of good-natured verbal and physical interaction from spectators, but short engagements had not allowed the phenomenon time to develop fully. However, because of *Fame* and the easy to obtain *The Rocky Horror Picture Show Audience Par-tic-i-pation Album*, along with intriguing stories in science fiction publications and film magazines, *Rocky Horror*'s reputation as an (unintentional) audience participation piece had escalated remarkably quickly.

Actor Mark Turnbull joined the company as Dr Scott in 1986 – the production often broke with tradition by having separate actors play Eddie and Dr Scott, and even doubled Eddie with the Narrator at one stage – and, despite warnings from friend and fellow actor Chris Marlowe, who was then playing Brad on the tour, he soon experienced his own baptism of fire:

'Chris is godfather to all of my boys, and still the best Brad that I've ever seen or worked with, a very undervalued actor in my opinion. Chris and I had a drink at the Arts Club and he said to me, "You do know what you're letting yourself in for, don't you?" I said, "No," and he replied, "It's mental," and went on to describe how, as an actor, you had to get used to having stuff thrown at you, how you had to evolve a completely different way of playing the piece. He advised against going into the audience, because an actress playing Magenta had been hit by an audience member once and the theatre had laid on security staff as a result.

'We had one week's rehearsal and I distinctly remember my first night; the roar when the tabs went up and the hail of stuff that descended onto the stage; not just rice, but full bags of rice. The audience had perfected the art of smuggling stuff into the theatre.

'It was quite honestly the most insane evening of my life,' Turnbull continues, energetically recalling his first experience of a 1980s *Rocky Horror Show* audience. 'When I came on there was pandemonium. I had to wait to say my line. I waited, and waited, and waited. I actually stepped out of character and shouted at the audience. There was silence and then a huge cheer; I thought, "Okay, there's a way through this." There was a phalanx of bouncers surrounding Frank for his entrance; there were bouncers stationed across the front of the stage. It was like being at a rock concert.'

Similar scenes greeted each and every performance as the tour progressed. Candles were lit and held aloft in their hundreds during 'Over at the Frankenstein Place'; enormous packets of rice (some of them unopened), enough to equip the largest wedding congregation a hundred times over, indiscriminately bombarded the occupants of the stalls; water was unleashed in torrents from gigantic pump-action super-soakers and large plastic detergent bottles, refilled at the theatre's wash-basins during the interval once their initial load had been fully discharged.

As if all of this wasn't enough of a danger to the actors (a live moving target may be harder to hit than a movie screen but it does tend to bruise and bleed more easily), as well as a frightening fire hazard in more ways than one, the returning fans – who soon began coming to multiple performances – started to scour the script for amusing and imaginative new ways to interact physically with the onstage antics. Their repertoire of props and missiles multiplied as the run continued, and, for the safety of expensive carpets and seating – not to mention the cast – increasingly stringent bag and body (though thankfully not cavity) searches resulted.

'The show constantly evolved,' elucidates Mark Turnbull. 'The audience kept coming up with new lines and the cast then generated one-liners in response to them, and the audience then developed responses to the responses.

'Actors who were new to the show had no idea; no idea at all. Karyn O'Neill, who played Janet, was shocked at being called a slut, but we all had to cope. We re-learnt timings to allow for call-backs. There were no microphones for dialogue in big venues and *Rocky* mania had hit, well and truly.

'I did a 24-week tour and quickly realised that the same faces kept turning up at different venues. I started to recognise fans from previous performances; they were following the show around the country. In that respect it was like being on a rock tour, which kind of compensated for all the madness. We had a huge pantechnicon with a giant Columbia face on the side, and even roadies who'd worked with rock bands like the Who. One of the laser boys, Andy Shaw, used to ride a Harley across the stage for Eddie's entrance. It was very rock 'n' roll.'

A very well-known British advertising campaign for Bounty, a chocolate bar filled with desiccated coconut, labelled its product 'The taste of paradise.' Henceforth, whenever Frank-n-Furter declared 'Paradise is to be mine' to his guests, a barrage of that very same choccie bar would emerge from the darkness of the stalls; a sea of calorific arrows from a battalion of chocoholic archers.

It was not safe to relax once the prevailing chocolate storm had subsided however. A subsequent line in the very same speech had the actors diving for cover once more, as a milk chocolate covered wafer bar, whose famous slogan had always been 'Have a break, have a Kit Kat' rattled loudly onto the stage like a hail of machine gun bullets in eye-catching red and white wrappers. Occasionally a chocolate bar called Picnic would also make an appearance on the stage at the point when the Narrator ended his pre-'Floorshow' speech with that very word.

The bombardment was seldom limited to water, rice and chocolate bars though. Any item that even remotely related to the dialogue, no matter how cryptic or obscure, might be employed by the show's resourceful devotees. Water pistols to simulate the rain storm was one thing, and rice during the wedding scene was expected, but theatre staff learned to remain especially vigilant at the utterance of lyrics such as Frank's announcement that his Charles Atlas-inspired man-made love-toy had 'Swallowed raw eggs'; a line penned innocently by Richard O'Brien well over a decade earlier.

'What a sucker you'd been' prompted the throwing of innumerable babies' dummies (or pacifiers as they are known in the United States); while the line 'The chips are down' would see attacks of frozen oven chips

5: MADNESS TAKES ITS TOLL

(French fries), sometimes still in their large sealed plastic bags, eliciting a complaint of 'These are rather limp; doesn't anybody have a hard one?' from a disappointed Frank-n-Furter, an enquiry rewarded by the occasional well-timed (and equally well-aimed) cucumber.

Although during US movie screenings it was Brad's cry of 'Great Scott' that traditionally summoned a mammoth assault of (ideally Scott's brand) toilet paper, for the British stage version it tended to be Frank's far less subtle exclamation of 'Oh shit,' at the sight of Dr Scott infiltrating his stronghold, that provoked a similar blizzard of bog rolls.

Even Columbia's 'Some people would give their right arm for the privilege' could, on occasion, be a precursor to the appearance of a (presumably fake; although one never knows) human arm on the stage. It was not unknown for the imaginative use of such objects to cause hilarity amongst the performers as they fought to keep control of what was fast becoming an uncontrollable situation.

Inevitably, things began to get out of hand, as the conduct of the crowd – like children allowed to play without ground-rules or parental discipline – quickly became more and more unacceptable. Completely random items, with no attachment to the dialogue whatsoever, were obviously being thrown around for the sheer hell of it, without any thought of the show's script at all; the most common being bags of flour.

'I hope it's self-raising,' was one local high school student's admittedly humorous riposte, as a half-empty bag of cloudy white powder landed directly on his crotch. But such witticisms only masked concern at an escalating and potentially dangerous turn of events that, if left unchecked, would (and indeed did) soon come to an explosive head.

Aspects of the staging were constantly revised as the tour progressed – the aforementioned motorcycle for Eddie's entrance; the freezer's traditional Coca-Cola illustration updated to a logo for trendy American beer Budweiser; a mock-up of the famous 'Aphrodite of Milos' ('Venus De Milo') statue (with a secret breast compartment, from which the Narrator would retrieve his hand-held microphone); and a rock star-worthy birth from a giant egg supplanting Rocky's previous patchwork assembly from an assortment of bandaged limbs (and other more personal body parts, of varying proportions, presented for Frank's approval). But it was the progressively unruly behaviour of the audience that necessitated a number of early changes.

One such modification occurred when the musicians left their traditional residence of the open – and thus vulnerable – orchestra pit and retreated to a safer permanent position backstage for the sake of their fragile instruments and breakable bodies. Then Frank-n-Furter's electrifying first appearance, one of the show's critical moments, was also compromised by the intimidating conduct of the crowd. In the beginning, when Jeffrey Longmore made his entrance, he would usually answer the servants' unified cry of 'Master!' with a deeply bellowed 'Yes,' pitched somewhere between Dame Edith Evans and then British Prime Minister Margaret Thatcher, from the rear of the auditorium, before strutting along the venue's central aisle, accompanied by the unmistakable strains of the thumping intro to 'Sweet Transvestite'. In the interests of actor safety, however, the character would later be forced to make a more traditional, though less exciting, theatrical entrance from the wings.

During the early 1986 leg of the tour, Frank-n-Furter was played by Bobby Crush. Notable for being the only performer ever to have their name on the Hanley production's posters – thanks to his stature as an eminent pianist and variety artist who had won TV talent show *Opportunity Knocks* on six occasions and been awarded Best New Artist of 1972 by the Variety Club of Great Britain – Crush, a wholly respectable old-school family entertainer, was a somewhat surprising casting choice, as Rayner Bourton noted in his 2008 book of *Rocky* memories:

'Much ground has been broken by *The Rocky Horror Show*, changing many people's attitudes to many previously taboo matters. I first became aware of how accepted, almost mainstream, *The Rocky Horror Show* had become when, in the mid-1980s on Radio 2's weekday afternoon programme, predominantly listened to by millions of middle-aged men and women, I heard host Gloria Hunniford interviewing housewives' favourite pianist Bobby Crush about playing a transvestite in *The Rocky Horror Show*. I couldn't believe it; how could such a clean boy, straight out of the middle of the road music publisher's catalogue, be playing Frank-n-Furter? Ozzy Osbourne yes, but Bobby Crush? I rang the station to express my disapproval of the sanitisation of the character, but I never got through, and my opinion remained unvoiced. I now understand my disapproval was misjudged; it was part of the show's evolution, its transition to establishment, to it becoming an institution.'

Some spectators remember an even greater security presence than usual for Crush's initial appearance as Frank-n-Furter; in fact several seem to recall him making his entrance through the auditorium flanked by burly security guards. It is likely that the company was taking no chances in an effort to avoid repercussions of an unpleasant occurrence that had dominated the local press a few months earlier.

'HOOLIGANS HALT CITY SHOW' the evening edition headline of *The Sentinel* – Stoke-on-Trent's daily local newspaper – had hollered on Saturday 9 November 1985. The following report revealed how the previous evening's performance of 'the outrageous rock musical' *The Rocky Horror Show* had been abandoned during its second half after 'water bombs, eggs, lumps of candle wax and metal spiked objects were pelted down onto the stage.' The article quoted a furious Paul Barnard, who 'branded the incident as malicious and said someone could have been seriously hurt.' It detailed how, due to hazardous conduct from certain patrons, the show had been temporarily stopped during the first half, 'to let them calm down,' but that further outbursts in the second act, which resulted in an actor being hit by an object thrown from the balcony, a dangerously flooded stage and copious amounts of water in close proximity to the electrical equipment, gave the management no choice but to prematurely end the performance.

'Audience participation we do not mind,' Barnard was quoted as saying, 'but we cannot tolerate actors being abused and having dangerous missiles hurled at them.'

Donning the good doctor's heels and hosiery for that particular leg of the tour was David Dale, a renowned female impersonator on the UK cabaret circuit, who had played the role in a previous production before audience participation had become such a formidable force. The deeply affecting experiences of the 1985 tour left him feeling troubled and uncomfortable with *Rocky* – a show he had previously enjoyed – and its 'fans', to the extent that he reportedly turned down a subsequent offer to understudy Frank for the prominent London revival in 1990.

In the weeks following the incident, witnesses recalled that water-bombs loaded with tin tacks – clearly intended to cause damage or injury, as thorough scrutiny cannot reveal even the tiniest reference to such objects in Richard O'Brien's script – had been relentlessly thrown at the stage by (as is often the case) a small group of troublemakers. While these people – like the hooligan element at a football match – do not deserve to be called fans and would not be recognised as such by the show's faithful followers, it is invariably the genuine and compliant supporters who suffer any resulting consequences of such regrettable actions.

This upsetting occurrence would actually cause irreparable damage to *The Rocky Horror Show*'s reputation in the UK, and its far-reaching repercussions persistently affected all future productions and the way in which devoted *Rocky* fans were viewed by subsequently wary theatre managers and their front-of-house staff.

As many venues enjoyed profitable return engagements, and the show commemorated 39 phenomenally successful weeks on the road during 1985, the Theatre Royal Hanley Plc was granted the UK touring rights for the foreseeable future; with the proviso that they would be revoked if at any time the show remained off the road for more than four successive weeks, including the traditional December and January pantomime season.

'We spent one Christmas and New Year at the Apollo in Manchester,' muses Mark Turnbull. 'On New Year's Eve, midnight came. We stopped the show; sang "Auld Lang Syne", then killed Eddie.'

With the production now playing some of the country's largest theatres, its understandably anxious producers concluded that, if it was to have an extended existence, this once modest little piece – which had originally been designed and staged for London's minuscule Theatre Upstairs and had died a painful death when transposed to New York City's cavernous Belasco – would need to be embellished and expanded. The simple, uncomplicated set, perfectly befitting Brian Thomson's 'B-movie for the stage' concept of the original, was given an ostentatious facelift – brash, flashy and distracting – instantly compromising the show's innocent subtlety. At the suggestion of producer Charles Deacon, a huge investment was made adding laser effects – henceforth mentioned on all posters and press advertising – that, in a desperate effort to justify the massive expenditure, would be used extensively throughout the show.

The effects worked best in the scenes of the castle's climactic blast-off for the planet Transsexual and the birth of Rocky Horror – a role now aptly filled by the well-oiled and muscular form of David Ian, a shrewd businessman who would later become a much-revered and powerful theatrical impresario. Conversely, however, over-use of the heavily-publicised lasers during the production would ultimately reduce their impact, as the show became increasingly reliant on the abundant use of such routine lighting effects rather than the strength and ingenuity of its script and songs.

With a view to anticipating, and even defusing, potentially volatile situations – the unpleasant and destructive events of November 1985 still an all-too-recent memory – the Narrator, by necessity, now assumed the role of host or a master of ceremonies, opening each performance with a sober caution about not throwing objects onto the stage: 'There's always one, and he's usually the pillock that gets thrown out; don't do it.

'We have stopped the show before,' he would solemnly advise, while competing with the obligatory chorus of 'Boring!' and a profusion of foul-mouthed insults from some in the impatient crowd, 'so please take heed of our warnings; they're only given once.'

With the over-excited spectators now hopefully in no doubt as to where they stood, the Narrator would lighten the mood with a touch of blatant schoolboy innuendo, as he sensibly advised against the use cameras or binoculars during the operation of the laser beams. 'We don't want you going blind,' he would proclaim cheekily. 'Well, not in that way.'

In the person of Peter Thorne, an accomplished actor whose playing age befitted the character, *Rocky*'s scholarly storyteller retained enough of his imposing dignity. When Marc Seymour assumed the position towards the end of 1987, however, the character changed completely; and the gloriously deadpan authority figure, lovingly created by Jonathan Adams in 1973, was sadly no longer recognisable. With a clown white face and bright red lips, recalling the disturbingly androgynous visage of *Cabaret*'s famously hermaphroditic MC (albeit without his intimidating menace), Seymour, who graduated to the Narrator's role via that of Transylvanian Ghoul and later Eddie, deviated from the scripted persona of an aloof commentator, wholly detached from the rest of the action, by playing the part as an overtly mischievous, sleazy, supercilious pervert. From kissing Rocky on the cheek and calling it a 'perk of the job' to gleefully squeezing Janet's breast and then sulkily protesting about receiving a well-deserved slap in the face for venturing his fingers to her nether regions – 'Bitch,' he would grumble petulantly, 'She didn't do that in rehearsal' – Seymour's Narrator seized every juvenile opportunity to playfully abuse and fondle the other players as they froze in tableau during his scene-linking orations. It is safe to say that Edgar Lustgarten's attitude toward such depraved deportment would have been disapproving to say the least.

Having played Dr Scott for the first few months of 1986, Mark Turnbull asked producer Paul Barnard to audition him for the part of Frank-n-Furter, but left the production when his request was denied. With the show missing his strong vocals, however, he was invited to rejoin the company – again as Dr Scott – in July the same year. 'When I wanted more money, the trade-off was taking on three covers,' recalls the actor, who consequently became understudy to Frank, Riff Raff and Brad in addition to his full time role. 'There were no rehearsals, I had to step straight back in.'

After playing Scotty for another year, Turnbull would finally assume the prestigious role of Frank-n-Furter full-time from November 1987. 'By '87 we all had hand-held mics,' he remembers, 'as that was the only way to work over the noise. So that gave us back some measure of control over the proceedings. I developed ways to deal with hecklers; normally they only want their 15 seconds of fame, so if they shouted a line and got a laugh, I'd let them have their moment of glory, then come back with a put-down to re-establish control. That usually got a cheer too, and we could then move on with the script. If the heckler persisted, we'd just ignore them. One of my favourite lines was, "I tell you, honey, they ruined a fine arsehole when they put teeth in your mouth".'

Upon being showered with a (soft, strong and thoroughly absorbent) cascade of toilet rolls, Turnbull would usually toss them back with a contemptuous cry of 'Worn by puppies, and thrown by dogs,' in reference to a long-running advertising campaign for the Andrex brand of toilet tissue, which famously featured a young Golden Labrador with a penchant for stealing the paper from the convenience at the most inconvenient moment.

'Sometimes the audience lines were ones you hadn't heard before, and some of them were genuinely funny and made you laugh,' Turnbull admits philosophically. 'If that happened, I'd lick my finger and paint an imaginary "One" in the air, signalling that the audience had got one up on me and acknowledging it. But, as an actor, you had to strike a fine balance between giving the audience what they wanted and getting on with the show. Otherwise, the actors could become seduced by the audience; they'd want to please, and they'd all end up becoming little Frank-n-Furters. This was a note often given by Viv after we'd been touring for a while and become a little blasé about the audience.

'I remember once when I was playing Frank at the Hexagon in Reading, when I was bombarded by bags of flour. I thought to myself, "Sod this for a game of soldiers," and walked off. Every night we had the Phantoms sweeping the stage between numbers just to get rid of the debris. God knows where all the chocolate went; rumour was that the band either ate it or sold it on.'

Though his memories of the tour are often truly affectionate, Turnbull admits that the thankless task of dealing with the crowd's unruly conduct night after night could get exceedingly tiresome: 'When it was good, it was a fabulous show. When it was bad, it was an ordeal. Typically the worst audiences were the late Friday and Saturday night shows when you got a lot of drunks. Often the theatre security simply removed the troublemakers, but, inevitably, many slipped through. I remember one night as Frank when a guy in the audience grabbed my ankle during "Sweet Transvestite" and wouldn't let go. The theatre hadn't provided any security at the front of the stage, no pit, so that the punter just leaned over and grabbed me by the ankles. It got to the point where I thought, "This is getting ridiculous; I can't move, and if I try to I'm going to fall and injure myself." I pulled him hard against the stage, and he let go. Sometimes we just cut the dialogue and went straight to the next number, as there was obviously more of a party going on in the audience. On a bad night, you just felt like the show had nothing to do with you.'

A frenzied following firmly established, comparable to that of its cinematic counterpart, and its reputation now rigidly ensconced in the public's consciousness, *The Rocky Horror Show*'s immediate outlook appeared cheerily optimistic. The increasingly affluent production had sustained 47 weeks on the road during 1986; a feat replicated the following year, though interrupted midway by a separate summer excursion to Israel, which included two weeks at the Cinerama in Tel-Aviv.

'That was totally weird,' reminisces Mark Turnbull, who played Dr Scott for the Israel dates opposite Jonathan Kiley's Frank. 'We went straight from the airport to a dump of a hotel. Then, the next day, we put our costumes on in order to meet the press at a smart hotel. We arrived in a truck that was blaring out 'The Time Warp' from huge speakers and that, as a result, stopped the traffic. We played the show in a massive discotheque. It had a capacity of four thousand, and they'd built a stage and a fly tower inside.

'I remember a bizarre radio interview. There were 12 of us being interviewed and it turned out to be forces radio, not a commercial station. Everywhere we went, there was very tight security. The show itself was quite novel for us, as it was the first time any of us had played the piece without audience responses; they just didn't know them. But it was so hot there; the make-up just ran off you, and we all had to take salt tablets to avoid dehydration.'

Turnbull also recalls an unforgettable open-air performance in a vast amphitheatre at the Sea of Galilee: 'The stage was actually a concrete bunker. There were no dressing rooms, and the entire fit-out had been done by candle light, as they'd forgotten to get us any generators.'

Fondly remembered by the company as an outstanding highlight of the entire tour, the three weeks in Israel during the July of 1987 was an experience that the subsequent fortnight in Peterborough could not quite live up to.

Given the unstoppable nature of the increasingly popular production, faithful British fans may have been forgiven the complacent presumption that the show would continue unaltered in its current form for the foreseeable long-term, much like the decade's perpetual tour of Andrew Lloyd Webber's *Joseph*. A level of shock and disbelief therefore greeted the startling news that Rocky's 1988 outing would be 'The Farewell Tour,' and that, while its fruitful run would resume unabated for the next seven months, the final performance would take place at its home base in Stoke-on-Trent during the first week of August.

Richard O'Brien's personal views about this particular touring version had never been a secret. Never shy about voicing his negative opinions, the author remained far more concerned with *The Rocky Horror Show*'s artistic integrity than with the tour's lucrative success, and he apparently deplored the direction in which Hanley had taken this once razor-sharp, dark little satire. It was widely reported that he considered it 'vulgar' and thought that it contained 'not enough horror, and too much showbiz.'

In conversation with Rob Cope for a UK science fiction fan publication in 1990, O'Brien claimed that the tour had 'smacked of amateur night out.' He criticised its poor production values – 'They only had a few fucking lasers; so what?' – and announced that he absolutely hated the set – 'Those painted canvas backdrops I detested so much; I'd have burnt them up.'

O'Brien also went on to attack the 'sloppy' casting process, which he said seemed to recruit young actors whose relative inexperience consequently allowed the audience to take over. He admitted that audience participation had become an established part of the show's appeal, but insisted that it should never sink to the level of pantomime, citing a particular low point from a performance he had attended in Bristol when the cast had allowed (and even actively encouraged) the crowd to drag them into a cheap, panto-style 'Oh yes it is – Oh no it's not' routine.

It is worth noting that posters for the tour's 1986 December engagement – showing the sacred Michael English Columbia face wearing a Santa Claus hat and a trio of cartoon Ghouls dragging a sleigh through the snow – unashamedly marketed the show as 'Manchester's alternative pantomime.'

O'Brien maintained that, while it might sound patronising, audiences actually appreciate being told where they stand – preferring the artist to take control and stipulate where the line is drawn – and specified that Frank has to deviously 'control and manipulate' everybody, both on stage and in the audience.

As a counterpoint to O'Brien's well-known less-than-favourable sentiments toward their beloved production, Hanley's Charles Deacon and John Farrow (producer and executive producer respectively) wrote a defensive editorial for the tour's final programme, justifying all of their creative decisions on the grounds of public demand – 'We do believe our *Rocky* of 1988 is some way on from the original *Rocky* – it has had to move with the times' – and enumerating overwhelming fan response as a more-than-adequate motive – 'As far as we as producers are concerned, if we succeed in giving you what you want, then we have achieved what is really important.'

In some ways, these words echoed Malcolm Sircom's assertions in his text for the brochure – 'It is this cult following that has turned the show into an adult pantomime, not the show itself that has become one' – and, while future productions would prove that the show did not need to sacrifice all of its ironic innocence, subtle sexuality and satirical B-movie caricature in order to remain an undemanding and interactive crowd-pleaser, its 1980s incarnation had unquestionably transmuted into an uncontrollable, almost unrecognisable, monster.

Notoriously pedestrian regional journalists would more often lazily appraise the infantile shenanigans of the exotically-attired audience rather than review the performance itself. The musical arrangements, once akin to the raw rock 'n' roll influences of Richard O'Brien's misspent youth, now sounded artificially electronic and excessively synthesised. On a nightly basis, the country's most majestic auditoria evoked the aftermath of a prison riot, a shameful mess of rice, water, flour, toilet paper and various, often unidentifiable, emissions. Unauthorised amendments to the dialogue – intended to imply the pretence of spontaneous ad-libs – merely came across as crass, tired and overly familiar; delivered in dispassionate haste without trace of wit, fervour or zeal.

And with the show's official programme notes preposterously declaring: 'The plot is largely irrelevant,' the protective author's fatherly

5: MADNESS TAKES ITS TOLL

condemnation of the production's direction is clearly understandable.

By now, rumours that Richard O'Brien was planning to stage a new production of *The Rocky Horror Show* in London's West End were flourishing. Therefore, while his disparaging remarks were no doubt genuinely heartfelt, it was believed by some that, as he presumably took a sizeable percentage of the tour's weekly earnings (which over four years would have accumulated considerably), the decision to withdraw the UK touring rights was probably influenced by this intention as much as by his well-publicised artistic scruples.

'There are now over one million fewer "virgins" since we started our tour in 1984 – sorry.' Such was the Theatre Royal Hanley's earth-shattering 'Special announcement' on the back of the large format souvenir brochure – available for purchase alongside the usual array of T-shirts, badges, key fobs and other merchandise of questionable quality – as the record-breaking run entered its final sell-out week; a week that incredibly marked the tour's eleventh visit to its Stoke-on-Trent base in four years. In fact, *Rocky* played Hanley with such startling regularity that in retrospect, given the usual attire of its male patronage, and in an age of equality, it seems odd that no-one ever had the foresight to install a permanent make-up mirror in the Gents' toilets.

Ticket-holders received a final-week presentation pack with their booking – containing a programme; the souvenir brochure; a certificate of attendance; an A3 colour photo of the company; and a voucher for a commemorative T-shirt, featuring the traditional Columbia face (now sporting a mournful red tear) and the legend 'Bye Bye Rocky' – and all were entered into a prize draw. Winners of the draw, along with fans who had attended the show at least once a week for the tour's duration, and those seeing all six performances of the final week, not only had their names printed in the programme but also received invitations to the exclusive cast and crew farewell party, taking place on the evening of Friday 5 August, immediately following the penultimate performance.

A memorable highlight of these bittersweet festivities was the one and only performance of *The Tacky Horror Show*, an affectionate parody of the Theatre Royal Hanley's historic production, conceived and performed by members of the venue's own front-of-house staff and volunteers. Introducing the 30-minute presentation, Peter Thorne – one of the tour's most popular Narrators – sneered comically, 'Who did you expect – Charles Gray? On this money, you'll have to make do with me.' He then read out a list of specially-prepared audience responses for the evening. Upon hearing the line 'Wait, I can explain,' the crowd was instructed to call out 'It had better be good; we don't want Bobby Crush back,' eliciting a mixed reaction from the audience and prompting Thorne to announce sheepishly, 'Oh, I quite liked him.'

Crush was not the only familiar name to come under such playful attack, however, as the parody's protagonists, Mad Dangers and Annette Spice, braved 'Typical Stoke-on-Trent weather' to look for help at a nearby edifice, which looked like 'a theatre for rich trustees.'

'The owner might be a Theatre Royal producer,' observed Annette, 'and you may never get paid' – a remark presumed by many to be a cheeky reference to Paul Barnard, who had been dismissed the previous year amid allegations of fraud and tax anomalies.

Ultimately, it appeared that our heroes had 'succeeded in visiting the Theatre Royal without seeing a member of staff wearing a *Rocky* T-shirt' – a genuine rarity at the time and thus an accurately observed slice of local satire – to witness the entrance of Rob Cope's Frank-n-Spurter. Like a traditional cod panto, *The Tacky Horror Show*, for all of its (occasionally uncomfortable) irreverence, was ultimately nothing more relevant than a fairly forgettable half hour of amateur dramatics and trivial lampoonery; although a number of ardent *Rocky Horror* fans in attendance felt that Cope, a talented local performer with a compelling singing ability and an appealing stage presence, would have made a convincing Frank in a professional production of *Rocky* itself.

Allocating seat numbers for the very last night of the tour in Hanley would prove a pointless exercise. From the moment the band played the unmistakable intro to 'Science Fiction Double Feature' and Julie Fox's raunchy Usherette swaggered boldly onto the stage, every member of the audience leapt from their seats, stampeded toward the front and stood for the entire performance as if attending an open-air rock concert. Numerous tales of the Theatre Royal's lovingly restored balcony moving as much as nine inches under the weight of several hundred over-enthusiastic Time Warpers that night might just be the stuff of local legend. But then again, they might not.

Thirty minutes of encores and speeches followed. John Farrow – jokily implying that he was actually speaking to Richard O'Brien (believed to be in Australia at the time) via his rather large and cumbersome state-of-the-art 1980s mobile 'phone – fanned the flames of the company's alleged grudge with the show's author by implicating the profoundly emotional audience. 'I can't tell them that,' he quipped curtly. 'I can't tell them it's a load of …' He then held out the phone for the expected overwhelmingly enthusiastic response as he yelled, 'Tell him what you think of the show.'

Subsequently revealing a supposedly genuine telegram, ostensibly received from O'Brien that very day, Farrow read, '"Thank you for four wonderful years. Thank you for half a million pounds",' and then paused for more uproarious applause before continuing, 'and he says, "When do I get the rest?"'

Boos, jeers and a surprising amount of abusive hostility greeted this last

5: MADNESS TAKES ITS TOLL

remark, with at least one clearly audible cry of 'Tell him to fuck off' from somewhere in the stalls.

With the benefit of hindsight, this admittedly short-lived fan animosity toward the man credited with creating their precious obsession seems somewhat extreme and peculiar. It was probably nothing more than an ignorant over-reaction to the consensus that he was mercilessly exterminating their beloved *Rocky*; a deed that, as far as the quality of future *Rocky Horror* productions was concerned, would ultimately turn out to be more of a rescue than an assassination attempt.

Eventually introducing producer Charles Deacon as 'the one man without whom ...,' Farrow was unable to resist yet another gibe by flippantly adding, 'apart from Richard O'Brien, who's too mean to come from Australia.'

Deacon sincerely thanked the fans for their continued unwavering support: 'We all share one thing in common, and that is we love *Rocky*.' He then promised that one day soon 'we'll meet again,' before surrendering the stage to Dr Frank-n-Furter (Mark Turnbull) for an obligatory rousing chorus of 'The Time Warp'.

An extended castle blast-off sequence – a suitable swansong for the lasers – climaxed with a black-out and a lone feather boa (picked up by a single spotlight) descending slowly onto the stage, accompanied by a tearfully melancholic final refrain of 'Superheroes'.

'Lost in time, and lost in space, and meaning,' sung melodically and dreamily from offstage – a poignant, tasteful and beautifully understated ending – ensured the desired effect of 'not a dry eye in the house.'

Definitely of its time, and fondly remembered by an entire generation of fans, many of whom got their first live *Rocky Horror* experience from this amiable yet shallow reworking, the Theatre Royal Hanley's interpretation remains an extremely important chapter in the history, success and continued development of a uniquely enduring theatrical phenomenon. The production almost single-handedly helped keep the receivers at bay for a number of years. With its passing, the theatre proceeded to be plagued by debt and the perpetual threat of closure before its eventual purchase by music tycoon Mike Lloyd in 1996. Sadly however, with the collapse of Lloyd's business empire four years later, shortly after the opening of the National Lottery-funded Regent Theatre literally just around the corner on Hanley's Piccadilly, the Theatre Royal's survival finally became impossible. The building was later used briefly as a Jumpin Jaks nightclub and cabaret venu, before ultimately closing its doors for good; its heyday as one of the country's finest live entertainment palaces now a constantly fading memory.

Two other noteworthy productions of *The Rocky Horror Show*, both of which toured several major European cities (excluding the United

Kingdom), opened towards the tail end of the decade. The first of these, produced by the Broadway Musical Company New York and directed by Johnny Worthy, ran between 1988 and 1990 and was a modest and good-natured production. With musical arrangements by the original's Richard Hartley, it remained true to the spirit of the show as conceived, despite its programme notes retaining the Hanley version's rather ignorant and unforgivable suggestion that 'The plot is largely irrelevant.'

Regardless of the unmistakable quality of the Broadway Musical Company's production, it was a second – wholly unrelated – European tour, launching in June 1989, that, for rather unsavoury reasons, would later end up snatching the headlines. Despite its production company being named as Dusseldorf-based Panda Productions (or 'Equity blacklisted Panda Productions' as the *Stage* newspaper would come to label them), even a fleeting glimpse at the show's programme – which featured production photos of flashy Hanley-esque costumes, settings and lasers – revealed more than a few familiar names from the recent UK tour.

Most conspicuously, there was producer Paul Barnard (now head of Panda Productions), as well as director Vivyan Ellacott, choreographer Loraine Porter, laser operator Andy Shaw, several musicians and, among its cast, Jonathan Kiley (a popular and highly acclaimed former Hanley Frank-n-Furter, once again reprising the coveted role), Marc Seymour as Eddie/Dr Scott, Peter Thorne as the Narrator, Christopher Marlowe as Brad and Andrew Ryan as Riff Raff. The production, though well received by audiences, eventually terminated prematurely due to managerial disputes and poor organisation.

Amongst the cast of a subsequent tour of Italy and France, again produced by Barnard's Panda Productions, was Mark Turnbull. '*Rocky*'s a strange drug when you're an actor,' he attests, justifying his decision to return. 'The show's a big part of the demolition of the career I should've had. Actors normally blow from one thing to another, but I stuck – or got stuck – with *Rocky*. It's like being a member of a club; as such, there's nothing like it. The whole routine of getting ready and getting dressed is fabulous. I used to buy my stilettos from Cover Girl in the Holloway Road. I never wore platforms, as I'm so tall; I always thought that my Frank would be more elegant in stilettos.'

However, as Turnbull confirms, the tour was once again beset with difficulties from the moment it opened: 'We rehearsed and set off for Milan. By the way, the narration was in Italian. Something felt wrong though. There were obvious signs of problems, particularly with the producers of that tour. There were obvious tensions in all sorts of areas with erratic behaviour and decisions.

'Opening night in Milan was an experience. All the audience turned up in furs, bedecked with jewels, and I swear you could hear a collective jaw

5: MADNESS TAKES ITS TOLL

drop when we started. They'd evidently come to see Shakespeare or something high-brow from a British company. We did two weeks in Milan, then Turin. Even La Cicciolina, the porn star turned politician, came to see us, and a news crew filmed the entire show.'

Despite sizeable audiences for the first few weeks, trouble began once the show got to Trieste. Turnbull remembers that the stage manager was fired and the cast stopped getting paid; while the company's failure to arrange accommodation for the subsequent venue resulted in the cast having to stay at a doss house in Trieste for a week:

'We went from one to two weeks in a venue to one to three nights. I threatened to walk, so I got paid, but then one day there was no tour bus to get us to the next venue.

'We took the train to Florence, where we appeared in a circus tent. We got to Thursday, which was pay day, and there was no money; but there was a full house. So I said, "Give the audience back their money and we'll do it for free." Barnard refused, so I took my make-up off, went back to the hotel and booked myself on the next flight; where I bumped into the others from the cast who'd evidently had the same idea as me.'

Upon returning to the UK, the understandably disgruntled cast was met by the next troupe of actors preparing to fly out to replace them.

Panda's reported failure to pay company wages on more than one occasion eventually incurred the anger of Richard O'Brien himself. According to the *Stage* newspaper, the author claimed that he was owed thousands in unpaid royalties and had even, in the words of one ex-employee, 'turned up at rehearsals and implored the actors not to go on tour.'

It was a rather gloomy conclusion to the eventful 1980s chapter of the *Rocky Horror* story.

As the BBC's 2006 'time-travelling' cop show *Life on Mars* – set coincidentally in 1973, the very year of *The Rocky Horror Show's* inception – and its 2008-2010 follow-up *Ashes to Ashes* – based in the '80s – would eventually demonstrate, those consecutive decades were lightyears apart in so many ways. The brutal and edgy 'a pint, a fag [that's 'cigarette' for American readers] and a punch-up,' three-day week reality of *The Sweeney's* no-nonsense coppers Regan and Carter had been unceremoniously usurped by the sports jackets with rolled up sleeves and designer sunglasses of Crockett and Tubbs, the image-conscious fashion-victim detectives of *Miami Vice*; a reflection of the latter decade's excessive 'greed is good' philosophy advocated by Michael Douglas's Gordon Gekko in Oliver Stone's 1987 movie *Wall Street*.

Culturally, the 1980s became known as 'the decade that taste forgot.' The decade of leg-warmers, shoulder pads, the mullet, the flat-top, Michael Jackson's Moonwalk, Reaganomics, Thatcherism, yuppies, Live Aid,

Rambo, Eddie Murphy, Arnold Schwarzenegger, alternative comedy, Stock, Aitken & Waterman, the video revolution and the Rubik's Cube.

Although its story and characters had emerged relatively unaffected, *The Rocky Horror Show* essentially escaped becoming an irrelevant period piece – and actually thrived as a work of crowd-pleasing entertainment – by morphing like some lycanthropic shape-shifter into something of a different animal.

Nevertheless, like the global climate, social trends and anxieties are in a constant state of transition, their sudden diversion often triggered without warning by the most unforeseen occurrences. As another unpredictable decade loomed, one burning question reared its head: with a new and deadly sexually-transmitted epidemic sensationally grabbing headlines around the world, and responsible 'safer sex' attitudes suddenly very much in vogue, could a frivolous little rock 'n' roll musical – famous for symbolically applauding the permissive gender experimentation and free-spirited carnal lifestyles of the 1970s – succeed in making the '90s suitably naughty?

6
I Wanted To Be Dressed Just The Same

'Are you dressing up?'

Tell anyone that you are going to see *The Rocky Horror Show* and it is likely you'll be asked this very question. Even those with little or no knowledge of the show's plot, characters or music will, more often than not, make such a predictable enquiry.

The implication is obvious. Even amongst the uninitiated, *Rocky's* rampant reputation precedes it.

Dressing as a figure from a much-loved film or TV show or in the style of an iconic pop star is a not uncommon element of fandom. However, while science fiction or fantasy fans may occasionally don their replica Starfleet uniform, Klingon battle armour or Hogwarts School of Witchcraft and Wizardry dress robes, it is a behaviour predominantly associated with die-hard Trekkers or movie geeks; and an activity that, regrettably, a judgemental mainstream society generally deems a bit sad or strange.

Rocky Horror, on the other hand, usually provokes an altogether different response. It has actually become unequivocally associated with such participatory rituals, with individuals from all walks of life and every age group – not just the show's most dedicated followers – eager to slip into something a little more revealing, and quite obviously a lot less comfortable, for a night at the theatre. From the butchest red-blooded male rugby player, happily squeezing his 48" Charlton Heston-like pecs into his diminutive girlfriend's scantiest size ten flimsies; a lady of advancing years, audaciously strutting her stuff in fishnet stockings and black leather bondage wear; a teenage hen party in cheap plastic devil horns and the slutty contents of an Ann Summers bargain bin; or a normally straight-laced, happily-married accountant, smartly attired in his best tailored jacket, formal shirt and tie, with just a pair of naughty French knickers and thigh-high PVC fuck-me boots to suitably finish the look. A phenomenon unique to this particular work of entertainment, the unscripted, unrehearsed exploits witnessed in the foyer, auditorium and theatre bars are often as much of a spectacle as anything occurring on stage.

Coming face to face with infatuated spectators adorned in homemade (often identical) duplications of the onstage costumes is merely one of the unconventional obstacles a *Rocky Horror* cast member might have to face. These days, seemingly obligatory interactive involvement from no longer quietly passive observers has become an expected ingredient of the *Rocky Horror* experience, and has made the piece even more famous as a participatory experience than as the groundbreaking work of contemporary theatre it once was.

Brad and Janet are rudely – yet somehow affectionately – designated 'Asshole' and 'Slut' by boisterous fans, and these uncouth nicknames are often bellowed loudly whenever the characters' names are uttered.

'I think perhaps you'd better both ...' the sinister Riff Raff slowly begins, upon first meeting the hapless young couple at the castle door. 'Fuck off,' commands the audience, before the seedy butler can finish his line with '... come inside.'

'The master is not yet married; nor do I think he ever will be,' the hunchbacked handyman reveals, shortly after Frank-n-Furter's show-stopping entrance. 'We are simply his ...' 'Slaves' is the crowd's flippant, but not entirely inaccurate, addition to the dialogue, leaving an incensed Riff Raff vehemently to spew the word 'servants,' as his copy of Richard O'Brien's lean libretto dictates.

While everyone on stage is a target for more than their fair share of unrestrained verbal abuse, the character most called upon to deal with an incessant onslaught of insulting profanity is the Narrator. 'It's true there were dark storm clouds,' he opines ominously, recounting the fateful night upon which the story takes place. 'Describe your balls!' the ever-charming audience demands defiantly, caring little about the actor's performance or the evidently impending doom and gloom implied by his character's sinister tone. This almost mandatory interruption leaves the once-respectable scholarly academic wide open to a now inescapable cheap joke at his expense, and gives his menacing description of the aforementioned storm clouds a completely different (and far less threatening) connotation than inferred in the written text. 'Heavy, black and pendulous,' is the onstage storyteller's scripted, and thus unavoidable, conclusion to the line in question.

As detailed in the previous chapter, in addition to the merciless vocal heckling, a huge amount of physical, often messy, prop-based participation has become exclusively synonymous with *The Rocky Horror Show*. Not just familiar but word perfect with the ins and outs of the scripted dialogue, fans have been known to bring along an arsenal of 'weaponry', occasionally even smuggling into the building (in sometimes intimate, and presumably uncomfortable, places) objects outlawed by theatre management and front-of-house security.

Throughout the fateful rainstorm, which drives the betrothed duo to Frank-n-Furter's citadel of carnal corruption, the audience traditionally fires water pistols to simulate the deluge; rice is thrown during the story's opening scene to evoke the aftermath of Ralph's and Betty's nuptials; rubber gloves are snapped (ideally in unison) when Frank-n-Furter, excited at the prospect of giving life to his perfect male plaything, does the same; toilet rolls are thrown indiscriminately around the auditorium at the moment Brad yells 'Great Scott,' and flashlights (once candles and cigarette lighters, in the days before most theatres sensibly prohibited this most obvious of fire hazards) are appropriately flashed during Brad's and Janet's 'There's a light' choruses of 'Over at the Frankenstein Place', metaphorically illuminating their historic walk to the castle.

How and why this happened, spontaneously and unexpectedly, has been argued and debated for as long as the *Rocky Horror* cult has existed. 'Maybe you shouldn't try to figure it out,' Susan Sarandon once offered shrewdly when quizzed about the unusual conduct exhibited by the film's devoted followers. 'Maybe it's just like love; you shouldn't try to figure it out, just enjoy it.' But, as indisputably wise as these words are, critics, theorists and theologians will always prefer to hypothesise endlessly and pretentiously about why an offbeat 1970s rock musical continues to provoke such bizarre conduct from sophisticated contemporary audiences; even when a definitive and satisfactory conclusion is impossible to reach.

In his 2007 book about *The Rocky Horror Picture Show*, Jeffrey Weinstock, Associate Professor of English at Central Michigan University, seemed to imply that those who create and yell out counterpoint dialogue, especially that which gives the illusion of anticipating or predicting a forthcoming scripted 'response' from an on screen character, are in some way harbouring a deep, dark desire to control the events of the film. The author noted that, with the movie being a permanent image, which remains fixed and unchangeable with every successive viewing, fans are fooling themselves with the deluded belief that their talkback is actually influencing the action on screen. Whether or not there is any truth to this extreme and possibly over-intellectualised theory, Weinstock may – by psycho-analysing the film's devoted followers in such a serious manner – be reading too much into their admittedly eccentric behaviour.

By studying its history, it may be just as logical to deduce that boredom, insomnia and an over-familiarity with the film itself were as much to blame for *Rocky Horror*'s notorious audience participation as anything more deep and meaningful.

After failing to make much of a dent at the box office on either side of the Atlantic, *The Rocky Horror Picture Show* had been considered a disaster, and a colossal embarrassment – probably as much for its unconventional attitudes and hedonistic content as its lacklustre financial takings – to its worldwide distributor 20th Century Fox. In the days before movies got a second chance at success with a subsequent home video release, the task of somehow salvaging this cinematic debacle was given to Tim Deegan, an eager-to-please 26-year-old advertising executive, who suddenly found himself shackled with trying to promote a *bona fide* box office bomb.

As previously noted, Fox had been wary of the film from the get-go, after a previous foray (or folly) into the world of glam rock horror a few months earlier. Brian De Palma's ambitious *Phantom of the Paradise* (1974), a lurid contemporary musical fusing the basic premise of Gaston Leroux's 1911 novel *The Phantom of the Opera* (and its numerous film adaptations) with the classic German legend of Faust. De Palma's film, with its colourful characters, a hint of *Frankenstein* and catchy – though hardly groundbreaking – rock tunes by Paul Williams, appeared on the surface to have instant cult appeal. But its failure further cemented an already accepted view that a cult movie cannot be intentionally manufactured. Finding what seemed to be a similarly confusing piece of puerile camp trash being assembled under their studio's name, Fox's recently appointed new senior management reputedly tried to stop production. Director Jim Sharman however was already beyond the point of no return and, despite being over budget to the tune of nearly a quarter of a million dollars, *The Rocky Horror Picture Show* was completed.

The film's memorable 'lips' image, accompanied by the unforgettable phrase 'A different set of Jaws' and the dripping blood title font, was used for one of its US one-sheet posters, generally referred to as Style A. The Style B one-sheet featured the bloody red title on a deep yellow background, along with a black and white photograph comprised of two still shots from the film – the 'Sweet Transvestite' throne scene and a self-conscious Brad and Janet in their virginal white underwear – plus a chorus kick-line of stocking-clad legs. A slogan across the top of the poster, reading 'He's the hero – that's right, the hero!!' – evidently referring to Frank-n-Furter – was undeniable proof that the Fox marketing department was clueless as to the subject of the picture and its intended audience. Unashamed hedonist, manipulator, sexual deviant, ego-maniac, blasphemer, drug addict, murderer, cannibal; Frank-n-Furter may be a lot of things, but a hero would hardly be one of the most obvious on anybody's list.

The flashy quad (horizontal) format poster used for the August 1975 UK release (and also the cover of the soundtrack album) featured a pop-art composite of Frank, Riff Raff and Magenta (with her Elsa Lanchester hairstyle from the movie's finale) against a red background, flanked by monochrome production stills set against blue and pink. These images were accompanied by various cheesy slogans – including 'Thrills & Chills,' 'Gorgeous Gals' and 'Lotsa Larfs & Sex' – that would probably have looked as at home on gaudy posters for a tacky 1970s British sex film as they would on ads for a '50s monster movie.

6: I WANTED TO BE DRESSED JUST THE SAME

Although *The Rocky Horror Picture Show* performed well in LA, following its 26 September 1975 official US premiere at the United Artists Westwood Theatre, the fact that it failed to excite audiences anywhere else on its initial theatrical release gave its humiliated studio and financially-wounded producers cause to drastically rethink their marketing strategy.

Though its pitiful takings were a disappointment, with mainstream audiences having harshly shunned the picture, Lou Adler was fascinated to learn from at least one small-town theatre manager that modest groups, made up of the same 40 or 50 people, were faithfully returning to see the film again and again every week. The suggestion that a cult following was, even then, already beginning to materialise was too intriguing to overlook.

Among the numerous things Fox found problematic about the film were its rather slow pacing when compared with the original stage show and its undeniably bleak ending. Various awkward revisions were therefore made to try to rectify such issues. Richard O'Brien suggested that the studio trim Richard Hartley's suitably mournful, but somewhat lengthy, instrumental intro for the song 'Superheroes' and cut immediately to Brad's vocal as soon as the castle had taken off. Clumsy editing, however, consequently led to the complete omission of Brad's and Janet's verses from most prints of the film, leaving the plot feeling more unresolved and perplexing than ever. The complete version would be released on video cassette in the UK in 1984, while years of pressure from ardent devotees would eventually lead to the reinstatement of this integral song for later US re-releases too, prompting a grateful acknowledgement from Jim Sharman in his 2008 memoir *Blood & Tinsel*: 'This original ending was thought too downbeat and was cut by the studio. Happily, it's been restored at the insistence of fans. Thanks, fans! The film doesn't make sense without it.'

After a further unsuccessful attempt by 20th Century Fox to open the movie as a drive-in attraction – this time as a double feature with *Phantom of the Paradise* (one of the very few logical choices for a suitable companion feature to *Rocky Horror* at the time) – Tim Deegan decided that its flagrant quirkiness might lend itself perfectly to the then-thriving midnight movie crowd. He approached Bill Quigley, publicist for the Walter Reade cinema chain, with a view to finding a suitable late night venue for the movie in New York.

Midnight movies had already become an accepted form of after-dark entertainment by the end of the 1960s, and out of the ordinary exploitation films such as Alexandro Jodorowsky's *El Topo* (1970); Tod Browning's controversial 1932 oddity *Freaks*; John Waters' notorious sleaze-fest *Pink Flamingos* (1972) and its 1974 follow-up *Female Trouble* (both featuring larger-than-life female impersonator Divine) proved a magnet for audiences with a curious taste for dark, disturbing and bizarre diversions.

The Rocky Horror Picture Show had its midnight opening at the Waverly Theatre in New York's Greenwich Village on 2 April 1976 – April Fools weekend seemed oddly appropriate given the nature of the film and its already tumultuous history – following in the footsteps of previous late night successes such as George A Romero's 1968 black and white horror opus *Night of the Living Dead*. Considering the nature of previous cult favourites on the so-called 'Werewolf Circuit', it would seem in hindsight that *Rocky Horror* could have been tailor-made for this cinematic graveyard shift. However, while the movie's eventual success would make a studio hero of Tim Deegan, 20th Century Fox and Lou Adler at first braced themselves for yet another failed crack at unleashing this apparently unmarketable motion picture.

In the beginning, many of *Rocky*'s midnight regulars were young and gay – the very target audience the film's promoters had been seeking, but did not realise they already had. Feeling shunned by conservative mainstream society, many of these people found themselves drawn inexorably to the strangely welcoming bosom of a dingy, foreboding, smoke-filled movie theatre during the forbidden hours of the morning, while those who inhabit the tiresome 'real' world of so called normalcy were slumbering, blissfully ignorant, in their cosy warm beds.

Rocky Horror's infamous audience participation reportedly began when Louis Farese, a young kindergarten teacher from the New York borough of Staten Island, felt overwhelmingly compelled to shout at the screen. It is generally accepted that, one night in 1976, just as Susan Sarandon's Janet Weiss futilely shielded her rain-soaked head with a newspaper, Farese, having already attended several midnight screenings of the film, was unable to resist impulsively yelling 'Buy an umbrella, you cheap bitch.'

Unsurprisingly, given the beer swilling, reefer smoking, insomnia suffering atmosphere, this unprompted addition to the soundtrack elicited a roar of approving applause from the mind-fucked, sleep deprived, after dark audience. Another early example of talkback – also reputedly created by Farese – was 'How strange was it?' in response to the Criminologist's allusion to Brad's and Janet's 'strange journey.'

In the weeks that followed, the size of the crowds increased phenomenally, and these lines of counterpoint dialogue were repeated enthusiastically, not just by Farese but in unison by the entire throng.

Regular *Rocky Horror* revellers at movie theatres throughout the United States quickly developed innumerable new responses to the script – some clever, some topical, some downright crude – and introduced props and physical participation to the proceedings. Some began attending screenings dressed as characters from the movie itself, and eventually fan performance groups – later to be known as shadow casts – were formed. These devotees began to act out their own intricately-rehearsed and

6: I WANTED TO BE DRESSED JUST THE SAME

immaculately-costumed versions of the entire film as it was concurrently projected onto the screen behind them.

Far from Jeffrey Weinstock's pseudo-intellectual supposition that any off-screen contribution to the filmed image exposed some kind of deep-rooted wannabe God complex amongst the participants, it is more likely that these people were simply having a little bit of rebellious juvenile fun. Indeed, an equally reasonable, yet far less weighty, explanation than Weinstock's might be found in the words 'Don't dream it, be it.' Frequently identified as some form of over-simplified message in the show itself – although a quick recall of the plot and the fate of its characters will verify that it isn't – the phrase no doubt struck a resounding subliminal chord with pubescent audiences; especially those with feelings of exile from their peer group, outsiders with feelings of confusion about sexuality, physical appearance or weight issues.

'Oh, fantasy free me' sings the sultry Magenta during her 'Time Warp' verse; while Frank-n-Furter later urges 'Give yourself over to absolute pleasure,' encouraging all-comers to embrace his hedonistic outlook on life. Fans of the film certainly took these sentiments to their hearts. Even if *The Rocky Horror Picture Show* itself had become an essential but almost secondary backdrop to the shenanigans of the audience, with a *bona fide* box office blockbuster having risen from the grave of their still-born celluloid catastrophe, 20th Century Fox could at last stop 'dreaming it' and finally, blissfully 'be it.'

In a 2005 interview for Stuart Samuels' film *Midnight Movies: From the Margin to the Mainstream*, Walter Reade publicist Bill Quigley noted: '*Rocky Horror* became such a phenomenon that the profits from *Rocky Horror* actually paid for the distribution overhead of the studio each year.'

In the same documentary, Lou Adler casually speculated about the film's unprecedented US box office takings to date: 'I'd be comfortable saying 175 million,' the typically laid-back mogul mused nonchalantly, as he possibly – and quite justifiably – smugly recalled the moment in 1974 when know-it-all studio heads had attempted to permanently halt production on this future cash cow at a time when the picture was just $200,000 over budget.

One feasible, but by no means exclusive, hypothesis as to *The Rocky Horror Picture Show*'s enormous success as a midnight movie is that it may be the only genuine cross-genre cult film. Pictures with comparable nerdy followings usually appeal to a particular faction of filmgoers, whereas *Rocky Horror* seamlessly unites and attracts fans of comedy, horror, science fiction, musicals, rock 'n' roll, camp and other genres. It also seems to draw those with differing tastes in music, from the hardest heavy metal to the most anodyne of lightweight pop, and from raw punk rock to MGM musicals and show tunes.

When queried for this book on their theories as to the secret of the show's continued success, several ex-cast members responded somewhat typically with the simple, yet rather unimaginative, answer, 'sex, drugs and rock 'n' roll.' Fans, on the other hand, when similarly questioned, were often more profound and inventive with their answers, regularly likening the experience to that of an adolescent rite-of-passage. 'There's a sense of investment and ownership because the fans made it what it is,' is how one such follower perceptively explicates the rabid devotion of *Rocky Horror*'s most fervent disciples.

Those with feelings of segregation, rejection and non-conformity repeatedly describe a sense of family and belonging in a world from which they would otherwise feel socially excluded. In a pitiless society, quick to judge and castigate those brave souls who dare to be different, *Rocky Horror* allows freedom of expression in a particularly harmless and innocent manner, refreshingly encouraging its followers to celebrate their diversity proudly. For some it provides an opportunity to experiment with cross-dressing, or a confused sexual identity, in safe, non-judgemental circumstances, while those with weight issues, an unconventional appearance or somewhat *avant-garde* leisure pursuits may well discover an essential sense of communal integration when elsewhere they might not.

'I've been involved in lots of fan communities before, but none feels like family in the way *Rocky* does,' attests one long-time devotee of the UK stage productions. '*Rocky* allows people with body issues or who are quite shy to be liberated. You do stuff you'd never imagine doing elsewhere. It gives you a safe space. It gives you a community where geeks are totally cool and where you won't get judged. *Rocky* accepts all; there's no body fascism.'

The idea of collective individualism has been used repeatedly as an effective marketing tool. The suggestion is that by wearing a particular 'badge' trademark – for example recognisable trendy clothing brands such as Levi Strauss, Abercrombie & Fitch, and Ralph Lauren – consumers believe that they are asserting their personal individuality, and consequently standing out from convention, while at the same time taking comfort from a sense of belonging to a community of like-minded individuals. The same can be said of football supporters who proudly wear the shirt of their chosen team, thus indicating that they are a partisan and have made a choice that is not universal, while concurrently binding themselves to other fans of that team in a way that little else could.

The same principle has more recently been given a 21st Century spin, thanks to the growth of the internet. The overwhelming popularity of social networking websites such as MySpace, Facebook and Twitter would imply that even the most reclusive and seemingly antisocial computer nerd is actually desperate for a sense of communal belonging. It is a delicious paradox that might actually go a long way to explaining the appeal of *The Rocky Horror Show* to its ever-growing army of devoted disciples. Perhaps in the interests of caution however, it should be noted that, while such readily available technology has certainly been instrumental in connecting innumerable like-minded individuals, certain negative repercussions have recently started to manifest themselves.

While probably more prevalent within the likes of the *Star Wars* and *Doctor Who* communities, the decidedly 21st century phenomenon of 'toxic fandom' and attitudes of one-upmanship amongst pop-culture afficionados – particularly disagreeable consequences of social media platforms granting everyone the means and opportunity to express conflicting opinions, no matter how disrespectful, condescending or extreme – had certainly begun to permeate *Rocky Horror* fan circles by the time of the show's 40th anniversary in 2013. During the 1970s and '80s – before the internet, e-mail and social media helped make being a pop-culture or sci-fi geek acceptable and mainstream – fan groups often felt closer, friendlier, and more intimate, primarily due to the dedication and effort required to seek out similarly-minded enthusiasts through fan clubs, printed newsletters, fanzines and hand-written correspondence. While purely a sign of the changing times, the technological advances which helped fans communicate easily and instantly on a global scale also generated an unpleasant culture of gatekeeping and elitism which, in recent years, has ironically made fandom feel considerably less like a family or community than it did in the days before the internet.

The aforementioned premise of collective individualism was touched upon by singer-actress and punk icon Toyah Willcox in programme notes she wrote for the show's twenty-fifth anniversary production in 1998. 'In 1975, I had black and pink hair, I lived in Birmingham, I was 17 years old and I thought I was alone in the world,' recollected the former '70s and '80s rock star, before going on to explain vividly the epiphany she experienced upon discovering a photograph of Little Nell as Columbia in *The Rocky Horror Picture Show*. 'It was a picture that penetrated my DNA. My life changed at this point and I knew I wasn't alone, and I actively sought my tribe.'

The very use of the word 'tribe' in this context reinforces the concept of collective individualism and coincides with similar views from countless other fans of the piece.

Well over a decade after she wrote this memorable editorial, Toyah – who had appeared with Little Nell and Richard O'Brien in Derek Jarman's surreal 1977 punk movie *Jubilee* (itself now something of an avant-garde cult favourite) – fondly recalls the first time she actually encountered *Rocky Horror* live on stage at the King's Road Theatre: 'Sometime in 1977 I was taken by some gay friends to see the show itself. They told me that I had to see it because it was "life-changing" and "theatre like you've never seen before." Well it was certainly a celebration. It was the first time I'd ever seen a cast come out into the audience and involve them, and it was obvious that the audience knew every word of the songs and the dialogue; and that was still quite early in the show's history.'

While the whole performance had an impact, the actress is still in no doubt as to which image had the most profound effect on her personally: 'For me the best moment was Little Nell's tap-dancing. It was a revelation and mind-blowing, because when I was 14 and taking tap lessons I never thought that tap could be cool; and she made it cool.'

'*The Rocky Horror Show* dared a generation to be different,' concluded Toyah's heartfelt reminiscences in the 1998 UK tour programme. 'It was "home" for a homeless generation, and we all met that night in the red velvet confines of an old music hall theatre on King's Road. It was great and we all were weird.'

In response to Patricia Quinn's 'What *did* you do, Richard?' on *The Rocky Horror Picture Show* DVD's audio-commentary, after she divulged that gentlemen from every conventional walk of life had periodically confessed to her that they had at one time or another donned fishnets and suspenders for an evening of *Rocky Horror* frivolity, O'Brien replied casually and succinctly: 'I released people from their kind of male-female polarised parameters.' It was a notion upon which he expanded for VH-1's *Behind the Music* in 2000:

'I think what I did was unleash a subliminal desire in people towards exhibitionism and narcissism; and unleash that joyous kind of sexuality that is always lurking under the surface. It taps into that part of the psyche that says, "Ooh, I'd love to be up there with a microphone, in high heels and a pair of fishnet stockings; singing some great rock 'n' roll songs, making love to everybody, and getting all the jokes and getting away with it. Yeah, that'd be groovy, wouldn't it?"'

'"Don't dream it, be it" is a great message,' ventured Susan Sarandon in her own corresponding VH-1 interview. 'And at a time when kids are having some sexual ambiguity, it's like a club where you can go, and all the kids that are left out or don't know what they're doing or are a little bit too odd to fit in their high school, instead of having to do something violent, they can put on this outrageous garb and go somewhere where they're accepted for who they want to be.'

With midnight movie madness firmly established at screenings of the film version – the phenomenon considered curiously newsworthy and already widely documented by the uncertain dawn of the 1980s – it was perhaps inevitable that such audience interaction would subsequently materialise, uninvited, at productions of the original *Rocky Horror* stage incarnation.

6: I WANTED TO BE DRESSED JUST THE SAME

However, while the throwing of rice, squirting of water and hurling of food items could likely cause damage to a cinema's screen and plush décor, resulting in a little inconvenient overtime for the venue's cleaning personnel and an understandably pissed off theatre manager, once live actors were brought into the equation, becoming potential targets for such unruly tomfoolery, the phenomenon became something different entirely.

There continues to be an ever-expanding divide between those who consider *Rocky Horror* to be nothing more than juvenile interactive theatre and purists who fervently refute such frivolous analyses. Although it is undeniable that such infantile participatory rituals saved the film from inescapable oblivion, the original stage version had been a stupendous audience-pulling hit long before spectators ever dreamed of shouting back at the action. Audience talkback began with the midnight movie screenings; it was never a part of the original *Rocky* game plan. And, in the eyes of many who helped bring the show to life in the first place, it still isn't.

Peter Blake and Daniel Abineri are two actors who, between 1975 and 1992, experienced very different manifestations of the show. Each portrayed Frank-n-Furter during *Rocky*'s original London engagement – Abineri also played the character with the very first UK touring company in 1979 – and then revisited the role for subsequent productions in the early '90s. Both found the show's audience participation in those later versions nothing less than an irritating ordeal.

'Each show was like a boxing match,' Abineri remembers sadly. 'The audience had utter contempt of, and for, the performances; they were more interested in who had the better costume – cast or audience.'

'Frank mustn't collaborate with audience participation,' the actor insists. 'He has to get on top of them. It's exhausting. I did use audience participation, but I hated it. I find it disrespectful. It's also very stressful when there are one thousand people shouting at you.'

Abineri has similarly unpleasant recollections of *Rocky Horror* audiences from when he toured with the show in New Zealand during the 1980s: 'The audience were actually trying to pull me off the ramp,' he laments. 'I ended up kicking out at people. It finished with 1,800 drunk Dunedin students rushing the stage at the finale.'

While this may sound like classic rock 'n' roll pandemonium, it is not the kind of anarchic behaviour a serious actor would expect, or should have to endure, on stage, especially when the consequences result in that actor never wanting to view any future *Rocky* performance. 'For that reason I would never see the show again,' Abineri declares sadly. 'Audience participation is so objectionable. I savour and nurture the memories I have and don't want them spoiled. I would go so far as to say that the fans have killed the show. It was unique and captured the zeitgeist of the '70s, and it's very different now; and worse for it.'

Fellow thespian Peter Blake eagerly shares this opinion: 'Sadly, I think it's become a parody of itself. It's turned into a three-ring circus with Frank as the lion tamer. They've tried to turn it into professional musical theatre and it's not. It shouldn't be. There was absolutely no need to re-invent this wheel because it wasn't broken. It's become pantomime and it's lost its soul as a result.'

'It's like when you take copies of a master tape,' agrees Jay Benedict, another early player from the King's Road production. 'It loses something in each generation and each translation. It's all got a bit camp of late, with all that rice throwing and joining in.'

New generations coming to the show since the early 1980s, of course, have never known it without such exuberant participation, which for them has now become an inextricable part of the *Rocky Horror* experience. 'And that's a shame,' Peter Blake persists passionately, 'because they're missing out on the original. I hate the hen parties that come along and spend the whole night screaming drunken comments. One night, during the time that audience participation had got out of hand with people throwing things, some idiot started spraying a super-soaker around. It hit the PA system, so I walked offstage down into the audience and physically removed her. I mean, that was dangerous; someone could've been electrocuted.'

But surely, these people have paid for their ticket. Are they not keeping actors in business and helping to keep *Rocky* alive? 'Yes, of course, but it spoils it for everyone else, including the cast. I do appreciate that there are new generations coming to *Rocky* and they have a different experience now; I just happen to prefer the original.'

Although clearly a staunch advocate of the show's earlier – pre-cult following – incarnations, Blake does, however, freely admit to having broken the sacred fourth wall by responding to the audience banter on occasion. 'You have to now,' he concedes. 'It's expected and has become part of the show. I limit my interaction though and tailor it to wherever it's playing. So, for example, I always tell the audience to shut up after Rocky's told me "Piss off", and the audience laughs at this.'

The actor justifies these actions by insisting: 'Frank has to reassert himself after Rocky's remark, or he'd lose his authority. When I was in Manchester I think I said something like "Be quiet, you mutinous mob of Mancunian minge-munchers," which seemed to go down well.'

Indeed it did; and, as Blake says, he often adapted this cheekily offensive put-down to accommodate whichever city the touring production was playing. In Stoke-on-Trent, for example, he called the audience 'Potteries plonkers' whilst in Birmingham they became 'Brummie bum-bandits.'

6: I WANTED TO BE DRESSED JUST THE SAME

With particular pertinence to this point, in his interview with Rob Cope in 1990 Richard O'Brien observed that an audience will passively accept almost any abuse that a performer chooses to throw at them. Having played Frank-n-Furter for several performances during the show's 1990 West End revival, the author selected the very same moment in the narrative to illustrate his point: 'I first of all called them reprobates. The next night I called them losers. The next night I called them deadbeats. By the time it got to the end of it, I called them a load of fucking deadbeats. "Listen up, you load of fucking deadbeats," and it's astonishing how much they will take, truthfully. And I think again that was an interesting exercise to see how much they would take off somebody actually coming at them.'

During the same discourse, O'Brien offered his own position regarding his creation's excessively vocal followers: 'Truthfully the lines aren't witty. If they're witty, that's fine, it's spontaneous; but we had one guy sitting in the front row one night who was just a complete fucking bore. He sat there, with his feet up, in the gear, but it was just boring, just so unfunny.'

'And there are some great lines,' the author admitted, before coining the unforgettable expression, which later became something of a cautionary watchword on *Rocky Horror* fan websites, 'Use wit, not shit.' Good advice, which certain members of the mainstream *Rocky* crowd would do well to heed.

There are performers, especially those who discovered *Rocky Horror* during or after the 1980s, who maintain an alternative attitude, actually embracing the spirit and eccentricity of the fans and the over-the-top ways in which they express their devotion to the show and its characters.

'I think everyone needs to accept audience participation,' says Anthony Topham, who assumed the roles of Eddie and Dr Scott for the 2005 European tour. 'The Rocky Horror Company needs to put bums on seats; so everyone should just go with it and give the fans what they want.

'Either do that or be strictly artistic; don't allow audience participation and risk alienating the fans,' Topham continues, implying that creative and artistic ambiguity, in terms of the way the show is presented and marketed, merely confuses its target audience. 'The show has a life of its own, so accept it. If people enjoy it for different reasons, that's okay. Either that, or just hire performing monkeys.'

However, it is not simply the case that those who played in the show prior to the birth of audience interaction consequently hated the development and those who appeared in later productions automatically accepted and celebrated it. David Bedella, who portrayed Frank-n-Furter more recently in the critically-acclaimed 2006/07 and 2009/10 UK touring productions, is amongst those who feel that a barrage of relentless irrelevant verbiage from an auditorium of loud-mouthed, overzealous, drunken punters can be extremely tiresome for a serious actor attempting to deliver an emotionally-centred performance.

'There were times when I fucking hated it,' he cringes. 'After a few months, it just becomes completely disheartening. Here's another wanker going for his 15 minutes of fame. There were nights when I was taking off my make-up; I'd look in the mirror and think, "Why am I doing this?" It was hard, very hard, and really made me consider going back. It's such a shame, because the true fans love the dynamics of the show, the highs and lows – and you want die-hard fans to be able to cry at the beauty of the moments we create near the end – but other people ruin it for them.'

By contrast, it appears that Anthony Topham genuinely relished his experiences of the show's interactive aspects; his fond memories and joyful enthusiasm for the piece are still infectiously palpable: 'As an actor in *Rocky* you can't afford to coast because of audience participation. The whole thing creates such an atmosphere and you really become wrapped up in it. No one show is ever the same, which is great for the cast. Anything can happen and anything goes – just like the B-movie it's written as.

'I always stayed backstage and found a place to watch the audience, because I just loved the atmosphere. That really built a buzz for the actors. Talking of atmosphere, I remember we performed in a Roman amphitheatre in Sicily. I looked out during "Over at the Frankenstein Place" and I could see two thousand people all holding up lights. That was amazing.'

Fittingly, the word 'atmosphere' rears its head time and again whenever people search for an appropriate noun to adequately express the electrifying experience of a live *Rocky Horror* performance. Interviewing Richard O'Brien in 1990, Rob Cope claimed to have seen most of the musicals playing in London's West End at that time – some of which were enormously successful long-running crowd-pullers – but claimed that none came close to having an atmosphere like that of *The Rocky Horror Show*. O'Brien's response was typically perceptive:

'It's probably what theatre used to be like before it became church-like and precious.

'The Victorians took a lot away from us. They took a lot of life away from us. Yes, the music hall was still on; but that was seen to be low life, as we become more middle class; *Rocky*'s probably closer to that experience than any other form of theatre. Rock 'n' roll of course, concerts, are close to it; but there's not an interaction, just shouting at the gods. The gods don't talk back very much, do they? They take the adulation, but, apart from the songs, it's a narcissistic experience, which is all for them. So yeah, *Rocky*'s got that going for it.'

'With the internet, kids are brought into the adult world so quickly these days,' ventures Toyah Willcox, 'but the show still retains its energy, its role as a rite-of-passage and its fun characters. When you look at the world we've made, with theme parks and such like, it slots right in. If it is like adult panto, that's fine; panto is a fantastic genre. It's how Shakespeare's plays started, and it's all encompassing and welcoming.

'The shouting out is all part of the event,' the actress-singer speculates, suggesting that an attempt to stage a totally straight production of *The Rocky Horror Show* today without any participation at all would result in audiences feeling cheated. 'Nowadays we're all performers; whether it's game shows, karaoke or posting comments on the internet. Look at the people who host *Eurovision* parties; you go there because you want to shout your opinion loudly and to be heard.'

A large proportion of actors, however, are not so enamored with such behaviour from conventionally more refined and courteous theatregoers. After all, for most professionally-trained and serious thespians, standing on stage in ripped fishnet stockings and 6" high heels, having 'Asshole' and other insulting profanities shouted at them by a mob of inebriated punters, was probably not their primary motivation for spending four long years at drama school.

In her 2006 book *A Stage Mother's Story: We're Not All Mrs Worthingtons!*, Hazel K Bell chronicled the theatrical career of her son Aidan, an actor who portrayed Riff Raff in several European productions of *The Rocky Horror Show* during the early 1990s. In one particularly memorable anecdote about a performance in Amstetten, Austria, the author told of how that show's Narrator – evidently an old-school showbiz veteran, unfamiliar with the unorthodox customs of this peculiar cult following – did not take kindly to the unexpected barrage of abuse emanating from a small but determined group of hardcore *Rocky* disciples in the stalls. Furious, he threatened to call the police and have the offenders removed if they did not sit and watch the show in respectful silence; an attitude that would hardly seem in keeping with *Rocky Horror*'s rebellious rock 'n' roll reputation.

Assuming the Narrator's role for the New York revival in the year 2000 was 1970s American talk show legend Dick Cavett, a seasoned professional who took any over-the-top audience involvement in his stride, choosing to adopt a far more laid-back approach and express jocular disdain toward the show's more ardent followers.

Upon being disparaged for his alleged lack of neck from the few members of the midnight movie crowd who could actually afford to shell out the undeniably steep $80 for a Broadway theatre ticket – all blissfully ignorant of the fact that their 'jokes' did not really work unless specifically directed toward the 'neck-less' figure of Charles Gray in the film version – Cavett patiently explained the remarks to the uninitiated who made up most of the high-brow New York audience. 'The actor playing the Narrator in the film appears to have no neck,' he clarified dryly and coolly to the bemused Broadway elite. His subsequent condescending remark was clearly aimed squarely at the overly vocal fans: 'Some of you may have realised that you're *not* at a film?'

With this unusual form of spectator involvement now being so widespread and synonymous with the work itself, it has become increasingly hard to separate the show from its religiously devoted fans. This is especially true of the media, which frequently finds it more interesting, amusing and newsworthy to focus on the outrageously dressed audiences than the piece of theatre that spawned them. What many do not realise or understand is that *The Rocky Horror Show* was never actually conceived as an audience participation piece, and, while the habit of calling out counterpoint dialogue, infantile jokes and foul-mouthed insults may add to the experience of an enjoyably undemanding evening at the theatre, it adds nothing at all to the satirically dry wit of the existing script.

Richard O'Brien has always been fond of pointing out to new casts that the show works best if played ironically straight. The jokes will take care of themselves, he insists, whereas over-playing the piece and hammering home the gags will destroy its subtlety and acerbic edge. It is undeniable that audiences would benefit from this approach too.

Some even fail to grasp the simple fact that the humour is already there. The script has a wealth of sharp, witty, subtle and sophisticated jokes that do not need blatant and puerile superfluities to make them funnier.
'Whatever happened to Fay Wray? That delicate satin-draped frame,' goes Frank-n-Furter's sincere lament to the object of King Kong's impossible desires. 'As it clung to her thigh, how I started to cry, 'cos I wanted to be dressed just the same.' The laugh is right there, dripping with irony; Frank's tender tribute ultimately exposing his fetishist cross-dressing craving to slip into Wray's sensual feminine attire. Intercepting Frank's gentle admission of "cos I wanted to be dressed ...' with a yobbish chorus of 'like a chicken!' not only kills an amusing lyrical punch line, but categorically demonstrates that the scripted version is by far cleverer and wittier. In recent productions, rambunctiously vocal fans have even responded to Frank-n-Furter's suggestion that the newly created Rocky is, 'Ready for the ultimate test,' with an unambiguous cry of, 'Anal'. The issue here, of course, is that Frank's scripted remark already carries this implication. The joke is already the whole point of the line, making such a blunt and far less witty punchline from the audience completely redundant.

That *Rocky Horror* has gained a reputation as perhaps the world's most famous audience participation piece continues to be both a blessing and a curse to its creators. The individuals responsible for marketing each new revival will, unsurprisingly, view the show's infamous interactive following as a goldmine of self-promotion. But, as a direct result, it has become increasingly difficult for directors to stage the piece as originally envisioned. Indeed, for the best part of the '80s and '90s, producers and directors had a tendency to craft and market their productions of *The Rocky Horror Show* to deliberately cater to its latter-day status as a camp, superficial, one-dimensional party piece. In many ways it was probably these producers – with the satisfying ker-ching of easy money drowning out any thought of artistic integrity – who were to blame for the show becoming such an out of control monster.

Unlike the irresponsible Victor Frankenstein of Mary Shelley's novel, however, Richard O'Brien was not only aware of the shortfalls of such deficient productions, he made it his mission to drag his beloved creation, kicking and screaming, back to the laboratory slab in order to carry out the painful but necessary corrective surgery it undoubtedly required. A conscious effort was made to respect and preserve the veracity of the script and its beloved characters, even if that meant – sacrilegiously in the eyes of some – altering or even deleting certain provocative lines of dialogue in order to discourage out of place talkback at inappropriate moments. While never wanting to put an end to audience interaction altogether (after all, the spirit and fervent devotion of its followers helps to make the *Rocky Horror* experience so exceptional), Christopher Luscombe, who helmed the 2006/07 UK tour (the story of which is still to come), believed that a healthy balance could be realistically achieved – a genuine symbiotic relationship between show and fans – that respectfully maintained and upheld the truth of the piece without sacrificing any of the fun.

In truth, *The Rocky Horror Show* has always been its own entity. It ran for the best part of a decade in London – with successful engagements in other cities around the world – long before revellers felt compelled to arrive in costume or shout obscenities at the cast. By being so stubbornly adamant that the show is all about themselves and their oh-so-amusing counterpoint dialogue, those who insist that audience participation is essential to the show's success are missing the fact that *Rocky* thrived without it as a renowned piece of must-see theatrical entertainment for years. Audiences lovingly embraced the original stage productions years before the curious and quirky unessential by-product of audience interaction came along and rescued the less successful movie version from cinematic oblivion. There is also the reality that the show continues to be an enduring crowd-pleaser in countries where audience participation has not established itself in the way that it has in America, mainland Europe and Great Britain.

Various versions of *Rocky Horror Etiquette* have been circulated by fan groups over the years, with internet chat rooms, forums and discussion boards continually awash with myriad opinions as to what constitutes appropriate and inappropriate participation. Verbal interaction with the film is generally considered more of an acceptable 'anything goes' kind of affair, it being impossible to disrupt or distress the actors once their performances had been captured on celluloid; the first DVD release in 2000 even included optional 'Participation Prompter' and 'Theatrical Experience' bonus features. It is, on the other hand, considered – by those with a genuine love for the show itself – extremely bad form to heckle a *Rocky Horror* stage production during its quieter, poignant and more thoughtful moments.

Brad's tender love ballad 'Once in a While', Frank's touching Fay Wray tribute during 'The Floorshow', the climactic death scenes and the show's powerfully cathartic dénouement are the most fitting examples. The climax of *The Rocky Horror Show*, if played correctly, can rival the most serious tear-jerking ending for sheer emotional punch. As Frank tenderly cradles Columbia's dying body in his arms, the heartbreaking impact of her selfless sacrifice can be irreversibly ruined by a flippant and thoughtless cry of 'Fuck her while she's still warm' from an ignorant loudmouth in search of a final cheap laugh at the expense of the script's sometimes overlooked tragic depth. It's not that the line itself isn't funny – it's certainly suitably irreverent – but it feels completely inappropriate given the emotional weight of the scene in question.

The fact that Brad Majors is seldom the biggest asshole in the theatre is an irony no doubt lost on the majority of offenders. After all, no self-respecting theatregoer would dream of heckling Shakespeare's 'star-crossed lovers' during their tragic final moments; just as it would never be expected for *Blood Brothers*' Mrs Johnstone to suffer such indignities as she gives her heartrending all for that revered musical's shattering finale.

A less disruptive, more press- and media-friendly side of the *Rocky Horror* cult – and certainly the one with which the public at large is most familiar – is undoubtedly the audience's penchant for dressing in costume to attend performances.

While the notion that it is in some way compulsory for those viewing the show to do so in costume is an odd misconception – one that has been known to deter shyer, less adventurous types from seeing *Rocky* in the first place – many do seize the opportunity to slip into something not usually associated with their dreary everyday existence.

The opening night of the latest touring version in any major city will inevitably impel the editor of the local rag to issue one of his or her eager-to-please young hacks with a camera to snap some titillating shots of the neighbourhood lads wearing their wife's, girlfriend's, or maybe even their mother's underwear, in an effort to amuse and bemuse the readers of the following day's edition.

6: I WANTED TO BE DRESSED JUST THE SAME

Though generally accepted that many of the earliest *Rocky* regulars were gay, once the fun, flamboyant nature of this new late night sensation was revealed by the media it quickly appealed to the straight community as well, who no doubt realised that they might be missing out on an exciting and liberating after dark experience.

'Why do straight people get off on it so much?' queried presenter Rhona Cameron during a discussion with Richard O'Brien on British television's late night *Gay Time TV* programme in 1996. The enquiry prompted a smart, though hardly Earth-shattering, response from the man who had probably spent much of his life fielding similar questions about his most enduring work. 'Because we do them a favour really,' he casually proclaimed. 'The Quentin Crisps of the world, they do everybody a favour; they cheer everybody up, they loosen the barriers.'

With this outlook in mind, it is easy to perceive that there is nothing to exclude anybody from enjoying *The Rocky Horror Show* – whatever their sexual preferences or political viewpoint – however conventional or unconventional a lifestyle they may lead.

'I think it's about letting people feel that they're not being judged and allowing them to express themselves,' suggests 2009/10 UK *Rocky Horror* tour actress Kara Lane. 'When you look at some of the fans in costume, take for example a lady wearing a basque, stockings and suspenders; she may not have the courage to wear that at any other point of her life. It makes me feel honoured to have been part of something that allows her to feel comfortable and sexy doing that. Or couples that come along, and the man might be a cross-dresser; *Rocky*'s something they can do together. It's harmless fun and acceptable for men to be dressed as women and for women to be as glamorous as they wish.'

With regard to his show having broken down barriers and made life easier and more bearable since its 1973 opening, Richard O'Brien stated in a 1991 television interview, 'I would go so far as to say that we probably created a climate where people like Boy George and Julian Clary can operate.' In his 2000 interview for VH-1, meanwhile, the author-composer emphatically declared, 'If I've in any way enabled people who've felt lost and uncomfortable about their nature to live in a happier world, then thank God I did something worthwhile on the planet.'

As already noted, in addition to its undisputed appeal to the gay community, particularly youngsters experiencing confusing feelings of adolescent self-discovery, *Rocky Horror* is probably a secure non-judgmental outlet for straight men with private cross-dressing tendencies, or at least those whose curiosity cannot be comfortably expressed fully in a regular public situation.

For ardent fans, the ritualistic donning of costume is much the same in principle as assuming the attire of a USS Enterprise bridge officer or a certain Time Lord's knitted scarf; but the very nature of *Rocky Horror*'s chosen apparel immediately provokes a different attitude from spectators because of established sexual or fetishist associations with such attire.

'The element of transvestism wasn't intended as a major theme,' Richard O'Brien revealed to Patricia Morrisoe in 1979, 'although it turned out to be one. Writing a transvestite into the play was a very naive judgment. Maybe there was a lot of subconscious feeling about that coming through.'

Yet, in retrospect, this naive judgment turned out to be O'Brien's masterstroke, as it allowed freedom of expression to flourish healthily, whilst encouraging otherwise conservative people to playfully cast aside their restrictive inhibitions.

'It allows people to access that part of themselves that wants to wear a dress,' observes Anthony Topham. 'That was true in the '80s and '90s. In recent UK tours, it's mirrored changes in society as it's become sane and normal to dress up.'

'One only has to observe the audience and what they get up to pre-show,' offers Christopher Luscombe, director of several recent *Rocky Horror* touring productions. 'If I was ever in a town and didn't know where the theatre was, all I had to do was look out for the *Rocky* fans and follow them from the railway station. Their night – and their outfit – has been planned. It's a big deal for them; they can let their hair down and wear the fishnets instead of the pinstripe. As such, it's a valuable release.'

'I think people are looking for permission to let the "themselves" out,' suggests David Bedella, another memorable Frank-n-Furter. '*Rocky* doesn't just give you that permission, it positively encourages you to be as crazy, raunchy and as seductive as you want to be; it lets people experience a whole other side of themselves.'

One particular *Rocky Horror* follower and self-confessed cross-dresser is quick to corroborate this view, explaining how the show offers an opportunity to comfortably acknowledge and flaunt one's feminine self in public: 'As I have always been a [transvestite], it was a great excuse to dress up and go out in public as Frank without being "read" by the public,' he candidly reveals. 'They just see me as someone dressing up for the show, but I'm doing it for real.'

Although he has on occasion dressed as other characters, this particular gentleman maintains a special affinity with Frank-n-Furter. 'I have developed him over the years with fantastic make-up and costumes, and it's not just what's on the outside, it has to come from within. I ooze the feminine side of me.'

Rocky Horror fans certainly like to make a big entrance. Surveillance of any theatre foyer 30 minutes or so prior to curtain up will reveal definite exhibitionist tendencies; maybe even a momentary craving for celebrity

6: I WANTED TO BE DRESSED JUST THE SAME

stardom, as the fellow in question is quick to confirm: 'Frank gets a lot of attention, which I absolutely love. It makes your night when everyone wants photos with you. I feel brilliant.'

Posing for photographs with like-minded attendees in the foyer prior to a performance has, for devoted fans and occasional audience members alike, become a fundamental part of the overall *Rocky* experience. It is therefore a massive shame that the kill-joy management of some venues have tended to go overboard with their in-house security, even to the extent of confiscating people's cameras at the door.

Like no other trip to the theatre, a night at *The Rocky Horror Show* is now an authentic social event, akin in many ways to a landmark birthday party or a family wedding. Thanks to the famed costume rituals of its audiences, it elicits a community spirit like no other dramatic work; of which pre-show photographs in the bars and foyer have become an integral ingredient – even more so with the rising popularity of social networking internet sites, where such images and experiences can be instantly shared with friends and associates.

Most viewers will be aware that the taking of pictures during any theatrical performance is in breach of copyright laws – while flash photography can also prove distracting to actors onstage – and is therefore prohibited within the auditorium. Hence, while the prudent searching of bags – in order to prevent potentially dangerous props from entering the theatre – is, in view of the rather unruly reputation of the show's post-'80s audiences, a sensible precautionary measure, physically removing cameras upon entry to the building is unnecessarily excessive. A warning not to take photos of the show itself would surely suffice – and usually does for many venues – while the alternative offered by some theatre personnel that, having reclaimed their cameras from the cloak-room after the performance, attendees could take their required photos at the end of the night (post-coitus as it were) is no adequate recompense. These photo opportunities are unquestionably a pre-show ritual; they are part of the buzz, the thrill, the anticipatory excitement of the evening. Attempting to take such pictures at the end of the night – when feathers are limp, eye make-up has run, bravado (amongst other things) has deflated and people's priorities are suddenly on the journey home or the location of the nearest drinking establishment – will never be the same.

In a 1991 television interview, in which he described the show as both 'a moral tale' and 'a cautionary tale,' Richard O'Brien offered his own theories as to the fanatical devotion of the most dedicated *Rocky Horror* followers, some of whom see the film and the show dozens, hundreds, even thousands of times. 'I think that in many ways it's become a kind of medieval mystery play of today,' he mused. 'And I think that's why those young people go to the cinema again and again and dress up. I think they've become the strolling players.'

Although a certain amount of costuming accompanies other cult films and television sci-fi shows – a lot of aficionados being typically creative and naturally artistic people – it could be argued that donning appropriately themed attire is actually the very heart of *Rocky Horror* fandom. While most members of the general public would be satisfied to turn up in an ill-fitting borrowed corset or that cheap, poorly stitched together French maid uniform from a local joke shop – and good for them for making an effort and dipping a fishnet-clad toe in the liberating waters of enticement – genuine enthusiasts take their costuming a lot more seriously.

Fans of the film spend untold hours and a lot of money dutifully reproducing exact replicas of the outfits seen on screen, avidly scrutinising close-up photos or freeze-frames on the DVD to get them just right. If that is not enough, there are websites offering helpful tips and reference material, the most well-known of which proudly calls itself the Anal Retentive *Rocky Horror* Costume List.

Those inclined toward the stage productions often have an even tougher job than adherents of the film, as designs and details will usually vary between each successive production. The most dedicated will be amongst the crowd on the opening night of the latest revival, studying or even sketching the new designs with a view to reproducing them as rigidly as possible. It is a testament to the dedication of the show's disciples that, unlike the film's costumes, which remain unchanged with every viewing, a stage tour may last only a year or two before those faithfully copied costumes might become obsolete; and all-new recreations will be needed for the next production.

One possible explanation, or part thereof, as to why UK audiences in particular so fervently embraced the phenomenon of audience participation – hitherto associated primarily with US screenings of *The Rocky Horror Show*'s celluloid spin-off – and applied it wholeheartedly to the live stage productions might be found in that most British of traditions, pantomime. While Richard O'Brien has, quite rightly, disputed allegations that the show is merely a pantomime for adults, there are definite parallels to be drawn between a typical panto audience and the spontaneous addition of unpremeditated participation to the *Rocky* legend. 'It feels like *our* pantomime' is how one long-time follower succinctly rationalises the show's appeal. 'Not the one your parents take you to; it feels naughty and subversive.'

Pantomime, the origins of which can be identified in, amongst other things, ancient Greek mime, French theatre and 16th Century Italian Commedia dell'Arte, has been a firmly established Christmas institution in the UK for hundreds of years. A typical modern pantomime – most major

6: I WANTED TO BE DRESSED JUST THE SAME

British theatres present one every year during the festive season – will loosely rework a classic fairytale and turn it into a childishly anarchic family-friendly farce, shoehorning in a few contemporary pop tunes as well as the odd A, B or Z-list celebrity, television personality or sports star to draw undemanding punters away from the festive TV offerings and leftover turkey.

Cinderella, Snow White and the Seven Dwarfs, Aladdin and *Dick Whittington* are generally considered the most archetypal pantomime stories, although *Babes in the Wood* (elements of which are abundantly evident in *The Rocky Horror Show*'s narrative) is also popular. As with all of the best ostensibly innocent works of family entertainment, there is usually a profusion of vaguely subversive ingredients thrown into the mix with the intention of eliciting hysterical laughter from blissfully oblivious children, while cheekily tormenting the unnecessarily uptight political correctness brigade. Custom dictates that the traditional figure of the kindly pantomime dame and Cinderella's cruel ugly sisters are played by men in grotesquely exaggerated make-up and outrageously comedic outfits. Fast and furious dialogue will be typically peppered with naughty jokes and double-entendres, designed to go well and truly over the kids' heads, although a blatant bum or boob reference will have the young 'uns rolling in the aisles. The beautiful princess will be romanced by a dashing hero or handsome prince, sometimes (though not always) played by another woman in tights and kinky boots, which could make their inevitable first kiss and spectacular finale nuptials seem possibly strange (or maybe oddly arousing, depending on your outlook) to anyone not prepared to suspend disbelief, kick their adult cynicism up the ass and buy into this make-believe world of theatrical fantasy.

Time-honoured audience participation plays a pivotal role in pantomime, with customarily established comebacks already known to the crowd long before they even purchase their tickets or take their seats. 'He's behind you,' yells the audience spontaneously as the devious villain stalks the hapless hero. They know the story, they know the ending; but still they return year after year for a slice of undemanding and uplifting escapism.

It has been acknowledged that children will happily listen to the same bedtime story night after night. Without delving too deeply into human or child psychology, maybe prior knowledge of the story and the promise of a predestined happy ending, guaranteed by countless previous readings, aids restful sleep by calming both mind and body. It is not unrealistic to suppose that this desire for comfortable and comforting familiarity does not stop with the arrival of adolescence; a reasonable rationalisation as to why individuals might be drawn to the same film or play even after multiple viewings.

'Oh no, she's not,' spit the vile ugly sisters, at the suggestion that

Cinderella is locked in the cupboard to prevent the gallant Prince Charming from finding her, working the enthusiastic young crowd into a frenzy. 'Oh yes, she is,' the spectators confirm excitedly through mouthfuls of half-chewed popcorn and sweeties, exposing the villains' dastardly plot and paving the way for the inevitable happy ending.

Probably the most significant, and often overlooked, difference between pantomime participation and that of *The Rocky Horror Show*, however, is that this active audience involvement is an integral and customary part of the traditional panto structure. Unlike with *Rocky Horror*, pantomime participation is deliberately written into the script and vigorously encouraged by the onstage performers.

Another notable aspect of the pantomime audience's conduct is the use of costume, and although most of those so attired are usually pre-schoolers dressed as Cinderella or Snow White – rather than a sex-craved extraterrestrial scientist and his scantily-clad attendants – it is nevertheless worthy of contemplation that these young supporters choose to express themselves by interacting with a work of theatre in this way. As impressionable and absorbent as the juvenile subconscious is, is it not logical to suppose that a fishnet future may already be predestined for some of those baby-faced Snow Whites?

Richard O'Brien's oft-quoted claim that *Rocky Horror* was simply a work of shallow juvenile entertainment with no significant message is an assertion he has been compelled to reassess over the years; and, while his claim that he wanted to write something 'any ten-year-old could enjoy' might shock the less liberally minded (in view of the show's sexual connotations), it is worth considering that every schoolboy loves a bit of smut. Let's face it, many a pubescent epiphany has probably been memorably initiated by a discarded stack of dog-eared wank mags, discovered amongst the dense foliage of an overgrown railway embankment or roadside hedgerow.

Rarely does the press for a *Rocky Horror* production stipulate a strictly 'adults only' stance, typically settling for an innocuous small-print caution, 'This show has rude parts.'

'I see people of all ages coming into the auditorium, and they all seem to go out happy,' avowed UK tour director Christopher Luscombe in 2006. 'It's very interesting, that; it seems to have very wide appeal.'

On its original cinematic release, *The Rocky Horror Picture Show* was given an 'R' rating by the Motion Picture Association of America (MPAA), which stipulated that viewers under the age of 17 would require an accompanying parent or adult guardian. In Australia, the film was rated 'M' (for 'Mature Audiences'), denoting that it was recommended for those over the age of 15. In the UK, it was given an 'AA' certificate. 'AA' had been introduced by the British Board of Film Censors (later to be known, slightly less provocatively, as the British Board of Film Classification) during an overhaul of their ratings system in 1970, and precluded anyone under the age of 14 from seeing a film with that certificate. Aside from its sexual themes, the *Rocky Horror* screenplay's single expletive – Frank-n-Furter's lyric 'A mental mind-fuck can be nice' during the song 'Wise Up Janet Weiss' – would have been enough for the BBFC to preclude pre-teens from seeing the film, with sexual swear words then generally considered strictly taboo in non-adult entertainment.

With another major revision of the UK ratings structure in 1982, the 'AA' certificate was replaced by '15' (no-one admitted under the age of 15), which became *The Rocky Horror Picture Show*'s UK rating until the early 1990s.

With the release of Tim Burton's *Batman* in 1989, a brand new '12' certificate was added to the BBFC's system, prohibiting anyone under that age from seeing a film carrying that particular rating; although in 2002 it would be amended to '12A', which meant that under-twelves now simply had to be accompanied by an adult.

In 1992, having noted that all of the film's limited number of UK prints had become extremely damaged and scratched after many years of regular late night screenings up and down the country, UK *Rocky Horror* fan club president Stephanie Freeman approached 20th Century Fox with a view to them producing a new print for the Transylvania '92 fan convention she was organising to take place in London that Hallowe'en. This version of the film would be the first cinematic (i.e. non-video) release to feature the song 'Superheroes' in its entirety, and would, because of this 'additional' scene, be regarded by the BBFC as a new film and thus subject to reclassification. As a result, *The Rocky Horror Picture Show* was now granted the less restrictive '12' certificate for subsequent UK cinema screenings; although '15' would remain its rating for video, DVD and Blu-ray releases.

In spite of its famously naughty adult content, which certainly caused jaws to drop in the 1970s, *Rocky Horror* has rarely been perceived as dangerous or seriously subversive. This view is supported by the broad-minded attitude of long-standing devotees who take their young children along to organised fan events and performances of the stage show. The frolicsome youth of the permissive society grew up to be understandably liberal parents. The free-spirited generation of the '70s and early '80s willingly imparted its own rite-of-passage upon its open-minded and impressionable offspring; and, while it is usually the norm to find one's parents' music and old-fashioned youth culture decidedly square, unhip and embarrassingly outdated, *Rocky Horror* is most definitely a very real exception.

Evidence to support this claim can be found not only at the show itself – which continues to attract a keen multi-generational audience – but also at informal social gatherings such as the UK fan club's annual picnic at Oakley Court (the 1974 filming location for *The Rocky Horror Picture Show*), where the next generation of enthusiastic adolescent *Rocky Horror* followers merrily mingle with middle-aged fans, many of whom bring along their own children. Devoid of dangerous preconceived notions of judgement or ridicule, boys are more than keen to raid their mum's make-up box and slip into a baggy Transylvanian tailcoat or a pair of oversized high heels, purely in the name of innocent dressing up fun. Cinderella's ball gown may have become a saucy French maid's apron and the glass slippers a pair of jewelled vaudevillian tap-shoes, but the spirit of fancy dress and pantomime remains the same.

Promoting his UK touring production in 2006, director Christopher Luscombe offered his personal theories as to the show's endurance: 'It's got all the fun of a big musical; the big emotions, the music, the witty dialogue, amazing look, all that. But I think it's a very profound piece; and that's why it has lasted really, because it tells us something about the human condition.

'Dress how you want to dress; be who you are; be authentic. Don't try and be what you think society wants you to be.'

While Luscombe's words are precisely on the nail, part of the brilliance of *The Rocky Horror Show*'s script is the way it underplays such insightful complexities by masquerading as a camp, sexy, playful romp. The witty messages, knowing irreverence and B-movie references are there, but none is pretentiously spelled out or hammered down the throats of the audience. It is more important for them to feel entertained, have fun, laugh and cry and rock in the aisles. Whatever else they take away from the experience is up to them.

It is a lesson that other gender-bending musicals might do well to heed. *Hedwig and the Angry Inch* (the story of a physically and emotionally scarred East German transsexual) and Jonathan Larson's Broadway hit *Rent* (a 1990s retelling of Puccini's *La Boheme*, updated for the AIDS generation) both feature vibrantly enjoyable music, appealing characters and interesting storylines, but somehow feel full of their own overblown self-importance and an unnecessary longing to spell out overly significant messages about gender pigeon-holing and confused sexuality. Even the comparatively frothy *La Cage Aux Folles* wears its *vive la différence* moral on its delicately effeminate sleeve.

By comparison, rather than striving to subvert or question conservative attitudes, Richard O'Brien's objective was simply to have fun with a lightweight concoction of comedy, horror, sex, drugs and rock 'n' roll.

The implications remain abundantly clear – *The Rocky Horror Show* continues to appeal to a massively mixed audience because it does not preach, alienate or threaten – and Jack Tinker's perceptive observations from his 1973 *Daily Mail* review of the original production are once again irresistibly evoked: 'It is far too jokey to ever be accused of practising the corruptions it pretends to preach.'

There have been copious academic studies, discussions and hypotheses endeavouring to explain the social and psychological reasons behind *Rocky Horror*'s uniquely excessive and compulsive participatory fanaticism; most of them far more serious and pompously long-winded than the suggestions offered here. After all, the purpose of this book is to explore the origins, history and continued evolution of the show itself – while celebrating its existence as a much-loved work of entertainment – rather than to attempt yet another pointless, pretentious and inevitably inconclusive study of fan psychology.

Though it is likely that much of the intellectual speculation may well hold some truth, like most conundrums of this nature, it is ultimately impossible to reach a definitive answer. Everybody with an interest in the subject (or indeed any subject) will harbour personal theories to explicate its appeal. Some might be plausible and stimulating food for thought; others just laughable, provocative, overblown nonsense.

Hence that simple and dismissive proposition once offered by actress Susan Sarandon – never just a pretty face – may, in the end, be the wisest, most rational and sensible conclusion after all:

'You shouldn't try to figure it out. Just enjoy it.'

7
Let's Do The Time Warp Again

The weather across most of Great Britain on Saturday 6 August 1988 was seasonally warm and pleasant. Glorious sunshine, often an intermittent luxury during a typical English summer, made the evening perfect for relaxing with a chilled beverage in the shady beer garden of a traditional British pub; or for enjoying the idyllic sunset, while strolling hand-in-hand with a loved one along an otherwise deserted sandy beach.

At the Theatre Royal Hanley, on the other hand, in the city centre of Stoke-on-Trent, the energised full-house audience, hot and sticky in their cheap satin lingerie, second hand tailcoats and treacherously high spiked heels, prepared themselves for the rapidly approaching bittersweet finale of what was now an indisputable classic of rock musical theatre.

It was the very last performance of the phenomenally successful four year tour of *The Rocky Horror Show*.

A monumental mass of mountainous mammaries, constantly threatening to burst free like some frighteningly fleshy avalanche from a multitude of ill-fitting corsetry, along with a cornucopia of variously proportioned gentlemen's trouser tackle, stuffed unceremoniously into the most minuscule of feminine panties (leaving little room for manoeuvrability, let alone modesty), shook with uncontrollable delight as the show's Narrator – the slender, clown white-faced Marc Seymour – made a teasingly exciting declaration.

Discovering his beloved fiancée in a compromising position with Frank-n-Furter's new muscle-bound plaything, Craig Deegan's rouge-cheeked, baby-faced and vulnerable Brad Majors delivered his customary scripted consternation for the final time: 'Janet,' he sobbed in over-the-top dismay. 'How could she? That's it. It's over.'

'Over? What was over?' posed Seymour's melodramatic Narrator, before deviating from the text with the most crowd-pleasing and perfectly timed ad-lib of the night: 'Not *The Rocky Horror Show*.'

Twenty-first Century teenagers, relentlessly updated by an incessant bombardment of modern communications technology, might find it inconceivable, but in the dark pre-internet days of the 1980s this seemingly innocuous quip (nothing more than uninformed speculation by the actor himself) was as close as its ravenous fans could have hoped for to an official affirmation that *The Rocky Horror Show* would definitely have a

7: LET'S DO THE TIME WARP AGAIN

future. And it sent them into a thunderous frenzy.

Apart from the occasional unsupported rumour, up-to-date news about the supposed West End production (or indeed the future of the show in general) was anything but forthcoming. It would be a few more years until the World Wide Web made the internet easily accessible to the general public as a convenient international information tool. Therefore, fan communication and social networking in 1988 was difficult at best. Frustrated by this situation – and with Sal Piro's New York based American fan club catering solely for fans of the movie version – a young lady from the south of England decided to approach Richard O'Brien with a proposal for launching a British *Rocky Horror* fan club.

After catching a late night screening of *The Rocky Horror Picture Show* on UK television in the mid-'80s, and subsequently tracking down the touring stage production during its final few months, Stephanie Monteath had become hooked, and it was her own irritation at the lack of accessible information about the show and its future that encouraged her to take personal ownership of the situation.

No stranger to the fickle faddy nature of fandom, Richard O'Brien was keen that, should he endorse the venture, TimeWarp (as it would be known) should not only be the only official UK *Rocky Horror* fan club, but that it should also be a long-term endeavour.

With O'Brien's blessing – along with that of 20th Century Fox and producer Michael White – Monteath, with her friend Amanda Langley, set about creating TimeWarp. Photocopied flyers were distributed to members of the audience during the final week of *The Rocky Horror Show* at the Theatre Royal Hanley, and the fan club's inaugural newsletter – forged on a trusty old typewriter and repeatedly Xeroxed, in the primeval days before personal computers and home printers became commonplace – went out to its first 43 appreciative members in October 1988.

Any early doubts O'Brien may have harboured about Monteath's commitment or the prolonged existence of the fan club itself would prove groundless. TimeWarp recruited thousands of active members and produced an informative and entertaining printed quarterly newsletter for the next 20 years, before continuing as an online newsletter from its sixty-ninth issue in 2009.

Stephanie Monteath married fellow *Rocky Horror* devotee David Freeman in 1990. Faithful fans of both stage and screen incarnations of *Rocky*, they appeared together as Riff Raff and Magenta in London's first and most famous *Rocky Horror Picture Show* fan shadow cast, Charming Underclothes (occasionally known jokily as the Charming Underclothes Nocturnal Theatre Society, the initials of which proudly formed one of the least subtle acronyms of all time). Based originally at the Screen cinema on Baker Street, which had first shown the film in February 1987, the troupe transferred to Leicester Square's Prince Charles cinema in July 1991, where weekly late night screenings would continue for the next ten years.

David Freeman launched the UK fan club's website (timewarp.org.uk) in 1997, and thanks to regular updates and the obvious devotion and infectious enthusiasm of its dedicated webmaster, it quickly became one of the most popular and certainly most informative *Rocky Horror* fan sites on the 'net.

Even as the British fan club was being born, plans were already underway for bringing a brand new production of *The Rocky Horror Show* to London's West End; although, at the time, most fans would have been completely oblivious as to the extent of these rather lengthy preparations.

Since taking on the role of Brad Majors in the original London and Japanese stage versions of the show – besides numerous other theatre, film and television appearances – Christopher Malcolm had started to make a name for himself as a theatrical producer. In 1986, with the Albery Theatre's 1980 revival of Rodgers and Hart's *Pal Joey* and a number of other successful productions already under his belt, he formed VIVA! Theatre Productions along with Jill Sinclair – sister of John Sinclair (the same names keep recurring) – and her husband Trevor Horn.

A serious motorcycle accident in 1987, which resulted in multiple leg and hip injuries, years of surgery and the subsequent need of a walking stick, may have somewhat hindered Christopher Malcolm's acting career, but it certainly didn't end it. In fact, for his recurring role as Justin in Jennifer Saunders' BBC sitcom *Absolutely Fabulous*, he seemed to use his pronounced limp and consequential cane as something of an endearing character trait.

Seeing a performance of the 1980s touring production, and noting how it had unexpectedly become a unique interactive theatrical experience since its modest beginnings at the Royal Court Theatre, Malcolm was convinced that *Rocky Horror* was a musical ripe for a major West End revival; an idea he eagerly proposed to a receptive Richard O'Brien.

In 1989, along with Howard Panter, then managing director of the Turnstyle Group and Independent Theatrical Productions Limited as well as a former director of Maybox Theatres Plc (London's second largest theatre-owning company during the 1980s), Malcolm and O'Brien formed Rocky Horror Limited (later to be known as Rocky Horror Company) to own and control the worldwide rights for all future stage productions of *The Rocky Horror Show*. From the outset, it was O'Brien's intention that the primary concern of the company – a subsidiary of which, Rocky Horror London, with Malcolm and Panter as joint directors, would be responsible for the proposed new West End incarnation – should be the quality and integrity of the show itself.

As previously noted, O'Brien had made no secret of his disdain for what he saw as the Theatre Royal Hanley's tawdry pantomime approach to the piece, and he was extremely keen for such artistic missteps to be avoided in the future. With this in mind, it was nevertheless agreed that, in order to survive amongst the West End's current crop of crowd-pleasing mega-budget extravaganzas, *Rocky* would have to grow from the unassuming experimental work that had first played the King's Road's dilapidated picture palaces nearly two decades earlier.

Although melodically sound, many musicals from the late '60s and early '70s – particularly *Hair* and even, to a degree, *Jesus Christ Superstar* – felt so very much of their time that they generally proved tricky to revive for contemporary audiences. While there was no doubt that *The Rocky Horror Show*'s score remained strong and timeless, the piece itself, which had famously started life with a minuscule budget on a postage stamp-sized stage in the tiniest attic theatre in Sloane Square, would now need to compete with breathtaking, multi-million pound musical spectaculars such as *Les Miserables* and some of Andrew Lloyd Webber's most enduring hits: *Cats*, *The Phantom of the Opera* and *Starlight Express*. A portion of the considerable budget for the latter – which had opened on 27 March 1984 – had been used to install a permanent 'race track' that snaked around the stalls and across the front of the circle of London's Apollo Victoria Theatre, allowing performers (representing model trains) to roller-skate at high speeds above the heads of the audience.

As undeniably perfect as it had been at the diminutive Theatre Upstairs, there was no way Brian Thomson's minimalist Odeon carpet and scaffolding ensemble could have realistically held its own against technically sophisticated excesses such as this or *Phantom*'s internationally famous chandelier drop, especially if it was to attract the crucial tourist trade in addition to local crowds. Therefore, with the Piccadilly Theatre on London's Denman Street as the chosen venue and the production scheduled to commence a fortnight of previews on Wednesday 4 July 1990, prior to the official opening night on Monday 16 July, set designer Robin Don created a gothic masterpiece easily worthy of Universal or Hammer in their classic horror heydays. An imposing practical wrought iron staircase dominated the upstage area, while dark and ominous 'stone' walls – bathed in a suitably eerie yellow-green glow, courtesy of lighting designer Nick Chelton – convincingly suggested the gloomy interiors of a creepy and foreboding Transylvanian castle.

Reflecting the show's significantly increased budget since its King's Road days was an authentic car (created, along with other props, by the appropriately named Acme company) for the fateful journey of Brad and Janet, and a huge transparent (and somewhat phallic) tubular dome, which would be flown in and out as required and used efficiently as Frank-n-Furter's laboratory equipment. Not only would this oversized test tube provide a practical focal point from which the newborn Rocky could emerge in all of his rippling glory, but it was also the method by which the victorious Riff Raff and Magenta would beam back to their home planet at the show's climax. Frank-n-Furter would make his 'Floorshow' entrance perched elegantly on a large crescent moon, while, in a nod to Brian Thomson's original King's Road design, the instantly recognisable red and white Coca-Cola logo once again adorned the door of Eddie's freezer.

With Robin Lefevre – then Associate Director of Hampstead Theatre, with several well-received provincial productions and West End transfers to his name – assuming directorial duties, Richard Hartley and Sue Blane returning as the show's musical director and costume designer for the first time in a decade, and Jonathan Adams adding a level of dignified sophistication and charm to the new company by reprising the role of the Narrator, which he had created 17 years earlier at the Theatre Upstairs, it was hoped that *Rocky Horror* might at last regain some of its original integrity.

'We had to sit down and say, "What did we have originally with *Rocky*? What were the elements that made it work?"' Richard O'Brien told Rob Cope in 1990. 'And it's very difficult to define. Because we didn't want to slavishly try and recreate what had gone before. It's like trying to get all the same people back to a party. And it doesn't work, does it? What was spontaneous was great. And you try and relive a spontaneous moment, and you're screwed.

'One of the things we felt was that the chemistry of the players was right in the first instance. It wasn't a question of trying to get people that were similar to each of the individuals, but trying to find people that would work together and form a new chemistry.'

Although O'Brien's belief that the chemistry of the ensemble should be a top priority was no doubt valid, the latest embodiment of *Rocky* would not be playing to a handful of shocked spectators in a musty old loft or a converted Chelsea flea-pit. The Piccadilly, with a seating capacity in excess of 1,200, was a major West End playhouse in the heart of London's bustling primary (and savagely competitive) theatre district.

Producers were understandably nervous.

The Rocky Horror Show had become an unexpected *avant-garde* hit in the early '70s by playing intimate old picture palaces.

The Piccadilly Theatre's most recent production had been the ill-fated *King* – a musical by Richard Blackford, Maya Angelou and Alistair Beaton, based on the life of martyred civil rights activist Martin Luthor King Jr – which had opened on Monday 23 April 1990 and closed, due to unspectacular business, just a month later on Saturday 26 May.

A top priced ticket for *The Rocky Horror Show*'s initial preview performances on 16 and 18 June 1973 had cost a mere 50 pence. Five years later, tickets at the King's Road Theatre, shortly before the show's very first West End transfer to the Comedy Theatre, had been priced at a fairly lofty (for the time) £1.25, £2.50, £3.25 and £3.75. By comparison, ticket prices for the show's 1990 West End opening at the Piccadilly Theatre would be £16.00, £17.50 and £20.00 for the stalls and royal circle, and £10.00, £12.50 and £15.00 for the dress circle.

When it opened in 1973, the show had nothing to prove. It was a frivolous bit of experimental fun for a troupe of largely unknown actors, and it had nothing to live up to. In 1990, on the other hand, it had everything to live up to, not least its own reputation. Consequently, other issues – largely promotional and financial – would this time play a large part in the *Rocky Horror* casting process.

With West End prices so high and a vast array of tempting alternatives playing in the area's numerous nearby venues, it is perhaps understandable that, whereas a perfectly cast troupe of talented unknowns had contributed immeasurably to the tacky B-movie charm of Jim Sharman's experimental 1973 production, those promoting and controlling the not inconsiderable funds for a major West End or Broadway presentation would be keen to secure a few familiar names off the telly to help attract mainstream audiences.

The crucial role of Frank-n-Furter in the new production went to Tim McInnerny. A talented character actor with a number of well-received straight dramatic roles to his name, McInnerny was nonetheless known primarily to British TV viewers for his portrayals of Lord Percy and Captain Kevin Darling in the BBC's popular historical comedy series *The Black Adder* (1983), *Black Adder II* (1986) and *Blackadder Goes Forth* (1989) and was certainly not an obvious choice for the lead singing role in a major West End rock musical.

As Richard O'Brien revealed to Rob Cope just over a month into the show's run at the Piccadilly, the casting of McInnerny as probably *Rocky Horror*'s most integral character was always going to be a gamble: 'Again that balance comes up, and comparisons,' the show's author explained. 'For instance, casting Tim McInnerny is a risk. And it's always a risk; it's a risk every night with Tim, because he's not a singer. It's an area he's not been involved in before, and he doesn't have a lot of experience in that area.'

Remaining positive, O'Brien went on to insist that such risks were not necessarily a bad thing, as they often helped to discourage the inevitable comparisons with previous interpretations. 'We had an awful lot of people who wanted to come along and audition for us,' he divulged, 'and they gave us clone-like auditions of Tim [Curry] and myself.'

Along with a multitude of other talented hopefuls, singer-actress Zalie Burrow attended a *Rocky Horror* casting call at London's famous Pineapple

Dance Studio: 'I'd left Guildford School of Acting in 1987 after a three-year Musical Theatre course. I got a call from my agent, out of the blue one day, for an audition for *Rocky Horror*.' She even recalls her choice of quirkily appropriate outfit for the day: 'I remember I wore a leather mini-skirt and I'd back-combed my hair violently. Very rock 'n' roll I thought.'

Also present at the audition was a high-spirited and confident actress, impressionist and voice-over artist by the name of Kate O'Sullivan. Both Burrow and O'Sullivan were recalled to the Piccadilly Theatre and ultimately cast amongst the show's minimal but vitally important ensemble.

'We both got understudy roles,' Burrow confirms, 'me as Columbia and Janet, and her as Magenta. We also had to be Phantoms.

'As Phantoms we had a fabulous time,' the actress divulges gleefully, confirming that their roles included the time-honoured pre-show stalking and spooking of the audience, a custom established by the cast of the original 1973 production:

'We wore these ripped trousers with fishnets underneath, coloured shirts with frilly fronts, and a stocking on our heads covered by a clear mask, so we looked like mannequins; very freaky. We had so much fun scaring the audience before the show began. We'd stand stock still in the loos, so that people thought we were tailors' dummies; and you'd hear women queuing up for the loo, saying to each other, "Do you think they're real or not?" Then we'd move and they'd scream. We'd hide in the theatre, behind the doors, and lie behind seats in the rows. Ian Good once chased a Japanese tourist around the theatre stalls. For some reason the Japanese screamed the loudest; it was hilarious.'

Sultry, dark-haired, doe-eyed New Zealand-born British actress Gina Bellman was cast as Janet Weiss, while comedian and actor Adrian Edmondson assumed the role of Brad Majors. In 1989, Bellman had played the title role in the BBC's sexually explicit (at least by 1980s UK television standards) four part serialisation of Dennis Potter's contentious 1987 novel *Blackeyes*, making her no stranger to erotic entertainment and on screen nudity. Edmondson, also not known as a singer (at least not in the conventional sense), was familiar to the public from his performances as part of Peter Richardson's alternative comedy troupe the Comic Strip, and in anarchic youth-orientated BBC sitcoms such as *The Young Ones* (1982-1984), *Filthy Rich and Catflap* (1986) and later *Bottom* (1991-1995) – shows that made him, from a marketing point of view, a bigger draw than Tim McInnerny. Hence the 1990 London revival would mark one of the very rare occasions where the actor playing Brad actually got billing over Frank-n-Furter on a *Rocky Horror* poster.

An interesting (yet perhaps inevitable, given the show's longevity) irony was that the new generation of *Rocky Horror* players now included those who had grown up as fans of the original production.

By the late 1980s, Linda Davidson was already a familiar face to British television audiences. She had made her debut appearance on BBC 1's flagship soap opera *EastEnders* on 5 March 1985, playing teenage punk and free-spirited single mother Mary Smith during the then fledgling show's fifth episode; and, over the next three years, her hard-hitting storylines involved drugs, delinquency, stripping and prostitution. Davidson's character finally departed the popular soap, with a memorably defiant two-fingered salute, on 26 May 1988, leaving the actress free to pursue other opportunities.

Given the *Rocky Horror* producers' apparent desire to secure bankable names – with Adrian Edmondson and Tim McInnerny already in the cast – it was something of a bitter irony that what they perceived as an unshakable public image as *EastEnders*' unmarried punk mum looked like costing Davidson a chance to play the one role she had dreamed of since childhood. In an article headed 'I'M THE *ROCKY HORROR* STAR THEY DIDN'T WANT' for the 29 July 1990 edition of the *People* newspaper, she revealed that ever since sneaking off to join the audience of *The Rocky Horror Show* during a school trip to London to see the musical *Grease* in the late 1970s she had been totally fixated with one character in particular: 'For four years I *was* Columbia. I adored her and went about pretending I was her all the time.' But the producers of the revival had persistently refused to let her even audition for the part. 'It was always "Here's Linda Davidson, ex-*EastEnders*, blah blah" – I hated it,' the petite but feisty young actress fumed. 'It wasn't until just three weeks before rehearsals started that the producers relented and finally let me have a go.

'I can't really believe I'm in the show. It's the best thing I have ever done in my life.'

Davidson's unquestionable passion for Columbia and *Rocky Horror* itself showed in her infectiously frenzied performance. Many fans noted that, with her effervescent demeanour and high-pitched squeals, she skilfully managed to channel Little Nell while at the same time making the part her own, and the gleeful sparkle in her eyes when meeting her own stage door groupies after each performance intimated that her infectious enthusiasm for the role was nothing less than absolutely genuine.

As Riff Raff, singer-actor-musician Edward Tudor-Pole provided a *bona fide* link to the legitimate British rock scene of the '70s. In 1974, Tudor-Pole formed the punk band Tenpole Tudor – perhaps best known for their rousing 1981 anthem *The Swords of a Thousand Men* – and in 1980 he appeared in *The Great Rock 'n' Roll Swindle*, director Julien Temple's bizarre and controversial pseudo-biopic of the Sex Pistols. It had been suggested that Tudor-Pole might replace John Lydon (aka Johnny Rotten) as the Pistols' front-man after Lydon openly and sensationally quit the line-up in

January 1978, although manager Malcolm McLaren eventually made the decision to disband the group instead.

According to Zalie Burrow, Tudor-Pole's performance caused quite a stir, even on the very first day of rehearsal. 'We rehearsed at St Xavier's church hall in Warwick Avenue, through a glorious summer,' she smiles reflectively. 'I remember the first read-through so vividly. Ed Tudor-Pole threw himself at his role of Riff with huge gusto, and leapt all over the available furniture while singing his opening number. He certainly made an impression, and this was just the read-through.'

Suitably sinister, intimidating and edgy, Tudor-Pole's insanely manic interpretation of Riff Raff at the Piccadilly Theatre was described favourably by Richard O'Brien (while speaking to Rob Cope in 1990) as 'Mad as a hatter; wonderfully so.'

The production would not be the last time that the actor would follow in O'Brien's frequently unpredictable footsteps. After fronting the first four series of Channel 4's cult postmodern game show *The Crystal Maze* between February 1990 and June 1993, and having gained enormous popularity with the public, O'Brien surprisingly decided to leave the show at the height of its success; after which Edward Tudor-Pole was chosen as a suitable replacement for what would be the programme's final two seasons in 1994 and 1995.

For what was to be *Rocky*'s first West End revival, it was decided that Michael English's widely recognisable Columbia image, which had served the show the world over for the better part of two decades, should be retired in favour of a fresh promotional campaign by Dewynters Plc – a prolific and acclaimed theatrical marketing company based in Leicester Square – along with brand new poster art by London's Shaun Webb Design.

The posters featured a black background with four pop-art style comic book images in separate boxes. This quartet of brightly coloured designs incorporated the head and shoulders of a pretty blonde girl (generally accepted to be Janet Weiss) in a 1950s-style black dress mottled with red and green flowers; a naked (from the waist up) muscular male torso; a pair of female thighs with a crotch barely covered by an extremely high-cut thong; and two non-gender specific legs (pictured from the knees down) clad in green leggings and black calf-length sci-fi boots, which stirred up memories of Alex Raymond's original *Flash Gordon* comic strips.

While many of the Piccadilly Theatre's posters would at first include all four of these icons, as well as the show's cast and production credits, the Janet image would be used on its own for others, including the cover of the subsequent cast album.

From the 1990 production onwards, a major permanent change to the show's advertising would be the significant addition of Richard O'Brien's

7: LET'S DO THE TIME WARP AGAIN

name above the title. This unambiguous declaration of ownership would prove immediately controversial with some of the show's original collaborators; among them Brian Thomson, who was not involved with the West End revival:

'I mean, "*Richard O'Brien's Rocky Horror Show*"! Give me a break,' he scoffed to Scott Michaels and David Evans for their 2002 book *Rocky Horror: From Concept to Cult*, before stressing how much of a group effort the formation of the original production had been.

Though Thomson's annoyance, seemingly shared by a number of others, was perhaps understandable to a certain degree – Jim Sharman having initially workshopped the show during rehearsal while encouraging his eager young company to submit ideas, jokes and lines of dialogue for inclusion – surely O'Brien's name above the title merely identified him as the author of the piece; which of course he was and always had been. The phrase 'Book, music and lyrics by Richard O'Brien' had appeared in all programmes and promotional literature since *Rocky*'s Royal Court debut; and since Lou Adler had chosen to brazenly showcase Tim Curry's name across posters for the 1975 Broadway production – with not even the tiniest of acknowledgements for the show's writer and composer – O'Brien might well be forgiven for feeling entitled to a certain level of protective ownership. After all, the words 'William Shakespeare's *King Lear*' might legitimately adorn the posters for any new staging of that particular dramatic landmark, yet no-one would ever presume them to be a claim that the Bard had mounted the first production all by himself.

Sue Blane's flawless costume designs would once again be integral to the look of *The Rocky Horror Show* and its characters. While it is arguable that almost anybody could feasibly throw the contents of a tacky backstreet lingerie store onto an eclectic bunch of actors for comedic effect, Blane somehow had an innate knack of making the look intrinsically sexy, cool and uniquely *Rocky Horror*, a skill that evidently eluded countless other designers. As a result, Blane would be repeatedly hired to provide costumes for each successive UK production mounted by the Rocky Horror Company, as well as several European tours, thus finding herself unavoidably linked with the show – a show she had at first tried to turn down in 1973 – for the rest of her career.

Christopher Porter – who would initially be credited as Costume Buyer in the show's programme, but would later become Costume Supervisor and ultimately Associate Costume Designer for future productions and tours – explains how his long association with Sue Blane and *The Rocky Horror Show* began:

'Well, it was strange the way it happened,' he smiles, clearly relishing the opportunity to quote the show's extraterrestrial mad scientist, 'My family moved us to Australia, and after I left school – in fact I think it might have been my final year at school – I went to see the first Australian production of *Rocky*. It was the first production that was licensed outside of the UK, and it changed my life.'

'It was an amazing performance,' Porter continues, recalling Reg Livermore's historic turn as Frank-n-Furter, 'A terrific cast, and a perfect situation too because it was an old run-down cinema. Brian Thomson built a catwalk into the auditorium – with playing areas in the scaffolding around the front of the stage – just like in the King's Road cinema. And they made it even more decrepit and rundown, which is kind of the best way to see the show. The jewel amongst the ruins.'

'Fast forward a few years down the line, I came back to the UK and, after going to art college, I started working in the theatre. I was working at Leicester Haymarket doing a production and they said, "Sue Blane is the designer on the next show." I was so excited that she was going to do this huge musical and I could work alongside her. She didn't let down in any area at all. She's a total delight to work with, and, at that time, probably one of the most famous and revered costume/set designers in the UK. So, I started working with her on this production as a buyer, and she liked me, and she kept asking me to come and work for her. Sue prefers to work with men; she is a demanding designer, but funny and collaborative too, where some are just dictators.'

After enjoying a good working relationship with Blane – as a buyer and assistant on several productions – Porter was hired in the same capacity for the high-profile West End revival of *The Rocky Horror Show* but would soon find himself promoted.

'The management thought I was too young and inexperienced and didn't want me to be the Costume Supervisor, so I became the assistant, with a dear friend Charlotte Bird as Supervisor,' he explains, 'And you know, within twelve months the Supervisor moved on to another project and I got the job.'

Much that had gone into making the original King's Road costumes so memorably perfect was revisited for the Piccadilly revival (once again, if it ain't broke...), albeit with a substantially higher budget.

Adrian Edmonson's Brad wore a variation of the original's blue plaid jacket, along with black trousers and white polo-neck pullover; while Gina Bellman found herself in Janet's white cardigan sweater and time-honoured pink dress. Stripped down to her 'charming underclothes' in Frank's laboratory, however, she would display a net underskirt with stockings and suspenders (consistent with 1950s fashions) rather than the cheap and simple white half-slip of previous Janets.

In accordance with the menacing gothic nature of Robin Don's set, Blane kept the costumes of the castle's occupants decidedly dark. This included Columbia, whose plain black tailcoat with silver waistcoat and shorts, though still in keeping with the Ruby Keeler tap-dancing iconography of the original concept, was pretty far removed from the showbiz glitz and never-ending sequins of Little Nell's familiar screen image.

Even Tim McInnerny's Frank-n-Furter had flat, no-nonsense tones with much less sparkle than Tim Curry and his immediate successors; and his hairstyle – long and straight, presumably to avoid comparisons with the loose curls of Curry's 1960s hippie style – made him look more like Nana Mouskouri than Marc Bolan.

Hairdo dilemmas were certainly not unique to Frank either, for, while Perry Bedden had favoured a heavily-lacquered black widow's peak, evocative of Christopher Lee's Dracula, many other stage Riff Raffs had found themselves shackled with the customary polished pate, often by way of an unconvincing rubber bald cap, thanks largely to the unshakable image of Richard O'Brien in the film version. Edward Tudor-Pole defied this convention quite spectacularly with shoulder-length black hair – plus a single off-centre white stripe – lacquered backwards (horizontal to his head) into an almost lethal looking point. To give Frank's scheming sibling servants a freaky family resemblance, Magenta (played by Mary Maddox) would also sport long dark hair – though without the stiffened spike of Tudor-Pole's Riff Raff – with a single white stripe.

For the most part, Frank-n-Furter's Machiavellian servants would be costumed in refined versions of their traditional butler and maid outfits. As well as the usual see-through chiffon wrap, however, Sue Blane's design for Magenta this time incorporated a boned conical bustier, similar to the so-called bullet bra distributed by famous underwear manufacturers such as Maidenform in the 1950s before the advent of Lycra a decade later completely revolutionised ladies' lingerie and made cones and boning in such garments redundant. It would be no surprise to learn that Blane's finger was well and truly still on the pulse (her 1973 costume designs had, after all, famously anticipated the look of punk), as this most 1950s of underwear fashions went on to enjoy something of a renaissance in the early '90s courtesy of Jean-Paul Gaultier's headline-grabbing costume designs for Madonna's Blond Ambition Tour.

Unlike the gold quilted designs seen in the film, the mutinous servants' spacesuit tunics for the show's denouement were of a flat metallic silver fabric, with thigh-high boots to finish the look; boots so high that, if truth be told, they sometimes obscured the fact that Edward Tudor-Pole was wearing the traditional stockings of his character's beloved planet.

As Eddie, Scottish actor Gordon Kennedy – who would later appear as psychotic android Hudzen-10 in a 1989 episode of *Red Dwarf* and as Little John in three series of the BBC's revamped version of *Robin Hood* between 2006 and 2009 – donned sleeveless biker leathers and cowboy boots similar to those of Meat Loaf's interpretation. Furthermore, in a sly reference to Jim Sharman's classic film version, the doomed object of Frank-n-Furter's dodgy experiments now wore a white T-shirt with the 'Denton: The Home of Happiness!' logo (as seen in the movie's churchyard scene) emblazoned across the front.

Rocky Horror himself, played by the suitably hunky Adam Caine, was given little more than a pair of tight mid-thigh-length Lycra cycling shorts, originally black but changed to a leopard-print later in the run, to preserve what little dignity the role traditionally allowed. Subsequent touring productions would revert to the more aesthetically pleasing gym trunks of previous incarnations.

Meanwhile, despite its initial failure at the worldwide box office, the show's celluloid adaptation *The Rocky Horror Picture Show* had gradually become something of a cinematic legend. Thanks in no small part to its well publicised status as a late night cult sensation, the film had played as a midnight show every Friday and Saturday at hundreds of movie theatres since the late 1970s – not just in the US, but all over the world – making it the longest sustained motion picture engagement in cinema history.

This unprecedented success would be commemorated in justifiable style on 20 October 1990 in the form a massive fifteenth anniversary convention. Held on Stage 14 at 20th Century Fox studios in Los Angeles (earlier in the week, the city's mayor, Tom Bradley, had officially proclaimed 18 October Rocky Horror Picture Show Day in honour of the movie's birthday), the event, hosted by US fan club president Sal Piro and attended by 3,000 devoted fans, also reunited many of the movie's stars. Although a family illness purportedly prevented Susan Sarandon from joining them, Richard O'Brien, Patricia Quinn, Little Nell, Barry Bostwick and Meat Loaf were present and correct to perform songs, relate anecdotes, share trivia, answer questions from fans and sign a few thousand autographs. Particularly exciting, given his unsubstantiated reputation for seemingly shunning the *Rocky Horror* limelight, was the news that Tim Curry – who, due to work commitments, had been unable to attend the tenth anniversary celebrations at New York's Beacon Theatre in 1985 – had agreed to appear at the fifteenth.

On the night itself, Curry – introduced excitedly by a beaming Richard O'Brien, who looked on in the manner of a proud father at his son's graduation – casually made his entrance accompanied by an impromptu rendition of the unmistakable intro to 'Sweet Transvestite' (played by the live onstage band), to the kind of thunderous ovation most often reserved for the music world's most revered rock gods. Grinning from ear to ear, he basked in the adulation of the fanatical crowd, before expertly manipulating them further – and metaphorically turning the applause up to 11 – by sensually purring the song's opening line, 'How d'ya do? I ...'

7: LET'S DO THE TIME WARP AGAIN

'It's so comforting to know there are so many people in this world sicker than I am,' Curry smoothly told the screaming masses, much to their collective delight. 'I think I'm the only person here tonight who doesn't look like me.'

A slew of officially licensed souvenir merchandise created specifically for the film's fifteenth anniversary included T-shirts; a lovingly produced soundtrack box set, released on both CD and cassette formats and including rare non-*Rocky* solo tracks from both Tim Curry and Little Nell as well as Barry Bostwick's never-before-released rendition of 'Once in a While', which had famously been cut from the film prior to its original 1975 opening; a three-issue comic book adaptation with artwork by Kevin VanHook; and *Creatures of the Night: The Rocky Horror Picture Show Experience*, Sal Piro's enthusiastically-written celebration of the movie's fans and unique midnight following, which he would follow up with a subsequent volume five years later.

On 8 November 1990, three weeks after this convention, *The Rocky Horror Picture Show* received its very first US home video release. Although it had been available on VHS and Betamax in the UK and Australia since 1984, Lou Adler had hitherto resisted issuing the film on video cassette in the United States, primarily to preserve its reputation and unique appeal by maintaining the popularity and exclusivity of its nationwide midnight screenings. Thus, on its initial release, the video – aimed largely at the rental market – carried the somewhat hefty retail price of $89.95. It was only made available to purchase at a more reasonable and fan-friendly sell-thru cost – somewhere between the $20 and $30 mark – a couple of years later. Similarly the film had occasionally been shown on late night television in various countries with very little fanfare, but its US TV debut on the Fox network on 25 October 1993 would be presented as a major event, with fan and shadow cast involvement, edited audience participation and the cooperation and assistance of Lou Adler and Sal Piro.

With the film version having made such a massive impression, particularly amongst adolescent audiences, and its oft-quoted dialogue now on a par with that of the likes of *Casablanca* and *Star Wars*, Richard O'Brien set about officially revising the stage show's script for the first time since he and Jim Sharman had collaborated on the movie's screenplay in 1974. Dialogue alterations for the 1990 West End revival at London's Piccadilly Theatre would therefore include the addition of several lines that had originally been written specifically for the screen version.

The most significant of these amendments was the reversal of the songs 'Sweet Transvestite' and 'The Time Warp' so that they now matched the order in which they had appeared in the film. As this meant that 'The Time Warp' would now be performed before Frank-n-Furter's entrance – and with the movie's chiming coffin clock not there to herald the song's introduction on stage – an additional line from Brad was added in place of the servants' original collective cry of 'Master!' Immediately after Riff Raff and his fellow minions reappeared, Brad now comforted his spooked fiancée before addressing the castle's inhabitants: 'Excuse me, hi, look if I could just use your 'phone, we'll move right along. I'm sure you've got a lot of things to do and a great evening planned.'

This line, while noticeably expository and a tad clumsy, served its purpose. Riff Raff simply replied with 'Oh yes, you've arrived on a rather special night; it's one of the master's affairs,' as he had in the film, and Janet's remark about Frank being lucky prompted Magenta's famous 'Yeah – he's lucky, I'm lucky, you're lucky, we're all lucky.' This in turn led perfectly into Columbia's 'All except Eddie' and subsequent dialogue from the show's original script, which introduced 'The Time Warp' as normal.

At the climax of the number, Brad gleefully enquired, 'Say, do you guys know how to Madison?' – another line from the Sharman and O'Brien movie screenplay that had not been present in the original stage version – and the thumping intro for 'Sweet Transvestite' then kicked in.

The victorious exchange between Riff Raff and Magenta prior to the castle's climactic blast-off had originally involved Magenta casually enquiring, 'I wonder if I remembered to cancel the milk,' and Riff answering, 'No matter, Magenta; activate the Transit Crystal.' O'Brien reworked this scene for the revival to include a rearranged version of Richard Hartley's atmospheric incidental music, a brief ethereal choral reprise of 'The Time Warp' and the triumphant former servants' dialogue from the film:

> RIFF RAFF: Our noble mission is almost completed, my most beautiful sister; and soon we shall return to the moon-drenched shores of our beloved planet.
>
> MAGENTA: Ah, sweet Transsexual, land of night. To sing and dance once more to your dark refrain; to take that step to the right.
>
> RIFF RAFF: But it's the pelvic thrust …
>
> ETHEREAL CHORUS: That really drives you insane …
>
> MAGENTA: And our world will do 'The Time Warp' again.
>
> RIFF RAFF: Activate the Transit Crystal.

Hartley's showdown music – used to great effect on screen as Rocky carried his fallen creator to the top of the RKO Pictures radio mast before being mercilessly gunned down by Riff Raff – had been wittily arranged in the style of Ennio Morricone's descriptive scores for many a spaghetti Western face-off. The resourceful composer re-scored it brilliantly for the West End revival as an emotionally-charged and powerfully-operatic piece, which gave Frank-n-Furter the affecting send-off he had always deserved.

Along with a number of other minor dialogue alterations – including the use of the *Picture Show*'s revised lyrics for 'I Can Make You a Man' – these modifications would remain in place for most subsequent officially licensed productions of *The Rocky Horror Show*. The UK version of the published libretto by Samuel French would not be completely altered accordingly, however, and while the switched order of 'The Time Warp' and 'Sweet Transvestite' was eventually acknowledged and included in a revised reprinting in 2004, Magenta's original 'I wonder if I remembered to cancel the milk' remained unchanged.

By comparison, the 1998/99 American edition of the script – published as part of French's Musical Library series in the US, where licensed local and independent productions of the show became much more frequent than in the UK – curiously contained all of the post-'80s dialogue amendments, as well as more detailed and specific stage directions than the leaner British edition.

In keeping with Jim Sharman's original B-movie intentions at the Royal Court and King's Road Theatres, the show's interval – added for the 1979 West End transfer to the Comedy Theatre and simultaneous UK tour – was removed for the duration of its engagement at the Piccadilly. Accordingly, punters were allowed to take drinks into the auditorium (in safe plastic glasses naturally), thus allowing *Rocky* fans on the front row to rest their beers on the stage itself. How's that for rock 'n' roll decadence?

While a pre-show screening of Jack Arnold's *Creature from the Black Lagoon* – presented in its original 3-D form, thanks to the insertion of cheap (though still collectable to fans) 3-D glasses in *The Rocky Horror Show*'s programme – further enhanced the 1950s creature feature ambience as the audience entered the theatre, it was clear that much had changed since the early '70s, including the attitudes and sexual politics of audiences.

A truly astonishing triumph of wit and creativity over a non-existent budget and the confines of a minuscule performance space, Jim Sharman's pioneering 1973 production had attracted King's Road sophisticates, as well as the hippest celebrities and pop icons of the time. Furthermore, the director's ploy of transferring his surprise hit to a converted condemned cinema in Chelsea instead of a conventional city centre playhouse cleverly added to the show's intrigue and word-of-mouth success. Conversely, the 1980s audiences for *The Rocky Horror Show*, itself transmogrified into a garish pantomime mockery of its former self, had consisted primarily of a perturbed post-punk youth, irritated by high levels of unemployment, uncomfortable Cold War tension and perhaps the subconscious knowledge that they might now be reaping the dire consequences of the previous generation's liberal sexual proclivities.

A deadly, incurable disease, spread mostly by way of unprotected sexual contact or intravenous drug use with a shared or unsterilised hypodermic, had quickly spelled the end of the blithe permissiveness that the seemingly carefree youth of the 1960s and '70s had so freely enjoyed. Since its discovery and identification in the early 1980s, Acquired Immune Deficiency Syndrome (AIDS), and the Human Immunodeficiency Virus (HIV) that causes it, had quickly become an epidemic and a key global health concern. That it seemed to be largely ignored by governments when it was wrongly believed to affect only homosexuals (it was ignorantly nicknamed 'The Gay Plague' at the time) must surely be cause for some weighty political debate in its own right; but once it was revealed to be a danger to all, typical knee-jerk panic began, with at least one newspaper supplement sensationally labelling the disease 'Public Enemy Number One'.

The British government launched its memorable 'Don't Die of Ignorance' crusade in 1986; the campaign included huge billboard posters, nationwide leaflet distribution and frighteningly effective television adverts (which made number 49 in Channel 4's *100 Greatest Scary Moments* TV compilation in 2003), in an attempt to equip the public with the facts (and inevitable myths) about this all-too-real new health menace.

Fifty-nine-year-old Hollywood leading man Rock Hudson (born Roy Harold Scherer Jr) became one of the first prominent celebrities to succumb to the disease when he passed away on 2 October 1985. Likewise, the music world would lose one of its larger-than-life legends when Freddie Mercury, the unforgettably flamboyant front-man to British rock band Queen, died of AIDS-related bronchial pneumonia on the evening of 24 November 1991 at the age of 45. The virus would ultimately be responsible for the untimely deaths of millions – famous and otherwise – in the years that followed.

It is not unreasonable to suppose that the naturally horny adolescents grudgingly thrust into this gloomy sexual landscape might have felt a degree of unconscious jealousy and bitterness toward their free-thinking, promiscuous and comparatively consequence-free predecessors. And for those wishing to revive a musical that had, for almost two decades, celebrated freedom of expression and sexual experimentation, there was suddenly the question of responsibility. Hence, in the amended script, a somewhat awkward condom reference was ham-fistedly shoehorned into the silhouetted bedroom scene between Frank and Brad.

'There's no crime in giving yourself over to pleasure, is there?' Frank would tease as usual, before waving an unrolled prophylactic over Brad's face and declaring parentally, 'Unless of course you forget to wear one of these.'

In future productions the humour of this gag would become increasingly cruder, with Frank pulling the supposedly used sheath from his (or Brad's) dick, and then sometimes even dangling it into his mouth or licking the 'cum-filled' end with his tongue in order to elicit further cheap laughs from the delightedly grossed-out crowd.

Even though there is little doubt that the instigators of a 1990s interpretation of *The Rocky Horror Show* were admirably showing a conscientious attitude by addressing – albeit somewhat jokily – a very serious and delicate health issue that had not even existed when the original production had been conceived, somehow the use of condoms never seemed to sit right within the frivolous and escapist context of the script. This is particularly pertinent when one considers Frank's self-centred arrogance and flagrant disregard for political correctness.

After all, while H G Wells' Martians had ultimately succumbed to deadly microscopic bacteria within the Earth's atmosphere, against which their alien bodies had no defence, is it not logical to assume that an intergalactic sexual predator such as Frank-n-Furter might, either by a natural resistance or highly advanced forms of inoculation, have long since become immune to the sexually transmitted infections of other planets?

With the subtle, sardonic satire of the original King's Road incarnation having given way to mindless pantomime high-jinks in just a few short years, director Robin Lefevre was faced with finding a balance that could stay true to the spirit of the original while retaining a hint of the broader send-up that had enticed the less demanding youthful audiences of the '80s. A fitting example perhaps could be found in Lefevre's (and choreographer Stuart Hopps') staging of Brad's heartfelt solo 'Once in a While'; a number that the Theatre Royal Hanley had found increasingly impossible to present as a sincere romantic ballad, due to the fact that audiences would not allow the actor to sing it without constant ill-mannered interruptions. For the Piccadilly production, Brad would sing the song fairly straight, with a fitting amount of truthful sentiment, accompanied by two Phantoms – usually the girls, unless one of them was required to cover one of the main roles – dressed in theatrically stylised white nurse's uniforms.

Zalie Burrow is quick to point out that the nurses themselves grew from the resourceful imagination of the actors – another of Jim Sharman's valuable techniques from 1973, eagerly encouraged for the revival by the show's author. 'Richard O'Brien embraced creativity amongst the cast,' she verifies, 'so we invented quite a few things. You might recall the nurses coming up through the floor, playing castanets and tambourine during

"Once in a While", or the nurse's outfits we wore for that number. We were always dreaming up ways to enlarge our roles. Now we were Phantoms *and* nurses. Result.'

Presented somewhere between supportive reassurance and gentle ridicule, this onstage backing for the emotionally damaged Brad could be genuinely touching; that is until the Phantom nurses mockingly turned around to reveal that the backs of their skirts were actually cut away to expose their naughty white French knickers – complete with a red sequinned heart symbol on one butt cheek – prompting a knowing chuckle from the audience, but without overly compromising the poignant honesty of the moment.

Any hopes the producers may have harboured that the outlandish and unruly audiences of the 1980s may have gone away – forgotten about *Rocky* and taken up football hooliganism as an alternative hobby perhaps – were swiftly dashed when the new production opened for its first preview performance on Wednesday 4 July 1990.

In spite of the show's reputation, Zalie Burrow reveals that no-one – least of all the director – was even remotely prepared for the astonishing audience conduct, which took all concerned completely by surprise. 'It was very exciting; but also terrifying,' she recalls with an unmistakable degree of affection. 'On opening night we could hear all this noise from front-of-house. And then when the iron curtain rose, it was unbelievable. The audience were chanting "Give us an 'R' … 'R'… Give us an 'O' … 'O'…" and so on. It was like a football crowd.'

As before, the audience participation did not stop at mere verbal interaction, however, as the unsuspecting new cast quickly discovered. 'The next thing was the rice,' Burrow continues. 'The audience hurled loads of it onto the stage, making the surface like a skating rink.'

Like the Hanley tour's Ghouls before them, the Piccadilly's Phantoms would now need to be suitably equipped to clear the stage of hazardous objects: 'We Phantoms were sent on with brooms. In fact Mary Maddox, who was playing Magenta, had a bad fall and was off for a while very early on in the run. That gave Kate [O'Sullivan] an opportunity to step up and play Magenta. She had a few minutes to do her costume and make-up, and – bam! – she was on.'

Showers of rice, water, toilet rolls and chocolate bars were accompanied by each and every tired old talkback line and heckle from the Theatre Royal Hanley tour and the 1983 *The Rocky Horror Picture Show Audience Par-tic-i-pation Album*. This behaviour – hitherto unheard of amongst the West End's famously cultured crowds – quickly necessitated bag searches, prop confiscation and hastily printed signs forbidding the throwing of any objects at the stage, and was astutely acknowledged by *Guardian* theatre critic Michael Billington who noted (not unfairly), 'A once pointed pastiche has turned into a yob's night out.'

Christopher Malcolm would later recall, in his programme notes for the 2006 UK *Rocky Horror* fan convention, his personal reaction to this unexpected and unprecedented audience involvement: 'In the first preview we were all alarmed by the force of the fans' accompaniment to the action, which essentially was a riot of noise and interruption! Myself and Howard Panter, co-producer, stalked the aisles and the back of the auditorium wondering if we would ever get to the end of the show, and indeed whether we would face a general walk-out by the actors in protest at the goings-on in the auditorium.'

Ultimately however, Malcolm continued, the cast seemed to thrive on the invigorating energy of the crowd. 'Who could not be moved by the sight of hundreds of lights being held aloft *en masse* during "Over at the Frankenstein Place?"' he pondered nostalgically.

This magnificent sea of lights stirs comparable emotions in Zalie Burrow, whose memories of the dedicated *Rocky Horror* followers and their incredible commitment are, for the most part, extremely fond: 'The show, really, belongs to the fans; it's their show. I always found the regulars to be very respectful, not rowdy or aggressive.' This, though, does not mean that things did not get out of hand now and again, as the actress is equally keen to point out: 'It was wonderful; most of the time. Sometimes, however, it became a bit of a competition, a free-for-all; almost a battle between cast and audience. On those occasions, on certain performances, I did feel frustrated, because the pace and timing of the show were destroyed. But then, the audience could create something really special. Like in "Over at the Frankenstein Place", it was so moving to see all the lights swaying out in the audience. It was a private moment between cast and audience; we were in a bubble, a magical little world within the theatre.'

Burrow also reveals that a company meeting was called early in the run to assess the unexpected level of distracting – and potentially dangerous – audience interaction: 'Everyone was shocked by the audience participation and wanted to air their views. Generally, I think people felt it was a positive two-way thing that we should embrace. The audience input soon became an integral part of the show; and in the midweek shows, where the audience weren't as experienced with their shouted responses, the show sometimes felt flat. Then there was no energy, and we loved the energy. The weekend shows were the best. So, it's a fine balance. Good audience participation you enjoy; but it can also destroy.'

A star-studded press night took place on Monday 16 July – according to various reports, famous attendees included Rik Mayall and Ruby Wax (both of whom had appeared in Jim Sharman's 1981 *Rocky Horror* spin-off movie *Shock Treatment*), Boy George, Steven Berkoff and Adrian Edmondson's actress-comedienne wife Jennifer Saunders – followed by a kitschy first night party at Stock's nightclub in the King's Road (a suitable nod to *Rocky*'s roots).

Reviews for the production were typically mixed. The *Guardian*'s Michael Billington, who had given the original production a rave in 1973, called the latest version an 'overpriced piece of commercialised camp,' but at the final count the positive almost certainly outweighed the negative and provided a number of suitably enthusiastic quotes for the theatre's front-of-house displays. 'Does it all still work, now that it has a double layer of nostalgia?' pondered the *Daily Telegraph*'s Charles Osborne, before concluding, 'Yes, I think it does.'

Predictably, a number of newspaper columnists decided to venture down the lazy journalistic route of concentrating on the fans' outrageous costumes and participatory antics rather than the production itself. Some even suggested that the 'show' put on by the audience was actually more entertaining than the one on the stage. 'More of an event than a show, the entertainment began a good half an hour before the scheduled start of the performance,' wrote Clive Hirschhorn for the 22 July edition of the *Sunday Express*, 'as a couple of hundred people, caparisoned only in suspendered fishnet stockings and corsets, made an endearing spectacle of themselves. Determined to have the time of their lives, they turned the Piccadilly's auditorium into an enormous fancy dress party, barely allowing the assembled cast on stage to get a song or word in.'

Although largely complimentary of the production itself, with particular kudos going to Robin Don's impressive set, Hirschhorn's review ended with yet more praise for the show's spectators: 'In the end, though, none of this really matters. It is an occasion when the audience are more important than the cast, and from this critic they get a rave.'

In her critique for the *Stage* newspaper, Pauline Loriggio adopted a more scholarly view of the show, as well as a more hostile view of the crowd's crude pantomime shenanigans: 'Fostering the absurd notion that they are more entertaining than on stage stylised sleaze, the little horrors in the auditorium are going to be a bit of a drag to Richard O'Brien's revival of *The Rocky Horror Show*.

'Now out of a rep cinema near you and into the Piccadilly Theatre, the camp groupies, having earned their place in the cult trade, prefer to drown out the proceedings with razor blunt wit. All would be better employed concentrating on the production in hand, which thankfully sticks as tightly to the strength of the work as Tim McInnerny's suspenders to his tights.'

In view of the publicity and fan speculation regarding Richard O'Brien's less than favourable opinions of *Rocky*'s 1980s manifestations, one actor in particular was more than a little shocked at finding himself cast in the latest West End revival. With the Theatre Royal Hanley production now a memory, and the aforementioned unpleasant

7: LET'S DO THE TIME WARP AGAIN

experiences with Panda Productions' subsequent European tour behind him, Mark Turnbull had understandably assumed that his personal involvement in the history of this enduring musical was finally over. As he has previously noted however, for many actors *Rocky Horror* is a show that never really goes away. Therefore, with two young mouths to feed and thousands of pounds in unpaid wages from the rogue Euro tour yet to materialise, the out of work actor learned that the Piccadilly Theatre urgently required an experienced Frank-n-Furter to understudy Tim McInnerny:

'Spookily my agent called and told me to get myself down to the Piccadilly Theatre. This was one week after the show had opened there. I said to him "Why? They don't want anything to do with us Hanley-ites".' Upon arriving at the Piccadilly later the same evening, however, Turnbull discovered that McInnerny was unexpectedly absent and Richard O'Brien was hurriedly getting into costume to go on as Frank. 'Richard wore his own frocks for the part, which was kind of sweet.

'I was introduced to Robin Lefevre, Chris Malcolm, Howard Panter and Richard and asked to audition. I chose to sing "Sweet Transvestite" and "I'm Going Home". They then told me to go and wait in the pub over the road. I was only there ten minutes before Robin came and told me to call my agent, and that I'd got a job as walk-on cover for Frank. He wanted me to watch Richard perform for the next two nights, so that I could learn the blocking. I had one rehearsal the following Monday at 9.00 am, which included choreography and two hours with the stage manager, and that was it.

'The final arrangement was, to my recollection, that I did two shows a week as the alternate Frank, and then any others for which Tim was indisposed. My costumes were made over the same weekend. I wore my own stilettos and threw away the head-dress they provided for "The Floorshow", and I took a lot of the trimmings off the frocks to get Frank back-to-basics.

'I was lucky to make quite a few appearances as Frank at the Piccadilly, which was a dream come true, as I'd always wanted to play a leading role on a West End stage.'

Turnbull also admits, however, that on occasion the galaxy's not so sweet transvestite caused him to suffer for his art:

'I actually hurt myself badly one night when on the cherry picker they used to extend Frank over the audience. It started to move before I'd got myself balanced and braced against the side, so I ended up wrenching all my back muscles just trying to stay on.

'I used to take a risk with the moon entrance for Fay Wray. There was a lap strap that you were supposed to wear, like a safety belt; but I never did, because after you'd been lowered you had to undo it in order to get off the moon, and I always felt that looked wrong. But it was scary getting on that thing about 50 feet up in the flies.'

Turnbull reveals that having the show's author around helped him to glean a profound insight into the mind behind the madness, as well as the fascinating characters it had conceived:

'I spent a couple of very pleasant interludes in the bar with him and he was very gracious and amusing. I came to realise that *Rocky* is his *Othello*, with Riff as Iago; this comparison I do remember, and I remember being incredibly touched by his descriptions of Riff's reasons for hating Frank. Actually, he's far more of a puritan than most people think. Whether he intended to or not, Richard wrote his own masterpiece with *Rocky*, and I suspect that it reflects his own obsessions. He was great when he used to direct the understudy rehearsals, because he'd give you all the nuances and timings for the characters that you'd never have got from a director who didn't have Richard's history and passion for the show."'

His back-to-basics approach for the character allowed Turnbull, whose previous experiences with the role had been the playful and superficial panto-style productions of the 1980s, to add some much needed depth and pathos to Frank-n-Furter's demise, a moment many other actors felt the need to send-up: 'I hated it that the actors were generally trying to play for laughs. It might sound odd, but actually the Hanley audience used to shut up for the death scenes; yet in London people were shouting out rubbish like "Fuck her while she's still warm," and Frank would pretend to sniff Columbia's muff just to get a laugh.'

With audience participation having obviously become an inescapable part of the show, Turnbull remembers that the management initially attempted various methods to try to calm things down: 'They removed trigger lines, anything to make it more like the King's Road show. They'd hold up signs to the audience saying things like "The Narrator is not boring," and no-one in the audience was allowed to stand up at all. It seemed they were trying everything they could to be different to Hanley; to be anti-Hanley.'

Though some may have been critical of the inadequate vocal abilities of a couple of the leads – a somewhat inevitable hazard of casting actors with limited singing experience primarily for their celebrity status – Turnbull insists that the backing vocalists – Zalie Burrow, Ian Good, Kate O'Sullivan, Paul Reeves and Stephen Thiebault in the Phantom and understudy roles – were all strong and accomplished singers: 'And the band was fabulous – Clem Cattini was a hero of mine, as one of the all time great British drummers, and Dave Brown was a fine MD. We had one of the best bands ever. They responded well to having someone who could sing Frank and really kicked.'

Another member of that impressive band line-up was Derek Griffiths –

7: LET'S DO THE TIME WARP AGAIN

already a veteran of the King's Road and Comedy Theatre productions – who, upon expressing his interest to Richard Hartley, was immediately hired to play electric and acoustic guitar for the show's run at the Piccadilly:

'He said he'd love to have me back,' Griffiths recounts excitedly, 'and said, "I've got Clem Cattini, is that okay?" "Is that okay! Clem's one of the best drummers on the planet. That guy's played on more number one hits than anybody."'

With Dave Brown already in place as musical director, Hartley was looking for talented musicians to fill the bass guitar and tenor sax positions and asked Griffiths if he had any recommendations. Griffiths suggested Alyn Ross, who had played bass for the Japanese production, and Geoff Driscoll, who had taken over saxophone duties in the King's Road when Phil Kenzie had left. 'Phil's still a mate,' adds Griffiths, 'and I knew he was living in LA. He'd gone over there to play with Al Stewart and then Rod Stewart, so he couldn't have done the gig.'

While the presence of Richard Hartley helped keep the score true to that of the original, certain factors – including the size of the venue, audience expectations and the natural progression of the rock musical genre itself – inevitably dictated a certain evolution in the way the songs were played, as Griffiths explains:

'At the King's Road it was very basic. We had an upright piano and no effects whatsoever. Compare that with the Piccadilly production, when we had synthesisers and sweeping orchestral strings. The music was all synthesised; and there was Clem, the original rock 'n' roll drummer. The music itself isn't taxing, so there's scope for improvisation; except for 'Time Warp', that keeps you busy as a guitarist. You know the famous intro; well Richard Hartley always insisted that it's played on the down stroke. It's easier for the guitarist to play it down and then up, but Richard insisted that it didn't sound right and he always wanted me to play only down strokes.

'The band was on a rampart on the stage. I think it was the first time that had happened and it started a trend. The cast liked to shin up the rampart and interact with us.'

Griffiths maintains that one thing that had definitely not changed since the old days was the genuine feeling of playful camaraderie enjoyed by *The Rocky Horror Show*'s ensemble: 'We used to have so much fun with the backing singers as well. They were stationed next to us. I remember Zalie Burrow and Kate O'Sullivan, when we were at the Piccadilly, mooning at us and the actors, trying to make people corpse. We had such a laugh; they were extremely naughty girls.'

This good-humoured allegation is corroborated by Burrow herself, who openly recalls this playful behaviour: 'The booth itself was encased in black felt; very cosy, if a little claustrophobic. We shared two microphones and it was boring after a while waiting for our harmony sections; so we used to mess around a lot. Don't tell the director – too late.

'Kate regularly had water fights with Brad before the show and I regularly undressed Geoff Driscoll when he was playing the sax overture and could do nothing about it,' Burrow confesses impishly; although she is keen to clarify that she never removed his underpants.

With the traditional mid-performance beer run to a nearby pub – which the band had enjoyed nightly during the show's King's Road engagements – no longer feasible in their new West End home, seasoned rock 'n' rollers Griffiths and Driscoll managed to find a comparable satisfactory alternative. 'We opened the show there by having champagne,' Griffiths declares, 'and decided as a band that we rather liked that; so we ordered a case to be delivered to us every week from then on. Driscoll was nominated champagne monitor and it was his job to refill our glasses during the show. He perfected the champagne run; when he wasn't playing, he'd shin down the scaffolding and race to the fridge in the backstage dressing room and bring back a cold bottle. We ended up with a bottle mountain in front of the band. When he had a deputy, he'd leave a note instructing him on his duties as champagne monitor.'

Like most hit West End musicals, the successful production soon spawned a cast recording. Arranged by Richard Hartley and recorded at London's A Major Studio and Westside Studios, and released on CD, cassette and a double vinyl LP by Chrysalis Records Ltd (distributed by EMI) in the autumn of 1990, this album marked the first time that a complete audio recording of *The Rocky Horror Show* in its entirety (dialogue included) had been made commercially available. Richard O'Brien's initial idea was for the album to sound in essence like a BBC radio play; *The Rocky Horror Radio Show* was in fact reportedly mooted as an early title suggestion before *Richard O'Brien's The Rocky Horror Show: The Whole Gory Story* (a bit more of a mouthful) was ultimately settled on instead.

Artistically the idea would prove only partially successful. The recording was very strong technically – the pitch-perfect musical tracks were pure vintage *Rocky* in all the right ways, thanks to the involvement of Richard Hartley and musicians (including Derek Griffiths and Geoff Driscoll) who clearly knew the show's background and understood its genre – but much of the dialogue was grossly overplayed by the actors (to an embarrassing degree in some cases). Performers' decisions to deliver particular phrases in oddly eccentric ways, whilst questionably emphasising certain words, came across as baffling and cringe-worthy at times. In addition, Tim McInnerny's limitations as a singer, sometimes conveniently veiled by the atmosphere and raw energy of a live theatrical situation, were exposed quite conspicuously by a polished studio recording. Another problem was the addition of newly-written expository lines, included on the album to explain some of the script's visual gags and situations to listeners unfamiliar with the show's action – for example Riff Raff's needlessly specific 'Master, on the monitor, we have a visitor *in a wheelchair,*' and Columbia's grating shriek of 'Let's get you out of these wet clothes' to Brad and Janet – all of which felt uncomfortably clumsy and superfluous.

While *The Rocky Horror Show* had regularly drawn sensationalist media hype since its 1973 debut, its publicity was on occasion a little more negative than perhaps its producers would have liked. One particularly memorable story that made UK newspaper headlines in the 1990s concerned an unpleasant incident involving actress Mary Maddox. According to press reports at the time, for her role as Magenta at the Piccadilly Theatre the unfortunate artiste had been supplied with make-up to which her skin was allergic. This had caused a violent reaction, resulting in a persistent dermatological condition.

Curiously the story did not appear to be limited to the British press, as a later, 26 May 1995, *Chicago Tribune* report (which also appeared on their website) told how Maddox, who had sued the Rocky Horror Company for damages, was ultimately awarded $301,100 in compensation.

'Mary Maddox sued the show's producers for negligence for making her use the ultraviolet orange greasepaint,' the article stated. 'It caused her eyes to swell and left her with irritant contact dermatitis, a chronic condition. "The last few years have been awful," Maddox said after the verdict at London's High Court. "It has been impossible for obvious reasons to pursue my career. The greasepaint used on me changed the skin tissue on my face forever."

'The court heard that she was only able to take up about a quarter of the roles she had been offered since developing the allergy,' the piece concluded, saying that, according to Maddox, her face was now unalterably allergic to water, making it impossible for her to swim or take a shower.

As Frank-n-Furter sleazily tells his increasingly dissentious domestic personnel, loyalty must be rewarded. And how exactly did the *Rocky Horror* producers choose to reward the loyalty of their devoted fans once Tim McInnerny's contract came to an end in October 1990?

Simple; they gave them Head.

Although he would later find fame as Rupert Giles in Joss Whedon's landmark fantasy drama series *Buffy the Vampire Slayer* and as the British Prime Minister in the BBC comedy sketch show *Little Britain*, charismatic English actor Anthony Head (aka Anthony Stewart Head) – born on 20 February 1954 in the inner city district of Camden Town in northwest London – was at the time known mostly for a series of successful TV adverts promoting Nescafe Gold Blend coffee (known in the US as Taster's Choice). As the charming actor smoothly reveals, however, a certain amoral alien scientist had infiltrated his subconscious from the moment he saw the original production of *The Rocky Horror Show* in 1970s Chelsea:

'I'd seen Peter Blake as Frank I think – in the King's Road – and later saw someone else, whose name I can't remember, who played it a bit more like John Inman in an end of the pier show. But somehow there was always the ghost of Tim Curry's definitive performance lurking in the background; and I got to thinking, "You know, there may be more to this." A voice in my head, some untapped part of me, was saying that I could bring something different to the role.

'Some time later, I was doing a play in the wilds of Clwyd in Wales, and I heard on the grapevine that they were auditioning for a production that was going on at the Piccadilly. There wasn't any way that I could get there in time; so I phoned my old agent and told her in no uncertain terms to beg, steal or borrow for me to be seen. Anyway she didn't do any of those things, and when I later saw a poster for the show I realised that the moment had gone, and I was really pissed off.'

Luckily for the actor whose Frank-n-Furter would quickly become a firm favourite amongst devoted long-term *Rocky* followers, Head was later asked to try-out as Tim McInnerny's successor:

'I jumped at it. I said, "*Yes*, please, I would kill to do it." So off I went to audition for Chris Malcolm and Richard O'Brien. I don't recall exactly whose place it was, but it was in someone's house. There was a spiral staircase in the kitchen and they asked me to make Frank's first entrance down this staircase. So I did and they went very quiet and looked at each other. I thought to myself, "You either just blew that out of the water or were completely crap."'

Clearly impressed, Malcolm and O'Brien nixed Head's concerns by immediately informing him that the part was his; and, with his first performance scheduled for Monday 29 October 1990 (just in time for Hallowe'en), the actor hurriedly set about making the now-familiar role his own.

This intended individuality was reflected in his choice of costumes, which he wanted to be unique to his Frank. There was a lot of delicate femininity involved – he wore his corset over a tatty lace teddy for example – and the actor decided to bypass the traditional green surgical gown in favour of a white 1940s nurse's uniform with a Red Cross emblem, pill box hat and huge rubber gloves:

'I remember in rehearsal chatting to Sue Blane about the costume. I didn't want to be a Tim Curry lookalike. Tim was unique and fabulous in the role, but what was the point of my simply copying him? I'm a great believer that you should do what you can to add something if you're covering a role, to bring yourself to it. Tim had nailed the sexual ambiguity of Frank – very masculine and, at the same time, very feminine – he is sexy to both men and women. I wanted to play with those elements a little more and bring something demonic to the role.'

Head was keen for some of this intended demonic intensity to involve a level of energetic physicality, possibly involving 'leaping' around the stage in a manner that might make Frank's customary footwear even more impractical and hazardous than usual:

'I also wanted to be very active – no, not just in a sexual way, but physically too – so I needed something more practical than platforms. I mean all those guys who've played him wearing platforms; you can't exactly leap around in those things and you risk life and limb if you try. So I opted for some little patent leather S&M ankle boots, although they ended up looking more like Victorian lace-ups. I wanted them pointy and with thin stiletto heels, but somebody pointed out, "The set's peppered with 15-millimetre holes, you'll keep catching a heel." So they ended up being a little chunkier than I'd have preferred. But Sue was very open to ideas and discussion; I think it was fun for her to play around with the brand a bit.'

Other costume deviations initiated by Head himself included the beautiful pink basque and impressive feather head-dress he wore for 'The Floorshow', and something a little more lacy and pleasing in place of the traditional black briefs:

'It was also my idea not to wear the classic cire pants. It's a matter of opinion, but I never thought they were very sexy. I suggested French knickers, something like Sally Bowles in *Cabaret*; decadent, sexy. Sue said if we were going down the '40s/'50s route, why not make it a teddy under the basque, which, as it turned out, had the bonus of being incredibly flattering as well.

'I was very fit at the time from all the leaping around. The set had a great staircase rising from stage level to the fly floor, some 30-odd feet, and I used to leg it up that, two to three stairs at a time; I did end up with firm buns.

'I was very fond of that costume, I must admit; I took it home with me,' the actor confesses, with a mischievous smirk.

While the presence of Frank (or at least that of his *avant-garde* attire residing in the bedroom cupboard) never adversely affected the relationship between Head and his long-term partner Sarah Fisher in any way, the actor blithely reveals that the unscrupulous doctor occasionally decided to amusingly remind them of his existence:

'When we did [the game show] *Celebrity Mr & Mrs*, they showed pictures of me in a very nice white linen shirt and Armani jacket; as Frank; and as the PM in *Little Britain* – in leather posing pouch and with a feather duster – and asked me which one Sarah would most fancy me in. Well, I chose Frank – I thought it was a trick question, okay – and she said, "Pardon? Since when have I asked you to run off and put on your basque and red wig for me?"'

Oddly enough, this wasn't the first time that the endearing deviant from the planet Transsexual had metaphorically come between the couple, as Head fondly and mischievously recounts. 'They gave me some four-inch heels to play with in rehearsals,' he smiles impishly. 'I took them home to practice, but when exactly do you whip 'em out and strut your stuff? One day I was hoovering while Sarah had gone shopping, and I thought I might as well try them on. I was behind the bed when I heard Sarah come back. When she came into the bedroom, I jumped into the wardrobe in embarrassment. She asked me why I was looking so furtive, and I literally came out of the closet in my heels.

'I have since taught both of my daughters to walk in heels; I have a bizarre sense of achievement about that. And when I was in *Buffy*, I designed my demon character's footwear to look like hooves; they were built up onto three-inch or so heels. I was walking onto set when Nick Brendon, who played Xander, called out, "Hey Tony, walk like Frank." So of course I did. Picture a six-foot-six horned demon swinging its hips across an LA car-park.'

With the generally accepted view that an overtly effeminate performance takes away much of the character's power and unpredictability, it is perhaps surprising to remember that Anthony Head's portrayal added quite a bit more camp than many of his predecessors. And yet, thanks to the talent, stage presence and unmistakable masculinity of the actor himself, he lost none of Frank's vitally important menace or danger.

'I loved the idea of '40s actresses,' the actor enthuses. 'That was what Frank would have watched and who he'd have wanted to be like; Fay Wray or Rita Hayworth. When I sang the Fay Wray lines, I'd come down on the moon with a black top hat and blonde wig like Marlene Dietrich. And when I did the "Your back's to the wall" speech, I was that actress, erm … Barbara Stanwyck, eyes and teeth.'

It is an interpretation that calls to mind the approach adopted by Reg Livermore, who had famously fashioned his Frank on Bette Davis for Jim Sharman's original Australian production at Sydney's New Arts Cinema in 1974. Indeed, while Anthony Head was playing the part, the Piccadilly's band would add a touch of 'Falling in Love Again', Dietrich's famous anthem from the 1930 film *Der Blaue Engel* (*The Blue Angel*) to the usual fanfare heralding Frank's 'Floorshow' entrance.

In response to being told of Peter Blake's notion that Frank-n-Furter is 'a space pirate who'll fuck anything and anyone,' Head has his own firm views about the kind of creature Frank should be. 'A space pirate? I think that's a bit romantic,' he declares smoothly. 'He's a lech. He's the ultimate showman, but there's nothing behind the show; he gets his henchmen to do all his work for him and he basically screws everything up, quite literally. Just look at his creations – disasters. He really is only interested in fucking. Can't help but like him though.

'I also used a ratty looking wig,' says Head, happy to elucidate further on his well-thought-out depiction of this fascinating classic character. 'I couldn't really play the part with my own short hair, so why not make a feature of it? I wanted Frank to be grungy and nasty, and have a wig that he'd have taken off at night without dressing it, filled with bugs and dreads and all sorts.

'I found a wonderful make-up stick called Elephant Grey, which gave me an extremely unpleasant pallor. I wanted it to look like Frank just slapped on more make-up every day; that he didn't take it off at night or anything, just added more and more layers. He's a pretty disgusting character really; a dirty little sod who's obsessed with sex.'

One actress clearly not convinced by this interpretation of the character is former King's Road Janet Weiss, Belinda Sinclair. 'I saw the production with Anthony Head. I hated it. I thought the whole thing was crude and vulgar,' she confesses, describing Tony's Frank as 'lascivious' when compared with Tim Curry's gentler, almost sweetly endearing, methods of seduction.

To the die-hard *Rocky Horror* fans of the early 1990s, however, Anthony Head was unquestionably the real deal. For one thing, he gleefully embraced audience participation in ways that Tim McInnerny – who at times appeared a touch intimidated and averse to it all – had not.

'Oh, I loved it. It was genius,' Head enthuses genuinely, as the noticeably vivid recollections keep coming. 'It gave the show an element of danger; you honestly didn't know what would happen from night to night, and it gave me incredible power as a character. But I think it was right to have only Frank and the Narrator answering back, while the other characters maintain the reality of acting inside the fourth wall. It stops the show becoming a free-for-all and allows the action to drive through. It's weird now to think of the original show not having that dynamic because there was no audience participation.'

Like the actors who had valiantly battled against unruly audience behaviour during the show's most wildly extreme and out-of-control period in the '80s, Anthony Head grabbed the bull by the balls (aiming for the horns would have been far too obvious and easy) and dared to confront – and even enjoy – this most unique of theatrical challenges. He remembers being encouraged in the beginning to prepare a 'phrase book' of stock responses and cutting remarks with which to arm himself against the inevitable barrage of constant heckling. In addition to those collected from friends in the business, a number of useful put-downs were found in the popular US comedy series *Cheers*, mostly amongst the caustic dialogue of acid-tongued Carla Tortelli played by Rhea Perlman.

'One of my favourites was, "Is that your head on your shoulders or did your neck just blow a bubble?"' Head chortles, before recalling that his absolute favourite of all was actually suggested by *The Rocky Horror Show*'s drummer Clem Cattini. In response to any gobby punter yelling out that in addition to his scripted 'naive charm' Eddie also had a big dick, Head could (after a considered pause) promptly hit back with his already cunningly prepared retort: 'Well I'm sure it would rattle in your mouth, dear.'

As an easily recognisable face from a well-known coffee commercial, it was inevitable that the actor would also find himself on the receiving end of the occasional coffee-themed witticism from time to time; to which he would usually respond with a move he hijacked from a rival brand's ad campaign. 'I'd just give them the wanker/coffee hand gesture in return,' he quips, 'although that's not actually from the ad I was in; that one was all Gareth Hunt's.

'Chris Malcolm said to me after the first week, "Great; the good news is you've got the audience put-downs off pat. Bad news is you've added about 20 minutes to the show."'

Head laughs as yet more memories flood back. 'So I reined it back and answered about 60 percent of the heckles. It reached a point where I could silence the back row of the balcony at the Piccadilly with a look; oh, the power. That worked well; apart from one night when we had a bunch of very drunken and rowdy sailors in. They knew you had to shout, but didn't know what to shout about, beyond just ... shouting. It wore thin quite quickly.'

This kind of thing had been a constant irritating danger since the show's audience participation rituals first began, and would continue to be so: those inebriated souls who turn up, blissfully ignorant of the show's cult following and traditional talkback, and – upon hearing the practised *Rocky* regulars shouting their tried and tested counterpoint dialogue – suddenly get the misguided idea that they are allowed to rudely heckle the cast with badly timed, ill-judged, irrelevant drunken twaddle.

'As the run at the Piccadilly went on,' continues Head, 'the more experienced fans found new answers to my answers, some of which were very intelligent and witty. There was one guy in particular who was incredibly inventive, and I always looked forward to what he would come up with next.

'It isn't for everyone though,' he concedes, in reference to the constant clamour from the audience. 'Someone who had not had such a great

7: LET'S DO THE TIME WARP AGAIN

experience with it saw me in Groucho's on my last night and said "It was horrible, wasn't it?" I was flabbergasted; I'd heard he hadn't enjoyed it, but all I could reply was "Er … no."'

An unashamed fan of the show, Head is unequivocal that Frank-n-Furter's first appearance remains the best theatrical entrance of all time, as he fondly remembers this enigmatic *alter ego* slowly coming to life on a nightly basis:

'He sort of filtered through in layers. As the make-up went on, then as the first pieces of costume – the teddy, the stockings – until there'd be a moment when I'd look into the mirror and there he was, smiling back at me. The final moment – when I had to cross the backstage area to climb the steps up to the band platform for the first entrance – the hips would inevitably start to sway and I knew he's truly arrived.

'Frank is just the best character to play. There is no better stage entrance in the world. When you hear the kick drum thumping out the beat and the audience starts stamping and clapping, it gives you such an adrenaline rush. You couldn't top the buzz you get playing Frank; not least because you get to sing some of the best rock 'n' roll ever written for a musical.'

As the show's second leg at the Piccadilly, which ran from the end of October 1990 until the following summer, saw most of the original ensemble leave the production for pastures new, Anthony Head's Frank-n-Furter would be surrounded by an infusion of fresh blood.

Actress and TV presenter Vicky Licorish assumed the role of Columbia after Linda Davidson's departure; Tim Whitnall supplanted Ed Tudor-Pole as Riff Raff; Ivan Kaye took over as Eddie/Dr Scott; Kate O'Sullivan became Magenta; and Glaswegian actor-comedian Craig Ferguson replaced Adrian Edmondson as Brad. A tall, confident and physically arresting performer, Ferguson – who, 15 years later, would succeed Tom Snyder and Craig Kilborn to become the third host of the CBS network's *The Late Late Show* on US television – helped return the square-jawed, broad shouldered look of the archetypal Hollywood hero to Brad Majors after Edmondson's somewhat more gawky and timid comedic approach.

While Zalie Burrow had understudied both Columbia and Janet on a number of occasions, she is happy to admit that, of the two roles, she felt a lot more comfortable as Janet: 'I played Columbia as awkward and geeky. She was a tough one for me, as I didn't feel she fitted me; so I went the geeky route. One night, Gina, who played Janet, was ill and I was her understudy. Richard O'Brien happened to be in that night and I was offered the part when Gina left.'

Though they had essentially been offered their respective dream roles for the production's second leg, Burrow and Kate O'Sullivan, now close friends, at first felt compelled to conceal the thrilling news from each other. 'Neither wanted to upset the other one,' says Burrow, 'as we both wanted the roles we had understudied so much.'

Unsurprisingly though, such overwhelming excitement would not be bottled up for too long: 'We shared the same dressing room, and I finally plucked up courage to tell Kate that I'd been offered the role of Janet. She said "I've been offered Magenta," and we both went wild. So I'd achieved my ambition of playing a West End lead.'

With Burrow and O'Sullivan fittingly promoted to Janet and Magenta, Julia Hampson and Penelope McGhie became the new Phantoms (and female understudies), while versatile stalwart character actor Peter Bayliss – remembered for his recurring role as Mr Dunstable in school-based 1960s sitcom *Please Sir!* and its spin-off series *The Fenn Street Gang* on UK television – stepped into Jonathan Adams' shoes as the show's long-suffering Narrator. An experienced veteran of theatre, film and television, Bayliss proved more than adept at dealing with *Rocky*'s now customary heckling, and, unlike Adams, even began to encourage the odd bout of interaction from the crowd, particularly during the quieter midweek performances.

'We used to have such a laugh amongst the cast,' smiles Anthony Head, echoing the feelings of cheerful company unification referred to by many a *Rocky Horror* alumnus. 'When I went down on Craig Ferguson, who played Brad, we used to crack up a lot; as you would, going down on Craig Ferguson. I loved Eddie Tudor-Pole as Riff, really manic. The irony is that he was a newbie at [the drama school] LAMDA and I was assigned as his mentor. Having met me, he walked straight out and went to RADA; I was responsible for that. Tim Whitnall I knew from *Godspell* at the Young Vic. I'd played Jesus in a touring production, and kept saying, "When we did it, we did it like this." Bless him, he finally cracked, after putting up with it for a week or so, and said, "Tone, *I'm* doing it now." Lesson learned.'

During his stint as Frank at the Piccadilly, Head – who had missed out on being involved with the production's cast album – released a remixed version of 'Sweet Transvestite' as a single (available as a shaped picture-disc, proudly depicting Head as Frank in all his glory, and as a CD maxi-single, as well as the then customary 7" and 12" vinyl pressings), produced and arranged by Zeus B Held, on the Chrysalis label.

A staunch advocate of Richard O'Brien's classic score, the actor is especially vocal with his praise for another of Frank's magnificent showstoppers:

'"I'm Going Home" is one of the greatest songs ever written for a stage show; so simple, yet so powerful. I used to pull off Frank's wig before singing it, leaving a crappy sweaty hairnet so that he became a figure of tragedy. Then, at the end, when he's got everyone's sympathy, I used to smile so that everyone realised that, yet again, Frank's played them. It's such a great song. I approached Chris Malcolm to see if I could record it as a single. The A&R guy at the record company said yes but wanted me to record "Sweet T" at the same time with another producer, and of course that's what ended up being released. I wanted to introduce the great British public to a relatively unknown torch-song, and they got a kind of up-tempo Lou Reed version of a song they already knew. Shame, as the record release happened to coincide with the return from the Falklands War. Would've been topical; one of those "coulda-woulda-shoulda" moments.'

Presented annually by the Society of London Theatre, the Laurence Olivier Awards (formerly the Society of West End Theatre Awards but renamed in 1984 after the legendary British actor) are a prestigious affair, and to be nominated in any category is a huge honour. That the Piccadilly Theatre's production of *The Rocky Horror Show* found itself with a nomination for Best Musical Revival – along with The Fantasticks at the famous Open Air Theatre in Regent's Park and an Opera North/Royal Shakespeare Company co-production of Jerome Kern and Oscar Hammerstein II's much admired *Show Boat* that had opened at the London Palladium on 25 July 1990 – was therefore a big deal.

Sue Blane was also nominated for the Best Costume Design award, but for her work on Richard Jones' original London production of Stephen Sondheim's *Into the Woods* at the Phoenix Theatre.

Hosting the ceremony, which was televised on 7 April 1991, Angela Lansbury described *Rocky Horror*, with a delighted chuckle and a suitably naughty glint in her eye, as 'A charming old-fashioned story. Boy meets girl, boy loses girl, boy and girl find instead one very sweet transvestite from Transsexual, Transylvania and a bewildering crowd of other assorted weirdoes, most of whom are in the audience.'

The eminent star of stage and screen then introduced an exuberant live excerpt from the production itself. 'The Time Warp', performed by members of the Piccadilly company – including Tim Whitnall, Kate O'Sullivan, Vicky Licorish and Peter Bayliss – culminated in a slow-motion camera zoom and freeze frame on an imposing Anthony Head, dressed in his full Frank-n-Furter regalia, and was undoubtedly one of the ceremony's highlights.

That it ultimately lost out to *Show Boat* was no great shock, but *Rocky*'s presence amongst such esteemed company could be viewed as an indication of its continued ability to charm the supposedly toffee-nosed theatrical establishment with its irresistible rock 'n' roll rebelliousness.

International tourism had seen a dramatic decline since the summer of 1990 as a direct result of unsettling global events. On 2 August 1990, hostile forces under the command of Iraq's president Saddam Hussein had invaded the neighbouring oil-rich state of Kuwait in the Persian Gulf, sparking an immediate international crisis that threatened the stability of the Middle East and the world's economy.

A six month period of economic sanctions and perilous negotiations ensued; but with Saddam ignoring a United Nations Security Council deadline to withdraw his troops from Kuwait, an international coalition led by the United States and Great Britain commenced a campaign of continuous air strikes against Iraq's capital Bagdad on the evening of 16 January 1991. These attacks paved the way for a massive coalition ground assault and the eventual liberation of Kuwait on 28 February.

Throughout the crisis, amid fears of terrorist reprisals against the West, many Americans in particular refused to fly overseas – something that persisted in the aftermath of the resultant war. A predictable knock-on effect was the depletion of theatre audiences in and around London's West End, which saw a succession of previously successful productions forced to close prematurely. One of these, the Piccadilly Theatre's revival of *The Rocky Horror Show*, ended its run on Saturday 22 June 1991, after that evening's rousing farewell performance.

It was perhaps no surprise to learn, however, that a new UK tour was already on the cards. A huge part of the show's continued success throughout the 1980s could be attributed to its week by week visits to the country's provincial playhouses. And so, with many fans unable to afford a trip to see the show during its year-long engagement in the nation's capital, it was again time to take *Rocky* to them.

Derek Griffiths remembers Christopher Malcolm inviting the band to dinner, during which he asked if they would like to remain with the show for the forthcoming tour. Griffiths laughs at the recollection of the band's response, as (fuelled by alcohol maybe?) they suddenly decided to try their luck and mischievously dictate terms: 'We replied, "Yeah, as long as you're paying us the West End rate." And he agreed.

'Touring with any show is quite relentless, but you got Sunday, Monday and half of Tuesday off whilst the show moved on to its next venue, so that made it more bearable.'

It should be noted that later UK touring productions would often play six nights a week (including two performances on Fridays and Saturdays), typically giving the cast only Sundays off before the production opened in the next city of the tour.

'The downside,' continues Griffiths, 'was that the band could be playing anywhere, from the flies to an orchestra pit, depending on the venue. Sometimes we were just stuck in a side room with a monitor.'

With Robin Lefevre unavailable, Christopher Malcolm himself took over directorial duties for the tour, although programmes would include the credit 'Based on the 1990 London production – Directed by Robin Lefevre.' This proved to be the beginning of a stint that would see Malcolm directing numerous productions of the show in the UK, Europe and

7: LET'S DO THE TIME WARP AGAIN

elsewhere – as well as overseeing and producing a large number of others around the world – almost continuously for the next 12 years.

Both Lefevre's and Malcolm's attitudes toward the show's required acting style were, according to Zalie Burrow, in complete harmony with Richard O'Brien's. 'I didn't know that Chris was the original Brad initially,' the actress confesses. 'Richard had said that he wanted the Piccadilly production to be truer to the original King's Road version. He was insistent that we play from the truth, not as caricatures. He told us to play for real, not for laughs. Chris was in agreement, as was Robin. They all came from the same place; play it for real and not for laughs and then it will be funny.'

In addition to those players staying on from the Piccadilly cast – including Burrow as Janet, Kate O'Sullivan as Magenta, Adam Caine as Rocky and former Phantom Paul Reeves stepping into the principal role of Brad Majors – the 1991/92 UK tour would see the welcome return of two celebrated Frank-n-Furters from the show's early days. Peter Blake resumed the role from the autumn of 1991 until the following summer, while Daniel Abineri took over in the autumn of 1992.

Having played opposite Anthony Head's Frank-n-Furter for several months, Zalie Burrow now found herself sharing scenes with Peter Blake and his distinctive take on the character. 'Blakey's very different,' she confirms warmly. 'Whereas Tony was quite precise and aware of getting all the little details right, Blakey's attitude was more like, "If your heel goes to the left and you stumble, so what?" He was all smudged red lipstick and shredded fishnets.'

Whereas Daniel Abineri had played Frank in a number of Australian and New Zealand productions since the end of the original London run, and thus had been privy to the disquieting rise of disorderly audience participation during the 1980s, Blake – now known to television audiences for his portrayal of self-absorbed fantasist Kirk St Moritz in BBC sitcom *Dear John* – found himself facing a completely different kind of *Rocky Horror* audience from those he had been used to.

Aside from the heckling and participation however – which the naturally quick-witted and acid-tongued actor had absolutely no trouble dealing with – *The Rocky Horror Show* itself seemed to have grown and metamorphosed from the intentionally grungy and charming little B-movie satire that Jim Sharman had mounted in hip and happening 1970s Chelsea.

In a 1992 interview with Gillian Christie for the TimeWarp fan club newsletter, Blake's attitude to the show's so-called evolution from grubby little rock show to mainstream musical theatre was characteristically blunt. 'There's all sorts of shit in the show now,' he growled. 'Attitudes have changed. It was never a fucking *musical*. 'The Time Warp' is all choreographed now; we never had a fucking choreographer. It's very hard to get the young kids in the show to understand what it's really about; they've all got it fifth-hand through the film.

'I remember sitting there at the first preview ever, with the ramp up in front and Pat Quinn doing the Usherette with pubes hanging out the sides of her knickers, really dirty and tacky like it's supposed to be. What's happened now, because it's become a big West End show, is that all the girls wear support tights because they're so fucking vain about their thighs.'

Derek Griffiths first noticed this change of attitude toward the show during its engagement at the Piccadilly. For the first time in its history, it appeared that some cast members had started to feel that they were perhaps bigger than the show itself. 'They just looked on it as a way to start their West End careers,' he laments despairingly, 'and that's wrong. Don't do that with *Rocky*. As an actor, you should look back on your time with *Rocky* with pride and as an end in itself, not as a springboard to something else.'

Well said that man.

'The production started to become too professional and glossy as well,' Griffiths continues, as if to echo Peter Blake's sentiments. 'The King's Road felt like you'd gone to a flea-pit cinema on a Sunday afternoon. You'd got those Ushers crawling under the seats and grabbing people's legs and scaring the crap out of them. People used to prod the Ushers before they moved, to see if they were real. What a laugh. But now, you couldn't do any of that because of bloody health and safety legislation and public liability.'

In spite of this shift in tone since the King's Road days, Griffiths is keen to point out that the closeness and feeling of kinship within the company remained untarnished throughout his two decade association with the show. 'It was a very close-knit community,' he reminisces happily. 'It felt just like a family. Howard Panter used to take us out to dinner. We had lots of after-show jam sessions. There were so many times that things went wrong, but we just got on with it. In Wales once, one of the tabs stuck and Peter Blake did a stand-up routine while they were trying to fix it. I think some of the newer, younger actors were a bit shocked by what they found. It was very *laissez-faire*; very rock 'n' roll. Those who'd grown up in theatre were shocked, but I grew up in a rock band, so I was used to just getting up and bollocking it out.'

The tour saw the reinstatement of the mid-show interval – which had been removed for the duration of the West End run as a nod to the B-movie conventions of Jim Sharman's original incarnation – as most regional venues traditionally required an intermission in order to sell refreshments (alcoholic and otherwise) to all those high-spirited thirsty punters who invariably arrived with their wallets bulging under the weight of hard-earned disposable income.

Furthermore, whether justified within the context of the story or not, one aspect of the show certainly benefitted from the recent West End production's questionable addition of a 'safer sex' approach to the Frank and Brad bedroom scene. As film director Mel Brooks had satirically yet rather astutely pointed out in *Spaceballs*, his 1987 big screen mockery of *Star Wars* and the space opera sub-genre it created, the world of tie-in merchandising was the area in which the capitalist producers of contemporary mainstream entertainment could actually expect to make the biggest bucks; as a foresighted George Lucas had cunningly demonstrated a decade earlier. As if to illustrate the uneasy truth of such inescapable cynicism, the licensors of *The Rocky Horror Show*'s collectable memorabilia promptly decided to capitalise on the production's newfound (though strangely incongruous) attitude of social responsibility by producing for the 1991/92 UK touring version – and numerous productions thereafter – cheaply manufactured (and perhaps slightly overpriced) souvenir condoms; surely their most indispensable items. Just as George Lucas's Ewoks had helped sell thousands of *Star Wars*-themed teddy bears to a whole generation of wide-eyed impressionable pre-PlayStation moppets, so *The Rocky Horror Show* proudly did its bit for sexual awareness.

Bearing the admittedly witty moniker Frankie's Johnnies – as well as the slogan 'Do your worst, interior one!', a droll but suitable paraphrasing of one of Frank-n-Furter's lines from the show's script – *Rocky*'s first souvenir packet of three contained a trio of flavoured (or rather 'Falvoured', as the conspicuously clumsy typo on the side of the box declared) coloured rubbers, which joined the programmes, T-shirts, posters and badges available in theatre foyers.

While it would perhaps be unrealistic – given its quirky adult content – to expect *Rocky Horror* to reach the dizzying heights of *Star Wars*, *Star Trek* or *Doctor Who* as a mainstream pop-culture phenomenon, the musical nevertheless spawned innumerable articles of souvenir memorabilia. Some of the most suitably peculiar items seen over the years included both male and female underwear, glittery nail varnish, cocktail stirrers, commemorative candles, teddy bears, a Frank-n-Furter rubber duck, and an 18-inch 'singing' Frank-n-Furter doll (produced by Spencer Gifts in 2001) that played 'The Time Warp' from the movie's soundtrack whenever a concealed button was compressed on its belly – although perhaps one of Frank's own songs from Richard O'Brien's score would have been more apposite.

Throughout the 1990s and beyond, Rocky Horror Company licensed and oversaw a multitude of high-profile productions of the show around the world, all with the 'Richard O'Brien's' prefix over the title, and usually under the watchful and protective gaze of Christopher Malcolm and O'Brien himself.

Australia's special love affair with the show – which had started in 1974 with the Harry M Miller and Jim Sharman Sydney production and persisted into the '80s with producer Wilton Morley's touring versions – would continue unabated throughout the 1990s.

Like Miller, who had dominated the Australian music and theatre scene in the '60s and '70s, Paul Dainty had become something of a self-made mogul, having presented innumerable concerts by the likes of Abba (who were famously huge in Australia), David Bowie, the Rolling Stones and Tina Turner, as well as a number of theatrical works and prestigious sporting events. He had purchased Melbourne's Comedy Theatre in 1978, and in 1992 decided that the venue should launch a new production of *The Rocky Horror Show*. This would open on 2 July 1992 and then commence an extensive tour of Australia and the Pacific Rim.

Thanks to the presence of many of the show's original team – including set designer Brian Thomson and musical director Richard Hartley, plus Daniel Abineri playing Frank-n-Furter as well as directing – the 1980s tours 'down under' had looked and felt very much like the show's original 1970s incarnation. Paul Dainty, however, felt that *Rocky* in Australia was overdue a facelift. He instigated a fresh look and a completely new production, which became known as *The New Rocky Horror Show* on posters and marketing material.

Heading the cast as the deliciously degenerate Frank-n-Furter was a charismatic young actor-singer by the name of Craig McLachlan. With his portrayal of Henry Ramsay between 1986 and 1989 in the popular Aussie TV soap opera *Neighbours*, McLachlan had achieved heart-throb status, both in Australia and in the United Kingdom (where the series had become something of a surprise phenomenon) before 'defecting' to the Seven Network's rival soap *Home and Away* in 1989.

'I'm sure people would think that I'd play Rocky or even Brad, but to me the challenge presented by Frank-n-Furter was just irresistible,' McLachlan said in his biography for *The New Rocky Horror Show*'s large format souvenir programme; a sentiment the playfully mischievous actor would echo repeatedly during promotional press interviews and chat shows, often with a characteristic glint in his eye as he gleefully slipped into character as Frank (sometimes to the evident unease of his interviewer, which McLachlan would blatantly exploit in the name of too-good-to-miss comedy value).

As evidenced by his passionately dynamic and unashamedly sensual performance, McLachlan fervently seized the role of Frank-n-Furter like the gift it truly is for a performer, and relished every sordid moment of it.

7: LET'S DO THE TIME WARP AGAIN

Director Nigel Triffitt, who also designed the show's costumes and economical but visually impressive set, had most recently helmed a successful revival of *Hair* in 1991, making *Rocky Horror* a rather appropriate follow-up; although, as he freely admitted on an episode of Australian current affairs programme *Real Life* in 1993, he had not been too familiar with the show before he actually signed up to direct it:

'I'd seen it vaguely in 1974 with Reg Livermore in it, and didn't think much of it. Had never seen the film. So came into it without a knowledge of the phenomenon of *The Rocky Horror Show* that existed in the '70s and '80s particularly. So really one had to try and find a way of reinventing it without throwing the baby out with the bath water.'

In the same *Real Life* feature, which erroneously described Richard O'Brien as an Aussie, actress and stand-up comedienne Gina Riley explained her approach to the character of Janet Weiss:

'I wouldn't have done it if someone had said to me "You have to do this exactly the way everyone else has ever done it before," because for an actor that's just not interesting at all. I just wanted to put a much more sort of comic element; I mean, they're incredibly sort of sexually repressed, and so I just took the ball and ran with that.'

Curiously, while Riley's broader comedic technique (wide-mouthed grins and over-the-top facial expressions, as evidenced by archival clips of the production on YouTube) often elicited appreciative laughter from the audience, it in many ways pushed the character – and the piece itself – away from the subtle satirical 'play it for real' style that Richard O'Brien had long championed as the correct and most effective method of performing the show. Even the look of her Jackie Kennedy-style jet-black 1960s wig was cartoony and larger-than-life (a couple of the production's subsequent Janets would revert to slightly more refined and understated coiffures), while Craig McLachlan's Frank-n-Furter eschewed a hairpiece altogether in favour of his own short, curly masculine locks. A number of characters were given a harder-edged look, most notably Eddie and Magenta, both of whom had silver studs abundantly incorporated into their costumes; while the overall appearance of Brad Majors (comedian Stephen Kearney was cast originally, although Glenn Butcher took over early in the Melbourne run) seemed to evoke the dork interpretation rather than the more apposite all-American hero type as previously discussed.

Besides recalling the reviled – by *Rocky Horror* purists and Richard O'Brien alike – overly exaggerated pantomime approach of 1980s British productions, it could be argued that this disproportionate departure from reality diminished both the horror and genuine sexiness of the show's situations by reducing them to the level of shallow camp comedy.

Sadly however, such analytical dissection of the performances and directorial approach mattered little to the mainstream audiences who (to the delight of the producers) eagerly flocked to the production, cementing its success and ensuring that the tour could look forward to a long and prosperous future.

Seasons followed in Sydney, Adelaide, Perth, Brisbane and Hong Kong, with a number of particularly noteworthy performers following Craig McLachlan into the hallowed high heels of Dr Frank-n-Furter. These included Marcus Graham; former *Neighbours* star and international pop sensation Jason Donovan, presumably seeking a drastic change of image after playing the title role in the enormously successful West End revival of the Andrew Lloyd Webber and Tim Rice hit *Joseph and the Amazing Technicolor Dreamcoat* at the London Palladium in 1991; and Dale Ryder, lead singer of celebrated Melbourne-based rock group Boom Crash Opera.

In 1995, with Stuart Devenie in the role of Frank (sporting a conspicuous Tin-Tin-style blond quiff), Paul Dainty opened the production in New Zealand in association with Stewart and Tricia Macpherson – who, along with Ken Cooper, David Fraser and John Griffiths, had produced the first New Zealand production (starring Gary Glitter) in 1978. Having premiered successfully at the Aotea Centre in Auckland on 2 February, the 1995 production went on to enjoy equally popular seasons in Christchurch and Wellington.

Cast recordings were released for both the 1992 Australian and the 1995 New Zealand tours; but, while the vocal talent for the two albums would be provided by the actual cast members from the respective stage productions, the songs inexplicably featured inappropriate modern musical arrangements, created specially for the recordings by Garth Porter, which were markedly different – and invariably inferior – to those played in the stage show itself.

In his programme notes for the 2006 UK *Rocky Horror* convention, dubbed the Denton Affair, Christopher Malcolm recalled journeying to Argentina in 1993 to direct a Spanish-language production of the show, during which it was noted that much had changed in the years since the celluloid version had first opened there. 'The cinema where the film had been playing in the '70s had been fire-bombed by anti-gay protesters,' he revealed, 'so we were unsure whether the theatre show would work; but they loved it in Buenos Aires.'

As the Berlin Wall came down in 1989, symbolically ending four and a half decades of Cold War anxiety between East and West, *The Rocky Horror Show*'s small but not insignificant contribution to the alleviation of tensions often associated with outmoded intolerant attitudes could also be experienced in other territories.

During the early 1990s, the Republic of South Africa found itself famously liberated from a prolonged period of lawful apartheid and extreme conservatism, which had been enforced by the country's ruling

7: LET'S DO THE TIME WARP AGAIN

National Party since 1948. In addition to racial segregation, the government's laws also prohibited homosexuality, pornography and many 'immoral' forms of entertainment from the West. As history will attest, however, outright proscription is rarely a successful eliminator. In fact, as evidenced by the rise of bootlegging, organised crime and illegal speakeasies in the United States during the era of alcohol prohibition in the 1920s, it often inspires a wholly opposite subversive attitude – the offending article and its supporters merely being driven underground – as societies generally tend to impudently defy any overly suppressive authority.

The Rocky Horror Picture Show had enjoyed a financially strong opening in South Africa. A 20th Century Fox publicity communication, dated 28 May 1976 (reprinted in Bill Henkin's *The Rocky Horror Picture Show Book* in 1979) announced that the movie had rapidly become the most successful American motion picture in South Africa since the advent of television. 'In 12 weeks at the Highpoint Theatre, Johannesburg, six weeks in Cape Town and four weeks in Durban, the picture has racked up a phenomenal box office gross of $162, 150,' the report stated; while other sources indicated that around a quarter of a million people had already seen the movie, garnering it a huge cult following, by the time it was prematurely withdrawn from circulation.

'In South Africa the album went double gold and then they banned the film,' Richard O'Brien told Alan Jones in a 1981 interview for *Starburst* magazine. The article went on to detail a wonderful anecdote, which it claimed was O'Brien's personal favourite *Rocky Horror* story at the time. According to the tale, whilst attending an illicit *Rocky*-themed costume party in an undisclosed South African conurbation, O'Brien had happened to answer a telephone call from a member of the local constabulary, who promptly notified him that they were on their way.

'O'Brien decided to make his excuses and leave, and not be the one to ruin the party atmosphere,' the piece continued. 'As he was walking down the street, a car pulled up to him, and two men in corsets and fishnet tights asked him if he knew where the *Rocky Horror* party was taking place. O'Brien said he did, but advised them not to go as it was about to be raided by the police. Whereupon one of the men said, "What do you mean? We *are* the police; we wanted to let everyone know we were coming."'

Time warp forward to more enlightened times, and South Africa's first ever production of *The Rocky Horror Show*, directed by Christopher Malcolm and with Jeremy Crutchley in the crucial role of Frank-n-Furter, opened at Cape Town's Nico Theatre on 3 April 1992, before moving to the Victory Theatre (formerly the Grove Cinema) in Johannesburg. Newly re-opened as a venue for live entertainment, the Victory's inaugural production had been a recent revival of the 1974 South African musical *Ipi N'tombi* by Bertha Egnos and Gail Lakier. And then *Rocky* arrived to shake things up a bit.

A colossal hit with newly-liberated South African audiences, the production – presented by Colin Law and Neil Lovegrove for Witchway Entertainment by arrangement with Rocky Horror Company Ltd – ran for 18 months, winning the annual FNB (First National Bank of South Africa) Vita Award for Best Musical of the Year along the way.

A promotional cast CD of the subsequent Silver Jubilee revival was recorded between 18 and 25 August 1997, an entire week before the production actually premiered at Johannesburg's Victory Theatre on 31 August that year.

Restaged and choreographed by Lynsey Shmukler-Jones and Ingeborg Hieber, and produced by Colin Law and Neil Lovegrove for Venture Capital, this twenty-fifth anniversary production, starring David Dennis as Frank-n-Furter, Leonard John Urbani as Brad and Samantha Peo as Janet, firmly established *The Rocky Horror Show* as a genuine force to be reckoned with in South Africa. Richard Hartley's musical arrangements, partially updated by Pete Moss, and Jay Jay Schoeman's costume designs, which added a couple of twee twists here and there while essentially remaining faithful to the iconic Sue Blane originals, kept the show true to its roots; and further revivals would follow.

A massively successful European tour produced by Ballett, Classic & Entertainment GmbH in Hannover and directed by Christopher Malcolm commenced in Wolfsburg, Germany in January 1996 – and would eventually run for an incredible ten years. With a look based very much on that of the 1990 London revival, recycling Robin Don's awe-inspiring set design from the Piccadilly, and with the peerless Sue Blane again providing the all-important costume designs, the production featured an appealing and confident young American actor by the name of Bob Simon in the role of Frank-n-Furter. Having already played the part in a 1993 US tour, Cleveland-born Simon effortlessly slipped back into the heels and fishnets, and, like Daniel Abineri and Peter Blake, would revisit the character on numerous subsequent occasions.

Being controlled by the Rocky Horror Company and directed by Christopher Malcolm, the European tour – which visited cities in Spain, Italy, Sweden, Finland, Denmark, Holland, Hungary, Luxemburg, Austria and all over Germany (another country that, like Australia, seemed to have developed a special bond with the show) – would also swap and share a number of performers with Malcolm's equally popular UK productions. These included Larissa Murray (who played Janet in Europe and the UK); Rachel Hale (Phantom and Janet in Europe and Janet in the UK); Michael Dalton, Ross O'Hennessy and Shane Cortese (Rocky); Nathan Taylor

(Phantom, Brad and Frank); Amanda-Jane Manning (Phantom, Janet and Usherette/Magenta); Bekki Carpenter (Phantom); Nicky Willson (Phantom in the UK and Columbia in Europe); and Jon Boydon, who after playing Brad (and understudying Frank-n-Furter) for the 2002/03 UK production would take over the role of Frank on the European tour.

Anthony Topham, who played Eddie/Dr Scott during the European production's final tour between December 2004 and November 2005, recalls the efficient process employed by resident director Paul Winterford (from Christopher Malcolm's original staging) to put the show together and speedily block and rehearse new actors into their roles. 'The two-week rehearsal formula is exactly like panto,' he attests firmly. 'Here's your blocking, learn your lines and you slot in around Frank, who is the pantomime dame.'

By the end of the decade, this rather superficial approach to the characters and story would come to be regarded as something of a worrying throwback to the less cerebral interpretations that Richard O'Brien had vehemently fought and disparaged in the late 1980s; a situation that would culminate in a change of management within the Rocky Horror Company and the engagement of a new director for the show itself.

Topham also discusses his own perception of the differences between the show's cult in the UK and that in mainland Europe: 'I think the European tour is different from the UK in that the show still represents something more underground in Europe. The venues are smaller, the audiences take the meaning more to heart and it drags in new teenagers who haven't seen the show before, especially goths – i.e. those who are not part of mainstream culture.'

Topham believes that such cultural differences and attitudes might go some way to explaining the show's hugely enthusiastic European following, particularly in Germany where a large number of independent productions were staged in addition to the tour: 'In Germany, for example, there's something about the show that suits the German sensibilities. They're more conservative generally, so the "Don't dream it, be it" theme really strikes a chord.'

This conformist national outlook, which undoubtedly resulted in a more well-behaved and regimented crowd than those attracted by British productions of the show, allowed for the sale and use of participatory props (usually prohibited by UK theatres) – including water pistols, rice and toilet rolls – without fear of damage to the venue or danger to the performers. Disciplined and respectful German audiences invariably seemed to use such items specifically at their proper point of reference in the script and, as a rule, would not direct them toward the stage.

'We found some interesting differences between audience participation around Europe,' Anthony Topham continues. 'For example, in Denmark and Holland they generally try to drown out the Narrator by booing. You know in the UK, whenever Dr Scott's name is mentioned, the audience shout "Sieg Heil"? Well, in Germany it's illegal to do that, so they just shout "Huh." Also, Greece was a funny experience because there were subtitles being projected across a screen so that the audience could follow the dialogue. It became difficult to act, as the audience would laugh at a point that wasn't funny, but you realised that they were laughing at a line they'd just read and you were a couple of lines ahead of them.'

Actress Ellie Chidzey, who played Magenta opposite Topham's Eddie/Dr Scott, admits finding the aforementioned formulaic two-week rehearsal procedure creatively limiting:

'Well, it's certainly restricting as an actor to have to copy the original characters, and I was a little concerned going into a show that I'd heard had "Satanist" followers; people who totally idolised Tim Curry and worshipped the show.

'It was like, "Here's the formula that works; this is how you do it." There was no discussing the characters – apart from with Brenden [J Lovett] who played Riff; he'd played it for years and we discussed the relationship between Riff and Magenta. He told me the show was a spin on Adam and Eve; but Paul Pecorino, who played Frank, said it was the story of a spoilt prince who'd been banished from his home planet, and the other characters were his servants and keepers.

'On our opening night, the audience absolutely roared when I came on as the Usherette, and I nearly broke out of character,' confesses the actress as she recalls her first encounter with *Rocky*'s unparalleled fan devotion. 'In Italy they had a [response] to every line of "Science Fiction" and I was so taken aback that I actually stopped singing for a couple of seconds. Sometimes it was frightening, but the majority of the time I treated it like feedback and just thought "How bloody brilliant." It forms a bond between the company and the audience. It's okay if you corpse, because you're all in on the joke. Once you've learnt your lines, you can start to have fun with it. For example, when we were in Greece, we made cracks about the Greeks inventing buggery. We got used to all the stuff that was thrown; rice, water, toast etc.'

'Eddie's entrance was always fun,' Anthony Topham declares, elaborating on his own approach to the production and likening his first appearance to the crazed whirling tornado of a certain popular Warner Bros cartoon character. 'I came on like Taz. You don't need method acting for that one. I deliberately tried not to be influenced by the film, which I'd seen many years before. I sang "Eddie's Teddy" gospel-style, which was nice. I loved watching Paul [Pecorino] playing Frank. His character is the only one who can drive the show; no-one else gets to take the reins. It's a

7: LET'S DO THE TIME WARP AGAIN

great skill to bring the audience in, rather than simply stepping out of character. Frank must not simply be a pantomime dame. He's a tragic figure, a Norma Desmond; he's had a wonderful life and it's all now falling apart, so the actor must find something deeper. He's got to make the audience admire, despise, love and hate his hedonism all at the same time.'

With the show commemorating a number of special anniversaries during the '90s, the decade would witness a plethora of celebratory productions across several countries.

Although there was no UK tour in 1993, a number of other territories paid homage to *Rocky Horror*'s twentieth year accordingly. A major twenty-first anniversary production – known on posters as *The Rocky '21st Birthday Party!' Horror Show* – toured the length and breadth of Britain a year later. Notable primarily for Patricia Quinn reprising her original role of Usherette/Magenta, this coming-of-age tour – which also featured Jonathon Morris (known for his portrayal of Adrian Boswell in Carla Lane's BBC1 sitcom *Bread*, which ran for seven series and 74 episodes between May 1986 and November 1991) as Frank-n-Furter, Sophie Lawrence (formerly *EastEnders*' Diane Butcher) as Janet, and actor and quiz show host Nicholas Parsons as the Narrator – received a sincere seal of approval from none other than *Daily Mail* theatre critic Jack Tinker, whose famous 1973 rave had encouraged the show's initial success.

In his 1994 review – headlined 'ROCKY '94 STILL WINS BY A KNOCKOUT' – which appeared in the Friday 8 July edition, during a mid-tour West End birthday engagement for the show at London's Duke of York's Theatre, Tinker fondly remembered all that had made that historic first night at the Royal Court's Theatre Upstairs so special. 'It was to be a unique night in the theatre because an outrageously persistent legend was born,' he wrote, before recalling his 1973 sentiments – 'One is in danger of merely applauding it without assessing it' – and then heaping deserved praise upon the latest version; albeit with a sensible and characteristically perceptive acknowledgement of the show's continued evolution:

'Well here I am still applauding it. But assessment becomes ever harder as its cult status overwhelms its original charm.

'Jonathon Morris of TV's *Bread* is a Frank-n-Furter of the '90s. There is none of the insouciant subtlety of Tim Curry's transvestite from Transylvania in Mr Morris's cut-and-thrust lasciviousness. It is an up-every-front performance for an up-every-front age. The fans adored him, his tongue flickering like a python and his body writhing in similar snake-like danger.

'Like the age we live in, where once the show was simply high camp, now it is raucously explicit. But to survive, everything must grow, even if it stubbornly refuses to grow up. And we who were there at its birth and its christening must not resent it becoming the property of others.'

Of Patricia Quinn, whom he described as 'having about her a Dietrich quality that defies anything as mundane as mere arithmetic,' he declared unambiguously, 'She is still simply stunning.'

With the 1994 anniversary production a huge hit – and with a number of other officially licensed *Rocky Horror* productions being staged in the UK for the first time since the early '80s – the show toured successfully for a further two years with various cast changes along the way. In 1995, the role of Frank-n-Furter was taken by former British figure skater Robin Cousins. Perhaps an unusual choice for the part – despite his previous dabbles with the world of musical theatre, with an on-ice production of Rodgers and Hammerstein's *Cinderella* and the role of Munkustrap in a UK tour of *Cats* – the one-time Winter Olympic champion (he won a gold medal for Great Britain at Lake Placid in 1980) had his own fully-formed opinion about who the intergalactic seducer should be, which was somewhat removed from that of Anthony Head's intentionally grotesque interpretation. Speaking with Stephanie Freeman in an interview for the TimeWarp fan club newsletter, he expressed an interesting personal (and perhaps debatable) view that Frank should actually be a lot more sophisticated, elegant and refined than might be suggested by the carefree, rough-around-the-edges distillation of previous actors.

'I was talking to Sue Blane about costumes,' Cousins revealed, 'and she was saying that she felt the costume should be a sort of thrown-together affair. And I thought, having read the script, this man has everything prepared just in case. Ready for when he is going to die; he is meticulous. My theory is that he is in great shape himself, almost a god; so the only thing he could do was create an equal. I play him very tight, very clean and together and meticulous.

'Frank came to the world, and the only thing he knows about Earth people are Hollywood B-movies – Swanson, Barrymore and the like. He'd have to be that together to have an act like "I'm Going Home" prepared.'

As if to give audiences an opportunity to make a direct comparison of two markedly different interpretations of the character, Anthony Head briefly returned to the role – to cover Cousins' temporary absence – for the tour's 1995 summer engagement at London's Duke of York's Theatre.

'I just kind of swanned in, straight into the role,' laughs Head, remembering his welcome return to the bizarre, yet comfortably warm, world of Frank-n-Furter and his cohorts. 'It was a young cast, and they'd come into town from a tour and were used to quite a genteel Frank. And I was a bit different.'

During his six weeks with the show at the Duke of York's, Head took part in a special midnight matinee – a one-off charity performance featuring a gathering of wild and untamed celebrity guest stars – in memory of Erin Palmer Lund, a friend's daughter who had died of a brain tumour at the age of only three on 15 June 1994:

'Nigel Planer was the Narrator [while] Shane Richie played Eddie – with his lyrics on a piece of paper in his hand – and brought a slightly-out-of-it Robbie Williams with him. It was literally just after the Take That split, and Robbie made his entrance coming up in the tube wearing a T-shirt, gold lame shorts and boots. Then there was Ian Bartholomew, who wore an operating gown with a split up the back – when he turned upstage he revealed his very bare bottom – and Rebecca Lacey and Belinda Lang escorted him on stage dressed as nurses. It was great fun, lots of ad-libs.'

1998 marked *The Rocky Horror Show*'s twenty-fifth year, and, with its popularity showing no signs of diminishing, Silver Jubilee productions began to spring up all over the world.

While the European tour continued – its posters acknowledging the anniversary accordingly, and with Sue Blane and her team creating dazzling silver versions of the characters' costumes for the ensemble's finale bows and curtain calls – a new UK production, from the Christopher Malcolm and Howard Panter company Rocky Horror (London) Limited in association with Birmingham Repertory Theatre, opened on Tuesday 24 March 1998. After an inaugural three-week run at the Birmingham Rep itself, this incarnation of *Rocky* would take to the road for what would eventually be the best part of two and a half years.

While Robin Don once again designed the sets, they were completely rethought and dramatically scaled down from the magnificent – yet hardly practical for touring purposes (as the 1991/92 tour had revealed) – gothic edifice he had created for the 1990 London revival. A crowd-pleasing and clearly keen Jason Donovan was cast as Frank-n-Furter – having gained ample experience of the role during the 1995/96 tours of Australia and New Zealand – and would make his entrance along a huge, tongue-shaped catwalk that extended lasciviously toward the audience via an enormous gaping mouth; vaguely evocative of the movie's classic 'lips' poster.

Since famously winning a high-profile libel case against *The Face* magazine for allegations about his sexuality in 1992, the usually affable Donovan, once thought of as the cleanest of clean-cut healthy young role models, had probably been in the news more for his much-publicised cocaine habit than for his no-longer-thriving pop career. In January 1995, he had collapsed from a drug-induced seizure at the Viper Room, the prominent Los Angeles nightclub partly owned at the time by Hollywood luminary Johnny Depp, outside which actor and former child star River Phoenix had died of an overdose on 31 October 1993.

In many ways, this made *The Rocky Horror Show* and its themes of sleaze and corruption a fitting vehicle for the former daytime soap idol, whose life had gone from approximating Brad Majors in the real world to ironically portraying Frank-n-Furter on stage. Rarely less than deliciously unpredictable, often switching from foul-mouthed viciousness (ferociously telling hecklers to, 'Suck my cock!') to eccentric spaced-out daydreaming in the blink of an eye, Donovan was never averse to using his position as Frank as a means of sportingly sending up his own public image. Hence a sprightly audience reference to Kylie Minogue, his former *Neighbours* co-star and past love, would be met with a straight-faced utterance of 'You should be so lucky ... lucky, lucky, lucky' – a cheeky allusion to one of Minogue's biggest '80s pop hits.

Even closer to the bone would be the response by Magenta (Laurie Brett) to Frank's histrionic faint after discovering Janet and Rocky being more than just passing acquaintances on his laboratory monitor. 'Master,' she would shout irritably, in a topical addition to the script, as Donovan's Frank lay prostrate on the stage, 'this is not the Viper Room.'

Along with the rather unimaginative phrase '25 Years Young', promotional material for the latest UK tour – which spawned an energetic live cast recording featuring Jason Donovan as Frank and another fan favourite, Nicholas Parsons, reprising his 1994 role as the Narrator – utilised the title *The New Rocky Horror Show*, first seen on ads for the 1992 Australian production, causing concerned and confused fans to worry that the producers might be planning an unwanted reimagining of an already perfect piece of theatre. Andrew Lloyd Webber had, after all, re-launched his long-running musical *Starlight Express* as *The New Starlight Express* in 1992, controversially adding five new songs while omitting 12 of its originals. Given that *The Rocky Horror Show* was structurally faultless, and that every song in its impeccable score was an acknowledged classic, the prospect of new musical numbers – even if they were written by Richard O'Brien – being inserted into the show was something of an unthinkable nightmare.

Thankfully, rather than a change to the show as written, the dubious use of the word *'New'* in the title merely indicated that it was a new production. Though still directed by Christopher Malcolm, with Richard Hartley's musical arrangements and Sue Blane's costume designs, the latest version had a new-fangled set, a change of musical director in the form of Peter Whitfield (from the European tour) and a different band line-up.

As with any form of pop-culture devotion, it had become usual for the actors (and their characters) in *Rocky Horror* to achieve a kind of rock star status amongst the show's most ardent followers, a trend first observed by the players during the original King's Road production and, in particular, its resultant Japanese tour. With this trend continuing into the '90s, another member of the company found himself achieving unexpected celebrity status as well as the actors.

Transferred from the European production along with drummer Paul Matthews, exuberant saxophonist Dave Webb would take to the stage at the top of the second act to belt out a rocking instrumental medley of popular hits from the score; a stunt that served as an upbeat entr'acte – previously unnecessary until the show had an interval added for touring productions – before the Narrator appeared to continue the story. On more than one occasion, the increasingly popular Webb found himself facing a front row populated entirely by 'clones' of himself, as a gathering of the show's regular groupies had speedily changed their costumes during the interval in favour of the bandana, black vest and tight leather trousers worn by the clearly thrilled musician. Inflatable or plastic toy saxophones would often complete the look for this jovial moment of good-natured hero worship.

The occasional hiatus aside – during which Glasgow-born TV presenter Ross King filled Frank-n-Furter's spangled platform heels with a portrayal more than a little reminiscent of fellow Scot Peter Blake's – Jason Donovan's association with the show climaxed officially with an eight-week season at London's Victoria Palace in 1999.

Possibly looking for an image change after an extended run in the West End production of the family-friendly saccharine musical *Summer Holiday* had resulted in him being saddled with the rather insipid epithet of 'the new Cliff Richard,' future tabloid bad boy Darren Day assumed the role of Frank for the autumn leg of the tour. While in many ways his make-up and characterisation resembled those of Donovan – albeit less erratic and not so dreamily spaced-out – Day's tendency to make headlines, thanks to his 'love rat' reputation and much-publicised on-off relationships with a string of celebrity females, was never going to be overlooked by *Rocky*'s creatively witty followers. Therefore, Riff Raff's assertion 'The master is not yet married' would often be met with an eager cry of 'He just keeps getting engaged' from the audience, which the good-humoured Day would typically take in his stride.

In Australia, producer Paul Dainty launched his own twenty-fifth birthday production on 29 July 1998 at Sydney's Star City, a massive casino, hotel and entertainment complex that had opened the previous year. Essentially a continuation of the hit Australian version that had already toured for much of the decade, the newest manifestation featured a number of returning players from the 1992 line-up, as well as comedian Tim Ferguson as Frank.

'I don't know why it's endured; I have no idea,' director and designer Nigel Triffitt confessed to Sydney's *Today Tonight* programme on the eve of the production's premiere, before positing his own theory as to the show's perpetual appeal. 'I assume it's because it's about sick people's sexual behaviour and the extremity of such; and all of the human race has some form of extreme sexual behaviour, hopefully.'

As the '90s drew to a close, overwhelming evidence for the unmistakable allure of such deviant extremities was becoming increasingly prevalent. This once-modest little rock musical's staying power and canny knack of transcending cultural trends, public taste and ever-changing fashions displayed not the merest hint of beginning to fade. *The Rocky Horror Show* was a genuine, critic-proof, monster hit wherever it played in the world.

That is, with one very notable exception.

The show's failure to win over audiences and stuffy critics at the Belasco Theatre in 1975 had hung like an eternal embarrassing albatross around the collective necks of its creators for nearly two and a half decades of otherwise gold-paved success. Almost any given write-up of *Rocky Horror* history would inevitably draw attention to its unforgettably shameful performance in New York, the very city that had subsequently embraced the film version and made it a midnight phenomenon.

With a new millennium fast approaching, the *Rocky Horror* movie now regarded by many as a big screen musical classic, and the world having entered an ever more technologically advanced digital age – making the eternal need for simple nostalgic diversions more important than ever – the time finally felt right for a once forsaken little rock 'n' roll show to receive a 21st Century make-over and be given a long overdue second chance.

The Rocky Horror Show was coming back to Broadway.

8
I'm Sure You're Not Spent Yet

Despite pedants arguing vehemently – and with sound logic – that the 21st Century did not actually commence until 1 January 2001, the world was always going to celebrate the dawning of a brand new millennium precisely 12 months earlier.

While doom merchants feared a disastrous global computer crash as a result of the much-touted Y2K millennium bug – which thankfully failed to materialise – millions rejoiced as the stroke of midnight heralded the beginning of the year 2000, and massive firework displays signalled the onset of a brand new century.

Ever since *The Rocky Horror Picture Show* – which celebrated its twenty-fifth anniversary in 2000 – had first proved itself a solid, though belated, box office hit at movie theatres across the United States, there had been periodic whisperings that the musical stage play that spawned it might one day make a historic return to Broadway.

Critics had blamed the show's New York failure in 1975 at least in part on producer Lou Adler's choice of venue. *The Rocky Horror Show* had been a hit as an unassuming experimental work in London, Los Angeles and elsewhere, evidently best suited to tiny fringe theatres and disused cinemas, and had consequently been overwhelmed, both visually and acoustically, when transplanted uncomfortably to the echoing vastness of 44th Street's opulent Belasco.

Adler's misguided decision to try to open the show at a substantially larger venue for its prominent New York debut can perhaps, from a certain point of view, be partially understood. After all, the Great White Way has never been primarily associated with modest experimental works. Quite the reverse in fact; it is best known for brash, brazen, brightly-lit, loudly-heralded spectaculars and visual extravaganzas.

By contrast, youthfully hip, cool and fashionably with-it Los Angeles audiences had embraced the shabby, intimate B-movie nature of the musical when it made its US debut at Lou Adler's Roxy Theatre in 1974, and the city still seemed clued in to its charms 25 years later.

A 1999 production with Frank-n-Furter played by David Arquette – star of tongue-in-cheek horror movies such as *Buffy the Vampire Slayer* (a lightweight 1992 comedy that inspired the edgier and wittier television series), Wes Craven's *Scream* franchise (which began in 1996) and 2002's

CGI-heavy giant spider romp *Eight Legged Freaks* – almost certainly benefitted from the bijou nature of its location at LA's Tiffany Theatre, a former West Hollywood picture house.

Nonetheless, custom would indicate that most Broadway theatregoers expect their musicals to be bright, loud and showily grandiose; in which case it would seem unlikely that *The Rocky Horror Show* could ever be staged completely faithfully, in its tried and tested traditional form of a subtle satirical send-up, for a largely complacent, set-in-its-ways, decadent New York crowd. Hence, while Rocky Horror Company and Richard O'Brien would be typically (and quite rightly) protective of their baby's integrity for its eagerly-anticipated 21st Century Broadway revival, an unprecedented level of imaginative reinvention would be needed if Lou Adler's mistakes, and the haunting memories thereof, were to be avoided.

With a quirky programme note – 'Time: Then and Now – Place: Here and There' – effectively situating the show's action in an unspecified dreamlike and timeless parallelism, the latest production would premier on Wednesday 15 November 2000 at the Circle in the Square on 50th Street in central Manhattan. Situated below street level and with a fairly modest seating capacity (for a legitimate Broadway theatre) of 650 – the Belasco by comparison could accommodate 967 – the venue was far better suited to the long-established needs of *The Rocky Horror Show* than its much grander previous New York home had ever been.

Built in 1970 and designed by architect Alan Sayles, the Circle in the Square had an unusual interior layout, being one of only two Broadway playhouses to boast a thrust stage rather than a conventional proscenium arch. This allowed the action to penetrate the fabled fourth wall by way of an extended runway and effectively involve the audience – arranged in a horseshoe-shaped arc, facing the players from three different directions – in much the same way as the King's Road Theatre's catwalk had in the 1970s. Furthermore, a specially erected false proscenium would appear to collapse away during the final chorus of 'Over at the Frankenstein Place', implying that Frank's fortress of turpitude had further enveloped the crowd.

A certain amount of re-education as to what actually constituted *The Rocky Horror Show* would also be required if an entire generation of midnight movie cultists was to be coerced into accepting their favourite story in a different medium.

In the US, more than anywhere else in the world, the screen adaptation of *Rocky Horror* had eclipsed the original stage version for well over 20 years, thanks in no small part to the peculiar shadow cast phenomenon – dedicated groups of fans organising themselves into faithful replicas of the film's ensemble and meticulously re-enacting the entire picture as it was simultaneously projected onto a movie screen behind them – with which it had become solely associated. In the eyes of most American cinemagoers, many of whom would have been unaware that the film itself had in fact been preceded by a hugely successful live musical play in London, LA and Sydney, this extraordinary amalgamation of filmed image and synchronised onstage mimicry had become the bastardised definition of *The Rocky Horror Show*.

Producer Jordan Roth – who mounted the Broadway revival by arrangement with Christopher Malcolm, Howard Panter, Richard O'Brien and the now firmly established Rocky Horror Company – acknowledged the enduring significance of the show on the pop-culture zeitgeist in his programme notes for the production's glossily produced souvenir brochure:

'*Rocky Horror* has been an important, life-expanding rite-of-passage for a lot of people. I took it as a great responsibility that we were given this opportunity to take it to the next level and create the ultimate production.

'*Rocky* didn't start as a big Broadway musical that became smaller,' Roth went on for the benefit of the unacquainted majority. 'It began as a small underground event that had a life of its own and grew larger. I wanted to give our audience a *Rocky* they had never seen before and theatre like they've never experienced; an event that is powered by the audience's energy.'

In the same piece, director Christopher Ashley, a devoted *Rocky Horror* groupie since adolescence ('The show has been permanently embedded in his psyche since the age of 14,' the programme declared), expressed his personal desire to put Richard O'Brien's ever-relevant 'Don't dream it, be it' concept at the centre of the production. '*Rocky* was such a formative experience for me,' he enthused. 'The idea that you can be whatever you want and let your imagination run wild is incredibly exciting.

'The notion that you can change and re-invent your life was very important to me when I was growing up. We all have options to explore, whether it's whom we sleep with or how we dress. It's all up to us.'

Although the new Broadway adaptation would make no attempt to emulate the distinguished screen version in terms of design – unlike a multitude of previous independent US productions – the marketing for the revival would cunningly use the film's recognised cult following to its advantage. Flyers and press ads would tease potential audiences and fans of the film with provocative statements such as 'You're *all* virgins to us' and 'You haven't seen it until you've seen it live,' while the show's traditional bloody font logo was slyly amended to feature an open mouth in place of the letter 'O' in the word 'Show' above an upright silver microphone with the word 'Live' written down it vertically in red block lettering.

Other crowd-comforting references to the show's celebrated celluloid counterpart were cleverly incorporated into the production by way of David Rockwell's incredible set design. Prior to the opening number, the show's Phantoms, attired as 1950s style audience members, alongside a number of similarly-dressed mannequins to infer the illusion of a larger crowd, occupied two front sections of theatre seating cleverly built into the set. During a brief overture, they would excitedly leap from their seats to recite the familiar 'Give me an "R"' chant often employed by the MC at midnight screenings of *The Rocky Horror Picture Show*, and encourage the audience to join in, before the seats themselves hydraulically flipped over to form a flat front portion of the actual performance area. This innovation served the dual purpose of cleverly referencing *Rocky's* late night double feature origins while at the same time acknowledging the famously interactive nature of the *Rocky Horror* movie.

Aware that most New York audience members would now be far more familiar with the piece as a film than as a live musical, several uses of filmed imagery were wittily integrated into the staging. Consequently, the first appearance of Brad (Jarrod Emick) and Janet (Alice Ripley) would be by way of a short black and white movie projected onto a huge upstage screen. The couple, standing outside their local church and joyously waving off their unseen newly-married high school friends, exited the picture at the side of the screen at the precise moment the living, breathing actors emerged from behind it. The illusion that the characters had left their own personal motion picture and crossed into the real world was, therefore, not only in keeping with the B-movie roots of the show's concept, but also an astute way of helping the regular midnight groupies of the *Picture Show* to accept that their beloved celluloid heroes had indeed left the screen and come to life.

This opening motif would be cleverly bookended by another specially-shot piece of film, projected during the Narrator's final 'And crawling on the planet's face ...' speech at the end of the show. This sequence showed Brad and Janet wandering through the teeming streets of present day Times Square, in their skimpy 'Floorshow' outfits, and pushing the wheelchair-bound Dr Scott through crowds of uninterested passers-by.

For his imaginative reworking of the pivotal creation scene, David Rockwell devised a bizarre metal framework onto which was secured the lifeless figure of Frank-n-Furter's unborn creature. The frame unfolded to form a large ring with Rocky, dressed head to toe in a strange sterile one-piece contamination-proof diaphanous polyester bio-suit, strapped to it in an X-shaped spread-eagled position – suggesting an odd *avant-garde* approximation of Leonardo Da Vinci's famous 'Vitruvian Man' – while the Phantoms plugged an assortment of umbilical tubes and wires into various practical sockets in his weird, though clearly scientific, attire. Accompanied by a spectacular strobe lighting effect, the framework would then be hoisted into the air by a chain and spun like a gyroscope as the band struck up the introduction to 'The Sword of Damocles'. With the gossamer bio-suit swiftly stripped away in a heartbeat, Frank-n-Furter's beautiful new creation would be unveiled in all of his flawless, oiled and glittered, perfection. However, as David C Woolard revealed in the March 2001 issue of *Entertainment Design* magazine, Christopher Ashley had actually intended for Rocky to be completely nude for his initial appearance. Pointing out that this would require actor Sebastian LaCause to be totally unclothed for the entirety of his first musical number – impractical, undignified and distracting in all the wrong ways – Woolard's suggested a 'birth sac' covering the character's nether regions, providing the director with his desired 'umbilical cord moment' while at the same time preserving the actor's modesty.

The flashy, overindulgent production values – pretty much mandatory for a major Broadway extravaganza, but slightly over-the-top and previously unnecessary for *The Rocky Horror Show* – were never more perfectly evident than in the formidable laser weapon wielded by the traitorous Riff Raff's at the show's climax. Traditionally depicted as a hand gun – such as a flashing toy store ray gun (in accordance with the cheap sci-fi movie values of the show's source material), a modified super-soaker sprayed silver or the film's 'American Gothic'-inspired chrome trident – David Rockwell's Broadway variation was nothing short of a high-tech interplanetary military field-gun emplacement. Rolled onto the stage, the cumbersome contraption would be literally mounted by Riff Raff, who straddled its considerable girth and then held onto its bicycle-style handlebars in order to unleash its deadly rays of anti-matter.

As with the 1990 *Rocky* revival in London's West End, producers of the new Broadway version would feel understandably pressured to employ a few recognisable names amongst the ensemble. The most familiar of these were '60s and '70s talk show legend Dick Cavett in the role of the Narrator and rock star Joan Jett (born Joan Marie Larkin), most famous for her hit 1981 cover (with her band the Blackhearts) of 'I Love Rock 'n' Roll' – originally recorded by British glam rock group Arrows in 1975 – making her Broadway acting debut as Columbia. Just as Little Nell had been allowed and encouraged to draw on her own personality for the part – ultimately making her the effervescent, squeaky, sequined, tap-dancing groupie adored by *Rocky Horror* fans the world over – so did Jett; which naturally skewed the character in an entirely different direction.

Clad in leather cut-offs, chains and fishnet, the shaven-headed and husky-voiced Jett made Frank-n-Furter's favourite groupie more an archetypal rock chick, while the character's trademark 'Time Warp' tap routine was summarily eschewed in favour of a more apposite (for Jett's Columbia) electric guitar solo.

Contractual restrictions would prevent Jett, still a prolific recording artist, from being involved with the production's cast soundtrack – understudy Kristen Lee Kelly provided Columbia's vocals for the album – although the recording would actually lose very little as a result, apart from Jett's aforementioned 'Time Warp' guitar solo and the opportunity for promoters to use her name to help sell the disc.

Cavett's unparalleled experience, laid-back conversational style of chat and innate quick wit (he had enjoyed a brief stand-up career in the early '60s) would stand him in good stead for effortlessly dealing with *Rocky*'s customary audience talkback, while immediately getting the crowd on his side. He did, however, develop a tendency to deviate from the script, sometimes for extended periods of time, particularly during his opening monologues at the top of both acts, in order to gossip and joke with the audience about current affairs, politics and assorted unrelated topics. It was a habit that, far from the Narrator's usual mandate of quickly silencing hecklers and keeping the narrative flowing, could painfully slow the action at times.

A curious casting choice perhaps was that of outspoken stand-up comedienne Lea DeLaria – whose 1993 appearance on *The Arsenio Hall Show* had been generally proclaimed the first appearance by an openly gay comic on a late night US talk show – in the role of Eddie/Dr Scott. The stocky DeLaria had no problem playing a masculine role – 'Twice as macho as Meat Loaf ever dreamed of being' was how local gay publication *New York Blade News* described her performance – and would wring every ounce of comedy from her forceful portrayal of Dr Everett Scott, who, with a single sinister leather gauntlet, black eye-patch and aggressively over-the-top German accent, might be best described as Dr Strangelove-plus. Nonetheless, her obviously female voice would prove bewildering to some, particularly those listening to the subsequent cast album without having seen the show and wondering why Meat Loaf's part from the movie was being sung by a woman.

In her biography for the show's playbill, the actress was quoted as wanting to thank director Christopher Ashley 'for helping her realise her life's dream to become one of Broadway's leading men.'

As Magenta, the husky-toned and shapely Daphne Rubin-Vega, known primarily for creating the role of HIV-positive heroin addict Mimi Marquez in the original New York Theatre Workshop and Broadway productions of *Rent* – Jonathan Larson's contemporary reworking of Puccini's *La Boheme* – complemented both Joan Jett's rock chick version of Columbia and gravel-voiced Raul Esparza's elegantly gothic and strangely sophisticated Riff Raff; while, with his striking peroxide blond flat-top and spasmodic facial twitches, the immensely confident and compelling Tom Hewitt put his own wildly unpredictable spin on the character of Frank-n-

Furter, a performance that would earn him the honour of a Tony Award nomination.

Sue Blane and Richard Hartley would receive fitting acknowledgements in the Broadway production's playbill as the show's original costume designer and musical orchestrator respectively. However, David C Woolard's take on the characters' costumes, evidenced in particular by Joan Jett's American punk interpretation of Columbia, was markedly different from Blane's in a number of ways. The post-apocalyptic, cyberpunk look of *Rocky*'s contamination-proof birth-suit, along with a generous use of wet-look vinyl, particularly on the Phantoms' predominantly black outfits and Frank-n-Furter's lustrous green lab gown, called to mind the visual sense of *The Matrix* (1999) and comparable modern science fiction films.

Whereas the scripted character of Frank-n-Furter – not to mention his indelible iconic status in stage and film musical history – provided a fairly fixed blueprint as to the nature of his general attire, dissimilarities between Woolard's costume designs and those of Sue Blane were predominantly noticeable in their style. Frank's fondness for fishnet stockings, high heels and ladies lingerie was still very much in evidence – and rightly so – but for the most part Woolard avoided Blane's softer approach in favour of a more aggressive edge, in keeping with the newly-added ostentatious Broadway boldness of the piece.

The time-honoured lace frontage of Frank-n-Furter's tatty sequinned basque, for example, was spurned in favour of seven short buckled straps that smartly adorned the front of a spangled item of impeccably-constructed refined corsetry. Further straps connected this glittery red and black garment to the studded collar that replaced the character's more customary pearl necklace. The peroxide flat-top enhanced the up-to-date fashion-conscious masculinity of the character, duly distancing it from the dark-curled locks of Tim Curry's possibly overly-familiar screen interpretation; while intentionally asymmetrical stockings (with traditional tight mesh on one leg and larger-holed designer netting on the other) provided a mismatched look that helped to symbolise Frank's unbalanced personality.

The designer's apparent fondness for buckled straps was also in evidence on the front of Riff Raff's waistcoat, suggesting a weirdly quirky straitjacket motif; while, in addition to the one worn by Tom Hewitt, Frank's beautifully constructed 'Sweet Transvestite' costume would have to be completely duplicated for each of the actors portraying male Phantoms (of which there would usually be three) as they taunted and mocked the distressed and confused Brad during 'Once in a While'. Appearing first in facsimiles of Janet's unquestionably feminine 1950s dress, ostensibly to provide tender backing vocals, the Phantoms then showed their true colours by perceptibly deepening their singing voices and tearing away their girlie frocks to reveal disturbing replicas of their extraterrestrial master's sleazily subversive apparel.

Appropriately, Magenta and Columbia, who would sing 'Science Fiction Double Feature' as a duet at the top of the show, were dressed for the number in crimson commissionaire-style uniforms with short pleated black skirts, opaque black tights, red pill box hats and large hand-held flashlights. This bell-hop look deviated dramatically from the Usherette's traditional button-through pastel-shaded dress of most previous *Rocky Horror* productions but perfectly fitted the classic image of a 1940s or '50s cinema doorperson.

Reviews of the show's opening night were decidedly mixed. On the upside, *Newsday*'s Linda Winer gave it a fanatical rave. 'AMAZING. Broadway finally got a rock musical right,' she enthused; a dazzling opening line that could have been tailor-made for a theatre awning, and one that quickly made its way onto subsequent posters and flyers for the production. 'And – dammit Janet – it's not just any musical, but *The Rocky Horror Show*, the mother-ship for the supreme midnight movie and cross-dressing, cross-generational cult classic.

'Imagine the pressure. Producer Jordon Roth – who just may be the young blood Broadway so desperately craves – and director Christopher Ashley have managed to be true to the demented good nature of the urtext that spawned decades of zealots. More, the team also has justified going live with an experience that cannot be enjoyed at the movies, no matter how deliriously interactive the audience gets. Unlike most Broadway adaptations of movie brands, this is done with imagination and brains, not tracing paper and cynicism.'

In contrast to Winer's overwhelming exuberance, a number of critics chose to focus more negatively on the inescapably long shadow cast by the film's notorious cult following, while others ventured down the tired old route of reviewing the now customary participatory antics of the fans rather than the performance in question.

'While it's not a trend one wants to see spreading pell-mell up and down Broadway (it might be a bit distracting to have audiences shrieking "Asshole!" at *Copenhagen*'s Niels Bohr), the raucous involvement of the folks in the seats gives a daffy boost to the appeal of this loving revival of O'Brien's musical, a flimsy but nonetheless durable spoof of a schlocky horror pic dressed up in a glitter-rock frock,' wrote Charles Isherwood for *Variety*, happily yielding to the light-hearted spirit of it all; while his opening evaluation referenced *Variety*'s write-up of the 1975 New York production as an acknowledgement of the diluting effect that 25 years of changing social attitudes had inevitably had on the piece itself:

'When it opened on Broadway a quarter-century ago, *Variety* succinctly

8: I'M SURE YOU'RE NOT SPENT YET

and colourfully described *The Rocky Horror Show* as "A garish, ear-assaulting musical put-on of pseudo-science and ambi-sex porno entertainment." Sounds fun, no? Twenty-five years on, Christopher Ashley's revival of Richard O'Brien's garish, ear-assaulting put-on of pseudo-science and ambi-sex porno entertainment is still quite a lot of fun; but it's not likely to send Mayor Rudolph Giuliani into a tizzy. Today, the musical nearly qualifies as wholesome family entertainment.'

'For many of those attending the revival of *The Rocky Horror Show*, which opened officially last night under Christopher Ashley's direction, these three-dimensional characters are merely effigies, like the plastic *Star Wars* action figures that accompany fast food purchases, stand-ins meant to recall the real thing," suggested the *New York Times*'s Ben Brantley, alluding to the Circle in the Square's collection of living breathing 'imposters' masquerading as the movie's legendary ensemble. 'The real thing, of course, is on celluloid,' he insisted. 'The cast of characters who live on and on in movie houses around the world in midnight showings of *The Rocky Horror Picture Show*. That's the 1975 cult film that was made from Richard O'Brien's cult stage musical that slayed 'em in London and got slayed on Broadway, where it has now been revived in a twenty-fifth anniversary production.'

'Think of the androgyny of Alice Cooper and early David Bowie meeting Peter Cushing and Hammer Films,' was Clive Barnes' on-the-nail summing up of the material in his otherwise rather indifferent two-star review for the *New York Post*; a write-up in which he noted that he had seen the original London production in the '70s. 'It was then bizarre, sweet and oddly charming,' he admitted, in a brief, but relatively accurate, potted history of the show's early years. 'Arriving on Broadway two years later in an ill-advised and pointless cabaret setting, it looked weird, preposterous and distinctly charmless, and went belly-up after 45 performances. But the movie, made the same year, managed to recapture something of the show's original ditsy naiveté, and developed its own dedicated following.'

The all-important charm of the original production had, according to Barnes' critique, been seemingly forgotten by the creators of the latest version: 'The current over-produced Broadway offering, directed by Christopher Ashley, clearly believes that nothing succeeds like excess and has piled encrustation upon ornamentation. For the unconverted, such as myself, it is all too much.'

Though far from a rave, however, Barnes' review did find time to praise a few of the performances, especially those of Frank-n-Furter's hapless young victims: 'Ripley and Emick are adorable as the none-too-reluctant lovers.'

Regardless of the generally mixed opinions of the critics themselves –

several questioned if the film's midnight groupies would be willing or able to afford the live version's hefty $79.50 ticket price – many commended the spirited cast, with Tom Hewitt, Jarrod Emick and, in particular, Alice Ripley, already a Broadway diva of considerable repute, emerging with a generous portion of the plaudits.

'Hewitt's hair is bleached blond, but otherwise his aptly luscious performance is evocative of Curry's mixture of flamboyant menace and snarling song,' declared *Variety*'s Charles Isherwood; while, for *USA Today*, Elysa Gardner wrote, 'As Frank, Tom Hewitt makes a glamorous and winningly droll drag queen,' and that, 'Jarrod Emick endows Brad with a forceful tenor and an endearing, deadpan jocularity, and Alice Ripley's Janet is a dizzy delight.'

'Jarrod Emick, with his Dick Tracy jaw and boy scout demeanour, makes a terrific, four-square Brad, while Alice Ripley is funny and sexy at the same time, not an easy accomplishment,' acknowledged Michael Kuchwara, drama critic for the Associated Press. 'Both show their considerable musical-comedy training, delivering their numbers with a skill that far outshines the material.'

'Alice Ripley as Janet stands out, not just for her delicious shuffle between coyness and lust, but also for the surprisingly seamless way in which she adapts her classically pure voice to the rude rhythms of the score,' said Fintan O'Toole for the *Daily News*, while *Variety*'s aforementioned Charles Isherwood described the actress herself as 'Pin-up pretty and dressed for the top of a wedding cake,' and her performance, 'Absolutely the freshest and funniest thing in the show; her wide-eyed comic asides as she traces Janet's transformation from sorority girl to sex kitten are priceless.'

Isherwood's assessment of Jarrod Emick's personification of Brad Majors brimmed with equal praise: 'Peering intently through square black frames that echo his square jaw, Emick is a model of '50s young American manhood and he's no slouch in gold leather heels either.

'They're the ones who really seem to be from another planet,' the incisive critic astutely observed of Brad and Janet, 'and they're played to perfection here.'

Curiously, in spite of the assertion by many that *The Rocky Horror Show* no longer had the power to shock or surprise desensitised and blasé 21st Century audiences, a few reviewers were unable to resist singling out a fairly mild and infinitesimally brief flash of bared female breasts during the show's second half. Dominantly straddling Rocky as 'Touch-a Touch-a Touch-a Touch Me', her lyrically powerful declaration of newfound sexual freedom, reached its sensual crescendo, Alice Ripley's Janet Weiss deftly unhooked the back of her bra with one hand and then swiftly held it aloft with the other; a decisively forthright action that physically embodied the character's symbolic liberation. With Rocky's hands at once grasping Janet's exposed breasts, and an immediate blackout plunging the theatre into momentary darkness, this barely perceptible moment was nevertheless criticised by some as being unnecessary or somehow out of context with the mood of the show.

That such an innocuous glimpse of naked female flesh could still get supposedly forward-thinking critics flustered was, given the show's playfully rebellious reputation, a positive thing; although, oddly enough, their somewhat prudish and uninformed viewpoint loses validity when one remembers Peter Blake's passionate comments about the grubby and grungy nature of the original King's Road production. Though not a sex show, as Richard O'Brien correctly reiterated on numerous occasions, *Rocky Horror* had always been naughty, sexy and rude. During its early years in particular, the show had never been ashamed of proudly exhibiting its fair share of partial nudity; a fact that seemed to be sometimes forgotten during its development from a tacky little rock show into a legitimate mainstream musical. In the first London production, for example, Columbia's rouged nipples would often be visible over the top of her loose-fitting low-cut top; while both she and Janet would wear the tiniest of bras for 'The Floorshow', over which their naked nipples would again be in plain sight.

According to Patricia Quinn on *The Rocky Horror Picture Show*'s DVD audio commentary, the mischievous Little Nell had always been a notorious exhibitionist, so her saucy habit of regularly flashing her intimate bits and bobs – several of her subsequent film roles involved an even greater level of unashamed nakedness – would probably have been entirely intentional. Similarly, while Susan Sarandon's famously impressive breasts managed to stay somehow well and truly contained by her hardworking brassiere (if ever an item of lingerie deserved stunt pay ...), Nell managed to brazenly reveal her nipples at a couple of moments during the film version too; once through a strategically placed slit in her pyjamas as she boldly scolds Tim Curry's Frank, and again during her opening verse of 'The Floorshow', when her sequinned corset evidently fails to fully restrain her ample assets.

Thus, thanks mostly to the skilful performance of the actress, the fairly harmless – though undeniably erotic – action of Alice Ripley's Janet boldly whipping off her bra, a mere heartbeat before a blackout completely obscured her implied seduction of Rocky Horror, was absolutely in accordance with the spirit of the show's innocently subversive past. Likewise, it was no more explicit or dirty than Barbara Windsor famously losing her bikini top during the family rated *Carry On Camping*'s fondly remembered early morning keep fit scene.

'I can complain that Alice Ripley's topless nanosecond is demeaning and gratuitous,' nit-picked the rather aptly-named Martin Denton in a short list of minor quibbles during his otherwise upbeat online review of the production for NYtheatre.com.

'Demeaning to whom?' would seem the most obvious question, especially given the final irony that years later, on an internet fan site for *Next to Normal* – a 2008 musical drama, for which she garnered overwhelming critical acclaim as well as the 2009 Tony Award for Best Performance by an Actress in a Musical – Alice Ripley divulged that the decision for Janet to cast off her top along with her inhibitions had in fact been her own. 'It was my idea for Janet to take off her bra,' the actress confessed casually, gamely addressing those excited fans who had joyfully boasted that they had seen her topless. 'Believe it or not, it was a character decision.'

Co-hosted by Nathan Lane and Matthew Broderick, the 55th Antoinette Perry Awards for Excellence in Theatre (commonly known as the Tony Awards) were broadcast by the CBS television network from New York's Radio City Music Hall on the evening of 3 June 2001. The Circle in the Square's production of *The Rocky Horror Show* was nominated in four categories – Best Revival of a Musical, Best Performance by a Leading Actor in a Musical (Tom Hewitt), Best Direction of a Musical (Christopher Ashley) and Best Costume Design (David C Woolard) – while the company performed a lively rendition of 'The Time Warp' as part of the ceremony.

In the end though, it was always going to be the year of *The Producers*. The smash hit musical adaptation of Mel Brooks' irreverent 1968 comedy film had opened to rave reviews on 19 April 2001 and had been nominated for 15 awards across 12 categories. It would go on to win 12 (one in each of its nominated classes), breaking the 37-year record held by Jerry Herman's and Michael Stewart's *Hello Dolly*, which had opened, rather poetically, at the same venue – the St James Theatre at 246 West 44th Street – and had won an astounding ten Tony Awards (including Best Musical) in 1964.

Thus, while it lost out, somewhat predictably, to *42nd Street* for Best Musical Revival, *The Rocky Horror Show* would be beaten by *The Producers* in all three of its other categories. Nathan Lane triumphed over his *The Producers* co-star Matthew Broderick (as well as *Rocky*'s Tom Hewitt) and accepted the Best Performance by a Leading Actor in a Musical gong for his celebrated portrayal of scheming theatrical entrepreneur Max Bialystock; Susan Stroman received the Best Direction of a Musical statuette, while her *The Producers* collaborator William Ivey Long took the Best Costume Design honour.

Though it eventually left the ceremony empty-handed, the very idea of a Tony Award-nominated *Rocky Horror* – one that had received positive reviews and spawned a slickly-produced cast recording – would have no doubt baffled the Big Apple's snooty theatrical establishment of 25 years previously, had they been watching from the antiseptic comfort of their care homes.

With the cast's contracts terminating in the summer of 2001, the producers momentarily resorted to a little unabashed stunt casting in order to help prolong public interest in the production. Thus, popular *Saturday Night Live* actress-comedienne-singer-impressionist Ana Gasteyer took over the role of Columbia; TV and Hollywood heart-throb Luke Perry (of *Beverly Hills, 90210* fame) briefly slipped into Brad's pristine undies; and political comedienne Kate Clinton commenced a week of Narrator duties at the beginning of July.

With Tom Hewitt and Raul Esparza both choosing to pursue other avenues, experienced Broadway leading man Terrence Mann joined the cast as Frank-n-Furter for the show's autumn leg, while Sebastian Bach, former lead vocalist with American heavy metal line-up Skid Row, took over as Riff Raff. Glossy new promotional posters, prominently featuring both these stars, were swiftly produced.

Soon, however, ominous global events would again have devastating repercussions on everything from the ever-precarious state of world peace and the worldwide economy to the relatively unimportant fate of a blithe Broadway musical.

When, on the morning of Tuesday 11 September 2001, militant Islamic extremists crashed two hijacked commercial passenger jets into the iconic Twin Towers of New York's World Trade Centre, ultimately reducing the entire structure and surrounding buildings to rubble and killing over 2,700 people, the world was irrevocably changed. In the immediate aftermath of the atrocities – the single most audacious act of extreme terrorism in history – US President George W Bush launched his famous War on Terror, while Rudolph (Rudy) Giuliani, then Mayor of New York City, at once urged his citizens to adopt a steadfast business-as-usual attitude as a message of defiance and reassurance to the watching world.

This policy included re-opening the city's theatres and entertainment venues as soon as possible – with particular emphasis on escapist musicals and optimistic comedies – in an effort to persuade the all-important tourist trade that New York was still a fun, safe and desirable destination. Fittingly, *The Rocky Horror Show* would be amongst the first productions to re-open.

Nevertheless, just as the economic effects of the 1990/91 Persian Gulf crisis and subsequent war had contributed significantly to the premature closure of the West End production at London's Piccadilly Theatre a decade earlier, it was widely perceived that irreversible damage had already been done, and with ticket sales failing to improve satisfactorily – despite a special programme of guest Narrators, which included Jerry

Springer, comedian Gilbert Gottfried, chat show host Sally Jessy Raphael and *avant-garde* illusionist duo Penn & Teller – the Broadway revival closed, after a respectable 437 performances, on Sunday 6 January 2002.

It may have taken a quarter of a century, but the original theatrical incarnation of *Rocky Horror* had at last acquitted itself and been proved worthy in the City that Never Sleeps.

The New Victoria Theatre, Woking, England; Saturday 14 July 2007. By introducing Christopher Luscombe, director of the latest UK production, as the man who had brought the show back from the dead, Richard O'Brien implied intriguing volumes about his suspected, but officially undeclared, opinion of the tour that had preceded it; particularly to overly curious *Rocky Horror* fans, ever eager to read all they could between the lines and then hypothesise endlessly on internet discussion boards.

The predecessor in question had been the much-publicised thirtieth birthday tour, known on posters and promotional material as *Richard O'Brien's Rocky Horror Big 30 Show* – presumably with the intention of the '30' being pronounced 'Three-Oh' as in, 'Uh oh, the Big Three-Oh' (which also conveniently rhymed with 'Show') as opposed to 'Thirty' (which did not) – with the word *'The'* conspicuously dropped from the title; the beginning of another annoyingly inexplicable marketing trend. After opening at the Churchill Theatre in Bromley on Friday 4 October 2002, the production toured the UK to record-breaking business for 14 successive months.

With the tour sponsored by Flares, a chain of 1970s-themed nightclubs, Sue Blane tailored her usual iconic costumes with an additional '70s twist incorporated here and there. Some of these modifications worked quite agreeably – for instance Janet in a pale lilac adaptation of her traditional pink dress and a corresponding Brad sporting a fetching wide-lapelled tuxedo with matching waistcoat, high-waisted flared trousers and a showy white ruffled shirt with dark bow tie – while others seemed to sit rather awkwardly with the usually timeless look of the piece. Probably the most conspicuous offender was the Usherette, whose white vinyl skirt and pink swirl-patterned baby-doll top proved too much of a deviation from the norm for many long-standing *Rocky* devotees, who soon made their feelings known via internet chat rooms and fan site forums. Whether or not these fan protestations made a difference would remain undisclosed, but, either way, within a few weeks the character's outfit was back to a more traditional pink front-buttoning cinema uniform; albeit one worn with tights (pantyhose) rather than the customary (and far more alluring) stockings and suspenders.

Other costume innovations, dictated by the restraining 1970s theme of the overall design, included a short hippie-style jacket with long light green fur and cheap store-bought deely-boppers for Columbia. The two girl Phantoms would both tease and support Janet during 'Touch-a Touch-a Touch-a Touch Me' – itself scored with an up-tempo '70s disco beat – while tackily attired in black net skirts and bras, forked tails and sparkling red devil horns.

In short, the initiative to acknowledge the show's origins by adding an obvious '70s retro look to the costumes had the adverse effect of merely dating a once ingeniously unique example of timeless brilliance by naively rooting it in history. What's more, an attempt to honour the genesis of the piece by switching 'Sweet Transvestite' and 'The Time Warp' back to their original, pre-'90s order within the narrative appeared to confuse and upset newer fans, many of whom had little or no knowledge of the show's background and continually evolving script. The situation proved unwinnable when, paradoxically, a subsequent U-turn several weeks into the run – most likely intended to rectify the situation by placing the songs back in their now more familiar film order – vexed purists of the original 1970s stage version.

Cast in the role of Frank-n-Furter for this Pearl Anniversary production was Jonathan Wilkes, an engaging young performer with a strong singing voice and a rascally wit. Born in the village of Baddeley Green in Staffordshire on 1 August 1978, Wilkes spent his formative years playing in and around the streets of nearby Hanley, city centre of Stoke-on-Trent; as an indirect result of which, being cast as Frank-n-Furter for the *Big 30* production would not be his first encounter with the weird and wonderful world of *The Rocky Horror Show*. During a local radio interview – as the tour paid a week-long visit to Stoke-on-Trent's Regent Theatre in January 2003 – he vividly recalled his incredulity (as a carefree, dirty-kneed, football-loving pre-teen) at witnessing scores of *Rocky* fans in fishnets and feathers heading *en masse* for the city's Theatre Royal in the late 1980s.

A keen footballer from an early age, Wilkes eventually abandoned his teenage ambition to play professionally when the allure of an entertainment-based vocation proved irresistible. A popular consensus seemed to be, however, that his career had been overshadowed in many ways by that of his lifelong friend Robbie Williams – who, after leaving boy band Take That in 1995, had gone on to achieve phenomenal superstardom as one of the world's most successful modern rock artists – which was a shame, given that Wilkes was fast becoming a talented and appealing entertainer in his own right.

On the tour's opening press night in Bromley, Williams – himself no stranger to the show's inimitable brand of participatory insubordination, having appeared as Rocky in the one-off charity performance at London's Duke of York's Theatre, opposite Anthony Head's Frank-n-Furter in 1995 – was amongst the crowd, offering fervent support to his friend and long-term housemate. When, as Wilkes entered for the laboratory scene, adorned in Frank's customary green surgical gown, torn fishnet stockings and platform heels, he was reportedly greeted with a cry of 'You are not coming back in the house dressed like that' from an unidentified heckler, fans instantly jumped to their own wishful conclusions regarding the likely identity of the culprit.

Eight months later, Williams joined the audience again as Jonathan Wilkes made his West End debut and *The Rocky Horror Show* began a fortnight's official birthday engagement at London's Queen's Theatre on 23 June 2003.

A natural joker, Wilkes clearly favoured an unrestrained comedic approach over edgy androgynous sensuality in his depiction of the character, playing it with exaggerated facial expressions and excessively effeminate mincing. Although castigated by some fans for supposedly having reduced Frank to the level of a camp pantomime dame (more Widow Twankey than Tim Curry perhaps), his tomfoolery proved popular with mainstream audiences, and the phenomenally profitable production purportedly broke the in-house box office record at a number of venues.

Amongst those reaping the financial benefits of this success was former King's Road Riff Raff and *Rocky Horror Picture Show* Transylvanian Perry Bedden, whose foresight to invest in the high-profile tour paid off handsomely. 'I actually made a lot of money out of that, as I was one of the backers for Chris Malcolm,' the actor declares cheerfully. However, he freely admits that he was not a fan of the creative approach taken by that particular incarnation of the show. 'I think it went downhill with the *Big 30* tour,' he confesses, echoing the sentiments of many aficionados that the Pearl Anniversary production, with its nightclub sponsorship, resultant drunken hen party target audience and barefaced encouragement of rowdy, over-the-top crowd interaction, had been marketed more as a party than a legitimate work of classic musical theatre, and had thus taken something of a lamentable backwards turn toward the broad end-of-the-pier-style frivolities of the show's 1980s incarnation. 'Jonathan Wilkes as Frank, goosing everyone on stage? Frank wouldn't do that,' Bedden concludes sorrowfully.

Another problem with the production from an artistic standpoint would be that of its sometimes debatable casting choices. With the principal ensemble largely made up of hard-working and talented professional thespians, a certain fanfare was made of the marketing ploy to have the Narrator played by different performers – some with very little prior dramatic experience – at different venues on the tour.

Whereas previous *Rocky Horror Show* productions had featured their fair share of TV soap performers – particularly in the UK and Australia – these were generally accomplished artists, whose acting abilities were not in doubt. The increasing popularity of so-called reality programmes such as *Big Brother*, on the other hand, had seen the rise of a rather more disturbing theatrical trend. The casting of these shows' ex-competitors – usually members of the general public from a non-entertainment background – in less than demanding two-dimensional pantomime roles was perhaps forgivable; but with the viewing public exasperatingly elevating such glorified game show contestants to celebrity status, promoters of more challenging stage productions also began to see their names as a profitable financial draw. Unfortunately, limited acting proficiency, coupled with a complete lack of the necessary skills and spontaneity required for dealing with the frequently riotous interaction from a typical *Rocky Horror* audience would often expose the shortcomings of such transparent and misguided stunt casting rather quickly.

While effectively encouraging multiple venue viewings, with devoted fans wanting to see as many different Narrators as they could, the casting of obviously inexperienced and unqualified players, as well as a variety of quiz show hosts, TV presenters, comedians and former politicians, was bound to result in performances of varying quality and merit. Nonetheless, even though it would be refreshing and easily perceptible whenever a genuine actor took the role for an engagement, those who emerged with the biggest plaudits were not always the most obvious. A case in point: the appointment of John Stalker, the Greater Manchester Constabulary's ex-Deputy Chief Constable, the second highest rank attainable in territorial British police forces, at certain venues was considered by some to be poetically sublime; akin to having a genuine criminologist recite the legendary plight of Brad and Janet and their fabled strange journey. Moreover, Stalker had occasionally hosted factual crime documentaries on UK television, further likening him to the immortal figure of Edgar Lustgarten.

Notwithstanding the judgement of its outspoken detractors, the thirtieth anniversary production had legitimate flashes of brilliance; the casting of Brad and Janet, for instance, crucial to the artistic veracity of any version, was quite superb. Fresh-faced, pretty and petite Katie Rowley Jones handled the all-important understated transition from small town repression to dominant emancipation with dexterous aplomb, while Jon Boydon's heroic broad shoulders and square-jawed confidence were unmistakably reminiscent of a young Christopher Malcolm in his King's Road glory days. In his capacity as Jonathan Wilkes' chief understudy, Boydon also proved remarkably adept at covering the part of Frank-n-Furter, and was later invited to assume the role permanently for several months on the European tour.

As Frank's enigmatic wheelchair-bound adversary Dr Everett Scott, the insanely energetic Drew Jaymson – with a cranium of wildly maniacal shock-headed grey hair, and looking as though he might have taken method acting to psychotically suicidal extremes by jamming his fingers into a live plug socket before each of his scenes – proved an outstanding fan favourite by deftly winning over many of those who had otherwise bad-mouthed the production as a whole. His inventive interpretation of Eddie, the archetypal rock 'n' roll Frankenstein's monster, as a twitchy schizoid zombie with independently functioning out-of-control mismatched body parts, was initially a masterwork of extreme physicality; one that, despite striking a definite chord with *Rocky* aficionados, appeared to have been puzzlingly toned down within a few weeks of the tour's opening.

Shortly after the stupendously successful *Rocky Horror Big 30 Show* – by all accounts the most profitable production yet mounted since the formation of the Rocky Horror Company – ended in the winter of 2003, Jonathan Wilkes, who had always appeared to be thoroughly enjoying himself on stage as Frank-n-Furter, assumed the role of Danny Zuko for a limited Christmas and New Year season of the musical *Grease* at the Palace Theatre in Manchester. When asked by autograph-seeking groupies at the stage door if he was enjoying being involved in another celebrated rock 'n' roll classic, he cheerfully replied in the affirmative; before quickly adding a touchingly honest footnote: 'But I'm missing Frank.'

After 14 years and no fewer than 15 productions across several countries, the thirtieth anniversary UK tour would prove to be Christopher Malcolm's swansong as director of *The Rocky Horror Show*, and indeed as a member of the Rocky Horror Company, the conglomerate custodian of the show's worldwide rights he had been instrumental in founding. Although the details surrounding the sudden cessation of his activities within the company would not be made public, speculative *Rocky* fans, always quick to jump to their own sensationalist conclusions, surmised (rightly or wrongly) that creative differences – possibly between Malcolm, whose experience and familiarity with the piece as a director would have been practically unrivalled by that time, and the show's author-composer – might have been a contributory factor.

Later, in his contribution to the programme notes for the Denton Affair, the 2006 UK *Rocky Horror* convention, Malcolm would provide – in a paragraph headed, rather portentously, 'DARKNESS HAS CONQUERED BRAD …' – a sincere and genuinely moving conclusion to his remarkable period of involvement with this landmark work of modern musical theatre: 'Personally I am very sad that my journey has ended. The show in all its incarnations was a backdrop for much that has happened in my everyday life, particularly through the last 15 years. I am also very unhappy that it finished on a sour note with a very close friendship of such long standing being ended, leaving me having to withdraw from the company that I helped bring into existence in 1989. I will say no more on this, as it's pointless to rake over cold embers, but I will say that the whole thing has profoundly affected my family's life since.'

While its accuracy would remain publically unconfirmed, one suggestion seemed to be that O'Brien had perhaps become disillusioned and irritated at the current intellectual and artistic state of the show, fearing, as did many of its most passionate and protective followers, that an archaic sense of cheap vulgarity – a throwback to the unsavoury superficiality of the '80s productions to which the show's author had expressed disdain – had again begun to infiltrate recent interpretations.

In an interview for Sydney's TEN News in 1998, in which he also proposed that the real secret of *Rocky*'s incredible longevity was without doubt the timeless potency of Richard O'Brien's music, a jovial Christopher Malcolm had condensed the show's primary subject matter into a single unambiguous holler directly into camera: 'Sex! It's true. It's about sex.' A humorous off-the-cuff statement it may have been – as well as a sure-fire way of selling the show to the masses – but this tongue-in-cheek proclamation would seem to be at odds with Richard O'Brien's aversion to the profusion of tacky smut and crudity that some directors have added to their productions of the show.

Anthony Topham's memories of cast performance notes, dictated by the author himself during the European tour, include his surprise at finding himself on the receiving end of a personal rebuke pertaining to this very issue: 'He criticised my Eddie for having groped Columbia's crotch. He told us not to touch the genital area, as the show's not about explicit sex. Which seemed strange to us, as we thought it was all about sexual freedom.'

From O'Brien's perspective, the prevention of such blunt crudity and the preservation of the show's artistic integrity and quality had been the Rocky Horror Company's raison d'être from the outset, and there was a feeling amongst some that the *Big 30* production, despite its financial success and nightly standing ovations, had perhaps betrayed this principle.

A number of fans had also noted that Christopher Malcolm's direction was maybe feeling a little formulaic and unoriginal of late, an argument given a certain credence by Anthony Topham's recollection that there had been a rigidly-adhered-to pantomime-style rehearsal formula in place when he joined the cast of the long-running European version in the November of 2004: 'By that time, Chris Malcolm knew he wouldn't be involved, so he became associate director, and he saw a couple of rehearsals and shows.' Topham confirms that, despite Malcolm still being credited officially as director of the tour, the staging for most scenes was by that point being handled by resident director Paul Winterford.

Whatever the reasons for his untimely exit, Christopher Malcolm's fundamental contribution to the evolutionary development and continued unwavering success of *The Rocky Horror Show* cannot be understated. From initiating the role of Brad Majors in Jim Sharman's inaugural production at the Theatre Upstairs in 1973 to being one of the first to recognise the potential of a major 1990s West End revival, his foresight and belief in the show was paramount to the formation of the Rocky Horror Company and helped lay the groundwork for every future production of this unparalleled work of theatre.

Like Richard O'Brien, Jim Sharman, Richard Hartley, Brian Thomson, Sue Blane, Tim Curry, Michael White, Lou Adler and an elite handful of others, Christopher Malcolm is deservedly assured an eternal place at the heart of the show's enduring legend; and, while he politely declined more than one invitation to be interviewed for this book, his heartfelt remarks for the Denton Affair's convention programme offer a perfect and poignant conclusion to his momentous chapter in *Rocky Horror* history:

'Many things have had to change, and now I am through the pain it cost me I would add here that I have no regrets at any decisions I made on behalf of the company and the shows I have been directly responsible for. I have enjoyed every production for what they turned out to be, and I have so many memories and so many friends made during those years that I shall cherish for the rest of my life. Nobody can take that away from me.'

Christopher Malcolm sadly passed away at the age of 67 on 15 February 2014. In addition to his unquestionable repute as a theatrical producer – not to mention that hugely important place in *Rocky Horror* history – he would leave behind a considerable legacy of acting roles in theatre, film and television, with appearances in TV shows – such as *Only Fools and Horses* and *Absolutely Fabulous* – and movies – notably *Superman III* (1983), *Labyrinth* (1985) and as rebel pilot Zev Senesca (Rogue 2) in 1980's *The Empire Strikes Back*, the second film in the original *Star Wars* trilogy – being remembered particularly fondly.

Joint producers of the *Rocky Horror Big 30 Show* had been listed in the tour programme as Christopher Malcolm Ltd (Malcolm's latest production company) and Ambassador Theatre Group in association with SPZ Entertainment Group (the company of Trevor Horn and Jill Sinclair) and Matthew Mitchell Ltd. Subsequent to Malcolm's 2004 departure, Sinclair – who had co-founded VIVA! Theatre Productions with Malcolm in 1986 – joined Howard Panter and Richard O'Brien as the third member of Rocky Horror Company's board, until an accident at home sadly left her in a prolonged coma. After that, O'Brien and Panter would remain the company's only recognised directors.

Production credits for the self-proclaimed 'Brand Spanking New Production' of *The Rocky Horror Show* in 2006 would be Howard Panter for Ambassador Theatre Group, David Ian for Live Nation (Theatrical) UK

8: I'M SURE YOU'RE NOT SPENT YET

Ltd, SPZ Entertainment Group and Rocky Horror Company.

Panter's formidable Ambassador Theatre Group, formed in 1992 with his business partner and future wife Rosemary Squire, had become a major force to be reckoned with in little over a decade. In December 2009, Panter and Squire would be named top of the *Stage* newspaper's annually compiled list of the one hundred most powerful people in UK theatre, while their 2009 acquisition of rival conglomerate Live Nation's UK venues for a reported £90 million would create, according to the *Stage*'s news and opinion editor Alistair Smith, 'a new theatrical superpower; the largest theatre operator of the modern era.'

'In the regions, especially, it dwarfs all competition,' Smith declared of ATG's extraordinary position, emphasising that the purchase had been 'the largest theatre deal since Andrew Lloyd Webber bought his London venues in 2000.'

In view of his alleged disapproval of the tawdry production values and superficiality of the show's thirtieth anniversary incarnation, it was widely accepted that Richard O'Brien was now keener than ever for the adoption of a serious back-to-basics approach for the next major *Rocky Horror* revival. Hence the most important gap left by Christopher Malcolm's exit was that of a suitable director; one who could not only bring a required edginess and an exciting fresh perspective to the proceedings but whose ideas and understanding of the script would, presumably, concur with those of its author.

The man chosen for the task was Christopher Luscombe. A graduate of Pembroke College, Cambridge, where he had studied English, Luscombe had been a member of the Cambridge Footlights – the eminent university theatrical society that had famously nurtured such luminaries as Peter Cook, Stephen Fry, Hugh Laurie, *The Hitchhikers Guide to the Galaxy* creator Douglas Adams and future *Monty Python* legends Graham Chapman, John Cleese and Eric Idle – before pursuing an acting career. Having gained considerable experience in London's West End, as well as with the Royal Shakespeare Company, National Theatre and UK repertory companies, he had turned to directing, helming a number of lauded productions, including the 2003 touring version of the Andrew Lloyd Webber and Don Black musical *Tell Me on a Sunday* (starring Denise Van Outen); Bath Theatre Royal's 2004 tour of Oscar Wilde's *The Importance of Being Earnest*; the musical horror-comedy *Little Shop of Horrors* for the West Yorkshire Playhouse; and *The Shakespeare Revue* at London's Vaudeville Theatre. These swiftly gained him a reputation as a versatile and noteworthy director.

With the first venues announced – the commencement of the tour scheduled for Thursday 16 March 2006 at the Theatre Royal, Brighton – the 'Brand Spanking New Production' angle was clearly being hammered home on the newly designed *Rocky Horror* promotional material. A likeness of Janet Weiss (with artwork credited to Leigh Gallagher) wearing a floral-patterned 1950s party dress, rather reminiscent of the pop-art style used to publicise the 1990 West End production, proudly adorned posters and flyers. A conspicuous departure from the *Big 30* tour's poster image of a slightly out of focus Frank-n-Furter lasciviously licking his parted lips, the return to a simple cartoon rendition of the show's I young heroine was a further indication of O'Brien's desire for a less brazen approach. Although often fun (for audiences and advertisers alike) to focus on the deliciously devious Frank-n-Furter – a seductive villain will always be irresistible in any context – it can be easy to forget that the show's primary protagonists are actually Brad and Janet. Later posters would enhance this view further with a photographic representation of the actors currently portraying the fated young couple in the production itself, as ads for some of the early '90s tours had done.

Speculative and largely uninformed gossip regarding potential casting for the production quickly hit the message boards on the UK *Rocky Horror* fan club's internet site. With the announcement of a new tour, forums that had been quiet for months suddenly shuddered back to life. As always, it seemed probable that the producers would seek at least one famous name in order to drive ticket sales, leading some to conclude – albeit a little prematurely – that a celebrity Frank might be on the cards. Jason Donovan's performance had, after all, proved to be a winner with both die-hard *Rocky* fans and general theatregoers. One rumour circulated by frenzied fans was that Glaswegian singer-songwriter Darius Danesh (born Darius Campbell-Danesh and sometimes known simply as Darius), who had shot to fame after appearances on the reality-documentary *Popstars* and talent show *Pop Idol* on UK television in 2001, and subsequently enjoyed successful West End runs as Billy Flynn in the musical *Chicago* in 2005 and 2006, was a possible candidate.

Nevertheless, director Christopher Luscombe's preferred choice was, at the time, relatively unknown but undoubtedly tailor-made for the role of the alluring alien scientist. Smooth, velvet-voiced and impossibly charismatic, Chicago-born David Bedella had garnered considerable attention – and the 2004 Laurence Olivier Award for Best Actor in a Musical – for his creation of the dual role of Jonathan Weiruss (the Warm-up Man) and Satan in the original production of the Richard Thomas and Stewart Lee show *Jerry Springer: The Opera*, a bizarre and irreverent musical satire that had courted controversy – for its abundance of coarse language, sexual content and alleged blasphemy – almost from its inception. Bedella's other recent credits included the transsexual title character in a London production of *Hedwig and the Angry Inch* and, in addition to supporting roles in movies such as Oliver Stone's 2004 epic *Alexander* and Christopher Nolan's *Batman*

8: I'M SURE YOU'RE NOT SPENT YET

Begins in 2005, he had become familiar to British television audiences as Dr Carlos Fashola in the sixth and seventh seasons of the BBC's fashionable medical drama series *Holby City*.

As fate would have it, the actor had appeared several years previously in a US production of *The Rocky Horror Show* and was, as a result, already rather familiar with the character of Frank-n-Furter. 'It was way back in 1991 in Connecticut,' he explains. 'There was a cast from New York who was performing the show there. Drew Scott Harris was directing it and also appearing as Frank. I had auditioned for him for a different show, and he asked me to cover Frank instead, as he couldn't play the last two matinees.'

This production would eventually be allowed to continue for a little longer than originally planned, thanks to a chance encounter with an undisputed *Rocky Horror* legend, as Bedella illuminates. 'Unbeknownst to me, Meat Loaf saw our production and, as a result, wanted to invest to keep it touring. He also decided to do a pre-show, which was great fun for us, if a bit hard on the actor playing Eddie. Can you imagine having to go on and sing "Whatever Happened to Saturday Night" after Meat Loaf had just hit it out of the park in the pre-show? Horrible.'

Bedella remembers that touring *Rocky Horror* with Meat Loaf for four months – sharing a dressing room and hanging out – was genuinely thrilling, as it gave him the rare opportunity of getting to know the man behind the myth: 'In that time I got to see the real guy; the dad who made peanut butter and jelly sandwiches for his kids and made time to brush his daughter's hair. He had his own musicians with him and his wife sang back-up, and at times it felt like being on the road with a rock band.'

Reflecting on this US tour, Bedella's only real regret was not being allowed to fully explore the character of Frank and, most importantly, infuse it with facets of his own pulsating personality. 'I'd seen the *Picture Show*, so the initial characterisation was based on Tim Curry, with a posh English accent,' he confesses, a little guiltily. 'I'm embarrassed to say that I copied Tim, but I was young.

'The director had very specific ideas about the varied personalities and colours of the character. He wanted each scene to represent a different Hollywood *femme fatale*. He used to say, "Okay, you play this scene like Joan Crawford, this one as Bette Davis, or Gloria Swanson's Norma Desmond, or whoever." He missed the fact that the intrinsic attraction of Frank is that *everyone* finds him sexy; even the men in the audience who may have never before considered such a thing. He's just such a sexy guy; and you can't be that if you're imitating Bette Davis. Well, at least, I couldn't.'

In the years that followed, Bedella came to recognise that the character, by its very nature, could be allowed to soar only if the actor let himself out, 'as opposed to Tim or some other fabulous diva'; and although he had auditioned unsuccessfully for the thirtieth anniversary UK tour in 2002, he brought everything he had learned during his time playing personality-driven dominant roles in *Hedwig and the Angry Inch* and *Jerry Springer: The Opera* to his audition for the 2006/07 production, and set about injecting something of himself into the role.

'I sang the finale from *Hedwig*,' the actor declares proudly, revealing how he used the audition to skilfully seduce *The Rocky Horror Show*'s eagerly receptive new director. 'I started by telling them a story. I said, "I want to do a song from *Hedwig* and it's important you know the context." So I gave them the information and finished by saying, "It's all about freeing those around you to be the most they can be. In the end it's yourself you're really freeing," under which the pianist had started the intro – we'd rehearsed this. At the end, Chris Luscombe seemed very excited and, I think, impressed. He said to me, "This is truly not necessary, but purely as a treat for me, would you sing one of Frank's songs." He's rather clever about how he words things. I sang "Sweet Transvestite" and it went down very well.'

Having evidently won over his prospective director in the first instance, however, the actor was not considered to be famous enough – in the eyes of those who controlled the money – and would ultimately have a painfully long wait before hearing whether or not he would be cast: 'The next day I got a text from Chris, which read, "Dear David. After seeing your show tonight, I believe in my heart that you're my Frank and I will fight to have you." I thought then that I'd got the role, but it took another four months for them to actually offer. I'm afraid it was the old story of producers thinking that a "name" in the role is the only way to make a show work. They kept telling me "Don't accept anything else without telling us first, but hold tight as we're still looking for a 'star'." Wow, how nice. They were looking at celebs and keeping me hanging on; so, after months of this, I drew the line and told them my waiting was over. Either we had a deal or I was moving on, and in the end they gave it to me.'

Theorising that backers might favour the not-unheard-of alternative of casting a recognised celebrity as Brad or Janet, other fan whisperings posited that Kym Marsh, a former member of the manufactured pop group Hear'Say, the creation of which had been documented by the *Popstars* TV series, had auditioned for the *Rocky* tour's producers while she had been appearing alongside previous Frank-n-Furter Jonathan Wilkes in the 2005/06 pantomime *Mother Goose* at Stoke-on-Trent's Regent Theatre.

Suspense and speculation were ended shortly thereafter with the official announcement that Suzanne Shaw (born Suzanne Crowshaw in Bury, Lancashire, in September 1981) had been signed to play the role. Another ex-member of Hear'Say, the attractive singer-actress had most recently been seen as Snow White – opposite Toyah Willcox as the Wicked Queen and none other than Richard O'Brien, making his pantomime debut as the Mirror King (and surreptitiously shoehorning a crowd-pleasing rendition of 'The Time Warp' in amongst the poisoned apples and diamond-mining dwarfs of the age-old fairy tale) – in Milton Keynes.

Shaw's ill-fated relationship with former UK Frank-n-Furter Darren Day, whom she met while appearing in the 2003 stage production of *Summer Holiday*, had resulted in the birth of their son Corey in 2004; a rare example of Janet actually having Frank's baby.

Amongst his earliest and fondest memories of the rehearsal period, David Bedella counts his first meeting with *Rocky Horror* costume guru Sue Blane, for whom he has the utmost respect: 'I'd met with Chris at the Globe to talk about the concept and how we both saw it, and then I went off to the Ambassador Theatre Group's offices – which back then were at the Duke of York's Theatre – to meet Sue, so that we could discuss the look of Frank.' After climbing the stairs to the Duke of York's second floor lobby, the actor found himself confronted by three tables – one of which, he remembers, had a tea set on it, while the others were covered with drawings and samples of fabric – and, of course, Sue herself: 'I became acutely aware of the fact that I was in the presence of the woman who'd created iconic theatre history. I felt a little overwhelmed, but she was lovely and we just chatted about the look and feel of Frank. We made all the big choices and created it there and then. Sue asked my opinion of different fabrics and, when I had chosen one she said, "Yes, brilliant; and I think we should use this piece to trim it," and we did the whole thing. It was wonderful.'

Bedella also recollects the cast's first encounter with Richard O'Brien, always keen to offer his support and advice: 'He came to the first day of rehearsal; gave us his blessing. We all had a laugh with him and then he went. He's such a social animal. He devours people, you know, but in a good way. He came on the road quite often and was there for the first night in many cities. He made himself at home in my dressing room. I got used to having him there; wearing his assortment of spectacular outfits and make-up, and always strumming his guitar.'

Presented as a fascinating two-page spread in the tour's souvenir brochure was the transcript of a conversation between O'Brien and Luscombe that took place during the show's rehearsal period. In this, Luscombe confirmed that while it was his intention for the production to appeal to new audiences he was equally keen to honour the hardcore fans who, he acknowledged, were extremely protective of the show. Wisely recognising the value of the fans' opinions, and realising that their initial reactions and invaluable insight could be creatively beneficial to director and cast alike, Luscombe contacted TimeWarp's Stephanie Freeman with a view to her inviting a select number of long-term fan club members along to an early non-costumed run-through.

There would be anxiety on both sides, with the players – most of them new to the show themselves – eager to please, and the fans – notoriously defensive and opinionated about their favourite obsession – nervously edgy.

Upon arriving at the rather inconspicuous rear entrance of the Union Chapel on Compton Avenue in the London district of Islington, the privileged and excited few were shown to the building's charming old-fashioned Studio Theatre; a moderately-sized space with a lot of character, often used for the purposes of theatrical rehearsal.

Facsimiles of classic science fiction movie posters, comic book adverts for Charles Atlas's Dynamic Tension bodybuilding programme and illustrated documents relating to all aspects of the script's infinite implications decorated the walls of the rehearsal room; an instant indication that the man the producers had entrusted with the creative advancement and continued survival of the *Rocky Horror* legend had an unmistakable understanding of the material. There was little doubt that here was a director who got it.

It is therefore somewhat ironic to learn that Luscombe's prior knowledge of the show's subplots and abundant pop-culture allusions was actually very limited. This level of intense research is simply typical of the way he would approach any directorial project. 'I'd never seen the stage show or the film before my involvement,' he freely confesses, insisting that, while such an admission might horrify a lot of fans, this unfamiliarity proved beneficially liberating and allowed him the freedom to approach the piece completely objectively, without pre-conceived ideas or baggage. 'I was able to immerse myself in the show and explore every aspect with a fresh perspective, long before we even got into a rehearsal room.'

Also in attendance at the run-through was Richard O'Brien – getting his own first taste of Luscombe's interpretation of his work – the presence of whom instantly increased the adrenaline levels of performers and spectators.

Despite the absence of sets and costumes for this non-dress rehearsal (although, wisely seizing every opportunity to practice in them, David Bedella did wear his high heels), Luscombe decided to explain very little to the fervent assembly beforehand, allowing them instead to use their imaginations to put the pieces together for themselves. He did admit, however, that, while his objective had been for the invited fans to give the rookie *Rocky* cast a pre-tour taste of the audience participation they would soon be subjected to on a nightly basis, he thought it might now be more worthwhile and enjoyable for them simply to watch and appraise the company's variation of the material and its characters.

8: I'M SURE YOU'RE NOT SPENT YET

Accordingly, the delighted devotees observed for the most part in reverential silence – beaming like thrilled children being treated to an exclusive tour of Santa's workshop – while intermittently throwing in the odd cry of 'Asshole' and 'Slut' at the appropriate moments, along with other examples of the most common talkback lines; most often at the expense of the visibly nervous Michael Aspel, the urbane and unassuming British radio and TV personality who, in just over a week, would have the uneasy honour of being the brand new production's first Narrator.

As the host of the UK version of the TV show *This Is Your Life* from 1987 until its cancellation in 2003, Aspel had been regularly seen clutching the large red book traditionally associated with the long-running programme's presenter; a prop that no doubt would have elicited a slew of predictable one-liners from *The Rocky Horror Show*'s faithful followers. Hence, as a preventative measure, Aspel would be one of the few Narrators not to carry the character's customary leather-bound dossier; a dossier that, like a kind of reassuring crutch, would typically have had his lines printed in it. Without this comfort blanket, the actor, unlike some Narrators, would have to be doubly sure that he had all of his scripted monologues memorised. Instead of the book, Aspel's Narrator would enter, dressed in a long brown raincoat, holding a newspaper, which he would hand to Janet – for the purpose of shielding her head from the rain – at the end of his first speech.

Fan reaction to the rehearsal was overwhelmingly positive. To their collective relief, the musical arrangements were completely true to the organic spirit of Richard Hartley's original intentions, while the characters had clearly been thought about, discussed at length and developed accordingly.

It was clear from the very beginning that Christopher Luscombe was coming at the piece from an entirely different angle than, say, Robin Lefevre, director of the 1990 London production, who to Zalie Burrow's recollection had spent very little time on character development: 'He was very laid-back. Very easy going. He didn't analyse the characters greatly; I think he felt that the actors would grow into the roles.'

While Jim Sharman had had the luxury of creating the show from scratch with very few expectations and nothing to live up to, *Rocky*'s latest director had the benefit – and associated pressure – of the show's 30-year history and established cult reputation (revered by some, reviled by others) to draw upon. Therefore, as a relative *Rocky Horror* novice without Christopher Malcolm's extensive experience of the material, Luscombe – a softly spoken yet profoundly perceptive director – was able to examine the piece with invigorating impartiality, wisely choosing to approach it as a profound and respectable work of legitimate modern theatre.

Kara Lane, a flame-haired and spirited young actress who would step into the role of Magenta when the production returned for a subsequent tour of the UK in September 2009, gives a concise and revealing summary of Luscombe's directorial technique and keen eye for detail: 'When we started rehearsals, we spent the first three days sat around the table just discussing the characters, reading the script through, understanding the meaning behind each line, working out the love triangles, back stories, why Riff kills Frank etc. It was very interesting and very important for us all to have the same understanding of everything, so that we could portray that on stage.'

Unlike Christopher Ashley, who had deliberately rejected the innocent rock 'n' roll B-movie motifs and completely re-imagined the look of the piece for the 2000 Broadway revival as a post-apocalyptic fetishist wasteland, Luscombe would prudently retain the classic composition of the show as envisioned.

As the glut of printed matter on the chapel theatre's walls would instantly divulge, his thorough research into the script's mythological themes and eclectic pop-culture references included examining such fundamentally relevant topics as the science fiction B-movie genre, the classic rock 'n' roll era, Charles Atlas's muscle plan adverts, and 1950s family values, which he discussed at length with his enthusiastic and enlightened young troupe of players at the beginning of the rehearsal period.

'I listened to the soundtrack and read the script so many times,' the director reveals. 'With every show I do, obviously I try to get to the heart of it if I can. I firmly believe that the role of the director is to serve the writer, and to be as true to the original creative impulse as possible. In that sense my approach would be the same with *Rocky* as with any play or musical, and that's why the room was plastered with posters and other things. Sci-fi is not really my bag at all, but watching those B-movies was my way of discovering the heart of the show.'

This level of immersion, as David Bedella is quick to make clear, went far deeper than simply acknowledging the all-too-obvious sexual connotations of the 'Don't dream it, be it' message: 'A lot of people, including directors and cast, fall short in thinking it's merely saying, "Get out there and have sex."

'It's more than that,' he insists, expounding the script's more metaphorical and philosophical issues. 'It's really saying that we all have the ability to live out our dreams and our eccentricities; but we must remember that our actions have consequences. Frank, after all, pays the ultimate price for his hedonism; and think of Brad and Janet and the effects of their own actions.

'Can they salvage their relationship? They have discovered that, though they're engaged to be married, they don't know each other at all.'

8: I'M SURE YOU'RE NOT SPENT YET

Luscombe would also observe the sometimes overlooked parallels between the startling final body count of this deceptively amusing little rock musical and the epically tragic and cathartic denouement of Shakespeare's *Hamlet*.

Even before the addition of costume and make-up, the sheer power of Frank-n-Furter's death scene, played refreshingly straight, packed an unexpectedly overwhelming punch. After many years of countless Franks melodramatically hamming up their dying moments in order to court easy, though highly inappropriate, laughter from their spectators, David Bedella's potently affecting performance and Christopher Luscombe's bold choice to play the moment for real – the desperately terrified Frank literally begging his reluctant guests for help as his once faithful servant steadily aimed his lethal laser – brought forth a few actual tears from the rehearsal's assemblage of fans.

The shrewd decision to present 'Once in a While' as an understated sombre love song, with Brad alone onstage and Janet singing harmony from a temporary position up on the band's platform, would also prove genuinely touching. Many productions from the 1980s onwards had felt the need to play this song for laughs, awkwardly demonstrating a rather self-conscious fear of truthful sentimentality. Alternatively, as with the show as a whole, playing the number for real not only emphasised the emotional beauty of the ballad itself, but also highlighted the gentle irony of Richard O'Brien's songwriting in ways that a transparently broad send-up never could.

In evidence right away was the fact that the much-publicised 'Return to Richard O'Brien's classic original script' – being touted at the time in the tour's marketing blurb – was actually no such thing. Rather, the script being employed was essentially the author-composer's officially revised version of the libretto – used initially for the 1990 West End revival and every subsequent major production – but with a quantity of prudent pruning. In a video statement on the show's official website, shortly before the commencement of the 2006 tour, O'Brien announced that they (presumably meaning himself and the director) had 'taken out all the "improvements."'

The distinctly ironic inflection on the word 'improvements' implied that O'Brien had encouraged the removal of various ad-libs and unauthorised routines that had slyly made their way into the show during the preceding 30 years or so and had then never gone away. These revisions included the elimination of the unbefitting condom gags during the bedroom shenanigans between Brad and Frank, the overly comedic death scenes and much of the unscripted interactive banter with the audience that some Franks had felt the need to indulge in.

O'Brien-approved dialogue deletions, which would prove highly contentious amongst aficionados who considered the script sacrosanct, included the removal of Rocky's 'Have you got any lip-gloss?' and an entire speech by the Narrator:

'If one is suffering the pangs of remorse for a sexual indiscretion, it would seem logical that the transgressor would be sympathetic toward a loved one caught committing a similar misdemeanour. But emotion is an irrational and powerful master, and from what Janet witnessed on the monitor, there seemed little doubt that she was indeed its slave.'

The decision to cut this undeniably profound speech, for no outwardly apparent reason other than pacing, was a huge shame, as the beautifully constructed monologue – an example of Richard O'Brien's writing at its most rhythmically poetic – managed concisely to illustrate the Narrator's well-bred articulacy and toffee-nosed pomposity in just a few cannily assembled words. The speech would be rightfully reinstated for the show's fortieth anniversary production in 2012/13, but would find itself dropped again for subsequent tours.

Also excised was the brief reprise of 'The Time Warp' and associated dialogue as Frank-n-Furter's triumphant former servants returned to their home planet; an exchange that (having been created for the film version) had admittedly not actually existed in the show's original script. Rather than reinstate the original's 'I wonder if I remembered to cancel the milk' line from Magenta, however, the latest production would utilise *The Rocky Horror Picture Show*'s dialogue (also used in most stage productions from 1990 onwards) up until Magenta's 'To sing and dance once more to your dark refrain.' It would then jump immediately to Riff Raff's order 'Activate the Transit Crystal' (a stage show line, which had not been used for the film) and the castle's blast-off, thus sneakily skipping 'The Time Warp' reference completely and keeping the moment (and hopefully the audience) appropriately sombre.

Brad's incredulous exclamation 'You mean?' and Dr Scott's subsequent explanation of the Sonic Transducer were also taken out. This not only omitted possibly the script's purest parody of an authentically clichéd '50s B-movie dialogue exchange, it also left Janet to expertly deduce the machine's interplanetary function from Scotty's rather vague description of it as an 'Audio Vibratory Physio-molecular Transport Device.'

Certain lines would also be deleted in order to help discourage inappropriate shout-outs from the audience, particularly during the show's final scenes, as Christopher Luscombe confirms. 'There's a very serious side to *Rocky*,' he declares decisively. 'It's more than just a party. In fact, if it had only been a party, it would have fizzled out long ago. There are key moments – like Frank's death and the Riff and Magenta scene at the end – that you don't want ruined by inappropriate shouts.'

The director also agrees that the notion of not shouting out anything from 'The Floorshow' onwards – a discipline encouraged by an increasing number of fans – would seem to be a good rule of thumb: 'There are some call-backs that are offensive and I wanted to get rid of some of the accretions that the show's gathered over time. It did feel like trying to turn an oil tanker at times though,' he elucidates, whilst confirming that Richard O'Brien had absolutely no objections to such tactical editing of his dialogue. 'He was very much behind the idea of getting back to seriousness. He felt it had got a little out of hand and had to be reined in. We had lots of discussion about the back-to-basics approach. I love serious comedy and I could see the weight in the script. There's also the music from which one can take the cue for the right emotional pitch, and that last sequence of the show is almost operatic.'

Unsurprisingly, the decisions of O'Brien and Luscombe to remove certain lines of classic dialogue would generate a degree of controversy and discussion on fan club message boards. Brad's realisation 'You mean you're going to kill him? What's his crime?' for instance, considered by many *Rocky* aficionados to be an essential example of character development, was shortened, with the integral enquiry 'What's his crime?' being removed to prevent cries of 'Over-acting' or 'Bad acting' from mouthy spectators; a retort that Luscombe, a former actor himself, found particularly disrespectful.

Likewise Frank's insistent 'Wait. I can explain' prior to 'I'm Going Home' was truncated to just the single word 'Wait' in the hope of thwarting the predictable yobbish tirade of 'It had better be good; you got shot last time' at what should have been an emotional dramatic moment.

Although still in place when the tour began, Riff Raff's 'Say goodbye to all of this, and hello to oblivion' would also be swiftly cut because it brought forth an outburst of out-of-place idiotic 'witticisms' from the crowd.

At the very beginning of the run, Riff Raff's invitation for the rain-soaked Brad and Janet to cross the castle's threshold would be delivered without the time-honoured gap between his welcoming 'I think perhaps you'd better both …' and its conclusion 'come inside,' a point where devotees would traditionally yell 'fuck off' at their unfortunate heroes. However, as would prove the case with other examples of tactically altered delivery of the script's inadvertent audience participation trigger lines, the crowd usually shouted the response anyway, resulting in drowned out incoherent dialogue on stage and confusion from the uninitiated members of the audience. The pause would therefore be reinstated, and some of the other 'danger' lines left unchanged. After all, it was not as though Luscombe was endeavouring to be a party pooper or trying to put an end to all of the show's established participatory fun. Rather, he and O'Brien were simply attempting to give control of the action back to those on the stage.

As previously discussed, several *Rocky Horror Show* productions of the 1980s had turned into chaotic free-for-alls – a real case of 'tail wagging the dog' – with the audience virtually running the show and the actors pandering to every vulgar puerile quip from the stalls. Consequently, the shining brilliance of the script itself had become something of a victim of its own success, metaphorically strangled by its own reputation. With the *Big 30* production, a large number of the show's long-standing followers had started to experience a disturbing sense of déjà vu, as the tour – sponsored by a trendy nightclub chain and marketed as little more than a great big fancy dress party – had been seen as actively over-encouraging talkback from the crowd.

'I'd heard that in previous productions it had been the actors' goal to get the biggest audience participation they could,' says David Bedella. 'You can't deny that generating audience participation means that the show is succeeding, but I think it's most important to make sure that the audience know the boundaries.' Furthermore, the actor is convinced that, in spite of their riotous insubordination, viewers actually like to feel that Frank is in control: 'They like to see him be mean to someone else in the audience. So I gave myself a bit of free rein, in character. Chris always said to us, "Don't start a tennis match; you'll lose. Speak only when absolutely necessary. If possible, do it with a look instead; ever the high road."' Hence, while Frank and the Narrator would still, quite rightly, be the only characters authorised to address the audience directly, Bedella would keep his unscripted responses to a minimum – generally using them only as a last resort – as a tactical means of keeping the narrative flowing and silencing the most troublesome offenders as quickly as possible.

At the same time, however, the genuinely unique nature of *The Rocky Horror Show* and the unparalleled connection it has with its audience were not lost on director Christopher Luscombe. His challenge was therefore figuring out how to balance the integrity and poignancy of the show's deeper and more solemn moments without losing the joyful party atmosphere that had become totally and exclusively synonymous with this particular musical. 'Initially I was probably too anxious about the whole carnival atmosphere,' he confesses. 'But I did then start to enjoy it. I realised that *Rocky* has become an event and it is wildly celebratory, so I thought, "So be it; let's celebrate that too." Actors always strive to develop a connection with the audience, and it's rare to be able to do that; but, with *Rocky*, it's real. The show is unique. The theatre can't be too precise a science; it has to have spontaneity, and I suppose I started to run with it.'

Even so, the director is quick to point out that he had some strict rules for the actors: 'I'd seen DVDs of other productions where I felt the actors allowed in too much participation and it got out of hand. I didn't want the

8: I'M SURE YOU'RE NOT SPENT YET

actors to respond to all the call-outs, but equally I didn't want them to speak at the same time or they lost their power. It's a question of allowing space for the audience in the way that you would for a laugh in a comic play.'

Luscombe is equally keen to declare, however, that this approach relies heavily on the audience playing the game too and not merely shouting incessantly, randomly and drunkenly throughout. He also feels that, while an actor might get understandably frustrated or annoyed at the audience's insubordinate heckling, it is important to consider how their character might feel about the situation and react accordingly. Specifically, he recounts an occasion on which David Bedella lost his cool with a particularly bothersome punter; and the advice he offered to help the actor deal with such incidents in the future:

'I saw him in his dressing room and suggested that, while David the actor might get angry, Frank should always rise above it. He had to treat the audience as if they were just flies buzzing around him; they might annoy him, but they couldn't hurt him. Nothing threatens Frank; he's far too powerful. After that he was fine; not only in the role, but he led from the front and made every night like a first night.'

Typical Bedella put-downs, which became crowd-pleasers in their own right, included 'This isn't the film, dear; we can hear you being a twat,' and 'Me sing; you listen,' which, thanks to his commanding presence and deeply authoritative tone, usually proved successful in silencing excessive hecklers.

This allowed the script's sharp satire and cleverly constructed humour, some of which had of late become lost in a quagmire of over-acting and unruly audience disruption, to get laughs again. Even those abundantly familiar with Richard O'Brien's script began to rediscover jokes they had long-since forgotten. 'Maybe I made a mistake in splitting his brain between the two of them,' Frank's moment of introspective self-doubt was a prime example, along with 'I'm sure you're not spent yet' and 'It's not easy having a good time.'

Bedella is also happy to say that some nights were refreshingly quiet from a participation point of view: 'That could be good, because then you could concentrate on the character. Without audience participation you had to remind yourself to play the piece and not the audience.'

Following the excited response to the open rehearsal run-through – which had ended promptly after the reprise of 'Science Fiction Double Feature' with a chance for the cast and fans to chat informally and discuss their views – feelings on the tour's opening night in Brighton were curiously mixed.

The beautifully-observed and ably-executed characterisations received an unreserved thumbs-up, and the thankfully old-school musical arrangements were deservedly applauded. But still, as the final curtain fell – and the scantily-clad congregation once again braved the nipple-hardening arctic winds of an out-of-season British coastal town – there emerged a lingering, unnerving, stomach-tightening realisation that something did not feel right.

While few would have questioned Christopher Luscombe's wise decision to play the heartbreaking sentiment and tragedy of the script's final scenes with truthful sincerity – without cheap and needless lampoonery – it generated the unanticipated conundrum of how to fulfil the carefree wants of a fun-loving, and now emotionally confused, throng of intellectually undemanding high-spirited revellers.

Traditionally the show would culminate with an instrumental rendition of 'Sweet Transvestite' or a medley of the score's most popular numbers during the ensemble's final curtain calls, before one last rocking repeat of 'The Time Warp' sent the elated audience out on an unmistakable high. Christopher Luscombe's cast, on the other hand, simply lined up without musical accompaniment to politely take their bows. On opening night, the fans (including those who had attended the rehearsal and unreservedly praised the production's cast and director a week earlier) applauded and cheered the outstanding performance along with the rest of the impressive first-night crowd. They then waited ... and waited ... and waited in patient anticipation for the customary final reprise of 'The Time Warp'.

It never came.

The audience – casual visitors as well as the show's dedicated regulars – seemed genuinely bewildered by this puzzlingly lacklustre denouement. Rather than the intelligent direction, the unmistakable excellence of the performances or the manifold merits of the production overall, the absence of a closing 'Time Warp' reprise was, somewhat worryingly, the most audible topic of conversation as the crowd exited the auditorium. Even those who had commended the production in rehearsal considered the evening's conclusion to be shockingly flat; a feeling that audiences should never expect to experience at the end of a *Rocky Horror Show* performance.

Contrary to the assumption of many fans, however, this lack of a final rollicking rock 'n' roll reprise was not actually a calculated effort to further emphasise the subdued solemnity of the story's conclusion, as the director explains: 'The thing about the reprise was simple. We had a limited rehearsal period, during which I obviously concentrated on the show itself. There are lots of options for the reprise; so I thought we'd just play the show as it was to the audience and see what the reaction was. After all, Richard didn't write the show with 'The Time Warp' reprised at the end.'

By the fourth performance – the 6.00 pm early evening matinee on Saturday 18 March 2006 – after using the first couple of nights to assess the atmosphere and overall disposition throughout the auditorium during and

8: I'M SURE YOU'RE NOT SPENT YET

after the show, the typically insightful director had decided that a recurrence of the show's most famous anthem was necessary after all, and the indispensable rock 'n' roll curtain call was reinstated. 'I sat in the audience and it was immediately obvious that something was needed,' he admits freely. 'So we rehearsed it and added it on the third night. So it was only two nights (three performances) without the reprise.'

The director's intuition was proved absolutely correct when, following the cast's customary bows, the instantly recognisable strumming intro began and (as Riff Raff) the grim-faced, glowering Iain Davey fixed his intensely piercing eyes on the screaming crowd and launched into the familiar opening verse:

'It's astounding. Time is fleeting. Madness takes its toll ...'

The auditorium erupted.

Communal hyperventilation at its most blissfully satisfying and an approving roar of ecstatic applause to rival any heard at even the most epic rock concert or sporting event confirmed the capability of a rousing rock 'n' roll reprise to provide a far greater cathartic release of powerfully pent-up passion than any mournfully heartrending downbeat conclusion could ever hope to do. And ironically it elicited more tears of emotion from the jubilant crowd.

Another concern was that of the invisible Usherette (which had absolutely nothing to do with Claude Rains). An unseen Shona White sang the reprise of 'Science Fiction Double Feature' from behind the scenes, while a baffled audience stared blankly at closed curtains and an empty stage, wondering where the hell she was.

To evoke the feeling of a black and white B-movie, Sue Blane had designed a beautiful dark silver-grey translation of the character's traditional uniform for the opening number; and with the ensemble wearing corresponding pink versions of their characters' outfits for the curtain calls, for the Usherette to have taken up her usual bookending position for the show's epilogue would have created a glaring costume continuity problem. Again, by the fourth performance of the week, Luscombe had elected to bring the character on stage for the song as convention dictated. Shortly thereafter the grey costume would be replaced by its pink counterpart for the rest of the tour, solving most, though not quite all, of the problem.

For her reappearance in previous incarnations, the Usherette would usually have been carrying her refreshments tray, as she had at the beginning of the show. In Luscombe's production, however, strangely bereft of this prop, she simply took a slow reflective stroll from stage left to stage right, her hands casually resting in the pockets of her dress, tearfully crooning the plaintive closing number. Once again, a purposely tender moment would be ruined by thoughtless hecklers, who, rather than embracing the poignancy of the song, immediately focused on the lack of ice-cream tray and began to rudely enquire as to its whereabouts. A later, typically clever, Luscombe epiphany would resolve this irritating issue. Rather than leave her entirely empty-handed, the director opted to have the Usherette enter clutching a long-handled broom so that she could gently sweep the stage as she sorrowfully sang. Not only did the idea make logistical sense – 1950s picture palace personnel would surely have been duty-bound, at the end of each evening, to brush the torn ticket stubs, cigarette butts and fallen popcorn from the sticky Coca-Cola-stained carpet – it also added volumes to the scene's wistfully melancholic mood.

A further Luscombe innovation introduced during the tour emerged from the realisation that the scene immediately following Columbia's drug-induced freak-out and consequential exit, prior to 'The Floorshow', marked the only instance in the script that the show's intergalactic trio – Frank, Riff Raff and Magenta – were alone together on stage. As a result, the director's inspired notion was to have David Bedella's imposing Frank-n-Furter suddenly drop his Earthling facade and authoritatively address his servants with a pronounced pseudo-Transylvanian accent, akin to that of Magenta. For the final scene, the mutinous Riff Raff delivered his lines with the same interplanetary intonation.

'That relates to the big decision we made about Frank having an American accent,' Luscombe recalls. 'I was delighted when I cast David as Frank, but we were faced with the issue of his accent. I think we'd all been influenced by Tim Curry to assume that Frank had an English accent, but, when I thought about it, the show is written in an American idiom. It parodies B-movies, which are a feature of American popular culture, and there are endless Americanisms in the script, so it made perfect sense that Frank should, in fact, have an American accent.

'Richard, after all, wrote the part before he considered Tim for the role, so there was no rule saying that it had to be an English accent. That is by no means a criticism of Tim, of course, whose performance was fabulous.

'So the American accent worked well with David's voice, naturally, but my question was, "So, if the aliens are posing as humans, and that's an act, then what would their real voices be?" Riff was using a posh English butler's voice and Magenta was an American good-time girl, but both of these were acts. There's the chilling moment when Frank drops his guard when he's with them, and why would they keep up the act when the three of them were alone? The choice of Transylvanian accent was so logical.'

Luscombe, who hired a dialect coach to help the actors hone their intergalactic inflections, feels that this particular creative character choice helped make the show 'Fresh – truer in a sense – and certainly special for those actors.'

With considerable thought and time having clearly gone into making

8: I'M SURE YOU'RE NOT SPENT YET

every plot point and character nuance as truthful as possible, a number of fans were puzzled by the anomalous sight of Brad and Janet joining in with the Phantoms and joyfully jiving along in the lab to Eddie's 'Hot Patootie'. It was a directorial decision deemed by some to be a misstep in the depiction of the naturally nervous, strait-laced young couple.

'We actually discussed that a lot,' admits Luscombe. 'Dramatically there's an issue, as there's a long sequence of them not actually doing very much. I wanted to make it look as if, hoping against hope, they felt that maybe it was a friendly party after all – albeit a strange one – and that Frank was actually going to be a great host, so they should try and join in. It was always meant to look as if they were joining in tentatively though, with Janet maybe more enthusiastic than Brad.'

Suitably debonair and eloquent in the role of the Narrator, Michael Aspel seemed not nearly as nervous as he had at the rehearsal a week before. With a full, vocally-enthusiastic audience to bounce off, he delightedly threw himself into the proceedings with fitting fervour.

David Bedella meanwhile majestically personified every crucial ounce of seductive charm and cross-gender appeal required of his demanding role as the wayward space invader. As Luscombe had argued, the early decision to retain his American accent for the character made perfect narrative sense, as not only had Frank's knowledge of Earth been supposedly gleaned from watching old Hollywood movies, but he was also trying to fit in to a middle-American environment.

'Well, the first thing – and Chris Luscombe always does this – was to work on the truth of the text,' Bedella expands. 'We spent a long time reading and re-reading everything Frank was saying and figuring out why. That gives you a rock solid foundation on which to build and work. Then, and only then, do you put the character through the filter of your own personality. However, we reached a stumbling block. Something wasn't right. After about ten minutes of speaking the text out loud we realised that the block was actually the timbre of my voice combined with the English accent – it was sounding too much like Tim Curry again. We discussed trying it with my native accent, slightly heightened to give a sense of self-importance, which was kind of cool and made sense to me, as the aliens would've adopted local accents where they landed on Earth. So we did, and it fell into place.'

The fact that his charismatic leading man had managed to effortlessly imbue the character with crucial aspects of his own naturally alluring personality was only too apparent to the show's instinctively perceptive director, as Bedella purrs softly: 'Chris said to me one day, "I didn't know when I hired you to play Frank that you *were* Frank. I've been watching you during rehearsals and you've systematically seduced the entire cast and crew." But I love that. I love how you can disarm people by being a little bit flirty. It's exciting when people know that you find them sexy, and I do find most people sexy. You know if you're playing Frank right when, with just the lift of an eyebrow, he can get you to lie down.'

Of Luscombe's directorial techniques and meticulous approach to the material, Bedella is unconditionally and wholeheartedly complimentary: 'He's fabulous. He's a sculptor more than a director. He's the finest I've worked with in 28 years. The great thing is that he was an actor before becoming a director so he's been there; he knows the actor's psyche. He understands the needs and insecurities of an actor. Also, he is the arbiter of good taste. He urged us always to "Keep it classy." He understood the level of innuendo in the script and the potential to play it dirty, but he always said to us, "Ever the high road in this world we create. Let the audience go down *that* road when they choose." Another of the great things about Chris was that all the cast knew their background stories; even the Phantoms knew why they'd come to live in the castle and why they followed Frank.'

'He makes you feel like you're the one coming up with all the ideas, when in actual fact he's just planting the seed and seeing what grows from that,' asserts Kara Lane (Magenta on the subsequent 2009/10 UK tour), illuminating further on the much-respected director's techniques. 'If it doesn't work, he'll either tweak it slightly so it does or suggest a different idea. I don't ever remember him telling anyone that they were wrong. He spoke to us all individually throughout rehearsals to ask us how we felt our character progress was coming along.'

Primarily famous for being a fifth of a somewhat anodyne and now defunct pop line-up, Suzanne Shaw was under particular scrutiny from the show's pernickety followers, particularly at the beginning of the 2006 tour. Not just a pretty face, however, the talented Miss Shaw had a varied assortment of other strings to her bow, including a considerable amount of previous acting experience and extensive dance training (as her biography in the *Rocky Horror* programme would attest), and her multi-layered, vivacious and touchingly honest portrayal of Janet Weiss silenced all but the most obstinate of cynics.

The angelically handsome and suitably toned Julian Essex-Spurrier – the absolute embodiment of Rocky Horror as envisaged – proved particularly ideal as the show's traditionally difficult to cast title character. Basically the 21st Century poster boy for all that the role demanded, the self-assured actor confidently nailed the all important self-absorbed vanity of the newly formed narcissist in addition to his endearing childlike innocence. Sporting his naturally dark locks in rehearsal, although he was bleached blond in time for opening night, Essex-Spurrier's reading of Rocky as the archetypal Californian surf-bum fitted the character like a well-worn pair of gym shorts.

8: I'M SURE YOU'RE NOT SPENT YET

While Eddie's pink T-shirt, regarded by many as a something of a wardrobe *faux pas*, would be switched for something a little more befitting of a juvenile delinquent rocker later in the run, Nathan Amzi's well observed and authentically enigmatic Dr Scott was the subtle antithesis of the *Big 30* tour's crazy wild-haired professor or Lea DeLaria's Dr Strangelove on acid (and hormones) interpretation on Broadway. Cunningly underplayed, without sacrificing the comedic ludicrousness of the character, and still conveying the detectable implication of a sinister hidden agenda, Amzi managed to deftly endow Frank-n-Furter's nemesis with a compelling and seldom seen believability.

The absence of a profusion of pre-show Phantoms prowling the auditorium before the performance would be one of Christopher Luscombe's more radical deviations from tradition. 'I'm not convinced about the traditional role they had,' the director muses. 'Although I'm sure it worked in a small converted cinema, it's not easy to create atmosphere with three or four actors in huge houses, and I think that actors can become diminished when they're in the audience. Also, I like a show to begin with the beginning – and those opening chords of "Science Fiction" are magical – rather than a sort of half-hearted start. The other thing is that I wanted to keep the audience cool and not excite them too much before the start; i.e. treat it like a normal musical, rather than us saying, "Go on – shout out."'

While the decision to keep the Phantoms out of the audience before the show certainly helped to provide the startling first chord of the Usherette's opening number with an added impact, it also reflected an unavoidable truth that the general perception of the Phantoms themselves had inevitably altered during the preceding 33 years. Since Jim Sharman and his historic first cast had been obliged to create them, primarily for practical reasons, the principle purpose of the show's Usher characters had developed from creepy and unpredictable silent horror figures – who would create an atmosphere of unease before the performance – into a much more active and perceptible role, functioning as understudies and onstage backing singers while also fulfilling certain stage management duties.

Although most (though not all) post '70s productions had kept the characters – who were typically billed as either Ghouls or Phantoms and rarely wore the distinctive translucent plastic masks anymore – the nature of the show's cult following, with many fans seeing a production innumerable times and becoming personally familiar with the players, actually lessened their impact dramatically. It would, after all, prove rather difficult for any serious actor to lurk and freak out an unsuspecting punter if they had an overly friendly fan clinging to their side on a nightly basis, asking what they'd bought from the shops that day, where they might be going after the show or if anything funny had happened backstage that evening.

'I like the idea of those Ushers,' admits former European tour Magenta Ellie Chidzey, in reference to the Phantoms' original incarnation. 'I think it should be scary; but the direction we were given was all about fun. Frank and Riff had to stay dark but the rest of us played it for laughs.'

While the Phantoms generally seemed to work best as barely-noticeable ghost-like background figures – quite literally phantoms – lurking in the shadows, quietly supporting and metaphorically commenting upon the action without detracting from or upstaging the principal characters, certain directors made the mistake of upsetting the balance of the piece by involving them far too much. Similarly, a problem with some productions would be the troublesome issue of Phantom overcrowding. As evidenced repeatedly, three or four would seem ideal, while more than six usually appeared to be too many. It is worth remembering that these characters were never a part of the original concept of the show, but were born out of a need for backing singers, understudies and genuine front-of-house personnel. Therefore, over-filling the stage with a veritable surplus of them, as some directors (possibly influenced by the film's controversial Transylvanians) have tended to do – utilising them as a kind of superfluous chorus – merely diminishes their shock value by creating a detrimental over-familiarity.

Compared with the number of progressively lavish and sophisticated productions of recent years, Christopher Luscombe's translation of the material was visually a relatively restrained affair, keeping it truer to the sense of the original but with an added slick polish, compliant with the up-market expectations of demanding modern theatregoers, as illustrated by Janet Bird's modest but resourceful set.

Stretching vertically between stage and fly-space, four upright ladders (represented in rehearsals by short unassuming pieces of wood on casters), rolled on from the wings as and when required, were used extensively to elevate performers and to hang props and additional scenery. These addenda included various items of laboratory equipment and an up-lit 'window' for Riff Raff's vocal contribution to the approach of Brad and Janet to the castle.

In accordance with the low-tech nature of the script's source material, as well as Frank-n-Furter's kitsch eccentricity, the integral life-giving scientific apparatus would – in what was hopefully a monumental diversion from anything Mary Shelley might have imagined – be bicycle powered.

With a combination of electrical jump leads, plastic cables connecting Rocky's brain to that of Eddie's corpse (hidden inside a white coffin, scrawled with recurrent graffiti of his own name in a mixture of different

8: I'M SURE YOU'RE NOT SPENT YET

handwriting styles, rather than the conventional deep freeze or Coca-Cola machine of most productions) and a grumpy Riff Raff pedalling as fast as his gangly legs would allow – and being thrashed accordingly by Frank's cat-o-nine-tails when that clearly was not fast enough – the latest embodiment of Rocky Horror would be heretically brought into existence.

A departure from the scripted stipulation of Frank-n-Furter's unborn creation being mummified in bandages – as seen in Hammer's *The Curse of Frankenstein* and any number of comparable horror films, in addition to *The Rocky Horror Picture Show* and countless *Rocky Horror* stage productions – and from the Broadway revival's spectacular spinning gyroscope, Julian Essex-Spurrier's well-oiled Rocky would be unveiled, wearing nothing but his customary boxing boots and leopard-print trunks, inside a large, inventively-illustrated quadrangular crate. In context with the script's pop-culture eclecticism, the life-size reproduction of a classic Charles Atlas magazine ad (complete with a monochrome photo of the great man himself), which boldly adorned the upright box's front-facing hinged lid, was accompanied by a small red, black and white circular logo incorporating the words 'Ahh Fix', a blatant parody of the famous British plastic model kit manufacturer Airfix, and the slogan 'Your own Charles Atlas Pick 'n' Mix: You get PROOF in the first 7 days – I can make this NEW MAN of you,' along with the cautionary 'WARNING: This Is Not A Toy' and a droll '1:1 SCALE' specification to complete the joke.

The self-assembly model kit motif would be amusingly continued as the box opened to reveal the spread-eagled Rocky attached to a 'plastic' rectangular frame, accompanied by a selection of shiny camp accessories, which included a pair of green glitter stilettos, a construction worker's yellow hard-hat, metallic pink cowboy boots and a brown and white cowhide-patterned Stetson.

The set design would make liberal use of crudely drawn shadow puppets (operated by members of the cast) to humorously display the carnal delights revealed by the laboratory's closed-circuit TV monitors, themselves hung temporarily from the set's movable ladders. The intentionally ridiculous cartoon nature of these uncomplicated figures allowed for comparatively graphic, though consequently hilariously inoffensive, depictions of Frank sodomising Brad and a dominant Janet straddling a perspiring Rocky.

A swift change of scenery for Dr Scott's entrance would theatrically shift the action from the laboratory to the kind of cosy drawing room, complete with fireplace and shabby *chaise longue*, that might have looked more at home in an ambitious amateur dramatics society's production of an Agatha Christie whodunit, without the characters having physically to travel anywhere as they did in the film version. Relocating the events of this pivotal scene from the laboratory, however, would require a slight alteration to one of Scotty's lines. The scripted reference to the lab's technologically advanced machinery – the wheelchair-using scientist's first clue that the castle's inhabitants might be of extraterrestrial origin – was changed to a slightly strange allusion to the chrome-plated cocktail shaker Brad now happened to be holding; an object that, despite its mundane commonplace appearance, Dr Scott somehow identified as being constructed from an unearthly metal.

Although the crucial seduction scenes were traditionally staged in silhouette, in accordance with Jim Sharman's original concept for the show, their presentation in a more unfettered fashion – making the actors' facial expressions fully visible to the audience, thus adding a whole new dynamic by increasing the comedy potential – had been experimented with in a number of high-profile productions; most notably Nigel Triffitt's 1992 Australian tour and the recent Broadway revival. Both these versions made use of voluminous bedclothes and strategic blackouts to conceal the disguised Frank-n-Furter's true identity until the opportune moment. By using another time-honoured theatrical convention – that of the upright bed – and thereby creating the impression that the audience was observing the action from above, Christopher Luscombe was able to reinvent the scene yet again and further exploit the humour.

With the beginning of the second half restructured slightly – the Narrator's speech now sandwiched neatly between the two bedroom scenes (with the character wearing a gentleman's bathrobe and carrying a lit candle) – the impact of the act's opening image would be fully highlighted.

Facing the audience, her head and shoulders above the covers, Suzanne Shaw's Janet writhed and moaned with blissful delight, her once virtuous face convincingly contorted in unmistakable ecstasy, as an unseen Frank-n-Furter demonstrated his well-practised oral abilities – in addition to an uncanny vocal impersonation of Brad Majors – beneath the sheets.

When the lights came up on the equivalent scene for Brad, his back would be to the audience, the rear of Janet's blonde hair visible over his shoulder. Struggling with the unfamiliar throes of passion – as well as getting to grips with the proverbial doggy position – and presuming he was fulfilling the womanly needs of his equally inexperienced young fiancée, the horrified all-American boy was stunned when the suspiciously loose wig came off in his hand and revealed instead the deviously shameless Frank-n-Furter.

'I have to say that Suzanne Shaw smells better than any human being on Earth,' David Bedella reveals candidly. 'She, Matt Cole and I were especially close. In rehearsal, I said to them, "Look, we need to agree how far we'll go in the sex scene," because, you know, you're in bed with these guys and you're simulating sexual acts, so you have a choice. As with all

8: I'M SURE YOU'RE NOT SPENT YET

acting, you can pretend or you can *live it*, and the audience can usually tell the difference. They both had such a clean, delicious smell; I wanted to eat them up. So we played the fuck scene as real as we dared, given the circumstances, and it was very sexy. Sometimes, waiting behind the bed for Act 2 to begin, we'd be chatting about nothing – stuff like, "Oh, did you see the such and such shop down the high street?" – and all the while I'd be caressing Suzanne's breasts or Matt's bulge. We didn't think twice about it, it was all so natural to be physical with each other, and it certainly got us in the mood for the next scene.'

In his write-up of the production for theatre website WhatsOnStage.com, reviewer Glenn Meads was clearly of the opinion that the casting decisions, as well as the company's choice of director, had certainly been the right ones, as far as getting the show back in line with its author's vision was concerned: 'The last time I saw Richard O'Brien's cult, camp classic musical it seemed to have lost its sex appeal and edgy sense of fun. Jonathan Wilkes' Frank-n-Furter was funny but not predatory enough. Something was missing and the whole concept looked tired. This new touring production has definitely got its mojo back.'

This revitalisation would be especially perceptible in the aforementioned expertly staged and executed bedroom scenes. They were seductively sexy without resorting to vulgar sleaze, and David Bedella's enticingly plausible cross-gender desirability readily endowed Frank with his requisite insatiability and dangerous allure. This, along with the touchingly truthful performances of his malleable teenage victims, gave the scenes – seldom scandalous to jaded modern audiences – a newfound and profoundly arousing comic naughtiness.

'Many have tackled this role, but none has nailed it quite like this,' read Meads' unashamedly adoring appraisal of Bedella's mesmeric performance. 'He oozes sex appeal, plays the homoerotic angles to the hilt and flirts with the audience at every opportunity. Fresh from his success as the Warm-up Man/Devil in *Jerry Springer: The Opera*, this gifted actor puts the sex back into *Rocky Horror* and the supporting cast step up a gear as a result.'

Christopher Luscombe upped the comedy of the bedroom sequence even more when the successful production returned to the road for a subsequent UK tour in 2009/10. With the apparent discovery of a couple of wayward pubic hairs – immediately following a brief bout of under-the-covers fellatio with his manly adolescent house guest – the expressively wide-eyed Bedella's immaculately-timed reactions reduced the audience to fits of uncontrollable hilarity at every performance. Mercilessly playing the fabled rule-of-three for all its worth, the actor would appear first to pick the pesky unwanted pubes from between his teeth, and then off his tongue, before ending the routine with a too-good-to-miss 'cat coughing up a fur ball' moment that never failed to slay the playfully shocked crowd. While this moment would be retained for subsequent productions of the show, other actors often failed to maintain the subtle truth of Bedella's performance and would typically overplay it for the sake of an easier laugh.

After the chorus choreography for 'The Time Warp' was reinvented for the 2006 production – by adding memorable 'clock-hands' arm movements to the famous 'Let's do the Time Warp again' refrain – a decision was made to revert to the more familiar party dance actions – which, although different from those seen in the original stage productions or on film, had somehow become established and habitual during the '80s and '90s – for the 2009/10 incarnation. Ironically, this was initially met with a level of resistance from a small proportion of *Rocky*'s most passionately devoted disciples.

'Jenny Arnold, the choreographer, asked Richard [O'Brien] if he was wedded to any of the original choreography,' explains Christopher Luscombe, 'to which he said no, so we were happy to move it on. The issue though with new choreography is that you break the connection between the stage and the audience if everyone's doing different versions of 'The Time Warp'. The funny thing was though that some long-term fans actually liked the new choreography, and I was barracked at the stage door for going back to the previous version.'

Of this mini-uprising, which culminated with an amusing (but no doubt heartfelt) protest on the tour's second night in Wimbledon on 18 September 2009 – with fans on the front row wielding colourful homemade placards demanding that Jenny Arnold's 2006 choreography be reinstated – Luscombe is dismissively philosophical. 'You can't please all the people all the time,' he smiles.

Additional tweaks for the tour's 2009/10 revival would include portable spotlights, used by Magenta (now played by Kara Lane) to illuminate Frank for his lyrical laboratory homage to Charles Atlas and by the Phantoms to emulate the effect of the legendary 20th Century Fox searchlights during Frank's introductory 'Floorshow' fanfare, which they would also chorally vocalise with powerful results; and Frank-n-Furter moaning lustfully as a clearly turned-on Magenta enjoyed a convulsively orgasmic climax whilst pulling the bloodied rubber gloves from her malevolent master's murderous hands.

Following a successful nine months on the road throughout 2006 – during which it had visited a multitude of the UK's most prestigious playhouses – Christopher Luscombe's well-received production enjoyed a five-week Christmas and New Year engagement at London's Comedy Theatre between 21 December 2006 and 28 January 2007. Strangely, while the rather romantic notion of *The Rocky Horror Show* having returned to the very theatre in which (after six years of playing fringe venues in the King's Road) it had made its West End debut in 1979 was not lost on its fans, the production's short-sighted promoters surprisingly failed to exploit the obvious marketing possibilities of such an event and thus made no reference to the historical significance of this rather momentous occurrence.

With Suzanne Shaw leaving the 2006/07 production upon completion of her agreed contract at the end of the Christmas/New Year West End run, Phantom and Understudy Sarah Boulton competently assumed the role of Janet in the interim until Hayley Tamaddon – known to UK television audiences as Delilah Dingle in ITV's long-running rural soap opera *Emmerdale* – brought her considerable comic aptitude to the part. Also joining the cast in 2007 was Richard Meek, whose finely-chiselled features and heroic poise supported an impeccably observed example of the Brad Majors archetype.

Norfolk-born Meek – who would go on to have a long association with the show in the ensuing years – was immediately praised by fans and critics for his truthful depiction of the character, an approach he feels benefited from an initial unfamiliarity with the show itself:

'I remember the audition process with great fondness,' the actor smiles, recalling a moment when director Christopher Luscombe had asked about his prior knowledge of this rather famous work, 'I had to embarrassingly admit that, in fact, I'd never seen the film, let alone the stage production, and that my knowledge musically of the show extended to doing the 'Time Warp' at discos growing up. As it turned out, Chris was delighted by this because I think it meant I was coming to the material with fully open eyes, without any prior knowledge of how it's been previously played, and so I came from a whole different perspective.'

The actor confirms that his sincere and earnest characterisation – an approach celebrated by fans and endorsed by Richard O'Brien's much-publicised opinions about *The Rocky Horror Show*'s most fitting acting style – came directly from the character's kitschy cinematic roots: 'I had no reference of how Brad had previously been played, but, doing my research on the 1950s – and the B-movies and classic sci-fi – his dialogue just read to me as an all-American guy, the sort of guy an all-American girl would want to take home to her parents. Strong physically, but not enough to be a hunk, and a sensitive side – demonstrated in 'Once in a While' – but not enough to make him a wimp or geek. I always feel like he has a bravado about him that he just cannot keep up.'

The company's well-judged casting decisions would continue with the tour's resurgence in 2009/10, which, in addition to the welcome return of David Bedella (and, later in the run, Julian Essex-Spurrier and Richard Meek), included the diminutive and naturally bubbly Ceris Hine as a frenziedly hyperactive and extremely popular Columbia.

'Richard O'Brien said he thought Ceris was the quintessential Columbia, the best since Little Nell,' Bedella reveals. 'And Kara [Lane] was the sexiest Magenta in the world. So many brilliant and subtle nuances. Like when Columbia was having her freak-out and approached the *chaise longue* where Magenta was lying on her back; as she got closer, Magenta raised her hips like a cat in heat, in an unconscious, uncontrollable, sexual reaction to the proximity of her playmate.'

The actor is full of equal praise for Glasgow-born Haley Flaherty, a versatile and appealing young actress whose expertly honest depiction of Janet's delicately perceptible ripening eclipsed even the first-rate performances of her immediate predecessors:

'Haley Flaherty is a brilliant actress to work with; every moment spontaneous, organic and so funny. She's also very grounded; she's the one I used to take my troubles to, and she had an uncanny ability to make me laugh on stage. The times in "Planet Schmanet" when she was pulling away from me instead of letting me grab her arms. And then she pointed into the wings – of course I looked around to see what she was pointing at, but she had tricked me. Her Janet was feisty and not letting Frank completely dominate her.'

'I started watching the *Picture Show* when I was about 12 and I absolutely loved it,' says Kara Lane, whose debut as Magenta also came in the 2009/10 tour. 'From the first time I watched the movie I was immediately drawn to the character of Magenta,' the actress reveals. 'I don't know exactly why I loved her so much; maybe it was because she was so sexy, mysterious, aloof yet charismatic, and had hair like mine. From then on I'd go to every fancy dress party as her, and managed to convince a surprising amount of my male friends to go with me as Frank.'

The vivacious Australian is convinced that her affinity with the character from an early age gave her added self-assurance when her chance to try-out for the show came along: 'Everyone said I'd be perfect as Magenta. I guess that gave me the confidence I needed in my auditions.'

Despite the practice being frowned upon by many in the industry, a number of successful *Rocky Horror* wannabes have admitted to attending their auditions in costume, and Lane happily justifies her decision to do the same: 'Normally I wouldn't dream of it, but for this one I figured that the audience go to see the show dressed as the characters all the time; why shouldn't I dress up if I'm actually going for the role? So I put on a corset, hot-pants, fishnets, very high heels, teased out my hair and wore false eyelashes and bright red lipstick. Christopher Luscombe later told me that when I entered the room I looked like some extraordinary creature from another planet.

'I had to sing "Science Fiction" first, and was asked to do the first verse

8: I'M SURE YOU'RE NOT SPENT YET

sweetly, innocently and as excited about the idea of watching these movies as possible; and the second verse sinfully and seductively. Then we did Magenta's verse in 'The Time Warp'. We stood around the piano and just played with different ways of singing it. At one point I sang a whole line up the octave, which surprised me as much as Neil Rutherford, the casting director; and the next minute we were practically rolling around on the floor with laughter. That certainly broke the ice.'

Of her personal approach to such an iconic figure, Lane admits to developing her interpretation of the character gradually as she relaxed into the role: 'In the beginning I think I played her very similar to how Pat Quinn played her; only because that's what was imprinted in my mind from all those hours of watching the movie. Then as rehearsals went on I started playing around with her a bit.

'My personal worry at first was that I still felt too human as Magenta,' the actress confesses, recalling that her naturally intuitive director was quick to provide essential inspiration. 'I can't even remember what he said to me, but suddenly I felt myself introducing a psycho element into the character. She was slightly mad with her expressions and body movements. I think Chris hypnotised me.'

In addition to making the occasional surprise stage appearance at the end of the show – always to the delight of the excited crowd – Richard O'Brien openly praised the production during several interviews, paying particular homage to the admirable cast and Christopher Luscombe's instinctive understanding of the script's affectionately kitschy style and underlying themes.

While the long overdue British premiere of his 1982 Australian-produced musical *The Stripper* during the summer and autumn of 2009 would make him unavailable to oversee the launch of the latest *Rocky Horror Show* tour, O'Brien declared in a conversation with *BBC Breakfast* that he knew he could relax knowing that the always dependable Luscombe and Bedella were once again involved.

When asked by host Paul O'Grady during the 20 October 2009 edition of Channel 4's *The Paul O'Grady Show* what he thought of the latest version, O'Brien was full of the same unreserved approbation: 'It's very good because it's got David Bedella in the lead again and he's fantastic; and directed again by Christopher Luscombe. And I know it's in safe hands when those two chaps are on board.'

In an interview for WhatsOnStage.com in April 2010, O'Brien offered his own rationale for what made Bedella's interpretation so special: 'Probably one of the finest actors we've ever had play Frank, because his economy is so good. His lack of working to prove that he's this character. He just has a real economy: a fabulous voice, great looking man, funny, sexy, charming and slightly dangerous.'

Despite having earned the trust and respect of the show's uncompromising author-composer, Bedella at first felt a degree of anxiety over experimental efforts he made to enhance and personally develop Frank's appearance for the latest leg of the tour: 'I felt at one stage that I wasn't getting the audience response that I was previously, and I couldn't figure out why, so I asked Chris Luscombe to come and see if I was doing anything different. He came to a matinee and told me straight away, "It's your make-up. It's changed and it's separated you from us." Interestingly, I had recently got a new dresser who had worked professionally as a tranny, and I asked him for make-up tips. He created a new look with a very heavy foundation and stunning make-up. When I turned around it looked like I was wearing a porcelain mask. It was gorgeous, but I hadn't realised that what I'd done was what trannies do; I'd used make-up to turn myself into a woman, and that's not Frank. As Chris said, "You've lost the look of a guy who's just grabbed a lipstick." It was too perfect. So I reverted to the previous make-up with lighter foundation, and even let some stubble show through to highlight the masculine features of my face, and – guess what – the response came back.'

The actor admits to feeling honoured at being asked to reprise the role, especially as Ambassador Theatre Group had reportedly received numerous requests for his return: 'It was a great way to come back to the show, feeling acknowledged and appreciated from the first production. Chris Luscombe and I were like schoolboys in the rehearsals. We kept running off to the corners and laughing to each other, saying, "Can you *believe* we're doing it again?" It was great fun.'

One thing the Luscombe-helmed production did inherit from its thirtieth anniversary precursor was the lucrative convention of employing multiple Narrators over the course of the tour.

Ex-New Zealand Prime Minister Sir Robert Muldoon may possibly have been the first prominent name to assume the role when he took to the stage at His Majesty's Theatre in Auckland in 1986, but the real era of employing an already-famous name to play *The Rocky Horror Show*'s pompous Narrator began in earnest with Nicholas Parsons in 1994. Not everyone supports the use of such barefaced stunt casting, however, as a saddened Daniel Abineri attests. 'I think the show's become a bit like reality TV now that they use celebrities,' he sighs. 'Having, for example, a celebrity Narrator takes away from the mystery.'

Ziggy Byfield, another of the original production's early participants, agrees: 'I do think the show has lost its soul,' he declares. 'The later productions really lost the show's heart. Directors shouldn't fiddle with an Englishman's view of American B-movies. It's lost that, to quote Frank "certain naive charm." I saw the Piccadilly production in 1990 with Adrian Edmondson as Brad; what an awful bit of casting.'

8: I'M SURE YOU'RE NOT SPENT YET

'The show's become highly polished in the last eight years or so, with famous actors,' notes Toyah Willcox disapprovingly. 'Originally everyone who was in it was slightly broken. They so didn't belong that they brought danger onto the stage; and that's where Richard [O'Brien] comes from.'

Although the likes of Craig McLachlan, Anthony Head and Jason Donovan proved that a celeb Frank-n-Furter could work very well, the character (and in fact the show) could go horribly wrong in the hands of a less accomplished artist. A challenging and complex role – sometimes massively underestimated by the uninitiated – the requirements for Frank-n-Furter include an inherent sexual magnetism, natural charisma and (for dealing with the often unpredictable indignities of audience participation) superior improvisational skills; and that is in addition to the obligatory strong singing voice, serious acting ability and physical stamina. While a celebrated showbiz luminary might guarantee ticket sales, it was never a secret that most fans would prefer to see the right unfamiliar actor playing the role than a well-known but ultimately miscast TV personality. Nevertheless, as an added box office draw, producers and promoters would habitually favour famous names in order to help generate that all-important revenue, and, in the case of *The Rocky Horror Show*, the character of the Narrator most readily suited this objective.

With a large case file inside which his scripted lines could be surreptitiously hidden, and very little interaction with the other characters, the part could be taken by different performers quickly brought in as and when required and rehearsed with negligible disruption to the rest of the company.

Even so, the assignment would not be entirely without challenge, with the role as conceived having changed considerably, from the 1980s onwards, from that of a wryly-observed Edgar Lustgarten parody to an authoritative master of ceremonies, charged with the unenviable task of keeping the boisterous crowds under control as well as relating the all-important story.

In his question-and-answer exchange with author Scott Michaels for the 2002 book *Rocky Horror: From Concept to Cult*, actor Christopher Biggins expressed his own interest in playing the character. 'I was never asked. But I would have loved to have been the Narrator at one of those revivals,' he merrily announced. When the UK fan club later asked its forum members to put forward suggestions for the part for the then forthcoming 2006 production, many of them quoted this interview, bringing the actor's inclination toward the role to the fore. And sure enough, with the announcement of the final casting, fans were delighted to learn that one of the tour's upcoming Narrators would indeed be Christopher Biggins.

Incidentally, this much-loved veteran of television, film and theatre had, in the same book interview, let slip his personal aversion to the notion of heckling at *The Rocky Horror Show*: 'I have to say that I went to see the last big revival at the Piccadilly Theatre and I hated it, because the audience interrupted so much that you didn't hear any of the show. I thought it was terrible. It's fine to do it in the cinema, but in the theatre, if you paid money to see it, I would be really angry.'

Such comments notwithstanding, Biggins – considered something of a legend in the famously participatory world of pantomime – did admit that such interactive feedback from the crowd might actually be good from the Narrator's viewpoint; and in the event he joyously embraced every aspect of spectator involvement, while his warm and jovial personality (both on and off stage) and sharp ad-lib skills, together with his naughty habit of purposely attempting to make his fellow cast members corpse, swiftly and effortlessly made him a firm favourite with *Rocky* audiences.

Already a major player in *Rocky Horror* history, thanks to his appearance as a Transylvanian in Jim Sharman's movie version, Biggins would later host a one-man charity concert performed by David Bedella in aid of the Terrence Higgins Trust at London's Leicester Square Theatre on Monday 2 March 2009, during which he would playfully boast that he had been in both *The Rocky Horror Picture Show* and *The Rocky Horror Show*. A claim he proudly declared Bedella would never be able to make, as he had been in only the latter.

The sight of a recognisable face, possibly best known for a different (perhaps more venerable) line of work, in the dignity-challenging position of *Rocky Horror*'s condescending Narrator – generally the show's most verbally abused and jokingly disrespected character – quickly spawned a comically acerbic put-down, to which performers could prepare their own personally relevant anticipatory responses.

'Over? What was over?' the Narrator would ask, as the script demanded, of the cuckolded Brad's impetuous declaration that his relationship with Janet was at an end.

'Your career!' would be the rapidly established wicked retort from the audience.

A few chose to passively resign themselves to this affront. For instance, as the majority of spectators, unaware of the ritual, jeered disapprovingly at the perpetrators of such an insulting remark, writer-actor Steve Pemberton – known for his offbeat characters in cult comedy series such as *The League of Gentlemen* and *Psychoville* on BBC television – calmed them with a comical look of defeat. 'No, they're probably right. I mean look at me; I'm wearing Christopher Biggins' hand-me-downs,' he would confess, mournfully; before pausing briefly and dolefully accepting his own self-denigrating final insult. 'And they fit.'

Some decided to react with playful hostility toward their abusers. Portly Liverpudlian television actor Michael Stark blasted hecklers with tried and tested old-school put-downs such as 'If you wanted to be in the show, you should have come to the fucking rehearsals,' which tended to have the desired effect; while distinguished Scottish actor Gerard Kelly responded to the jokey exclamation of 'Your career!' with an explosive, yet seamlessly eloquent, diatribe of tongue-in-cheek abuse. 'Listen,' he roared, haughtily, 'you're sitting out there in the dark with two thousand strangers. I'm up here on a stage, with a microphone, surrounded by lights. God has a plan. You're not in it. Shut it.'

As a sad postscript to his appearance in the show, Kelly, having already assumed Narrator duties in Edinburgh and Aberdeen during the summer of 2010, died of a brain aneurysm at the age of just 51 on 28 October of the same year, shortly before he was due to play the role again in his home city of Glasgow.

An even 'angrier' interpretation of the Narrator was that of writer-actor Reece Shearsmith, who played the part for a week-long run in his home city of Hull in 2010. A recognisable face from films such as John Landis' darkly amusing *Burke and Hare* (2010) – which, by coincidence, featured Tim Curry in the supporting role of Professor Alexander Munro – in addition to multiple character roles alongside Steve Pemberton in the BBC's *The League of Gentlemen* and *Psychoville*, Reece countered the *Rocky* audience's customary career slur with a furiously heated retort. 'Oh, fuck off,' he snapped harshly, brilliantly feigning shock and irate disgust. 'My career? I've got a fucking BAFTA.

'What have you got?' he mercilessly challenged the culprits, going on to propose that their most outstanding asset would, in all likelihood, be a grotty council house, 'covered in shit,' located in a reputedly disreputable part of town. The locals of course, recognising the reference, roared approvingly.

By contrast, cheery celebrity chef Ainsley Harriott's comeback to this habitual example of audience repartee incorporated a playful product placement for his personally-endorsed range of convenience cuisine. 'Thank God for couscous, eh?' he would beam rascally, instantly producing a sachet that bore his name and visage, as the crowd cheered with favourable recognition. The cheeky star amplified this routine for subsequent appearances on the tour by opening his jacket, in the manner of a dodgy backstreet watch dealer, to reveal the entire range pinned to the lining, further promoting his wares with an excitedly persistent plea of 'Eight lovely flavours.'

While actors, on the whole, adhered to the lines as written, apart from the occasional aside, comedians and those practised in fronting talk shows and quiz programmes often seemed inclined to deviate, perhaps a little self-indulgently, from the text, as Dick Cavett had demonstrated in the New York revival.

One of the Broadway production's guest Narrators, in November 2001, was irreverent stand-up comic, film actor and prolific voiceover artist Gilbert Gottfried. In addition to lending his distinctive gravelly vocal talents to bad-tempered wisecracking parrot Iago in the Walt Disney animated classic *Aladdin* (1992), plus its straight-to-video sequels and spin-off TV series, and appearing in movies such as 1987's *Beverly Hills Cop II*, Gottfried was notorious for his subversively edgy comedic style that frequently involved such touchy subjects as race, politics and sensitive global affairs. Mere weeks after the harrowing events of 11 September, he was blithely joking about the leader of the organisation responsible for the devastating attacks in the very city in which they had occurred. There is of course a place for such controversial, yet tension-alleviating, humour; and to Gilbert Gottfried that place was apparently in the middle of a light-hearted, escapist, rock 'n' roll fantasy. 'Next week the celebrity Narrator will be Osama bin Laden,' he proclaimed merrily, while the audience laughed uneasily. 'He loves musical theatre. He's a cold-blooded killer, but he used to be a choreographer.'

With regard to the ethnicity of black actor James Stovall who, as one of the production's Phantoms, might on occasion have been required to understudy the role of Dr Scott, then being played by Jason Wooten, Gottfried found it similarly irresistible to point out the obvious irony, given the character's implied political affiliations: 'Last night the German guy in the wheelchair was off sick, and they had his understudy playing. And his understudy's black,' the provocative comedian announced, joking naughtily, 'Black people make me nervous enough; but a black Nazi ... I was terrified.'

During her stint as the Narrator in December of the same year, eminent chat show host Sally Jessy Raphael for the most part remained faithful to the words as written, but was at first thrown slightly by the time-honoured request 'Describe your balls!' from the crowd; most probably yelled automatically by fans of the film not used to seeing a woman in the role. With a wry smile, the clearly amused, but completely professional, daytime TV icon quipped dryly, 'Was anyone else hurt in the accident?'

Of course, by permitting temporary guest stars, particularly stand-up comedians and television presenters, to do their own schtick – sometimes even betraying the make-believe nature of the characters by directly identifying the artists portraying them – producers risked compromising the sincerity of the script, to a level analogous with excessive and uncontrolled audience participation.

As Richard O'Brien, and any number of the show's most intuitive directors, would no doubt attest, failing to play the piece for real can seriously diminish its value as a work of drama. Whereas it might satisfy the self-indulgent compulsions and attention-seeking insecurities of the speaker by eliciting the desired momentary mirth, unprompted tangential soliloquising seldom benefits the existing script.

O'Brien kept the show's dialogue short, sharp and snappy for a reason. It fuelled the crucial cinematic rhythm and rapid tempo of the original production, giving its early anxious audiences little time to think, let alone relax.

A disciplined professional actor would most likely accept that everything required will, in some way, have already been provided by the writer; thus allowing the players to concentrate on performance, motivation and characterisation. Conversely, by slowing the pace, interrupting the plot and needlessly embellishing the script, invasive ad-libbing and spontaneity – often associated with an impulsively inventive stand-up comedian – will usually just impair the innate wit of the piece itself.

Disorderly audience participation would continue to be a nuisance; although David Bedella notes that it did seem to diminish a little between the 2006/07 tour and its 2009 revival, giving him a chance to relax and focus on his performance to a far greater extent than before. 'On the first tour, we spent most of our time training the audience,' he declares unequivocally. 'It was still such an adult panto in 2006/07. Instead of playing Frank, I was thinking, "How am I going to regain control? How am I going to quiet them?" So I couldn't give my all to the role. This time around, the audience knew that things had evolved, and it became a joy to perform. I could concentrate on the character and embrace the audience participation because it didn't overpower the show. The audience understood the pay-off; do this, and get a better Frank. It gave me the freedom to soar.'

Knowing that O'Brien and Luscombe were making a serious attempt to return control of the action to those on stage, as well as hoping to minimise the level of unsuitable indiscriminate heckling, passionate *Rocky Horror Show* enthusiasts called – via fan club message boards and internet chat sites – for etiquette; and at the beginning of the 2006 tour they had begun urging devotees to keep their talkback sparing and witty.

Though opinions varied to some extent, the show's most ardent admirers seemed to agree that, while audience participation was an established, fun and totally unique aspect of the show's continued appeal, the on stage performance should always remain the primary focus and that heckling during the script's touchingly emotional moments – most notably Brad's gentle ballad 'Once in a While', the tragic death scenes and the melodically downbeat final numbers (Frank's poignant, 'Whatever happened to Fay Wray?' verse in 'The Floorshow', 'I'm Going Home', 'Superheroes' and the reprise of 'Science Fiction Double Feature') – was unacceptable.

Observing one night that Richard Meek, the actor playing Brad at the time, appeared visibly frustrated and dispirited by constant moronic heckling – persistent cries of 'Asshole', 'Get your cock out' and the like – during 'Once in a While', an equally dismayed David Bedella made the decision to halt the show momentarily and openly address the issue with the audience:

'I could see from the wings he was completely disheartened, so, when I came on immediately after, instead of starting into the "How maudlin" dialogue, I said "Now what made you think it was okay to shout out all through his song? It's a ballad for Chrissakes. You don't shout out during a ballad. Now, let's all apologise to Richard. Ready? We're sorry Richard ... Now shut the fuck up."'

It was also acknowledged that many of the worst offenders – usually motivated by anarchic high spirits and excessive alcohol consumption – would probably be occasional attendees whose enthusiasm for the show might be limited to its once yearly (at most) visit to their local theatre; as opposed to members of the hardcore *Rocky Horror Show* fan base who eagerly followed each successive touring production from city to city and generally accepted and embraced the need for a sensible balance between the show's scripted dialogue and their own disruptive verbal intrusions.

Therefore, while familiar with the show's widespread reputation as an interactive party piece, most occasional attendees – that is those not following hardcore fan opinion on internet message boards – would be ignorant of its extremely protective aficionados and their strict views on the differences between appropriate and inappropriate participation.

'Sometimes the show became all about the audience participation,' Kara Lane remembers despairingly. 'It was a very hard balance to get right. All the dedicated fans seemed to know how far was too far. It was usually the random drunks who wouldn't quite get the concept of the audience participation and think it was fine to just shout out anything – or even just scream long sounds (not even words) – and spoil it for the rest of the audience.

'One thing that Chris managed to do was teach us some techniques that helped us actors control the shout-outs. In previous productions the audience participation became so bad that the actors found it hard just to get through the show. The great thing about our production is that, with Chris's help, the majority of the time the audience participation was a lot more controlled, and so complemented the show rather than took over it. The first few times we started getting quieter audiences – which seemed to depend on the town rather than the day of the week – we were very put off and didn't really know how to take it. Then Chris reminded us that that's how we'd rehearsed the show, so to treat it as a great opportunity to really focus on our characters and telling the story, which of course won them over in the end anyway.'

While it has been noted that most staunch *Rocky Horror Show* followers would happily observe appropriate etiquette so far as audience participation was concerned, it remains unlikely that dialogue delivered through gritted teeth and a palpable look of frustrated annoyance on the face of a visibly exasperated performer would ever be enough to deter the most excessively vociferous of offenders.

Devoid of all respect for the rhythmically sporadic 'tennis match' associated with traditionally tolerable *Rocky* talkback, persistent hecklers – blissfully unaware that those irately rolling their eyes onstage might not actually be enjoying the constant rudeness and interminable interruptions to their thoughtfully crafted performance – would almost certainly misinterpret the eventual exasperated cry of 'Shut the fuck up' as an ironic show of appreciation.

However, even though the insubordination and indiscriminate conduct of the riotously loud-mouthed spectators of the recent thirtieth anniversary tour had been blamed by many fans for the excessively intolerable levels of boorish, undisciplined and over-the-top heckling that had arisen during the first leg of Christopher Luscombe's far more refined and thoughtful 2006 production, it was by no means the only suspect.

In 1999, a company known as Sing-a-long-a Productions had enjoyed a number of hugely successful UK screenings of *The Sound of Music* – Robert Wise's ever-popular 1965 screen version of the Rodgers and Hammerstein stage musical – by adding on screen lyrics, in order for the audience to join in with the songs, and encouraging attendees to dress as the characters. Nazis, nuns and lederhosen made the film ripe for camp costume possibilities; although long-time *Rocky Horror* fans were immediately shaking their collective heads in disbelief at the misguided souls who believed that dressing up and shouting at a movie screen was a new idea. The success of the Sing-a-long-a *Sound of Music* screenings – which quickly grew into fully structured party nights, complete with an onstage host, organised costume contests and regimentally controlled audience participation – led the company to consider contenders for similar shows. It would not be long before they turned their attentions to that most obvious of candidates, *The Rocky Horror Picture Show*.

'The Campest Cult Classic of all time gets the Sing-a-long-a treatment it's been SCREAMING for!' declared the ads. A questionable statement at best, given that *The Rocky Horror Picture Show* – a movie that had enjoyed copious amounts of spontaneous audience participation and a much-publicised cult following for 25 years without need of on screen lyrics or regimentation – would probably top most people's list of films that did not need anything even remotely resembling the 'Sing-a-long-a treatment'.

A typical Sing-a-long-a *Rocky Horror Picture Show* screening would begin with a host, dressed in a slipshod approximation of a *Rocky Horror* costume – a far cry from the lovingly-reproduced precise duplicates of Sue Blane's creations that regularly adorn most passionate fans and dedicated shadow cast members – introducing the proceedings. Although the choice of host might vary from venue to venue, one particular individual's apparent unfamiliarity with the film – and the relationships of its characters – before the projector had even warmed up was embarrassingly noticeable. Wearing black fishnets, leather skirt and a rubber bald cap, the lady in question proudly announced that she was Riff Raff's sister; a declaration that led many fans to question whether or not she had actually even seen the movie she was about to introduce. As anyone familiar with the plot of the picture would know, not only did Riff Raff already have a sister – another of the film's principal characters, with whom he shared a very special relationship – but a large proportion of the audience would probably be dressed as her.

In addition to hijacking much of the film's long-established talkback, developed over many years by its famously inventive fans, and teaching variations thereof to the bemused crowd at the beginning of the evening (so that no-one would feel left out, eh kids?), the ever-so-helpful Sing-a-long-a people issued prop bags containing the likes of party-poppers, playing cards and a newspaper. They then inexplicably encouraged people to contemptuously 'boo' Riff Raff whenever he appeared on screen. Why? Who knows? Probably to make all self-respecting *Rocky Horror* fans tear their hair out in frustrated bewilderment. The pre-show would not be complete of course without a demonstration of the choreography for one of the film's beloved songs.

'The Time Warp'? Of course not, that would be far too obvious. No, these baffling people had their own inane little arm movements so that everyone could join in with … 'Eddie's Teddy'!

Even before their debut, the Sing-a-long-a *Rocky Horror* screenings created controversy amongst the film's hardcore fan base. Online rumours that, should they prove successful, Fox would grant Sing-a-long-a exclusive rights to all future UK screenings of the movie – thus putting an end to the fan-led shadow cast screenings that had been instrumental in making the picture the enduring success it had long-since become – provoked anger from passionately protective *Rocky Horror* followers.

While this eventuality never occurred – Sing-a-long-a shows and periodic independent screenings being allowed to co-exist after all – Sing-a-long-a Productions' idiosyncratic approach to *Rocky*'s already recognised participation clearly had an undesirable effect on the stage show's audiences.

Infuriatingly, the Sing-a-long-a compere's habit of advising the crowd to shout, 'Asshole' and 'Slut' at Brad and Janet whenever they appeared on screen and *every* time their names were mentioned (including during the songs) – rather than just once or twice, as the generally accepted decorum of the live version advocated – would soon, to the chagrin of actors and fans alike, pervade auditoriums playing host to the touring stage productions.

In the years since Ziggy Byfield, Christopher Malcolm, Belinda Sinclair and other British cast members had appeared on stage in the first Tokyo production in 1975, *The Rocky Horror Show* had remained phenomenally popular in Japan, with both the stage and film versions continuing to draw considerable crowds.

During the mid-1990s, Japanese rock singer and guitarist Rolly Teranishi (often credited simply as Rolly), himself a long-time *Rocky* fan, had eagerly assumed the role of Frank-n-Furter for an extensive tour of the country and garnered a fervent fan following along the way. He revisited the character for another successful Japanese revival in 1999; while a high-profile 2011/12 touring production – with Rolly this time playing the role of Eddie – would be accompanied by the welcome release of the first ever Japanese language *Rocky Horror Show* cast recording.

Meanwhile, after a strangely conspicuous ten year absence from the Australian stage, *The Rocky Horror Show* made a much-heralded return to Sydney's Star City casino and entertainment complex with the premiere of a brand new production, co-produced by Howard Panter (for Ambassador Theatre Group) and Paul Dainty (for Dainty Consolidated Entertainment), on 12 February 2008; although this version would not enjoy the same staying power as the show's previous manifestations 'down under'.

The latest revival, directed by Gale Edwards, starred celebrated recording artist iOTA – winner of multiple theatre awards, including the prestigious Helpmann Award for Best Male in a Musical, for his vibrant lead performance in the Australian production of *Hedwig and the Angry Inch* – in the role of Frank-n-Furter, ably supported by Paul Capsis and Tamsin Carroll as Riff Raff and Magenta, and the effervescent Sharon Millerchip as Columbia.

Giving the production a brighter, glitzier and more vibrantly showy feel than the sleazy gothic tackiness of earlier incarnations, lighting designer Damien Cooper appeared to have eschewed the show's traditional cheap horror movie aura in favour of complementing Dale Ferguson's colourful sets with dazzlingly flashy showbiz pizzazz. Nonetheless, even vaguely concealed by flamboyant phantom featherage, the giant mobile phallus that Frank rode onto the stage for his 'Floorshow' entrance may have been rather anomalous with the author's aversion to overly explicit sexual imagery over suggestive subtlety.

While retaining a basic suggestion of their iconic forebears, the intricately detailed costumes created by Julie Lynch – particularly those of

Frank-n-Furter and his entourage – exhibited a spectacularly elaborate showiness and theatrical artificiality, which in some ways seemed to distance them from the truthfulness Richard O'Brien had repeatedly insisted was crucial to the piece. A number of these designs were, however, memorably spectacular. Columbia's meticulously complex red, white and blue sequined number, for example, implied an outrageously jazzy exaggeration of Britain's Tiller Girls or the famous New York Rockettes; and the three-dimensional miniature of the RKO Pictures radio mast perched on top of an off-centre pill box hat on the Usherette's head was an inspired detail.

Initially announced as a forthcoming national tour, taking in Melbourne, Brisbane, Adelaide and Perth after its much-publicised Sydney debut – with all five cities listed on the tour's website, souvenir T-shirts and merchandise – the production would fold prematurely, and without explanation, after its engagement at Melbourne's Comedy Theatre in the autumn of 2008.

Better received was a major new European tour, produced by Michael Brenner (for BB Promotion GmbH) in association with Howard Panter (for Rocky Horror Company Limited), which visited cities in Germany, Austria and Switzerland to much acclaim. Helming this production, which previewed on Tuesday 28 October 2008 (just in time for an official Hallowe'en press launch) at the Admiralspalast, an impressive pre-war entertainment venue located on Berlin's bustling Friedrichstrasse, was English director Sam Buntrock.

While it may not have been particularly imaginative or exciting, the uncomplicated poster design – a reproduction of the classic bloody font logo set against a plain black background, accompanied by the succinctly accurate slogan 'Bad, Bizarre and Bloody Brilliant!!' – was remarkably arresting. The huge glass-framed posters overlooking Berlin's Schönefeld Airport, and the gigantic dripping blood lettering dominating the side of the theatre, plainly visible to passengers arriving into the city by train, made *Rocky*'s presence in the German capital impossible to ignore.

As with recent UK tours, the Narrator would be portrayed by different locally-known celebrities throughout the run. For the Berlin performances it was German film and television actor Martin Semmelrogge, known to international audiences for his supporting roles in Wolfgang Peterson's epic 1981 World War II submarine drama *Das Boot* and Steven Spielberg's multi Oscar-winning *Schindler's List* (1993).

Although Sam Buntrock's cast spoke their dialogue in English – except for the Narrator, who delivered his lines in his (and the audience's) native tongue – verbal participation was relatively minimal and unproblematic, probably due in part to the (in this respect advantageous) language barrier and in some way to the courteous and well-mannered German audiences lacking the shameful hooligan element synonymous with British crowds. This thankfully allowed the text to be restored to its entirety, including the lines that Christopher Luscombe had cut to discourage unruly audience participation at inappropriate moments.

Visually much darker than either Luscombe's UK production or the colourfully extravagant lightshow of Gale Edwards' Australian revival, Buntrock's interpretation, smartly designed by David Farley, called to mind the classic Universal horror movies of the 1930s, as well as German Expressionism associated with the silent era. Films such as *Der Golem*, released in 1920 and directed and co-written by Paul Wegener, who also starred as the monstrous clay ogre of the title; Robert Wiene's *Das Kabinett des Doktor Caligan* (known to English speaking audiences as *The Cabinet of Dr Caligari*), also from 1920; and the 1922 masterpiece *Nosferatu: Eine Symphonie de Grauens* (English title: *Nosferatu: A Symphony of Horror*), generally accepted to be the first (unofficial) screen adaptation of Bram Stoker's *Dracula*, directed by the legendary F W Murnau; a film-maker whose influence on original *Rocky Horror* director Jim Sharman had been acknowledged.

Though also very different from the look of Christopher Ashley's overstated Broadway reinterpretation, Buntrock's version made effective use of filmed imagery in much the same way, beginning with a tone-setting preview montage, consisting of historical consumer ads (Corny popcorn, the Auto Dicer Food Chopper, Sheen hair wax and T-Ketchup) and nostalgic old film previews. This sci-fi geek's utopia included the fast-paced original trailer for Jack Arnold's *Tarantula* (1955), a film referenced directly in the Usherette's melodious prologue; the 1957 exploitation quickie *Daughter of Dr Jekyll*, starring Gloria Talbot and *Tarantula*'s John Agar; the memorably creepy promo for the 1960 spine-chiller *Village of the Damned*, a minor classic of the genre, based on the 1957 book *The Midwich Cuckoos* by British novelist John Wyndham, author of *The Day of the Triffids*; and 1957's *The Unearthly*, starring John Carradine and wrestler turned (not very good) actor Tor Johnson in the oh-so-challenging role of large lumbering bald bloke.

Watched by a reclining Dr Frank-n-Furter (Rob Morton Fowler), seen in silhouette behind the screen – cleverly establishing the character's fondness for cheesy old Earth movies before the scripted show had even commenced – the coming attractions dissolved into an immense celestial star field, as a plaintive piano introduced a gentle interpretation of 'Science Fiction Double Feature'. A leisurely camera zoom toward a slowly spinning Earth, during the Usherette's wistfully hypnotic rendition of the opening number, ultimately revealed the globe to be a pedestal for a disproportionately large model of a small white church. This section of film climaxed with an obvious miniature tree in the grounds of the church comically falling over, and being quickly "replanted" by a colossal human hand, as Brad (Chris Ellis-Stanton) and Janet (Ceri-Lyn Cissone) made their entrance onto the stage, accompanied by four (two male and two female) Phantoms dressed as gleeful wedding guests.

A projection of burning celluloid, followed by the inevitable film break and the caption 'Reel Missing' caused the silhouetted Frank finally to leap to his feet and strike a momentary defiant pose – hands on hips – before stomping off tersely at the end of 'Damn it. Janet.'

Film was also used for the climactic castle blast-off sequence; a moment that – exploiting lighting, pyrotechnics and models – had already been realised in numerous imaginative ways over the years. For the 1975 *Rocky Horror* movie, Brian Thomson – constrained by budgetary restrictions – had been forced to abandon his plans for a detailed scale replica of Frank-n-Furter's residence, in favour of the infinitely cheaper option of a cut-out photograph of the building. Plainly visible in the finished film, vaguely shrouded by an inadequate veil of smoke, the real house would be clearly still in place behind its gravity-defying photographic replica. Janet Bird's innovation for Christopher Luscombe's 2006 UK tour was, if anything, even less high-tech, as a suitably-lit miniature castle was simply passed between Phantoms across the darkened stage to simulate its launch and subsequent journey through the cosmos.

Rather than show the entire castle lifting off, Sam Buntrock's production employed an inventive black and white shot of a gyroscopically-spinning flying saucer – not dissimilar to Klaatu's interplanetary vessel in *The Day the Earth Stood Still* (1951) or special effects maestro Ray Harryhausen's iconic stop-motion invaders in *Earth Versus the Flying Saucers* (1956) – rising stylishly from the burnt out shell of the now empty castle and hurtling into the stratosphere, implying that the castle had perhaps been a form of camouflage for the alien craft, rather than being the vehicle itself as in most previous incarnations of the show. As with the opening images of the small-town church and globe, the obviously miniature castle – which now perched on top of said globe for the Usherette's emotive reprise of 'Science Fiction' – and accompanying 'toy' spaceship created the deliberately cheap and tacky look of a low budget Hollywood monstrosity.

David Farley made a few departures from the norm with his costume designs too. Riff Raff (Stuart Matthew Price) and Magenta (Maria Franzén) complemented each other with a sophisticated suggestion of stylistic Victorian elegance – Riff accessorising with a pair of John Lennon-style spectacles with circular green lenses – while, in place of the time-honoured gym trunks, Rocky (Andrew Gordon-Watkins) wore long, tight metallic gold trousers, laced up the sides.

Shunning the usual reveal, Frank made his initial entrance without his customary opera cloak. Instead he would appear in an upstage doorway atop an imposing staircase, silhouetted by creative rear lighting, wearing a Marlene Dietrich top hat and curly blonde wig. After his descent – his traditional attire already in full view – he would quickly remove the hat and wig to expose his shorter, more masculine, peroxide locks at the appropriate moment; while his household attendants gathered around a flickering antique projector and donned hand-held classic masquerade masks for the line 'We could take in an old Steve Reeves movie.'

With an intricately-choreographed feather fan routine, 'The Floorshow' became a stylishly chic burlesque chorus number. Overlooked by a crudely-painted New York skyline, temporarily pinned to the back of the stage, Frank – wearing a slinky outfit approximating Fay Wray's 'Delicate satin-draped frame', which would be torn away to reveal white basque and stockings for the song's 'wild and untamed thing' section – lounged on a gorilla's paw throne at the forced-perspective peak of an artistically rendered downstage caricature of the Empire State Building.

In selecting 'The Floorshow' outfits for his guests – who, in another interesting departure from the norm, would be attired in non-matching outfits – the hedonistic extraterrestrial narcissist appeared to have raided an eclectically kinky dressing up box. Most memorable were Janet's sexy wet-look black-and-red latex corsetry (with buckled front straps) and rubber stocking boots, plus whip and miniature top hat – which, by completely contrasting actress Ceri-Lyn Cissone's delicate 'butter wouldn't melt' features, would concur perfectly with her crucial character arc – and Rocky in a skimpy variation of a 1920s bathing beauty costume in pastel pink with matching lace parasol (used provocatively during his choreography) and wide-mesh fishnet stockings.

While previous productions had witnessed their share of light-haired Frank-n-Furters, the elegantly striking Maria Franzén's cascading blonde tresses gave Magenta – most often presented as a cool and mysterious brunette or a fiery redhead – a rather atypical look.

Unlike *Hair*, which in accordance with the peacenik hippie movement it fervently celebrated had a definite political standpoint, *The Rocky Horror Show* never openly involved itself with such weighty concerns. Nor would such overly-intellectual stimuli have felt appropriate within the outwardly jokey ambience of the piece. Even Dr Scott's intimated Nazi leanings were typically dealt with in a playfully inoffensive comic book manner, while esoteric details – such as Frank's '4711' tattoo and the red triangle on his surgeon's gown – appeared to be even less significant. Nonetheless, whether deliberate or not, director Sam Buntrock's Aryan alien quartet – Frank, Rocky, Riff Raff and Magenta noticeably sported fair skin and bleached locks, while the show's Earthlings all had darker hair – in a production that mainly toured cities in Germany and Austria, appeared to present an interesting subversive subtext for anyone who might wish to observe it.

This rather interesting idea – that a personal design decision might invoke thought-provoking political suppositions not consciously intended by the writer – was touched upon by Richard O'Brien in his discussion with Christopher Luscombe for the 2006 UK tour brochure. 'In somewhere like South Africa, that would have been extremely provocative,' he said of the notion that a cast made up entirely of black actors, save for a Caucasian Brad and Janet, could have altered the usual perception of the piece entirely.

Buntrock also showcased the script's sensationally absurd horror elements in gloriously melodramatic fashion. Rocky's pivotal birth scene, for instance, was achieved by means of an effective blend of animation and ingenious sleight of hand. Observed in silhouette through a hospital curtain, drawn around a raised podium in the laboratory, Frank's embryonic creature appeared to grow from a suspended Pyrex test tube into which the obsessed scientist had poured a combination of chemicals. Accompanied by suitably foreboding music, a spindly, limb-like appendage crept disturbingly from the top of the glass cylinder, like a grotesquely profane five-fingered serpent, rapidly expanding into a fully-formed human arm before the audience's very eyes. A sinister tinkling of breaking glass allowed a foot and a leg to grow likewise from the bottom of the tube, promptly joined by a head and the outstanding requisite limbs. With the rest of the receptacle finally shattering, as the increasingly burly torso broke free, the freshly grown experiment dropped to the floor of the platform; with the real actor now sneakily replacing the clever special effects trickery. The fruits of Frank's and Riff Raff's labours then slowly stood up, drew back the flimsy partition and launched into a superb rocking arrangement of 'The Sword of Damocles', concluding one of the most memorably inventive creation sequences in *Rocky Horror Show* history.

Honouring the show's gory Hammer horror origins, Jack Edwards' leather-clad Eddie sported a suitably gruesome make-up effect, with half his brain (Rocky having been given the other half of course) fully exposed through a gaping hole in the side of his head. The luckless ex-delivery boy suffered yet more graphic humiliation, as, having chased him onto Rocky's birth podium at the climax of 'Hot Patootie', Frank pulled across the surgical screen between himself and the audience (some homicidal maniacs clearly value their privacy) and viciously slaughtered his victim, again in silhouette – evidently one of the director's favourite visual devices – with a large butcher's knife, copious spurts of bright red blood appearing to splash the pristine white curtain in a recognisable nod to *Psycho*'s legendary shower murder.

8: I'M SURE YOU'RE NOT SPENT YET

The production's attention to detail could be quite stimulating. Following her enlightening boudoir encounter with Frank-n-Furter – observed in shadow through gossamer bed drapes, as in the *Rocky Horror* movie – noticeable lipstick kiss marks adorned Janet's body, as well as the gusset of her not so virginal white panties; Frank clicked his heels together three times on the final line of 'I'm Going Home', upholding the tradition of *Wizard of Oz* references favoured by Jim Sharman; and old movie-style credits were projected onto the screen (a truly brilliant idea) during the closing song.

The understandably traumatising effects of Eddie's brutal death upon Columbia – one of her lovers being mercilessly slain by another before her delicate adolescent eyes – were thoughtfully acknowledged and explored during the course of the second act. Actress Kelly Winter played the pre-'Floorshow' scenes as a drunken wreck constantly clutching a half-empty bottle of Jack Daniel's and glaring angrily at Frank, her ruined eye make-up now a cartoon racoon's visage of dried tears and smeared mascara.

Staged within these circumstances, 'Once in a While' – sung by Brad to this heavily inebriated and depressed young soul – took on a hitherto unexplored poetic significance, equating the miserable groupie's heartrending plight with that of the confused and emotionally wounded hero.

Evoking the atmospheric shadowy nightmares of both *Caligari* and *Nosferatu*, the rebellious Riff Raff and Magenta – now impressively 12 feet tall, with their legs and means of motorisation hidden by the exceptionally long robes of their high-collared grey, green and black space outfits – glided eerily and gracefully onto the stage like a bizarre gothic hybrid of Murnau's emaciated vampire Count and *Doctor Who*'s twisted megalomaniacal genius Davros (creator of the infamous Daleks).

Though it differed markedly from that of Christopher Luscombe, Sam Buntrock's intrinsic understanding of Richard O'Brien's material was immediately apparent. Accordingly, aside from the occasional glaring misstep – such as a massively misguided and cringe-worthy comedic death for Columbia (a huge error of judgment, considering the cannily pitched emotional truth in evidence elsewhere) – the director delivered a smartly-conceived and competently-executed interpretation of the show.

Considering the musical excellence of both Luscombe's UK version – above all, the exquisite vocal talents of a flawless on stage ensemble and a perfectly coordinated band of gifted musicians – and Buntrock's 2008 European adaptation – specifically a number of pleasing orchestrations, particularly 'The Sword of Damocles' and 'Once in a While', and Stuart Matthew Price's stunningly held final note at the end of Riff Raff's contribution to 'Over at the Frankenstein Place (which brought forth joyful nightly applause) – it remains an enormous disappointment, and a source of endless irritation amongst fans, that neither production generated a cast recording.

With the odd costume amendment, a small number of staging revisions and a couple of slightly modified musical arrangements, the European production would be revived in the summer of 2011 – a two- or three-year gap between tours being common in order to maintain public interest and keep the show fresh for new audiences – with Rob Morton Fowler and Kerry Winter reprising their roles as Frank and Columbia and a company of eager new faces making up the rest of the ensemble.

The English Stage Company, based at the Royal Court Theatre in London's Sloane Square, commemorated its fiftieth anniversary in 2006 with an impressive season celebrating its most beloved, groundbreaking and fondly-remembered works. Intellectuals and pretentious theatre buffs promptly began falling over themselves to praise the company's most revered and influential productions. Amongst them, quite predictably, was *Look Back in Anger*. Having premiered at the Royal Court on 8 May 1956, John Osborne's gritty working class character piece – which spawned a dour 1959 film adaptation starring Richard Burton – may not have been unanimously lauded right away, but it was responsible for initiating the 'angry young man' sub-genre, while setting a trend for a wave of equally grim 1960s kitchen sink dramas, and becoming a universally respected work of British theatre in its own right. Undoubtedly the critics' preference for the most seminally important play of the preceding 50 years, *Look Back in Anger* would be selected for special honours during the respected company's Golden Anniversary year.

When it came to the People's Choice however – a public poll to determine the most enjoyed production during the organisation's first half century – the hugely admired Mr Osborne's work would not be at the top of the list. Nor would Samuel Beckett's *Endgame*, first produced in 1957; Edward Bond's *Saved*, the subject of a famously significant censorship battle and contentious prosecution in 1965; or *Death and the Maiden* by Ariel Dorfman, which debuted at the Royal Court on 9 July 1991 and would be followed three years later by a screen version directed by legendary film-maker Roman Polanski and starring prominent Hollywood A-listers Sigourney Weaver and Ben Kingsley. Applauded works each and every one; and all eligible for consideration, along with every other production mounted at the Royal Court Theatre throughout the English Stage Company's long and eventful history.

Nevertheless, unlike stuffy drama critics, theatre analysts and pretentious journalists – all of whom would likely have been most displeased with the eventual outcome of the all-important public vote – it appeared that the general population had a rather different definition of enjoyment.

9
Sensual Daydreams To Treasure Forever

That *The Rocky Horror Show* spawned a vast and enduring legacy is unquestionable. A plethora of camp rock shows followed in its sensually sequinned and pioneering footsteps. Even if perhaps their plots were not directly influenced by *Rocky Horror* itself, cult musicals such as *Bad Boy Johnny and the Prophets of Doom* (written by recurring Frank-n-Furter Daniel Abineri in 1986 and first presented in 1989 with Russell Crowe in the lead role), *Saucy Jack and the Space Vixens*, *Hedwig and the Angry Inch* and *Repo: The Genetic Opera* (the film version of which, often marketed along the lines of '*Blade Runner* meets *The Rocky Horror Picture Show*,' starred ex-West End Frank-n-Furter Anthony Head as the title's twisted and tormented repossessor of vital organs), undoubtedly owed a large debt of gratitude to the plucky revolutionary spirit of Richard O'Brien, Jim Sharman and their enterprising team of talented rock 'n' roll activists.

Countless attempts to recapture *The Rocky Horror Show*'s seamless fusion of science fiction, gothic horror, rock music and ironic wit would result in an excess of less successful works in the decades that followed. But, as the ever astute Richard O'Brien noted on many occasions, if the formula could be easily replicated, a wealth of wannabe author-composers would be continually making fistfuls of easy cash.

With the picture having gained a cult following in the years since it achieved the dubious (and arguable) title 'Worst Movie of All Time,' it is perhaps unsurprising to learn that, in the wake of *Rocky Horror*, there was more than one attempt at adapting Edward D Wood's 1956 schlock sci-fi clunker *Plan 9 from Outer Space* into a stage musical. As well as parodying the original film's wobbly sets, dreadful dialogue and unintentionally hilarious acting, the musical versions readily exploited its director's famous predilection for ladies' clothing. A rock 'n' roll, cross-dressing, science fiction B-movie spoof; now why does that sound so familiar?

Despite its built-in blend of memorably awful lines, camp characters, cross-dressing and an outrageous science fiction plot, however, the work of the late Ed Wood failed to make any kind of noticeable impact on the hit-and-miss world of musical theatre.

On 6 May 1982, another musical based on a much-loved cult horror cheapie premiered Off-off-Broadway at the WPA (Workshop for the Players' Art) Theatre; one that, unlike the ill-fated *Plan 9* adaptations, would fare much better with mainstream theatregoers.

With a book and lyrics by B-movie aficionado Howard Ashman and music by Alan Menken, *Little Shop of Horrors* incorporated elements of the classic theatrical horror-comedy *Arsenic and Old Lace* and the oft-told Sweeney Todd legend, and combined them with a pastiche of catchy 1960s-style tunes, forbidden romance and lashings of ghoulish black comedy. Upon re-opening Off-Broadway at the Orpheum Theatre in New York's East Village on 27 July of the same year, the show ultimately ran for five years and 2,209 performances, becoming the most financially successful Off-Broadway production in history. The subsequent, Cameron Mackintosh-produced UK version, which opened on Saturday 1 January 1983 at London's Comedy Theatre, scooped the London *Evening Standard* Award for Best Musical, just as *The Rocky Horror Show* had done a decade earlier.

Ashman and Menken based their musical on film-maker Roger Corman's popular Faustian fable *The Little Shop of Horrors* (1960), a micro-budgeted black and white tongue-in-cheek horror movie that the director famously made in just two and a half days in order to resourcefully utilise an already existing set (left over from a previous production) before it was torn down.

The plot of Corman's film, penned by screenwriter Charles B Griffith and shot for a mere $30,000, revolves around naive and clumsy florists' shop assistant Seymour (played by Jonathan Haze), whose self-cultivated hybrid plant becomes a massive public sensation, thus saving the ailing Skid Row store of Gravis Mushnick (Mel Welles) from financial ruin. Unfortunately, this seemingly ideal and lucrative situation has one minor (and very sinister) drawback. The plant thrives only on a constant diet of fresh human blood. Seymour therefore finds himself reluctantly compelled to provide a steady supply of delicious arterial fluid by way of various questionable and grisly methods, thus sowing the seeds for his own unavoidable destruction.

Corman's film became an enduring cult hit – referred to by some as *The Rocky Horror Picture Show* of its day – and was delightfully cheap, blackly comic and undeniably witty. Much of the humour in Griffith's joyfully irreverent and acid-sharp screenplay has easily stood the test of time, too, remaining genuinely amusing decades later.

With his script for the musical version, Howard Ashman, a fan of Corman's film, remained respectful of the original while improving and tightening its overall structure, fleshing out the relationships of the main characters and wisely omitting a few of the superfluous ones.

The original picture intimated that nerdy shop assistant Seymour (his surname has been variously listed as Krelboin, Krelboined or Krelbourne in countless reviews and reference books, probably due to its being difficult to hear clearly on the cheaply-recorded soundtrack and only the character's first name appearing in the on screen credits) had grown the flesh-eating plant himself and christened it Audrey Junior after the shop's other assistant, the ditzy but well-meaning Audrey Fulquard (Jackie Joseph), with whom he was secretly infatuated. Ashman developed the romantic relationship between Seymour (whose last name is definitely Krelborn in the musical) and Audrey, and promoted one of the original film's incidental characters, a sadistic dentist named Dr Phoebus Farb (changed to Orin Scrivello DDS for the musical), to the role of Audrey's viciously controlling, leather-jacketed motorcyclist boyfriend. This provided much opportunity for comedy and gave the character a show-stopping rock 'n' roll entrance number of his own, while considerably upping Seymour's motivation for wanting the scene-stealing villain dispatched and chopped into plant food.

Revealed to be of extraterrestrial origin rather than a home-grown creation of the tale's hapless hero, the musical's plant, which Ashman's script called Audrey 2, was brought to life on stage by way of a series of impressive puppets – built in a range of sizes to signify its substantial growth as its food supply increased – designed and created by Martin P Robinson. A crowd-pleasing character in its own right, Audrey 2 became a hilariously hip, foul-mouthed, jive talking, soul singing, show-stealing botanical menace that would triumph in the end by devouring almost all of the human cast.

Surviving this multiple bloodbath was the three-girl Greek chorus of Ronette, Chiffon and Crystal – drolly named after fashionable all-girl pop groups of the 1960s – who sang the show's apocalyptic yet curiously catchy and upbeat finale 'Don't Feed the Plants', as the faces of Audrey 2's unlucky victims were revealed as backing singers in its suddenly blooming flowers.

Characters deleted from Ashman's reworking of Corman's story included Seymour's overbearing hypochondriac mother; a pair of investigative detectives, one of whom, Sergeant Joe Fink (Wally Compo) had also provided the original film's off-screen narration; a constantly mourning Jewish housewife named Mrs Shiva (mentioned briefly in the musical adaptation but never actually seen) whose enormous family appeared to be dropping like flies (thus necessitating repeated visits to the florists); and the memorable Bourson Fouch (cult movie stalwart Dick Miller), a man whose peculiar dietary habits also called for regular trips to Mushnick's cut-price flower shop.

A big budget film version of the musical, directed by Frank Oz and released by Warner Bros in 1986, notably reinstated the original film's most famous subsidiary character. The role of Wilbur Force, a masochistic dental patient, had been brought to life in Roger Corman's movie by a young Jack Nicholson in one of his earliest screen appearances. Actor-comedian Bill Murray – of *Caddyshack* (1980), *Stripes* (1981) and *Ghostbusters* (1984) fame – recreated the character, renamed Arthur Denton, for the musical remake.

As originally shot, the climax of the movie mirrored that of the show, with Audrey 2 gulping down both Audrey and Seymour before spreading its gargantuan progeny across the United States and attacking its landmarks in a spectacular, special effects-heavy finale. However, whereas the conclusion of *The Rocky Horror Picture Show* had remained refreshingly faithful to the downbeat denouement of the original stage incarnation, negative test audience scores for *Little Shop of Horrors* in 1986 resulted in hasty reshoots. Director Frank Oz controversially scrapped the final scenes – which reportedly cost a hefty $5,000,000 – in favour of a brand new 'happy' ending in which Seymour faced off against and ultimately triumphed over his photosynthetic nemesis as it defiantly belted out 'Mean Green Mother from Outer Space', an up-tempo rock number written especially for the film by Ashman and Menken.

The movie performed disappointingly at the box office but eventually found a dedicated following on video and, like its black and white predecessor, became a cult favourite. Its radically altered ending, however, would ultimately confuse subsequent theatre audiences, many of whom would be more familiar with TV showings of Frank Oz's screen adaptation and therefore unaware that the stage version's doom-laden finale actually came first.

In a similar vein (pun acknowledged and feverishly embraced) was *Zombie Prom*, a tongue-in-cheek parody of 1950s teen culture with music by Dana P Rowe and a book and lyrics by John Dempsey. After debuting in Florida at Key West's Red Barn Theatre in 1993, an Off-Broadway production of the musical, directed by Philip William McKinley, opened in New York at the Variety Arts Theatre on 9 April 1996; while a 36-minute short film version, directed by Vince Marcello and starring American drag queen RuPaul (full name RuPaul Andre Charles) as haughty high school principal Miss Delilah Strict, premiered in 2006.

Zombie Prom breathed macabre new life into the age-old 'good girl falls for bad boy' premise of innumerable '50s and '60s pop songs – notably the Shangri-Las' 1964 hit 'Leader of the Pack' – by giving it a cheeky horror movie twist. At the behest of her impossibly strait-laced parents, sweetly wholesome Toffee, a popular student at Enrico Fermi High School, is pressured into dumping her wrong-side-of-the-tracks delinquent boyfriend Jonny Warner, an adolescent rebel without a cause, whose stubborn insistence on dropping the customary 'h' from his first name has upset the status quo of the small town local community. After committing suicide by hurling himself into the nearby Francis Gary Powers nuclear power plant, the distraught Jonny is unexpectedly resurrected by Toffee's love and inconsolable grief. Inexplicably emerging from his school locker – performing a raucous rock 'n' roll number entitled 'Blast from the Past' – this green-faced, gruesomely disfigured, motorcycle-riding greaser is unmistakably a direct descendent of the unfortunate Eddie, *Rocky Horror*'s putrid ex-delivery boy.

While the no-nonsense Miss Strict threatens to cancel the senior prom if Jonny defies the school's rigid 'No Zombies' policy by attending – thus allowing the show to touch on racial tolerance and civil rights issues in a frothier and more jocular manner than the likes of John Waters' *Hairspray* – it is her own less than squeaky clean past that promises to catch up with her in the final scenes.

With its simple melodies, witty lyrics and amusing dialogue (peppered with corny one-liners, B-movie clichés and a healthy irreverence) *Zombie Prom* – which became a popular choice for the end-of-year musical at many American schools – was another worthy addition to *The Rocky Horror Show*'s legacy.

As well as a multitude of original works, *Rocky* would also be followed by a flood of so-called jukebox musicals; shows that, rather than containing musical numbers composed for the piece itself, utilised existing rock and pop songs, loosely linking them together by way of an often rather shallow plot to form an enjoyable, but frequently undemanding, evening's entertainment. Noteworthy examples have included the phenomenally successful *Buddy: The Buddy Holly Story* – which featured the many hits of its titular rock 'n' roll icon – and *Priscilla: Queen of the Desert* – a bright and energetic stage show, strikingly designed by *Rocky Horror*'s Brian Thomson and based of Stephan Elliott's camp 1994 road movie *The Adventures of Priscilla: Queen of the Desert*. With a score made up of '60s and '70s disco classics (some of which worked better than others within the context of the show), the stage version of *Priscilla* premiered at the Lyric Theatre, Star City, in Sydney on Saturday 7 October 2006. With its Sydney debut a success, subsequent productions opened in London, Auckland, New York and elsewhere, and prompted some audience members to attend performances in drag, albeit on a scale not even approaching that of *Rocky Horror*.

The promoters of many other camp post-*Rocky* musicals would actively encourage costuming amongst their audiences in somewhat paradoxical attempts to try to force cult followings upon such projects. *The Rocky Horror Show*, of course, never had to resort to such strained marketing tactics; its participatory rituals were entirely spontaneous, unplanned and unexpected.

Arguably the best, and certainly the cleverest, of the increasing number of rock 'n' roll jukebox musicals was *Return to the Forbidden Planet*, an engaging hit that skilfully reworked the plot of MGM's 1956 science fiction classic *Forbidden Planet* (itself based on Shakespeare's *The Tempest*) while mixing in a collection of familiar rock tunes from the 1950s and '60s – including the Safaris' 'Wipe Out', Jerry Lee Lewis's 'Great Balls of Fire' (aptly used during the rocket ship's encounter with a life-threatening storm of asteroids), the Beach Boys' 'Good Vibrations' and Bobby 'Boris' Pickett's 1962 novelty favourite 'Monster Mash' – along with an abundance of recognisable lines (and comic paraphrasing of such) from several of the Bard's most well-known plays, making it immediately intellectually superior – and yet, ingeniously, unpretentiously accessible – when compared with most outwardly superficial and lazy jukebox efforts.

Conceived by Coventry-born writer-director Bob Carlton, Artistic Director for London's Bubble Theatre Company between 1979 and 1984 and latterly Artistic Director for the Queen's Theatre, Hornchurch in Essex, *Return to the Forbidden Planet* began its life – in a tent, no less – at the Bubble Theatre during the mid-'80s. A modest experimental piece (the way in which so many eventual cult classics begin), the show continued to be revised and reworked during the next few years, and was re-launched at Liverpool's Everyman Theatre and then London's Tricycle Theatre before finally opening in the West End at the Cambridge Theatre on 18 September 1989.

Unlike the 1956 film, which had merely borrowed the premise of its storyline and very little else from *The Tempest*, the musical reinstated many of Shakespeare's original character names – hence Dr Morbius and Robby the Robot once again became Prospero and Ariel – while Carlton cheekily called his heroic and unflappable rocket ship commander Captain Tempest. Unmistakably intentional nods to the show's sci-fi B-movie origins included conspicuously undisguised hairdryers masquerading as ray guns, clearly visible wires operating the mentally-conjured monster from the id, and a performer on roller-skates representing the automated Ariel.

A thoroughly enjoyable crowd-pleaser it may have been, but, as previously noted, *Return to the Forbidden Planet* comprised already-existing pop songs rather than original compositions. Thus its triumph at the 1989/90 Laurence Olivier Awards, where it picked up the all-important Best New Musical honour – sensationally trumping the celebrated *Miss Saigon* – came as a shock to a large number of critics.

In 2009, Bob Carlton would direct the first UK production of a little-seen musical from the early 1980s. Featuring characteristically witty lyrics by Richard O'Brien, complemented by Richard Hartley's typically captivating tunes, *The Stripper* – based on a 1961 pulp novel by Carter Brown (the pen name of British-born Australian crime writer Alan G Yates,

9: SENSUAL DAYDREAMS TO TREASURE FOREVER

of whom O'Brien was a fan) – had been the outcome of a request by the Sydney Theatre Company for the two Richards to write and compose them a brand new musical.

The result, which followed the fortunes of an investigative detective, Lieutenant Al Wheeler, played by Terence Donovan (father of Jason), and his relationship with an exotic dancer by the name of Deadpan Delores, was originally mounted in Australia in 1982 with *Rocky Horror* set designer Brian Thomson assuming directorial duties; although its inception – apparently not helped by creative conflicts observed during rehearsals – would be something of a troubled one.

In the years immediately following the midnight re-launch of *The Rocky Horror Picture Show*, fans had become increasingly aware of a seemingly irrevocable clash of personalities between Brian Thomson and Richard O'Brien – not that either ever tried to make a secret of it – and, in an interview with author David Evans, which took place on Friday 5 May 2000 and appeared in the book *Rocky Horror: From Concept to Cult*, Thomson suggested that this had likely been fuelled by artistic differences on the set of *The Stripper*. An admirer of Carter Brown's original book, it seemed that O'Brien had reverently adapted it into a lengthy and rather laborious libretto. According to Thomson, the actors were having trouble with the monotonous dialogue, and, as director, he felt the script needed to be pared down and simplified in order to make it snappier and more practical

'It really needed condensing,' Thomson told David Evans. 'The dialogue was very repetitive, and so I started working on it. Richard O'Brien wasn't having any of it. He refused to have his script touched and got really pissed off. In the end, I refused to have him in the theatre.'

Creative differences about the dialogue aside, few could deny that, true to usual form for O'Brien and Hartley, *The Stripper*'s catchy and melodic songs did not disappoint. A particular highlight was 'Planning My Big Exit', an affecting final ballad sung by Robyn Moase as the dying Delores, which was easily comparable to Dr Frank-n-Furter's similarly tender farewell. Despite the show's short engagement – reportedly just five weeks – the production did spawn a now very hard to come by vinyl cast recording, much sought-after by today's ardent *Rocky Horror* collectors.

Though the high standard of his songwriting remained consistent, O'Brien had found more than once that trying to repeat *The Rocky Horror Show*'s unprecedented success was a frustrating and irritatingly impossible task. His musical *T Zee* – an earlier attempt to duplicate the elusive winning formula, with the obvious camp potential of Edgar Rice Burroughs' Tarzan legend in place of *Rocky*'s science fiction B-movie lore – opened at the Royal Court Theatre on 10 August 1976 and reunited several familiar faces.

Past *Rocky* alumni Richard O'Brien as Eugene De Lyle, Belinda Sinclair as Alison Dare and Kimi Wong doubling as Jay and a Mutant joined the likes of Paul Nicholas as Bone Idol (another typically droll O'Brien name), Warren Clarke (who had previously appeared with O'Brien at the Royal Court in Jim Sharman's well-received production of Sam Shepard's *The Unseen Hand*) as T Zee, Diane Langton as Princess La and Julian Littman as a Mutant to make up a talented ensemble. Other instantly noticeable *Rocky Horror* names in the programme included producer Michael White, Richard Hartley, composing and arranging the score in addition to playing keyboards, and Brian Thomson and Sue Blane once more handling the set and costume design duties. Michael English again designed an eye-catching poster – a large central skull flanked by a long-haired naked female beauty and a beefy Rocky Horror-alike – while photos were accredited to the incomparable Mick Rock.

Critic W Stephen Gilbert – who three years earlier had showered *The Rocky Horror Show* with unreserved enthusiasm, calling it 'Near perfect late-night diversion: hilarious, nostalgic, flattering, spoofy, hectic, loud and daft' – was not so forthcoming with the praise when called upon to review the team's latest effort for *Plays and Players* magazine in October 1976. 'T Zee looks so thin and mean that one goes back to one's enjoyment of *Rocky Horror*, fearful of the temptation to rewrite history and say it wasn't so,' he bewailed, intimating that inevitable comparisons with its groundbreaking predecessor might have been partly responsible for the new show's downfall – especially without the element of surprise, undoubtedly one of *Rocky*'s trump cards at the time of its startling debut.

Presented at 10.30 pm in the cramped and seedy attic space of the Theatre Upstairs, *Rocky Horror* had been a deliciously naughty late night guilty pleasure. Consequently, the attempt to follow it with a legitimate mainstream work – no matter how saucy or intentionally irreverent – appeared somewhat manufactured, formulaic and unavoidably contrived. 'It's later and wiser now,' Gilbert lamented, in a write-up that came over as regretful and apologetic, as though having to admit to being let down by his heroes had left this early champion of the O'Brien and Hartley partnership with feelings comparable to remorse. '*T Zee* at 9.00 in the Court's main auditorium is rather as if the Marcels had released, say, "There's a Small Hotel" as a follow-up to "Blue Moon" in the wake of the Beatles' transformation of the pop landscape.'

Gibert's analysis of Nicholas Wright's directorial skills, as compared with those of the famously inventive and resourceful Jim Sharman, was also less than favourable. The staging of *T Zee* was, the critic opined, 'Prey to false starts and dead ends; or, at least, it allows false starts and dead ends to reveal themselves all over the project.' Although he complimented the vocal talents of Belinda Sinclair and, in particular, Diane Langton, he

9: SENSUAL DAYDREAMS TO TREASURE FOREVER

felt that the combined abilities of a strong company were not nearly adequate to save the piece from a very short theatrical life and subsequent oblivion. 'The application of the cast is not enough to hide the emptiness of the project,' he concluded gloomily, as if sorrowfully aware that he might be hammering the last rusty nail into the coffin of *The Rocky Horror Show*'s first true successor. 'And the audience, resolutely unmoved throughout, file out at the end as silent as if from a funeral. *T Zee* is a melancholy event – an anachronism, all camped up and nowhere to go.'

Similar disappointments were to follow.

Richard O'Brien's *Disaster*, with music composed and adapted by Richard Hartley ('From a moderately unoriginal idea by Brian Thomson' read an under the title addendum in the programme) and a cast featuring *Rocky Horror*'s Patricia Quinn, Christopher Malcolm and Jonathan Adams as well as O'Brien himself, was presented by London's Institute of Contemporary Arts (ICA) in 1978, but its somewhat misguided title would prove depressingly prophetic.

Top People, another little known O'Brien project, opened at the Ambassador's Theatre in the West End in 1984, but reportedly closed again within a week. Ouch.

In another collaboration with Richard Hartley, O'Brien composed a trio of memorable musical numbers for Australian director Philippe Mora's *The Return of Captain Invincible*, a 1983 spoof superhero movie. This starred Alan Arkin, Christopher Lee and Kate Fitzpatrick (who had played the role of Magenta in Jim Sharman's 1974 production of *The Rocky Horror Show* in Sydney) and achieved something of a cult success during the mid-1980s.

O'Brien extensively reworked the script of *The Stripper* for Bob Carlton's UK production, which premiered at the Queen's Theatre, Hornchurch on Friday 28 August 2009. This version featured Jonathan Wrather as detective Al Wheeler, Emma-Jayne Appleyard as Deadpan Delores, Jack Edwards and Chris Ellis-Stanton (who had appeared as Eddie/Dr Scott and Brad respectively in the 2008/09 European tour of *The Rocky Horror Show*) as Harvey Stern and Steve Loomis, and O'Brien himself in the relatively small role of Mr Arkwright. He cut several of the show's original songs and at least one character, while adding new numbers, penned by himself and Hartley, to the score.

'I said to Richard that this was a chance to write some more rock 'n' roll,' O'Brien revealed in an interview for the production's programme, 'but when I started to think about it, I realised these characters were more likely to listen to Ella Fitzgerald and Sinatra and drink whisky; a slightly more grown-up and jaded bunch. The songs are deliberately puerile, but they also comment on the hypocrisy and exploitative nature of the genre.'

While the show was quite well-received, particularly amongst followers of O'Brien's work, many British fans who had already heard the 1982 Australian cast recording seemed to prefer the original's somewhat more rock 'n' roll arrangements.

'They were paperback pulp fiction,' said O'Brien of Carter Brown's work, during the same interview. 'Reading matter – I won't call them literature – written for undereducated adolescent males, a bit like the James Bond books, the only difference being that James Bond was written by a man who went to Eton. But the writing is just as puerile, but also just as enjoyable and very much targeted at men – the girls in both of them are always slightly available and big breasted and all that stuff.'

Following its debut in Hornchurch, the UK production of *The Stripper* embarked upon a criminally short mini-tour, limited to just Milton Keynes and Glasgow, after which its creators would assess the public's response before deciding whether or not to make further rewrites and changes for another potential re-launch in the future. In an online promotional video for the 2010 UK tour of *The Rocky Horror Show*, O'Brien let slip that one possible innovation to *The Stripper*, which he seemed to still think of as a work in progress, might be a change of title. He suggested *Drop Dead Delores* as a promising alternative.

O'Brien elucidated further during an interview on Radio New Zealand later the same year, in which he divulged that, while its short UK tour had proved that there was an audience for such a musical, he and Hartley had already rewritten parts of its script and score in response to its reception. 'We've reworked it, and it's off to find a good first class director,' he revealed, confirming that one song had already been removed and another added. 'And when we get the first class director, he can get the other people – first class people – a designer and whatever.'

Another reworked, and somewhat scaled-down, UK production of *The Stripper* – this one directed by Benji Sperring, with cabaret style seating and a cast of five – would open for a five-week summer engagement at London's St James Theatre on 7 July 2016, suggesting that both O'Brien and Hartley continued to regard the piece as something of a work in progress and had not yet given up on it.

Having successfully launched *The Stripper* in the UK for Richard O'Brien and the Ambassador Theatre Group, the Queen's Theatre, Hornchurch was given the rare opportunity to stage its own four-week repertory production of *The Rocky Horror Show* during the summer of 2011. The endeavour would prove interesting and challenging, particularly as the theatre's company of resident players, known as cut to the chase… (in lower case) and formed by Bob Carlton in 1998, was a troupe of actor-musicians. The multi-talented performers would therefore play their own instruments (most could play at least two) in character, eliminating the necessity for the conventional separate band. This arrangement, which had worked perfectly for *Return to the Forbidden Planet* – that particular musical having been conceived that way in the first place – would prove divisive amongst hardcore *Rocky Horror* fans. With the show's dialogue so cinematically sparing and economical, a great deal of important characterisation and subtle motivational business needed to happen between the lines – a sly look here, a facial tick there – which proved undoubtedly tricky with Riff Raff playing an electric violin, Magenta on sax and Janet frequently blowing into her trumpet.

An inventive set, designed by Mark Walters, incorporated instantly recognisable visual references to *The Rocky Horror Picture Show* – including 'Denton: The Home of Happiness!' billboards in the opening scene's churchyard and a reproduction of Grant Wood's 'American Gothic' painting above the door of the castle's vestibule – in addition to a montage of adroitly-selected science fiction movie clips pertaining to the Usherette's opening number. This perfectly-pitched design helped curb some initial fan concern by immediately capturing the B-movie feel of the piece, as well as Richard O'Brien's original intentions; while one noteworthy face in the nine-strong cast (Phantoms and understudies were also economically absent from this translation of the show) was that of Julian Littman as the Narrator.

As the Queen's Theatre's musical director, Littman was also responsible for arranging the show's beloved and iconic songs for the production. The actor had begun a long association with Richard O'Brien when he had appeared as a Mutant in the ill-fated *T Zee* at the Royal Court Theatre in 1976, while 30 years later he assumed the role of Dr Everett Scott in the one-off *Rocky Horror Tribute Show* in May 2006, again at the Royal Court. Littman's interpretation of the Narrator, channelling the distinctive intonation of both Orson Welles and Vincent Price, was a refreshing return to the character's Edgar Lustgarten roots after years of stunt casting had witnessed a long line of celebs pretty much playing themselves.

While it was felt by some that the unsettling actor-musician dynamic had indeed impeded some of the plot's essential character nuances, not to mention Richard O'Brien's oft-repeated 'play it for real' mandate, the strength of the show as written, along with a spirited and enthusiastic cast – Littman's Narrator, Tom Jude's quivering Riff Raff and Simon Jessop's hysterical turn as a manic and rather Dr Strangelove-esque Dr Scott in particular – made it a phenomenally successful four-week run for a struggling independent theatre.

In 1990, with *The Rocky Horror Picture Show* celebrating 15 triumphant years as the world's longest-running and most popular cult movie, 20th Century Fox announced that they were to produce a direct sequel, entitled *Revenge of the Old Queen*, from a new script by Richard O'Brien.

As previously recounted, although *Shock Treatment*, the unsuccessful

1981 follow-up to *The Rocky Horror Picture Show*, had borne no relation to the events of the first picture, O'Brien had initially composed the majority of its songs as part of a screenplay entitled *Rocky Horror Shows His Heels*, which would have continued the first film's chronology with a scientifically-revived Frank-n-Furter and Janet Weiss pregnant with his child.

'*Shock Treatment* was a disaster,' the author declared openly during his interview with Rob Cope in 1990, in which he implied that shoehorning the songs into a totally unrelated story, instead of making the film for which they had been written, had been a misguided decision by Jim Sharman, and that going down that particular route had proved to be a mistake. 'The soundtrack of *Shock Treatment* is great,' he avowed proudly, 'and if you listen to the soundtrack, you can see the potential the film could have had; and it didn't have that because we got sidetracked by Jim Sharman. In fact he has to take complete responsibility for sidetracking us, and we have to take complete responsibility for going along with it, for allowing him to do that.

'We should've gone with the first draft,' he continued. 'It would have been much better. We should've developed the first draft, as opposed to saying no.

'He said, "I don't want to do more of the same." In which case, at that moment, we should've said, "In that case, Jim, you go and do your film, the films you want to do; but we want to do this."

'That's what we should have done. But we didn't do it. God knows why, but we didn't.'

Revenge of the Old Queen would apparently ignore the events of *Shock Treatment* and take up the *Rocky Horror* story 15 years later, with Riff Raff returning to his home planet of Transsexual in order to answer for his crimes and explain the disappearance of Frank-n-Furter to the queen (widely rumoured to be Frank's mother).

'Riff Raff'll be in it,' the author confirmed. 'Riff Raff is the scapegoat, so he has to be in basically; 'cos he has to take the blame, and he has to be booted and cajoled, and the worm turning again.'

While it remains a writer's prerogative to secure a meaty role for himself or herself, a humorous statement printed in the souvenir booklet that accompanied *The Rocky Horror Picture Show*'s fifteenth anniversary DVD box set, written by Richard O'Brien in the first person from Riff Raff's perspective, seemed to indicate that Patricia Quinn would not be afforded the same privilege. 'The real story of what happened in that house is known only by me and my late sister, and obviously she's no longer talking,' the piece announced cryptically, leading fans to wonder how far the psychopathic handyman might have gone in order to cover his tracks and silence any witnesses.

9: SENSUAL DAYDREAMS TO TREASURE FOREVER

Ultimately such speculation would go unanswered. Although the TimeWarp fan club's 1992 *Rocky Horror* convention brought confirmation from Zalie Burrow and Kate O'Sullivan – two actresses who had featured in the recent West End revival of *The Rocky Horror Show* and its subsequent tour – that they had provided vocals for demo recordings of a couple of new songs for the proposed new film's score, entitled 'The Moon Drenched Shores of Transylvania' and 'Never Let Your Daughter Date an Alien' (the first of which later turned up online, thus confirming its existence), the project remained in pre-production hell for several years before appearing to have been cancelled.

Burrow happily demonstrates that she can still recall some of the lyrics from the unmade sequel's score, revealing a few tantalising snippets of what could have been: "'Never let your daughter date an alien, you don't know where they've been,'" she intones nostalgically, confirming that the words would have been true to O'Brien's signature ironic wit. "'It's terrifying getting tactile with a Martian pterodactyl. You get no sympathetic touches when they've got you in their clutches ...'"

While *Revenge of the Old Queen* was considered dead and buried by the end of the 1990s, O'Brien's earlier premise for a 'monster rises from the grave' type of sequel – abandoned in favour of *Shock Treatment* – would not be forgotten. In 2001 it was announced that he had been redeveloping some of the themes explored in his original treatment for *Rocky Horror Shows His Heels* – particularly the idea of Janet being pregnant with Frank-n-Furter's baby – and was planning to incorporate them into a new *Rocky Horror* sequel for the stage. Though officially untitled, this work would, for a while, be unofficially christened *Rocky Horror: The Second Coming* by fans.

A number of other personal projects would periodically interrupt the author's progress on the venture. *Disgracefully Yours*, a one-man (and three backing singers) stand-up show, featuring O'Brien as the sardonic singing demon Mephistopheles Smith – a devilish evangelist blithely promoting a new and improved Hell as the afterlife destination of choice (a character O'Brien had already debuted at TimeWarp's *Rocky Horror* convention on Hallowe'en 1992) – played a well-received season at the Edinburgh Festival during the summer of 1995, followed by a short run of 21 performances at London's Comedy Theatre in March 1996; *Absolute O'Brien*, a solo album of self-penned compositions (labelled 'cool jazz' as opposed to rock 'n' roll) was released on CD in 1999; and, as already noted, the reworked UK version of his melodramatic musical detective story *The Stripper* opened in Hornchurch in 2009.

It would be fair to point out that a lot of fans hold the view that *The Rocky Horror Show* ought to remain a one-off self-contained story; that the fate of Brad and Janet beyond the Narrator's closing 'Lost in time, and lost in space, and meaning' speech should be eternally ambiguous; and that untold revivals of the timeless original, or even a brand new Richard O'Brien musical completely unrelated to the events and characters of *The Rocky Horror Show*, would be infinitely preferable to any kind of direct sequel.

However, rumours that the author-composer was continuing to work on the script for the follow-up persisted. The conversation between O'Brien and director Christopher Luscombe transcribed in the souvenir brochure for the 2006 UK tour of *The Rocky Horror Show* dropped further hints about its development.

'Brad is one of those old-fashioned protective men,' said Luscombe, clarifying his approach to the characters for the latest touring production. 'He's always telling Janet that everything's going to be okay because he's by her side. Yet if anybody's equipped to deal with the experience it's Janet. And ultimately Brad learns a lot from Frank. I suspect he'll be a good husband, because of what he's experienced.'

'Not according to what happens in my Part 2, he won't,' O'Brien replied, cunningly refuelling fan intrigue with one deliberately vague sentence.

'We'll save that for next year,' was Luscombe's even more cryptic response, before he quickly changed the subject.

While this led many *Rocky* enthusiasts to conclude that an inaugural production of the new sequel might be on the verge of being mounted – probably with Luscombe directing – the assumptions again proved premature.

During a live on stage talk about the history of *Rocky Horror* at London's South Bank Centre on the evening of Sunday 4 September 2011, O'Brien and long-time collaborator Richard Hartley divulged that, even though a solid draft of the sequel's first act did exist, its second half had been the subject of continual rewrites for many years, and neither was yet satisfied with the work as a whole. Promisingly, O'Brien made it clear that he would not want to see a production of the show mounted in any form until he felt sure that the script and the score were right.

However, while this declaration from the author would seem to once again cut short any notion of a new *Rocky Horror Show* stage sequel, it was not in fact the end of the story, as an already existing spin-off was about to be unexpectedly resurrected.

In the wake of its initial big screen release and meagre box office takings, *Shock Treatment* – Jim Sharman's 1981 cinematic follow-up to *The Rocky Horror Picture Show* – had, slowly but surely, gained a legitimate cult following in its own right. While not even close to that of its predecessor's midnight event status, the fact that a spin-off very few had actually seen (or even heard of) could gather its own separate loyal fan base was a noteworthy achievement.

9: SENSUAL DAYDREAMS TO TREASURE FOREVER

One particularly outspoken and unashamed supporter of *Shock Treatment* was British film critic Mark Kermode, who repeatedly described it as one of his favourite cult films. On the evening of Saturday 17 September 2011, Kermode presented a gala screening of the movie as part of the second annual New Forest Film Festival at Brockenhurst College in Hampshire, England.

During a pre-screening Q&A, before an assemblage of faithful *Shock Treatment* fans – many of them dressed as characters from the movie – the evening's special guest Richard O'Brien described the film – the very film he was there to introduce – as 'Deeply, deeply flawed'.

'There's a lot wrong with it,' he insisted, 'the storyline is exceptionally muddy, exceptionally difficult to follow'; and, while he praised the songs – arguing that the score was possibly even better than that of *Rocky Horror* – and the efforts of the cast, declaring that his on screen co-stars were all, 'Doing as well as they could with the rather inept storyline,' (a comment which drew an appreciative chuckle from the captivated crowd) – it was abundantly clear that the overall product had been a huge disappointment to its typically unassuming writer-composer.

Nevertheless, when asked by Kermode if – in light of its recent reassessment and newfound appreciation – it was likely that *Shock Treatment* would ever be turned into a stage production, O'Brien was not unreceptive to the idea:

'With our knowledge of reality TV, and this idea that fame is more important than talent,' he conceded, 'I think we could actually turn it into a good stage show.'

The ever-astute author acknowledged, however, that it would perhaps be more prudent for another writer and creative team to adapt the piece for such a venture. 'So often you can't see the wood for the trees,' he admitted, 'I think probably it would need somebody else with wit and intelligence to come in and do that.'

Therefore, when it was announced in early 2015 that Tarquin Productions and director Benji Sperring would be mounting the very first official stage production of *Shock Treatment* at the King's Head Theatre Pub in the London Borough of Islington, it became apparent that O'Brien had finally found the 'wit and intelligence' that he felt the piece required. However, as revealed in an article for the 16 April 2015 edition of the *Stage* newspaper, the project had been a long time coming. The piece declared that Sperring had first approached O'Brien – with the proposal of turning *Shock Treatment* into a stage production – ten years previously, shortly after the director had graduated from the director's course at the Central School of Speech and Drama:

'"He kept putting me off, saying it was the wrong time, but I went back to him again and again," says the director. "Eventually he invited me to explain what I wanted to do with the show and last year I got the 'Let's do it' call I'd been waiting for."'

The enthusiastic young director also recalled how, like so many others, his experience of seeing a certain classic rock 'n' roll musical at a young age had been a massive influence during his adolescence: '"I saw *The Rocky Horror Show* at the Birmingham Hippodrome when I was 15 or 16 and it was a revelation. It literally changed my life. I'd grown up in a repressed, single-parent family where sexuality wasn't discussed. So it was life-affirming for me to find that the feelings I'd been having were normal, that guys could love guys, women could love women, it wasn't all as clear-cut as I'd been led to believe. We sat at the side of the stage, in a box, and at one point Jonathan Wilkes, who was playing Frank-n-Furter, looked up and winked at me and I felt like the most special person in the audience. I've never forgotten that."'

In the same article for the *Stage*, Richard O'Brien explained his reasons for finally allowing the much criticised and often misunderstood *Rocky Horror* follow-up to be staged theatrically for the first time:

'"We were waiting for someone to come along who believed in the work. Hearing the ideas of this young company, they saw the potential and the possibilities of something that has waited patiently on the shelf for many years. It was our ideas that created the work originally, but it is their ideas that have shaped it to what it will become."'

Whereas O'Brien's faultless script for *The Rocky Horror Show* – which had benefitted instantly from its slender B-movie structure and economical use of dialogue – would continue to be praised decades after the show's memorable 1973 opening, *Shock Treatment*'s detractors (O'Brien included) had immediately found its screenplay (co-written by O'Brien and director Jim Sharman) to be a rather overblown, disjointed mess. The challenge of adapting this imperfect screenplay into a witty, coherent and engaging stage play would go to Tom Crowley. In 2008, this aspiring writer-performer had taken a new 'Writing, Directing and Performance' university course in the UK city of York, although he believes that much of his education actually came from the extracurricular societies that he joined during his time there:

'The Drama Society staged nine plays per term in their Drama Barn venue and I wrote my first play, *Shed* – to be staged there – and directed it myself,' he reflects, '*Shed* was the script I sent to the Royal Court Theatre's literary department that got me accepted onto the Royal Court Young Writers Programme in 2012.'

For his part in the King's Head Theatre's Trainee Director Scheme in 2013, Crowley assumed the roles of Assistant Stage Manager on director Adam Spreadbury-Maher's adaptation of Giuseppi Verdi's 1859 opera *Un Ballo In Maschera* (*A Masked Ball*) – the events of which would be

9: SENSUAL DAYDREAMS TO TREASURE FOREVER

imaginatively relocated to the updated setting of a Swedish furniture superstore in Wembley – and Assistant Director for Robin Norton-Hale's London production of Liz Lochhead's critically acclaimed *Mary Queen of Scots Got Her Head Chopped Off*.

'This consolidated my involvement with the theatre after I'd got to know the team a bit through my friend Rachel Lerman, who was a producer there for many years,' the writer explains.

'After the trainee scheme, I worked the box office for a while to support the lifestyle of hedonism and vulgarity to which I had become accustomed, and I think just being around helped me to stay in the team's thoughts. There was a big change of management at the theatre around the end of 2014 and the start of 2015, with half of the team leaving to become a touring company and the other half staying to run the venue, with Adam Spreadbury-Maher staying on as Artistic Director.'

With a view of cementing a fresh identity for the King's Head – originally founded by Dan Crawford in 1970 and purportedly London's second oldest operating pub theatre – Spreadbury-Maher proposed a 'From Screen to Stage' season, incorporating an immersive adaptation of Irvine Welsh's 1993 novel *Trainspotting* – itself the inspiration for Danny Boyle's acclaimed 1996 film of the same name – and Benji Sperring's stage premiere of *Shock Treatment*.

'Adam asked if I'd be interested in applying for the job of adapting the latter, and, of course, I said yes please,' Tom Crowley elaborates, 'After that, I was sent the partially-unused screenplay for *The Brad and Janet Show* and the shooting script of *Shock Treatment*, and told to study up and come to a meeting with Benji, bringing a few thoughts on how I'd bring it to the stage.'

'As I recall, I believe I came to the meeting with a general idea that we should slim down the cast size and the complexity of the film's many subplots; but that really it was up to Benji what he wanted to do with the material, as the stage production was his baby. I think all of that endeared me to him as a potential writer, particularly the last part.'

Consequently, the task of reworking the piece for an intimate performance space at the back of a London pub began with a substantial cull of the film's innumerable surplus characters, which would see the movie's excessive ensemble reduced to a cast of just seven performers. Although this drastic decision would initially have fans of the film lamenting the loss of certain beloved characters – especially the enigmatic Austrian game show host, gourmet chef and questionable psychiatrist Bert Schnick, memorably brought to life in the film by the legendary Barry Humphries – it would significantly ground the show's narrative and allow the story to focus primarily on three very different (and largely dysfunctional) couples – Brad and Janet Majors, Ralph and Betty

Hapschatt, and Cosmo and Nation McKinley – as well as primary antagonist and chief manipulator Farley Flavors.

'When we began working on the adaptation, we had a brief synopsis which I believe Benji had put together and got approved by O'Brien and Hartley in advance,' reveals Crowley, 'So we were starting from a mutually agreed position.'

The writer confirms that this pre-approved treatment already had a number of key changes in place, chiefly the aforementioned omission of Bert Schnick – who would nevertheless be referenced verbally by other characters, thus confirming his existence within the show's universe – and the film's shock reveal that Brad and Farley were in fact twin brothers:

'It was sad to lose Bert, of course,' he admits, 'Benji and I discussed Bert early on, and while Barry Humphries is absolutely excellent in the film – and a blind, loudly-dressed Teutonic celebrity chef is an undoubtedly inspired concept for a character – we couldn't justify making room in the script and the budget for another character. We decided instead to put all of that stage presence and Frank-n-Furter-esque pizzazz into Farley, who, in the film, is a much more mysterious and sinister figure.'

'It was quite helpful to remove the "I am your brother" twist, and focus solely on Farley as an agent of temptation and corruption to Janet, with Brad as the damsel in distress,' the writer adds, whilst also acknowledging that the identical twins aspect of the film's plot would have been considerably more challenging to achieve in a theatrical setting:

'I love Cliff De Young as both Brad and Farley,' he declares, 'but we couldn't have an actor double on stage in the same way. If we'd gone down that route, [the musical number] 'Duel Duet' would have involved some incredibly speedy quick-changes.'

While few would question the talents of Cliff De Young and Jessica Harper – their performances in *Shock Treatment* remain undeniably solid – many felt that they were not the same characters viewers had met in the first film. Therefore, when it came to the stage version, one very wise decision would be to make the protagonists unmistakably recognisable as *Rocky Horror*'s Brad and Janet, a couple audiences already knew and cared about.

'If *Shock Treatment* is fundamentality a battle for Janet's soul, as we see in the film, then we need to set up the stakes of that battle,' Crowley explains, 'Brad and Janet love each other, truly, but they're having trouble seeing eye-to-eye and aren't certain whether they've chosen the right path in life; experiences many couples go through. This makes them both ideal prey for hybrid TV producer/televangelist Farley, who offers not only fame and fortune, but also purpose.'

'It's hard to recall exactly what decisions were made at which points, as the adaptation was an ongoing conversation throughout, but I remember that my main driving instinct when I began my work on the script was that it seemed crucial that we set out clearly that this was the same Brad and Janet that we met in *Rocky Horror*, that this was a direct sequel, and that we were going to see that same couple's relationship develop and encounter difficulties along the way.'

Creating such continuity for Richard O'Brien's hapless young couple would be achieved early on by Xylona Appleton's simple costume design, which eschewed the 1980s power suit – worn by Jessica Harper's Janet in the movie version – in favour of a plain, vaguely frumpy, bored housewife variation of Janet's familiar mid-century attire from *The Rocky Horror Show*. As history started to repeat itself, and Janet's self-confidence and suppressed sexuality again began to take control, this conventionality would be contrasted by a short, slutty, white vinyl nurse's uniform and of course the show-stopping little black dress. Additionally, hilarious new lines of dialogue – such as Janet declaring that she and Brad had, 'Been through so much together; infidelity, homicide, aliens, fishnet stockings... and that was just the engagement party' – neatly tied the two stories together, whilst serving as joyous little call-backs to the events of *Rocky Horror*.

Other fan-pleasing sharp new lines included the likes of 'What is your Majors malfunction?', 'Wake up and smell the Rohypnol', and 'We didn't get where we are today by leaving incriminating fingerprints on dangerously modified medical equipment', while the script also instated 'Trust me, I'm a doctor' – the 1981 film poster's celebrated satirical tagline – as a spoken declaration from Dr Cosmo McKinley. Another welcome innovation would be the inclusion of some electro-shock therapy ('of the most humane variety,' insists an increasingly unhinged Cosmo), which – although alluded to in Richard O'Brien's ultimately discarded screenplay for *The Brad and Janet Show* – had been bizarrely absent from a film called *Shock Treatment*.

Even more crucially, Tom Crowley's exceptionally sharp script developed the motives and psychology of Ralph Hapschatt quite dramatically. Not only did Brad's and Janet's High School friend – the wedding of whom had served as the original catalyst for their own engagement and subsequent strange journey – now have a thirst for fame which possibly even surpassed that of Janet, but, by making it abundantly clear that his adoration for Farley Flavors was more than mere hero worship, a confused sexuality became an integral component of his character's arc. As well as adding weight to the matter of the Hapschatts' marriage problems, and with the removal of Janet's jingoistic dad, Harry Weiss, from the proceedings, this development allowed 'Thank God I'm a Man' – Richard O'Brien's brilliantly ironic ode to misogynistic, flag waving bigotry – to be fittingly transferred to the repressed Ralph. Even more appropriately, Ralph's story now climaxed with a lively rendition of 'Breaking Out', the rousing rock anthem originally intended to be sung by Rocky Horror as he rose from the ashes at the beginning of *Rocky Horror Shows His Heels*, O'Brien's previous attempt at a *Rocky Horror* follow-up. Having been forced to commit the cardinal sin of not advancing the plot – by being relegated to an extraneous performance by the on screen band Oscar Drill and the Bits in the *Shock Treatment* movie – this fantastic song was finally given the relevance it craved and deserved, with lyrics such as 'I've been a lifetime on deposit, and that's a long time in the closet' now feeling much more pertinent.

Although its screenplay had been derided by many, the most consistently praised aspect of *Shock Treatment* had always been its songs, with O'Brien and Hartley delivering their usual high standard of clever catchy tunes.

'The main thing that hit me was how good the songs were,' says Tom Crowley, recalling the first time he viewed the film, 'I couldn't believe more people weren't talking about those songs.'

With this is mind, most of the numbers would remain largely unaltered for the stage production, although, due to the scaled down cast, some would have their lyrics amended accordingly and be assigned to different characters.

'Both O'Brien and Hartley were incredibly supportive of the project,' Crowley confirms, 'O'Brien more distantly so, as he was already living in New Zealand, but he sent numerous e-mails to the team to wish us well and congratulate us on our advance press and, later, good reviews.'

'Hartley, however, was incredibly hands-on and available to us,' the writer continues, emphasising the vital collaboration between the movie's composer and the stage version's Musical Director Alex Beetschen as they embarked on the, 'Staggering challenge of condensing the film's explosive rock 'n' roll tunes down to a small band in a tiny pub theatre.'

'I didn't get to spend a huge amount of time with Hartley,' he confesses, 'But he seemed uniformly charming, intelligent and helpful.'

For the stage adaptation, the most lyrically reworked song would be 'Looking For Trade'. Originally written by Richard O'Brien as he was putting together *Rocky Horror Shows His Heels* – his first crack at a *Rocky Horror* sequel – in 1978, the number would have reportedly seen a recently revived Frank-n-Furter hunting for young virgin boys, whose blood he required in order to prevent his body from decomposing (due to an error in the resurrection process); hence the lyric 'I need some young blood, I need it now'. It is fair to say that, without this context, the song had felt somewhat shoehorned into what eventually became *Shock Treatment*. With new lyrics – written by Crowley (in collaboration with Alex Beetschen) – the song became 'Looking For Fame', which better fitted the themes of the

9: SENSUAL DAYDREAMS TO TREASURE FOREVER

story by highlighting Janet's rabid new thirst for stardom.

'One of the film's greatest points is its uncanny prediction of reality television as we know it now – rivalled only by Nigel Kneale's *The Year of the Sex Olympics* – so it seemed important to preserve the film's lessons about the vapidity, corruption and danger of quick-'n'-easy fame, and add to those the observations we've been able to make, with the benefit of hindsight, here in the early part of the 21st century,' Crowley continues, defending the ultimately justified decision to revise this particular song in order to amplify its relevance to the plot, 'We needed Janet's temptation to cleave closer to the central theme of the show as we saw it.'

As evidenced by the original production of *The Rocky Horror Show*, a small cast in a rather compact performance space would undoubtedly be subject to an amplified level of critical scrutiny. The correct balance of highly talented performers was therefore an essential ingredient of the show's potential success.

In the pivotal role of Janet Majors, the vivacious Julie Atherton – already a musical star of some repute, with a number of solo albums and several West End and touring credits to her name (including an acclaimed turn as Kate Monster and Lucy the Slut in the 2006 London debut of the hit 2003 Broadway musical *Avenue Q*) – would skilfully convey both likeable vulnerability and ruthless ambition, whilst never letting the audience forget who they were supposed to be rooting for. Likewise, as Brad – victim of the McKinley's malevolent malpractices and titular electro-shock therapy – Ben Kerr brought a truthful susceptibility to a role which, in terms of *Shock Treatment*'s plot at least, could perhaps be perceived as less significant, and thus more of a challenge in many ways, than that of his high-flying wife. An added reprise of 'In My Own Way', with a sombre arrangement and appropriately emotional lyrics, provided a connection to Janet's rendition of the song earlier in the show and brought Brad's story to a satisfying conclusion.

Subsequent to *Shock Treatment*'s run at the King's Head, Kerr would join the cast of the 2015/16 UK tour of *The Rocky Horror Show*, as one of the production's four onstage Phantoms. The position would also require him to understudy the part of Brad in the event of the principal actor being indisposed for any reason. Therefore, when he actually did cover the role – at Manchester's Opera House on Thursday 7 January 2016 – Ben Kerr became the first actor to have played Brad Majors in officially licensed professional productions of both *The Rocky Horror Show* and its follow-up; a small, but undeniably noteworthy, *Rocky Horror* landmark.

While most would concede that, as a primary villain, *Shock Treatment*'s Farley Flavors lacked a great deal of Frank-n-Furter's deliciously mesmerising charisma and sexual magnetism, the enigmatic manipulator had a compelling presence nonetheless. Whilst clearly still pulling everybody's strings, the stage incarnation of Farley – no longer just a 'Fast Food King' – now appeared to own not just all of Denton's businesses, but the entire town itself. This sly comment on the 21st century's 'Mr Corporation' mentality blatantly expanded the narrative's observations on modern consumerism, probably best exemplified in the film by the brilliantly satirical 'Bitchin' in the Kitchen' (another terrific example of Richard O'Brien's distinctively witty flair as a lyricist).

For the first three weeks of the show's seven week run at the King's Head, Farley would be played by Australian actor-writer-comedian Mark Little. Known primarily for his role as Joe Mangel in the popular television soap opera *Neighbours*, as well as his highly praised performance in the one-man West End stage show *Defending the Caveman* (which won a prestigious Laurence Olivier Award in 2000), Little's winning personality and enthusiastic performance as Farley – which made up for his noticeable limitations as a singer – was duly embraced by audiences.

For the remainder of the run, the role would be taken by Pete Gallagher, an appealing and prolific stage actor with a resounding singing voice and the charisma to match. No stranger to Richard O'Brien's wonderfully weird world, having memorably played the dual role of Eddie and Dr Scott in the 21st anniversary UK tour of *The Rocky Horror Show* in 1994 – the celebrated production which famously starred Jonathon Morris as Frank-n-Furter, Sophie Lawrence as Janet, and the legendary Patricia Quinn reprising her original role of Magenta – Gallagher was a welcome addition to the *Shock Treatment* cast. At well over six feet tall, the striking actor had given Eddie in particular the suitably imposing look of a classic Frankenstein's monster, and his impressive stature and rock star qualities were a perfect fit for the overbearing authoritarian Farley Flavors.

As The Twins Macabre – an already established ghoulish and unsettling comedy double act – Adam Rhys-Davies and Nic Lamont had garnered critical acclaim and something of a cult following on the UK comedy and cabaret circuit in the roles of homicidal ten-year-old psychopaths Maurice and Ivy Macabre, making them the ideal choice for *Shock Treatment*'s devious siblings Cosmo and Nation McKinley, to which they brought a suitably strange, sleazy and darkly comedic creepiness. With their expert comic timing and unmistakable chemistry, the talented duo, dressed in formal pressed white shirts, dark ties and shiny black trousers (an interesting departure from Sue Blane's clinical green medical uniforms from the original film version) – sexy and sinister in equal measure – infused their characters with a remarkably funny and fascinating oddness, making them entirely their own whilst cannily retaining the essential essence of those created on film by Richard O'Brien and Patricia Quinn.

Somewhat akin to *The Rocky Horror Show*, the limited number of players dictated that there were no peripheral characters, as all were now vital to

9: SENSUAL DAYDREAMS TO TREASURE FOREVER

advancing the events of the story. With no Bert Schnick, for example, scheming charlatan practitioners Cosmo and Nation would play a much larger role in both the script itself and Farley's overall plan. Similarly, while no longer coupled with the film's Judge Oliver Wright, a spirited performance from Rosanna Hyland would see the resourceful and resilient Betty Hapschatt independently solving the mysteries, exposing the villains and helping to reunify Brad and Janet, making her, in many ways, the sole voice of sagacious reason in this otherwise completely mad world.

Portraying Betty's estranged, narcissistic, confused and desperately ambitious husband, Ralph – a role expanded enormously for the stage version – the effervescent Mateo Oxley turned in a delightfully camp, unrestrained and at once crowd-pleasing performance, embracing weirdly appropriate hints of Jim Carrey's eccentric title character from the 1994 comedy film *Ace Ventura: Pet Detective.*

The fact that *Rocky Horror* had started life as a modest fringe production in a tiny location – only to be adapted into a fairly major motion picture – and the sequel was now going through a reversal of the same process was lost on no-one. The uncomplicated set design by Tim Shortall – bare white walls, dominated by an ominously oversized version of the customary 'On/Off Air' light box, perfectly fusing typical TV studio conventions with the unhealthy sterility of a clichéd sanatorium – brilliantly suited the piece whilst adequately reflecting *Rocky*'s humble beginnings. In keeping with its cinematic origins – as well as *The Rocky Horror Show*'s original Theatre Upstairs production – the show would also be presented without an intermission, a decision which served the frenetic pace and non-stop rock 'n' roll feel of the piece enormously.

When *Shock Treatment: The Musical* – as it was known on posters and other promotional material – opened at the King's Head for its first preview performance on Friday 17 April 2015, the first few rows of its eager full house audience were occupied largely by dedicated *Rocky Horror* and *Shock Treatment* aficionados, many of them costumed accordingly.

'We knew that we'd have fans in costume, and we were even fairly sure that we'd have a large number of fans in *Shock Treatment*-specific costumes, who knew the songs,' declares Tom Crowley, 'But we couldn't have predicted the joy we felt at our first preview, when all the Cosmos and Nations turned up in force and belted out 'Denton USA' along with the cast. That was quite something.'

Indeed, while customary lyric boards were held aloft for the opening number's chorus – in the style of an actual television company's easy manipulation of its studio audience – primarily for the benefit of the show's largely conventional theatre crowd, hardcore fans immediately revealed that, for them at least, such cheesy pantomime tactics were completely unnecessary, as – to the surprise and delight of the company –

they proceeded to boisterously sing along to each and every song from O'Brien's and Hartley's rich and enduring score. By the time the appropriate company reprise of 'Little Black Dress' rounded off the evening, the entire audience was on its feet, singing and cheering with jubilant approval. Fans – even those costumed as the likes of Nurse Ansalong and Bert Schnick (characters which had been cut from the stage adaptation) – embraced this fresh new take on *Rocky Horror*'s often overlooked spin-off right away, and even found themselves accepting the controversial decision to drastically condense the cast to just seven players. Having wrestled with such choices during the writing process, Tom Crowley happily admits that this instant fan validation came as quite a relief:

'That was, for me, the greatest challenge: make sure the fans don't miss Bert. My greatest vindication came after the first preview, when an audience member – who had literally come dressed as Bert – told me that losing him from the show was acceptable.'

After a week of previews, the production opened officially to the press on 22 April 2015, and, while some criticised a few technical acoustic issues, most reviewers seemed to agree with the enthusiastic opinions of the hardcore fans.

'Richard O'Brien's talent for subversive social satire thrives in this lively adaptation for the small stage,' was Paul Vale's adroit summing up for his four (out of five) star review in the 30 April 2015 edition of the *Stage* newspaper; while, in her write-up for Westendwilma.com, Lisa Theresa Downey-Dent declared – not entirely accurately – that, 'It is a common consensus that *Shock Treatment* is ignored if not despised by *Rocky Horror* lovers,' before continuing eagerly, 'but this production could turn the tables. Characters, storytelling and incoherencies have all been tightened and condensed into a still insane, but somehow coherent, massively entertaining show that makes the audience care for the plight of all characters,'

'*Shock Treatment* is a must-see musical, impossible to be more critical about,' Downey-Dent enthused, proclaiming excitedly, 'Had someone offered, I'd have stayed for the second performance an hour later without hesitation.'

For Britishtheatre.com, Stephen Collins' largely positive online review praised the set design, script adaptation and performances – particularly that of the much-lauded Julie Atherton – although, like several others, he was compelled to point out Mark Little's shortcomings as a singer. Perhaps most interestingly, whilst praising the performance of Ben Kerr, Collins likened Brad's situation to that of Christ awaiting the crucifixion, possibly perceiving even deeper profundities than the script's generally acknowledged themes of obsessive TV habits, toxic fame, corporate greed

9: SENSUAL DAYDREAMS TO TREASURE FOREVER

and modern consumerism.

'In hindsight,' Collins' astute three-star write-up concluded, 'O'Brien's 1981 script is strangely prescient, especially with its focus on quick fix solutions, the wide-reach and unstoppability of reality television and that fact that, despite the passage of time, individuality and acceptance are not universal concepts. So, while there is a real sense that this show is just shits and giggles, there is an underbelly of social comment which is worth reflection.'

Considering such generous reviews and audience acclaim, it was extremely disappointing to many that – for reasons which would remain undisclosed to the public (a practice which, as always, succeeded only in fuelling speculation and the online rumour mill) – a subsequent revival or West End transfer, which many devotees had hoped for, never materialised. Likewise, no licensed cast album would be produced, leaving fans with nothing but dodgy bootleg recordings as a means of preserving and reliving the show's many pleasures.

Marketing for the King's Head Theatre Pub's debut production of *Shock Treatment: The Musical* exploited the film's established 'Not a sequel, not a prequel, but an equal' approach quite proudly – with the phrase 'For the first time on stage, The Rocky Horror Show sequel – prequel – equal' (the words 'sequel' and 'prequel' being unceremoniously crossed out), accompanied by the ominous phrase 'The doctor will see you now…', adorning posters, flyers and press ads – and the all-too-short run was a popular hit with audiences.

While the provocative tagline proved to be a useful and enduring promotional tool, however, many would probably argue, quite reasonably, that *The Rocky Horror Show* remained a perfect one-off, and, as such, would never have an equal. Nevertheless, thanks to the lasting brilliance of O'Brien's and Hartley's outstanding songs, Benji Sperring's perseverance and resourceful direction, and Tom Crowley's witty and efficient script adaptation, most would agree that it now had a more than worthy sequel.

As well as various unrealised sequels and spin-offs, rumours of a possible made-for-TV film remake, tentatively titled *The Rocky Horror Birthday Show*, to be produced by music channel MTV in association with Lou Adler, began about a year before *The Rocky Horror Picture Show*'s thirtieth anniversary.

The thought that a station aimed primarily at the mainstream teen market might be behind a new version of a movie celebrated largely for its sexually subversive themes had *Rocky Horror* followers up in arms. Alarm bells began ringing in earnest when an online survey asked fans their opinions on such speculative whisperings as a made-for-television remake possibly omitting the bedroom scenes and Frank's seduction of Janet and Brad (an integral part of the plot), removing 'Touch-a Touch-a Touch-a

Touch Me' (Janet's defining musical moment), excluding the song 'Superheroes', kicking off the action in a place other than the town of Denton (why?) and, worst of all, having Frank-n-Furter (to be played, according to some news reports, by bizarre shock-rocker Marilyn Manson) depicted this time as a brilliant and famous plastic surgeon living in a posh modern penthouse, thus inexplicably eschewing the archetypal mad scientist and crusty gothic castle of Richard O'Brien's knowingly clichéd intentions.

Thankfully, this misguided debacle did not materialise, but the fact that such outrageous ideas were mooted in the first place gave a frightening indication of what might happen should creative and artistic decisions be left to those with no understanding of the subject matter.

Remake rumours reared their dubious head once more – this time with widespread announcements in the international press – in July 2008. The Thursday 14 July edition of the UK's *Daily Mirror* reported that, although the new MTV/Sky Movies co-production would use Richard O'Brien's and Jim Sharman's original screenplay for *The Rocky Horror Picture Show* as its basis, O'Brien himself would not be involved.

'Anger fuels and distorts my outlook on the whole thing,' the author-composer told the *Independent* newspaper. 'When the stage show first went to the US, Lou Adler arranged the sale of the film rights to Fox. I wanted to take the contracts home to read, but was hurried into signing them. After signing something I hadn't read, sure enough I found out I was going to be marginalised. It made Fox $360,000,000, keeping them afloat for years. Lou made a conservative profit of about $20,000,000; whereas I've made less than a million.'

It is perhaps worth noting that Adler's stamp of ownership on the ever-popular *Rocky Horror* movie would be further indicated by the fact that, on the Blu-ray edition released to commemorate the picture's thirty-fifth anniversary in 2010, his name curiously now preceded Michael White's on both the US and UK versions of the film, whereas White's had hitherto been first on all UK prints and video releases.

To the consternation of *Rocky Horror* purists, a number of reports suggested that the alleged forthcoming remake was to include new musical numbers, leading an understandably puzzled O'Brien to question how the makers planned to find new songs without the artistic input of the show's original composer. Some fans rationalised that, hopefully, such rumours might indicate simply the possible reinstatement of 'Superheroes', excised from early prints of the original movie, and Brad's gentle love ballad 'Once in a While'.

Meanwhile, Lou Adler himself – who the *Daily Mirror* reported would executive-produce the new version with Gail Berman – told the press: 'The *Rocky Horror* phenomenon has reincarnated itself in numerous ways since

9: SENSUAL DAYDREAMS TO TREASURE FOREVER

its birth. Our hope has always been that each new endeavour and rebirth will expose new audiences to *Rocky Horror* and expand its fan base.'

Adler clearly had this outlook in mind when, with all notion of a remake again shelved for the time being, he sanctioned a crossover between *The Rocky Horror Picture Show* and the youth-orientated television show *Glee*.

Airing on the Fox network in the autumn of 2009, the first season of *Glee* - created by Ryan Murphy, Brad Falchuk and Ian Brennan - had become something of a minor TV sensation. While many of a certain age may have perceived it as little more than *Fame*-lite, the colourful series, set primarily at the fictional William McKinley High School, struck a resounding chord amongst young adolescents and prepubescent girls in particular, and a second season was swiftly commissioned.

Directed by Adam Shankman, *The Rocky Horror Glee Show* was transmitted as the fifth episode of the second season on 26 October 2010, after being heavily promoted as the series' Hallowe'en special.

Shankman had not only helmed the joyous 2007 screen adaptation of the Broadway musical smash *Hairspray* (itself based on cult director John Waters' 1986 film of the same name) but had appeared as a reluctant werewolf in the lightweight movie parody *Monster Mash* (aka *Frankenstein Sings*) in 1995, making him no stranger to camp comedy horror and quirky rock 'n' roll mayhem; and its healthy celebration of diversity and eccentricity, coupled with an eclectic ensemble of misfit characters, ought to have made *Glee* the perfect choice for an amalgamation with *Rocky Horror*. In addition to entertaining guest appearances by Barry Bostwick and Meat Loaf in supporting roles, the episode featured cover versions of seven of Richard O'Brien's classic songs - all performed, with varying degrees of artistic achievement, by members of the *Glee* cast - and an impressive onstage mock-up of *The Rocky Horror Picture Show*'s laboratory set. However, a somewhat contrived plot - in which glee club director Will Schuester (Matthew Morrison), fuelled by an ulterior motive of attracting the attentions of McKinley High guidance counsellor Emma Pillsbury (Jayma Mays), pressures his reluctant cast of irritatingly self-conscious and neurotic students into staging a production of *The Rocky Horror Show* as their school musical - lets it down drastically.

The episode concluded with Will, having recognised the selfishness of his intentions, deciding to cancel the production in order to spare the collective embarrassment of his apprehensive cast, thus reducing the entire *Rocky Horror* aspect of the story to a pointlessly irrelevant MacGuffin. So much for sticking it to the man.

Furthermore, with the series' family audience no doubt uppermost in the minds of the writers and the prominent network, the script plays things far too safely by inexcusably toning down the lyrics to both 'Sweet

Transvestite' (the word 'Transsexual' being senselessly altered to 'Sensational' even though 'Transvestite' remains intact) and 'Touch-a Touch-a Touch-a Touch Me' (a song Jayma Mays purportedly asked to sing in the episode, having previously performed it for her original *Glee* audition); casting a female character in the role of Frank-n-Furter; and sanitising all of *Rocky*'s most pertinent themes.

'This play is terrible,' sneers acid-tongued cheerleading coach Sue Sylvester (the glee club's arch nemesis, played with relish by a scene-stealing Jane Lynch) upon witnessing one of the show's baffling rehearsals. Were it ever performed in this form – with illogical direction, infinite plot liberties, a blatant disregard for the differences between *The Rocky Horror Show* and *The Rocky Horror Picture Show* (the front cover of Will's script clearly reads '*The Rocky Horror Show*' whereas Rocky himself appears to be depicted as being mute, as he is in the *Picture Show*), characters (notably Magenta and Columbia) being infuriatingly doubled-up as a means of giving every main cast member a lead part in the show, and the coherent structure and continuity of Richard O'Brien's narrative becoming virtually nonsensical – even *Rocky Horror*'s most dedicated enthusiasts might be inclined to agree with her.

Far from *Rocky*'s finest hour, *The Rocky Horror Glee Show*, with its unforgivable sanitisation of the original show's sexual ambiguity, free-spirited humour and edgy rock 'n' roll sensibilities, gives the overall impression of a massive missed opportunity. Speaking to the press in New Zealand shortly after the episode premiered, Richard O'Brien reportedly expressed his disappointment and bewilderment at its dilution of *Rocky*'s core themes. In the end, though, the programme – lightweight, colourful and trivial though it may have been – no doubt served its intended purpose of raising awareness of the original, with both the episode and its strategically-released soundtrack CD introducing the *Rocky Horror* phenomenon to a brand new teen (and pre-teen) market just in time for the October 2010 debut of *The Rocky Horror Picture Show* on high-definition Blu-ray disc. For 20th Century Fox, who owned the rights to both *Glee* and *The Rocky Horror Picture Show*, the situation would be the epitome of win-win.

Considerably more satisfying – certainly from an artistic and cerebral perspective – was 'Creatures of the Night', a 2005 instalment of the CBS network's weekly crime drama *Cold Case*. Originally broadcast on the evening of 1 May 2005, the episode saw the series' regular team attempting to crack the unresolved murder of a Philadelphia hotel doorman by the name of Mike Cahill (played by Zack Graham) in 1977. It appears that the crime might be the handiwork of an incarcerated serial killer who, as the story opens in 2005, may be on the verge of being released on a technicality if it cannot be irrefutably proved that he was responsible for Cahill's

9: SENSUAL DAYDREAMS TO TREASURE FOREVER

untimely demise. In accordance with the series' regular structure, flashbacks of past events are interwoven into the present day narrative.

Set against the frivolous world of *The Rocky Horror Picture Show*'s midnight movie scene at its absolute zenith in the late '70s, the plot makes use of the *Rocky* cult's rite-of-passage themes and playful decadence by deftly utilising them as part of the stimulus for the vicious actions of its disturbed and excessively pious killer. Raised by an overbearing, regimented and devoutly religious father with a military background and a firm belief that uniforms should be respected, the troubled Roy Brigham Anthony (Alex Ball) is revealed to have become conflicted and confused by his feelings towards a free-spirited young waitress (played by Laura Leigh Hughes in the modern day portion of the episode and Claire Coffee for the 1977 scenes) with whom he worked, as well as the seemingly sordid and sinful late night world of *Rocky Horror* to which she introduced him. This, along with his increased resentment toward Cahill's blasphemous attitude and apparent disrespect for his doorman's uniform, had impelled the increasingly schizophrenic Roy to commit the first of a series of murders; all of which had involved victims in uniform.

With a convincing recreation of *The Rocky Horror Picture Show*'s customary midnight madness, Barry Bostwick moodily portraying the present day incarnation of the condemned serial killer – seen being re-incarcerated, accompanied by the plaintive strains of 'Over at the Frankenstein Place' from the movie's soundtrack, at the end of the episode – and a clever use of *Rocky*-style head-shots and bloody font cast names as its closing credits, the makers of *Cold Case* produced a suitably reverential and intelligent *Rocky Horror* homage.

While it could never hope to boast anything even remotely approaching the number of tributes and parodies bestowed upon the likes of mainstream movie and television franchises such as *Star Wars*, *Star Trek* and *Doctor Who*, *Rocky Horror* has nonetheless enjoyed its share of references in contemporary pop-culture – a clear acknowledgment of any work's intransigence and mythic status – affirming its evolution from underground cult to an established household name.

Perhaps unsurprisingly, given the pop-culture savvy wit of its creator and head writer Joss Whedon, the television incarnation of *Buffy the Vampire Slayer* – which ran for seven phenomenally successful seasons between March 1997 and May 2003 – made a couple of (fairly low key) references to Richard O'Brien's enduring classic. In 'Anne' – the first episode of the series' third season, originally broadcast on 29 September 1998 – an incidental character named Lily (played by Julie Lee) is seen wearing a T-shirt with *The Rocky Horror Picture Show*'s distinctive 'Denton: The Home of Happiness!' image on it. A more blatant allusion would be heard in 'Band Candy' – the same season's sixth episode – written by Jane

Espenson and first aired on 10 November 1998. 'Let's do the Time Warp again,' mutters the incredulous Buffy (Sarah Michelle Gellar) upon discovering that the town's entire adult population has reverted to an adolescent state of mind after consuming the strange candy of the episode's title.

In 'Too Old to Trick or Treat, Too Young to Die', a third season Hallowe'en episode of the Fox network's popular sitcom *That '70s Show*, broadcast on 31 October 2000, foreign exchange student Fez (played by Wilmer Valderrama) appears dressed throughout in the manner of Dr Frank-n-Furter, while two characters in WB's *Sabrina: The Teenage Witch* are seen preparing for a screening of *The Rocky Horror Picture Show* in the episode 'Some of My Best Friends are Half-Mortal', first shown during the show's fifth season on 10 November the same year.

Meat Loaf, now a legitimate rock star in his own right, assumed guest duties on NBC's long-running weekly comedy show *Saturday Night Live* on more than one occasion, but it was an on screen reunion with his *Rocky Horror* co-star Tim Curry on the evening of 5 December 1981 that would prove legendary. During the evening, Curry, who hosted that week's episode, performed the famous innuendo-laden *Zucchini Song* (known in the UK as *The Marrow Song*) in the style of a Victorian musical hall act and also appeared as Mick Jagger – often cited as one of the inspirations for his flamboyant, peacock-strutting interpretation of Dr Frank-n-Furter – complete with an over-the-top cod cockney accent, in an extended (in truth rather overlong and laboured) lampoon of a one-man television special. The evening's highlight however – at least as far as *Rocky Horror* fans were concerned – was a short, fast-paced, two-handed skit, in which Curry and Meat Loaf, obviously enjoying themselves immensely, appeared in a spoof commercial as the brash proprietors of Tim and Meat's One-Stop *Rocky Horror* Shop, selling satirically overpriced 'official' *Rocky Horror* props – water pistols, newspapers and toast (for just 'eight bucks a slice' they announce excitedly) – to the midnight market, while affectionately sending up their own roles in the whole *Rocky* cultural phenomenon.

'The movie made millions of dollars,' notes a grinning Curry.

'Yeah, but Tim and I, we didn't make a dime,' Meat laments, prompting Curry's sly reply:

'Speak for yourself.'

'Hey man; like, you got paid?' a comically astonished Meat then queries hastily, suddenly feigning shocked exasperation.

As if in ironic illustration of the endless money-making possibilities seized by studios and avaricious movie producers, another of the sketch's jokes – the availability of 'licensed' *Rocky Horror* costumes and the *Official Rocky Horror Guide Book* (ostensibly outlining the details of talkback lines and audience participation) – would actually become a reality several

9: SENSUAL DAYDREAMS TO TREASURE FOREVER

years later.

Stabur Press published *The Official Rocky Horror Picture Show Audience Par-tic-i-pation Guide* (the real one) in 1991. Written and compiled by Sal Piro and Michael Hess, the book featured an entire transcript of the film's screenplay, interspersed (in bold type) with the most widely-accepted lines of counterpoint audience dialogue, as well as a catalogue of collectable *Rocky Horror* merchandise and promotional items, which at the time (in the days before the internet) proved absolutely invaluable to collectors.

Licensed off-the-shelf *Rocky Horror* costumes and wigs for four of the film's characters – Frank-n-Furter, Riff Raff, Magenta and Columbia – became commercially available in 2001, although they appeared to be rather cheaply made and were of a significantly inferior quality to most intricately-detailed and lovingly-constructed fan-made reproductions of Sue Blane's immortal creations.

Whereas the sketch featuring Tim and Meat's One-Stop *Rocky Horror* Shop became a fan favourite, it was by no means the only – or indeed the first – *Rocky Horror* television parody. A year earlier, on 12 December 1980, the ensemble of *Fridays*, ABC's short-lived (from 11 April 1980 to 23 April 1982) rival to NBC's *Saturday Night Live*, had broadcast an extended parody entitled *The Ronny Horror Show*, in which then US president Ronald Reagan (played by John Roarke) was irreverently portrayed as *Rocky Horror*'s Dr Frank-n-Furter.

Like Tim Curry and Meat Loaf, Susan Sarandon proved she was not above mocking her own role in *The Rocky Horror Picture Show* when she appeared in a sketch alongside fuzzy felt-faced vampire puppet character the Count on PBS's ever-popular children's series *Sesame Street*. In this skit, while seeking shelter from the customary deluge, the mismatched couple find themselves at the typically imposing doorway of a foreboding gothic castle. In accordance with his name, the Count urges Sarandon to continually knock on the door (so that he can count the knocks) despite it being all too clear that there is no-one home. The punch line comes when her numerically-obsessed companion reveals that the castle is actually his own home. He knew all along that there was nobody inside to answer the door, but wanted to keep counting how many times she knocked. As one might expect, although rain-soaked, out of breath and acting with puppets, the Academy Award-winning beauty effortlessly emerges with her dignity completely intact.

Rocky Horror fans would, for obvious reasons, also latch onto an otherwise fairly innocuous moment in *The Witches of Eastwick*, director George Miller's 1987 film adaptation of John Updike's satirical post-feminist novel, in which Sarandon's newly-sexually-awakened character Jane is venomously called 'slut' by a disgusted bystander.

A second season episode of ABC's *The Drew Carey Show*, appropriately titled 'New York and Queens', screened on 14 May 1997, saw the programme's four central characters arriving dressed as *Rocky* characters at a midnight movie screening, only to be faced with a line of outrageously attired drag queens and the horrendous revelation that the once regular screenings of *The Rocky Horror Picture Show* have been superseded by *The Adventures Of Priscilla: Queen Of The Desert*. An elaborate dance-off between suitably attired *Rocky* and *Priscilla* fans is ultimately broken up by the arrival of local law enforcement and the arrest of several members of the rebellious rabble (including Carey himself, wearing Brad's white charming underclothes) who find themselves thrown unceremoniously into the back of a waiting police van.

During the 1990s, an odd postmodern status symbol seemed to be a mention on Fox's ever-popular animated show *The Simpsons* – the *Star Wars* movies had been honoured with innumerable references over the years – and *Rocky Horror* was finally awarded the privilege during the eighteenth episode of the series' sixth season on 5 March 1995.

In the episode 'A Star is Burns', the character Dr Hibbert – dressed in full Frank-n-Furter fishnets and corsetry – arrives at the local movie theatre to discover that a gala event, the Springfield Film Festival, is in full swing. Chuckling to himself, the portly doctor good-naturedly acknowledges his embarrassing *faux pas* by proclaiming 'I thought they were playing *The Rocky Horror Picture Show* tonight,' before giggling cheerfully; a brief but entirely fitting tribute from one triumphant 20th Century Fox franchise to another.

Other memorable examples of *Rocky Horror* being singled out for mention in popular culture included Simon Pegg's infuriated outburst about the shortcomings of 'The Time Warp' (and its countless admirers) in *Spaced*, an offbeat postmodern British sitcom co-written by Pegg, Edgar Wright and Jessica Stevenson, which ran for two series on Channel 4 between September 1999 and April 2001. In many ways a UK answer to the 1990s' twentysomething slacker culture – celebrated in such films as Kevin Smith's low budget cult classic *Clerks* (1994) – *Spaced* followed the day to day fortunes of grungy flatmates Daisy Steiner (Stevenson), a hopelessly underachieving wannabe journalist, and Pegg's computer game-obsessed sci-fi geek and comic book nut Tim Bisley. Bored and irritated by a mind-numbingly tedious flat-warming party thrown by Daisy in the show's second episode (first screened on 1 October 1999), Pegg's eternally cynical and exasperated Tim finally storms out angrily when *Rocky*'s familiar anthem – Edward Tudor-Pole's rocking rendition from the 1990 London cast album no less, as opposed to the bland synthetic cover versions often heard at real parties – materialises on the stereo amongst the evening's unimaginatively anodyne music selections.

'They were playing 'The Time Warp', Mike; I hate "The Time Warp,"'

9: SENSUAL DAYDREAMS TO TREASURE FOREVER

he snarls, furiously and disgustedly, to his stocky, gun-fixated best friend (played by the likeable Nick Frost). 'It's boil-in-the-bag perversion for sexually-repressed accountants and first year drama students with too many posters of *Betty Blue*, *The Blues Brothers*, *Big Blue* and *Blue Velvet* on their blue bloody walls.'

In spite of its inflammatory assessment of the song and its countless devotees, most *Rocky Horror* fans would be good-natured and graciously self-aware enough to accept this undeniably articulate tongue-in-cheek tirade as suitably hilarious and comically perceptive.

Another brief but notable *Rocky Horror* reference occurred in the Hallowe'en episode of the cult Al Murray and Richard Herring comedy series *Time Gentlemen Please*, broadcast on UK satellite channel Sky One between 2000 and 2002. Primarily a sitcom vehicle for the opinionated, xenophobic and misogynistic Pub Landlord – comedian Murray's popular stage *alter ego* – the programme, known for its abundance of running gags and silly catchphrases, as well as its quirky and memorably well-realised supporting characters, managed to reference two of Richard O'Brien's timeless musical numbers during 'The Pub that Forgot Time ...', an episode first shown on 30 October 2000.

'Damn it. Janet,' snorts Rebecca Front's scatterbrained and eccentric brewery rep Ms Vicky Jackson, exasperatedly correcting herself for yet again forgetting the name of Julia Sawalha's outspoken Australian barmaid. At once recognising her unintentional mention of the song's title, and clearly amused by it, she laughs, 'Damn it. Janet. Do you get it? Like in *Rocky Horror*,'' before chirpily singing the familiar refrain 'Let's do the Time Warp' and asking 'Have you seen it?'

'No!' the other characters irately retort in unison, in accordance with another of the series' running gags; none of them ever recognises her ceaseless pop-culture references, and they always appear keen to belittle her by rebuffing them instantly.

In addition to such references on television, *Rocky Horror* would find itself mentioned in the occasional cinematic work too. Whereas the significance of its place in Paul Mazursky's *Willie & Phil* (1980) and, in particular, Alan Parker's *Fame* (1980) has already been well documented, there are a number of other notable – though perhaps less well-known – examples. An unseen character by the name of Tony Rocky Horror is discussed by Samuel L Jackson and John Travolta in Quentin Tarantino's *Pulp Fiction* (1994); and a couple of drag queens named Peaches 'n' Cream (played by Stephen Spinella and Alec Mapa) disastrously botch an audition by executing a painfully slapdash, under-rehearsed and farcical dance routine to the strains of 'The Time Warp' (from *The Rocky Horror Picture Show*'s soundtrack recording) in 2004's *Connie and Carla*, a cheery gender-bending comedy directed by Michael Lembeck. This film, whose title characters (engagingly portrayed by Nia Vardalos and Toni Collette), having unwittingly witnessed a murder, hide out from the mob by disguising themselves as female impersonators (thus becoming girls dressed as men dressed as girls) and seeking sanctuary in a Los Angeles gay bar, could be perceived in many ways as an updated female retelling of Billy Wilder's 1959 classic *Some Like it Hot*, one of cinema's truly seminal cross-dressing movies.

In 1985, a mere ten years after immortalising his iconic performance as Frank-n-Furter on celluloid, Tim Curry played the lead role in the British TV movie *Blue Money*, a comic crime caper made by London Weekend Television. In one scene, while attending a Come as Your Favourite Movie Star costume party, Curry's character (dressed as Fred Astaire in top hat and tails) passes a background extra attired in the unmistakable manner of *Rocky Horror*'s Dr Frank; a fleeting throw-away visual gag that, to *Rocky* and Curry fans, would become a treasured moment.

Amongst the handful of modern movie blockbusters that have made, often quite subtle, references to *Rocky Horror* are the successful *Men in Black* films, director Barry Sonnenfeld's science fiction comedies, which starred Tommy Lee Jones and Will Smith as K and J (or Kay and Jay as they would be listed in the films' credits), members of a secret US government agency assigned to monitor and police extraterrestrial activity on Earth. A brief scene in the 1997 original featured a close-up of a non-speaking character with a memorably striking visage that instantly called to mind an exaggerated approximation of Richard O'Brien's Riff Raff; while in the 2002 sequel *Men in Black 2* a classic 'lips' poster for *The Rocky Horror Picture Show* could be clearly glimpsed over Will Smith's shoulder during an integral sequence in a contact's attic.

Following his hysterical 'Time Warp' tirade in *Spaced*, Simon Pegg would again make reference to *Rocky Horror* in his screenplay (co-written with Edgar Wright) for the 2004 comedy zombie movie *Shaun of the Dead*. In a line excised from the released film, but still included on its commercially available soundtrack CD, grouchy housemate Pete (played by Peter Serafinowicz) dismisses an accusation from Shaun (Pegg) that he has in the past sold marijuana by retorting coolly 'Yeah, once; at college, to you. I did a lot of stupid things at college, Shaun. I dressed up as Frank-n-Furter, I drank Snakebite and Black, I slept with a fat girl; it doesn't mean I want to do any of them for a living.'

More recently, three of the unfortunate female characters in *Halloween 2*, director Rob Zombie's 2009 sequel to his 2007 reboot of John Carpenter's 1978 slasher classic, wore replicas of *The Rocky Horror Picture Show*'s Frank-n-Furter, Magenta and Columbia costumes for much of the movie's blood-spattered final act.

2009 also marked the release of MGM's lightweight remake of their

9: SENSUAL DAYDREAMS TO TREASURE FOREVER

1980 urban musical fable *Fame*; and, like its grittier R-rated predecessor, the new family-friendly version would include a nod to a certain midnight movie phenomenon. While auditioning for a place at the renowned High School for the Performing Arts in New York City, the character Joy (played by spunky Anna Maria Perez de Taglé) gives a feisty rendition of Columbia's defiant dressing down of Frank-n-Furter. Observing with a perceptible smile, which would seem to indicate his recognition of both the speech itself and the wannabe actress's potential, Charles S Dutton's drama teacher Mr Dowd remarks dryly, 'Wow; you're fearless, aren't you?'

'Some say annoying,' the young hopeful glumly confesses; to which Dutton's character affirms sincerely:

'You know, it's possible to be both.'

That the *Fame* remake, directed by Kevin Tancharoen, should incorporate such a blatant nod to *The Rocky Horror Picture Show* is entirely fitting, and would appear to be a knowing acknowledgement of the importance of the 8th Street Playhouse sequence in Alan Parker's original. Those scenes not only highlighted the integral rite-of-passage experienced by the character Doris (Maureen Teefy), they also opened up the *Rocky Horror* cult to a wider and much more diverse audience in the early 1980s, augmenting its appeal considerably and helping to ensure its unwavering permanence within the modern pop-culture zeitgeist.

Even more recently, writer-director Stephen Chbosky adapted his 1999 coming-of-age epistolary novel *The Perks of Being a Wallflower* for the screen, with Logan Lerman, Emma Watson and Ezra Miller putting in perceptive performances as its trio of troubled and misunderstood teens. Shot in and around the US city of Pittsburgh during 2011 and released the following year, the film, like the book on which it was based, features a number of key scenes involving members of a local *Rocky Horror Picture Show* shadow cast. With *Rocky Horror* again playing its customary role in such works as an allegorical rite-of-passage, these crucial sequences, which faithfully and lovingly recreated the midnight *Rocky* scene of the early '90s, were shot at the Hollywood Theater in Dormont, Pennsylvania. In addition to some of their regulars being invited to appear in the movie as *Rocky Horror* audience members, Pittsburgh's actual shadow cast, known as Junior Chamber of Commerce, would be acknowledged in the film's closing credits for their cooperation and involvement. Chbosky's sensitive direction and obvious affection for the material ensured that *The Perks of Being a Wallflower* would be the most significant and positive use of the *Rocky Horror* phenomenon in a mainstream motion picture since Alan Parker's original 1980 version of *Fame*.

Another notable use of *The Rocky Horror Picture Show* in contemporary literature would show up amidst the myriad of pop-culture references in author Ernest Cline's debut novel *Ready Player One*. Published in 2011, the book centres on a dystopian future, in which – in order to escape their gloomy Orwellian reality – much of the population regularly retreats into the OASIS, a virtual world where any fantasy can be played out by way of a technologically-enhanced extended reality. In one sequence, the primary protagonists – by way of their OASIS avatars – attend a screening of *The Rocky Horror Picture Show* on a virtually-realised version of the planet Transsexual, even taking on the exact appearances of the movie's Eddie and Columbia in order to perform in a shadow cast. Given *Rocky Horror*'s irrefutable prominence in the world of interactive entertainment, it seems fitting that Cline should have made it a significant element of a science fiction story which focuses on the possible future of such immersive escapism. While Steven Spielberg's 2018 film adaptation altered or omitted some of the book's cerebral elements and set pieces – including the *Rocky Horror* scene – in favour of faster pacing and flashy cinematic visuals, it still included a reference (albeit a much more subtle one) with the iconic lips featuring amongst numerous patches sewn onto the jacket worn by Helen Harris (played by Lena Waithe), the real-world identity of OASIS avatar Aech.

Furthermore, as if to underscore the influence of *Rocky Horror* in the modern pop-culture arena, Cline would again reference the film (and the character of Columbia) in his much-anticipated follow-up novel *Ready Player Two* (published in November 2020).

These days, of course, it is not only in the mainstream where a respectable brand might expect to find itself exploited, sometimes quite unscrupulously, by another artist. In a world where literally nothing would appear to be sacrosanct, just about every successful modern movie is likely to have had at least its title subjected to the indignities of the X-rated parody.

In addition to the very well-known *Flesh Gordon* (1974), other pornographic rip-offs of famous Hollywood hits have included such delightful spoof titles as *The Sperminator* (1985); *Pornocchio* (1987), with the immortal tag line 'It's not his nose that grows'; *Edward Penishands* (1991), which unlike Tim Burton's much-admired 1990 fantasy *Edward Scissorhands* actually spawned several sequels; and *Shaving Ryan's Privates* (2003). Hence, given its recognised sexual themes, it should come as no surprise to learn that the unashamedly kitsch *The Rocky Horror Picture Show* actually inspired more than one hardcore reworking by the prolific adult movie industry. Probably the first, and arguably most famous, of these was director Loretta Sterling's *The Rocky Porno Video Show*, released uncut on videotape in the US by 4-Play Video in 1986.

Young married couple Tommy (Tom Byron) and Tammy (Bionca, an 'exciting new sex star' according to the video cover) find themselves stranded in a particularly unrealistic rainstorm, probably achieved by the state-of-the-art special effects technique of a slack-jawed guy in a baseball cap standing off camera with a garden hose. Seeking refuge at a nearby residence (the non-existent budget does not even allow us to see whether or not it is a castle, as we are shown little more than a section of wall and a close-up of a rather unremarkable door), the newlyweds are invited inside by an overacting odious manservant (Francois Papillon), whereupon they fall prey to the salacious advances of intergalactic sex fiend Mistress Tantala and her sleazy alien entourage.

Aside from the bloody font lettering on its cover and posters (but not the on screen title of the film itself), *The Rocky Porno Video Show* neither looks nor feels like *Rocky Horror*, although its theme song is admittedly quite memorable (given that it pretty much just lifts the tune of 'Sweet Transvestite' and adds its own ludicrous lyrics), and the cheap sets and tacky laboratory equipment (a bog-standard buzzing plasma ball seems to be the most scientifically high-tech item) might have looked at home in one of Edward D Wood's science fiction travesties. The plot (such as it is, this being a hardcore porn film) has little to do with that of *The Rocky Horror Show*, and the grotesque mistress of the house, with her huge breasts and crazily back-combed, infinitely lacquered hair, bears absolutely no resemblance to Frank-n-Furter in either appearance or characterisation.

Populated largely by unappealing people indulging in obnoxious sex, with practically no artistic merit whatsoever, *The Rocky Porno Video Show* is a cheaply produced mess, completely devoid of comedy or erotic appeal; and it is unlikely that even the most hardened (wahey, missus) connoisseur of porn would find it even remotely titillating.

As its title might suggest, director Kovi Istvan's *Funky-Fetish Horror Show*, shot in Budapest, Hungary, in February 2002 and released as Volume Six of the Private video label's Pirate Fetish Machine DVD series, takes a more sado-masochistic approach to *Rocky*'s basic premise. Though little more than another hardcore shag-fest, *Funky-Fetish Horror Show* (the on screen title's hyphen is absent from the DVD cover and promotional material) makes the odd attempt to reference its source here and there, even paraphrasing snippets of its dialogue. In addition to the disembodied lips that open the film, Brad (Csoky Ice) and Janet (Michelle Wild) brave another obviously fake downpour and approach the castle (definitely identifiable as a castle, albeit a rather modern one, in this version) via a familiar looking 'Enter At Your Own Risk!!' sign. Inside they are welcomed by a sex-crazed host – described in the DVD's production notes as 'Time Travelling Transylvanian Transvestite Frank 'n Fuckter (Steve Holmes), resplendent in black stockings and cape' – and are then quickly re-attired in kinky BDSM lingerie, perilously high spiked stilettos and an assortment of vinyl and latex bondage wear. As far as anything resembling a story goes, however, that's about it; the rest of the picture is just the usual bombardment of crude and unimaginative fucking and sucking, made even more difficult to watch by an overuse of ultra-violet make-up, neon lighting, smoke effects and dizzying camerawork.

At least *The Rocki Whore Picture Show: A Hardcore Parody*, directed by Brad Armstrong and released on DVD by Wicked Pictures in 2011, is a little more commendable. Whereas its profusion of explicit sex scenes, tediously slow pacing and painfully bad acting – typical for a porn movie – hardly help to distinguish it from any number of other uninspired made-for-video skin flicks of the last three decades, its inventive production values and resourceful costume designs (which cleverly evoke the look of *The Rocky Horror Picture Show* without being wholly accurate reproductions) and an apparent fondness for the movie on which it is based actually make this particular pornographic rip-off worthy of attention by genuine *Rocky Horror* aficionados.

Having already stopped their car in the customary torrential downpour on a deserted country road, in order to indulge in a spot of obligatory hardcore nookie, fresh-faced (but clearly not so innocent) newlyweds Brad (Rocco Reed) and Janet (Jessica Drake) find themselves in an all-too-familiar situation.

'You are now officially lost,' they are politely informed by their vehicle's female-voiced GPS satellite navigation system. 'Goodbye.' It's a nice gag that, like Janet also acknowledging that her cell phone has no signal, neatly addresses the technological advancements that have occurred since *Rocky Horror*'s original Brad and Janet first set off on their fateful night out.

Wrongly assuming that they have been sent by an adult casting agency, a creepy bald-headed butler named Stiff Staff (Randy Spears) – who, it later transpires, more than lives up to his name – invites the unfortunate couple into the castle of Frank-n-Beans (Mac Turner), a cross-dressing porn director. Spears, who has something of a Boris Karloff look about him, manages to keep his character reasonably sinister under the circumstances, while Turner makes a fairly commendable attempt at mimicking Tim Curry's landmark performance. In fact the film's puerile character names are not a million miles away from the same level of unashamedly juvenile wit that dreamt up Riff Raff and Frank-n-Furter.

The haphazard script merely borrows the basic premise of the original while discarding several key plot elements (and with a run time of over two and a half hours, it is a damned sight longer than it as well). For instance, unlike their mainstream counterparts, this Brad and Janet do not seem quite so virginal, and both sport obvious tattoos. Likewise, Frank-n-Beans has somehow managed to create Rocki (Puma Swede) – a statuesque blonde female with unfeasibly large breasts, whom he delightedly refers to

9: SENSUAL DAYDREAMS TO TREASURE FOREVER

as 'The epitome of porn-tastic perfection personified' and 'The next generation in porn superstars' – even though he does not appear to possess any scientific knowledge or originate from another planet.

Being a straight porn movie intended for the heterosexual market, any actual sex in the picture – aside from the obligatory girl-on-girl action (there's a routine lesbian scene between Vagina (Nicki Hunter) and Euphoria (Alektra Blue), the film's equivalent of Magenta and Columbia, and Janet services Rocki with an enormous red strap-on) – is fairly customary in nature. Though completely unexpurgated and explicit, Frank's seduction of Janet looks a lot like its precursor from *The Rocky Horror Picture Show*. Brad, on the other hand, finds himself at the mercy of Mona (Kaylani Lei) and Lisa (Annie Cruz), Frank-n-Beans' insatiable twin make-up girls, who, after painting his face in the manner of Barry Bostwick's distinctive white and red 'Floorshow' visage, treat their 'victim' to a lengthy three-way before Frank even arrives on the scene. To its credit, the script makes a bit of an effort to remain true to the sexual ambiguity of Frank-n-Furter's roots by hinting that Frank-n-Beans does at least have something of an amorous interest in Brad. Stiff Staff, however, calls his master away before anything scandalous can occur between the two men.

A bonus feature on the DVD's second disc includes footage of Armstrong and members of his cast promoting their then forthcoming film and recruiting extras to play Transylvanians at a thirty-fifth anniversary convention of *The Rocky Horror Picture Show* in Los Angeles, hinting that the director at least may actually be a fan of the real thing. Furthermore the script makes a couple of curious meta-references to *Rocky*'s cult following and participation rituals. When Frank-n-Beans proposes a toast, he is suddenly required to dodge two slices of grilled bread that inexplicably fly towards him from off-camera, as he gives the wheelchair-bound T P Scott (aging porn legend Ron Jeremy) an accusing look. There are numerous toilet paper gags throughout the film; and, as a seductive Frank entices Janet with the promise of guaranteed 'Satis... faction' – a cheeky pilfering of Frank-n-Furter's teasing 'Antici... pation' – she implores him 'Say it' during the tantalising mid-word pause, just as genuine *Rocky Horror* midnight revellers urge their Frank to do on a regular basis.

The picture also attempts to emulate *Rocky*'s songs. Of course the filmmakers were never going to be allowed to use Richard O'Brien's highly respected music for a hardcore porn rip-off – surely they did not believe otherwise – and so, with poor lip-syncing, out of tune singing and crude lyrics that do not scan properly, the songs in question emerge as embarrassingly ghastly knock-offs of the superlative originals. 'The Time Warp' becomes 'Orgy' ('Let's have an Orgy again' sing the awkward ensemble in a badly choreographed dance number right before the wafer thin plot collapses altogether in favour of the film's climactic group sex sequence) and there are no prizes for guessing what the words 'Touch-a Touch-a Touch-a Touch Me' are altered to.

With the word *'Parody'* conspicuously appearing as part of the film's title and Rocki being deliberately spelt with an 'I' (a fact referenced directly by Frank-n-Beans during his introductory number) for no apparent logical or narrative reason beyond that of differentiating it from the title it is lampooning, it is not difficult to sense the company's nervousness about potential lawsuits materialising from the direction of *The Rocky Horror Picture Show*'s copyright holders. It is significant that a pretty comprehensive disclaimer appears both on screen at the beginning of the film itself and on the back cover of the DVD:

'The Rocki Whore Picture Show: A Hardcore Parody is a parody motion picture. It is not sponsored by, endorsed by, or affiliated with Twentieth Century Fox Film Corporation, the original creators of *The Rocky Horror Picture Show*, any predecessor or related work, or the holders of any related music or other intellectual property rights therein.'

Phew, talk about covering your ass. The final irony is that, while Richard O'Brien, Lou Adler and 20th Century Fox would no doubt object (quite understandably) to its very existence, *The Rocki Whore Picture Show: A Hardcore Parody*, in spite of its terrible songs, clumsily structured plotting and seemingly never-ending barrage of explicitly-depicted sex acts, appeared to exhibit considerably more reverence and affection for its source material than either *The Rocky Horror Glee Show* or the promised small screen remake of *The Rocky Horror Picture Show* itself, which, after years of rumour and development hell, would eventually emerge to something of a mixed reception.

Marketed as a 'television event', *The Rocky Horror Picture Show: Let's Do The Time Warp Again* (to give it its full, rather convoluted, title) was first transmitted in the US on the Fox network on Thursday 20 October 2016.

At the time, the practice of broadcasting specially staged and reworked live adaptations of popular musicals had become something of a winning trend. *Peter Pan Live!* and *The Wiz Live!* – aired on 4 December 2014 and 3 December 2015 respectively – had attained satisfactorily high viewership for NBC, and the network would achieve similar success with their 7 December 2016 production of *Hairspray Live!*, while Fox scored their own ratings hit with *Grease Live!* on the evening of Sunday 31 January 2016.

Whether or not Fox considered the option of giving their new version of *The Rocky Horror Picture Show* the live broadcast treatment – as well as their reason for ultimately not choosing that route – would not be publically disclosed. However, with the problematical issue of the stage and film rights being controlled by completely different companies, there remains the possibility that, although an obvious choice for such an endeavour, such complicated issues may have prohibited the development

9: SENSUAL DAYDREAMS TO TREASURE FOREVER

of a live TV adaptation of *Rocky Horror* even if the idea had been proposed.

With the on screen Producer credit occupied solely by John Ryan, Lou Adler (co-producer of the original 1975 movie) would receive billing as an Executive Producer, along with Gail Berman and director Kenny Ortega, while Adler's son – musician and record producer Cisco Adler – produced the soundtrack album and its re-orchestrated versions of Richard O'Brien's classic songs.

'It was huge, it was heavy,' Cisco candidly told Josh Chesler, in an interview for *LA Weekly* in October 2016: 'For me, it was a duty, and I always like a challenge. I was like, "Fuck yeah, I'll do a musical with 21 songs and 10 singers and a million fans who hold this property so precious that they can't wait to tear it to pieces." That sounds like a puzzle I want to figure out. As a musician and a producer, it was an epic mountain that felt amazing to climb.'

As for the film's director, with musical films, pop promos and concert tours to his name – working with such luminaries as Cher, Gloria Estefan and Michael Jackson – Kenny Ortega certainly had the credentials. He had begun his film career as a choreographer on the 1980 musical fantasy *Xanadu* (starring Olivia Newton-John and Hollywood legend Gene Kelly), and subsequently provided choreography for the likes of *Ferris Bueller's Day Off* (1986) and *Dirty Dancing* (1987) amongst others. Ortega made his directorial debut for Walt Disney Pictures in 1992 with historical musical drama *Newsies* (aka: *The News Boys*), before helming cult Hallowe'en favourite *Hocus Pocus* (with Bette Midler, Sarah Jessica Parker and Kathy Nijimy) which came out in July 1993, and Disney's three original *High School Musical* movies (in 2006, 2007 and 2008 respectively).

Early publicity for the project declared that, while it would be re-imagined visually, the sacred dialogue of Richard O'Brien's and Jim Sharman's beloved screenplay would remain intact (a fact that fans duly applauded). Even so, confirmed reports that (although he would receive his customary screenplay and composer credits) O'Brien himself would be given no creative input or involvement in the new production angered and upset the devoted *Rocky Horror* fan community, causing resentment and unease before the cameras even rolled. Nevertheless, in his interview for *LA Weekly*, Cisco Adler endeavoured to stir up enthusiasm within the sceptical fan base: 'As people start seeing this film and hearing this record, those fans of the original are going to realise we made this for them,' he declared, 'It's not about making another version of the movie; it's an homage to forty years of the cult classic and all of the iterations it's had.'

Initially, many devotees conceded that the opening scene at least – staged in and around a stylised gothic castle (the filming location of which was actually the famous Casa Loma in Toronto, Canada), with a reproduction of the original movie's Transylvanian flag flying above it–

had shown promise. Eschewing the iconic 'lips' imagery, in favour of the more time-honoured Usherette concept – thus cannily uniting the stage and screen incarnations of *Rocky Horror* (an idea highlighted by the scene's final close-up of the Usherette's rouged lips) – the building itself appeared to double as a huge luxurious movie theatre – the name 'Castle' and the words 'Midnight Madness' and 'Science Fiction Double Feature' shining brightly over its entrance. The unashamedly meta sequence also featured a motley assortment of punters, seen purchasing tickets, procuring the customary popcorn and settling into the stalls during the opening number. Whilst obviously a fitting allusion to the 1975 film's devoted midnight audiences, it is also worth noting that Jim Sharman had employed precisely the same idea in 1981's *Shock Treatment*, as the on screen television audience – a blatant metaphor for *The Rocky Horror Picture Show*'s interactive disciples – took their seats at the beginning of the movie.

As the Usherette, American singer-songwriter Ivy Levan – dressed in a suitably short, sexed-up, grey variation of a traditional commissionaire style uniform (with red fishnet stockings and underwear) – delivered a dreamily arranged rendition of 'Science Fiction Double Feature', while classic posters and advertisements for the song's many movie references adorned the walls and foyer of the character's beloved picture palace. Although Levan's contemporary vocal affectations felt conspicuously at odds with Richard O'Brien's deliberately uncomplicated rock 'n' roll pastiche (a fault shared by several other members of the cast), the orchestrations for 'Science Fiction Double Feature' remained fairly consistent with the sentiment and overall ambience of *Rocky Horror* as conceived.

Following this imaginatively creative opening, however, the film's direction and design descended into fairly pedestrian territory, constantly flaunting inferior recreations of Jim Sharman's and Brian Thomson's ingeniously resourceful ideas.

As the newly married Hapschatts and their wedding congregation had not appeared in the original stage incarnation – the show picking up the action with Janet having already caught the bride's bouquet – it could be argued that the churchyard scene was entirely unessential to the new version. With the opening title sequence seamlessly fading in on the church spire and the camera pulling back to reveal the wedding, Jim Sharman's direction and Peter Suschitzky's cinematography had immediately made the original film – an adaptation of a famously modest theatre piece – feel appropriately cinematic whilst incorporating Brad's and Janet's introduction into the scene as a whole. Conversely, Ivy Levan's 'Science Fiction Double Feature' culminated with a flash of lightning, followed by a sudden black-out – typical of made-for-TV movies, which frequently have to incorporate obvious visual fades in order to accommodate the obligatory commercials – before simply cutting to the church spire and the next scene. As a result of this abrupt edit, Kenny Ortega's adaptation might have worked better if it had omitted the redundant wedding scene – which in this version noticeably slowed the action – and cut straight to Brad and Janet's opening dialogue. Even the original's provocative American Gothic image was pointlessly repeated with an incognito Riff Raff and Magenta (in this case Reeve Carney and Christina Milian) again assuming the roles of church caretakers. However, while Brian Thomson's simple white wooden church – thriftily constructed in the autumn of 1974, with little more than a fake frontage and limited funds, in the middle of a muddy field in the South East of England – had effectively called to mind the rustic middle American farmhouse of Grant Wood's celebrated painting, the new version's church had a wider façade and more conventional brickwork, making it entirely the wrong shape and time period for the reference to work.

Resisting, for some reason, the opportunity to put their own spin on the characters of Brad and Janet – either by their own choice or from a directorial decision – Ryan McCartan and Victoria Justice, for the most part, seemed to merely copy the performances of Barry Bostwick and Susan Sarandon, even down to imitating vocal inflections and replicating pauses between the lines. Therefore, while the players clearly tried their best, they ultimately appeared ill at ease, struggling noticeably with Richard O'Brien's deceptively complex characters. McCartan, in particular, seemed to have difficulty getting the hang of the required, and notoriously tricky, ironic B-movie acting style (which the intuitive Bostwick and Sarandon had achieved instinctively), opting instead for awkwardly exaggerated pauses and overly simplified melodramatic delivery.

At the time of the film's broadcast, many critics praised the casting of trans-actress Laverne Cox – known primarily to television audiences for her recurring role as Sophia Burset in the long-running comedy-drama prison series *Orange is the New Black*, which ran for seven seasons on the streaming service Netflix between 2013 and 2019 – as Dr Frank-n-Furter. Understandably, in a constantly developing, forward-thinking society, the issue of gender identity, sexuality and inclusion had become a considerably more topical and sensitive subject in the media and elsewhere in the decades following *The Rocky Horror Show*'s pioneering debut in 1970s Chelsea. However, notwithstanding the undeniably important matter of representation, many pointed out that, by portraying Frank – a character who, despite originating from a planet called Transsexual, had typically been depicted as a bi or pansexual man – as prima facie a woman (trans or otherwise), several plot discrepancies had been created. Aside from lyrics such as 'I'm not much of a man by the light of day' and 'I'm just a sweet transvestite' no longer making sense – with further confusion arising from characters referring to Frank as 'She' and 'Her' and yet still calling her 'Master' – the biggest shift was that the major concept of Brad's implied heterosexist 1950s attitudes being challenged by his pleasurable homosexual liaison with the outwardly masculine Frank – fundamental to his character arc and the central themes of the show itself – had, in effect, been nullified.

'There's no shock value to that character being a woman, because she looked like a glamorous, lovely woman,' proposes veteran *Rocky Horror Show* actor Kristian Lavercombe, 'And there was no reason for them [Brad and Janet] to be scared or shocked by her; and I think that completely changed the storyline.'

Over the years, numerous stage actors had been allowed to put their own slant on the character of Frank-n-Furter. However, as far as the celluloid version was concerned, Tim Curry's performance cast an undeniably long shadow, and, while clearly enjoying herself in the role, Laverne Cox's mannerisms, intonation and facial expressions – which sometimes seemed to cross the line between simple imitation and grotesque parody – left viewers in no doubt that she had clearly been influenced by his perfectly pitched, iconic portrayal.

For the new film, Curry himself assumed the role of the Criminologist – listed as 'The Narrator/Criminologist' in the end credits – bringing a significant element of class and much-needed *Rocky Horror* heritage to the piece. With his speech and movement impeded dramatically by the effects of a debilitating stroke – which he had suffered in 2012 – Tim shared his scenes with a peculiar, sour-faced butler character (played by Canadian actress Jayne Eastwood), who demonstrated the steps of 'The Time Warp' and turned the pages of *The Denton Affair* dossier for the impaired actor.

Although the film would receive negative criticism for many of its creative decisions and certain casting choices, numerous fans praised the standout performances of Annaleigh Ashford and Adam Lambert. Ashford – who, rather than copying Little Nell's iconic vibrant, squeaky-voiced portrayal – played Columbia as a bored petulant teen with a punk-inspired costume that was something of a refreshing departure from the original film's prominent gold sequined tailcoat. The words 'Frankie Fan' and a denim square – featuring a pair of crudely painted red lips – on the back of her studded black leather jacket added to the meta approach of the piece by suggesting that, as well as her love for Frank and Eddie, the groupie might also be a fan of *The Rocky Horror Picture Show* itself.

Since the death of their legendary front-man Freddie Mercury in November 1991, British rock band Queen had successfully collaborated with other vocalists: Paul Rodgers (between 2004 and 2009) and Adam Lambert from 2011 onwards. With a spectacular, though somewhat nonsensical, entrance – crashing his motorcycle through the upstairs

9: SENSUAL DAYDREAMS TO TREASURE FOREVER

laboratory's window – and looking like a cross between a cadaverous Elvis and a zombie James Dean, Lambert's established rock star status and dynamic theatricality allowed him to fill Eddie's well-worn biker boots with ease. In fact, upon seeing his scene-stealing performance, many lamented the fact that the flamboyant star had not played Dr Frank-n-Furter, a role for which he seemed tailor-made.

Like Ryan McCartan and Victoria Justice, a number of the film's other cast members appeared to be avoiding creative character choices – perhaps feeling a little intimidated by the enormity of taking on such beloved roles – opting instead to merely replicate the performances of their predecessors.

Some viewers observed that stage and screen legend Ben Vereen seemed oddly reserved as Dr Everett Scott, squandering the fundamental B-movie satire and comedic opportunities offered by such a rich gift of a character; while, as Rocky Horror himself, the appealing Staz Nair – sporting knee-length baggy gold gym shorts (somewhat less saucy than the tight-fitting 'budgie smugglers' of Rayner Bourton's or Peter Hinwood's incarnations of the character) – looked the part in every way, his startled, stiff-legged performance felt a little restrained until he was finally allowed to cut loose during 'The Floorshow'. Following in the hallowed footsteps of author Richard O'Brien – certainly a reason to feel intimated – Reeve Carney brought a suitably sinister menace to the critical role of Riff Raff, but struggled a little with the more enigmatic, paranoid complexities of the character; and, although clearly having fun as Magenta, the sincerity of Christina Milian's performance was hindered by a costume which might have looked more at home in a bad amateur production.

In truth, the costumes as a whole, provided by the renowned William Ivey Long – whose celebrated work had featured in numerous Broadway musicals, including 2001's *The Producers* (and its subsequent 2005 film adaptation), *Hairspray* in 2002, the 2003 revival of *Little Shop of Horrors* and 2007's *Young Frankenstein* – came over as misguidedly pristine and polished – lacking the essential rips, dust, cobwebs and overall truth of their 1975 precursors – which added immeasurably to the new film's flaws. The genius of Sue Blane's designs for the original stage and screen incarnations of *Rocky Horror* helped to ground the ostensible absurdity of Richard O'Brien's characters by giving them a sense of authenticity. Along with Brian Thomson's ingenious production design and Terry Ackland-Snow's inventive art direction, Blane's costumes had given the original movie a fitting Hammer horror aesthetic which perfectly befitted the rationale of Jim Sharman's direction. In short, they looked like the clothes these people would wear if they actually existed in the real world; they felt genuine, lived in and rough around the edges. Conversely – and in spite of interviews suggesting that he definitely understood the B-movie roots of the piece and its characters – William Ivey Long's curious design choices for the 2016 version had the look of showy Hallowe'en costumes, almost as if the characters themselves were having a fancy dress party.

Similarly, production designer Peter Cosco and art director Michaela Cheyne gave the piece the look of a garish pop music promo, rather than the more appropriate classic horror movie vibe of the 1975 movie. Too much pop and not enough rock was also a common criticism of the updated musical arrangements. For the most part, however, the brilliance of O'Brien's compositions and Richard Hartley's unrivalled original orchestrations were thankfully still recognisable, and at least the addition of a 'shoop shoop' intro for 'The Floorshow' and 'na-nana-na-na-na-na' choruses for 'Hot Patootie' remained in keeping with the 1950s rock 'n' roll influences of *The Rocky Horror Show*'s score.

The most contentious exceptions seemed to be Frank-n-Furter's songs. Controversially tailored for Laverne Cox's modern diva style, their attempts to be quirky and contemporary conflicted awkwardly with the rest of Richard O'Brien's classically simple rock 'n' roll compositions. With a dubiously slow and dreamy intro, and complete lack of a strong bass line – robbing the number and Frank's all-important entrance of any impact whatsoever – 'Sweet Transvestite' became the worst offender in this respect.

Kenny Ortega's background in musicals and promotional pop videos was almost certainly a contributing factor to the film being somewhat over-crowded and over-choreographed. When approaching the 1975 version, Jim Sharman realised that O'Brien's tacky little rock show had little in common with a typical musical, and chose therefore to focus on character, motivation and performance while, quite rightly, leaving the intentionally minimal choreography basic and unsophisticated.

The Transylvanians – never an element of *The Rocky Horror Show* on stage – were added by Sharman, against the wishes of Richard O'Brien, as a means of filling the screen during 'The Time Warp' and laboratory sequences, but their uniformed appearance, and the director's innate skill at keeping them under control within the confines of a scene, prevented this ensemble from ever pulling focus from the principal actors or the plot. Ortega's Transylvanians on the other hand were permitted to over-populate Frank-n-Furter's domain with irrelevant and pointless dancing at every opportunity, spilling over into every segment of the story. Furthermore, while Sharman had the good sense to rid the castle of these superfluous extraterrestrial partygoers before the intricate plot thickened with the arrival of Dr Scott and Riff Raff's crucial eleventh-hour coup, Ortega let them run riot throughout; partying into the night, hijacking 'Wild and Untamed Thing', and, worst of all, eliminating all emotional poignancy from the script's tragically dark ending.

In addition to its opening 'Science Fiction Double Feature' sequence, the

9: SENSUAL DAYDREAMS TO TREASURE FOREVER

film admittedly boasted a small number of other interesting ideas and Easter eggs for *Rocky Horror* aficionados to enjoy. *Rocky Horror Picture Show* fan club president Sal Piro made a cameo appearance as the Hapschatts' wedding photographer; the inscription on a headstone in the churchyard clearly read 'Mary Shelley – 1797–1851 – There Is A Light'; another gravestone in the same scene bore the name 'Price' (presumably a tribute to the legendary horror movie actor who had famously attended the first London performance of *The Rocky Horror Show* at the Royal Court's Theatre Upstairs in 1973); the banner inside the castle now displayed the phrase '41st Annual Transylvanian Convention' in honour of the 1975 film's astonishing durability; Brad and Janet appeared to be dancing the Madison during 'Hot Patootie'; Columbia amusingly sucked a lollipop through a strategic slit in her surgical mask; and the newborn Rocky emerged from a box of ice, somewhat akin to the original stage production's Coca-Cola machine.

Another intriguing suggestion was that of Magenta now appearing to call the shots, with the henpecked Riff Raff apparently her subordinate, an idea best exemplified by the moment in which she held up hand-written cue cards next to the T.V. monitor for her anxious brother to read as he nervously explained to Frank-n-Furter the circumstances of Rocky's escape from the lab.

Despite these, all too rare, flashes of ingenuity however, most devotees agreed that this superficial, made-for-television reworking was miscast, poorly designed and severely flawed. Falling somewhere between a legitimate remake and a weird self-aware celebration – whilst failing to make any real impact as either – *The Rocky Horror Picture Show: Let's Do The Time Warp Again* seemed unsure of its own identity. Its sanitised tone, not helped by the rules and moral constraints of television, led some to compare it to the often derided *Rocky Horror* episode of *Glee* from a few years earlier. Others noted that it had gone down an unsuitably peculiar Disney route – abandoning the essential raw rock 'n' roll and subversive edginess of the original work in favour of brightly lit sets and unnecessarily elaborate dance numbers – which had given it the wholly inappropriate look and feel of the decidedly bland *High School Musical* films.

While the world around it changed dramatically – both culturally and politically – in the decades following *The Rocky Horror Show*'s rather modest birth, the themes and cultural works that had inspired it – and its perpetually youthful author-composer – remained as potent as ever. A number of the movies Richard O'Brien had name-checked in 'Science Fiction Double Feature' were consequently granted the dubious honour of, invariably inferior, Hollywood remakes.

Producer Dino De Laurentiis's lavish 1976 update of *King Kong*, directed by John Guillermin, which relocated the dizzying all-action finale from the Empire State Building to the recently-unveiled twin towers of New York City's World Trade Centre had its merits, as did Peter Jackson's rather overlong and self-indulgent 1930s-set reworking of the story that premiered worldwide in 2005. Enjoyable as they are, though, neither comes close to capturing the heart, magic and technical finesse of the beloved 1933 classic.

A concept considered tantamount to cinematic sacrilege, and thus derided by science fiction aficionados for decades, had been the idea of remaking *The Day the Earth Stood Still*. Nevertheless, such a task would eventually be attempted by director Scott Derrickson and released in 2008 by 20th Century Fox; although the result became something of a disjointed incoherent shambles. Entirely removed from Michael Rennie's autocratic, yet warmly compassionate, alien emissary, Keanu Reeves' hard-hearted and stone-faced Klaatu seemed to miss the mark entirely; a muddled screenplay by David Scarpa eschewed the integral Cold War premise of the immaculately-structured and intellectually stimulating 1951 movie in favour of a relevant, though shoddily executed, ecological message; while a wholly inappropriate overabundance of flashy computer-generated visual effects seriously overshadowed the essential human and political drama that made Robert Wise's original such an outstanding and important film.

With Mary Shelley's eternally pertinent themes transcending generations and providing fuel for innumerable screen adaptations of variable quality, the cinema's fascination with the legend of Frankenstein continued unabated.

1974's gloriously titled *Frankenstein and the Monster from Hell*, Hammer Films' final foray into the macabre world of Peter Cushing's increasingly obsessed Baron (this time with David Prowse as an extremely grotesque, yet pitiable, ape-like creature), was a suitably bloody and morbid swansong for the series. Nonetheless, Hammer's famous gore quotient had already been surpassed a year earlier by writer-director Paul Morrissey's decidedly gruesome and conspicuously camp *Flesh for Frankenstein*, co-produced by Andy Warhol (alternative titles included *Andy Warhol's Flesh for Frankenstein* and *Andy Warhol's Frankenstein*) and released – in 3-D no less – just as *The Rocky Horror Show* was vibrantly re-energising London's King's Road.

The film's rather mixed-up plot involves a plan by the tenacious Baron Frankenstein (played by a wonderfully sordid and unapologetically theatrical Udo Kier) to construct both male and female humanoid creatures in an effort to breed a perfect Serbian super race. Although their crudely-pieced-together bodies blatantly betray their creator's less than sophisticated sewing skills, the results of this fanatical scientist's labours are, like Dr Frank-n-Furter's burly blond plaything, rather fine-looking physical specimens. With the Baron apparently sharing an incestuous marriage with his sister (Monique van Vooren) – the mother of his two creepy children, who, in the aftermath of the film's climactic bloodbath, would appear to be on the verge of continuing daddy's profane experiments – and the Greek gymnasium look of his spacious tiled laboratory preceding that of *The Rocky Horror Picture Show* by more than a year, this particular *Frankenstein* adaptation actually shares more in common with Richard O'Brien's musical than most.

While generally perceived as a dark send-up, the picture's copious over-the-top examples of dismemberment, disembowelling, bountiful nudity, necrophilia and other perverse sexual intimations saw it banned as a 'video nasty' in Britain during the 1980s. Perhaps unsurprisingly, it later gained something of an affectionate cult following.

Post *Rocky Horror*, Tim Curry showcased his luxurious singing voice with a quartet of solo albums – *Read My Lips* (1978); *Fearless* (1979); *Simplicity* (1981); and finally *The Best of Tim Curry* (1989) – in addition to several well-received concert appearances, although he would continue to be embraced primarily for an extensive array of diverse character roles – serious and light, comedic and straight – in theatre, film and television.

The actor was nominated for a Tony Award for his 1981 performance as Wolgang Amadeus Mozart in Peter Shaffer's *Amadeus* on Broadway – the winner being Sir Ian McKellen for his portrayal of the scheming Antonio Salieri in the same production – and his exhilarating Pirate King in the 1982 London run of Gilbert and Sullivan's *The Pirates of Penzance* is still fondly remembered.

The acclaim garnered for his inspired Broadway depiction of Mozart was scarcely surprising, given that the gifted and intelligent actor had previously recreated another real life artistic genius in ITC Entertainment's ambitious six-part historical television drama *Will Shakespeare* (aka *Life of Shakespeare* and *William Shakespeare: His Life and Times*), a production that also featured Ian McShane as Christopher Marlowe and Nicholas Clay as the Earl of Southampton, and was first broadcast on ATV (Associated Television) in June 1978.

Rarely cast as a cinematic leading man, Curry specialised in an almost never-ending list of scene-stealing supporting roles. Roles such as malevolent supernatural circus clown Pennywise in the 1990 TV mini-series of Stephen King's *It*; Dr Yevgeniy Petrov in the Cold War submarine thriller *The Hunt for Red October* (1990), which starred Alec Baldwin, Sean Connery and Sam Neill; *Muppet Treasure Island*'s memorable Long John Silver in 1996; the hilariously smarmy hotel concierge of John Hughes' *Home Alone 2: Lost in New York* (1991); the conniving Rooster in the 1982 film version of the hit Broadway musical *Annie*; *Congo*'s bizarrely accented (another of his apparent specialities) Herkermer Homolka in 1995; enigmatic disc jockey Johnny LaGuardia in *Times Square* (1980), director Allan Moyle's New York-based modern fable; and, almost unrecognisable (until he speaks) – thanks to the incredible prosthetic make-up designed by Peter Robb-King (who also served as chief make-up artist on *The Rocky Horror Picture Show*) and Rob Bottin – as the Lord of Darkness in director Ridley Scott's 1985 mythical adult fantasy *Legend*.

Additionally, Curry has had the oft-repeated distinction of being the one worthwhile highlight of an otherwise mediocre movie. Notable examples include *National Lampoon's Loaded Weapon 1* (1993), a second-rate spoof of the popular *Lethal Weapon* films, starring Emilio Estevez, Samuel L Jackson and William Shatner; 2001's irredeemable horror parody *Scary Movie 2*; and the children's fantasy adventure *The Secret of Moonacre* in 2008.

The actor has also been a prolific voiceover artist for a seemingly inexhaustible catalogue of animated features, cartoon shorts, computer games and audio books.

In December 2004, Eric Idle and John Du Prez premiered a new comedy musical at Chicago's Shubert Theatre, with a prominent cast that included David Hyde Pierce, Hank Azaria, Sara Ramirez and, in the lead role of King Arthur, Tim Curry. Directed by Mike Nichols and sub-headed 'A new musical lovingly ripped off from the motion picture *Monty Python and the Holy Grail*', the original New York production of *Monty Python's Spamalot* became a Broadway triumph after it transferred there the following February. The celebrated production was then nominated for 14 Tony Awards, of which it won three, including Best New Musical. Tim Curry made the *Python* team's translation of Arthur: King of the Britons – a character played in the original 1975 movie by the idiosyncratically eccentric Graham Chapman – completely his own; a world-weary cynic with more than the merest hint of the actor's own apparently disenchanted outlook.

Although frequently the product of unsubstantiated hearsay, Curry's resentment toward the media's unyielding over-association of him with his performance as Dr Frank-n-Furter became notorious amongst *Rocky Horror* devotees as the initially unsuccessful film version began to pick up business on the midnight circuit. In a chapter entitled 'Artistic Limitations' for his 1996 book *Toxic Fame: Celebrities Speak on Stardom*, author and entertainment journalist Joey Berlin included a remarkably pertinent quote from the actor:

'Here I am, a moderately articulate person with some experience of the world, and more often than not there is still a photograph of Dr Frank-n-Furter affixed to almost everything I have to say, largely because it's another way of getting a pair of legs and suspenders and garters onto the

9: SENSUAL DAYDREAMS TO TREASURE FOREVER

page of a family newspaper to astonish and amuse. That gets pretty old after a while because it's sloppy and it's cheap and it's unsparing. But so is fame.'

Considering the myopic fixation favoured by numerous writers and critics with a single, almost 40-year-old movie role, Curry's frustrated yearning for a wider appraisal of his entire – extremely prolific and varied – body of work feels wholly warranted. And yet, under closer scrutiny, his apparent disassociation of himself from Frank-n-Furter, as well as an alleged aversion to the *Rocky Horror* phenomenon as a whole, would appear to have been unfairly exaggerated.

In the 1999 BBC Radio 2 documentary *Let's Do The Time Warp Again*, the eloquently well-spoken actor openly rationalised his personal decision to shun the fame and publicity machine for the whole of his career, after having already witnessed a number of friends and associates ('Icarus figures,' as he aptly called them) tragically destroying themselves as a result of merciless celebrity lifestyles. Ironically, Frank-n-Furter's ultimate fate at the climax of *The Rocky Horror Show* could easily be viewed as a warning against such decadent excesses. During the same interview, however, Curry refreshingly expressed palpable affection and gratitude for the character and the show that had helped launch his career.

On the evening of Sunday 19 June 2005, attired in a manner befitting a far more conventional physician (specifically a starched white coat) and with tongue planted firmly in cheek, Curry took to the stage and, by way of a couple of cheeky references, cheerfully invoked the immortal memory of the wayward Transsexual scientist during a sketch for the doctors-and-nurses themed fifteenth incarnation of *Broadway Bares*, an annual comedy-burlesque charity revue that helps raise funds for the US theatre community's Broadway Cares/Equity Fights AIDS organisation.

When *Spamalot* opened at London's Palace Theatre on 30 September 2006, Curry returned to the role of King Arthur for a three-month West End season – his first time performing on a British stage in two decades – giving most UK *Rocky Horror* fans their first ever opportunity to see one of their most elusive heroes in the flesh. Though initially a little reticent about confronting their idol at the stage door, thanks largely to whispered horror stories about his supposed hatred of all things *Rocky*, most were pleasantly relieved to find him receptive, charming and more than happy to pose for photographs and sign those all-important items of *Rocky Horror* memorabilia.

As indicated by interviews and numerous appearances at fan events, *The Rocky Horror Show* continues to have a profound and lasting effect on a good proportion of its early collaborators – Patricia Quinn, Little Nell, Rayner Bourton, Susan Sarandon, Barry Bostwick and Meat Loaf among them – many of whom appear to be fiercely proud and outspoken champions of all that this rather extraordinary work of entertainment represents.

Furthermore, many of those interviewed for this book remain connected to *Rocky* in a variety of special and deeply personal ways.

'I do have some fabulous memories,' says Daniel Abineri of his numerous appearances as Frank-n-Furter throughout the '80s and early '90s. 'One was playing opposite Richard O'Brien at a midnight matinee in Sydney, on behalf of Amnesty International. He was playing Riff and when he sang "The darkness must go …" I got goose bumps all over. Another was the last night at the Comedy [in London]; Johnny Rotten was in the front row and Steve Strange was in a box, clad in his "Fade to Grey" outfit.'

In keeping with the unabashed narcissism of Frank-n-Furter himself, many actors are openly forthcoming in admitting their own self-absorbed feelings of rock god status once inside his sequinned corset and rhinestone-encrusted shoes; an attitude that to some degree helps explain the character's ongoing appeal on both sides of the curtain.

'I just love the end of "Sweet Transvestite,"' grins David Bedella, joyfully recalling how, at some performances, the rapturous screaming of the crowd at the climax of Frank's first number would literally last for several minutes. 'The audience wouldn't even let you start the next line. I'd stand there, bathing in it. It was like an outpouring of love, and you could almost feel the waves of adoration. I used to stand there and think, "Thank you, God." That part of the show was a highlight even on bad days.'

'I guess I didn't realise it at the time, but *Rocky* was one of the most important times of my performing life,' confesses Mark Turnbull, his sentiments corresponding completely with so many others whose time on Earth has been enriched by this one-of-a-kind work of entertainment. 'Playing Frank allowed me to be all the things on stage that I'm not in everyday life – to be desirable, sexy, witty and stylish, and to experience the kind of audience reaction that only a rock star can have – which is pretty nice for a very un-famous actor like me.'

'I must admit, that first night when the audience went wild, I just couldn't help smiling,' recalls Kara Lane of her very first entrance as the Usherette on the 2009 UK tour. 'I thought my face might crack. As a theatre actor I thrive on reaction; it's a kick. And with *Rocky* you can't help but feel that, for this one time in your life, you're a star.'

Even incidents that resulted in actual physical injury seem to be fondly remembered through rose tinted spectacles. 'I do recall being interviewed on radio about Frank,' Daniel Abineri discloses, 'and I was asked if I'd ever fallen over on the heels. I hadn't, so I told them so; and then, that very night, I was feeling a bit cocky and ended up ruining my knees for the

9: SENSUAL DAYDREAMS TO TREASURE FOREVER

show.' The accident occurred when the actor forcefully dropped to his knees as he delivered the line 'It would probably be a one-way ticket to the bottom of the bay,' during Frank's dramatic laboratory monologue – only to find himself in excruciating pain. 'I ended up getting water on the knee and was in agony,' he winces. 'I certainly couldn't do that move again. All those performances in heels have left me with problems with my hips, pelvis and hamstrings; I now have to wear special shoes to help my physiotherapy. My hamstrings are permanently tight, due to my calf being raised in heels for so long. I have suffered physically for the show, like the night Rocky did a cartwheel and kicked one of my front teeth out.'

Abineri is not the only performer to have suffered for his art and shed blood in the name of *Rocky Horror*, as David Bedella vividly recounts: 'Our last night in Woking, I was getting all the red stuff on for "The Floorshow". It's a fast change and I had to run each night to make it to the moon on time. I was coming around the corner from the quick change area and collided with Susie, one of our crew. The top of her head smashed right into my face and bam ... my nose was broken. Biggins was seated in Frank's green chair in the wings and he said he could hear the crack of the cartilage when we hit. Luke, our stage manager, grabbed me by the arm and said "You can't go on." I kept running, saying "I gotta go, that's my music." The curtains opened and when the light hit me I could see the blood on my own nose and could feel blood running to my upper lip. I knew I had red gloves on, so I just kept dabbing and mopping with my hands while singing "Whatever happened to Fay Wray?" and somehow made it through the end of the show.'

Incredibly, it appeared that some spectators had actually interpreted Bedella's resilience and professionalism in the face of this genuine bodily harm as simply another premeditated facet of an intensely calculated performance: 'My friend Jaye Jacobs – Donna from *Holby City* – was in the house that night,' the actor continues, 'and she told me, after the show, she thought it was the most brilliant acting choice ever. She looked at me, sniffling and wiping my nose, looking slightly out of it, and she thought, "Look at him, he's coked out of his mind." Brilliant.'

Mark Turnbull meanwhile calls to mind a rather strange occasion when, during his time with the UK tour of *The Rocky Horror Show* in the 1980s, he was invited to go along in costume and address the morning assembly at a local junior school: 'They asked me to go dressed as Frank, so I turned up and took a seat on stage with the rest of the teaching staff. The headmaster introduced me and handed over to me. Well, I hadn't been briefed on what they expected, so there was a bit of an awkward silence. Then I told them that I'd come in character from a show that was playing locally, and said that I was playing a character who was a transvestite; and I asked if anyone's dad, maybe, was a transvestite.' Turnbull remembers that, after another slightly awkward moment, a solitary hand in the midst of the crowd slowly rose into the air. 'I dread to think what happened to that poor little kid afterwards,' he cringes. 'He probably got teased mercilessly. After assembly I went for tea and biscuits with the head; it was totally bizarre.'

Turnbull then smiles as a further amusing anecdote springs to mind; this one concerning an incident that took place during one of the tour's engagements in Scotland: 'I remember one night in Glasgow when Kinny Gardner, a native Scot, decided to play Riff with a Scottish accent. He got barracked, as the audience thought he was taking the piss out of them; they thought he was a jumped up Englishman trying out a Scots accent.'

'It's funny, but, whenever I dream, my dreams are always about the show,' reveals a reflective Zalie Burrow. 'It has a power and it stays with you.'

The actress goes on to suggest that *Rocky Horror* has something of a six-degrees-of-separation vibe going for it, as she fondly recalls that Caroline Noh, one of the King's Road production's early Magentas, taught her at drama school. 'As soon as you meet an actor who has done *Rocky*, you are a member of a very special club,' she declares, further emphasising the notion of 'the *Rocky* family', a concept repeatedly referred to by loyal fans and ex-cast members alike: 'I bumped into Gordon Kennedy [Eddie/Dr Scott in the 1990 revival] and his kids recently in McDonald's. We decided that we would say we bumped into each other in Soho House, so much more appropriate; oh well, our secret's out. Kate [O'Sullivan, 1990/91 Phantom/Magenta] and I are still very close, probably because she married my brother. So we're aunties to each other's kids and were each other's bridesmaids.'

Following their unforgettably joyous time with *The Rocky Horror Show* in London and on tour around the UK, Burrow and O'Sullivan also maintained their professional and personal association with members of the production's band: 'In fact we've all stayed in touch and we have a function band called the Rocky Band,' Burrow announces happily.

The actress's lasting affection for the show's original Narrator, an actor who revisited the role 18 years later for the 1990 West End revival at the Piccadilly Theatre – and who passed away on 13 June 2005 at the age of 74 – is also very much in evidence. 'Jonathan Adams was divine,' she smiles. 'He used to invite me and Kate over for afternoon tea for years after our time in *Rocky* finished. I remember eating Greek salad in his garden; it was always Greek salad. He was a great artist and had these amazingly detailed medical drawings on the walls. He gave me a tape recording of him performing "Baa Baa Black Sheep" in different styles [Adams' party piece, which he had also used as his audition for the original *Rocky Horror Show* at the Royal Court in 1973], which was random and utterly brilliant.

9: SENSUAL DAYDREAMS TO TREASURE FOREVER

He was a one-off and I often think of him with huge fondness.'

Another former Janet with endless praise for the show's very first Narrator is Belinda Sinclair. 'Jonathan Adams was fabulous; easily the best Narrator,' she affirms. 'He was like a kindly uncle telling the story. He didn't try to get gags out of the script. Nowadays the Narrators try to be in the show and take part; Jonathan stood outside of it and just told the story. He got laughs of course, but he didn't deliberately go for them.

'I must say, I feel like a bit of a maiden aunt going to see the young casts now. But, as an actor, how do you top *Rocky*? It was a huge part of our lives; we just didn't realise it at the time.'

When asked if he might consider assuming the role of the Narrator in a future production, Anthony Head – one of the most memorable and popular Frank-n-Furters of the 1990s – is optimistically open-minded. 'Yes, I would, but I'd have to find something new to bring to it,' he avows enthusiastically. 'The Narrator is pretty much a blank page. As long as he drives the show, there's nothing set in stone. I'd happily go to see the new tour, as I love the show and it's always good to see new interpretations. I did see a Hungarian production when I was filming in Budapest. The narration was shared by two large women dressed as British bobbies, and Dr Scott had Catherine wheels attached to his wheelchair.'

Pondering possible reasons for the sheer staying power of an almost 50-year-old theatrical piece in the wake of countless forgotten shows from the same era, Head is typically expressive and reverential. 'It's a free spirit,' he declares. 'It's not like *Phantom* or *Les Mis*, which clunk along like unstoppable machines. It allows people to be what they want to be. It's enabling; it lets you strut your stuff, and good on you madam or sir for doing it. The audience all go out on a high; and, of course, it's got that music – the best rock 'n' roll ever written for the stage. I think the other thing is that the fans kind of own it. I started to recognise certain fans who kept returning, and the atmosphere at the stage door was simply joyful. It wasn't just about getting autographs; more a feeling of, "I was here."'

'I don't think there's one single thing that you could point to; it's a combination of things,' suggests Mark Turnbull, whose own suppositions – including the idea of a pride of ownership amongst the show's most ardent followers – concur closely with those of his fellow Frank. 'To start with, the music's fabulous; there's not a duff song in the show. Secondly, the show allows you to be – and feel – sexy, but not in an overtly sexual way. It allows you to be something else, something a bit outrageous. In that sense, it's like music fashion, like the New Romantics were. Importantly, it allows the fans to have a sense of ownership of something. Also, it doesn't take itself seriously. It's derivative, yet Richard tapped a vein that others could enjoy. It is a masterpiece; not Shakespeare, yet very potent. Finally, it's the sort of show that you come out of on a high.'

Actor Jay Benedict, meanwhile, is unequivocally clear and articulately comprehensive about why he feels the show struck such a nerve with audiences. 'Dead simple,' he proclaims, with palpable exuberance mounting from his perpetual passion for the piece. 'It's sex and drugs and rock 'n' roll. It's a get down and dirty, no happy ending kind of a show. It's not a traditional boy meets girl, there's fight over her honour and a happy ending. *The Rocky Horror Show* turned that on its arse. The straight guy gets turned. Instead of heterosexuality, there's bisexuality. It's a degenerate show that appeals to the lowest common denominator in people. It had all the right ingredients and the audience was totally absorbed. They were mesmerised and reverential. Don't forget that it started in a pre-AIDS world off the back of *Hair*, hippies, T-Rex and Bowie.'

'Somehow it touches people,' offers Belinda Sinclair, positing her own theories as to the show's continued durability. 'They can identify with the good versus evil story. It's a rock 'n' roll panto; it's *Babes in the Wood* with a dame. I don't think the music can be bettered; it's very simple and feels so familiar to you. The show's got everything; comedy, sex, rock 'n' roll. Really, there's no need to change the message, unlike *Hair* – where it was centred around the Vietnam War and would need to be updated for the Iraq War – there's no need to change it, because it's got an essential innocence.'

With the show as initially conceived becoming something of a victim of its own success, particularly during the 1980s – thanks largely to its growing reputation as an extravagantly outrageous and interactive social experience – directors of later productions had to find ways of balancing the essential story-driven innocence and simplistic naiveté of its author's original intentions with the increasingly over-the-top grandiose theatrics and unrestricted vulgarity demanded by uncompromisingly broadminded modern day audiences.

'It's not so much theatre-going, it's party-going, isn't it?' was Richard O'Brien's own hypothesis as to *Rocky*'s unwavering appeal to contemporary viewers, while speaking on Radio New Zealand in 2010; an experience he implied was singularly unique to this particular theatrical piece:

'It's people going out to have a good evening; a good night out, as opposed to, "We're going to the theatre." And I like that.

'And in this day and age, you want a bit of a return on your investment, don't you? And to come out of the theatre feeling a lot better than you did when you went in is pretty damned good.'

On the whole, most fans would probably agree that, while the show should always live up to, and preferably surpass, such requirements – and that the uncomfortable removal and alteration of certain sections of its classic dialogue (in order to discourage bothersome heckling at inappropriate moments) has on occasion been unjustifiably excessive – the piece itself, rather than its colourful and often overexcited audience, should remain the show's driving force. These days, however, attendees reserve the right to squeeze into ill-fitting corsetry and shout questionably timed obscenities at the unfortunate cast members; all in the name of the aforesaid 'good night out.'

Changing attitudes and constantly escalating expectations – not to mention much larger budgets – have seen *The Rocky Horror Show* grow from a little bit of unassuming late night rock 'n' roll fun into a polished, lavishly produced, mainstream musical, often misread by ignorant reviewers as merely a backdrop for childishly asinine audience shenanigans. Nonetheless, the most perceptive of directors and designers continue to realise that maintaining the essence and integrity of the piece as envisaged by Richard O'Brien and Jim Sharman is still the technique most likely to make the show work.

'It's supposed to be tacky, shabby and all covered in dust and crap,' states Neil McCaul. 'It must be rough and ready. It should borrow heavily from the silent movie/film noir genre. Above all it must be sinister; I don't get all the camp stuff that's crept in. Think Max Schreck in *Nosferatu*. It should be interesting and fun, but also dangerously vicious. I think the venue helps. The King's Road Theatre was rough; in winter it could be minus ten degrees in the corridor. There was lots of illness there.

'The first time I saw it I remember the sheer wallop and impact it had. Especially Frank. Here was this hefty bloke; you'd no idea where the hell he came from, but he was shockingly alien. Tim Curry had this amazing rock baritone singing voice and this ridiculous accent, straight out of the Women's Institute – but filthy dirty.'

During an interview with British TV presenter Matthew Wright on his morning discussion programme *The Wright Stuff* on 15 August 2009, Richard O'Brien theorised that a lack of expectation or long-term potential had, as much as anything else, most likely added immensely to the show's astonishing success and longevity. 'It was just going to be fun,' he emphasised. 'I think that element comes over; I really believe it. Nobody had any idea about any of its potential; three weeks' fun and that was it. And I think it shows every time the show plays; that comes across somehow.'

Writing for the Daily Mirror in 1990, Hilary Bonner also identified this unpretentious fun aspect as a major factor in the show's continued popularity.

'It is almost impossible to describe *The Rocky Horror Show* without making it sound terrible. The truth is it is actually rather wonderful,' Bonner declared boldly; an assessment which, while sounding at first like something of a backhanded compliment, was really rather astute and unmistakably affectionate.

'Most important of all, it is fun – and the theatre can do with a lot more of that,' the journalist concluded, casually identifying a key reason for the show's wide mainstream appeal and continued adoration. While its themes reflected the liberalisation and changing attitudes of the late '60s and early '70s – homosexuality had not been decriminalised in Britain until 1967, just one year before the relaxation of theatrical censorship – they did so in a playfully inclusive and accessible manner, with no out-of-place antagonism or outwardly opinionated political stance.

It is this lighthearted accessibility which, probably above all else, keeps *Rocky Horror*'s appeal continually relevant, fresh and cross-generational; and while there is little doubt that a large number of critics might have preferred *Look Back in Anger* or a comparable work of 'proper' serious drama to have been selected by the Royal Court Theatre's People's Choice vote in 2006, *The Rocky Horror Show*'s victory – by an overwhelming majority – and the derisory way in which the news was reported by some implied a lot more about snobbery and the British class divide than most would have dared to acknowledge.

Enjoyed and admired by many journalists and showbiz academics the show may be, but it is with the general public that it has always inspired devotion, passion, and – it must be said – feelings not dissimilar to love.

There had been an indication that the winning selection would be performed again, for one night only, at the Royal Court itself; a prospect that seemed too good to miss for most long-standing *Rocky* fans, who – networking via the UK fan club – at once began urging each other to cast their votes on the Royal Court's website.

With all votes counted and *Rocky Horror* easily the clear winner, however, it was announced that the celebratory performance would not be a warts-and-all recreation of the show's humble inaugural production (with shabby Odeon carpet, minimalist scaffolding set and a solitary cable microphone). Instead, it was to take place in the main house as opposed to the impractically small Theatre Upstairs, in the form of a prestigious charity gala concert appropriately labelled *Richard O'Brien's Rocky Horror Tribute Show*.

With proceeds going to the global human rights organisation Amnesty International, tickets came in a range of prices – £50, £100, £200 and £350 – just a little bit higher than the 25p and 50p charged for *The Rocky Horror Show*'s first preview performance on 16 June 1973. Nevertheless, the show's ardent supporters, determined to be present at a genuine once-in-a-lifetime celebration of their beloved obsession, would not be deterred. With the £350 price tag for a front stalls ticket well beyond their means, most *Rocky Horror* followers settled for a £50 seat, placing them in the upper circle; a position that, given the compact venue's rather intimate

9: SENSUAL DAYDREAMS TO TREASURE FOREVER

interior, would not actually result in a limited view of the action.

After very little rehearsal, a fact that bequeathed the evening a suitably raw spontaneity, the gala, directed by Christopher Luscombe with musical direction by Mark Warman, took place on the evening of 3 May 2006 at 8.00 pm.

'We had so little time to get that together,' confirms Luscombe. 'On one hand we had an amazing line-up, a great MD and band; but, on the other, the cast availability was very patchy. We had odd sessions with individuals, but our first and only run-through was on the day itself. It was quite scary, and that's why there was an edge to it, but it was great fun to do.'

In the days leading up to the performance, it was rumoured that tickets, having quickly sold out shortly after going on sale, had been exchanging hands for as much as £800 on the internet, prompting Richard O'Brien to informally request that sellers donate half their profits to Amnesty International.

The chosen concert format encompassed all of the show's songs, linked by specially-written narration showcasing the author's distinctive sardonic wit; and the never-to-be-repeated all-star ensemble featured former cast members from the show's 33-year history, along with a number of celebrity guest stars.

A host of familiar British names – actor-presenter Tony Slattery, future *Rocky Horror Show* tour Narrator Steve Pemberton, presenter and broadcaster Jamie Theakston, former Frank-n-Furter Robin Cousins and *Rocky Horror* legends Christopher Biggins and Rayner Bourton – assumed the role of the Narrator for one night only, appearing individually and intermittently throughout the performance to introduce each song and, in the absence of the script's customary dialogue, to tell the story.

Richard O'Brien began the evening with a sincere tribute to *Rocky's* original producer, himself comfortably ensconced in the stalls, who received an entirely deserved early ovation: 'Before we start, I want to say a very special thank you to one person who's sitting amongst you. A person who struggled with illness recently. In fact he was seen wrestling with the Grim Reaper down Sunset Boulevard, stopping only briefly for a couple of G & Ts and a quick dip at the Beverly Hills Hotel. Michael White, our producer.'

When the performance was released on DVD a couple of years later, it was in a severely truncated form, which, while still including the songs, shamefully denied viewers the chance to hear O'Brien's respectful tribute to Michael White, as well as many of the night's more amusing one-liners. For example, O'Brien's accurate revelation that *The Rocky Horror Show* had been translated into a plethora of languages, 'including Hebrew and Icelandic,' provided a neat set up for a memorably droll gag, disappointingly absent from the DVD version. 'That was an interesting production,' he quipped dryly, with his usual puckish smile, leaving a perfectly timed pause before his smartly delivered punch line: 'The text was in Hebrew; the songs were in Icelandic.'

Guest performers for the tribute performance included Patricia Quinn – ever happy to champion the *Rocky* cause – enchantingly opening the show with her sweetly innocent trademark rendition of 'Science Fiction Double Feature'; Kraig Thornber, fondly remembered by fans as Riff Raff in the show's twenty-first birthday tour, slithering back into the deviously twisted form of the hunchbacked extraterrestrial handyman with ease; and, most thrilling of all, Little Nell, who flew to London for the rare and historic opportunity of joining O'Brien and Quinn to perform 'The Time Warp' – in the building where it all began – as the evening's finale.

Taking in the beautiful sunshine of a tranquil summer evening, the typically affable Nell posed for pictures, signed autographs and effortlessly charmed fans outside the theatre – while taking almost as many photos with her own camera – until a few minutes before the performance was due to commence.

Anthony Head sang most of Frank-n-Furter's numbers, justifiably bringing down the house with 'Sweet Transvestite', while West End luminary Michael Ball took over for 'The Floorshow' and an emotionally charged rendition of 'I'm Going Home.'

It was not the first time since his last stint in the show itself that Head had been required to re-inhabit the character that seemed to fit him so comfortably. He had slipped contentedly back into a very familiar outfit – his own costume from the 1990 West End revival – to take part in a celebrity karaoke special, as part of twenty-fifth anniversary celebrations for *The Rocky Horror Picture Show*, televised by US music channel VH-1 in 2000. 'When I arrived, they invited me up to sort through some bits of costume, and I said "No thanks, I've brought my own,"' he smiles naughtily. 'To my chagrin, Eric McCormack, the guy who plays Will in *Will & Grace*, had already bagged "Sweet Transvestite" and "I'm Going Home", so I was left with "Planet Schmanet". It went down well though.'

Actor-comedian Adrian Edmondson gladly returned to the role of Brad Majors, the character he had played at the Piccadilly Theatre in 1990, for the majority of the Royal Court's *Tribute Show*, with special guest Stephen Gately, of popular Irish boy band Boyzone, taking to the stage for 'Once in a While'. Gately (who later died from a previously undiagnosed heart condition at the age of just 33 on the morning of 10 October 2009) delivered a beautifully-balanced and tender version of Brad's soul-baring ballad; and the fact that he managed to nervously fluff the opening lyric – ironically the title of the song – and instead commence the number with the beginning of its subsequent line somehow added to the under-rehearsed

9: SENSUAL DAYDREAMS TO TREASURE FOREVER

charm of the whole night.

The part of Janet was shared for the evening by ex-*EastEnders* actress Sophie Lawrence, who had assumed the role for the show's twenty-first anniversary production in 1994, and Joanne Farrell, a blonde bombshell with a dynamite voice, who had played her on the 1995 UK tour.

Everyone appeared to be having fun. The never-less-than-engaging Christopher Biggins jollily bumbled his way through some of the Narrator's (more intricate than normal) monologues. He noticeably messed up his lines for 'The Time Warp' – to his own amusement as much as everyone else's – while his hilariously botched attempts to get his usually quite dexterous tongue around the phrase 'Audio Vibratory Physio-molecular Transport Device' (traditionally one of Dr Scott's lines) provided much mirth for all concerned. The esteemed veteran of stage and screen also sniggered as he read Richard O'Brien's newly-written description of Dr Scott's fateful arrival at the castle. 'We are not told how he affects an entrance,' he smirked knowingly, as he bluntly enunciated another irreverently comic addition to the text that would sadly be deleted from the subsequent DVD release: 'But we must assume that he doesn't shinny up any drainpipe ... as he is in a wheelchair.'

Rayner Bourton, meanwhile, clearly relished the chance to narrate the laboratory scene, vividly and articulately annunciating the dramatic birth of the show's title character, the very role he had proudly created more than three decades earlier. 'A body lies on an operating table,' he roared gleefully, with suitably sinister wild-eyed intensity. 'Wires and tubes are attached to the bandage-swathed figure. Switches are switched; levers pulled. Electricity courses through cables, and the corpus delectable twitches and spasms with life.'

Having appeared with Richard O'Brien and Little Nell in Derek Jarman's *Jubilee* in 1977, self-confessed *Rocky* fan Toyah Willcox was asked to play Magenta for the *Tribute Show* by O'Brien himself; an invitation she accepted without hesitation. 'I was thrilled,' she gushes genuinely. 'It was a stunning opportunity to plug into the origins of the show and I loved every minute. It must have been a nightmare for Richard because everyone was trying to get stage time and was telling him what to do. And you don't tell Richard O'Brien what to do. He was happy to let mistakes and experimentation become part of the show, as he did originally.'

With typical gusto, Toyah – whose reminiscences and thoughts on *The Rocky Horror Show* had appeared in the 1998 UK tour programme – visibly threw herself into the proceedings with her usual fervour, even if, like Biggins, she did manage to stumble over some of her 'Time Warp' lyrics in the understandably adrenaline-fuelled excitement.

Several years on, the actress has her own ideas as to why she found the experience so intensely enjoyable: 'I think because I'm the kind of person

Magenta was written for. You have to be non-conformist and have a certain rough-edged anarchy.' She also says she would readily return to the role for a future production should the opportunity arise. 'I love the part, and I'd do it because I think that Richard needs friends around him,' she ventures, recalling fondly her memories of appearing with *Rocky*'s author-composer in pantomime at the Milton Keynes Theatre in 2005: 'I liked him immensely. He's very human, not surrounded by a posse of "yes" people; so I know that, if he asked me to do it, I'd be asked for the right reason.'

In keeping with the austerity of the venue and the benefit's selected charity, the *Tribute Show*'s cast wore mostly black smart-casual attire for the evening, although some opted to incorporate the odd *Rocky Horror* twist here and there – the Franks wore appropriate make-up, jewellery and accessories, Toyah donned an eccentric black tutu, and the suitably buff Gary Amers stripped to the waist and applied a liberal layer of glitter to his well-oiled torso in order to portray Rocky – while the low key set, simply consisting of a large *Richard O'Brien's Rocky Horror Tribute Show* title card, flanked by two smaller Amnesty International logos, along with an on stage band and backing singers, was aptly unassuming.

Although a number of subsequent press reports would make reference to the fact that, for the *Tribute Show*, audience participation and unruliness had been kept to a minimum by the powers that be, a brief examination of internet message boards and *Rocky Horror* fan forums would have shown them that, prior to the evening in question, a conscious decision to this effect had already been collectively taken by the show's ardent followers.

Out of respect for O'Brien and this extraordinary commemorative performance, the fans themselves had decided that, while attending in costume was deemed acceptable – and dancing to 'The Time Warp' was law – they would all voluntarily refrain from any of the now-traditional verbal participation and heckling for the duration of the concert.

It had, after all, been the show's devotees whose loyal votes had secured its privileged place as the People's Choice. The true fans had genuine affection for *The Rocky Horror Show* – it meant something special and personal to each and every one of them – and they were eager to rejoice and pay it the homage it was due.

Even before the installation of the Riff Raff Statue in Hamilton in 2004, it had long been acknowledged that, while Elvis Presley's faithful disciples had Graceland in Memphis, Tennessee, as a recognisable mecca, so *Rocky Horror* devotees were blessed with the two Courts. That is the Royal Court Theatre in London's Sloane Square, where Jim Sharman's inaugural production of *The Rocky Horror Show* had debuted during the hot and sticky summer of 1973, and Oakley Court, the majestic mansion on the banks of the River Thames in Berkshire, where location filming for *The*

9: SENSUAL DAYDREAMS TO TREASURE FOREVER

Rocky Horror Picture Show had taken place in the cold wet autumn months of 1974.

While countless Elvis fanatics will no doubt make at least one pilgrimage to his stately Memphis home during their lifetimes, the man himself shuffled off his mortal coil in 1977, leaving his followers with the inescapable truth that none will ever get the chance to see their idol performing live again. It is here that *Rocky Horror* devotees have a definite edge over their Presley-worshipping counterparts.

On 3 May 2006, the one-night-only *Rocky Horror Tribute Show* climaxed with Richard O'Brien, Patricia Quinn and Little Nell together on stage at the Royal Court Theatre, the actual birthplace of *Rocky Horror*, belting out an exhilarating rendition of 'The Time Warp' to the overwhelming delight of every authentic fan in the building. They were, of course, joined by a remarkable and unique line-up that included Rayner Bourton (the original Rocky Horror himself), Anthony Head (one of the show's most beloved Frank-n-Furters), Adrian Edmondson, Michael Ball, Toyah Willcox and Stephen Gately.

Emotionally fulfilling and genuinely special, the performance was ultimately praised by most critics – aside from the most obstinate of not-to-be-swayed *Look Back in Anger* supporters, that is – with several recognising that the Royal Court, having possibly become rather staid and self-important in the decades since *Rocky* first rocked its rickety rafters, had, for once, allowed itself to let its hair down, kick up its heels and remember what it was like to have a bit of fun.

In the end, it would be just as well that all concerned had had such a bloody good time; as, with some of the hastily scribbled signs in the foyer stating that *Rocky Horror* had come home 'For the first *and last* time,' the possibility of the venue's management and the company's austere custodians ever letting their guard down again would seem somewhat unlikely.

10
And I Realise I'm Going Home

Aiming his fearsome triple-barrelled laser weapon in the direction of any Earthling foolish enough to conspire against him, the devious Riff Raff, vengeful ambassador from the planet Transsexual, watches menacingly over tourists and sightseers on Hamilton's Victoria Street.

A plaque beneath this bigger-than-life-sized bronze effigy bears the character's name, in the customary dripping blood font, flanked by two sets of the stylised lips associated with *Rocky Horror* movie posters and press ads. Under this lies a tasteful explanatory inscription: 'It's Astounding! Where we stand is the birthplace of *The Rocky Horror Picture Show*. On this site stood the Embassy Theatre, the home of Hamilton's late night double feature picture show, and *the* barber shop where Richard O'Brien cut hair and daydreamed from 1959 to 1964.'

The idea of building a monument to commemorate the life and achievements of *The Rocky Horror Show*'s illustrious creator began in the mind of writer-director and sometime councillor Mark Servian. A staunch supporter of culture and the arts in the city, and a little disenchanted by that which he called 'Hamilphobia' or 'cultural cringe' – the feeling that Hamilton, with its apathetic cow town image, was somehow deemed inferior to Wellington as a desirable visitor destination – Servian envisaged something not only of which Hamiltonians could be proud, but also a shrine for faithful followers of the *Rocky Horror* phenomenon, a previously unexploited area of potential tourism.

It had never been a secret that O'Brien considered New Zealand his home, as, although he had not actually been born a Kiwi, he and his siblings had grown up in the country; and his brother and sister still lived there. In 2000, he had been featured on an episode of the Qantas Airlines-sponsored *Coming Home* programme on New Zealand television, for which he had revisited his family's first New Zealand home – 16 Kitchener Street in the Hamilton suburb of Claudelands – as well as his former schools in Tauranga. Standing on a leafy and idyllic suburban street outside his beloved childhood home for the first time in 46 years, as a wealth of memories clearly raced to the surface, O'Brien appeared genuinely overwhelmed, likening the feeling, rather poetically, to being in a time warp.

10: AND I REALISE I'M GOING HOME

During the programme, he found himself reunited with now-retired Hamilton hairdresser Stan Osborne and his wife Olga, for whom he had served as a teenage apprentice in the late 1950s and early '60s; and it was during this reunion with the Osbornes – a couple he had not seen for 25 years – that O'Brien emotionally revealed a newfound desire to come back to the country for good. He divulged that he was currently in the process of purchasing two and half acres of land near the pastoral town of Katikati as his retirement plan, and would be signing the documents that very weekend.

He spoke warmly of New Zealand's truly classless society – the absolute antithesis of the vulgar social rat race he had found waiting for him in 1960s Britain – while expressing a heartfelt longing to return indefinitely to the beautiful land of his childhood. A longing that, to *Rocky Horror* aficionados, would make the lyrics to 'I'm Going Home', Frank-n-Furter's affecting farewell torch-song, resonate ever more deeply.

Mark Servian's wish was for Hamilton to pay tribute to Richard O'Brien in an authentic 'local boy makes good' kind of a way. Nevertheless, while his proposal for a statue had the immediate backing of numerous Hamiltonians, many of whom shared Servian's view that the city needed to lighten up, broaden its cultural horizons and embrace the 21st Century, it was met with fierce resistance from those who felt that honouring a musical that seemed to celebrate cross-dressing, gender confusion and sexual diversity would create an unhealthy image for their homely community.

Some feared that this unassuming tranquil neighbourhood might consequently turn into a hotspot for sexual deviants or perhaps be branded 'tranny town' by outsiders, especially as the statue, designed by Greg Broadmore, sculpted by Brigitte Wuest and constructed by Richard Taylor's and Tania Rodger's Weta Workshop – the multiple award-winning special effects company behind such films as Peter Jackson's blockbusting *The Lord of the Rings* trilogy, his 2005 remake of *King Kong*, and James Cameron's record-breaking science fiction epic *Avatar* (2009) – was to depict Richard as Riff Raff in his extraterrestrial national dress – complete with stockings, high-heeled ankle boots and short quilted tunic – from *The Rocky Horror Picture Show*'s final scenes, rather than the more conventional butler's outfit he had worn for the majority of the film.

Other concepts had been considered and initially sketched by Weta – including one of Riff in his traditional hunchbacked handyman garb, lurking next to a mock-up of the Sonic Oscillator in Frank-n-Furter's laboratory, and another of him in his spacesuit on a stylised version of the famous RKO Pictures' radio mast – before the final design was agreed upon.

An eventual council vote came back with 12 in favour and two against; after which Hamilton City Council agreed to contribute $25,000 to the $125,000 bronze sculpture. Other benefactors included the Perry Foundation and the Riff Raff Public Arts Trust, while the Waikato Museum of Art and History would handle the actual installation of the piece on behalf of Hamilton City Council.

Those opposed to the project were councillors Jocelyn Marshall and Roger Hennebry; and, while both stood by their moral objections, Hennebry expressed additional concerns that the statue's unconventional attire and associated ambiguous sexuality might encourage bigoted vandalism.

In spite of the opposition, around five thousand supportive Hamilton revellers, a small but enthusiastic number of them costumed in suitably risqué *Rocky Horror* apparel, joined the festivities, and danced to 'The Time Warp', as O'Brien's bronze likeness – officially known as the Riff Raff Statue – was finally unveiled at the stroke of midnight on Friday 26 November 2004; a glittering event that was covered extensively by local TV and radio stations.

'Most of the finger-wagging comes from people who haven't seen the show,' O'Brien told interviewer Mark Sainsbury on *An Evening with Richard O'Brien*, a one-off New Zealand TV special first broadcast in 2008 in which he sang a few of his own songs while candidly talking about his life and career. 'And actually they say "We" as if they've been elected as the spokespersons of Hamiltonians.

'Apparently, *Rocky*'s going to attract homosexuals to the city,' he laughed, rolling his eyes despairingly, with a characteristic wry smile, before adding cheekily, 'You should be so lucky.'

This prompted Sainsbury to read a portion of a letter, written to the local press, expressing the concerns of one the statue's detractors: 'Do we want to become another homosexual mecca, rather than a beautiful, productive peaceful and family-oriented city?' 'What idiocy,' responded the still smiling O'Brien, noting that some had even been opposed to the name Riff Raff itself and the seedy images it supposedly conjured up. As he noted, one worried citizen had actually been compelled to write to a local paper saying that he had researched the definition of the term 'riff raff' in more than one dictionary and discovered that it described someone or something rather undesirable.

'It's a literary and theatrical device to give a character a name that tells us about the character,' O'Brien explained patiently. 'In Jacobean comedy, we have the name Face, the Alchemist. Face tells you everything about this person; duplicity. We have ladies; we have Sneerwell and Teasel, and names like this. They tell us something about a character and they allow us to enjoy the character on a deeper level. Uriah Heep; what a wonderful name that is. It's a made up name by Dickens, but immediately you think of a urine-sodden dung heap, don't you?'

The actor-author-composer also addressed the likelihood of his scantily-clad bronze effigy becoming an embarrassing potential magnet for alleged

10: AND I REALISE I'M GOING HOME

unsavoury types with his usual articulacy. 'As for attracting transvestites and transsexuals and transgendered people and gay people to Hamilton, on the premise that there is this theme inside the piece, it's nonsense,' he maintained vehemently, reiterating the view that *Rocky Horror* shared its most fundamental thematic principles with the Old Testament's Genesis story. 'If I'd taken the second major story in the Bible, which is Kane slaughtering his brother Abel, and written that as a musical and played the role of Kane – and you built a statue of me in the role of Kane – by the same premise it's going to attract murderers to the city,' he argued rationally, 'and murderers who kill their brothers; they're all going to flock in. What a load of nonsense.'

'Being a bronze erection?' O'Brien quipped, in response to Sainsbury's enquiry about how it felt to be honoured with a statue, upon the very site where once had stood Hamilton's Embassy cinema – a place where, as a teenage Bodgie, he had spent numerous hours captivated by the late night science fiction double features that would one day inspire his wonderfully kitschy masterpiece. 'It's humbling,' he declared, with an unmistakable air of genuine humility, as if the awesome enormity of such a tribute and its connected connotations had just hit him. 'It's absolutely wonderful, isn't it? It's absolutely extraordinary. And it's so beautiful; Weta Workshops [sic] have done such a wonderful job. Hamilton should be very pleased just to have that piece of bronze. It is beautifully rendered; beautifully, artistically put together.

'Imagine if it hadn't been,' he joked. 'I'd still have had to have the smile on my face, wouldn't I? And go "Oh, isn't it marvellous?" But when they took the top off that, and you go, "Oh my god, that's fantastic."

'I don't deserve it,' he added with sudden solemnity, his tone turning slightly severe and meekly poignant. 'I really don't truly deserve it; I've done nothing in my life to deserve that. But I'm very grateful.'

The spontaneous applause from the assembled studio audience that greeted this sincerely self-effacing statement implied that those in attendance had no doubt whatsoever that, despite his diffidence, their own local rock 'n' roll hero not only deserved such an accolade but had most assuredly earned it.

As Mark Servian had hoped, the Riff Raff Statue quickly became a Hamilton tourist attraction, with innumerable *Rocky Horror* fans and casual visitors alike gathering to pose with it for photographic mementos. The bronze figure spawned an official website (featuring a live 24-hour webcam) and acquired its own social network identity on the internet with over two and a half thousand Facebook friends (and counting). Meanwhile Servian, rather fittingly, exploited his brainchild for a subsequent local election campaign, by way of business cards featuring his name and an image of the Riff Raff sculpture next to a surprisingly touching slogan: 'I owe this guy my life – Vote for him.'

For decades, literally scores of larger-than-life individuals would be put forward – by innumerable sources – as plausible inspirations for the character of Frank-n-Furter. Alice Cooper, Mick Jagger, David Bowie, Joan Crawford, Bette Davis, Richard III, Ivan the Terrible, Cruella De Vil; the bizarre inventory of rock stars, Hollywood divas and literary villains is as endless as it is eclectic. However, in a conversation with Dominic Wells, which appeared in the Tuesday 18 August edition of *The Times* newspaper in 2009, the man who had conceived the character more than a quarter of a century before offered another, rather more surprising, suggestion.

His own mother.

'He's a drama queen really,' was Richard O'Brien's concise summation of Frank. 'He's a hedonistic, self-indulgent voluptuary, and that's his downfall.'

According to Wells, it was upon adding the term 'ego-driven' to his list of Frank's unpleasant traits that O'Brien's voice suddenly trailed off, as he began to recognise elements of someone a lot closer to home in his self-seeking, tyrannical, extraterrestrial creation. 'I was going to say a bit like my mother,' he admitted softly.

Intriguingly, the implication that his mother's desire to disassociate herself from her proletarian roots may have been a contributing factor in the decision to relocate the family to New Zealand in 1952 also seemed to unfold during this illuminating discussion.

'My mother was an unpleasant woman,' the typically forthright O'Brien continued, with what the eloquent columnist described as 'sudden venom'. 'She came from a working class family; wonderful people, not much money, under-educated but honest, a great moral centre of honesty and probity. And she disowned them. She wanted to be a lady. And consequently became a person who was racist, anti-Semitic. It's such a tragedy to see someone throwing their lives away on this empty journey, and, at the same time, believing herself superior to other people.

'I loved her, but stupid, stupid woman, she wouldn't understand the value of that. She was an emotional bully. And sadly, all of us, my siblings and I, are all damaged by this. She was bonkers, my mother, and I think by saying that I'm allowing her to be as horrible as she was without condemning her too much.'

In the same touchingly truthful and enlightening piece – in which Wells' aptly described him as 'Small but elegant, like a cashmere jumper washed on too high a heat. His porcelain features, sardonic smile and shaved head strip two decades from his 67 years' – O'Brien revealed that, having been made to feel odd and isolated by cruel societal pigeon-holing for much of his life, he had, just a few years previously, 'stepped into the abyss' and, in his own words, gone 'completely crackers.'

10: AND I REALISE I'M GOING HOME

Although he had casually, and quite cryptically, touched upon personal feelings of sexual segregation in his programme notes for various tours of *The Rocky Horror Show* – 'I was born of woman, begat by man, my parents actually, and whilst the battle of the sexes has roared on without any sign of cessation, I have been caught between the enemy lines and confined to a life in no-man's land ever since. Should intelligent protoplasm continue to be polarised in this way? I, for what may well be selfish reasons, say, "I don't think so, matey"' – he clarified this viewpoint far more extensively in his 2009 interview for *The Times*:

'All my life, I've been fighting never belonging. Never being male or female. And it got to the stage where I couldn't deal with it any longer. To feel you don't belong ... to feel insane ... to feel perverted and disgusting ... you go fucking nuts. If society allowed you to grow up feeling it was normal to be what you are, there wouldn't be a problem. I don't think the term "transvestite" or "transsexual" would exist; you'd just be another human being.

'I'd been fighting going to therapy, treating what I was as though it were some kind of illness to be cured. But actually, no, I was basically transgender, and just unhappy.

'I lost the plot. Paranoid delusions; the works. It was at the time when Bush and Blair ruled the fucking world, and trying to claw my way back to sanity I saw no standard norm. I wanted to get back to normal, but where's the benchmark of sanity? I was drowning and couldn't find a surface.'

The revelation that the man whose much-loved *magnum opus* helped to relax conservative sexual attitudes – and continues to help many a confused adolescent come to terms with his or her own sexuality and self-worth – should have felt so bewildered and psychologically detached is an upsetting thought to all who admire both the man and his work.

And yet, thanks largely to the unconditional love of his devoted children – especially an emotionally-inspiring telephone call from his eldest son Linus in Canada – it was an experience from which O'Brien concluded he had ultimately emerged a happier human being with a greater acceptance of himself:

'There is a continuum between male and female. Some are hard-wired one way or another. I'm in between. Or a third sex I could see myself as quite easily.'

Speaking on Radio New Zealand in 2010, O'Brien indicated that finally being able to feel that it was acceptable to discard all personal pretence concerning who he was had made him more centred. He declared calmly that he was now happier than he had ever been:

'I'm two years away from my three-score year and ten. I'm still looking rather sexy. My children love me. And I'm allowed to be myself. If I get an invitation to an official kind of a function – a starchy function that says "black tie" – they generally put on the bottom of the invitation, "Not you, Richard." And that's kind of nice.'

Asked if he had ever wondered how differently his life might have turned out had he remained in New Zealand and not made that fateful decision to return to England during the 1960s, O'Brien proposed that such alternative historical journeys could not be retrospectively contemplated, philosophically adding that if he had not been born transgender – and therefore not suffered the lasting pain and confusion it had caused him – he would never have conceived *The Rocky Horror Show*.

Following his visit to New Zealand in 2000 for Qantas Airlines' *Coming Home* programme, Richard had planned to retire to the land in which he had spent the best part of his formative years. As he had failed to submit an application before the official cut-off age of 55, however, some speculated that he would not actually qualify for permanent residency or citizenship. Nonetheless, as reported by the *New Zealand Herald* on 9 June 2010, Dr Jonathan Coleman, the current Minister for Immigration, refuted speculation that O'Brien's application had already been turned down. 'Nothing has been received, so there is nothing to decline,' he stated. New Zealand Prime Minister John Key – who, it transpired, had attended late night screenings of *The Rocky Horror Picture Show* during his youth – later told the press that any such application would be considered, along with all such requests, in accordance with its individual merits. Then, in August 2010, it was reported that Associate Immigration Minister Kate Wilkinson had relaxed the usual age criteria for O'Brien – not uncommon for cases involving special circumstances (and, after all, very few applicants would likely have written a hit rock musical or had a bronze likeness erected in their honour) – and that the first stage of his application for permanent residency had been rubber stamped.

Subsequently, in a story headlined '*Rocky Horror* creator to become real Kiwi' in its 30 November 2011 edition, the *Waikato Times* reported that Richard O'Brien would at last be officially registered as a New Zealand citizen on Wednesday 14 December 2011.

'Now I belong,' the 69-year-old actor-writer-composer smiled proudly. 'I've been claimed for many years. It really is nice to belong.'

At the ceremony itself – a low key affair that took place at the City Council Reception Lounge in Hamilton – O'Brien was among 50 residents to be formally inaugurated as newly-recorded citizens.

Once more (with feeling), a sentimental remembrance of the momentous lyrical refrain from Frank-n-Furter's moving final melody would seem particularly apposite:

On the day I went away;
(Goodbye) Was all I had to say;

10: AND I REALISE I'M GOING HOME

(Now I) Want to come again and stay;
(Oh my) Smile and that will mean I may;
I've seen blue skies through the tears in my eyes;
And I realise I'm Going Home.

Upon receiving his Certificate of Citizenship, and literally beaming with joyful contentment, New Zealand's newest citizen courteously thanked the Mayor of Hamilton, Julie Hardaker, who customarily welcomed him to the country.

'All official now,' she chirped.

'God bless, thank you,' Richard quietly replied, with sincere emotion.

Showing his certificate to the press after the ceremony, he confessed to being at a loss for words. Acknowledging it a rare occurrence to find himself thus inarticulately humbled, he recalled that, even as a ten-year-old boy – first arriving in the country with his family early one morning in 1952 – he had at once felt as though he was home.

'I am really lost for words,' he repeated, with a perceptible lump in his throat, 'because it's so wonderful; and it's the fulfilment of a journey.'

In August 2012, it was reported by local press in New Zealand that O'Brien had announced his engagement to long-term partner Sabrina Graf – whom he had first met in London, while she had been visiting from Germany, ten years previously – and that they planned to marry in April 2013.

When Hammer Films departed Bray in November 1966 – relocating the bulk of their production to the celebrated Elstree Studios in Borehamwood, Hertfordshire, just outside London – it left the future of their former home in an almost perpetual state of uncertainty. Certainly Bray's glory days were over, especially after Hammer sold the studio in 1970; and, while it continued to host the occasional feature film – most notably *The Rocky Horror Picture Show*, with model and miniature work for Ridley Scott's *Alien* (1979) also being shot there during the summer of 1978 while principal photography was taking place 30 miles away at Shepperton Studios in Surrey – the site was subsequently used chiefly as a rehearsal venue for pop music promos and television productions.

More recently, it was reported by BBC Berkshire that, unable to stay abreast of modern technological advancements and in the face of increasingly tough competition from the likes of other major UK studios (such as Pinewood and Shepperton), the owners of the site, Bray Management Limited, along with Windsor and Maidenhead council, had on Wednesday 4 July 2012 approved a plan for a major redevelopment of the land occupied by this once great and iconic British film studio.

'The main studio buildings will be knocked down, with a new media centre also being built,' the report stated – words that would no doubt fill every dedicated Hammer and *Rocky Horror* devotee with shock, revulsion and utter dismay – while confirming that, as a Grade II listed building, Down Place itself would be converted back into a private residence.

This heartbreaking revelation not only seemed to signal the genuine end of an era for British film with agonising finality, it painfully hammered every last nail into its coffin, and – as if to make doubly certain that the ever-tenacious Count Dracula would never again be able to open the lid with his clawed, gnarled fingers and rise from the grave – metaphorically poured six feet of industrial-strength concrete on top of it.

However, after several years of inactivity, reports began to circulate that filming had commenced on a number of new productions – with the likes of director Dexter Fletcher's colourful 2019 Elton John biopic *Rocketman* (which starred Taron Egerton as the famously flamboyant rock star) and, somewhat appropriately, a three-part reworking of *Dracula* (developed for television by Mark Gatiss and Steven Moffat), which aired on BBC 1 and Netflix in January 2020, being shot at the studio – suggesting that Bray had refused to stay buried after all.

Meanwhile, the renovation of Oakley Court – which had been reduced to little more than a dilapidated shell since falling into an even worse state of disrepair after the cessation of Hammer's dealings with Bray – began in 1979.

Rather than the inside of the building being redesigned and refurnished from scratch, much of the original furniture and plaster was lovingly and painstakingly restored to its former glory, exploiting the stately grandeur of the existing interiors wherever possible, particularly in places such as the library and the drawing room. This scrupulous attention to and respect for the house's history would prove a blessing for fans of *The Rocky Horror Picture Show*, as several well-known locations for many of the film's scenes would remain instantly recognisable. Aside from the exterior appearance of the edifice itself, the main entrance hall – including the magnificent staircase used for Magenta's memorable entrance down the banister – would provide a jaw-dropping introduction and the first of many photo opportunities for visiting *Rocky Horror* and Hammer film devotees. Thanks to Patricia Quinn's unforgettable and much-loved first appearance as Frank-n-Furter's enigmatic maid, that most hallowed of banisters would continue to brave the indignities of innumerable legs and backsides of all shapes, sizes and genders for years to come.

Though it bears little resemblance to an upright coffin with a sinister human skeleton inside it, a magnificent grandfather clock has periodically taken pride of place, somewhat fittingly, on the self-same spot as the one whose chimes accompanied Riff Raff's unforgettable introduction to 'The Time Warp'; and, while Frank-n-Furter's wrought iron elevator – constructed as a prop for the movie – has long since vacated the premises,

10: AND I REALISE I'M GOING HOME

the ghosts of Riff Raff and his sultry sister, elbow-sexing their way toward the adjoining chamber and its colourful chorus of Transylvanians (filmed on a soundstage next door at Bray Studios and incorporated into the number via Graeme Clifford's seamless editing) might still be imagined by those relaxing in the softly-lit bar that now occupies the room in question.

The building's iconic stone griffins – seen in a number of movies and television productions shot at the location during the '50s, '60s and '70s – also remain an integral part of the building's ambience, providing yet another essential photo opportunity for *Rocky Horror Picture Show* obsessives. Some fans have been known to take along their own homemade 'Enter At Your Own Risk!!' signs, attaching them (temporarily of course) to the imposing wrought iron gates in order to recreate Brad's and Janet's fateful first encounter with the castle of Dr Frank-n-Furter.

During the extensive conversion process, several luxurious suites were incorporated into the original mansion, while the majority of the rooms were housed in two specially-added extensions, known as the Riverside and Garden Wings. After two years and a sum of £5,000,000, Oakley Court opened to the public as a beautiful, high-status four-star hotel on Saturday 7 November 1981.

A third annexe was unveiled in June 1997. Known as the Courtyard Wing, this extension incorporated an additional 22 air conditioned bedrooms, along with a health and fitness club consisting of a swimming pool, spa, sauna, steam room, solarium, gymnasium (should Rocky Horror himself ever feel the need to stop over) and beauty treatment rooms; while two tennis courts and a nine-hole golf course were also added to the premises.

Even then, however, the hotel was not allowed the luxury of resting on its considerable laurels, as, two years later, the Boathouse – a purpose-built meeting room for up to 25 guests – was unveiled on the banks of the River Thames itself.

As the 21st Century dawned, the establishment's in-house publicity described the hotel in justifiably grand terms: 'Now with its former splendour and beautiful setting of 35 acres of landscaped gardens on the banks of the Thames, Oakley Court ranks as one of the outstanding (prestigious) hotels of this country.'

Not bad for a once ramshackle ruin that, on the big screen, had famously doubled as the menacing gothic dwellings of Count Dracula, Baron Frankenstein and Dr Frank-n-Furter.

In the summer of 2006, having previously planned and executed three hugely successful UK *Rocky Horror* conventions during the 1990s – known officially as Transylvania '92, Transylvania '94 and Transylvania '99 – Stephanie Freeman decided to organise something a little different. The idea was to hold a more relaxed and informal gathering for fans, as opposed to the usual heavily-structured and guest-driven conventions. Inspired by the Narrator's scripted line 'This was to be no picnic,' a peaceful and informal outdoor buffet in the grounds of Oakley Court seemed a fitting idea.

A special room rate, agreed by the hotel, incorporated an overnight stay in one of the many luxurious bedrooms, food and soft drinks for the picnic itself and a full English breakfast the following morning. Attendees would be allowed plenty of free time to chill out, explore the building – the actual Frankenstein Place from the movie they worshipped – and don their costumes accordingly for essential photo opportunities. As a special bonus, the Freemans organised a late night screening of *The Rocky Horror Picture Show* at the very location where it had been filmed almost 32 years previously; an occasion made even more momentous by the unexpected arrival of Richard O'Brien earlier in the evening. O'Brien, in a perceptibly laid-back and sociable mood, chatted nonchalantly with overawed fans, signed numerous autographs, posed for photos and finally introduced the movie itself before heading off into the night.

The event, dubbed *The Rocky Horror Picnic Show*, was a popular success. The hotel's employees and regular guests took the unusual presence of several dozen scantily-clad picnickers in good spirits, and the sunshine was glorious – although provision had been made for an indoor picnic should the unpredictable British weather make an attempt to spoil the festivities. Another event was swiftly organised for the following summer; after which the TimeWarp fan club's *Rocky Horror Picnic Show* became an annual happening, impressively attracting a greater number of fans each year. With Oakley Court being a prominent and tastefully refined hotel and conference venue, it would quite rightly be considered unacceptable for doting *Rocky* disciples to turn up in costume at any time other than these specially organised yearly fan club events; but once the TimeWarp picnics had been accepted and established, they became a more than satisfactory annual outlet for such devotion.

Directly ahead of the building's breathtaking entrance hall, which today provides the hotel's main lobby area, is the room in which the movie's gruesome dinner scene was shot, and, while the doors and the table were replaced during the refurbishment, the interior of the room remains instantly recognisable. For an optional supplement during the early evening of the 2007 fan club picnic, Stephanie Freeman arranged a recreation of this memorable movie moment by way of an evening meal for a limited number of attendees in the room itself, regrettably without Riff Raff's and Magenta's eccentric serving techniques or Eddie's freshly butchered corpse under the table.

In 2008, with TimeWarp celebrating its twentieth anniversary as the UK's one and only officially sanctioned *Rocky Horror* fan club, Stephanie Freeman commissioned a faithful reproduction of the *Picture Show*'s black and white

10: AND I REALISE I'M GOING HOME

Transylvanian flag – complete with its distinctive RKO style lightning flash – which the management kindly agreed to fly in place of the hotel's customary red, white and blue UK Union Flag for the duration of the weekend. Like the picnic itself, this would become a yearly tradition; and while the specially made one-off flag was mistakenly flown upside-down by hotel personnel in 2008, the error would be rectified the following year. The unmistakable monochrome colours of the planet Transsexual then reclaimed their rightful place in the skies of Windsor, over Frank-n-Furter's magnificently imposing domicile, for three or four days every August.

Between 27 August and 10 October 2010, Christopher Luscombe, director of the most recent UK tours of *Rocky Horror*, oversaw a production of the show at the COEX Artium in the Gangnam district of Seoul, South Korea. While the piece had been successfully staged in Korea on previous occasions – a 2001 production had even spawned an agreeable CD cast recording – the newest embodiment, which starred American-born Juan Jackson as Frank-n-Furter and used the latest British incarnation as its basis, would be the first English language version to play in the country.

Assuming the role of Riff Raff in Seoul – alongside Jackson's striking Frank-n-Furter – would be Kristian Lavercombe – a multi-skilled and versatile Welsh-born actor who, like Richard O'Brien, had been raised and educated in New Zealand. No stranger to the world of *Rocky Horror*, Lavercombe had previously appeared in three independant productions which no doubt gave him an advantageous understanding of the show and its characters:

'When I was about 21, maybe 22, I somehow got cast as Frank in a small festival production,' the actor explains. 'I understand that somebody had known one of the producers or people who hold the rights to *Rocky*, and that's how they got hold of it. And it was in New Zealand; I think they thought no-one would see it. And they probably didn't see it. So, it was only on for a couple of weeks. You know, a little, small taster. But I did that, and I had a blast. I had an absolute blast.'

'And I just thought Frank-n-Furter was such an amazing role. I'd done quite a lot by age 21, but the character was so wild, I thought, and had so little restrictions of what you could do. And then I absolutely adored the other characters.'

'That was like a pro-am production where I was paid, but there were some amateurs in the thing as well,' Lavercombe elaborates, 'New Zealand has this programme thing where it's a mixture of professional and amateur people. And then the next one was a professional production, where I got cast as Brad, and again I really loved it, and the audiences were really interesting. And that was all in New Zealand and I had a great time doing that; and I did that for maybe about three or four months. And then, a few years after that, I got asked by the same director who directed me initially in the first *Rocky Horror* to come back into a different town and play Frank-n-Furter again; so I played Frank-n-Furter then for another production. Again, that was a semi-pro production. And so it was a show that just kept on popping into my life every now and again.'

Kristian's association with *The Rocky Horror Show* would continue several years later, when a friend happened to mention that there was an audition in Auckland the next day for a production opening in South Korea on 27 August 2010:

'My agent didn't hear about it at all, so I literally just found out about it the night before and went,' he recalls, 'Actually, I was lucky because I don't think the audition notices went out to a lot of people, because they didn't go to the agents. And, as a result, at the auditions there was a real mishmash of people there who weren't very experienced; and, when the audition woman came out and went, "Okay, girls, if you'd like to get your heels on… and, guys, if you'd like to get your heels on as well," I was the only guy that brought heels, so I stood out from the crowd anyway.'

Ironically, for the actor whose name would ultimately become as synonymous with the character as the likes of Richard O'Brien, Perry Bedden and Sal Sharah, the one role that Lavercombe had not intended to try-out for was Riff Raff, a fact he had initially intended to declare at the audition:

'I was going to go in and say, "I've done these, I'm prepared. I only heard about it last night. I know the show really well; I can sing anything from the show." And I had planned on saying, "Anything apart from Riff Raff, 'cause I'm actually a light baritone, I'm not a tenor, and I know Riff Raff is really high, so I'm never gonna be able to sing that." But, when I went in, I stopped myself from saying that, as it's a little bit negative; and Chris [Luscombe] went, "Oh well, we'll get you to sing Riff Raff," because, ironically, what I didn't know was that was the role they hadn't really cast yet.'

'I thought, because I've done a couple of different roles, then I'd actually make a really good Swing; I could play Frank, and I could play Brad, and maybe I can play somebody else,' the actor continues genially, 'I wasn't expecting to play Riff Raff at all. So, then I got it, and then I was like, "Oh my god, how am I going to sing this every night?" Because it's a full-on sing, and even when I was practicing at home, I was like, "I don't know how I'm gonna do it."'

As Kristian recollects, following the New Zealand audition, the company then rehearsed the show in Sydney, Australia, prior to its opening in South Korea.

'It was a Chris Luscombe production which Chris didn't actually direct, because he wasn't available,' he points out, explaining that, in Luscombe's absence, Associate Director Michael Howcroft simply took the reins instead:

'He directed that in the style of Chris, because they were just repeating the exact production.'

With the production running concurrently in the UK, however, Kristian recalls that a replica of Janet Bird's acclaimed set had to be constructed from photographic references, which resulted in various inconsistencies:

'It looked the same, but it was all slightly different from what the people in the UK were used to,' the actor smiles, revealing how, by replicating exactly the scenery and props from backstage images of the UK production, the Korean crew's attention to detail provided at least one particularly amusing anomaly: 'I think they took a photo of the props table, and it's my understanding that David Bedella had an inhaler on the props table; and they'd actually made an inhaler. A *fake* inhaler. That turned up on the props table as well; so, Mike [Howcroft] came across and said, "What is that? There's no inhaler in the show." But then they showed the photo, and it was David Bedella's.'

After completing its six-week engagement in Seoul, the production re-opened in New Zealand at the Civic, a theatre in the Edge Performing Arts and Convention Centre in Auckland. Aptly assuming the role of the Narrator for the New Zealand dates would be none other than Richard O'Brien himself, who, when asked by the press if he felt the piece could still be considered suitably risqué for contemporary audiences, was typically dismissive about his creation's subversive reputation. 'It never really was,' he replied. 'It only appeared that way. It was, and remains, a lovely juvenile distraction.'

Though he had on occasion played other characters in the show – Frank, Eddie, the Usherette, and, of course, Riff Raff – taking on the role of its supercilious storyteller allowed the author the opportunity personally to invite his audience – by way of his own script – to join him on that rather famous strange journey of his own invention. For devotees of the show, this might be comparable to witnessing William Shakespeare reciting one of his celebrated soliloquies or Charles Dickens declaring to an avid crowd, 'Old Marley was as dead as a doornail.' Or, to give it a more up-to-date, and perhaps less pretentious, pop-culture perspective, the equivalent of George Lucas personally verbalising the opening crawl from *Star Wars* or J K Rowling reading aloud her description of Harry Potter's first arrival at Hogwarts before an assemblage of open-mouthed admirers.

The production followed its two-week run in Auckland with limited seasons at Wellington's St James Theatre and the Isaac Theatre Royal in Christchurch before moving to the Esplanade Theatre in the Republic of Singapore for a fortnight in January 2011, where a number of cast members from the recent UK tour – including Richard Meek as Brad and Haley Flaherty as Janet – joined the company.

'This big, bad rock musical-turned-classic finally finds its way past the censors into Singapore,' declared the local edition of *Time Out* magazine, pointing out that the 1975 film version had been banned there until 2003 'because of its sexual and masochistic content.'

During his question-and-answer session at a 2011 *Rocky Horror* convention in London, Richard Meek revealed that – with male homosexual practises and depictions thereof still illegal in Singapore – the pivotal bedroom scenes in particular had been toned down for the show's engagement in the city.

In anticipation of *The Rocky Horror Show*'s Ruby Anniversary – with Sunday 16 June 2013 marking exactly 40 years since the very first preview performance rocked the rafters of the Royal Court's tiny Theatre Upstairs (three nights before its official opening on 19 June) – a revamped UK touring production opened at the Theatre Royal, Brighton in December 2012.

As this particular embodiment of the show was to commemorate such an enormous landmark in *Rocky Horror* history, the producers of the latest incarnation – presented by Howard Panter for the Ambassador Theatre Group – secured a few bankable names to help sell the production to mainstream theatregoers. This time, however, unlike certain previous instances of so-called stunt casting, each of the players in question would have a legitimate musical theatre pedigree.

With a number of stage roles already under his belt, including stints as Teen Angel in the UK tour of *Grease* and Parson Nathaniel in the smash hit arena production of Jeff Wayne's musical version of *The War of the Worlds*, Welsh recording artist Rhydian Roberts (usually billed professionally as just Rhydian) – the popular runner-up of the 2007 series of ITV talent show *The X-Factor* – was cast as Rocky for the first three months of the run; a period that would see the hard-working singer concurrently playing his own solo concert dates.

As the Narrator, British character actor Philip Franks immediately proved himself adept at handling the now customary talkback from the show's most ardent fans – snappily responding with an array of humorous put-downs and witty comebacks – while somewhat refreshingly revisiting the character's roots by making him more of a snooty Edgar Lustgarten type intellectual with a crushed velvet smoking jacket and a disapproving demeanour.

Endowed with a natural stage presence and a powerful singing voice, and having recently played the lead in Andrew Lloyd Webber's prominent arena tour of *Jesus Christ Superstar* – opposite Tim Minchin as Judas and former Spice Girl Melanie C as Mary Magdalene – the charming Ben Forster assumed the role of Brad Majors for the initial leg of the much-publicised new *Rocky Horror* tour. The televising of *Superstar*'s casting process as a 'public vote' primetime talent show on ITV had already given Forster a considerable fanbase of his own, which no doubt the promoters of *Rocky* hoped to take advantage of; and the talented actor easily endowed Brad with all of the square-jawed, broad-shouldered B-movie heroics required of the character.

Playing the part of Janet Weiss would be Roxanne Pallett, an attractive and spirited young actress from the North West of England. Although best known to British TV viewers as Jo Sugden – a role she played from August 2005 until December 2008 – in the popular ITV soap *Emmerdale*, it is no stretch to suppose that Pallett's brief but memorable appearance in the 2010 giant crocodile gore-fest *Lake Placid 3* might have helped prepare her for *The Rocky Horror Show*'s ironically straight-faced monster movie acting techniques; and the plucky actress boldly threw everything into her vigorous and well-judged depiction of Janet's all-important emancipation.

Immediately following Pallett's scheduled departure from the production in May 2013, the role of Janet would be assumed by the engaging and personable Dani Harmer, a former child star – known primarily to UK television audiences for her recurring role as Tracy Beaker in the BBC TV adaptations of Jacqueline Wilson's popular chldren's stories – whose cheerful and endearing personality would make her an immediate fan favourite both on and off stage.

While his award-winning performance as free-spirited drag queen Felicia (stage name of the character Adam Whitely) in the West End production of *Priscilla: Queen of the Desert* – which ran at London's Palace Theatre between March 2009 and December 2011 – confirmed that accomplished musical theatre star Oliver Thornton was already no stranger to camp cross-dressing roles, the actor wisely decided to go his own way with Frank-n-Furter, instead of simply imitating what others had done with the role. This approach would help assuage the concerns initially expressed by some *Rocky* devotees – largely on the strength of his *Priscilla* persona alone – that he might be a little too effeminate to convey the crucial masculinity and irresistible sexual omnipotence essential to Frank. While there may indeed have been a hint of the drag queen about Thornton's portrayal of the crazed alien scientist, however, it manifested itself as the more dominant and commanding variety – veiled suggestions of Hollywood divas such as Joan Crawford, Bette Davis and Gloria Swanson, whether intentional or not, have never been at odds with the role as originally envisaged – and, by the end of 'Sweet Transvestite' on the first night of the run, his theatrically manic, sinuously elegant and unpredictably histrionic interpretation of *Rocky*'s much-loved mad doctor had the audience eating out of his hand.

Also joining the cast were Joel Montague, in the crucial dual role of the doomed Eddie and his enigmatic uncle Dr Everett Scott, and Abigail Jaye, a wonderfully expressive musical theatre performer, as a suitably sultry and mysterious Magenta. An agreeable and fitting idea would see her Usherette, at the end of 'Science Fiction Double Feature', personally drawing back the shabby old cinema curtain to invite the audience, quite literally into the bygone B-movie world of Brad and Janet.

In addition to this exciting company of talented newcomers, the line-up included a couple of familiar *Rocky* faces. The terrific Ceris Hine – already a fan favourite from the 2009/10 UK tour – made a particularly welcome return to the role of Columbia; while the dynamic Kristian Lavercombe – who had played Riff Raff in the production that had toured South Korea, New Zealand and Singapore in 2010/11 – now treated UK audiences to his energised and wildly expressive interpretation of the resentful hunchbacked manservant.

'After the Singapore season of that tour, I moved to London, and happened to be around when the next UK tour came up,' Lavercombe explains, 'I got asked if I'd like to audition for it. On that occasion Chris Luscombe asked me to come in and have sing through with Stuart Burt who was head of casting for ATG, as he'd never seen me before. I did that and thankfully Stuart was also keen to have me in the production.'

With expectations riding higher than ever, this 'All New 40th Anniversary Party Production' (as flyers and posters labelled it) gave director Christopher Luscombe the opportunity to revisit his already acclaimed vision of the piece and – while, most importantly, remaining true to the spirit of the show as envisaged by Richard O'Brien and Jim Sharman – add a few new ideas to help keep the show fresh and exciting.

As an adored work of entertainment, *The Rocky Horror Show* had, in the course of nearly 40 years, become the very embodiment of the well-known maxim 'If it ain't broke, don't fix it.' Hence, after getting so much right with his previous take on the piece – which had pleased not only audiences and critics but also the show's notoriously protective author-composer – many felt, quite rightly, that to change things now, just for the sake of it, would have been a huge mistake.

As was explained in the new production's programme notes, in approaching Christopher Luscombe to revisit *Rocky Horror* – no doubt realising that the show's devoted audiences now had certain expectations, many of which were probably crucial to its continued success as a lucrative crowd-pleaser – the producers had 'stressed that the baby was not to be thrown out with the bathwater.'

'They wanted me to retain my vision of the show, but to give the fans new elements to enjoy,' the director revealed., 'But when you bring in a new designer and a new choreographer, that process tends to happen automatically. We're talking about detail rather than any broad brushstrokes, and I'll leave it to the audience to spot the innovations for themselves.'

While a couple of the show's classic musical arrangements were reworked slightly (some more successfully than others), and the look of Sue Blane's iconic costumes remained largely unaltered from those of previous

10: AND I REALISE I'M GOING HOME

productions, the most remarkable and successful innovation would be a clever, yet astoundingly simple, new set. Created by award-winning designer Hugh Durrant, the efficiently theatrical construction allowed scenes to switch quickly between the castle's sumptuous vestibule (adorned with rare artefacts and oversized replicas of stuffed animal heads heads; as if to emphasise Brad's description of the residence as 'some kind of hunting lodge for rich weirdoes') to the white tiled sterility (and eccentric scientific equipment) of Frank's laboratory, by way of rotating panels in the 'walls'. Furthermore, in a blatant and entirely apposite reference to the *The Rocky Horror Show*'s B-movie heritage, the semi-circular design incorporated a giant silver filmstrip motif across the entire length of the set – in front of the band's platform – through which Magenta and Columbia would appear as they voyeuristically observed 'Touch-a Touch-a Touch-a Touch Me' and Janet's seduction of Rocky Horror himself.

For what was (quite worryingly to some fans) blatantly advertised as a 'Party' production – a marketing strategy which, while no doubt successful in selling tickets to the masses, might be considered a little obvious and uninspired – Christopher Luscombe was faced with the almost impossible task of balancing the extremely welcome back-to-basics approach he had instigated for his 2006/07 version with the overtly camp and glitzy aspects demanded by the wild and untamed mainstream who frequently made up the bulk of show's nightly audience.

As might be expected from a director who clearly understood the rich complexities of Richard O'Brien's multi-layered script, the sinister between-the-lines motivations and subtle nuances of the characters – as well as the poignant depths of the show's more emotional moments – were once again given much thought and consideration.

In particular, played with absolute truth and intensity were Brad's tender solo 'Once in a While'; Frank-n-Furter's 'Whatever happened to Fay Wray?' portion of 'The Floorshow' – for which, seated on the front of the stage mere inches from a captivated audience, Oliver Thornton would enjoy his very own Judy Garland moment, somewhat akin to that of Tim Curry during 'I'm Going Home' in *The Rocky Horror Picture Show* – and the calamitous heartbreak of the final scenes.

The flipside to this was a perceptibly more relaxed attitude towards a few of the show's more frivolous aspects. This outlook was underscored by a crowd-pleasing decision to allow the hitherto haughty Narrator – who had remained, quite noticeably, fully and modestly attired through to the very end of Luscombe's previous take on the piece – to boldly whip off his formal trousers (thanks to the wonders of Velcro) in the manner of a male stripper, revealing fishnet stockings and black stilettos for the evening's final 'Time Warp' reprise.

The choreography for 'The Time Warp' would again find itself the subject of controversy and backlash at the beginning of the tour. With 2012's novelty dance party hit 'Gangnam Style' (by South Korean recording artist Psy) and its promotional video fresh in the public's consciousness, the cast's final refrain of 'Let's Do The Time Warp again' – led by a wide-eyed, maniacally grinning Riff Raff – during the show's undisputed showstopper would be accompanied by the more recent song's signature horse riding and lasso 'cowboy' dance instead of the customary 'Time Warp' arm movements. Defensive *Rocky Horror* fans immediately took to the internet and social media with the legitimate argument that Richard O'Brien had, with 'The Time Warp', knowingly parodied 'The Twist', 'The Loco-Motion' and other 1960s dance crazes, and that the addition of a cheap reference to a far more recent novelty hit was an insult to its status as both a witty parody and a classic party dance in its own right. Soon afterwards, the welcome choice was made to drop the inappropriate 'Gangnam Style' moves from 'The Time Warp' choreography.

According to publicity blurb for this fortieth anniversary production, during its four incredible decades on the planet *The Rocky Horror Show* had been translated into more than 20 languages and been performed to phenomenal acclaim in over 30 countries. As noted by a joyous Richard O'Brien – when he and Richard Hartley joined the on stage cast to face an overwhelming ovation from the euphoric opening night throng at Brighton's Theatre Royal on Thursday 20 December 2012 – for a show expected to have run its natural course after a limited three-week engagement at the Royal Court in 1973, one might say it had done rather well.

For the show's actual 40th anniversary in June 2013 – '40 & Fabulous!' the posters brazenly declared – the production found itself enjoying a particularly busy week at Manchester's Palace Theatre. In addition to the birthday performance itself – which took place officially on Wednesday 19 June – several special events were organised by Rocky Horror Company and Ambassador Theatre Group to celebrate the show's astonishing achievement and to thank the most avid *Rocky Horror* fans for their loyalty and continued support.

A fun but nonetheless rigorous open audition – led by director Christopher Luscombe, choreographer Nathan M Wright and Dance Captain Andrew Ahern – earlier in the year had selected two *Rocky Horror* devotees (Matthew Atkins and Jenna Watkinson) to rehearse (with the tour's Resident Director Simon Greiff) and perform their own rendition of 'Damn it. Janet' in front of the full house crowd at the end of the show's evening performance on Tuesday 18 June. From an enthusiast's perspective, however, the highlight of the week took place on the morning of Saturday 22 June, as a gathering of the show's most ardent devotees was treated to an informal Q&A with Christopher Luscombe, a 'Time Warp' dance tutorial with Nathan M Wright and Andrew Ahern, and an in-depth discussion and tour of the set with Company Stage Manager Phil Sykes and set designer Hugh Durrant. Durrant's contribution to the morning was particularly pleasing, as he had brought along his beautifully detailed original miniature model of the set for fans to appreciate, photograph and admire appropriately.

While it had long been accepted that 20th Century Fox's strict copyright regulations effectively prohibited any video release of a *Rocky Horror Show* stage performance, it had on occasion been noted by Richard O'Brien that, under the right circumstances, a one-off live broadcast would be permitted.

While no such opportunity had been seized during the show's 40th anniversary year in 2013, it was announced in the summer of 2015 that a limited two-week run at London's 786-seat Playhouse Theatre – with Richard O'Brien as the Narrator (a role he had previously played in New Zealand in 2010) – would indeed incorporate such a momentous event. While an upcoming UK tour – set to commence at the Theatre Royal, Brighton on Thursday 17 December 2015 – would see celebrated West End performer Liam Tamne stepping into Frank-n-Furter's hallowed heels, fan favourite David Bedella returned to the role for the brief London run.

In addition to Bedella, the London cast would incorporate a combination of *Rocky* veterans – Haley Flaherty as Janet, Kristian Lavercombe as Riff Raff, Ben Forster as Brad, Jayde Westaby as Usherette/Magenta and Rachel Grundy as a Phantom – and some of the actors who had been cast for the upcoming 2015/16 tour; Dominic Andersen as Rocky, Sophie Linder-Lee as Columbia, and Ben Kerr, Will Knights and Hannah Malekzad as Phantoms).

Of particular note was Richard Meek – known primarily to UK theatregoers as one of the show's most popular Brads – deftly taking on the dual roles of Eddie and Dr Scott. Unlike many actors – who often play Frank-n-Furter's wheelchair-bound nemesis as a broad comedic caricature or an over-the-top Dr Strangelove clone – Meek refreshingly approached the role of Dr Scott with the same level of authentic sincerity as he had Brad Majors:

'When I play comedy roles, I have always come at it from a truthful angle,' he declares, 'Playing things for real allows the text to be funny if it actually *is* funny. For example, the "Audio Vibratory Physio-molecular..." line, I always played "Ha, there you go, see; I know what I'm talking about" and I think, for me, that was better than playing for laughs.'

With regard to *Rocky*'s notoriously vocal – and occasionally unruly – British audiences, the presence of the show's much-loved writer-composer as its traditionally contemptuous Narrator gave the London performances an edgy new dynamic. Whilst obviously basking in the prolonged, rapturous applause which greeted his character's first entrance each night, O'Brien's barely concealed disdain for some of the production's now infamous audience shout-outs would provide a new level of amusement as he could not help but point out the superfluous nature of this counterpoint dialogue. For instance, whenever – during the Narrator's pre-'Floorshow' monologue – his scripted line, 'And just a few hours after announcing their engagement, Brad and Janet had both tasted...' was met with the expected, unsubtle chorus of, 'Frank's cock,' from the exuberant crowd, the script's author would complete the line as written, 'Forbidden fruit,' before adding solemnly, 'Frank's cock was implied.'

Similarly, on the occasion any foolhardy heckler was brave enough to meet this particular Narrator's query of, 'What was over?' with the now customary cry of, 'Your career,' they would invariably find themselves on the receiving end of a barrage of hostile jeering from an audience clearly on the side of the show's beloved author. Once this unfriendly cacophony had subsided, O'Brien would calmly address the heckler with a satisfied reply of, 'You haven't though this through, have you?'

With the 17 September charity performance and live cinema broadcast set to raise money for Amnesty International, a clever and appropriately tasteful limited edition T-shirt was produced especially for the show's two-week West End run. This black shirt (with faded yellow lettering) featured the organisation's instantly recognisable candle surrounded by barbed wire logo – symbolising the light of hope shining through the constraints of oppression – accompanied by the poignantly apposite *Rocky Horror Show* lyric 'There's a light in the darkness of everybody's life', seemingly emerging from a shadow.

In the days prior to the much-anticipated livestream, a procession of trucks and large vans – housing outside broadcast equipment, and conspicuous by the enormous parabolic dishes on their roofs – gathered outside the Playhouse. With the gala charity performance – in aid of Amnesty International – scheduled to be beamed live to more than 600 cinemas across the UK and Europe on the evening of Thursday 17 September, nothing would be left to chance. Therefore, one of the week's earlier performances – that of Tuesday 15 September – was also filmed in its entirety. This not only served as a rehearsal for the cameras and film crew but could also be used as a back-up should any technical problems occur with the live transmission on the Thursday.

Numerous shots of patrons entering the theatre along a Hollywood-style red carpet were also filmed on the Tuesday. This footage was then edited to form a short section which could be passed off as live and precede a brief pre-show of TV presenter Mel Giedroyc interviewing members of the audience before the Thursday night's show.

Giedroyc would also be one of five special guest Narrators – the others being Stephen Fry, Emma Bunton, and previous West End *Rocky Horror Show* cast members Adrian Edmondson and Anthony Head – sharing the role with Richard O'Brien for one night only.

10: AND I REALISE I'M GOING HOME

There had been some concern that, with the performance being broadcast live, any particularly obnoxious or distasteful shout-outs from the audience might sully this rare opportunity to present the production to such a huge universal audience. Overall, however, the hardcore fans in the theatre limited their exuberant vocalisations to the traditional heckles which had (for better or worse) become almost a part of the show. In fact, when one solitary voice did indeed interrupt Frank-n-Furter's clearly emotional query, 'Whatever happened to Fay Wray?' with a boorish holler of, 'She shagged King Kong,' – breaking the tender poignancy of this beautiful moment – actor David Bedella responded firmly with an unambiguous reply of, 'Me sing, you listen,' before winking at the audience and singing the line again.

In addition to clearly defining the boundaries – something Bedella had always excelled at when it came to *The Rocky Horror Show*'s unique relationship with its audience – this allowed the moment to be cut from a subsequent edited version of the performance. In accordance with contractual conditions, this amended edition – which omitted all of the pre-show and interval filler, removed some of the more intrusive audience interaction and tightened up various shots and camera angles – could be transmitted a number of times on several international TV arts channels – such as Sky Arts in the UK, BBC America in the US, and SBS (the Special Broadcasting Service) in Australia – within a sixty day period, whilst still being classified as a live broadcast.

A huge success, *Rocky Horror Show Live* (the word 'Live' was featured prominently in large yellow letters beneath the usual show logo, unequivocally differentiating it from the movie) topped the daily UK cinema box office for 17 September 2015, reportedly raising more than £600,000 for Amnesty International, the same charity which had benefitted from the Royal Court's *Rocky Horror Tribute Show* in 2006.

In May 2016, it was reported that Howard Panter and Rosemary Squire had stepped down as joint chief executives of Ambassador Theatre Group – the theatrical juggernaut they had founded in 1992 – with corporate CEO Mark Cornell assuming leadership duties of the business with immediate effect. As detailed by the *Stage* newspaper, Panter and Squire would continue to be shareholders and board members whilst retaining (non-executive) director roles within ATG. As part of the deal, they also purchased Trafalgar Studios – formerly London's Whitehall Theatre – which would subsequently become the heart of Trafalgar Entertainment (a new company co-founded by Panter and Squire in 2017) and re-open as the Trafalgar Theatre in July 2021 after major restoration and refurbishment. The *Stage* also confirmed that Panter would 'remain chairman and producer of *The Rocky Horror Show* worldwide'.

Having outlaid a significant amount – both financially and artistically – for their '40th anniversary party production', Rocky Horror Company would certainly make the most of their investment during the ensuing decade. Not only would the set and overall staging remain the same for each successive UK tour, but the production would also venture overseas. The 2014 and 2018 Australian tours – the former of which saw Craig McLachlan returning to the role of Frank-n-Furter for the first time in over twenty years – would employ Christopher Luscombe's direction, Nathan Wright's choreography and Hugh Durrant's set, but with a predominantly local cast.

A South African tour – which visited the Artscape Opera House, Cape Town between 6 December 2019 and 12 January 2020 and Teatro at Montecasino, Johannesburg from 17 January to 1 March 2020 – also used the same set, and a feeling of overfamiliarity with the production (particularly in the UK) led some fans to call unsuccessfully for the show's design and direction to be refreshed. It was felt that this self-proclaimed 'party production' was backsliding towards the camp, over-the-top, broad pantomime approach of the Theatre Royal Hanley and *Big 30* productions of the 1980s and early 2000s, something Christopher Luscombe's acclaimed 2006 revival had skilfully and purposely managed to avoid.

By eschewing the raw rock 'n' roll tackiness of *The Rocky Horror Show*'s experimental origins, in favour of slick and polished modern musical theatre conventions, the latest version began to feel a little too sophisticated and over-choreographed, with even the deliberately simple 'Time Warp' gaining unnecessary extra arm movements, and a brief but superfluous dance break being added to 'Hot Patootie – Bless My Soul'. Furthermore, despite obvious visual allusions to its Hammer horror roots, Hugh Durrant's colourful set was, in many ways, the antithesis of the dark, eerie, gothic domicile created by Robin Don for the 1990 West End revival, while the bright, unrestrained lighting design did little to emphasise the essential horror aspects of the show.

As publicity material encouraged audience participation and interaction far more blatantly than had the previous production – in 2006 director Christopher Luscombe had made a determined effort to ensure that the actors and the story remained in control – the balancing act between the 'grume, gunpowder and gusset' of Barry Humphries' famous review of the King's Road production for *Punch* magazine and the 'Guaranteed party' attitude of the show's contemporary marketing campaigns became even more precarious.

Conflicting drastically with the stuffy Edgar Lustgarten origins of the character, the Narrator often came over as something of a stand-up comedian, frequently deviating from the scripted lines with out of character vulgarity or current affairs-based satire, which, while invariably eliciting the desired hilarity from the audience, took them out of the story far too regularly. Similarly, the traditionally horrific moment in which a clear plastic bag containing the dismembered limbs and organs of the recently murdered

Eddie is revealed by the manic Frank-n-Furter was now played for laughs, with the characters frantically throwing the bag to each other whilst screaming hysterically in a comedic manner, and Columbia's drug-induced freak-out had become excessively protracted and needlessly self-indulgent.

The consensus amongst fans was that this more superficial approach was perhaps in accordance with the desires of the production company, whose emphasis on *Rocky*'s interactive, dress-up and sing-along elements would seem comparable to those of shallower and far more frivolous musicals which, in an increasingly competitive theatrical market, would likely be the show's primary competition at the box office.

As the production's artistic choices continued to divide purists – who understood and respected the piece itself as a unique work of classic theatre – and the mainstream for whom the show was merely a backdrop for their boozy costumed festivities, a particular crowd-pleasing constant across each successive tour was the presence of Kristian Lavercombe, who found himself returning to the role of Riff Raff for the UK, Australian and South African engagements, whilst becoming something of an ambassador for the show and a popular fan favourite along the way.

Recalling that his original two-day 'dance, acting and singing' audition for the 2010 South Korean production was the most extensive, Kristian points out that each subsequent audition processes was an entirely different experience:

'Me being cast as Riff Raff has never been a guaranteed thing. Every production starts off with a clean slate. And there have been a few times where it almost didn't work out,' the actor declares frankly, 'However, going through an audition process isn't generally called for, as when you've been in a production you've already proven that you can perform the material. The creative team have seen me perform Riff Raff hundreds of times – they know my performance inside and out – and in an audition process you just go through material from the show. Me auditioning to the people who taught me the role would be a redundant process.'

'The first Australian tour I did, we were told that the UK tour would be finishing, and a new Australian production would be starting up with an all-new cast,' Lavercombe recalls, referring to the 2014 Australian tour, which would commence following the conclusion of the UK's 2012/13 (40th anniversary) tour and would be the first to re-use that production's set. 'However, I was in the unusual situation that was the only member of the UK cast that could legally work in Australia – without a special visa – because of my New Zealand citizenship, so I asked to be considered. Then, when they struggled to find someone appropriate from the people who auditioned, I was cast. Then, in the following Australian productions, they were pretty much on-going, so I just continued on where I left off.'

'In South Africa, they had originally cast a South African actor to play

Riff Raff, and I wasn't offered it. Then that actor pulled out of half the season because his wife was pregnant, so they asked me to do the second half of the tour. Then he pulled out of the tour completely and I replaced him to do the whole thing.'

As Lavercombe elaborates, repeatedly revisiting this complex alien character for consecutive tours, saw him developing various aspects of the character over time; his make-up design being a prime example: 'I just gradually evolved it without realising,' he confesses, 'I don't consciously change anything major; but you look back and go, "Oh, I've actually changed."'

The actor posits that this evolution of the character's grim visage may stem from not having been given a proper make-up brief for Riff Raff when he first played the role, and therefore having to experiment with the look of the character over time. 'I just made it up myself,' he admits, 'And I shouldn't have. Now I look back on it, it just wasn't right; although, at the time, it felt right. But now I look back and I go, "Oh, that's wrong," and it keeps on evolving.'

'I do like looking in the mirror as a character and not seeing myself. I like to see the character,' he declares, 'I think the make-up was too full-on in the past. But I've gone through whole stages of ageing him up and not ageing him up and doing lots of different things and changing the way he looks.'

'If there's something I don't do, then I'm certainly like, "Oh, there's something going on here." And sometimes I can forget, and go, "Why doesn't it look like Riff Raff?" And I think it's usually the eyebrows; because I do the eyebrows last, and he's got bushy eyebrows,' Lavercombe continues, elaborating further on his nightly make-up ritual, and recalling an early decision to base his look on a photo of another actor's interpretation of the character, which ultimately proved misguided.

'I can't remember who was playing it,' he confesses, 'They had this quite full-on blocky kind of eyebrows, and I think I took inspiration from that initially; but it was wrong because I think he looked a bit too drag. It looked a bit too draggy – like a bit too Frank-n-Furtery – so then I made them a bit bushier and that's kind of stuck for me now. The eyebrows don't really change too much now.'

'As I'm with him longer, I just know him better,' the actor concludes philosophically.

Christopher Porter – another notable recurring name in the programmes – supervised the costume department for every major UK touring production (and several international tours) of *The Rocky Horror Show* from the 1990/91 West End revival onwards, even continuing his association with the show when Christopher Luscombe took over directorial duties in 2006:

'It's an unusual situation with Chris Luscombe, Sue [Blane] and I, because he was hired after they decided to replace the previous director,

10: AND I REALISE I'M GOING HOME

which was a big deal,' Porter elaborates, illuminatingly, 'Usually what happens in theatre is a director chooses his own team. Because Sue and Richard Hartley are bound up in the history of *Rocky Horror*, Richard [O'Brien] said, from day one, "I'm staying loyal to Sue Blane and Richard Hartley" – and anybody else that was one of the original team and who wanted to be involved – so we stayed with the production, but normally the director would choose his own costume designer.'

The logical decision to retain the show's original costume designer for the show's 2006 reworking was, as Porter confirms, wholeheartedly supported by Rocky Horror Company's perceptive Head of Production Meryl Faiers: 'In Sue and my case, the producers insisted we come with the package. As Meryl said, "We would be fools to ditch Sue Blane's designs; they are iconic, and part of the reason people come and dress up."'

By its very nature, Porter's role within the production team would be more active and hands-on than that of the show's legendary costume designer:

'Sue's situation has changed, in that she's now nearly 75, so she doesn't travel very much, and I fill in that gap for her during production periods,' he explains, 'I go to the production, I look at it, I make notes, we talk about it. She sees it when it gets near her and sometimes I join her. She allows me a lot of freedom within that.'

'A lot of people seem to think that my job is to make the costumes. I can't even sew,' Porter confesses, 'So, I am the one choosing what the shoes look like, or which person we'd get to make those costumes, who makes the hats, the jewellery, who paints the jackest and sews the knickers. My role is more of drawing up and sourcing things. Then we move into the wigs and make-up area, which I oversee, but obviously we have a wig and make-up supervisor. *Rocky* comes from a time when designers did everything. These days, they have different designers for different areas; so you'd have a set designer, a costume designer, and then you'd have a wig designer and a make-up designer. So, it's very complicated to pull it all together to one cohesive look. In the old days when we did this, Sue did it all, but she didn't do the sets on *Rocky*. She is a set designer, but she didn't do *Rocky Horror*.'

These comments illustrate how the show continued to develop and expand from a cheap and tacky rock 'n' roll piece into a slick mainstream musical, not just from its original 1973 incarnation at the Royal Court – where Sue Blane's entire costume budget had been around £200 – but also from its first major London revival in 1990, which, in spite of its sophisticated West End trappings, still retained something of a thrifty rock 'n' roll vibe:

'The costumes were originally mostly begged, borrowed or stolen from other shows at the Royal Court or things Sue and I were doing,' Porter admits, 'But also a lot of the costumes were just bought off the shelf. So, you'd go to department stores, Oxfam, hardware stores or Woolworth's and adapt something to use. But today it's nearly all manufactured, the whole show is pretty much made from scratch. We have a decent budget, and we're not afraid to spend it.'

While clearly a fan of the show, Porter is completely frank about his main reasons for staying with the *Rocky Horror* productions for more than three decades:

'I stay with it now primarily because I owe it to Sue,' he freely confesses, 'It's given me a good life for 32 years. Sue would be lost without me really. She would have to find someone else; she would find that very difficult. It's a big income for her, *Rocky Horror* worldwide. I'm pleased to do it because she's a very talented person.'

Christopher Porter's working relationship with the show's legendary costume designer is undoubtedly one of mutual admiration and trust, with Blane open to his suggestions should the need for changes to the designs arise:

'It usually comes out of necessity, where we can't get items that we need any longer, so I have to rethink it. If I can't come up with a solution, then I would 'phone Sue and say, "Well, what do you think?" and Sue would say, "Well, can you get me fabric samples? Give me options." And I'll get the samples and send them on to her, and we'll talk about them.'

'She relies on me to keep it true to her vision,' Porter continues, 'That, and also the fans, control the way the show looks really. I say the fans *control* it because, as you know, the fans dress up, and, if we change the design too much, something that they've been working on for twelve months to wear to a show suddenly becomes redundant and they're furious. I love to see what the fans come up with and how they interpret a design. Sometimes it's inspired lunacy.'

'I'll probably stick around until Sue decides that she doesn't want to do it anymore, and then I'll go as well. Not that I want to; I still get a lot of pleasure from doing it. It's a very handsome production, and Sue's design is outstanding.'

Porter also commends the production's accomplished director and their collaborative working relationship:

'Chris is a very thorough person. Having been an actor, he senses what performers need. That's why actors love working with him,' he affirms, 'I enjoy working with Chris. We have a laugh, and he appreciates the little tweaks I make with the costumes. He makes suggestions. I turn him down. We come to an agreement. If I think it's a good change, then we'll make the change. We get along very well, he's very collaborative and he listens. The producers and Richard didn't want someone who would go off on a tangent, wasting money on unsound concepts for the hell of it.'

Having also enjoyed a prolific career with London's prestigious Royal

10: AND I REALISE I'M GOING HOME

Opera House for over twenty years, Porter admits that, while rock 'n' roll B-movie horror and classical ballet and opera might sound wholly incompatible, the two worlds often collide:

'I take influences from *Rocky Horror* and I put it on stage in an opera if needs want,' he smiles, recounting such a situation with a lavish 2023 production of composer Sergei Prokofiev's *Cinderella*, 'They were trying to come up with a solution for the Ugly Sisters. And they said we need some sort of boa, but we can't make it out of feathers, and we can't make it out of this and we can't make it out of that, so what can we do? And I thought, well, we could make it like the boas that we make in *Rocky Horror*. They're just made of gossamer. That original idea of Sue's; it came from Sue seeing something that strippers wore because they couldn't afford expensive fabrics or feathers, they made them out of cheap fabric and net. So, someone said, "Let's do that," so it's just gone into a new production of *Cinderella*.'

Thanks to the skimpy nature of the *The Rocky Horror Show*'s iconic costumes, the often embarrassing or amusing issue of wardrobe malfunctions – a predicament most actors will have encountered at some point – remains a constant possibility, no matter how slick or sophisticated the production:

'Wardrobe malfunctions happen all the time in a show that requires people to remove most of their clothes,' Porter acknowledges, 'We do have to be very careful about what underwear we give the girls and boys so that they are 'contained', shall we say. We also have to try and subtly say, "You know, you've got to keep yourself tidy down below." The same goes for the boys; suddenly you've got acres of hair, and that's not pretty. Or people that think they need an extra bit of padding, coming out with a couple of pairs of socks stuck down their knickers or bras. I mean, that's even more distracting. When you're in a dressing room, you look in the mirror and you think that looks okay; but then the minute you step out on stage looking like that, you just look weirdly distracting.'

With *The Rocky Horror Show* just under eighteen months away from its 50th anniversary, news broke on 20 January 2022 that rock god (and *Rocky Horror* legend) Meat Loaf had died suddenly at the age of 74, a sombre reminder that, while the show itself may have achieved immortality, its stars were sadly not afforded the same privilege.

As friends and industry insiders began paying their respects to this genuine rock 'n' roll icon, and with the cast of *Bat Out of Hell* – a lavish touring jukebox musical which used the songs of Meat Loaf's friend and frequent collaborator Jim Steinman as the basis for its score – performing their own tribute during the finale of their evening performance on 21 January, *The Rocky Horror Show*'s 2021/22 UK touring company also marked his passing in an appropriate manner. Before the cast took their final bows at the Palace Theatre, Manchester on the evening in question, actor Stephen

Webb (in the role of Frank-n-Furter) gave a brief but befitting speech and – as the cast launched into their usual rousing reprise of 'The Time Warp' and 'Sweet Transvestite' – yelled poignantly, 'Meat Loaf, this one's for you.' As the late great rock legend himself once sang: not a dry eye in the house.

On a more celebratory note, having played several roles over multiple productions and tours, Kristian Lavercombe would achieve a major milestone on Tuesday 15 March 2022, with that evening's show at the Grand Opera House in York marking his 2000th *Rocky Horror Show* performance. As he specified on social media at the time, this remarkable achievement included '6 as Narrator, 43 as Frank-n-Furter, 72 as Brad Majors and 1879 as Riff Raff' and was commemorated by the company and his cast mates, who presented the actor with a specially commissioned cake featuring a photo (printed onto the icing) of him in action as Riff Raff, along with the words '2000 performances'. Furthermore, it was estimated that – barring illness or cancelled shows – his total number of performances would have reached around 2360 by the time of the show's 50th anniversary in June 2023, making Kristian Lavercombe the longest-serving *Rocky Horror Show* actor by a considerable margin.

A sudden announcement in October 2022 revealed that pop icon and *Rocky Horror Show* veteran Jason Donovan – still in great shape at the age of 54 – would be slipping back into fishnets and heels to play Frank-n-Furter for a new Australian tour, opening at Sydney's recently renovated Theatre Royal in February 2023. *Rocky Horror* itself may have started life as an experimental fringe theatre production over 10,000 miles away in London, but the show's undeniable antipodean heritage – its original director and set designer were Australians, as was one of its stars, and its British-born author-composer had been raised in New Zealand – made a Sydney launch for its highly anticipated 50th anniversary celebrations feel entirely appropriate.

Donovan – who had last played the role of Frank almost twenty-five years earlier during the show's 25th anniversary tour of the UK, a run which had culminated in the spring of 1999 with a limited West End engagement at London's Victoria Palace theatre – would be joined by Australian radio host and TV personality Myf Warhurst, taking on the crucial role of the Narrator for the Sydney 2023 dates.

'I am thrilled to be coming home next year to be part of the legendary *Rocky Horror Show*, and in its 50th Anniversary production no less,' an enthusiastic Jason declared to the press shortly after the tour was announced, indicating that his obvious admiration for the piece had not diminished since he had last donned Frank's fishnets, 'From the very first performance in London those years ago, Richard O'Brien created a show from the wilds of his imagination with incredible music that has now stood the test of time, and an awesome energy that befits its accolades and its endurance.'

Although labelled the '50th Anniversary Production' on ads – which also featured the same shot of actress Ceris Hine as Columbia which had now been a staple of the show's posters and marketing for ten years – and described in the official press release as a 'brand new Australian production', this new touring version would once again use Hugh Durrant's familiar ten-year-old set design, dashing the hopes of speculative fans who had hoped for a fresh redesign to suitably commemorate the enormity of *The Rocky Horror Show*'s 50th birthday.

For this particular Australian incarnation, however, with the 2021/22 UK tour extended into 2023 – its logo tweaked slightly to now include the phrase 'Celebrating 50 years of fun' – the same set could not simply be transported overseas as it had been previously. A replica of Durrant's 40th anniversary set was therefore constructed – again causing fans to lament the missed opportunity for a redesign – albeit with the occasional twist to befit its Australian location. The most immediately obvious of these, for anyone familiar with the UK tour's set, would be the exotic animal heads hanging on the walls of Frank's 'hunting lodge for rich weirdos'. In the UK, these walls displayed the heads of a crocodile, a mandrill and a dodo, whereas the Australian version would see a flamingo, a big cat, a crocodile and a shark exhibited instead, giving audiences on both continents the opportunity to spot subtle differences between the two sets.

The 50th anniversary tour of *The Rocky Horror Show* opened in Sydney on 14 February 2023 to standing ovations and mostly positive reviews, many of which praised Jason Donovan's triumphant return to the role of Frank-n-Furter whilst addressing the continued relevance of what some, in the more liberal and forward-thinking world of the 21st century, might consider to be an outmoded 1970s period piece. Writing online for Broadwayworld.com, Jade Kops observed: 'While *Rocky Horror Show* has become almost 'mainstream' in the contemporary landscape of less shock value associated with a man in a corset and fishnets, this work still remains a firm favourite as an escapist piece of theatre with a fun soundtrack, iconic choreography and amusing parody of bygone eras. This is well worth seeing for the new cast and the opportunity to see Jason Donovan return to the role.'

'At 50, *The Rocky Horror Show* looks rather more fit and fabulous than it did aged 40,' wrote Jason Blake in his three and a half (out of five) star review for Limelight Magazine, 'A decade ago, with Craig McLachlan in the role of Frank-n-Furter, the show (which I experienced in this venue) came across like a cheap pantomime, brought low by McLachlan's relentless showboating. The *Rocky* brand is Teflon to a large extent, but one imagines O'Brien – who guards his intellectual property fiercely – and the creative team led by director Christopher Luscombe saw the necessity in a hard reboot.'

'Gracing Frank with touches of faded silver screen glamour (Gena Rowlands came to mind while watching him),' Blake continued, 'Donovan maintains just the right degree of elasticity in his performance, an ability to give us the impression Frank is running the show without tripping the rhythm of the production – something McLachlan notably failed to do.'

As if to emphasise the validity of this particular Australian revival, it was announced shortly after the production premiered that the performance on the evening of Thursday 30 March 2023 would be streamed live to Australian cinemas, and, while a 28 October 2021 livestream of the UK touring production had failed to generate the same level of hype or publicity as the landmark 17 September 2015 West End broadcast, a press announcement from Marc Allenby – CEO of Trafalgar Releasing – appeared to indicate that this screening of the Australian production was being recognised as something of a big deal:

'We're delighted to be celebrating the 50th Anniversary of *The Rocky Horror Show* with a live broadcast from Theatre Royal Sydney to cinemas across Australia. This is our first live broadcast from an Australian venue and it's fantastic to be working with the team at the theatre and our partners within the Trafalgar Entertainment Group to bring one of the world's favourite musicals to cinema audiences across the continent for the first time.'

Following the highly praised launch of the latest Australian tour – and with special events and commemorative performances taking place in cities around the world throughout the year – 2023 would see this pioneering musical horror show celebrating half a century of continued success in suitably saucy rock 'n' roll style.

Whereas tastes frequently vary with the passage of time – up-to-the-minute trends constantly dictated by the latest fashion flux – certain stories remain timeless. In a world increasingly ruled by the advances of modern science and the latest technological innovations, it would appear that classic thematic elements – such as those of self-discovery, the hero's journey and the perpetual struggle of good versus evil – and the lessons they teach remain eternally archetypal. The ceaseless appeal of Shakespeare's works, the enduring Frankenstein myth, Charles Dickens' *A Christmas Carol* and most fairy tales, for instance, would seem to corroborate humanity's intrinsic need for basic moral and philosophical allegory thinly concealed within the framework of outwardly frivolous leisure diversions.

Such tales will always withstand being retold again and again. And *The Rocky Horror Show* is clearly such a story.

'I think it moves people as well as making them laugh. It touches on something profound, and at a deeper level than just a party night out,' director Christopher Luscombe rationalises. 'It feels like it serves a useful purpose for people.

10: AND I REALISE I'M GOING HOME

'That's perhaps hard for us in the theatre to relate to, as we deal in make-believe all the time; we dress up for a living.'

It is safe to say that *Rocky Horror*'s contribution to the world of rock is easily comparable to that of its place in the history of musical theatre; it certainly bridges the gap between the two more successfully than anything before or since.

While the cultural significance of *Hair* – and any number of comparable works – has been debated endlessly by historians and intellectual critics for decades, *Rocky Horror* is sometimes still dismissed as inconsequential and puerile. And yet, while the infantile behaviour of some of its latter-day audiences may have contributed immensely to such dismissively condescending attitudes, the piece itself remains without equal. There really is nothing quite like it.

To echo the sentiments of Dr Frank-n-Furter, it would seem abundantly clear that *The Rocky Horror Show* is most definitely not spent yet; and as this extraordinary musical celebrates 50 years of continued popularity – an astounding achievement by any standard – it looks set to go on delighting and enthralling not only its millions of already-devoted followers, but untold future generations, who have yet to discover its irresistible charms.

There is, after all, no crime in giving yourself over to pleasure.

Bibliography and Selected Sources

ROCKY HORROR BOOKS

The Rocky Horror Show (Libretto) – Book, Music & Lyrics by Richard O'Brien – Samuel French Ltd – ISBN 0 573 08055 0 – 0000 1 8308 – 1983 UK Edition
The Rocky Horror Show (Libretto) – Book, Music & Lyrics by Richard O'Brien – French's Musical Library, Samuel French Inc – ISBN 0 573 68112 0 – 1998/99 US Edition
The Rocky Horror Show (Libretto) – Book, Music & Lyrics by Richard O'Brien – Samuel French Ltd – ISBN 0 573 08055 0 – 2004 Revised UK Edition
The Rocky Horror Scrapbook – Designed by Brian Thomson – Starfleet Productions Inc – 1979
The Rocky Horror Show Book 1973 – 1987 – James Harding – Sidgwick & Jackson Ltd – ISBN 0 283 99388 X – 1987
The Rocky Horror Picture Show Book – Bill Henkin – Hawthorn/Dutton – ISBN 0-8015-6436-0 – 1979
The Official Rocky Horror Picture Show Audience Par-Tic-I-Pation Guide – Sal Piro and Michael Hess – Stabur Press Inc – ISBN Trade Paperback 0-941613-16-X – 1991
Creatures Of The Night: The Rocky Horror Picture Show Experience – Sal Piro – Stabur Press Inc – ISBN Trade Paperback 0-941613-12-7 – 1990
Creatures Of The Night II: More Of The Rocky Horror Picture Show Experience – Sal Piro – Stabur Press Inc – ISBN Trade Paperback 0-941613-75-5 –1995
The Rocky Horror Picture Show Original Movie Script – The Movie Script Library '20th Anniversary Edition' – OSP Publishing Inc – ISBN 1-56693-315-3 – 1995
Cosmic Light: The Birth Of A Cult Classic – Jim Whittaker – Acme Books/Jim Whittaker – 1998
Rocky Horror: From Concept To Cult – Scott Michaels & David Evans – Sanctuary Publishing – ISBN 1-86074-383-8 – 2002
Rocky Horror – Mick Rock – Schwarzkopf & Schwarzkopf – ISBN 3-89602-666-6 – 2005
Cultographies: The Rocky Horror Picture Show – Jeffrey Weinstock – Wallflower Press – ISBN 978-1-905674-50-3 – 2007
The Rocky Horror Show: As I Remember It – Rayner Bourton – MyBookyBook – ISBN 978-0-9562724-0-9 – 2009

BIBLIOGRAPY AND SELECTED SOURCES

Music On Film: The Rocky Horror Picture Show – Dave Thompson – Limelight Editions – ISBN 978-0-87910-387-3 – 2012
The Rocky Horror Picture Show 15th Anniversary (Booklet included with *The Rocky Horror Picture Show* fifteenth anniversary soundtrack box set) – Ode Sound & Visuals/Lisa Kurtz Sutton – R 71011 Ode – 1990
The Rocky Horror Picture Show Shooting Script – Jim Sharman & Richard O'Brien (Facsimile of 1974 shooting script for *The Rocky Horror Picture Show*, including script amendments dated 9/12/74 and reproductions of original shooting schedules dated 24/9/74) – HS Hollywood Scripts/Enterprise House, London

OTHER BOOKS

House Of Horror: The Complete Hammer Films Story – Edited by Allen Eyles, Robert Adkinson and Nicholas Fry (with additional revisions in 1994 by Jack Hunter) – Lorrimer Publishing Ltd/Creation Books – ISBN 1 871592 40 2 – 1973 (Revised 1994)
Hammer Films: The Bray Studios Years – Wayne Kinsey – Reynolds & Hearn Ltd – ISBN 1 903111 44 7 – 2002
A Thing Of Unspeakable Horror: The History Of Hammer Films – Sinclair McKay – Aurum Press Limited – ISBN 978 1 84513 348 1 – 2007
The Illustrated Frankenstein – John Stoker – Westbridge Books (A Division of David & Charles) – ISBN 0 7153 7924 0 – 1980
It's Alive! : The Classic Cinema Saga Of Frankenstein – Gregory William Mank – A S Barnes & Company Inc – ISBN 0-498-02592-6 – 1981
The Illustrated Frankenstein Movie Guide – Stephen Jones – Titan Books – ISBN 1 85286 524 5 – 1994
The Science Fiction And Fantasy Film Handbook – Alan Frank – B T Batsford Ltd – ISBN 0 7134 2726 4 – 1982
The Horror Film Handbook – Alan Frank – B T Batsford Ltd – ISBN 0 7134 2724 8 – 1982
Forrest J Ackerman's World Of Science Fiction – Forrest J Ackerman – Aurum Press Limited – ISBN 1 85410 573 6 – 1997
The Definitive Encyclopedia Of Science Fiction – David Pringle (General Editor) – Carlton Books/Colour Library Direct – ISBN 1-85833-815-8 – 1996
Revenge Of The Creature Features Movie Guide – John Stanley – Creatures At Large Press – ISBN 0-940064-04-9 –1988 (Third Revised Edition)
The Making Of King Kong – Orville Goldner & George E Turner – A S Barnes & Co Inc – ISBN 345-25826-6-495 – 1975
King Kong: The History Of A Movie Icon – From Fay Wray To Peter Jackson – Ray Morton – Applause Theatre & Cinema Books – ISBN 1-55783-669-8 – 2005
Nightmare Of Ecstasy: The Life And Art Of Edward D Wood Jr – Rudolph Grey

– Feral House – ISBN 0-922915-24-5 – 1992
The I Was A Teenage Juvenile Delinquent Rock 'N' Roll Horror Beach Party Movie Book: A Complete Guide To The Teen Exploitation Film 1954-1969 – Alan Betrock – Plexus Publishing Limited – ISBN 0-85965-195-9 – 1986
The Films Of Roger Corman: Brilliance On A Budget – Ed Naha – Arco Publishing Inc – ISBN 0-668-05312-7 – 1982
The Little Shop Of Horrors Book – John McCarty & Mark Thomas McGee – St Martin's Press – ISBN 0-312-01784-7 – 1988
Buffy The Vampire Slayer: The Watcher's Guide Volume 2 – Nancy Holder with Jeff Mariotte and Maryelizabeth Hart – Pocket Books – ISBN 0-671-04260-2 – 2000
Carry On Laughing: A Celebration – Adrian Rigelsford – Virgin Books – ISBN 1 85227 554 5 – 1996
The Life Of Python – George Perry – Pavilion Books Limited – ISBN 1-85793-441-5 – 1994
Keeping The British End Up: Four Decades Of Saucy Cinema – Simon Sheridan – Reynolds & Hearn Ltd – ISBN 1 903111 21 8 – 2001
Come Play With Me: The Life And Films Of Mary Millington – Simon Sheridan – FAB Press – ISBN 0-9529260-7-7 – 1999
To Hell And Back: An Autobiography – Meat Loaf (with David Dalton) – Virgin Books – ISBN 1 85227 880 3 – 1999
Chapters And Chances – Reg Livermore – Hardie Grant Books – ISBN 1-74066-170-2 – 2003
Blood & Tinsel: A Memoir – Jim Sharman – The Miegunyah Press – ISBN 978-0-522-85377-3 – 2008
Collage Of A Life: Memoirs Of An Artist, Actor And Humorist – Jonathan Adams – Silver Link Publishing Ltd – ISBN 978-1-85794-3 – 2008
A Stage Mother's Story: We're Not All Mrs Worthingtons! – Hazel K Bell – HKB Press – ISBN 0-9552503-1-5 – 2006
King's Road: The Rise And Fall Of The Hippest Street In The World – Max Decharne – Weidenfield & Nicolson – ISBN 0 297 84769 4 – 2005
The Oakley Court, Windsor: The Story Of… Windsor's Most Iconic Hotel – Jake H. Roche – www.jakerochebooks.co.uk – 2016
The Art Of Illusion: Production Design For Film And Television – Terry Ackland-Snow with Wendy Laybourn – The Crowood Press – ISBN 978-1-78500-343-1 – 2017
American Gothic: A Life Of America's Most Famous Painting – Steven Biel – W W Norton & Company – ISBN 0-393-05912-X – 2005
It's Behind You: The Story Of Panto – Peter Lathan – New Holland Publishers Ltd – ISBN 1 84330 736 7 – 2004
Toxic Fame: Celebrities Speak On Stardom – Joey Berlin – Visible Ink Press – ISBN 0-7876-0874-2 – 1996

BIBLIOGRAPY AND SELECTED SOURCES

MAGAZINES

Rocky Horror Picture Show Official Magazine – Collector's Edition 1979 – Blake Publishing Corp
Plays And Players – August 1973 – Volume 20 No 11 Issue No 239 (published monthly by Hansom Books)
Plays And Players – December 1973 – Volume 21 No 3 Issue No 243 (published monthly by Hansom Books)
Plays And Players – October 1976 – Volume 24 No 1 Issue No 276 (published monthly by Hansom Books)
Starburst –July 1981 – Issue 36 Volume 3 Number 12 (published monthly by Marvel Comics Ltd)
Fangoria – October 1981 – Issue 15 Volume 3 (published six times a year by O'Quinn Studios Inc)
The Oldie – 4 March 1994 – Issue 54 (published fortnightly by Oldie Publications Ltd)
The Musicals Collection – Grease – 1994 – Issue 23 (fortnightly part-work published by Orbis Publishing Limited/DeAgostini)
The Musicals Collection – The Rocky Horror Show – 1995 – Issue 41 (fortnightly part-work published by Orbis Publishing Limited/DeAgostini)
The Musicals Collection – Hair – 1996 – Issue 62 (fortnightly part-work published by Orbis Publishing Limited/DeAgostini)

VIDEO AND DVD

The Rocky Horror Picture Show 2-Disc Edition (Region 1) '25 Years of Absolute Pleasure!' – 20th Century Fox Home Entertainment – 2000574 – 2000 (US release)
The Rocky Horror Picture Show 2-Disc Edition (Region 2) '25 Years of Absolute Pleasure!' – 20th Century Fox Home Entertainment – F1-SGB 01424DVD – 2001 (UK release)
Shock Treatment '25th Anniversary Edition' (Region 1) – 20th Century Fox Home Entertainment – 2006 (US release)
Richard O'Brien's Rocky Horror Tribute Show (Region 2) – NVC Arts/Warner Music Entertainment – 50-51865-0799-2-7 – 2008
An Evening With Richard O'Brien (DVD-R) – Amazon.com/Thinking Room Productions Ltd – 2008 (New Zealand release)
Midnight Movies: From The Margin To The Mainstream – Metrodome – MTD5291 – 2007 (UK release)

TELEVISION

Behind The Music: The Rocky Horror Picture Show – VH-1 – VH-1 (USA) – First broadcast 31 October 1999
Walk On The Wild Side – Granada Television – Granada Television/ITV network (UK) – 1999 (produced and directed by Daniel Abineri)
Coming Home (With Qantas) (New Zealand) – 2000
100 Greatest Scary Moments – Channel 4 (UK) – First broadcast 25-26 October 2003 (presented by Jimmy Carr)
100 Greatest Sexy Moments – Channel 4 (UK) – First broadcast 29 November 2003 (presented by Anna Chancellor)
100 Greatest Musicals – Channel 4 (UK) – First broadcast 26-27 December 2003 (presented by Denise Van Outen)

RADIO

Let's Do The Time Warp Again – BBC Radio 2 (UK) – 1999

INTERNET

www.timewarp.org.uk (The Official UK *Rocky Horror* Fan Club)
www.rockyhorror.co.uk (*Rocky Horror* Company)
www.rocky-horror-show.de (2008/09 and 2011/12 European Tour)
www.atgtickets.com (Ambassador Theatre Group)
www.rockyhorror.com (*The Rocky Horror Picture Show* – The Official Web Site)
www.rockypedia.com
www.cosmosfactory.org (Cosmo's Factory – US *Rocky Horror* fan site)
www.rockymusic.org (RockyMusic – The Musical World of *Rocky Horror*)
www.rockyhorrorcostumelist.info (The Anal Retentive *Rocky Horror* Costume List)
www.ozrockyhorror.com (*Rocky Horror* Australia)
www.robcrusade.com (The Richard O'Brien Crusade – Richard O'Brien fan site)
www.riffraffstatue.org
www.anthonyhead.org (The Official Anthony Head Web Site)
www.arthurlloyd.co.uk (The Music Hall and Theatre History Web Site)
www.royalcourttheatre.com
www.shubertorganization.com
www.kmtheatre.co.uk (Official Kenneth More Theatre Web Site)
www.overthefootlights.co.uk
www.officialtheatre.com (London Theatre Guide)
www.whitelight.ltd.uk (The UK's Premier Supplier of Creative Lighting)

BIBLIOGRAPY AND SELECTED SOURCES

tobysimkin.com
castalbums.org
www.whatsonstage.com
www.bbc.co.uk/news
www.sunlive.co.nz
www.radionz.co.nz (Radio New Zealand)
www.youtube.com

In addition to the sources listed above, the programmes and souvenir brochures from numerous *Rocky Horror* stage productions, and the sleeve and liner notes from several cast recordings and soundtrack albums, proved invaluable.

Gallery

A selection of photographs and ephemera from fifty years of *Rocky Horror*.

'It was great when it all began' – programme cover from the very first production of *The Rocky Horror Show* at London's Royal Court Theatre Upstairs in June 1973.

GALLERY

148 King's Road, London (site of the former Classic cinema, Chelsea) photographed in 2006.

279 King's Road, London (site of the former King's Road Theatre) photographed in 2006.

A strange journey – UK *Rocky Horror Show* tour ad on the side of a bus in Edinburgh 2010.

Duke of York's Theatre, London 1994.

Piccadilly Theatre, London 1990, *Rocky Horror Show* West End revival.

Piccadilly Theatre, London, *Rocky Horror Show* 18th Birthday performance June 19th 1991.

GALLERY

Oakley Court – Room 112 – Richard O'Brien Suite (photo: Carol Mulhern)

Piccadilly Theatre, London 1990.

Theatre Royal, Hanley August 1988.

Theatre Royal, Hanley, England August 1988 – final performance aftermath.

GALLERY

Victoria Palace Theatre, London 1999.

Queen's Theatre, London 2003.

Queen's Theatre, London 2003 – Big 30 Birthday Cake.

Rocky Horror Show European tour 2008 – Berlin.

GALLERY

Rocky Horror Show promo tram, Sydney, Australia 2008 (photo: David White)

'Over at the Frankenstein Place' – the magnificent Oakley Court in Windsor, England; the original filming location for Frank-n-Furter's castle in *The Rocky Horror Picture Show*.

Rocky Horror Show European tour 2008 – show dos and don'ts in German.

Rocky Horror Show UK tour 2006 – No room for ambiguity here.

Rocky Horror Tribute Show, Royal Court Theatre, London May 3rd 2006.

GALLERY

Royal Court Theatre, London 2006.

Union Chapel, Islington, London (where rehearsals for the 2006 UK tour of *The Rocky Horror Show* took place).

The former Theatre Royal, Hanley, England (a far cry from its glory days) photographed in 2013.

Palace Theatre, Manchester, England during the show's 40th birthday week in June 2013.

GALLERY

Theatre Royal, Hanley August 1988 'Eddie's Teddy'.

Theatre Royal, Hanley August 1988 'Floorshow'.

Theatre Royal, Hanley August 1988. Julie Fox (Magenta) and Lorinda King (Columbia).

GALLERY

Theatre Royal, Hanley August 1988. Paul Critchlow (Riff Raff) and Julie Fox (Magenta).

Theatre Royal, Hanley August 1988. Paul Critchlow (Riff Raff) and Julie Fox (Magenta).

Theatre Royal, Hanley August 1988. Sue Cotter (Janet) and Paul Critchlow (Riff Raff).

GALLERY

Richard O'Brien *Disgracefully Yours*, London April 1996.

Richard O'Brien *Disgracefully Yours*, London April 1996.

During rehearsals for the very first Japanese production in 1975 (photo: Belinda Sinclair).

Judy Lloyd (Columbia) and her future (real life) husband Christopher Malcolm (Brad) during rehearsals for the very first Japanese production in 1975 (photo: Belinda Sinclair).

The Rocky Horror Show opens in Tokyo, Japan 1975 (photo: Belinda Sinclair).

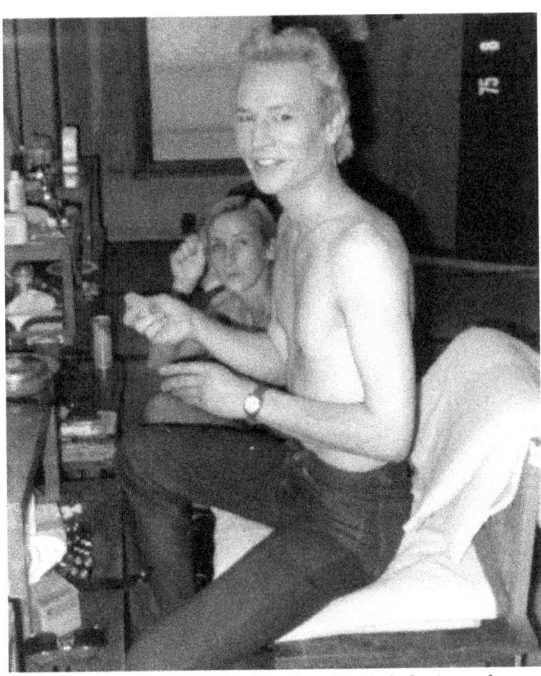

Judy Lloyd (Columbia) and Ziggy Byfield (Frank-n-Furter) during rehearsals in Japan 1975 (photo: Belinda Sinclair)

GALLERY

Belinda Sinclair (Janet) and Ziggy Byfield (Frank-n-Furter) sign autographs for fans in Japan 1975 (photo: Belinda Sinclair).

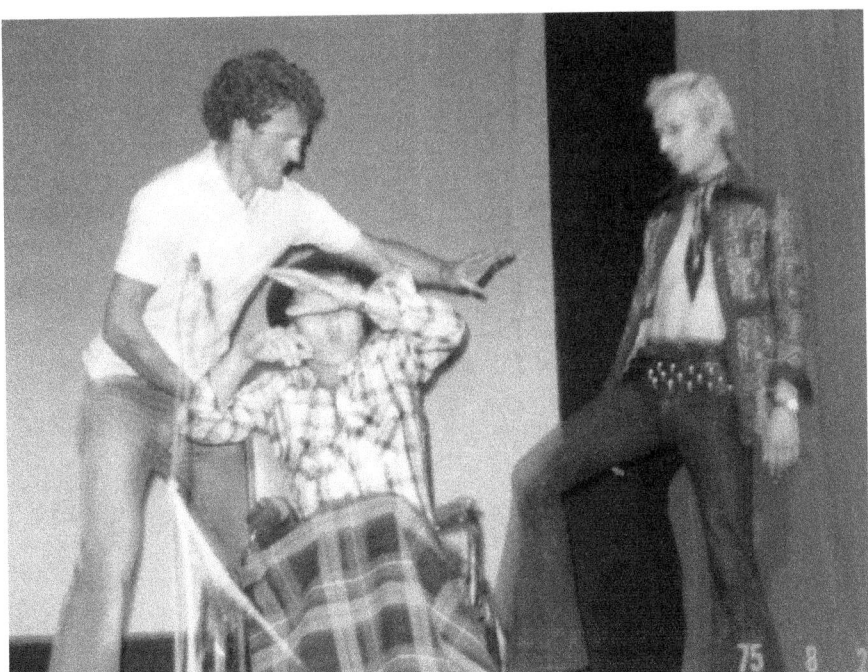

Christopher Malcolm (Brad), Neil McCaul (Dr Scott) and Ziggy Byfield (Frank-n-Furter) rehearse one of the show's pivotal scenes in Japan 1975 (photo: Belinda Sinclair).

Charming Underclothes – UK *Rocky Horror Picture Show* fan shadow cast – Prince Charles Cinema, London (early 1990s) (photo: David Freeman).

GALLERY

Return to Transylvania – Richard O'Brien and Patricia Quinn at Oakley Court in 1992; their first return visit since they filmed the movie there in 1974 (photo: David Freeman).

The Denton Affair (UK *Rocky Horror* convention), Manchester 2006 – Patricia Quinn (the original Magenta) meets members of the cast of the 2006 UK touring production (photo: Rob Bagnall).

Rio Cinema, Dalston, London – October 2018 – Richard O'Brien joins David and Stephanie Freeman and an international fan shadow cast to celebrate 30 years of the TimeWarp fan club (photo: David Freeman).

GALLERY

UK fans at the show.

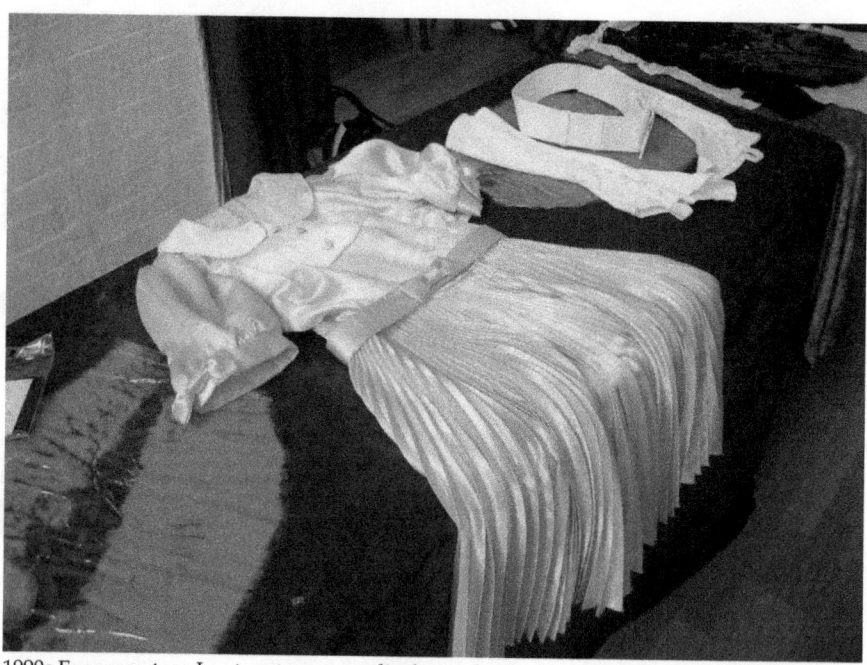
1990s European tour Janet costume – on display at the Denton Affair 3 convention in London July 2011.

Original corset worn by actress Julie Fox (Magenta) for the final curtain call during the 1988 leg of the Theatre Royal Hanley's UK tour.

Usherette costume worn by Julie Fox on the 1988 leg of the Theatre Royal, Hanley's UK tour.

GALLERY

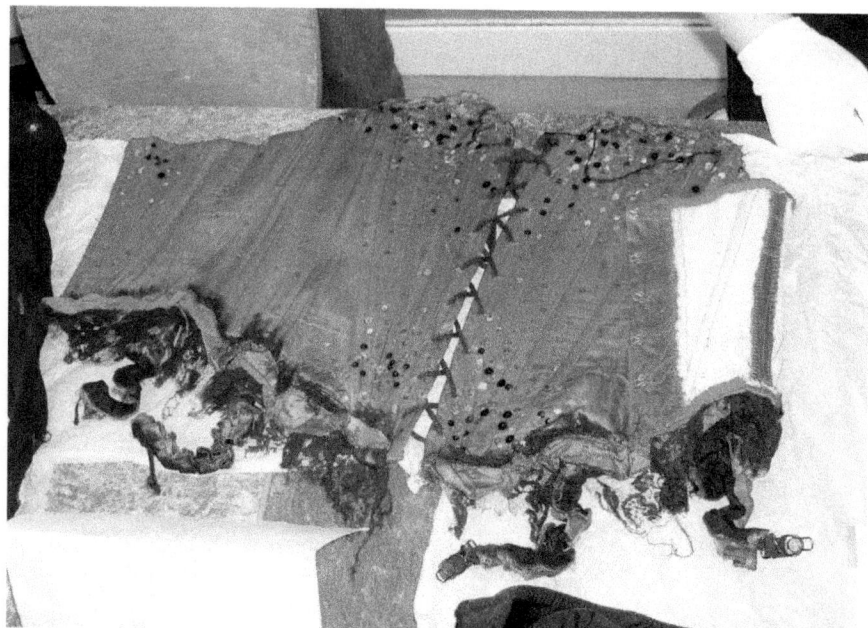

'Floorshow' corset worn by Tim Curry in the 1975 Broadway production of *The Rocky Horror Show* at the Belasco Theatre, New York City.

Usher's mask from the King's Road Theatre 1976. Purchased by Phil Barden from the actor Neil McCaul (photo: The Rocky Horror Phenomenon)

Poster from the King's Road Theatre, London 1973.

Programme – Classic cinema, Chelsea 1973.

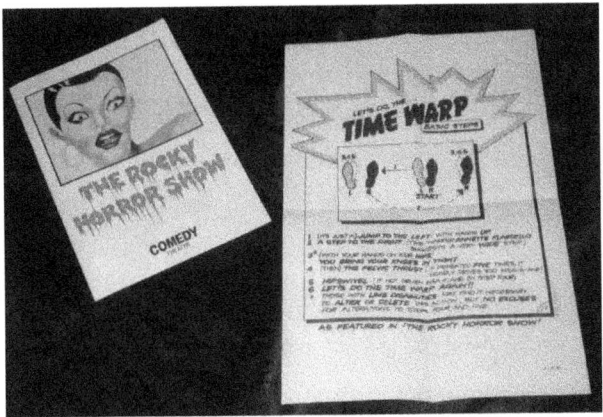

Programme and mask from the show's US debut at Lou Adler's Roxy Theatre in Los Angeles in 1974.

Programme and Time Warp instructions from the show's West End debut at London's Comedy Theatre in 1979.

GALLERY

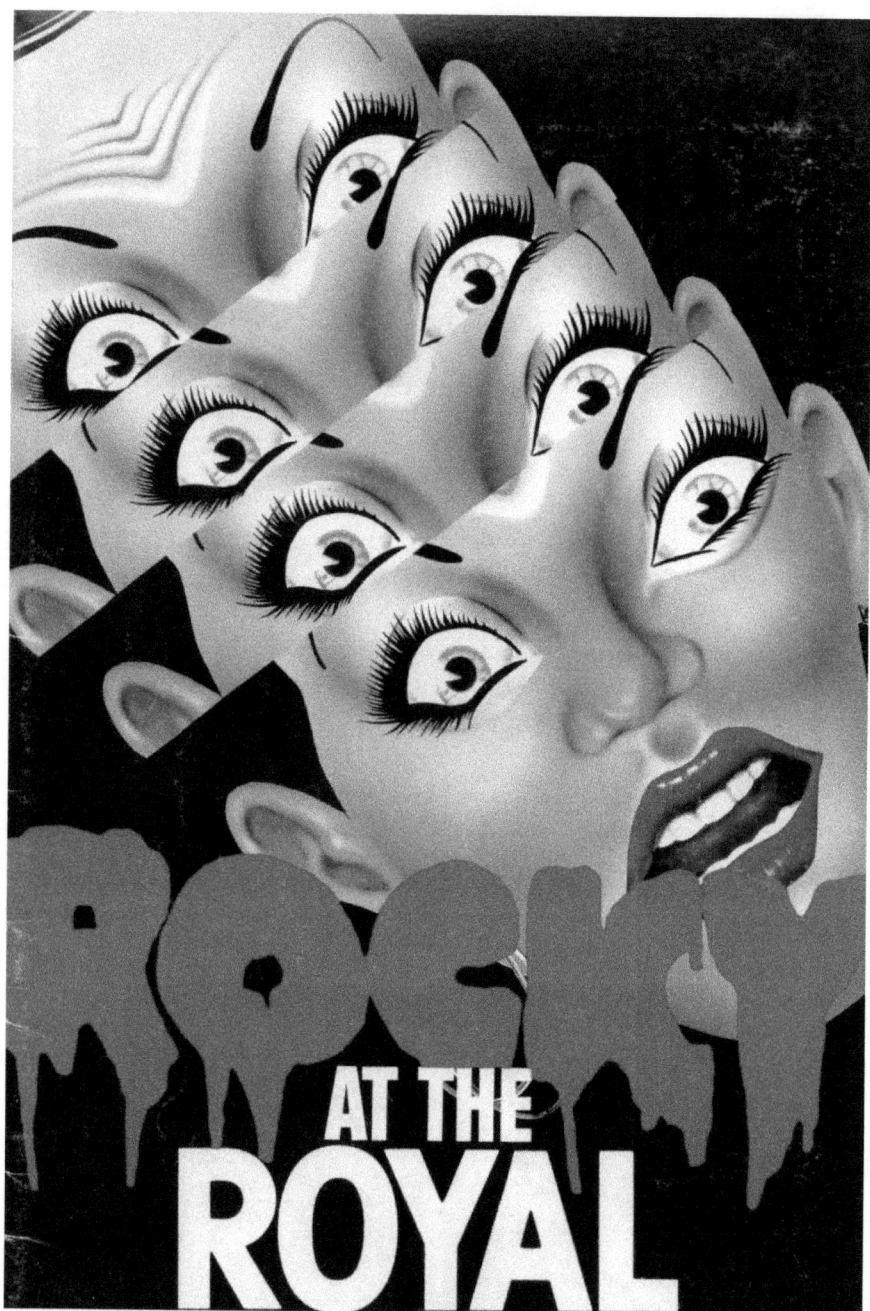

Programme from the 1981 Australian production at the Theatre Royal, Sydney.

Several programmes from the European tour which ran for ten years between 1996 and 2005.

Poster for the 2010 South Korean production directed by Christopher Luscombe.

Programme – Coliseum Theatre, Oldham, England 1981.

GALLERY

Programme – Forum Theatre, Wythenshawe England 1983.

Programme – Finland 1995.

Programme – South Africa 1997-1998.

Programme – Hungary 2000.

Programme – Lab Theater, Minneapolis, USA 2011.

Original London cast LP 1973.

7" vinyl single – Belinda Sinclair (1975 Turkish pressing).

GALLERY

7" vinyl single – Belinda Sinclair (1979 UK pressing).

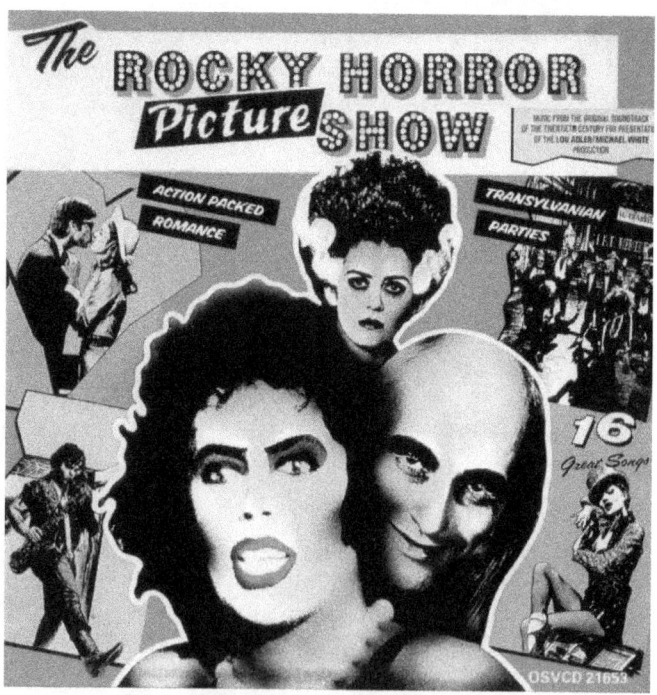

Original Motion Picture soundtrack LP 1975.

1991 Icelandic cast.

1992 Australian cast.

GALLERY

1995 Finnish cast.

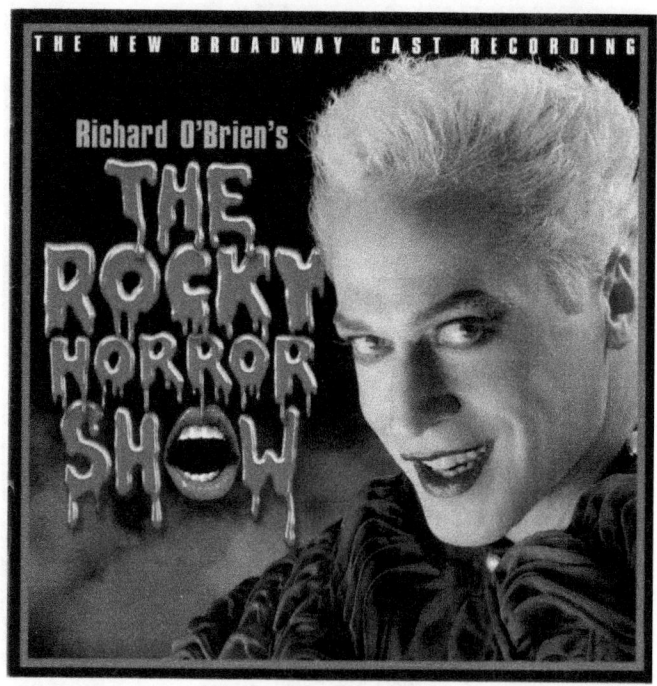

2000 Broadway revival cast.

2001 Peruvian cast.

2010 Icelandic cast.

GALLERY

2011-2012 Japanese cast.

Original Brazilian cast LP 1975.

Original Norwegian cast LP 1977.

London West End revival cast LP 1990.

GALLERY

7" vinyl single – Belinda Sinclair (1975 Japanese pressing).

Richard O'Brien's solo album 1999 (US cover image).

2018 Icelandic cast.

The Steinway Pianola Meets Rocky Horror LP 1980.

GALLERY

7" vinyl single – Ziggy Byfield (released in Japan 1975).

7" vinyl single – Anthony Head 1991.

Shaped vinyl picture disc version of Anthony Head's 1991 recording of 'Sweet Transvestite'.

The Rocky Horror Show PC game.

The Rocky Horror Show Amstrad Computer Cassette Tape Game
from Alternative Software. 1985.

The *Rocky Horror* Trivia Game produced by USAopoly 2006.

Trio of *Rocky Horror Picture Show* action figures produced by Vital Toys in 2000.

Set designer Hugh Durrant's original 2012 miniature model for the 40th anniversary production of *The Rocky Horror Show*.

Frank-n-Furter rubber duck produced by Celebriducks.

'Talking' Frank-n-Furter doll produced in 2001 by Spencer Gifts in a limited run of 30,000 (with every fan hoping to find number 4711).

GALLERY

Rocky Horror Hearse produced by Eddie Stringer to promote touring productions of the show (photo: Eddie Stringer).

Riff Raff Statue, Hamilton, New Zealand (photo: David White).

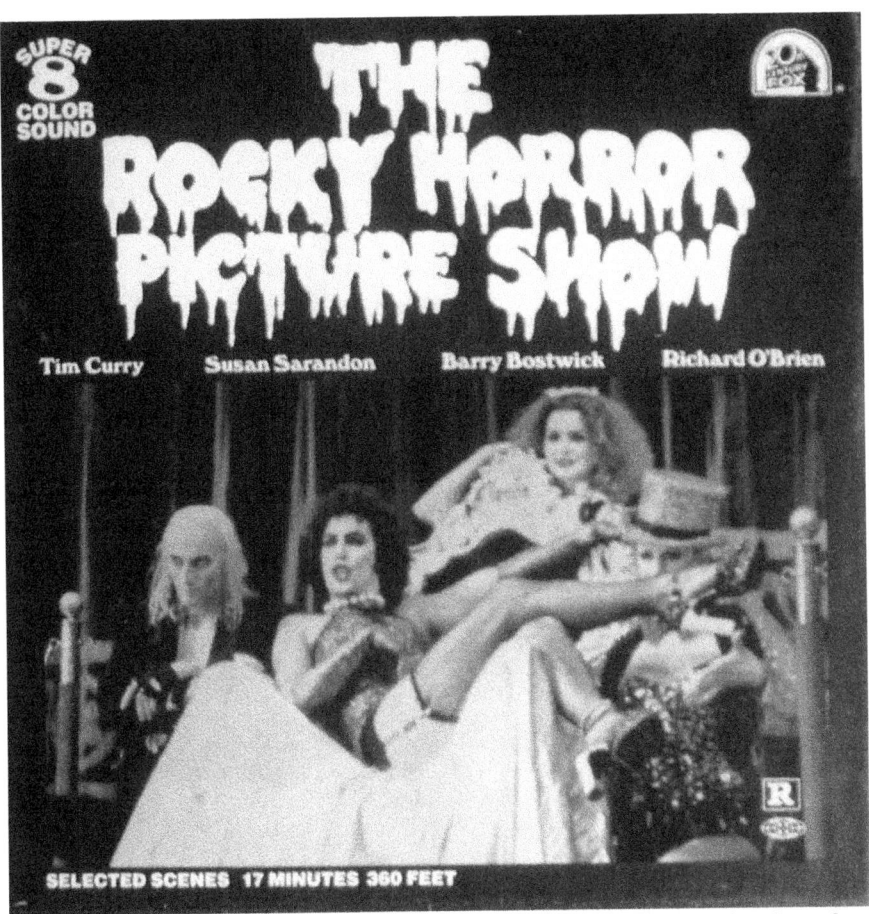

Blast from the past! *The Rocky Horror Picture Show* (or 17 minutes of it at least) on Super 8.

GALLERY

The Rocky Horror Picture Show on Betamax – UK 1984.

The Rocky Horror Picture Show Italian DVD 2011.

The Rocky Horror Picture Show German HD Blu-ray disc 2013.

GALLERY

A 2008 Japanese re-release of *The Rocky Horror Picture Show* on DVD.

The Rocky Horror Picture Show sample laserdisc release from Japan. 1985.

Index

2001: A Space Odyssey   134
20th Century Fox   95-97, 99, 109, 113, 117, 121-123, 126, 128, 170, 177, 179-180, 204-208, 226, 230, 241-242, 270, 323, 335, 354, 369-371, 373, 375, 383, 391, 426, 442
42nd Street   291
8th Street Playhouse, New York 164-165, 180, 185, 378
Abba   267
Abbott and Costello Meet Frankenstein 20
Abineri, Daniel   11, 88, 90, 158-161, 166-170, 212, 264, 267, 271, 327, 344, 395-396, 443
Abominable Dr Phibes, The   55
Absolute O'Brien   356
Absolutely Fabulous   231, 299
AC-DC   33
Ace Ventura: Pet Detective   366
Ackland-Snow, Terry   109, 111, 388, 441
Adams, Douglas   300
Adams, Jonathan   43, 57, 101, 104, 118, 137, 146, 150, 191, 233, 261, 352, 397-398, 441
Addams Family, The   184
Adler, Cisco   384
Adler, Lou   80-81, 84, 88, 90-91, 95-96, 100, 117, 122-124, 165-166, 173, 179-180, 206-208, 238, 242, 280-281, 299, 368-370, 383-384, 477
Adventures of Priscilla: Queen of the Desert, The   87, 348, 375
Adventures of Ulysses, The   103
Affleck, Ben   136
After Worlds Collide   136
Ahern, Andrew   425
Aladdin   182, 224, 331
Albery Theatre, London   92, 231
Alexander   301
Alexandra Theatre, Birmingham 185
Alien   134, 171, 414
All About Eve   74
Allen, Woody   24
Allman, Sheldon   32
Amadeus   392
Ambassador's Theatre, London 352
Amers, Gary   405
Amicus   102
Amzi, Nathan   151, 318
Andersen, Dominic   426
Andrews, Dana   30, 135
Andy Warhol's Frankenstein 391
Andy Warhol's Pigs   42
Angelou, Maya   233
Angels   76-77
Annie   392
Ansorge, Peter   56
Antony and Cleopatra   64
Apollo Theatre, Manchester 190
Apollo Victoria Theatre, London 232
Applause   74
Appleton, Xylona   362
Appleyard, Emma-Jayne   352
Are You Being Served?   141
Argento, Dario   175
Arkin, Alan   352
Armageddon   136
Armstrong, Brad   381-382
Armstrong, Louis   84
Arnold, Jack   19, 133-134, 244, 338
Arnold, Jenny   323
Arquette, David   14, 280
Arsenic and Old Lace   345
Arsenio Hall Show, The   285
Art of Illusion: Production Design for Film and Television, The   109, 441
Ash, Leslie   176
Ashes to Ashes   200
Ashford, Annaleigh   387
Ashley, Christopher   282, 284-285, 287-288, 291, 307, 338
Ashman, Howard   345-347
Askwith, Robin   22, 147
Aspel, Michael   306, 316
Astaire, Fred   377
Atherton, Julie   364

INDEX

Atkins, Matthew 425
Atlantic City 100
Atlas, Charles 53-55, 58, 71, 116, 187, 305, 307, 320, 323
Atwill, Lionel 32, 133
Avatar 408
Avenue Q 364
Avildsen, John G 100
Azaria, Hank 393
Babes in the Wood 136, 157, 182, 224, 399
Bacall, Lauren 72, 74-75
Bach, Sebastian 292
Bad Boy Johnny and the Prophets of Doom 344
Bad Girls 70
Badham, John 33
Bakaitis, Helmut 28
Baldwin, Alec 392
Ball, Alex 372
Ball, Michael 403, 406
Balmer, Edwin 136
Bande a Part 52
Barbarella 114
Bardo 183
Barnard, Paul 183, 189-190, 192, 197, 199-200
Barnes, Clive 288
Barry, Gene 136
Barry, Jeff 38
Barrymore, Drew 126
Barrymore, Lionel 275
Bartholomew, Ian 276
Bat Out of Hell 82, 434
Batman Begins 301-302
Bay, Michael 136
Bayliss, Peter 261-262
BBC 33, 43, 51, 70, 76-77, 83, 99, 101, 125, 141, 148, 163, 200, 231, 234-236, 240, 253-254, 264, 274, 302, 326, 329-330, 394, 414-415, 422, 428, 443
Beach Boys, The 33, 84, 349
Beacon Theatre, New York 241
Beast Must Die, The 102
Beatles, The 33, 36, 80, 351
Beaton, Alistair 233
Beckett, Samuel 120, 343

Bedden, Perry 54, 66-67, 79-80, 105-107, 124, 159, 167-168, 176, 240, 295, 419
Bedella, David 11, 142, 214, 221, 301-302, 304-305, 307-308, 311-312, 315-317, 321-327, 329, 332-333, 395-396, 420, 426, 428
Beetschen, Alex 363
Behind the Music 37, 129, 149, 211
Belasco Theatre, New York 122-124, 191, 279-281, 474
Belasco, David 122
Belgravia Theatre, London 36
Bell, Hazel K 216, 441
Bellman, Gina 235, 239
Benedict, Jay 74, 76, 78-79, 213, 399
Benighted 31
Berkley, Busby 40, 112
Berkoff, Steven 248
Berlin, Joey 393, 441
Berman, Gail 369, 384
Bernhardt, Sarah 46
Bertolucci, Bernado 146
Best of Tim Curry, The 392
Betty Blue 376
Beverly Hills Cop II 331
Beverly Hills, 90210 292
Beyond the Valley of the Dolls 52, 61, 95
Big Blue 376
Big Bopper 93
Big Brother 296
Biggins, Christopher 105, 146, 328-329, 396, 402, 404
Billington, Michael 146-147, 247, 249
Bionca 379
Birmingham Repertory Theatre 276
Bisson, Alexandre 37
Black Adder, The 234
Black Sabbath 33
Black, Don 300
Blackadder Goes Forth 234
Blackadder II 234
Blackeyes 235
Blackford, Richard 233
Blade Runner 344

510

Blair, Ian	38	Bray Studios	20, 97-98, 111, 416, 440
Blake, Jason	436-437		
Blake, Peter	11, 24, 92, 103-105, 137, 159-160, 212-213, 255, 257, 264-265, 268, 271, 290	Bread	274
		Breakfast, BBC	148, 326
		Brecht, Bertholt	24-25, 33
Blake, Susie	91-92	Brennan, Ian	370
Blatty, William Peter	34	Brenner, Michael	337
Bless Me Father	159	Bresslaw, Bernard	24
Blob, The	18-19	Brett, Laurie	277
Bloch, Robert	141	Bride of Frankenstein	30-31, 109, 114
Blood & Tinsel	44	Briggs, Raymond	163
Blood Brothers	183	Broadmore, Greg	408
Blue Angel, The	257	Broadway Bares	394
Blue Money	377	Broderick, Matthew	291
Blue Velvet	376	Brooks, Mel	109, 266, 291
Blue, Alektra	382	Brown, Carter	349-350, 353
Blues Brothers, The	376	Brown, Dave	251-252
Boheme, La	227, 285	Brown, Gaye	105
Bohr, Niels	287	Brown, Pendleton	166
Bolan, Marc	32, 59, 93, 240	Browne, Coral	54-55
Bond, Edward	37, 54, 343	Browning, Tod	20-21, 206
Bonner, Hilary	400	Bruce, Angela	24, 70, 76, 94
Bonnes, Les	48	Buck Rogers	132
Boom Crash Opera	269	Buddy Deane Show, The	53
Boot, Das	337	Buddy: The Buddy Holly Story	348
Bostwick, Barry	14, 33, 81, 100, 116, 118, 120, 151, 175, 241-242, 370, 372, 382, 386, 394	Buffy the Vampire Slayer	254, 257, 280, 372-373, 441
		Bugsy Malone	164
Bottom	235	Bundrick, John Douglas	96
Boulton, Sarah	324	Bunton, Emma	427
Bourton, Rayner	11, 41, 44, 58, 61-63, 66-69, 72, 82, 89-90, 103, 143, 146, 149-150, 152, 176, 189, 388, 394, 402, 404, 406, 439	Buntrock, Sam	337-342
		Burgess, Anthony	60
		Burke and Hare	330
		Burns, Keith	183
		Burroughs, Edgar Rice	350
Bowie, David	32, 58-59, 61, 64, 69, 88-89, 118, 158, 169, 267, 288, 399, 411	Burrow, Zalie	234-235, 237, 246-248, 251-253, 260-261, 264, 306, 356, 397
		Burt, Stuart	423
Bowles, Anthony	35	Burton, Richard	343
Boy George	220, 248	Burton, Tim	18, 226, 379
Boydon, Jon	272, 296	Butcher, Glenn	268
Boyle, Danny	360	Butterworth, Peter	24
Boyle, James	109	Bux, Ishaq	105
Boyzone	403	Byfield, Ziggy	11, 69-72, 74, 77-78, 84, 89-90, 92, 160, 176, 327, 336, 467-469, 496
Brad and Janet Show, The	172, 360, 362		
Bradbury, Ray	133		
Bradley, Tom	241	Byron, Tom	379
Brantley, Ben	288		
Brantley, Betsy	176		

INDEX

Cabaret 42, 191, 256
Cabinet of Dr Caligari, The 338
Caddyshack 347
Cage Aux Folles, La 227
Caine, Adam 241, 264
Calcutt, Stephen 105
Caldwell, Mark 41-42, 112
Cambridge Theatre, London 349
Cameron, James 170, 408
Cameron, Rhona 220
Cammell, Donald 97
Campbell, Nell 175, see also Little Nell
Campbell, Ross 45
Capra, Frank 133
Capsis, Paul 336
Carlson, Richard 133
Carlton, Bob 349, 352-353
Carney, Reeve 386, 388
Carpenter, Bekki 272
Carpenter, John 35, 134, 377
Carradine, John 338
Carrey, Jim 178, 366
Carrie 35
Carroll, Leo G 134
Carroll, Tamsin 336
Carry On Camping 147, 149, 290
Carry On Cowboy 23-24
Carry On Screaming 23
Carry On Sergeant 23
Casablanca 133, 242
Casey, Warren 33
Casino Royale 24
Casting the Runes 135
Cat People 113
Cats 183, 232, 275
Cattini, Clem 251-252, 259
Cavern, The 79
Cavett, Dick 216, 284-285, 330
Cecil, Hugh 105
Celebrity Mr & Mrs 256
Celestia Fox 102
Chaney Jr, Lon 20, 132
Channing, Dave 38
Chapman, Graham 300, 393
Chapters and Chances 85, 168
Charles, Thomas 37

Chbosky, Stephen 378
Cheech and Chong 80
Cheers 259
Chelton, Nick 232
Cher 384
Chesler, Josh 384
Cheyne, Michaela 389
Chicago 301
Chidzey, Ellie 273, 319
Chitty Chitty Bang Bang 127
Christie, Gillian 264
Christmas Carol, A 437
Chudleigh, Arthur 37
Churchill Theatre, Bromley 293
Cissone, Ceri-Lyn 339-340
Citizens Theatre, Glasgow 47-48, 63
Claire, Imogen 105, 176
Clarke, Warren 351
Clary, Julian 220
Clay, Nicholas 392
Cleese, John 300
Clerks 375
Client, The 100
Clifford, Clare 66, 75-76
Clifford, Graeme 118, 151, 416
Cline, Ernest 379
Clinton, Kate 292
Clive, Colin 20, 32
Clockwork Orange, A 60
Cochran, Eddie 44
Cocker, Joe 31
Coffee, Claire 372
Cold Case 371-372
Cole, Matt 321
Coleman, Jonathan 413
Coliseum Theatre, Oldham 166, 181, 481
Collette, Toni 377
Collins, Rufus 29, 105, 107, 176
Collins, Stephen 367-368
Coltrane, Robbie 161
Come Play With Me 146
Comedy Theatre, London 68, 77, 94, 150, 159-161, 167, 234, 244, 252, 267, 323, 337, 345, 356, 477
Comic Strip Presents..., The 163
Coming Home 407, 413, 443
Compo, Wally 346

Conde, Eduardo 91
Confessions of a Pop Performer 21
Congo 392
Connery, Sean 102, 136, 392
Connie and Carla 376
Conquest of Space 136
Conroy, Mike 172
Cook, Peter 300
Cooke, Sam 80
Cooper, Alice 32-33, 39, 59, 92, 288, 411
Cooper, Damien 336
Cooper, Ken 269
Cope, Rob 86, 142, 144, 194, 197, 214-215, 233-234, 237, 355
Copenhagen 287
Copperfield, David 161
Corman, Roger 126, 345-347, 441
Cornell, Mark 428
Coronation Street 92
Coronet Theatre, California 32
Corre, Sadie 105
Cortese, Shane 271
Cosco, Peter 389
Cosmic Light: The Birth of a Cult Classic 10, 45, 49, 73, 121, 123, 152, 439
Cousins, Robin 275, 402
Covington, Julie 14, 43-44, 47, 64
Cowan, Tony 105
Cox, Laverne 386-387, 389
Crabbe, Larry 'Buster' 132
Craven, Wes 280
Crawford, Dan 360
Crawford, Joan 32, 302, 411, 422
Creature from the Black Lagoon 133
Creeping Unknown, The 21
Cross of Iron 25
Crowe, Russell 14, 169, 344
Crowley, Tom 359-364, 366-368
Cruickshank, Harriet 47, 62
Crush, Bobby 189, 196-197
Crutchley, Jeremy 270
Cruz, Annie 382
Crystal Maze, The 237

Culture Club 162
Cure, the 163
Curry, Tim 11, 14, 24, 41-43, 45, 47-49, 51-52, 54, 63, 65, 71, 73-75, 81-84, 86, 89-90, 92-93, 96, 99, 101, 103, 107, 110, 112-115, 118, 120, 123, 125-126, 142, 160, 175, 234, 238, 240-242, 255, 258, 273-274, 286, 289-290, 295, 299, 302, 315-316, 330, 373-374, 377, 381, 387, 392-394, 400, 424, 474
Curse of Frankenstein, The 21-22, 109, 171, 320
Curse of the Demon, The 135
Curtiz, Michael 133
Cushing, Peter 21-23, 32, 34, 102, 127, 131, 144, 171, 288, 391
Da Vinci, Leonardo 107, 117, 283
Dainty, Paul 267, 269, 278, 336
Dale, David 185, 190
Dale, Jim 24
Dalton, Michael 271
Dalton, Timothy 126
Damiano, Gerard 60
Damien: Omen 2 170
Damned, the 163
Danesh, Darius 301
Daniels, Phil 176
Dark City 126
Dark Star 134
Daughter of Dr Jekyll 338
Davey, Iain 314
Davidson, Linda 236, 260
Davis, Bette 32, 74, 85-86, 168, 257, 302, 411, 422
Day After, The 163
Day of the Triffids, The 135, 338
Day the Earth Stood Still, The 9, 18, 35, 113, 131, 134, 339, 391
Day, Darren 14, 278, 304
De Gaulle, Charles 98
De Laurentiis, Dino 103, 126, 390
De Palma, Brian 34, 175, 177, 205
De Young, Cliff 118, 175, 361
Deacon, Charles 182, 191, 195, 198
Dead Man Walking 100

INDEX

Dean, James — 388
Dear John — 264
Death and the Maiden — 343
Debbie Does Dallas — 149
Deegan, Craig — 229
Deegan, Tim — 205-207
Deep Impact — 136
Deep Throat — 60
Defending the Caveman — 365
Dekker, Albert — 179
DeLaria, Lea — 285, 318
Dempsey, John — 347
Denberg, Susan — 144
Deneuve, Catherine — 118
Dennis, David — 271
Denton, Martin — 291
Depp, Johnny — 18, 276
Derr, Richard — 136
Derrickson, Scott — 391
Devenie, Stuart — 269
Devil Rides Out, The — 102
Devine, George — 37
Devlin, Johnny — 44
Diamond, Gillian — 41
Diamonds Are Forever — 102
Dick Whittington — 224
Dickens, Charles — 45, 184, 409, 420, 437
Dietrich, Marlene — 257, 275, 340
Diffring, Anton — 102
Dirtiest Show in Town, The — 38
Dirty Dancing — 384
Disaster — 352
Disgracefully Yours — 356, 464
Disney — 24, 32, 331, 384, 390
Ditko, Steve — 25
Divine — 206
Dobell, Linda — 76
Doctor Strange — 25
Doctor Who — 210, 221, 266, 342, 372
Doctor X — 27, 133
Don Giovanni — 51
Don, Robin — 232, 239, 249, 271, 276, 429
Donnelly, Jamie — 81, 123, 130

Donovan, Jason — 14, 170, 269, 276-278, 301, 328, 350, 435-437
Donovan, Terence — 350
Dorfman, Ariel — 343
Douglas, Angela — 24
Douglas, Michael — 200
Downey-Dent, Lisa Theresa — 367
Dr Cyclops — 179
Dr Strangelove — 150, 285, 318, 354, 426
Dracula — 20-22, 34, 130, 147, 240, 338, 415
Drake, Jessica — 381
Drew Carey Show, The — 374
Driscoll, Geoff — 77, 252-253
Drop Dead Delores — 353
Du Prez, John — 393
Duke of York's Theatre, London — 274-275, 294, 304, 447
Duran Duran — 162
Durrant, Hugh — 424, 426, 429, 436, 500
Dutton, Charles S — 378
Dylan, Bob — 73
Earth Versus the Flying Saucers — 339
EastEnders — 236, 274, 404
Eastwood, Clint — 134, 142
Ed Wood — 18
Eddie's Teddy — 70-71, 273, 335, 460
Edmondson, Adrian — 175, 235-236, 248, 260, 327, 403, 406, 427
Edward Penishands — 379
Edwards, Gale — 336, 338
Edwards, Jack — 341, 352
Egerton, Taron — 415
Egnos, Bertha — 271
Eight Legged Freaks — 281
Eisenstein, Sergei — 32
Ekland, Britt — 80
Ellacott, Vivyan — 181-183, 199
Elliott, Stephan — 348
Ellis-Stanton, Chris — 339, 352
Elvira — 126-127
Elvira: Mistress of the Dark — 126
Elvira's Haunted Hills — 126-127
Embassy Theatre, Hamilton — 18, 22, 407
Emden, Walter — 36-37

Emick, Jarrod	283, 288-289	Fischer, Stephen	183
Emmanuelle	146	Fisher, Sarah	256
Empire Strikes Back, The	299	Fisher, Terrence	144
Endgame	343	Fitzgerald, Ella	352
English Stage Company	37, 343	Fitzgibbon, Martin	38
English, Michael	68, 87, 121, 123, 183, 195, 237, 351	Fitzpatrick, Kate	29, 86, 352
		Flaherty, Haley	325, 420, 426
Enton, Boni	81, 123	*Flash Gordon Conquers the Universe*	132
Eskimo Nell	146	*Flash Gordon*	114, 119, 132, 237
Esparza, Raul	285, 292		
Esplanade Theatre, Singapore	420	*Flash Gordon's Trip To Mars*	132
Essex-Spurrier, Julian	317, 320, 324	*Flesh for Frankenstein*	391
Estefan, Gloria	384	*Flesh Gordon Meets The Cosmic Cheerleaders*	83
Estevez, Emilio	393		
Evans, David	63, 238, 350, 439	*Flesh Gordon*	379
		Fletcher, Dexter	415
Evans, Edith	189	*Flock of Seagulls*	162
Evening with Richard O'Brien, An	409	Fonda, Henry	136
Ever After: A Cinderella Story	126	*Forbidden Planet*	134, 349
Everett, Rupert	140	*Forrest Gump*	40
Evergreen	46	Forrest, Brett	160
Everyman Theatre, Liverpool	349	Forster, Ben	421, 426
Evita	44	Forum Theatre, Wythenshawe	482
Exorcist, The	34-35	Fosse, Bob	40
Eyen, Tom	38, 46	Fowler, Rob Morton	338, 343
Eyre, Judith	184	Fox, Julie	197, 461-462, 473
Faiers, Meryl	432		
Faithful, Marianne	45-46, 185	Fox, Robert	161
Falchuk, Brad	370	Francis, Anne	134
Fame	40, 164-165, 180, 185, 363, 370, 376, 378	Francis, Freddie	135
		Frankenstein and the Monster from Hell	391
Fangoria	171-173, 442	*Frankenstein Created Woman*	144
Farese, Louis	207	*Frankenstein Sings*	32, 370
Farley, David	338-339	*Frankenstein*	20-21, 31, 109-110, 130, 145, 147, 171, 205, 392, 440
Farrell, Joanne	404		
Farrow, John	195, 197-198	Franks, Philip	421
Fearless	392	Franzen, Maria	339-340
Feldman, Marty	109	Fraser, Antonia	56
Female Trouble	206	Fraser, David	269
Fenn Street Gang, The	261	*Freaks*	20, 206
Ferguson, Craig	260-261	Frederick's of Hollywood	40, 54
Ferguson, Dale	336	Freeman, David	230-231, 469-471
Ferguson, Tim	278		
Ferris Bueller's Day Off	384	Freeman, Stephanie	226, 275, 304, 416-417
Fighting Prince of Donegal, The	24		
Fillinger, Johan	91	French, Dawn	161
Film Talk	42, 112	*Fridays*	374
Filthy Rich and Catflap	235	Friedkin, William	34

INDEX

Frift, Dick 111
Front, Rebecca 376
Frost, Nick 376
Fry, Stephen 300, 427
Fullenwider, Fran 105
Funky-Fetish Horror Show 380
Gallagher, Leigh 301
Gallagher, Pete 365
Gambon, Michael 102
Garbo, Greta 40
Gardner, Ava 40, 103
Gardner, Elysa 289
Gardner, Kinny 397
Garland, Judy 106, 424
Garr, Teri 109
Gaskill, Bill 54
Gasteyer, Ana 292
Gately, Stephen 403, 406
Gatiss, Mark 415
Gaultier, Jean Paul 40, 240
Gay Time TV 220
Gellar, Sarah Michelle 373
Genet, Gene 48
Gere, Richard 33
Ghostbusters 347
Giedroyc, Mel 427
Gilbert and Sullivan 392
Gilbert, W S 36
Gilbert, W Stephen 53, 351
Girls on Top 161
Giuliani, Rudolph 288, 292
Give the Gaffers Time to Love You 42-43
Glee 370-371, 383, 390
Glitter, Gary 59, 90, 269
Godard, Jean Luc 52
Godspell 26, 43, 97, 127, 183, 261
Goldstone, John 148
Golem, Der 338
Good, Ian 235, 251
Goodfellas 177
Gordon-Watkins, Andrew 339
Gottfried, Gilbert 293, 331
Grabham, Mick 95
Graf, Sabrina 414
Graham, Marcus 269
Graham, Zack 371

Gray, Charles 02-103, 119, 137, 174, 196, 216
Grease Live! 383
Grease 33-34, 64, 81, 91, 100, 127, 164, 169, 236, 297, 383, 421
Great Rock 'n' Roll Swindle, The 236
Greene, David 97
Greenwood, Joan 161
Gregory, Frank 166
Greiff, Simon 425
Griffith, Charles B 345
Griffiths, Derek 77-79, 90, 93, 251-253, 263, 265
Griffiths, John 269
Groening, Matt 161
Grosund, Kari Ann 91
Grundy, Rachel 426
Grundy, Sydney 37
Guillermin, John 391
Gulliver's Travels 179
Hair 24-29, 41-43, 49, 51, 64-65, 69-70, 74, 78, 84, 88, 92, 181, 232, 268, 340, 399, 438, 442
Hairspray Live! 383
Hairspray 53, 348, 370, 388
Hale, Rachel 271
Haley, Bill 33, 58, 61
Halloween 2 (2009) 377
Halloween (1978) 35
Hall-Say, Richard 97
Hamlet 30, 154, 160, 308
Hammer 20-24, 35, 97-98, 102, 105, 109, 131, 135, 146, 148, 171, 232, 288, 320, 341, 388, 391, 414-415, 429, 440
Hammerstein II, Oscar 27, 31, 33, 262, 275, 334
Hampson, Julia 261
Hampstead Theatre, London 233
Haness, Abigail 81
Hanks, Tom 40
Hanley Theatre Royal, London 181-185, 189-190, 194-199, 229-230, 232, 246-247, 249-251, 429, 451, 459-463
Hardaker, Julie 414

Harders, Jane — 29, 86
Hargreaves, Roger — 184
Harmer, Dani — 422
Harper, Jessica — 175, 177, 361-362
Harriott, Ainsley — 330
Harris, Drew Scott — 302
Harry, Debbie — 88
Harryhausen, Ray — 339
Hartley, Dori — 142
Hartley, Richard — 35, 38, 45-46, 57, 95-96, 104-105, 122, 165, 167, 171, 179, 199, 206, 233, 243, 252-253, 267, 271, 277, 286, 299, 306, 349-353, 357, 361, 363, 367-368, 389, 425, 432
Haskin, Byron — 135
Hawkins, Jack — 102
Hawks, Howard — 114
Hawtrey, Charles — 24
Hayworth, Rita — 257
Haze, Jonathan — 345
Head, Anthony — 11, 14, 254-262, 264, 275, 294, 328, 344, 398, 403, 406, 427, 443, 496-497
Hear'Say — 303
Hedwig and the Angry Inch — 153, 227, 301, 303, 336, 344
Held, Zeus B — 261
Hello Dolly — 291
Helpmann, Robert — 127
Hendrix, Jimi — 33
Henkin, Bill — 270, 439
Hennebry, Roger — 409
Henry, Lenny — 161
Henson, Jim — 45
Herman, Jerry — 291
Hermine — 37
Herring, Richard — 376
Hess, Michael — 374, 439
Heston, Charlton — 202
Hewitt, Tom — 285-286, 289, 291-292
Hieber, Ingeborg — 271
High School Musical — 384, 390
Highpoint Theatre, Johannesburg — 270
Hillyer, Terence — 160
Hine, Ceris — 324, 423, 436
Hinwood, Peter — 103, 388

Hirschhorn, Clive — 249
His Majesty's Theatre, Auckland — 327
Hitchcock, Alfred — 120, 140
Hitchhikers Guide to the Galaxy, The — 300
Hocus Pocus — 384
Hodges, Mike — 126
Hoffman, Dustin — 42, 104
Holby City — 302, 396
Holden, William — 113
Holly, Buddy — 33, 93, 162, 348
Holmes, Steve — 380
Home Alone 2: Lost in New York — 392
Home and Away — 267
Hope, Julian — 160, 165
Hopper, Tobe — 34
Hopps, Stuart — 246
Horn, Trevor — 231, 299
Horror of Dracula, The — 22
Horror of Frankenstein, The — 145
House of Usher — 126
House of Wax — 55
House on Haunted Hill — 55
Howcroft, Michael — 419-420
Howson, Julia — 184
Hudson, Rock — 245
Hughes, John — 392
Hughes, Laura Leigh — 372
Humphries, Barry — 28, 71, 174, 360-361, 429
Hunger, The — 118
Hunniford, Gloria — 189
Hunt for Red October, The — 392
Hunt, Gareth — 259
Hunter, Nicki — 382
Husebo, Knut — 91
Huston, Anjelica — 126
Hyland, Rosanna — 366
I Walked With a Zombie — 113
I Was a Teenage Frankenstein — 18
I Was a Teenage Werewolf — 18
I'm Sorry, The Bridge is Out, You'll Have to Spend the Night — 32
Ian, David — 191, 299
Ice, Csoky — 380
Idle, Eric — 300, 393
Importance of Being Earnest, The — 300
Ingram, Lindsay — 105
Inigo Pipkin — 45

INDEX

Inman, John	141, 255
International Velvet	159
Into the Woods	262
Invasion of the Saucer Men	18
Invisible Boy, The	134
Invisible Man Returns, The	20
Invisible Man, The	20, 31, 132
iOTA	336
Ipi N'tombi	271
Irvin, Sam	126
Isherwood, Charles	287, 289
Istvan, Kovi	380
It Came from Outer Space	19, 133, 136
It	392
Ivan the Terrible Part 1	32
Jabara, Paul	29, 103-104, 143
Jackson, Michael	200, 384
Jackson, Peter	391, 408, 440
Jackson, Samuel L	376, 393
Jacobs, Jaye	396
Jacobs, Jim	33
Jagger, Mick	45, 62, 64, 96, 373, 411
James, M R	135
James, Sid	24
Jan and Dean	80
Jarman, Derek	103
Jarvis, Graham	81-82, 123
Jaye, Abigail	422
Jaymson, Drew	296
Jeremy, Ron	382
Jerry Springer: The Opera	301, 303, 322
Jessop, Simon	354
Jesus Christ Superstar	26, 28-29, 35, 45, 69, 84, 88, 91-92, 103, 106, 127, 143, 183, 232, 421
Jett, Joan	14, 284-286
Jodorowsky, Alexandro	206
Joe	100
John, Elton	415
Johnson, Darlene	174
Johnson, Dave	90
Johnson, Tor	338
Jones, Alan	86, 270
Jones, Katie Rowley	296
Jones, Richard	262
Jones, Tommy Lee	377
Joseph and the Amazing Technicolor Dreamcoat	26, 29, 92, 181, 194, 269
Joseph, Jackie	346
Jubilee	126, 210, 404
Jude, Tom	354
Julissa	91
Justice, Victoria	386, 388
Kahn, Madeline	109
Karloff, Boris	20-21, 31-32, 91, 145, 381
Kaye, Ivan	260
Kearney, Stephen	268
Keel, Howard	135
Keeler, Ruby	50, 145, 240
Keister, George	122
Kelly, Gene	384
Kelly, Gerard	330
Kelly, Kristen Lee	285
Kemp, Lindsay	47
Kennedy, Gordon	240, 397
Kenneth More Theatre, Ilford	181, 183, 443
Kenright, Bill	181
Kent, Trevor	87
Kenzie, Phil	96, 252
Kermode, Mark	358
Kern, Jerome	31, 262
Kerr, Ben	364, 367, 426
Key, John	413
Kick Up the Eighties, A	161
Kier, Udo	391
Kilborn, Craig	260
Kiley, Jonathan	193, 199
Kimi and Ritz	70
King Kong	9, 30, 113, 133, 217, 390, 408, 428, 440
King Lear	238
King	233
King, Carole	88
King, Jonathan	61
King, Ross	278
King, Stephen	34, 392
King's Head Theatre Pub, London	358, 368
King's Road Theatre	10, 67, 74-77, 89, 91, 103, 106, 110, 158-159, 210, 234, 244, 281, 400, 446, 474-475

Kingsley, Ben	343	Lefevre, Robin	233, 246, 250, 263-264, 306
Kiss	91		
Kneale, Nigel	21, 364	*Legend*	393
Knights, Will	426	Lei, Kaylani	382
Koga, Yuzuro	89-90	Leicester Square Theatre, London	329
Kops, Jade	436	Lembeck, Michael	376
Kramer vs Kramer	172	Lennon, John	339
Kramer, Jonathan	42	Leone, Sergio	114
Kristel, Sylvia	146	Lerman, Logan	378
Kubrick, Stanley	60, 134, 150	Lerman, Rachel	360
Kuchwara, Michael	289	Leroux, Gaston	205
La Rue, Danny	90	*Let's Do the Time Warp Again*	33, 43, 51, 83, 99, 101, 125, 229, 383, 390, 394, 443
Labow, Hilary	107, 174		
LaCause, Sebastian	284	*Lethal Weapon*	393
Lacey, Rebecca	276	Levan, Ivy	385
Ladd Jr, Alan	122	Leventon, Annabelle	105
Lake Placid 3	422	Lewington, Bill	49
Lakier, Gail	271	Lewis, Jerry	137
Lambert, Adam	387-388	Lewis, Jerry Lee	349
Lamont, Nic	365	Licorish, Vicky	260, 262
Lanchester, Elsa	114, 156, 205	*Life of Shakespeare*	392
Landis, John	330	*Life on Mars*	200
Lane, Carla	274	Linder-Lee, Sophie	426
Lane, Kara	130, 156, 220, 306, 317, 323, 325-326, 333, 395	*Little Britain*	254, 256
		Little Eva	53
Lane, Nathan	291	Little Nell	45, 50, 54, 57, 62-63, 68, 88, 98-99, 103, 108, 124, 175, 210-211, 236, 240-242, 284, 290, 325, 387, 394, 403-404, 406
Lang, Belinda	276		
Langley, Amanda	230		
Langton, Diane	176, 351		
Lansbury, Angela	72, 262	*Little Richard*	18, 33, 42, 44
Larson, Jonathan	227, 285	*Little Shop of Horrors*	300, 345, 347, 388, 441
Last Tango in Paris	146		
Late Late Show, The	260	Little, Mark	365, 367
Laurie, Hugh	300	Littman, Julian	351, 354
Lavercombe, Kristian	387, 418-419, 423, 426, 430-431, 435	Livermore, Reg	84-87, 90, 168, 239, 257, 268, 441
		Lloyd Webber, Andrew	26, 29, 44, 181, 183, 194, 232, 269, 277, 300, 421
Law, Colin	271		
Lawrence, Sophie	274, 365, 404	Lloyd, Judy	89-90, 466-467
Leachman, Cloris	109	Lloyd, Mike	198
League of Gentlemen, The	329-330	Lochhead, Liz	360
Leakey, Phil	21	Logan, Andrew	79
Ledger, Peggy	105	London Palladium	127, 262, 269
Lee, Christopher	21-23, 34, 102, 109, 127, 131, 145, 240, 352	Long, William Ivey	291, 388
		Longden, Robert	103
Lee, Julie	372	Longmore, Jeffrey	166, 181-182, 189
Lee, Stan	25		
Lee, Stewart	301		

INDEX

Look Back in Anger 37, 343, 401, 406
Lord of the Rings 408
Lorenzo's Oil 100
Loriggio, Pauline 249
Lovegrove, Neil 271
Lowe, Arthur 159
Lubin, Arthur 133
Lucan, Arthur 140
Lucas, George 60, 119, 266, 420
Lugosi, Bela 18, 20, 22, 140
Luscombe, Christopher 130, 154-155, 218, 221, 225, 227, 293, 300-301, 303-319, 321-327, 332, 334, 338-339, 341-342, 357, 402, 418-419, 423-425, 429, 431, 436-437, 480
Lustgarten, Edgar 43, 57, 102, 138, 192, 296, 328, 354, 421, 429
Lydon, John 236
Lynch, Jane 371
Lynch, Julie 336
Lyric Theatre, Sydney 348
MacArthur, Jeanie 89-90
MacDermot, Galt 24
Mackintosh, Cameron 160, 345
MacNeil, Colin 49
Macpherson, Tricia 269
Maddox, Mary 240, 247, 254
Madonna 40, 240
Maids, The 48
Malcolm, Christopher 43, 51, 81, 88-90, 99, 104, 159, 176, 231, 248, 250, 255, 259, 261, 263-264, 267, 269-272, 276-277, 282, 295-300, 306, 336, 352, 466, 469
Malekzad, Hannah 426
Mamas & the Papas 80
Mamma 37
Man from U.N.C.L.E., The 134
Mann, Terrence 292
Manning, Amanda-Jane 272
Manson, Marilyn 369
Mapa, Alec 376
Marcello, Vince 347
Marlowe, Christopher 186, 199, 392
Mars, Antony 37
Marsh, Kym 303
Marshall, Jocelyn 409
Marvel Comics 25, 442
Mary Queen of Scots Got Her Head Chopped Off 360
Mates, Rudolph 136
Matthews, Jessie 46
Matthews, Paul 278
Maurey, Nicole 135
Mayall, Rik 161, 175, 248
Mays, Jayma 370-371
Mazursky, Paul 185, 376
McCartan, Ryan 386, 388
McCaul, Neil 89, 159, 161, 400, 469, 474
McCormack, Eric 403
McDowell, Roddy 103
McGhie, Penelope 261
McHugh, Dion 166
McInnerny, Tim 234-236, 240, 249-250, 253-255, 258
McKay, Sinclair 20, 440
McKinley, Philip William 347
McLachlan, Craig 14, 267-269, 328, 429, 436-437
McLaren, Malcolm 88, 237
McLean, Don 93
McNamara, Des 89
McShane, Ian 392
Meads, Glenn 322
Meat Loaf 14, 24, 82, 88, 90, 93, 96, 101, 110, 116-117, 123, 126-127, 151, 241, 285, 302, 370, 373-374, 394, 434-435, 441
Meek, Richard 324, 333, 420-421, 426
Melanie C 421
Mellinger, Frederick 40
Men in Black 2 377
Men in Black 377
Mendelssohn, Felix 95
Menkin, Alan 345
Mercury, Freddie 245, 387
Merman, Ethel 40
Merry, Sue 118
Metal Mickey 176
Metalious, Grace 51
Meteor 136
Meyer, Russ 52, 95

MGM	40, 134, 208, 349, 377
Miami Vice	200
Michaels, Scott	63, 238, 328, 439
Michelangelo	109, 112
Middleton, Charles	132
Midler, Bette	384
Midnight Cowboy	42
Midnight Express	164
Midnight Movies: From the Margin to the Mainstream	99, 104, 117-118, 125, 156, 208, 442
Midsummer Night's Dream, A	95, 107
Mighty Joe Young	113
Milford, Kim	82, 103, 166
Milian, Christina	386, 388
Miller, Barry	164
Miller, Bill	81
Miller, Dick	346
Miller, Ezra	378
Miller, George	374
Miller, Harry M	84
Millerchip, Sharon	336
Millington, Mary	146, 441
Milner, Anthony	105
Milton Keynes Theatre	405
Minchin, Tim	421
Minogue, Kylie	170, 277
Miserables, Les	183, 232
Miss Saigon	183, 349
Mistress Tantala	380
Moase, Robyn	350
Moffat, Steven	415
Monster Mash	32, 349, 370
Montague, Joel	422
Monteath, Stephanie	230
Monterey International Pop Festival	80
Monty Python and the Holy Grail	393
Monty Python	126, 300, 393, 441
Moon, Keith	96
Moore, Kieron	135
Mora, Philippe	352
Morley, Robert	167
Morley, Wilton	167, 169-170, 267
Morricone, Ennio	244
Morris, Jonathon	274, 365
Morrisoe, Patricia	30, 35, 39, 47, 49-50, 221
Morrison, Matthew	370
Morrissey, Paul	42, 391
Moss, Pete	271
Mother Earth	69
Mother Goose	303
Moyle, Allan	393
Mozart	51, 148, 392
Mr Men	184
Mr Smith Goes to Washington	133
Muldoon, Robert	170, 327
Mummy, The	20
Muppet Treasure Island	392
Murnau, F W	52, 338, 342
Murphy, Ryan	370
Murray, Al	376
Murray, Bill	347
Murray, Larissa	271
Myron	109
National Lampoon's Loaded Weapon 1	393
National Velvet	159
Ned Kelly	97
Neighbours	170, 267, 269, 277, 365
Neill, Sam	392
New Rocky Horror Show, The	267, 277
New Starlight Express, The	277
New York Dolls	33
Newman, William	123
News Boys, The	384
Newsies	384
Newson, Jeremy	107, 174
Newton-John, Olivia	127, 384
Next to Normal	291
Nicholas, Anna	76
Nicholas, Paul	26, 351
Nichols, Mike	393
Nicholson, Jack	175, 347
Nico Theatre, Cape Town	270
Nielsen, Leslie	134
Night of the Demon	135
Night of the Living Dead	108, 207
Nightmare on Elm Street, A	146
Nijimy, Kathy	384
Niven, David	24
Nixon, Richard Milhous	119

INDEX

Noh, Caroline 75, 397
Nolan, Christopher 301
Norton-Hale, Robin 360
Norve, Ivor 91
Nosferatu 52, 338, 342, 400
Not I 120
O'Brien, Richard 10-11, 16, 23-30, 32-36, 38-47, 49-54, 56-58, 61, 68-71, 77, 81, 83, 85-86, 88, 91-93, 97, 99, 103-105, 107-108, 112, 114-117, 119-121, 123-129, 131-132, 135-139, 142-145, 147-150, 152, 154-158, 160, 162, 166, 169, 171-179, 184-185, 187, 190, 194-198, 200, 203, 206, 210-211, 214-215, 217-218, 220-223, 225, 227, 230-231, 233-234, 237-238, 240, 241-243, 246, 249-250, 253, 255, 260-261, 264, 266-268, 270, 272, 277, 281-282, 287-288, 290, 293, 298-301, 304-305, 308-310, 312, 322-326, 328, 331-332, 337, 341-342, 344, 349-359, 361-363, 365, 367-372, 376-377, 382-386, 388-390, 392, 395, 399-414, 417-420, 423-427, 432, 435-436, 439-440, 442-443, 450, 464, 470-471, 494
O'Brien, Willis 133
O'Dea, Judith 108
O'Grady, Paul 326
O'Hagan, Paddy 45, 54, 57, 70, 73, 150
O'Hennessy, Ross 271
O'Neill, Karyn 187
O'Sullivan, Kate 235, 247, 251-253, 260-262, 264, 356, 397
O'Toole, Fintan 289
O'Toole, Peter 24
Oakley Court 97-98, 108, 111, 117, 227, 405, 415-417, 441, 450, 454, 470
Obermeyer, Pamela 105
Odyssey, The 103
Oh! Calcutta! 26, 38, 68, 122
Oklahoma 27
Old Curiosity Shop, The 45
Old Dark House, The 31
Old Mother Riley Meets the Vampire 140
Oliver Twist 184
Olivia! 184
Olivier, Ernest 98, 108
On The Buses 20
One Hundred and one Dalmatians 32
Only Fools and Horses 70, 299
Open Air Theatre, London 262
Opportunity Knocks 189
Orange is the New Black 386
Orpheum Theatre, New York 345
Orr, Mary 74
Ortega, Kenny 384, 386, 389
Ortiz, Hector 91
Orton, Joe 141
Osborne, Charles 249
Osborne, John 37, 343
Osborne, Stan 22, 408
Osbourne, Ozzy 189
Osmond, Jimmy 41, 90
Othello 251
Otto & Windsor Ltd 100
Oxley, Mateo 366
Oz, Frank 346-347
Paddick, Hugh 141
Paige, Elaine 64
Pal Joey 231
Pal, George 73, 135-136
Palace Theatre, London 26, 45, 106, 394, 422
Palace Theatre, Manchester 297, 425, 434, 459
Pallett, Roxanne 422
Pankhurst, Christabel 70
Panter, Howard 231, 248, 250, 265, 276, 282, 299-300, 336-337, 421, 428
Papillon, Francois 380
Paragon, John 126
Parker, Alan 164, 180, 376, 378
Parker, Sarah Jessica 384
Parren, Chris 90
Pars, Ole 91
Parsons, Nicholas 14, 274, 277, 327
Paul O'Grady Show, The 326
Pavilion Theatre, Glasgow 185
Payne, Laurence 184
Peckinpah, Sam 25

Pecorino, Paul 273
Pegg, Simon 375, 377
Pemberton, Steve 329-330, 402
Penn & Teller 293
Peo, Samantha 271
Perez de Tagle, Anna Maria 378
Performance 97, 127
Perkins, Anthony 140
Perks of Being a Wallflower, The 378
Perlman, Rhea 259
Perry, Luke 292
Peter Pan Live! 383
Peterson, Cassandra 126
Peterson, Roger 93
Peterson, Wolfgang 337
Pettigrew, Yasmin 43, 50, 74-75, 76
Peyton Place 51, 150
Phantom of the Opera, The 68, 132, 184, 205, 232
Phantom of the Paradise 127, 175, 178, 205-206
Phipps, Max 87
Phoenix Theatre, London 262
Phoenix, River 276
Piccadilly Theatre, London 232, 232-235, 237, 239, 242, 244, 246-247, 249-250, 252, 254-255, 257, 259-265, 271, 292, 397, 403, 448-450
Pickett, Bobby 'Boris' 31-32, 349
Pidgeon, Walter 134
Pierce, David Hyde 393
Pink Flamingos 206
Pipkins 45
Pirates of Penzance, The 392
Piro, Sal 165, 176-177, 180, 230, 241-242, 374, 390, 439
Pit and the Pendulum, The 126
Plan 9 from Outer Space 18, 344
Planer, Nigel 276
Planet of the Apes 170
Playbirds, The 146
Playhouse Theatre, London 426-427
Playhouse Theatre, Nottingham 24
Please Sir! 261
Poe, Edgar Allan 126
Polanski, Roman 343
Pop Idol 301

Pop, Iggy 88
Popstars 301, 303
Pornocchio 379
Porter, Christopher 238-239, 431-434
Porter, Garth 269
Porter, Loraine 181, 199
Poseidon Adventure, The 95
Potter, Dennis 235
Presley, Elvis 18, 23, 27, 29, 33, 44, 50, 70, 79, 93-94, 145, 162, 169, 184, 388, 405-406
Price, Stuart Matthew 339, 342
Price, Vincent 20, 55, 57, 127, 354, 390
Priestley, J B 31
Prima Donna 183
Prince Charles Cinema, London 231, 469
Priscilla: Queen of the Desert 87, 167, 348, 422
Procol Harum 95-96
Producers, The 291, 388
Prokofiev, Sergei 434
Prowse, David 145, 391
Proyas, Alex 126
Psycho 140, 341
Psychoville 329-330
Pulp Fiction 376
Quadrophenia 176
Quatermass Experiment, The 21
Queen 88, 245, 387
Queen's Theatre, Hornchurch 352-354
Queen's Theatre, London 295, 452-453
Quigley, Bill 206, 208
Quinn, Patricia 11, 46, 49, 55, 57, 70, 76, 81, 93-94, 99, 103-104, 107-108, 111, 114, 121, 124, 130, 175, 179, 211, 241, 265, 274-275, 290, 326, 352, 355, 365, 394, 403, 406, 415, 442, 470-471
Rabbit 96
Rado, James 24
Ragni, Gerome 24
Rains, Claude 20, 30, 55, 132, 314
Ramirez, Sara 393
Ramones, The 33
Randall's Thumb 36

INDEX

Raphael, Sally Jessy   293, 331
Raven, The   126
Ray, Man   120
Raymond, Alex   126, 237
Read My Lips   392
Reade, Walter   206, 208
Ready Player One   379
Ready Player Two   379
Reagan, Ronald   163, 200, 374
Real Life   268
Rebecca   184
Reckford, Barry   42
Red Barn Theatre, Florida   347
Red Dwarf   70, 240
Redman, Amanda   160
Redwood, Manning   174
Reed, Lou   31-32, 89, 158, 262
Reed, Rocco   381
Reeves, Keanu   391
Reeves, Paul   251, 264
Reeves, Steve   50, 144, 340
Regent Theatre, Stoke-on-Trent   198, 294, 303
Removalists, The   37
Renet, Sinitta   176
Rennie, Michael   30, 55, 131, 391
Rent   227, 285
Repo: The Genetic Opera   344
Resistible Rise of Arturo Ui, The   24, 33, 155
Return of Captain Invincible, The   352
Revenge of Frankenstein, The   135
Revenge of the Old Queen   354-356
Rhys-Davies, Adam   365
Rice, Tim   26, 29, 44, 181, 269
Richard III   32
Richard, Cliff   163, 278
Richardson, Jiles Perry   93
Richardson, Tony   63, 97
Richie, Shane   276
Rietty, Robert   102
Riley, Gina   268
Ripley, Alice   283, 288-291
RKO   108, 113, 133, 243, 337, 408, 418
Robbins, Tim   100
Robb-King, Peter   121, 393
Roberts, Rhydian   421
Robertson, Wybrow   37
Robin Hood   240
Robinson, Ann   137
Rock Horroar   39
Rock Horror Show   91
Rock, Mick   88, 351, 439
Rocketman   415
Rocki Whore Picture Show: A Hardcore Parody, The   381, 383
Rockwell, David   283-284
Rocky Horror Birthday Show, The   368
Rocky Horror Double Feature Video Show, The   96, 98, 110
Rocky Horror Picture Show, The   417, 424, 439-440, 442-443, 454, 469, 499, 503-507
Rocky Horror Picture Show: Let's Do The Time Warp Again, The   383, 390
Rocky Horror Show, The   9-16, 19, 28, 31-32, 38-39, 41, 43-44, 48, 51, 53, 55, 57, 59-64, 67, 73-74, 76-78, 80-81, 84, 87-91, 93-97, 100-101, 103-104, 110, 114, 122, 124, 129, 131, 134, 143, 146-147, 149, 153, 157-159, 161-162, 165-166, 169, 174-176, 180-185, 189-190, 193-194, 196, 198, 200-203, 210-211, 215-220, 222-225, 227, 229-233, 236, 238-239, 244, 246, 249, 252-255, 259, 262-264, 266-271, 276-277, 279-282, 284, 287-289, 291-292, 294-295, 297, 299, 302-303, 306, 311, 323-324, 327-329, 336, 340, 344-345, 348, 350-353, 356-357, 359, 362, 364-366, 368, 370-371, 380, 386, 389-391, 394, 396-397, 399-402, 404-405, 407, 412-413, 419, 421-425, 428-429, 431, 434, 436-439, 442, 445, 447-449, 453-456, 458, 467, 474, 497-498, 500
Rocky Horror Show: As I Remember It, The   41, 143, 149, 439
Rocky Horror Shows His Heels   171, 173, 175-176, 355-356, 363
Rocky Horror Tribute Show   354, 401, 403-406, 428, 442, 457
Rocky Horror: From Concept to Cult   63, 238, 328, 350
Rocky Horror: The Second Coming   356

Rocky Monster Show, The 184
Rocky Porno Video Show, The 379-380
Roddam, Franc 176
Rodger, Tania 408
Rodgers and Hammerstein 27, 33, 275, 334
Rodgers and Hart 231
Rodgers, Paul 387
Rodgers, Richard 27, 33, 231, 275, 334
Roeg, Nicolas 97
Rogers, Jean 132
Rogers, Peter 23
Rolling Stones, The 33, 84, 97, 267
Romero, George A 35, 108, 207
Ross, Alyn 252
Rossiter, Leonard 24-25
Roth, Jordan 282, 287
Rotten, Johnny 236, 395
Round the Horne 141
Roundhouse Theatre, London 26
Rowe, Dana P 347
Rowlands, Gena 437
Roxy Music 33
Roxy Theatre, Los Angeles 81, 84, 90, 93, 95-96, 122-123, 280, 477
Royal Court Theatre, London 35-37, 55, 62-63, 67, 91, 96-97, 104-105, 120, 138, 176, 231, 238, 244, 274, 343, 350-351, 354, 359, 390, 397, 401, 403, 405-406, 421, 425, 428, 457-458
Royal Court's Theatre Upstairs, London see Theatre Upstairs, London
Royalty Theatre, London 26
Rubin-Vega, Daphne 285
RuPaul 347
Rush, Barbara 133
Russ Abbot's Madhouse 91
Russell, Willy 183
Rutherford, Neil 326
Ryan, Andrew 199
Ryan, John 384
Ryder, Dale 269
Sabrina: The Teenage Witch 373
Sainsbury, Mark 409-410
Samuel French 41, 138, 185, 244, 439
Samuels, Stuart 208

Sarah B Devine 46
Sarandon, Chris 100
Sarandon, Susan 14, 100-101, 118, 120, 127, 175, 204, 207, 211, 228, 241, 290, 374, 386, 394
Saturday Night Fever 33, 164
Saturday Night Live 101, 292, 373-374
Saucy Jack and the Space Vixens 344
Saunders, Jennifer 161, 231, 248
Saved 37, 343
Saville Theatre, London 24
Sawalha, Julia 376
Sayer, Philip 84
Sayles, Alan 281
Scales of Justice, The 43
Scarpa, David 391
Scary Movie 2 393
Schindler's List 337
Schoedsack, Ernest B 179
Schoeman, Jay Jay 271
Schreck, Max 400
Schwartz, Stephen 26
Scorcese, Martin 177
Scotland Yard 43
Scott, Bruce 83, 90, 96, 122-123, 152
Scott, Janette 135
Scott, Ridley 134, 171, 393, 414
Scott, Tony 118
Scream 280
Sea, The 54
Sebastiane 103
Secret of Moonacre, The 393
Sekely, Steve 135
Sellers, Peter 24
Semmelrogge, Martin 337
Serafinowicz, Peter 377
Servian, Mark 407-408, 410
Sesame Street 45, 374
Sex Pistols, The 88, 162-163, 236
Seymour, Marc 191-192, 199, 229
Shadow and Evil in Fairy Tales 157
Shaffer, Peter 392
Shaftesbury Theatre, London 24

INDEX

Shail, Gary 176
Shakespeare Revue, The 300
Shakespeare 15, 30, 32, 51, 64, 107, 134, 148, 200, 216, 219, 238, 308, 349, 392, 398, 420, 437
Shankman, Adam 370
Shannon, Frank 132
Sharah, Sal 419
Shark, Lorelei 121-122
Sharman, Jim 10, 28-29, 35-39, 41-47, 49, 51-54, 57, 61, 64, 66, 68-69, 71, 82-87, 89, 94-97, 99-101, 103-110, 112-114, 116-121, 123-125, 127, 138-139, 148-152, 158, 160, 162, 168-169, 171-176, 178, 205-206, 234, 238, 241-244, 246, 248, 257, 264-265, 267, 299, 306, 318, 321, 329, 338, 342, 344, 351-352, 355, 357, 359, 369, 384-385, 388-389, 400, 405, 423, 440-441
Shatner, William 393
Shaun of the Dead 377
Shaving Ryan's Privates 379
Shaw, Andy 187, 199
Shaw, Suzanne 303-304, 317, 321, 324
Shearsmith, Reece 330
Shed 359
Shepard, Sam 35, 104, 351
Shirley Thompson Versus the Aliens 28-29, 36, 87
Shmukler-Jones, Lynsey 271
Shock Treatment 174-179, 248, 354-368, 385, 442
Shortall, Tim 366
Shoulder to Shoulder 70
Show Boat 31, 262
Show De Terror De Rocky, El 91
Shubert Theatre, Chicago 393
Simkin, Toby 141
Simmons, Gene 91
Simon, Bob 271
Simplicity 392
Simpsons, The 161, 375
Sims, Joan 24
Sinatra, Frank 352
Sinclair, Belinda 24, 27, 64-65, 71, 89-91, 100, 258, 336, 351, 398-399, 465-469, 487-488, 494
Sinclair, Jill 231, 299
Sinclair, John 27, 61, 231
Siouxsie and the Banshees 163
Sircom, Malcolm 184, 195
Skid Row 292, 345
Slattery, Tony 402
Smith, Dick 118
Smith, Kevin 375
Smith, Will 377
Snow White and the Seven Dwarfs 32, 65, 224
Snyder, Tom 260
Some Like it Hot 377
Sondheim, Stephen 262
Sonnenfeld, Barry 377
Sound of Music, The 88, 334
Spaceballs 266
Spaced 375, 377
Spamalot 393-394
Spandau Ballet 162
Spears, Randy 381
Sperminator, The 379
Sperring, Benji 353, 358, 360-361, 368
Spice Girls, The 126
Spiceworld 126
Spielberg, Steven 122, 337, 379
Spinella, Stephen 376
Spreadbury-Maher, Adam 359
Springer, Jerry 14, 292-293
Squire, Rosemary 300, 428
St Cyr, Lili 40-41
St James Theatre, London 353
St James Theatre, New York 291
St James Theatre, Wellington 420
St Trinian's 140
Stage Mother's Story: We're Not All Mrs Worthingtons!, A 216, 441
Stalker, John 296
Stanfill, Dennis 122
Stanwyck, Barbara 257
Star Trek 152, 220, 266, 372
Star Wars 60, 119, 164, 170, 210, 242, 266, 288, 299, 372, 375, 420
Starburst 86, 270, 442
Stardust, Alvin 14

526

Stark, Michael	329	Teefy, Maureen	64
Stefano, Joseph	141	*Tell Me on a Sunday*	300
Steiner, Max	133	*Tempest, The*	134, 349
Stevenson, Jessica	375	Temple, Julien	236
Stewart, Al	252	Temple, Shirley	145
Stewart, James	133	Teranishi, Rolly	336
Stewart, Michael	291	*Texas Chain Saw Massacre, The*	34
Stewart, Rod	252	*That '70s Show*	373
Stigwood, Robert	29, 35, 103	Thatcher, Margaret	163, 189, 200
Stoker, Bram	20-22, 147, 338	Theakston, Jamie	402
Stone, Oliver	200, 301	Theatre Athenee, Paris	48
Stovall, James	331	Theatre Royal, Bath	300
Straker, Peter	74-75	Theatre Royal, Brighton	300, 421, 425-426
Strange, Glenn	20	Theatre Royal, Sydney	167, 435, 437, 454, 478
Strange, Steve	395		
Streiner, Russell	108	Theatre Upstairs, London	37-38, 42-43, 47, 51, 54, 62, 64-68, 74-75, 92-93, 102, 105, 110, 137-139, 147, 149-150, 191, 232-233, 274, 299, 351, 366, 390, 401, 421
Strickfaden, Kenneth	109		
Stripes	347		
Stripper, The	326, 349-350, 352-353, 356		
		Thelma and Louise	100
Stroman, Susan	291	Then, Tony	105
Stulberg, Gordon	95, 113, 122	Thesiger, Ernest	31
Summer Holiday	278, 304	*They Came from Denton High*	39, 171
Sunset Boulevard	113	Thiebault, Stephen	251
Surprises du Divorce, Les	37	*Thing From Another World, The*	114
Suschitzky, Peter	121, 385	*Thing of Unspeakable Horror: The History of Hammer Films, A*	20, 440
Suspiria	175		
Swanson, Gloria	32, 113, 275, 302, 422	*This Is Your Life*	306
		Thomas, Richard	301
Swede, Puma	381	Thomson, Brian	28, 30, 35-36, 38-39, 45, 51, 55, 65, 67, 87, 94-95, 97-98, 104, 107-110, 112-113, 120, 128-129, 138, 159, 165, 167, 174, 177, 191, 232-233, 238-239, 267, 299, 339, 348, 350-352, 385-386, 388, 439
Sweeney, The	200		
Swift, Jonathan	179		
Sykes, Phil	426		
T Zee	176, 350-352, 354		
Tacky Horror Show, The	196-197		
Take That	276, 294	Thornber, Kraig	403
Talbot, Gloria	338	Thorne, Peter	191, 196, 199
Tamaddon, Hayley	324	Thornton, Billy Bob	136
Tam-Lin	103	Thornton, Oliver	422, 424
Tamne, Liam	426	*Threads*	163
Tancharoen, Kevin	378	Thurm, Joel	100
Tarantula	134-135, 338	Tiffany Theatre, Los Angeles	281
Tarzan	66, 350	*Time Gentlemen Please*	376
Taylor, Elizabeth	40	*Times Square*	393
Taylor, Nathan	271	Tinker, Jack	58, 61, 66, 227, 274
Taylor, Richard	408		
Tebelak, John-Michael	26	*To Hell and Back*	82

INDEX

Today Tonight	278	Valderrama, Wilmer	373
Toeman, Claire	176	Vale, Paul	367
Toguri, David	102, 146, 165, 167	Valens, Ritchie	93
Tomb of Ligeia, The	126	*Valley of the Dolls*	52, 61, 95
Tommy	127	Van Outen, Denise	300, 443
Tooth of Crime	104	van Vooren, Monique	392
Top People	352	VanHook, Kevin	242
Topham, Anthony	214-215, 221, 272-273, 298	Vardalos, Nia	377
Topo, El	206	Vaudeville Theatre, London	300
Tourneur, Jacques	135	Vega, Gonzalo	91
Towering Inferno, The	95	Verdi, Giuseppi	359
Toxic Fame: Celebrities Speak on Stardom	393, 441	Vereen, Ben	388
Tracey Ullman Show, The	161	*Vertigo*	120
Trafalgar Theatre, London	428	VH-1	37, 46, 101, 129, 149, 211, 220, 403, 443
Trainspotting	360	Vicious, Sid	162
Transformer	89	Victoria Palace Theatre, London	278, 435, 452
Travolta, John	33, 127, 376	*Victoria Wood: As Seen on TV*	91
T-Rex	33, 399	Victory Theatre, Johannesburg	270-271
Tricycle Theatre, London	349	*Village of the Damned*	338
Triffitt, Nigel	268, 278, 321	Voight, John	42
Triplett, Sally Ann	183	von Franz, Marie-Louise	157
Truman Show, The	178	Waithe, Lena	379
Truman, Roy	72	*Walk on the Wild Side*	48, 88, 443
Tudor-Pole, Edward	236-237, 240, 260-261, 375	*Wall Street*	200
Turn Him Out	36	Walters, Mark	354
Turnbull, Mark	185-187, 190, 192-194, 198-200, 250-251, 395-398	*War of the Worlds, The*	14, 135-136, 421
Turner, Mac	381	Warman, Mark	402
Turner, Tina	267	Waters, John	53, 206, 348, 370
Twins Macabre, The	365	Watkinson, Jenna	425
Tyler, Liv	136	Watson, Emma	378
Tynan, Kenneth	26	Wax, Ruby	161, 174-175, 248
Tyrell, Ralph	28	Wayne, Jeff	421
Ullman, Tracey	14, 161	Weaver, Sigourney	343
Ultravox	162	Webb, Dave	278
Un Ballo In Maschera	359	Webb, Rita	21, 146
Unearthly, The	338	Webb, Shaun	237
Universal	20-21, 31, 109, 130-132, 162, 171, 232, 338	Webb, Stephen	434-435
Unseen Hand, The	35, 37, 43-44, 104, 351	Wegener, Paul	338
Updike, John	374	Weinstock, Jeffrey	204, 208, 439
Urbani, Leonard John	271	Weir, Peter	178
Vadim, Roger	114	Welles, Mel	345
		Welles, Orson	24, 354
		Wells, Dominic	411

Wells, H G	14, 132, 135, 246	Wilson, Jacqueline	422
Welsh, Irvine	360	Windsor, Barbara	146-147, 290
West Yorkshire Playhouse	300	Winer, Linda	287
Westaby, Jayde	426	Winstone, Ray	176
Westwood, Vivienne	88, 162	Winter, Kelly	342
Weta	408, 410	Winterford, Paul	272, 298
Whale, James	20-21, 31, 109-110, 114, 132, 141	Wise, Robert	131, 334, 391
		Witches of Eastwick, The	374
Wheatley, Dennis	102	*Wiz Live!, The*	383
Whedon, Joss	254, 372	*Wizard of Oz, The*	86, 105-106, 139, 342
When the Wind Blows	163	*Wolf Man, The*	20, 130, 132
When Worlds Collide	73, 135	*Women in Revolt*	42
Whistler, James McNeill	117	Wong, Kimi	24, 27, 29, 53, 70, 105, 126, 351
White, Michael	38, 44, 57-58, 61, 63, 68, 73, 75, 80, 84, 96, 122, 160-161, 165, 173, 230, 299, 351, 369, 402		
		Wood, Edward D	18-20, 344, 380, 440
		Wood, Grant	108, 114, 177, 354, 386
White, Shona	314	Wood, Mrs John	37
White, Trevor	103	Wood, Natalie	136
Whitehall Theatre, London	428	Woods, Harry M	46
Whitfield, Peter	277	Woodstock	80
Whitnall, Tim	260-262	Woolard, David C	284, 286, 291
Whittaker, Ian	109	Woolf, Henry	105, 107
Whittaker, Jim	10, 45, 49-50, 73, 83, 96, 121-123, 152, 439	Wooten, Jason	331
		Worthy, Johnny	199
Who, the	96, 176, 187	Wrather, Jonathan	352
Wicker Man, The	80	Wray, Fay	30, 77, 113, 133, 217, 219, 250, 257, 332, 340, 396, 424, 428, 440
Wiene, Robert	338		
Wild, Michelle	380		
Wilde, Oscar	300		
Wilder, Billy	113, 377	*Wright Stuff, The*	400
Wilder, Gene	109	Wright, Edgar	375, 377
Wilkes, Jonathan	14, 294-297, 303, 322, 359	Wright, Matthew	400
		Wright, Nathan M	425, 429
Wilkinson, Kate	413	Wright, Nicholas	37, 351
Will & Grace	403	Wuest, Brigitte	408
Will Shakespeare	392	Wylie, Philip	136
Willcox, Toyah	176, 210-211, 215, 304, 328, 404-406	Wyndham, John	135, 338
		Xanadu	384
Williams, Esther	112	*X-Factor, The*	421
Williams, Kenneth	24, 141	*Year of the Sex Olympics, The*	364
Williams, Paul	205	*You Only Live Twice*	102
Williams, Robbie	276, 294-295	*Young Frankenstein*	109, 184, 388
Williamson, David	37	*Young Ones, The*	163, 175, 235
Willie & Phil	185, 376	Ziehm, Howard	83
Willis, Bruce	136	*Zombie Prom*	347-348
Willson, Nicky	272	Zombie, Rob	377
Wilson, Barrie James	95		

About the Authors

ROB BAGNALL
Rob Bagnall was born and raised in Staffordshire, England, and is an actor, writer and B-movie enthusiast. Having never grown out of a childhood love of old monster movies, classic mythology, saucy humour and rock 'n' roll, his discovery of *The Rocky Horror Show* during a typically misspent adolescence was a joyous inevitability; and one which became a lifelong passion. The original 2013 edition of *Still the Beast is Feeding* – his first published book – was the culmination of decades of devotion to a very special rock 'n' roll musical.

PHIL BARDEN
Once upon a time an impressionable teenager with long hair and red Kickers walked into a crumbling cinema in the King's Road. The rest is history.

www.ingramcontent.com/pod-product-compliance
Lightning Source LLC
Chambersburg PA
CBHW051030160426
43193CB00010B/892